COMPREHENSIVE CURRICULUM
of Basic Skills

6

American Education Publishing™
An imprint of Carson-Dellosa Publishing LLC
Greensboro, North Carolina

American Education Publishing™
An imprint of Carson-Dellosa Publishing LLC
P.O. Box 35665
Greensboro, NC 27425 USA

ISBN 978-1-60996-335-4

03-070131151

TABLE OF CONTENTS

TABLE OF CONTENTS

MATH

APPENDIX

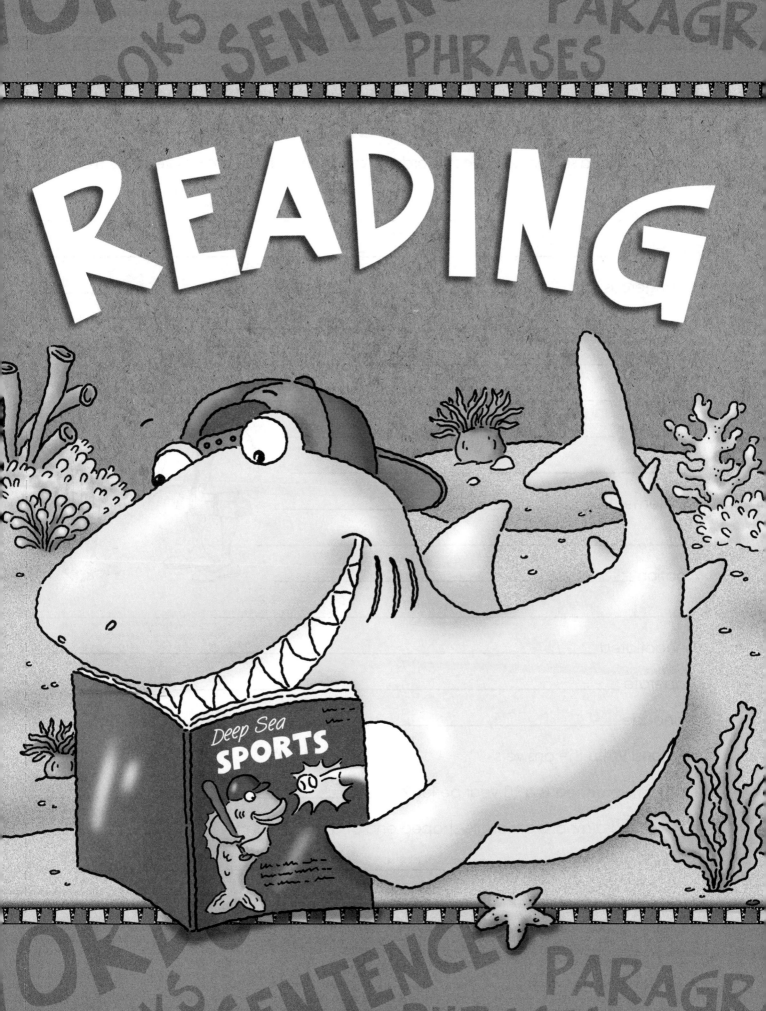

Name: _____

Spelling: Words With ā

Directions: Write a sentence for each word. Use a dictionary if you are unsure of the meaning of a word.

1. favorite _____

2. gable _____

3. dangerous _____

_____

4. patient _____

_____

5. lakefront _____

_____

6. statement _____

_____

7. nation _____

_____

8. negotiated _____

9. operate _____

10. decade _____

Directions: Write the answers.

11. Which word means a 10-year period? _____

12. Which word means a triangle-shaped end of a building's roof? _____

13. Which word means arbitrated? _____

Name: _____

Spelling: Words With ē

Directions: Write a sentence for each word. Use a dictionary if you are unsure of the meaning of a word.

1. niece _____

2. meaningful _____

3. conceited _____

4. baleen _____

5. field _____

6. disease _____

7. reactivate _____

8. peony _____

9. seafaring _____

10. theme _____

Directions: Write the answers.

11. Which word is a summer-blooming flower?

_____

12. Which word is a type of whale?

_____

13. Which word means an illness?

_____

Grade 6 - Comprehensive Curriculum

Name: _____

Spelling: Words With ī

Directions: Write a sentence for each word. Use a dictionary if you are unsure of the meaning of a word.

1. bisect _____

2. identify _____

3. frightened _____

4. glider _____

5. idol _____

6. library _____

7. pipeline _____

8. hieroglyphic _____

9. rhinoceros _____

10. silent _____

Directions: Write the answers.

11. Which word means to be scared?

_____

12. Which word means to divide into two sections?

_____

13. Which word is an animal?

_____

14. Which word is a type of ancient writing?

_____

Name: _____

Spelling: Words With ō

Directions: Write a sentence for each word. Use a dictionary if you are unsure of the meaning of a word.

1. clothing _____

2. slogan _____

3. total _____

4. stethoscope _____

5. voltage _____

6. stereo _____

7. protein _____

8. negotiate _____

9. locust _____

10. locomotive _____

Directions: Write the answers.

11. Which word is an insect?

   _____

12. Which word means a train?

   _____

13. Which word means a listening device
    to hear the heart?

   _____

14. Which word means to bargain?

   _____

Name: _____

Spelling: Words With ū

Directions: Write a sentence for each word. Use a dictionary if you are unsure of the meaning of a word.

1. universe _____

2. cruise _____

3. absolute _____

4. influence _____

5. unanimous _____

6. vacuum _____

7. putrid _____

8. incubate _____

9. peruse _____

10. numerous _____

Directions: Write the answers.

11. Which word means to read carefully?

_____

12. Which word means that everyone is in agreement?

_____

13. Which word means a sea voyage taken for pleasure?

_____

14. Which word means to keep eggs warm until they hatch?

_____

Spelling: Words With ō

Directions: Write a sentence for each word. Use a dictionary if you are unsure of the meaning of a word.

1. clothing _____

2. slogan _____

3. total _____

4. stethoscope _____

5. voltage _____

6. stereo _____

7. protein _____

8. negotiate _____

9. locust _____

10. locomotive _____

Directions: Write the answers.

11. Which word is an insect?

    _____

12. Which word means a train?

    _____

13. Which word means a listening device to hear the heart?

    _____

14. Which word means to bargain?

    _____

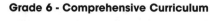

Name: _____

Spelling: Words With ū

Directions: Write a sentence for each word. Use a dictionary if you are unsure of the meaning of a word.

1. universe _____

2. cruise _____

3. absolute _____

4. influence _____

5. unanimous _____

6. vacuum _____

7. putrid _____

8. incubate _____

9. peruse _____

10. numerous _____

Directions: Write the answers.

11. Which word means to read carefully?

_____

12. Which word means that everyone is in agreement?

_____

13. Which word means a sea voyage taken for pleasure?

_____

14. Which word means to keep eggs warm until they hatch?

_____

Name: _____

Spelling: I Before E, Except After C

Use an **i** before **e**, except after **c** or when **e** and **i** together sound like long **a**.

Examples:
    relieve
    deceive
    neighbor

Exceptions: weird, foreign, height, seize

Directions: Write **C** in the blank if the word in bold is spelled correctly. Draw an **X** in the blank if it is spelled incorrectly. The first one has been done for you.

i before e,
except after c,
or when sounding like a,
as in "neighbor" and "weigh"

_C_ 1. They stopped at the crossing for the **freight** train.

_____ 2. How much does that **wiegh**?

_____ 3. Did you **believe** his story?

_____ 4. He **recieved** an A on his paper!

_____ 5. She said it was the **nieghborly** thing to do.

_____ 6. The guards **seized** the package.

_____ 7. That movie was **wierd**!

_____ 8. Her **hieght** is five feet, six inches.

_____ 9. It's not right to **deceive** others.

_____ 10. Your answers should be **breif**.

_____ 11. She felt a lot of **grief** when her dog died.

_____ 12. He is still **greiving** about his loss.

_____ 13. Did the police catch the **thief**?

_____ 14. She was their **cheif** source of information.

_____ 15. Can you speak a **foreign** language?

Grade 6 - Comprehensive Curriculum

Spelling: Words With ie and ei

Many people have trouble remembering when to use **ie** and when to use **ei**. The following rules have many exceptions, but they may be helpful to you.

Rule 1: If the two letters are pronounced like **ē** and are preceded by an **s** sound, use **ei**, as in receive.

Rule 2: If the two letters are pronounced like **ē**, but are not preceded by an **s** sound, use **ie** as in believe.

Rule 3: If the two letters are pronounced like **ā**, use **ei** as in **ei**ght and v**ei**n.

Rule 4: If the two letters are pronounced like **ī**, use **ei** as in h**ei**ght.

The sound **s** could be produced by the letter **s** as in **single** or the letter **c** as in **cease**.

Directions: Write the words from the box on the lines after the spelling rule that applies.

veil	brief	deceive	belief	niece
reindeer	yield	achieve	height	neighbor
grief	ceiling	weight	vein	seize

Rule 1: _____

Rule 2: _____

Rule 3: _____

Rule 4: _____

Directions: Complete the sentences with words that have the vowel sound shown. Use each word from the box only once.

1. My next-door (**ā**) _____ wore a long (**ā**) _____ at her wedding.

2. Will the roof hold the (**ā**) _____ of Santa's (**ā**) _____ ?

3. My nephew and (**ē**) _____ work hard to (**ē**) _____ their goals.

4. I have a strong (**ē**) _____ they would never (**ē**) _____ me.

5. For a (**ē**) _____ moment, I thought Will would (**ē**) _____ the game to me.

6. The blood rushed through my (**ā**) _____ .

7. What is the (**ī**) _____ of this (**ē**) _____ ?

Name: _____

Spelling: Words With ûr and ôr

The difference between **ûr** and **ôr** is clear in the words **fur** and **for**. The **ûr** sound can be spelled **ur** as in f**ur**, **our** as in j**our**nal, **er** as in h**er** and **ear** as in s**ear**ch.

The **ôr** sound can be spelled **or** as in f**or**, **our** as in f**our**, **oar** as in s**oar** and **ore** as in m**ore**.

Directions: Write the words from the box on the lines to match the sounds.

florist	plural	ignore	courtesy	observe
survey	research	furnish	normal	emergency
tornado	coarse	flourish	source	restore

ûr _____

_____

ôr _____

_____

Directions: Complete the sentences with words that have the sound shown. Use each word only once.

1. We all get along better when we remember to use (**ûr**) _____.

2. My brother likes flowers and wants to be a (**ôr**) _____.

3. What was the (**ôr**) _____ of the (**ûr**) _____ for your report?

4. He waved at her, but she continued to (**ôr**) _____ him.

5. For a plural subject, use a (**ûr**) _____ verb.

6. Beneath the dark clouds a (**ôr**) _____ formed!

7. Firefighters are used to handling an (**ûr**) _____ .

8. When will they be able to (**ôr**) _____ our electricity?

9. How are you going to (**ûr**) _____ your apartment?

Spelling: Words Beginning With sh and th

Directions: Write a definition for each word. Use a dictionary if you are unsure of the meaning of a word.

th

1. shallow: _____

2. thimble: _____

3. shear: _____

4. sheriff: _____

5. thermal: _____

6. throttle: _____

7. shingle: _____

8. shot put: _____

9. thrifty: _____

10. shoreline: _____

11. threaten: _____

12. thyroid: _____

sh

Directions: Use two of the above words in sentences.

13. _____

_____

14. _____

_____

Name: _____

Spelling: Words Beginning With ch

Directions: Write a definition for each word. Use a dictionary if you are unsure of the meaning of a word.

1. chimney: _____

2. china: _____

3. cheetah: _____

4. charity: _____

5. channel: _____

6. chandelier: _____

7. challenge: _____

8. chairman: _____

9. champion: _____

10. cheddar: _____

11. chime: _____

12. chisel: _____

Directions: Write the answers.

13. Which word is a tool for shaping wood?

_____

14. Which word is a type of cheese?

_____

15. Which word is an animal?

_____

Grade 6 - Comprehensive Curriculum

Name: _____

Spelling: The Letter Q

In English words, the letter **q** is always followed by the letter **u**.

Examples:
   question
   square
   quick

Directions: Write the correct spelling of each word in the blank. The first one has been done for you.

1. qill   _____ quill _____

2. eqality   _____

3. qarrel   _____

4. qarter   _____

5. qart   _____

6. qibble   _____

7. qench   _____

8. qeen   _____

9. qip   _____

10. qiz   _____

11. eqipment   _____

12. qiet   _____

13. qite   _____

14. eqity   _____

15. eqator   _____

16. eqivalent   _____

17. eqitable   _____

18. eqestrian   _____

19. eqation   _____

20. qantity   _____

Name: _____

Spelling: Words With kw, ks and gz

The consonant **q** is always followed by **u** in words and is pronounced **kw**. The letter **x** can be pronounced **ks** as in **mix**. When **x** is followed by a vowel, it is usually pronounced **gz** as in **example**.

Directions: Write the words from the box on the lines to match the sounds shown.

expense	exist	aquarium	acquire	request	exact
expand	exit	quality	excellent	quantity	quiz
exhibit	squirm	expression			

kw _____

_____

ks _____

_____

gz _____

Directions: Complete the sentences with words that have the sound shown. Use words from the box only once.

1. We went to the zoo to see the fish (**gz**) _____ .

2. I didn't know its (**gz**) _____ location, so we followed the map.

3. The zoo plans to (**kw**) _____ some sharks for its

   (**kw**) _____ .

4. Taking care of sharks is a big (**ks**) _____ , but a number of people

   have asked the zoo to (**ks**) _____ its display of fish.

5. These people want a better (**kw**) _____ of fish, not a bigger

   (**kw**) _____ of them.

6. I think the zoo already has an (**ks**) _____ display.

7. Some of its rare fish no longer (**gz**) _____ in the ocean.

Name: _____

Spelling: Words With Silent Letters

Some letters in words are not pronounced, like the **b** in **crumb**, the **l** in **yolk**, the **n** in **autumn**, the **g** in **design** and the **h** in **hour**.

Directions: Write the words from the box on the lines to match the silent letters. Use a dictionary if you are unsure of the meaning or pronunciation of a word.

condemn	yolk	campaign	assign	salmon
hymn	limb	chalk	tomb	foreign
resign	column	spaghetti	rhythm	solemn

n _____

l _____

g _____

b _____

h _____

Directions: Write words from the box to complete these sentences.

1. What did the teacher (**g**) _____ for homework?

2. She put words in a (**n**) _____ on the board.

3. When she finished writing, her hands were white

   with (**l**) _____ .

4. The church choir clapped in (**h**) _____

   with the (**n**) _____ .

5. While I was cracking an egg, the (**l**) _____ slipped onto the floor.

6. Did the explorers find anything in the ancient (**b**) _____?

7. My favorite dinner of all is (**h**) _____ and meatballs.

8. Do not (**n**) _____ me for making one little mistake.

Name: _____

Spelling: Words With ph or kn

The letters **ph** produce the same sound as the letter **f**. When the letters **kn** are together, the **k** is silent.

Directions: Write a definition for each word. Use a dictionary if you are unsure of the meaning of a word.

1. photographer: _____

2. knowledge: _____

3. knee: _____

4. telephone: _____

5. knock: _____

6. phonics: _____

7. physician: _____

8. knife: _____

9. pharmacy: _____

10. knight: _____

11. knit: _____

12. pheasant: _____

Directions: Write the answers.

13. Which word is a place to buy medicine?

_____

14. Which word is a synonym for doctor?

_____

15. Which word names a bird?

_____

Name: _____

Spelling: Words With gh or gn

Directions: Use the clues and the words in the box to complete the crossword puzzle.

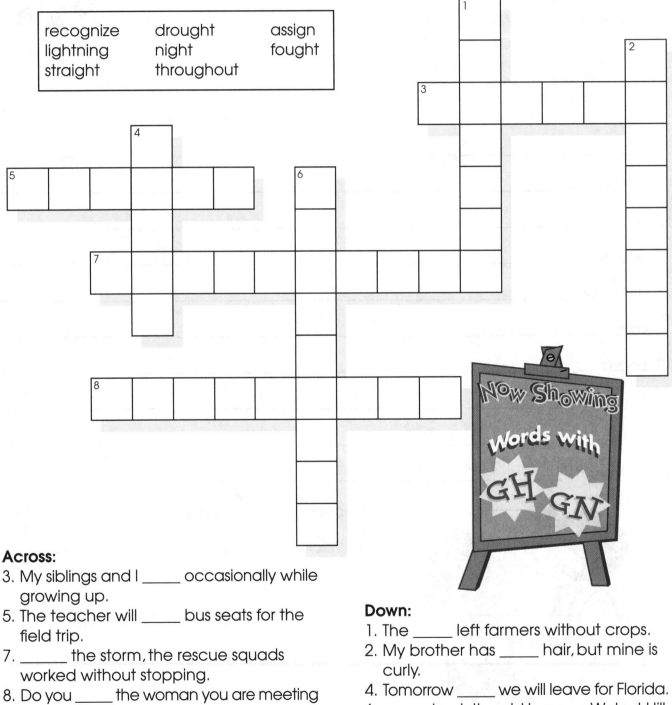

recognize	drought	assign
lightning	night	fought
straight	throughout	

Across:

3. My siblings and I _____ occasionally while growing up.
5. The teacher will _____ bus seats for the field trip.
7. _____ the storm, the rescue squads worked without stopping.
8. Do you _____ the woman you are meeting for lunch?

Down:

1. The _____ left farmers without crops.
2. My brother has _____ hair, but mine is curly.
4. Tomorrow _____ we will leave for Florida.
6. _____ struck the old barn on Walnut Hill.

Root Words

A **root word** is the common stem that gives related words their basic meanings.

Example: Separate is the root word for **separately**, **separation**, **inseparable** and **separator**.

Directions: Identify the root word in each group of words. Look up the meaning of the root word in the dictionary and write its definition. The first one has been done for you.

1. colorless, colorful, discolor, coloration

    Root word: _____ color _____

    Definition: __ any coloring matter, dye, __

    _____ pigment or paint _____

2. creator, creation, creating, creative, recreate

    Root word: _____

    Definition: _____

3. remove, movement, movable, immovable, removable

    Root word: _____

    Definition: _____

4. contentment, malcontent, discontent, discontentment

    Root word: _____

    Definition: _____

5. pleasure, displeasure, pleasing, pleasant, unpleasant

    Root word: _____

    Definition: _____

6. successor, unsuccessful, successful

    Root word: _____

    Definition: _____

Name: _____

Greek and Latin Roots

Many word patterns in the English language are combinations of Greek or Latin words. When you know what part of a word means, you may be able to figure out the meaning of the rest of the word. For example, if **cycle** means "circle or wheel" and **bi** means "two," then you can figure out that **bicycle** means "two wheels." **Root words** are the words that longer words are based on. For example, duct, which means "to lead," is the root of **conduct** or **induct**. Look at the chart below. It has several root words and their meanings on it.

Root	Meaning	Example	Definition
act	to do	interact	to act with others
aqua	water	aquatint	dyed water
auto	self	automobile	to move oneself
centi	a hundred	centennial	one hundred years

Directions: Look at each word equation below. The meaning of one part is shown in parentheses. Consult the chart of root words to find the meaning of the other part. Write the meaning in the blank. Combine the two meanings. Write the dictionary definition in the space provided.

1. react re (again) + act _____to do_____ = _____again to do_____

   Dictionary definition: _To act or do again_____

2. automatic auto _____ + matic (having a mind) = _____

   Dictionary definition: _____

3. transact trans (across) + act _____ = _____

   Dictionary definition: _____

4. centimeter centi _____ + meter (meter) = _____

   Dictionary definition: _____

5. aquanaut aqua _____ + naut (sailor) = _____

   Dictionary definition: _____

Name: _____

Root Words

Root	Meaning	Example	Definition
cede	to go	supercede	to go beyond
cept	seize	intercept	to seize during
duce	lead	deduce	to find the lead
fer	carry	interfere	to carry into
port	carry	transport	to carry across
spect	to look	inspect	to look in
tain	to hold	obtain	to gain by action
vene	to come	convene	to come to start

Directions: Complete the exercises below.

1. precede   pre (before) + cede _____to go_____ = _____before to go_____

   Dictionary definition: __to be, go or come before_____

2. report   re (again) + port _____ = _____

   Dictionary definition: _____

3. intervene   inter (between) + vene _____ = _____

   Dictionary definition: _____

4. induce   in (in) + duce _____ = _____

   Dictionary definition: _____

5. retrospect   retro (backward) + spect _____ = _____

   Dictionary definition: _____

6. refer   re (again) + fer _____ = _____

   Dictionary definition: _____

7. retain   re (again) + tain _____ = _____

   Dictionary definition: _____

8. concept   con (with) + cept _____ = _____

   Dictionary definition: _____

Prefixes

A **prefix** is a syllable added to the beginning of a word to change its meaning. The prefix **re** means "back" or "again," as in **re**turn. **Pre** means "before," as in **pre**pare. **Dis** means "do the opposite," as in **dis**appear. **In** and **im** both mean "not," as in **im**possible. (These two prefixes also have other meanings.) **Com** and **con** both mean "with," as in **com**panion and **con**cert. Use **im** and **com** with words that start with **p, b** or **m**. Use **in** and **con** with words that begin with a vowel or other consonants.

Directions: Match each word from the box to its definition.

disbelieve	recite	connotation	impolite	preview
impatient	distrust	configuration	prevision	incomplete
invisible	dislike	confederate	recover	compassion

1. share another's feelings ——————————

2. not finished ——————————

3. another meaning ——————————

4. become normal again ——————————

5. take away confidence ——————————

6. look to the future ——————————

7. arrangement of parts ——————————

8. say from memory ——————————

9. ally ——————————

10. hate ——————————

11. look at ——————————

12. rude ——————————

13. in a hurry ——————————

14. doubt ——————————

15. not seen ——————————

Directions: Add the rest of the word to each prefix in these sentences. Use words from the box only once. Be sure to use the correct form of the word.

16. When he re_____ from his cold, Jeff was im_____ to get back to work.

17. Jonah stared at the ghostly figure with dis_____ and dis_____.

18. I'd like to re_____ that poem, but my memory of it is in_____.

19. She was very im _____ during the movie pre_____.

Name: _____

Prefixes

A **prefix** is a syllable added to the beginning of a word that changes its meaning. The prefixes **in**, **il**, **ir** and **im** all mean **not**.

Directions: Create new words by adding **in**, **il**, **ir** or **im** to these root words. Use a dictionary to check that the new words are correct. The first one has been done for you.

Prefix		Root Word		New Word
1. _____il_____	+	logical	=	illogical
2. _____	+	literate	=	_____
3. _____	+	patient	=	_____
4. _____	+	probable	=	_____
5. _____	+	reversible	=	_____
6. _____	+	responsible	=	_____
7. _____	+	active	=	_____
8. _____	+	moral	=	_____
9. _____	+	removable	=	_____
10. _____	+	legible	=	_____
11. _____	+	mature	=	_____
12. _____	+	perfect	=	_____

Prefixes

The prefixes **un** and **non** also mean **not**.

Examples:
    Unhappy means not happy.
    Nonproductive means not productive.

Directions: Divide each word into its prefix and root word. The first one has been done for you.

		Prefix	Root Word
1.	unappreciated	un	appreciate
2.	unlikely	_____	_____
3.	unkempt	_____	_____
4.	untimely	_____	_____
5.	nonstop	_____	_____
6.	nonsense	_____	_____
7.	nonprofit	_____	_____
8.	nonresident	_____	_____

Directions: Use the clues in the first sentence to complete the second sentence with one of the words from the box. The first one has been done for you.

9. She didn't reside at school. She was a __nonresident._____

10. He couldn't stop talking. He talked _____

11. The company did not make a profit. It was a _____ company.

12. She was not talking sense. She was talking _____

13. He visited at a bad time. His visit was _____

14. No one appreciated his efforts. He felt _____

15. He did not "keep up" his hair. His hair was _____

16. She was not likely to come. Her coming was _____

Prefixes

The prefixes **co**, **col**, **com**, **con** and **cor** mean "with" or "together." The prefixes **anti**, **contra** and **ob** mean "against."

Directions: Write each word's prefix and root word in the space provided.

Word	Prefix	Root Word
coexist	co	exist
concurrent		
correlate		
codependent		
antigravity		
contraband		

Directions: Use the words from the chart above to complete the sentences.

1. When airplanes fly very high and then quickly drop down, they cause an

   _____ affect.

2. Materials that are illegal are called _____ .

3. A dog and a cat can _____ in the same house if they get along well.

4. Events that happen at the same time are _____ .

5. When two people rely on each other, they are said to be _____ .

6. The textbook will _____ with the teacher's lectures.

Name: _____

Prefixes

The prefixes **epi**, **hyper**, **over** and **super** mean "above" or "over." The prefixes **under** and **sub** mean "under."

Directions: Write each word's prefix and root word in the space provided.

Word	Prefix	Root Word
hyperactive	hyper	active
overanxious	_____	_____
superimpose	_____	_____
epilogue	_____	_____
underestimate	_____	_____
subordinate	_____	_____

Directions: Use the words above to complete the following sentences.

1. A photographer could _____ one image on top of another.

2. The _____ of the book may tell additional information about the story.

3. All the other children settled down for the night except the boy who was _____ .

4. He could not sleep because he was _____ about the upcoming trip.

5. The company's president told his _____ to take over some of the responsibilities.

6. Just because you think you are weak, don't _____ how strong you could be.

Numerical Prefixes

Some prefixes are related to numbers. For example, in Latin **uni** means "one." The prefix **mono** means "one" in Greek. The chart below lists prefixes for numbers one through ten from both the Latin and Greek languages.

Number	Latin	Example	Greek	Example
1	uni	university	mon, mono	monopoly
2	du	duplex	di	digress
3	tri	tricycle	tri	trio
4	quad	quadrant	tetro	tetrameter
5	quin	quintuplets	penta	pentagon
6	sex	sexennial	hex	hexagon
7	sept	septuagenarian	hept	heptagon
8	oct	octopus	oct	octagon
9	nov	novena	enne	ennead (group of nine)
10	dec	decade	dec	decimal

Directions: Complete the exercises below.

1. unicycle   uni _____ + cycle (wheel) = _____

   Dictionary definition: _____

2. monogram   mono _____ + gram (writing) = _____

   Dictionary definition: _____

3. sextet   sex _____ + tet (group) = _____

   Dictionary definition: _____

4. quadrant   quad _____ + rant (part) = _____

   Dictionary definition: _____

5. decigram   dec _____ + gram (gram) = _____

   Dictionary definition: _____

Name: _____

Review

Roots	Meanings	Prefixes	Meanings
fer	carry	dis	separate
graph	write	epi	upon, above
rupt	break	ex	out
tend	stretch	in	in
vade	go	trans	across

Directions: Complete the exercises below.

1. invade   in _____ + vade _____ = _____

   Dictionary definition: _____

2. disrupt   dis _____ + rupt _____ = _____

   Dictionary definition: _____

3. transfer   trans _____ + fer _____ = _____

   Dictionary definition: _____

4. extend   ex _____ + tend _____ = _____

   Dictionary definition: _____

5. epigraph   epi _____ + graph _____ = _____

   Dictionary definition: _____

Directions: The prefixes **mono** and **uni** both mean one. Write each word's prefix and root in the space provided.

Word	Prefix	Root
monorhyme	_____	_____
monosyllable	_____	_____
unilingual	_____	_____
uniparental	_____	_____
unilateral	_____	_____

Suffixes

A **suffix** is a syllable added to the end of a root word that changes its meaning.

When a word ends in silent **e**, keep the **e** before adding a suffix beginning with a consonant.

Example: amuse + ment = amusement

Exception: argue + ment = argument

When a word ends in silent **e**, drop the **e** before adding a suffix beginning with a vowel.

Example: amuse = amusing

Exceptions: hoeing, shoeing, canoeing

Directions: Write **C** on the blank if the word in bold is spelled correctly. Draw an **X** in the blank if it is spelled incorrectly. The first one has been done for you.

__C__ 1. She was a woman of many **achievements**.

_____ 2. He hated to hear their **arguments**.

_____ 3. Do you want to go **canoing**?

_____ 4. He kept **urgeing** her to eat more dessert.

_____ 5. She was not good at **deceiving** others.

_____ 6. He **rarely** skipped lunch.

_____ 7. Would you repeat that **announcment**?

_____ 8. Bicycle **safety** was very important to him.

_____ 9. Their constant **argueing** got on my nerves.

_____ 10. He found that **shoeing** horses was not easy.

_____ 11. The sun felt hot as they were **hoeing**.

_____ 12. She was so **relieveed** that she laughed.

Name: _____

Suffixes: Words Ending in Y

If a word ends in a vowel and **y**, keep the **y** when you add a suffix.

Example:
    bray + ed = brayed
    bray + ing = braying

Exception: lay + ed = laid

If a word ends in a consonant and **y**, change the **y** to **i** when you add a suffix unless the suffix begins with **i**.

Example:
    baby + ed = babied
    baby + ing = babying

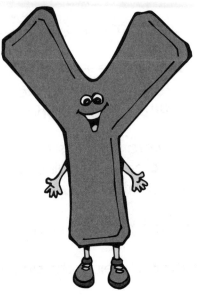

Directions: Write **C** in the blank if the word in bold is spelled correctly. Draw an **X** if it is spelled incorrectly. The first one has been done for you.

_C_ 1. She was a good student who did well at her **studies**.

____ 2. Will you please stop **babiing** him?

____ 3. She **layed** her purse on the couch.

____ 4. Both the **ferrys** left on schedule.

____ 5. Could you repeat what he was **saying**?

____ 6. He was **triing** to do his best.

____ 7. How many **cherries** are in this pie?

____ 8. The cat **stayed** away for two weeks.

____ 9. He is **saveing** all his money.

____ 10. The lake was **muddier** than I remembered.

____ 11. It was the **muddyest** lake I've ever seen!

____ 12. Her mother **babied** her when she was sick.

Name: _____

Suffixes: Doubling Final Consonants

If a one-syllable word ends in one vowel and consonant, double the last consonant when you add a suffix that begins with a vowel.

Examples: swim + ing = swimming   big + er = bigger

Directions: Add the suffixes shown to the root words, doubling the final consonants when appropriate. The first one has been done for you.

1. brim   +   ing   =   *brimming*
2. big   +   est   =   _____
3. hop   +   ing   =   _____
4. swim   +   er   =   _____
5. thin   +   er   =   _____
6. spin   +   ing   =   _____
7. smack   +   ing   =   _____
8. sink   +   ing   =   _____
9. win   +   er   =   _____
10. thin   +   est   =   _____
11. slim   +   er   =   _____
12. slim   +   ing   =   _____
13. thread   +   ing   =   _____
14. thread   +   er   =   _____
15. win   +   ing   =   _____
16. sing   +   ing   =   _____
17. stop   +   ing   =   _____
18. thrill   +   ing   =   _____
19. drop   +   ed   =   _____
20. mop   +   ing   =   _____

Name: _____

Suffixes: Doubling Final Consonants

When two-syllable words have the accent on the second syllable and end in a consonant preceded by a vowel, double the final consonant to add a suffix that begins with a vowel.

Examples: occur + ing = occurring   occur + ed = occurred

If the accent shifts to the first syllable when the suffix is added to the two-syllable root word, the final consonant is not doubled.

Example: refer + ence = reference

Directions: Say the words listed to hear where the accent falls when the suffix is added. Then add the suffix to the root word, doubling the final consonant when appropriate. The first one has been done for you.

1. excel   +   ence   = _____excellence_____
2. infer   +   ing   = _____
3. regret   +   able   = _____
4. control +   able   = _____
5. submit   +   ing   = _____
6. confer   +   ing   = _____
7. refer   +   al   = _____
8. differ   +   ing   = _____
9. compel   +   ing   = _____
10. commit   +   ed   = _____
11. regret   +   ing   = _____
12. depend   +   able   = _____
13. upset   +   ing   = _____
14. propel   +   ing   = _____
15. repel   +   ed   = _____
16. prefer   +   ing   = _____
17. prefer   +   ence   = _____
18. differ   +   ence   = _____
19. refer   +   ing   = _____
20. control +   ing   = _____

EXCEL + ENCE = EXCELLENCE

Name: _____

Suffixes

A **suffix** is a syllable added to the end of a word that changes its meaning. Some suffixes change nouns into adjectives.

Examples: fool — **foolish** nation — **national**

Other suffixes change adjectives into adverbs.

Examples: foolish — **foolishly** national — **nationally**

Directions: Match the root words with words from the box.

personal	stylish	obviously	professional
typical	childish	practical	medical
permanently	ticklish	additional	critical
gradually	physical	musical	

1. tickle _____
2. critic _____
3. add _____
4. person _____
5. child _____

6. grade _____
7. practice _____
8. physician _____
9. permanent _____
10. medic _____

11. type _____
12. music _____
13. style _____
14. obvious _____
15. profess _____

Directions: Circle the word or words in each sentence that are a synonym for a word from the box. Write the word from the box on the line. The first one has been done for you.

16. Knowing how to cook is a (useful) skill.   ___**practical**___

17. The lake slowly warmed up.   _____

18. Clearly, I should have stayed on the path.   _____

19. That is a fashionable outfit.   _____

20. Wanting your own way all the time is for little kids.   _____

21. Getting lost is common for me.   _____

22. My grades are a private matter.   _____

Name: _____

Suffixes: "ion," "tion" and "ation"

The suffixes **ion**, **tion** and **ation** change verbs into nouns.

Examples: imitate + **ion** = imit**ation**   combine + **ation** = combin**ation**

Directions: Match each word from the box with its definition.

celebration	solution	imitation	exploration	selection
reflection	conversation	population	invitation	suggestion
combination	decoration	appreciation	definition	transportation

1. a copy   _____   9. choice   _____

2. talking   _____   10. a party   _____

3. a request   _____   11. the answer   _____

4. the meaning   _____   12. people   _____

5. a search   _____   13. a joining   _____

6. mirror image   _____   14. new idea   _____

7. cars, trucks   _____   15. thankfulness _____

8. ornament   _____

Directions: Write the correct forms of the words in the sentences. The first one has been done for you.

16. **transport**   How are we ___transporting___ our project to school?

Did anyone arrange ___transportation___ ?

17. **decorate**   Today, we are _____ the classroom.

We brought the _____ from home.

18. **solve**   Have you _____ the problem yet?

We need a _____ by the end of the day.

Name: _____

Suffixes: "ment" and "ity"

The suffixes **ment** and **ity** change verbs and some adjectives to nouns.

Examples: treat — **treatment**   able — **ability**

Directions: Circle the word or words in each sentence that are synonyms for words from the box. Write the word from the box on the line. The first one has been done for you.

equipment	responsibility	activity	
accomplishment	adjustment	ability	treatment
assignment	personality	achievement	appointment
popularity	astonishment	advertisement	curiosity

1. The workers are bringing in their (machines.)   _**equipment**_

2. Whose duty is it to take out the trash?   _____

3. Do you know our homework for tonight?   _____

4. I could see the surprise in his face.   _____

5. Ken is happy with his new position.   _____

6. I was filled with wondering.   _____

7. She lists one achievement in particular.   _____

8. Look at the exercise on page 16.   _____

9. The way you get along with others is part of your character.   _____

10. I heard that commercial a hundred times.   _____

11. Amy has a strong athletic skill.   _____

12. Jason's kindness led to his acceptance by his friends.   _____

13. I need to make a change in my schedule.   _____

14. That is quite an accomplishment!   _____

15. The doctor is trying another way to help my allergies.   _____

Name: _____

Suffixes

The suffix **less** means **lacking** or **without**. The suffix **some** means **full** or **like**.

Examples:
    Hopeless means without hope.
    Awesome means filled with awe.

Directions: Create new words by adding **some** or **less** to these root words. Use a dictionary to check that the new words are correct. The first one has been done for you.

Root Word		Suffix		New Word
1. heart	+	less	=	heartless
2. trouble	+	_____	=	_____
3. home	+	_____	=	_____
4. humor	+	_____	=	_____
5. awe	+	_____	=	_____
6. child	+	_____	=	_____
7. win	+	_____	=	_____

Directions: Use the clues in the first sentence to complete the second sentence with one of the words from the box. The first one has been done for you.

8. Her smile was winning and delightful. She had a _____ winsome _____ smile .

9. The mean man seemed to have no heart. He was _____

10. She never smiled or laughed. She appeared to be _____

11. The solar system fills me with awe. It is _____

12. The couple had no children. They were _____

13. He had no place to live. He was _____

14. The pet caused the family trouble. It was_____

Name: _____

Suffixes: "ship," "ful" and "ist"

Directions: Write the meaning of each word on the line. Use a dictionary if you are unsure of the meaning of a word.

1. biologist: _____

_____

2. citizenship: _____

_____

3. companionship: _____

_____

4. archaeologist: _____

5. typist: _____

6. scholarship: _____

7. doubtful: _____

8. hopeful: _____

9. dictatorship: _____

10. chemist: _____

11. principalship: _____

12. artist: _____

13. spiteful: _____

14. professorship: _____

15. geologist: _____

Suffixes: "ance" and "ence"

Directions: Write words from the box to complete the sentences. Use a dictionary if you are unsure of the meaning of a word.

ance

performance	experience
correspondence	reliance
evidence	sequence
maintenance	absence
dependence	insurance

ence

1. The daycare position required _____ working with children.

2. During her _____ , a friend phoned each night with homework assignments.

3. My grandmother is known for her self- _____ .

4. The alphabet is a _____ of 26 letters.

5. A letter to my penpal is called long distance _____ .

6. The circus advertised a 2:00 P.M. _____ .

7. Many people have a great _____ on calculators for math.

8. Fortunately, most homeowners in the flooded area carried _____ .

9. The police gathered _____ in hopes of solving the burglary.

10. _____ of football and baseball fields requires much time and effort.

Suffixes

The suffix **ment** means the **act of** or **state of**. The suffixes **ible** and **able** mean **able to**.

Directions: Create new words by adding **ment** or **able** to these root words. Use a dictionary to check that the new words are correct. The first one has been done for you.

Root Word		Suffix		New Word
1. rely	+	able	=	reliable
2. retire	+	_____	=	_____
3. sense	+	_____	=	_____
4. commit	+	_____	=	_____
5. repair	+	_____	=	_____
6. love	+	_____	=	_____
7. quote	+	_____	=	_____
8. honor	+	_____	=	_____

Directions: Use the clues in the first sentence to complete the second sentence with one of the words from the box. The first one has been done for you.

9. Everyone loved her. She was ___loveable (also lovable).___

10. He had a lot of sense. He was _____

11. She committed time to the project. She made a _____

12. He always did the right thing. His behavior was _____

13. The tire could not be fixed. It was not _____

14. They would not buy the car. The car was not _____

15. He gave the reporter good comments. His comments were _____

16. She was ready to retire. She looked forward to _____

Review

Directions: Add one of the prefixes, suffixes or combining forms to a word in the box to complete each sentence. Use the definition in parentheses as a clue.

ian   ous   ship   an   ist   extra   trans   pre   micro   super

friend	music	geology	sensory	America
paid	wave	market	atlantic	danger

1. The _____ has a huge selection of fruits and vegetables. (large food store)

2. The first _____ flight was a remarkable feat in the history of aviation. (across the Atlantic Ocean)

3. The woman claimed that she knew the future because of her _____ capabilities. (beyond the normal senses)

4. When mailing your payment, please use the _____ envelope. (paid in advance)

5. Mrs. Johnson studied the violin for many years to become the accomplished _____ she is today. (person skilled in music)

6. The _____ oven is a modern-day convenience. (operating with extremely small electromagnetic waves)

7. Lightning is the most _____ part of a storm. (characterized by danger)

8. They raised the _____ flag over their campground in a gesture of patriotism. (belonging to America)

9. The Native Americans would often smoke a peace pipe as a sign of _____ . (the state of being friends)

10. Dr. Stokes is the finest _____ at the university. (one who is skilled at geology, the study of the earth's crust)

Review

Directions: Add suffixes to change these nouns into adjectives.

Searching **Suffixe**

1. person_____   music_____   child_____

Directions: Add suffixes to change these adjectives into adverbs.

2. permanent_____   obvious_____   gradual_____

Directions: Add the prefix **pre, un, in, re** or **con** to each word and use the word in a sentence.

3. search _____

4. join _____

5. compatible _____

6. wrap _____

7. school _____

Directions: Add the suffix **ish, ment, ion, ship** or **ful** to each word and use the word in a sentence.

8. square _____

9. invent _____

10. force _____

11. replace _____

12. chairman _____

Directions: Add suffixes to make the noun forms of these verbs.

13. select _____   16. imitate _____

14. decorate _____   17. reflect _____

15. invite _____

Review

Directions: Spell these silent **e** words correctly.

1. achievments _____

2. canoing _____

3. amuseing _____

4. urgeing _____

Directions: Add the suffixes to these words ending in **y** and spell them correctly.

5. baby + ies = _____

6. stay + ed = _____

Directions: Add the suffixes and spell these one-syllable words correctly.

7. hope + ing = _____

8. stop + ing = _____

Directions: Add the suffixes and spell these two-syllable words correctly.

9. recur + ing = _____

10. defer + ence = _____

Directions: Spell these words correctly by inserting **ie** or **ei**.

11. h __ __ ght

12. ch __ __ f

Directions: Circle the **q** words in each row that are spelled correctly.

13. quip   qeen   qick   quit

14. qestion   equator   quiet   qart

15. squirrel   sqare   squirm   sqeak

Name: _____

Analyzing Words and Their Parts

A **syllable** is a word or part of a word with only one vowel sound.

Directions: Fill in the missing syllables. Use words from the box. Write the number of syllables after each word. The first one has been done for you.

expense	exist	aquarium	acquire	request
exact	expand	exit	quality	excellent
quiz	quantity	expression	exhibit	squirm

1. ex <u>c e l</u> lent (3)

2. _____ squirm ( )

3. _____ act ( )

4. _____ quiz ( )

5. aquar ___ um ( )

6. ac _____ ( )

7. quali _____ ( )

8. _____ it ( )

9. ex _____ sion ( )

10. _____ ist ( )

11. _____ quest ( )

12. ex _____ it ( )

13. _____ pense ( )

14. _____ pand ( )

15. quan _____ ty ( )

Directions: Write words that rhyme. Use the words in the box.

16. fizz _____

17. resist _____

18. fact _____

19. fence _____

20. sand _____

21. it's been sent _____

22. this is it _____

23. made for me _____

24. reflection _____

25. worm _____

26. fire _____

27. best _____

28. fit _____

A **root word** is a common stem which gives related words their basic meaning.

Directions: Write the root word for the bold word in each sentence.

29. I know **exactly** what I want. _____

30. Those shoes look **expensive**. _____

31. She didn't like my **expression** when I frowned. _____

32. We went to the train **exhibition** at the park. _____

Dividing Words Into Syllables

Directions: Divide these words into syllables by putting a hyphen (-) between each syllable. The first one has done for you.

1. multiplication

   _mul-ti-pli-ca-tion_____

2. discover

   _____

3. ultimate

   _____

4. transfer

   _____

5. continent

   _____

6. follow

   _____

7. British

   _____

8. American

   _____

9. president

   _____

10. discrimination

    _____

11. spectacular

    _____

12. commercial

    _____

13. probability

    _____

14. country

    _____

15. casual

    _____

16. political

    _____

17. wrestle

    _____

18. basketball

    _____

19. particular

    _____

20. cereal

    _____

21. picture

    _____

22. plumber

    _____

23. personal

    _____

24. sentence

    _____

Synonyms

A **synonym** is a word that means the same or nearly the same as another word. **Example:** mean and cruel.

Directions: Circle the word or group of words in each sentence that is a synonym for a word in the box. Write the synonym from the box on the line. The first one has been done for you.

florist	courtesy	research	emergency	flourish
plural	observe	furnish	tornado	source
ignored	survey	normally	coarse	restore

1. The children seemed to (thrive) in their new school.   **flourish**

2. Her politeness made me feel welcome. _____

3. The principal came to watch our class. _____

4. Are you going to fix up that old house? _____

5. Six weeks after the disaster, the neighborhood looked as it usually did. _____

6. What was the origin of that rumor? _____

7. The cyclone destroyed two houses. _____

8. She neglected her homework. _____

9. The material had a rough feel to it. _____

10. Did you fill out the questionnaire yet? _____

Directions: Select three words from the box below. Write a sentence for each word that shows you understand the meaning of the word

plural	flourish	source	restore	observe	furnish	research

_____

_____

_____

Antonyms

An **antonym** is a word which means the opposite of another word.

Example: hopeful and discouraged

Directions: Circle the word or group of words in each sentence that is an antonym for a word in the box. Write the antonym from the box on the line.

nuisance	considerate
delicate	frivolous
entrance	shiny
divide	parallel
success	valley

1. It seemed as though we'd never make it to the top of the butte.

   _____

2. Rosa thought the woman was rude to the store clerk.

   _____

3. The two streets run perpendicular to each other.

   _____

4. The school carnival was a total failure due to the stormy weather.

   _____

5. Be sure to wash this sturdy sweater with other heavy items.

   _____

6. The third grade class worked hard learning to multiply.

   _____

7. The exit was blocked by a table.

   _____

8. The purchase of the coat was quite practical.

   _____

9. The teacher wrote that Colin was a joy to have in class.

   _____

10. The stone in her ring was dull and cloudy.

   _____

Spelling: Homophones

Homophones are words that sound the same, but have different spellings and different meanings.

Examples: night and knight, fair and fare, not and knot

Directions: Complete each sentence with the correct homophone. Then write a sentence using the other homophone. Use a dictionary if you don't know the meaning of a word. The first one has been done for you.

1. eight
   ate

   I <u>ate</u> two cookies.

   <u>Joanie had eight cookies!</u> _____

2. vein
   vain

   Since the newspaper printed his picture, Keith has been self-centered and _____ .

   _____

3. weight
   wait

   We had to _____ a long time for the show to start.

   _____

4. weigh
   way

   He always insists that we do everything his _____ .

   _____

5. seize
   seas

   The explorers charted the _____ .

   _____

6. straight
   strait

   It is sometimes difficult to draw perfectly _____ lines freehand.

   _____

7. principle
   principal

   The _____ summoned the student body to the auditorium for a special program.

   _____

8. their
   they're

   I'm sure _____ meeting us at the park rather than at home.

   _____

Name: _____

Vocabulary Building: Homographs

A **homograph** has the same spelling as another word but a different meaning. The two words are often different parts of speech.

Directions: Write the definition from the box for the bold word in each sentence.

con' tract	n.	an agreement to do something
con tract'	v.	to reduce in size, shrink
des' ert	n.	dry land that can support little plant and animal life
de sert'	v.	to abandon
Po' lish	adj.	of or belonging to Poland
pol' ish	v.	to smooth and brighten by rubbing
proj' ect	n.	a proposal or undertaking
pro ject'	v.	to send forth in thoughts or imagination

1. Iron is one of the metals that **contracts** as it cools.

   _____

2. You will have to sign a **contract** before I can begin work on your house.

   _____

3. The **desert** seems to come to life in the evening when the animals come out in search of food.

   _____

4. I hope you will not **desert** your friends now that they really need your support.

   _____

5. She will **polish** the stone and then use it to make a necklace.

   _____

6. The **Polish** people have been courageous in their struggle for freedom.

   _____

7. **Project** yourself into the world of tomorrow with this amazing invention!

   _____

8. I started this **project** on Monday, but it may be weeks before I finish it.

   _____

Name: _____

Vocabulary Building: Homographs

Directions: After each sentence, write the meaning of the bold word. Write another sentence using a homograph for the word.

1. The owner of the pet store tied a bright red **bow** around the puppies' necks.

Meaning: _____

Sentence: _____

2. Today, fewer pipes are made from **lead**.

Meaning: _____

Sentence: _____

3. Marcia's new house is very **close** to ours.

Meaning: _____

Sentence: _____

4. Please **record** the time and day that we finished the project.

Meaning: _____

Sentence: _____

5. It takes only a **minute** to fasten your seatbelt, but it can save your life.

Meaning: _____

Sentence: _____

6. I cannot **subject** the animal to that kind of treatment.

Meaning: _____

Sentence: _____

Multiple Meanings

Directions: Use a dictionary to write the meaning of the bold word in each sentence. Be sure the meaning fits the context of the sentence and the part of speech. The first one has been done for you.

1. Rosa will **graduate** *summa cum laude*.

   <u>to receive an academic degree</u>

2. The **graduate** looked for suitable employment.

   _____

3. The woman balanced her purse on the **counter**.

   _____

4. The boss **countered** the employee's request for a large raise.

   _____

5. Julio Mentarre will **conduct** the orchestra tonight.

   _____

6. Metal **conducts** electricity.

   _____

7. His **conduct** was questionable in that situation.

   _____

8. Please **file** these reports today.

   _____

9. The principal asked the students to leave in single **file**.

   _____

10. "Please hand me a **file**," said the woodworker to his daughter.

    _____

Vocabulary Building: Multiple Meanings

Directions: Use a dictionary to choose the correct definition for each bold word. The first one has been done for you.

1. My grandfather always has his **spectacles** perched on his nose.

   Meaning: <u>lenses worn in front of the eyes to aid vision</u>

2. The Fourth of July fireworks display was an amazing **spectacle**.

   Meaning: _____

3. We enjoy a rugged vacation, staying in a hunting **lodge** rather than a hotel.

   Meaning: _____

4. Don't let the baby have hard candy, because it could **lodge** in his throat.

   Meaning: _____

5. Termites will **bore** through the rotten wood in our basement if we don't have it replaced.

   Meaning: _____

6. That television show could **bore** even a small child!

   Meaning: _____

7. Don't **resort** to lies just to get what you want!

   Meaning: _____

8. The **resort** is packed with tourists from May to September each year.

   Meaning: _____

Name: _____

Vocabulary Building: Multiple Meanings

Directions: Read each sentence, then write another sentence using a different meaning for the bold word.

1. The prince will **succeed** his mother as ruler of the country.

   _____

2. All through the National Anthem, Johnny was singing in the wrong **key**.

   _____

3. There has been only a **trace** of rain this month.

   _____

4. I can't get involved in a **cause** in which I don't really believe.

   _____

5. It is very important to get plenty of **iron** in your diet.

   _____

6. A police officer can **issue** a warning to those disturbing the peace.

   _____

7. There is a mayoral candidate from each of the major political **parties**.

   _____

8. You can take that **stack** of newspapers to be recycled.

   _____

9. The judge will likely **sentence** the offender to a year in prison.

   _____

10. The lawyer made a **motion** to have the charges dropped.

   _____

Name: _____

Reading Skills: Classifying

Classifying is placing similar things into categories.

Example: January, May and **October** can be classified as months.

Directions: Write a category name for each group of words.

1. accordion   clarinet   trumpet   _____

2. wasp   bumblebee   mosquito   _____

3. antique   elderly   prehistoric _____

4. chemist   astronomer   geologist   _____

5. nest   cocoon   burrow   _____

Directions: In each row, draw an **X** through the word that does not belong. Then write a sentence telling why it does not belong.

1. encyclopedia   atlas   novel   dictionary

_____

2. bass   otter   tuna   trout

_____

3. sister   grandmother   niece   uncle

_____

4. bark   beech   dogwood   spruce

_____

5. pebble   gravel   boulder   cement

_____

6. spaniel   Siamese   collie   Doberman

_____

Name: _____

Reading Skills: Classifying

Directions: In each row, draw an **X** through the word that does not belong. Then write a word that belongs.

1. monkey   lion   zebra   elephant   dog   _____

2. daisies   roses   violets   ferns   pansies   _____

3. paper   pear   pencil   eraser   stapler   _____

4. sister   cousin   father   aunt   friend   _____

5. hand   mouth   shirt   foot   elbow   _____

6. shy   cry   happy   angry   sad   _____

7. puppy   dog   kitten   cub   lamb   _____

8. red   blue   color   yellow   purple   _____

9. Earth   Jupiter   Saturn   Pluto   Sun   _____

10. sink   bed   desk   dresser   lamp   _____

Directions: Name each category above.

1. _____   6. _____

2. _____   7. _____

3. _____   8. _____

4. _____   9. _____

5. _____   10. _____

Name: _____

Reading Skills: Classifying

Directions: Write three things that would belong in each category below. The first one has been done for you.

1. mammals

   _____whale_____   _____horse_____   _____elephant_____

2. rainforest animals

   _____   _____   _____

3. capital cities

   _____   _____   _____

4. oceans

   _____   _____   _____

5. occupations

   _____   _____   _____

6. Native American tribes

   _____   _____   _____

7. wars

   _____   _____   _____

8. planets

   _____   _____   _____

9. track and field sports

   _____   _____   _____

10. famous Americans

   _____   _____   _____

Types of Analogies

An **analogy** shows similarities, or things in common, between a pair of words. The relationships between the words in analogies usually fall into these categories:

1. **Purpose**   One word in the pair shows the **purpose** of the other word (scissors: cut).

2. **Antonyms**   The words are **opposites** (light: dark).

3. **Part/whole**   One word in the pair is a **part**; the other is a **whole** (leg: body).

4. **Action/object**   One word in the pair involves an **action** with or to an **object** (fly: airplane).

5. **Association**   One word in the pair is what you think of or **associate** when you see the other (cow: milk).

6. **Object/location** One word in the pair tells the **location** of where the other word, an **object**, is found (car: garage).

7. **Cause/effect**   One word in the pair tells the **cause**; the other word shows the **effect** (practice: improvement).

8. **Synonyms**   The words are **synonyms** (small: tiny).

Directions: Write the relationship between the words in each pair. The first two have been done for you.

1. cow: farm   _____ object/location _____
2. toe: foot   _____ part/whole _____
3. watch: TV   _____
4. bank: money   _____
5. happy: unhappy   _____
6. listen: radio   _____
7. inning: ballgame   _____
8. knife: cut   _____
9. safe: dangerous   _____
10. carrots: soup   _____

Writing Analogies

Once you have determined the relationship between the words in the first pair, the next step is to find a similar relationship between another pair of words.

Examples:
   Scissors is to **cut** as **broom** is to **sweep**.
   Black is to **white** as **up** is to **down**.

Scissors cut. Brooms sweep. The first analogy shows the **purpose** of scissors and brooms. In the second example, up and down are **antonyms**, as are black and white.

Directions: Choose the correct word to complete each analogy. The first one has been done for you.

1. **Sky** is to **blue** as **grass** is to
   A. earth   B. green   C. lawn   D. yard   _____green_____

2. **Snow** is to **winter** as **rain** is to
   A. umbrella   B. wet   C. slicker   D. spring   _____

3. **Sun** is to **day** as **moon** is to
   A. dark   B. night   C. stars   D. blackness   _____

4. **5** is to **10** as **15** is to
   A. 50   B. 25   C. 30   D. 40   _____

5. **Collie** is to **dog** as **Siamese** is to
   A. pet   B. kitten   C. baby   D. cat   _____

6. **Letter** is to **word** as **note** is to
   A. tuba   B. music   C. instruments   D. singer   _____

7. **100** is to **10** as **1,000** is to
   A. 10   B. 200   C. 100   D. 10,000   _____

8. **Back** is to **rear** as **pit** is to
   A. peach   B. hole   C. dark   D. punishment   _____

Analogies of Purpose

Directions: Choose the correct word to complete each analogy of purpose. The first one has been done for you.

1. **Knife** is to **cut** as **copy machine** is to

   A. duplicate   B. paper   C. copies   D. office   __duplicate__

2. **Bicycle** is to **ride** as **glass** is to

   A. dishes   B. dinner   C. drink   D. break   _____

3. **Hat** is to **cover** as **eraser** is to

   A. chalkboard   B. pencil   C. mistake   D. erase   _____

4. **Mystery** is to **clue** as **door** is to

   A. house   B. key   C. window   D. open   _____

5. **Television** is to **see** as **CD** is to

   A. sound   B. hear   C. play   D. dance   _____

6. **Clock** is to **time** as **ruler** is to

   A. height   B. length   C. measure   D. inches   _____

7. **Fry** is to **pan** as **bake** is to

   A. cookies   B. dinner   C. oven   D. baker   _____

8. **Bowl** is to **fruit** as **wrapper** is to

   A. present   B. candy   C. paper   D. ribbon   _____

Name: _____

Antonym Analogies

Directions: Write antonyms for these words.

1. run: _____

2. start: _____

3. laugh: _____

4. dependent: _____

5. young: _____

6. North: _____

7. sink: _____

8. success: _____

9. combine: _____

10. laugh: _____

11. polluted: _____

12. leader: _____

13. fascinate: _____

14. man: _____

15. awake: _____

16. begin: _____

17. increase: _____

18. reverse: _____

19. enlarge: _____

20. East: _____

21. rural: _____

22. amateur: _____

23. patient: _____

24. rich: _____

25. empty: _____

26. fancy: _____

27. introduction: _____

28. modern: _____

Directions: Write two antonym analogies of your own.

29. _____

_____

30. _____

_____

Grade 6 - Comprehensive Curriculum

Part/Whole Analogies

Directions: Determine whether each analogy is whole to part or part to whole by studying the relationship between the first pair of words. Then choose the correct word to complete each analogy. The first one has been done for you.

1. **Shoestring** is to **shoe** as **brim** is to

   A. cup   B. shade   C. hat   D. scarf   _____hat_____

2. **Egg** is to **yolk** as **suit** is to

   A. clothes   B. shoes   C. business   D. jacket   _____

3. **Stanza** is to **poem** as **verse** is to

   A. rhyme   B. singing   C. song   D. music   _____

4. **Wave** is to **ocean** as **branch** is to

   A. stream   B. lawn   C. office   D. tree   _____

5. **Chicken** is to **farm** as **giraffe** is to

   A. animal   B. zoo   C. tall   D. stripes   _____

6. **Finger** is to **nail** as **leg** is to

   A. arm   B. torso   C. knee   D. walk   _____

7. **Player** is to **team** as **inch** is to

   A. worm   B. measure   C. foot   D. short   _____

8. **Peak** is to **mountain** as **crest** is to

   A. wave   B. ocean   C. beach   D. water   _____

Name: _____

Action/Object Analogies

Directions: Determine whether each analogy is action/object or object/action by studying the relationship between the first pair of words. Then choose the correct word to complete each analogy. The first one has been done for you.

1. **Mow** is to **grass** as **shear** is to

   A. cut   B. fleece   C. sheep   D. barber   _____sheep_____

2. **Rod** is to **fishing** as **gun** is to

   A. police   B. crime   C. shoot   D. hunting   _____

3. **Ship** is to **captain** as **airplane** is to

   A. fly   B. airport   C. pilot   D. passenger   _____

4. **Car** is to **mechanic** as **body** is to

   A. patient   B. doctor   C. torso   D. hospital   _____

5. **Cheat** is to **exam** as **swindle** is to

   A. criminal   B. business   C. crook   D. crime   _____

6. **Actor** is to **stage** as **surgeon** is to

   A. patient   B. hospital   C. operating room   D. knife   _____

7. **Ball** is to **throw** as **knife** is to

   A. cut   B. spoon   C. dinner   D. silverware   _____

8. **Lawyer** is to **trial** as **surgeon** is to

   A. patient   B. hospital   C. operation   D. operating room _____

Analogies of Association

Directions: Choose the correct word to complete each analogy. The first one has been done for you.

1. **Flowers** are to **spring** as **leaves** are to

   A. rakes   B. trees   C. fall   D. green   _____fall_____

2. **Ham** is to **eggs** as **butter** is to

   A. fat   B. toast   C. breakfast   D. spread   _____

3. **Bat** is to **swing** as **ball** is to

   A. throw   B. dance   C. base   D. soft   _____

4. **Chicken** is to **egg** as **cow** is to

   A. barn   B. calf   C. milk   D. beef   _____

5. **Bed** is to **sleep** as **chair** is to

   A. sit   B. couch   C. relax   D. table   _____

6. **Cube** is to **square** as **sphere** is to

   A. circle   B. triangle   C. hemisphere   D. spear   _____

7. **Kindness** is to **friend** as **cruelty** is to

   A. meanness   B. enemy   C. war   D. unkindness   _____

8. **Pumpkin** is to **pie** as **chocolate** is to

   A. cake   B. dark   C. taste   D. dessert   _____

Name: _____

Object/Location Analogies

Directions: Write a location word for each object.

1. shirt: _____

2. milk: _____

3. vase: _____

4. screwdriver: _____

5. cow: _____

6. chalkboard: _____

7. shower: _____

8. cucumbers: _____

9. silverware: _____

10. car: _____

11. pages: _____

12. bees: _____

13. money: _____

14. salt water: _____

15. dress: _____

16. ice cream: _____

17. table: _____

18. medicine: _____

19. dog: _____

20. basketball: _____

21. bed: _____

22. roses: _____

23. dishwasher: _____

24. toys: _____

25. cookies: _____

26. bird: _____

27. seashells: _____

28. asteroids: _____

Grade 6 - Comprehensive Curriculum

Name: _____

Cause/Effect Analogies

Directions: Determine whether the analogy is cause/effect or effect/cause by studying the relationship between the first pair of words. Then choose the correct word to complete each analogy. The first one has been done for you.

You caused this...and now look at the effect!

1. **Ashes** are to **flame** as **darkness** is to

   A. light   B. daylight   C. eclipse   D. sun   ____eclipse____

2. **Strong** is to **exercising** as **elected** is to

   A. office   B. senator   C. politician   D. campaigning   _____

3. **Fall** is to **pain** as **disobedience** is to

   A. punishment   B. morals   C. behavior   D. carelessness   _____

4. **Crying** is to **sorrow** as **smiling** is to

   A. teeth   B. mouth   C. joy   D. friends   _____

5. **Germ** is to **disease** as **war** is to

   A. soldiers   B. enemies   C. destruction   D. tanks   _____

6. **Distracting** is to **noise** as **soothing** is to

   A. balm   B. warmth   C. hugs   D. music   _____

7. **Food** is to **nutrition** as **light** is to

   A. vision   B. darkness   C. sunshine   D. bulb   _____

8. **Clouds** are to **rain** as **winds** are to

   A. springtime   B. hurricanes   C. clouds   D. March   _____

Name: _____

Synonym Analogies

Directions: Write synonyms for these words.

1. miniature: _____
2. wind: _____
3. picture: _____
4. quiet: _____
5. run: _____
6. cloth: _____
7. mean: _____
8. cup: _____
9. sweet: _____
10. difficult: _____
11. obey: _____
12. plenty: _____
13. scent: _____
14. sudden: _____

15. gigantic: _____
16. rain: _____
17. cabinet: _____
18. loud: _____
19. leap: _____
20. jeans: _____
21. kind: _____
22. dish: _____
23. feline: _____
24. simple: _____
25. beautiful: _____
26. scorch: _____
27. story: _____
28. thaw: _____

Directions: Write two synonym analogies of your own.

29. _____

_____

_____

30. _____

_____

_____

Name: _____

Reading Skills: Fact or Opinion?

A **fact** is information that can be proved. An **opinion** is information that tells how someone feels or what he/she thinks about something.

Directions: For each sentence, write **F** for fact or **O** for opinion. The first one has been done for you.

___F___ 1. Each of the countries in South America has its own capital.

_____ 2. All South Americans are good swimmers.

_____ 3. People like the climate in Peru better than in Brazil.

_____ 4. The continent of South America is almost completely surrounded by water.

_____ 5. The only connection with another continent is a narrow strip of land, called the Isthmus of Panama, which links it to North America.

_____ 6. The Andes Mountains run all the way down the western edge of the continent.

_____ 7. The Andes are the longest continuous mountain barrier in the world.

_____ 8. The Andes are the most beautiful mountain range.

_____ 9. The Amazon River is the second longest river in the world—about 4,000 miles long.

_____ 10. Half of the people in South America are Brazilians.

_____ 11. Life in Brazil is better than life in other South American countries.

_____ 12. Brazil is the best place for South Americans to live.

_____ 13. Cape Horn is at the southern tip of South America.

_____ 14. The largest land animal in South America is the tapir, which reaches a length of 6 to 8 feet.

Reading Skills: Fact or Opinion?

Directions: Read the paragraphs below. For each numbered sentence, write **F** for fact or **O** for opinion. Write the reason for your answer. The first one has been done for you.

(1) The two greatest poems in the history of the world are the *Iliad* and the *Odyssey*. (2) The *Iliad* is the story of the Trojan War; the *Odyssey* tells about the wanderings of the Greek hero Ulysses after the war. (3) These poems are so long that they each fill an entire book.

(4) The author of the poems, according to Greek legend, was a blind poet named Homer. (5) Almost nothing is known about Homer. (6) This indicates to me that it is possible that Homer never existed. (7) Maybe Homer existed but didn't write the *Iliad* and the *Odyssey*.

(8) Whether or not there was a Homer does not really matter. We have these wonderful poems, which are still being read more than 2,500 years after they were written.

1. __O__ Reason: This cannot be proven. People have different opinions about which are the greatest poems.

2. _____ Reason: _____

3. _____ Reason: _____

4. _____ Reason: _____

5. _____ Reason: _____

6. _____ Reason: _____

7. _____ Reason: _____

8. _____ Reason: _____

Chilies

Directions: Read about chilies. Find the one opinion in each passage and write it on the lines.

Chilies are hot or sweet peppers. They are part of the "nightshade" family of plants that also includes potatoes and tomatoes. Potatoes and tomatoes taste better than chilies, though.

Opinion: _____

_____

Chilies were originally grown in Central and South America. By the 15th century, Europeans were cooking with them and drying them to use as a spice. European dishes taste better now than they did before chilies were used in them.

Opinion: _____

_____

Although it is really a Mexican recipe, every intelligent American loves *chili con carne*. It is made with spicy meat, beans and chilies. Today, most Americans call that dish "chili."

Opinion: _____

_____

Some people think that all chilies are hot. Therefore, they never eat any of them. What a silly belief! There are many different kinds of red, yellow and green chilies. Even red chilies can be sweet.

Opinion: _____

_____

Carol's Country Restaurant

Directions: Write in the corresponding numbered blank below whether each numbered sentence gives a fact or an opinion.

(1) I have visited Carol's Country Restaurant seven times in the past 2 weeks. **(2)** The meals there are excellent. **(3)** They often feature country dishes such as meatloaf, ham with scalloped potatoes and fried chicken.

(4) Owner Carol Murphy makes wonderful vegetable soup that includes all home-grown vegetables. **(5)** It's simmered with egg noodles. **(6)** Another of my favorite dishes is Carol's chili. **(7)** I'm sure it is the spiciest chili this side of the Mississippi River. **(8)** Carol says she uses secret ingredients in all her dishes.

(9) Whether ordering a main dish or a dessert, you can't go wrong at Carol's. **(10)** Everything is superb.

(11) Carol's Country Restaurant is on Twig Street in Freeport. **(12)** Prices for main entrees range from $5.95 to $12.95.

1. _____
2. _____
3. _____
4. _____
5. _____
6. _____
7. _____
8. _____
9. _____
10. _____
11. _____
12. _____

CAROL'S COUNTRY RESTAURANT

TODAY'S SPECIAL

Carol's Chili

Carol

CHILI

Review

Directions: Write 5 sentences that are facts and 5 that are opinions.

Facts:

1. _____
_____

2. _____
_____

3. _____
_____

4. _____
_____

5. _____
_____

Opinions:

6. _____
_____

7. _____
_____

8. _____
_____

9. _____
_____

10. _____
_____

Reading Skills: Cause and Effect

A **cause** is the reason something happens. The **effect** is what happens as the result of the cause.

Directions: Read the paragraphs below. For each numbered sentence, circle the cause or causes and underline the effect or effects. The first one has been done for you.

(1) All living things in the ocean are endangered by humans polluting the water. Pollution occurs in several ways. One way is the dumping of certain waste materials, such as garbage and sewage, into the ocean. (2) The decaying bacteria that feed on the garbage use up much of the oxygen in the surrounding water, so other creatures in the area often don't get enough.

Other substances, such as radioactive waste material, can also cause pollution. These materials are often placed in the water in securely sealed containers. (3) But after years of being exposed to the ocean water, the containers may begin to leak.

Oil is another major source of concern. (4) Oil is spilled into the ocean when tankers run aground and sink or when oil wells in the ocean cannot be capped. (5) The oil covers the gills of fish and causes them to smother. (6) Diving birds get the oil on their wings and are unable to fly. (7) When they clean themselves, they are often poisoned by the oil.

Rivers also can contribute to the pollution of oceans. Many rivers receive the runoff water from farmlands. (8) Fertilizers used on the farms may be carried to the ocean, where they cause a great increase in the amount of certain plants. Too much of some plants can actually be poisonous to fish.

Worse yet are the pesticides carried to the ocean. These chemicals slowly build up in shellfish and other small animals. These animals then pass the pesticides on to the larger animals that feed on them. (9) The buildup of these chemicals in the animals can make them ill or cause their babies to be born dead or deformed.

Name: _____

Reading Skills: Cause and Effect

Directions: Read the following cause-and-effect statements. If you think the cause and effect are properly related, write **True**. If not, explain why not. The first one has been done for you.

1. The best way to make it rain is to wash your car.

   <u>It does not rain every time you wash your car.</u>

2. Getting a haircut really improved Randy's grades.

   _____

3. Michael got an "A" in geometry because he spent a lot of time studying.

   _____

4. Yesterday I broke a mirror, and today I slammed my thumb in the door.

   _____

5. Helen isn't allowed to go to the dance tonight because she broke her curfew last weekend.

   _____

6. Emily drank a big glass of orange juice and her headache went away.

   _____

7. The Johnsons had their tree cut down because it had Dutch elm disease.

   _____

8. We can't grow vegetables in our backyard because the rabbits keep eating them.

   _____

Review

Directions: Write **Fact** or **Opinion** to describe each sentence.

_____ 1. Hurricanes are also known as typhoons.

_____ 2. Hurricanes are the worst natural disasters.

_____ 3. All hurricanes begin over the ocean near the equator.

_____ 4. All people are concerned about pollution.

_____ 5. Pesticides should never be used.

_____ 6. Many colonists died due to lack of food and sickness.

_____ 7. Kites are the best gift to give a child.

_____ 8. The names of Columbus' three ships were the *Niña*, the *Pinta* and the *Santa Maria*.

Directions: If the sentence demonstrates a logical cause and effect relationship, write **Yes** on the line. If the sentence is illogical, write **No**.

_____ 1. I ate fish and got sick, so all fish will make me sick.

_____ 2. The farmer began practicing crop rotation, and his crop yield improved.

_____ 3. I know how to swim, so I cannot possibly drown.

_____ 4. While learning to ski, Jim broke his leg.

_____ 5. The river overflowed its banks and caused much damage.

_____ 6. The Cincinnati Reds won 100 games last year, so they probably will this year.

_____ 7. Because I started using a new toothpaste, I will make more friends.

Name: _____

Reading Skills: Personification

When an author gives an object or animal human characteristics, it is called **personification**.

Example: The dragon quickly <u>thought</u> out its next move in the attack on the village.

Thought is a human process and not associated with mythical creatures, therefore; the dragon is personified in that sentence.

Directions: In the following sentences, underline the personification.

1. The cave's gaping mouth led to internal passageways.

2. The tractor sprang to life with a turn of the key.

3. The lights blinked twice and then died.

4. Crops struggled to survive in the blistering heat, hoping for rainfall.

5. The engine of the car coughed and sputtered as if it wanted to breathe but couldn't.

6. The arrow flew through the air, eyeing its target.

7. Snowmen smile from the safety of their yards.

8. Four-year-old Stephanie's doll sipped tea delicately.

Directions: Write a sentence that personifies the following objects.

1. flower _____

2. stuffed animal _____

3. car _____

Reading Skills: Symbolism

Symbolism is the use of something to stand for (symbolize) something else.

Example:

The elderly woman held the pearl necklace in her wrinkled hand and thought back on her life. Many years had gone by since her husband had given her the necklace, as many years as there were pearls. Some of the pearls, she noticed, were darker than others, just as some years in her life had been darker than other years.

The pearl necklace symbolizes the life of the elderly woman. Each pearl stands for a year

in her life, and the necklace represents the many years that have passed.

_____

Directions: Write what is being symbolized in the paragraph on the lines below.

The refugees boarded the small ship with high hopes. They had to believe that their destiny was to find the New World and seek shelter there. A few dared to dream of the riches to be found. For them, the boat itself looked like a treasure chest waiting to be discovered.

_____

_____

_____

For 12-year-old Sam, the basketball court was the best place to be. In Sam's neighborhood, crime ran rampant, and it was the one safe place for kids like Sam to play. Sam spent most nights at the court, practicing lay-ups, jump shots and three-point shots. Sam worked hard because for him it wasn't just a sport, it was a golden key.

_____

_____

_____

Name: _____

Reading Skills: Idioms

An **idiom** is a phrase that says one thing but actually means something quite different.
Example: Now that's <u>a horse of a different color</u>!

Directions: Write the letter of the correct meaning for the bold words in each sentence. The first one has been done for you.

a. forgive and make up	**f.** pressed tightly together
b. fact kept secret for fear of disgrace	**g.** relatives and ancestors
c. something that dampens excitement	**h.** rudely ignored
d. get acquainted, become less formal	**i.** excessive paperwork
e. treated like royalty	**j.** people were gossiping

_g_ 1. There is a pirate and a president in our **family tree**.

_____ 2. The Johnsons went through a lot of **red tape** to adopt their baby.

_____ 3. Sophia gave me the **cold shoulder** when I tried to talk to her this morning.

_____ 4. The big homework assignment threw a **wet blanket** over my plans for an exciting weekend.

_____ 5. At a party, Judy likes to **break the ice** by having her guests play games.

_____ 6. **Tongues were wagging** when the principal called Chet into his office.

_____ 7. There were five people **sandwiched** into the back seat of the car.

_____ 8. She viewed her poor background as **a skeleton in her closet**.

_____ 9. Let's forget our past mistakes and **bury the hatchet**.

_____ 10. When the mayor came to visit our school, we **rolled out the red carpet**.

Name: _____

Reading Skills: Idioms

Directions: Use the following idioms in a sentence of your own. Then tell what the phrase means in your own words.

1. raining cats and dogs

a. _____

b. _____

2. going to the dogs

a. _____

b. _____

3. barking up the wrong tree

a. _____

b. _____

4. hit the nail on the head

a. _____

b. _____

5. went out on a limb

a. _____

b. _____

6. all in the same boat

a. _____

b. _____

7. keep up with the Joneses

a. _____

b. _____

Name: _____

Reading Skills: Denotations and Connotations

Sometimes two words can be similar, yet you would not substitute one for the other because they each suggest different feelings.

Denotation means the literal or dictionary definition of a word.

Connotation is the meaning of a word including all the emotions associated with it.

For example, **job** and **chore** are synonyms, but because of their connotations, anyone would choose to do a job instead of a chore.

Directions: Circle the word in each group with the most positive connotation.

Example:

task	old	retort
(job)	mature	respond
chore	antiquated	react

remainder	haughty	conversational
remnants	cheeky	wordy
residue	proud	talkative

excessively	relaxed	shack
grossly	lazy	hovel
abundantly	inactive	hut

curious	swift	scamp
prying	hasty	rascal
nosy	speedy	hoodlum

Reading Skills: Denotations and Connotations

Directions: Replace the bold word in each sentence with a word that has a more positive connotation.

Example:

shut
He ~~slammed~~ the door when he left.

The dog's energy was **uncontrollable**.

We hoped to settle our **fight** peacefully.

The mother **reprimanded** the children when people began to look at them.

The children **gossiped** at lunchtime.

The girl **scribbled** a hasty note to leave behind.

Our conversation ended **abruptly** when the phone rang.

The principal was a **severe** man.

The boy **snatched** the toy from his baby brother.

The couple **rejected** their offer of help.

Dad reminded me to clean my **disastrous** room.

Similes and Metaphors

A **simile** compares two unlike things using the word **like** or **as**.

Example: The fog was **like** a blanket around us. The fog was **as** thick **as** a blanket.

A **metaphor** compares two unlike things without using the word **like** or **as**.

Example: The fog was a blanket around us.

"The fog was thick," is not a simile or a metaphor. **Thick** is an adjective. Similes and metaphors compare two unlike things that are both nouns.

Directions: Underline the two things being compared in each sentence. Then write **S** for simile or **M** for metaphor on the lines.

_____ 1. The florist's shop was a summer garden.

_____ 2. The towels were as rough as sandpaper.

_____ 3. The survey was a fountain of information.

_____ 4. Her courtesy was as welcome as a cool breeze on a hot day.

_____ 5. The room was like a furnace.

Directions: Use similes to complete these sentences.

6. The tornado was as dark as _____

7. His voice was like _____

8. The emergency was as unexpected as _____

9. The kittens were like _____

Directions: Use metaphors to complete these sentences.

10. To me, research was _____

11. The flourishing plants were _____

12. My observation at the hospital was _____

Name: _____

Vocabulary Building: Similes

A **simile** is a figure of speech comparing two things using **like** or **as**.

Example: The child was as quiet as a mouse.

Directions: Read the following paragraph. Underline the similes.

The kittens were born on a morning as cold as ice. Although it was late spring, the weather hadn't quite warmed up. There were five kittens in the litter, each quite different from its siblings. The oldest was black as deepest night. There was a calico that looked like Grandma's old quilt. One was as orange as a fall pumpkin, and another was orange and white. The runt was a black and gray tiger. She was as little as a baseball and as quick as lightning to fight for food. The kittens will soon become accepted by the other animals as members of the farm.

Directions: Using the following words, create similes of your own.

Example: piano—The piano keys tinkled like a light rain on a tin roof.

1. fire _____

_____

2. thunderstorm _____

_____

3. ocean _____

_____

4. night _____

_____

5. rainforest _____

_____

6. giraffe _____

_____

Name: _____

Vocabulary Building: Metaphors

A **metaphor** is a figure of speech that directly compares one thing with another.

Example: As it set, the sun was a glowing orange ball of fire.

The sun is being compared to a glowing orange ball of fire.

<u>sun</u>   <u>glowing orange ball of fire</u>

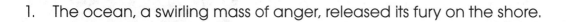

Directions: Underline the metaphor in each sentence.
Then write the two things that are being compared on the lines.

1. The ocean, a swirling mass of anger, released its fury on the shore.

   _____   _____

2. He was a top spinning out of control.

   _____   _____

3. The heat covered the crowd, a blanket smothering them all.

   _____   _____

4. I fed my dog a steak, and it was a banquet for her senses.

   _____   _____

5. The flowers in the garden were a stained glass window.

   _____   _____

Name: _____

Vocabulary Building: Metaphors and Similes

Directions: Underline the metaphors in the following sentences. Then rewrite each sentence using a simile.

1. She is a playful child, a real kitten!

   _____

2. Life today is a merry-go-round.

   _____

3. His emotions were waves washing over him.

   _____

4. His childhood was an image in a rearview mirror.

   _____

Directions: Write the meanings of the following sentences.

1. His mind was as changeable as spring weather.

   _____

2. His demand was like a clap of thunder.

   _____

3. There was joy written on the children's faces on Christmas morning.

   _____

Grade 6 - Comprehensive Curriculum

Name: _____

Reading Skills: Generalizations

A **generalization** is a statement or rule that applies to many situations or examples.

Example: All children get into trouble at one time or another.

Directions: Read each paragraph, then circle the generalization that best describes the information given.

Although many people think of reptiles as slimy, snakes and other reptiles are covered with scales that are dry to the touch. Scales are outgrowths of the animal's skin. Although in some species they are nearly invisible, in most they form a tile-like covering. The turtle's shell is made up of hardened scales that are fused together. The crocodile has a tough but more flexible covering.

Every reptile has scales.

The scales of all reptiles are alike.

There are many different kinds of scales.

The reptile's scales help to protect it from its enemies and conserve moisture in its body. Some kinds of lizards have fan-shaped scales that they can raise up to scare away other animals. The scales also can be used to court a mate. A reptile called a gecko can hang from a ceiling because of specialized scales on its feet. Some desert lizards have other kinds of scales on their feet that allow them to run over the loose sand.

Scales have many functions.

Scales scare away other animals.

Scales help reptiles adapt to their environments.

A snake will periodically shed its skin, leaving behind a thin impression of its body—scales and all. A lizard sheds its skin too, but it tears off in smaller pieces rather than in one big piece. Before a snake begins this process, which is called molting, its eyes cloud over. The snake will go into hiding until they clear. When it comes out again, it brushes against rough surfaces to pull off the old skin.

Snakes go into hiding before they molt.

Reptiles periodically shed their skin.

A lizard's skin molts in smaller pieces.

Reading Skills: Generalizations

Directions: Identify which statements below are generalizations and which are specific. Write **G** for generalization and **S** for specific.

_____ 1. We want to have lots of good food for the party.

_____ 2. Jenna gave me three pink shirts and two pairs of jeans.

_____ 3. Americans are generous and friendly.

_____ 4. There are ten more female teachers than male teachers at our school.

_____ 5. She wants me to buy watermelon at the grocery store.

_____ 6. She will never believe anything I say.

_____ 7. I got poison ivy because I didn't watch out for the foliage on our hike.

_____ 8. My mom is the best mom in the world.

_____ 9. I get depressed every time the weather turns bad.

_____ 10. The team is so good because they work out and practice every day.

_____ 11. Cats are so bad-tempered.

_____ 12. My dog has a good temperment because he's had lots of training.

_____ 13. Our football team is the best this county has ever seen.

_____ 14. I love the feel of rain on my skin, because it's cool.

_____ 15. That classroom is always out of control.

Name: _____

Reading Skills: Skimming and Scanning

Skimming is reading quickly to get a general idea of what a reading selection is about. When skimming, look for headings and key words to give you an overall idea of what you are reading.

Scanning is looking for certain words to find facts or answer questions. When scanning, read or think of questions first.

Directions: Scan the paragraphs below to find the answers to the questions. Then look for specific words that will help you locate the answers. For example, in the second question, scan for the word **smallest**.

There are many different units to measure time. Probably the smallest unit that you use is the second, and the longest unit is the year. While 100 years seems like a very long time to us, in the history of the Earth, it is a smaller amount of time than one second is in a person's entire lifetime.

To describe the history of the Earth, scientists use geologic time. Even a million years is a fairly short period in geologic time. Much of the history of our Earth can only be speculated by scientists before it was written down. Some scientists believe that our planet is about 4,600 million years old. Since a thousand million is a billion, the Earth is believed to be 4.6 billion years old.

1. What kind of time is used to describe the history of the Earth?

   _____

2. For the average person, what is the smallest unit of time used?

   _____

3. In millions of years, how old do some scientists believe the Earth is?

   _____

4. How would you express that in billions of years?

   _____

The Author's Purpose

Authors write to entertain, inform or persuade. To entertain means to hold the attention of or to amuse someone. A fiction book about outer space entertains its reader, as does a joke book.

To inform means to give factual information. A cookbook informs the reader of new recipes. A newspaper tells what is happening in the world.

To persuade people means to convince them. Newspaper editorial writers try to persuade readers to accept their opinions. Doctors write health columns to persuade readers to eat nutritious foods.

Directions: Read each of the passages below. Tell whether they entertain, inform or persuade. (They may do more than one.) Give the reasons why.

George Washington was born in a brick house near the Potomac River in Virginia on Feb. 11, 1732. When he was 11 years old, George went to live with his half-brother, Lawrence, at Mount Vernon.

Author's Purpose: _____

Reason: _____

When George Washington was a child, he always measured and counted things. Maybe that is why he became a surveyor when he grew up. Surveyors like to measure and count things, too.

Author's Purpose: _____

Reason: _____

George Washington was the best president America has ever had. He led a new nation to independence. He made all the states feel as if they were part of the United States. All presidents should be as involved with the country as George Washington was.

Author's Purpose: _____

Reason: _____

_____

Name: _____

Llamas

Directions: Read each paragraph. Tell whether it informs, entertains or persuades. One paragraph does more than one. Then write your reason on the line below.

A llama (LAH'MAH) is a South American animal that is related to the camel. It is raised for its wool. Also, it can carry heavy loads. Some people who live near mountains in the United States train llamas to go on mountain trips. Llamas are sure-footed because they have two long toes and toenails.

Author's Purpose: _____

Reason: _____

Llamas are the best animals to have if you're planning to backpack in the mountains. They can climb easily and carry your supplies. No one should ever go for a long hiking trip in the mountains without a llama.

Author's Purpose: _____

Reason: _____

Llamas can be stubborn animals. Sometimes they suddenly stop walking for no reason. People have to push them to get them moving again. Stubborn llamas can be frustrating when hiking up a steep mountain.

Author's Purpose: _____

Reason: _____

Greg is an 11-year-old boy who raises llamas to climb mountains. One of his llamas is named Dallas. Although there are special saddles for llamas, Greg likes to ride bareback.

Author's Purpose: _____

Reason: _____

_____

Now use a separate sheet of paper to inform readers about llamas.

Name: _____

Roller Coasters

Directions: Read each paragraph and determine the author's purpose. Then write down your reason on the line below.

Roller coaster rides are thrilling. The cars chug up the hills and then fly down them. People scream and laugh. They clutch their seats and sometimes raise their arms above their heads.

Author's Purpose: _____

Reason: _____

The first roller coasters were giant slides made of ice in Russia. That was more than 300 years ago! The slides were about 70 feet high, and people had to climb steep ladders to reach their tops. Riders got into carts and slid down very fast. Then they climbed the ladders again. Early roller coasters were more work than fun.

Author's Purpose: _____

Reason: _____

The first roller coaster in America was built in 1884. It cost only a nickel to ride the "Switchback Gravity Pleasure Railway" at Coney Island in New York. Roller coasters did not become very popular until the late 1920s.

Author's Purpose: _____

Reason: _____

Have you ever ridden a giant roller coaster? Some of the most famous ones in the world include the "Mamba" at Worlds of Fun in Kansas City, Missouri; the "Ultra Twister" at Six Flags Astroworld in Houston, Texas; and the "Magnum" at Cedar Point in Sandusky, Ohio. Roller coasters are fun because they have thrilling twists and turns. Some go very high and some turn upside down. Everyone should go on a roller coaster at least once in his or her life.

Author's Purpose: _____

Reason: _____

_____

Now use a separate sheet of paper to persuade people to ride roller coasters.

Review

Directions: Follow the instructions for each section.

1. Write a paragraph about a sport in which you are informing your audience.

_____

_____

_____

_____

_____

2. Write a paragraph about the circus in which you are entertaining your audience.

_____

_____

_____

_____

_____

3. Write a paragraph about the desire for a later bedtime in which you are persuading your audience.

_____

_____

_____

_____

_____

_____

Multiple Choice

Multiple choice questions are frequently asked on tests. Such questions include three or four possible answers. When answering a multiple choice question, first read the question carefully. Then read all the answers that are offered. If you do not know the correct answer, eliminate some of the ones you know are wrong until you have only one left. Remember these points when taking multiple choice tests:

1. Answers that contain phrases such as **all people**, **no one** or **everybody** are probably not correct. For example, a statement such as "all children like candy" is probably not correct because it allows for no exceptions. If there is one child who does not like candy, the statement is not correct. However, if you know that more than one answer is correct and the last choice in the group is "all of the above," then that phrase is probably the correct answer.

2. Answers that contain words you have never seen before probably are not correct. Teachers don't expect you to know material you haven't studied.

3. Answers that are silly usually aren't correct.

4. When two of the answers provided look nearly the same, one of them is probably correct.

5. Always check your answers if there is time.

Directions: Answer the questions about multiple choice tests.

1. The first thing you should do during a multiple choice test is _____

   _____ .

2. When you are reading the possible answers to a multiple choice question and you know the first one is right, should you immediately mark it without reading the

   other answers? _____

   Why or why not? _____

3. Write three phrases that might tell you that an answer is probably not correct.

   _____

   _____

   _____

Name: _____

True/False

True/false tests include several statements. You must read each one carefully to determine if it is right or wrong. Remember these tips:

1. Watch for one word in the sentence that can change the statement's meaning from true to false or vice versa.

2. Words such as **all**, **none**, **everybody** or **nobody** should alert you that the answer may be false. Using these words means that there are no exceptions.

3. There are usually more true answers on a test than false ones. Therefore, if you have to guess an answer, you have a better chance of answering right by marking it "true."

4. Always check your answers if there is time.

Directions: Answer the questions about true/false tests.

1. List four words that can alert you that a question is false.

   _____

2. One word in a sentence can

   _____ .

3. If you must guess an answer, is it wiser to guess true or false? _____

4. True/false tests are made up of several _____ .

5. Can you do well on a true/false test by only skimming each statement? _____

6. If the word "everybody" is in the statement, is the answer probably true or false? _____

7. When the word "all" appears in the statement, is the answer probably true or false? _____

8. What should you do last when taking a true/false test?

   _____

Fill-In-the-Blank

Fill-in-the-blank tests are more difficult than true/false or multiple choice tests. However, there may be clues in each sentence that help determine the answer. Look at this example:

The _____ of the United States serves a _____ -year term.

Can you tell that the first blank needs a person? (The answer is "president.") The second blank needs a number because it refers to years. ("Four" is the answer.) Think about these other tips for taking fill-in-the-blank tests:

1. Always plan your time wisely. Don't waste too much time on one question. Check the clock or your watch periodically when taking a test.
2. First read through the entire test. Then go back to the beginning and answer the questions that you know. Put a small mark beside the questions you are not sure about.
3. Go back to the questions you were not sure of or that you didn't know. Carefully read each one. Think about possible answers. If you think it could be more than one answer, try to eliminate some of the possible answers.
4. Save the most difficult questions to answer last. Don't waste time worrying if you don't know the answer to a question.
5. Sometimes you should guess at an answer because it may be right. There are some tests, though, that deduct points if your answer is wrong, but not if it is left blank. Make sure you know how the test will be scored.
6. Review your test. Make sure you have correctly read the directions and each question. Check your answers.

Directions: Answer the questions about fill-in-the-blank tests.

1. Fill-in-the-blank tests may have _____ in each sentence that help you figure out the answer.

2. Always plan your _____ wisely when taking a test.

3. Should you try to answer a question as soon as you read it?_____

4. Should you answer the hard or easy questions first? _____

5. If you are not sure of a question, you should _____ beside it.

Name: _____

Matching

Matching tests have two columns of information. A word
or fact from one column matches information in the
other. Read these tips to help with matching tests:

A
B
C
D

1. Look at one question at a time. Start with the first word
   or phrase in one of the columns. Then look at the
   possible answers in the other column until you find
   the correct one. Then go to the next word or phrase
   in the first column. If you don't know the answer to
   one question, skip it and go back to it later.

2. If there are several words in one column and
   several definitions in the other column, it is often
   easier to read the definition first and then find the
   word that goes with it.

3. Carefully read the directions. Sometimes one column on a matching test is longer than
   the other. Find out if there is one answer that won't be used or if an answer in the
   opposite column can be used twice.

4. Check your answers if there is time.

Directions: Answer the questions about matching tests.

1. Matching tests have how many columns of information? _____

2. If one column has words in it and the other column has definitions in it, which one

   should you look at first to make the test easier? _____

3. To eliminate confusion, you should look at _____ question at a

   time.

4. Do the columns on a matching test always have the same number of things

   in them? _____

5. Are there ever items left unmatched on a matching test? _____

6. Does it matter if you look at the right or left column of a matching test first? _____

Essays

Essay questions give you a chance to demonstrate what you have learned. They also provide the opportunity to express your opinion. Although many students think essay questions are the most difficult, they can be the most fun. Remember these tips when writing the answer to an essay question:

1. Think about the answer before you write it. Take time to organize your thoughts so that you can better express yourself.
2. Write a few notes or an outline on a piece of scrap paper or on the back of the test. This helps remind you what you want to write.
3. State your answer clearly. Don't forget to use complete sentences.
4. Review the answer before time runs out. Sometimes words are left out. It doesn't take much time to read through your essay to make sure it says what you want it to say.

Directions: Use these essay-writing tips to answer the following question in the space provided.

What is your favorite type of test? Give several reasons why.

_____

_____

_____

_____

_____

_____

_____

_____

_____

Review

Directions: Complete each question about tests.

1. Four steps for writing an answer for an essay test include:

   1) _____

   2) _____

   3) _____

   4) _____

2. In a matching test, it is sometimes easier to read the _____ and then match it with a word from the opposite column.

3. One column on a _____ may be longer than the other.

4. Tests that require you to fill in the blanks may provide _____ in each statement.

5. Always _____ answers if there is time.

6. Certain words such as **none** and **all** should alert you that an answer may be _____ .

7. There are usually, but not always, more _____ statements on a true/false test.

8. If **everybody** or **everything** is used in one of the answers for a _____ , it is likely that that answer is not right.

9. If two possible answers for a multiple-choice question sound nearly the _____ , one of them is probably correct.

10. If two answers to a multiple choice question appear to be correct, the answer could be one that says _____ .

Comprehension: Fun With Photography

The word "photography" means "writing with light." "Photo" is from the Greek word "photos," which means "light." "Graphy" is from the Greek word "graphic," which means "writing." Cameras don't literally write pictures, of course. Instead, they imprint an image onto a piece of film.

Even the most sophisticated camera is basically a box with a piece of light-sensitive film inside. The box has a hole at the opposite end from the film. The light enters the box through the hole—the camera's lens—and shines on the surface of the film to create a picture. The picture that's created on the film is the image the camera's lens is pointed toward.

A lens is a circle of glass that is thinner at the edges and thicker in the center. The outer edges of the lens collect the light rays and draw them together at the center of the lens.

The shutter helps control the amount of light that enters the lens. Too much light will make the picture too light. Too little light will result in a dark picture. Electronic flash—either built into the camera or attached to the top of it—provides light when needed.

Cameras with automatic electronic flashes provide the additional light automatically. Electronic flashes—or simply "flashes," as they are often called—require batteries. If your flash quits working, a dead battery is probably the cause.

Directions: Answer these questions about photography.

1. From what language is the word "photography" derived? _____

2. Where is the camera lens thickest? _____

3. What do the outer edges of the lens do? _____

_____

4. When is a flash needed? _____

_____

5. What does the shutter do? _____

_____

_____

_____

Comprehension: Photography Terms

Like other good professionals, photographers make their craft look easy. Their skill—like that of the graceful ice skater—comes from years of practice. Where skaters develop a sense of balance, photographers develop an "eye" for pictures. They can make important technical decisions about photographing, or "shooting," a particular scene in the twinkling of an eye.

It's interesting to know some of the technical language that professional photographers use. "Angle of view" refers to the angle from which a photograph is taken. "Depth of field" is the distance between the nearest point and the farthest point that is in focus in a photo.

"Filling the frame" refers to the amount of space the object being photographed takes up in the picture. A close-up picture of a dog, flower or person would fill the frame. A far-away picture would not.

"ASA" refers to the speed of different types of films. "Speed" means the film's sensitivity to light. The letters **ASA** stand for the American Standards Association. Film manufacturers give their films ratings of 200ASA, 400ASA, and so on to indicate film speed. The higher the number on the film, the higher its sensitivity to light, and the faster its speed. The faster its speed, the better it will be at clearly capturing sports images and other action shots.

Directions: Answer these question about photography terms.

1. Name another term for photographing. _____

2. This is the distance between the nearest point and the farthest point that is in focus in a photo.

   _____

3. This refers to the speed of different types of film. _____

4. A close-up picture of someone's face would

   ☐ provide depth of field.   ☐ create an ASA.   ☐ fill the frame.

5. To photograph a swimming child, which film speed is better?

   ☐ 200ASA   ☐ 400ASA

101

Comprehension: Photographing Animals

Animals are a favorite subject of many young photographers. Cats, dogs, hamsters and other pets top the list, followed by zoo animals and the occasional lizard.

Because it's hard to get them to sit still and "perform on command," some professional photographers refuse to photograph pets. There are ways around the problem of short attention spans, however.

One way to get an appealing portrait of a cat or dog is to hold a biscuit or treat above the camera. The animal's longing look toward the food will be captured by the camera as a soulful gaze. Because it's above the camera—out of the camera's range—the treat won't appear in the picture. When you show the picture to your friends afterwards, they will be impressed by your pet's loving expression.

If you are using fast film, you can take some good, quick shots of a pet by simply snapping a picture right after calling its name. You'll get a different expression from your pet using this technique. Depending on your pet's disposition, the picture will capture an inquisitive expression or possibly a look of annoyance, especially if you've awakened Rover from a nap!

Taking pictures of zoo animals requires a little more patience. After all, you can't wake up a lion! You may have to wait for a while until the animal does something interesting or moves into a position for you to get a good shot. When photographing zoo animals, don't get too close to the cages, and never tap on the glass or throw things between the bars of a cage! Concentrate on shooting some good pictures, and always respect the animals you are photographing.

Directions: Answer these questions about photographing animals.

1. Why do some professionals dislike photographing animals? _____

_____

2. What speed of film should you use to photograph quick-moving pets? _____

3. To capture a pet's loving expression, hold this out of camera range. _____

4. Compared to taking pictures of pets, what does photographing zoo animals require?

_____

_____

Generalization: Taking Pictures

A **generalization** is a statement that applies to many different situations.

Directions: Read each passage and circle the valid generalization.

1. Most people can quickly be taught to use a simple camera. However, it takes time, talent and a good eye to learn to take professional quality photographs. Patience is another quality that good photographers must possess. Those who photograph nature often will wait hours to get just the right light or shadow in their pictures.

   a. Anyone can learn to use a camera.

   b. Any patient person can become a good photographer.

   c. Good photographers have a good eye for pictures.

2. Photographers such as Diane Arbus, who photograph strange or odd people, also must wait for just the right picture. Many "people photographers" stake out a busy city sidewalk and study faces in the crowd. Then they must leap up quickly and ask to take a picture or sneakily take one without being observed. Either way, it's not an easy task!

   a. Staking out a busy sidewalk is a boring task.

   b. "People photographers" must be patient people and good observers.

   c. Sneak photography is not a nice thing to do to strangers.

3. Whether the subject is nature or humans, many photographers insist that dawn is the best time to take pictures. The light is clear at this early hour, and mist may still be in the air. The mist gives these early morning photos a haunting, "other world" quality that is very appealing.

   a. Morning mist gives an unusual quality to most outdoor photographs.

   b. Photographers all agree that dawn is the best time to take pictures.

   c. Misty light is always important in taking pictures.

Generalization: Camera Care

Directions: Read each passage and circle the valid generalization.

1. Professional photographers know it's important to keep their cameras clean and in good working order. Amateur photographers should make sure theirs are, too. However, to take good care of your camera, you must first understand the equipment. Camera shop owners say at least half the "defective" cameras people bring in simply need to have the battery changed!

   a. Cameras are delicate and require constant care so they will work properly.

   b. Many problems amateurs have are caused by lack of familiarity with their equipment.

   c. Amateur photographers don't know how their cameras work.

2. Once a year, some people take their cameras to a shop to be cleaned. Most never have them cleaned at all. Those who know how can clean their cameras themselves. To avoid scratching the lens, they should use the special cloths and tissues professionals rely on. Amateurs are warned never to loosen screws, bolts or nuts inside the camera.

   a. The majority of amateur photographers never bother to have their cameras cleaned.

   b. Cleaning a camera can be tricky and should be left to professionals.

   c. It's hard to find the special cleaning cloths professionals use.

3. Another simple tip from professionals is to make sure your camera works before you take it on vacation. They suggest taking an entire roll of film and having it developed before your trip. That way, if necessary, you'll have time to have the lens cleaned or other repairs made.

   a. Check out your camera before you travel to make sure it's in good working order.

   b. Vacation pictures are often disappointing because the camera needs to be repaired.

   c. Take at least one roll of film along on every vacation.

Generalization: Using a Darkroom

The room where photographs are developed is called a "darkroom." Can you guess why? The room must be dark so that light does not get on the film as it is being developed. Specially colored lights allow photographers to see without damaging the film. Because of the darkness and the chemicals used in the developing process, it's important to follow certain darkroom safety procedures.

To avoid shocks while in the darkroom, never touch light switches with wet hands. To avoid touching chemicals, use tongs to transfer prints from one chemical solution to another. When finished with the chemicals, put them back in their bottles. Never leave chemicals out in trays once the developing process is complete.

To avoid skin irritation from chemicals, wipe down all countertops and surfaces when you are finished. Another sensible precaution—make sure you have everything you need before exposing the film to begin the developing process. Any light that enters the darkroom can ruin the pictures being developed.

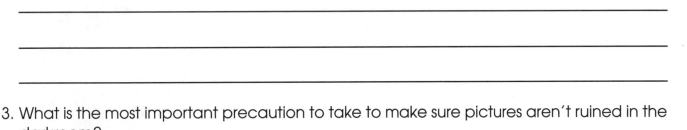

Directions: Answer these questions about using a darkroom.

1. Which generalization is correct?

   a. Developing pictures is a time-consuming and difficult process.

   b. It's dangerous to develop pictures in a darkroom.

   c. Sensible safety procedures are important for darkroom work.

2. Write directions for working with photography chemicals. _____

   _____

   _____

   _____

3. What is the most important precaution to take to make sure pictures aren't ruined in the darkroom?

   _____

   _____

   _____

Review

Directions: Circle the missing word for each sentence.

1. The Greek word _____ means writing.

   a. photos

   b. amateur

   c. graphic

2. The distance between the nearest point and the farthest point in a photo is called the _____.

   a. graphic

   b. shooting

   c. depth of field

3. _____ refers to the angle from which a photograph is taken.

   a. Photos

   b. Angle of view

   c. Lens

4. The _____ of the film is its sensitivity to light.

   a. tripod

   b. amateur

   c. speed

5. The speed of different types of film is called _____.

   a. professional

   b. amateur

   c. ASA

6. The _____ of the camera collects the light rays and draws them together at the center.

   a. shutter

   b. lens

   c. ASA

7. Taking a picture is often referred to as _____.

   a. shooting

   b. graphic

   c. speed

Main Idea/Recalling Details: Kites

Kites are a familiar sight on breezy fall days. They come in a great variety of sizes, colors and designs. It is not known who invented kites, but kites have been flown since the beginning of recorded history. While today children and adults use them for recreation, throughout history kites have had other uses.

In the United States, kites have been used in weather and other scientific research experiments. Before airplanes and weather balloons, the National Weather Service had kites carry weather instruments as high as 4 miles above the earth. In addition, the United States military used kites for observing the enemy and sending messages between troops.

In other countries, kites had cultural and religious importance. The ancient Chinese flew kites over their homes to drive out evil spirits. The Chinese still enjoy kites so much that one day each year they celebrate Kites' Day.

On some Pacific islands, kites were thought to have spiritual qualities. They were believed to symbolize both sides of nature—life and death. On some Polynesian islands, kites were used as protection against evil. These kites were often shaped like birds and used as soaring messengers to the heavens. In Hawaii, kites were also used to establish land ownership. A kite was released in the air, and a claim was given for the area where it came down.

Directions: Answer these questions about kites.

1. The main idea is:

    ☐ Kites come in a great variety of sizes, color and designs.

    ☐ While today kites are used for recreation, throughout history they have had other uses.

2. Besides recreation, name two ways kites have been used in the United States.

    1) _____

    2) _____

3. What country celebrates a holiday called Kites' Day? _____

4. How did Hawaiians use kites to decide land ownership? _____

    _____

Comprehension: Aerodynamics

Kites are able to fly because of the principle of aerodynamics. This big word simply means the study of forces that are put into action by moving air. Three main forces work to keep a heavier-than-air kite flying—lift, gravity and drag.

This is how it works: The flying lines, or strings, are attached to the kite to hold it at a slant. The wind pushes against the underside of the kite. At the same time, the wind rushes around the edges of the kite and "drags" some of the air from the upper side. This creates a partial vacuum there. The push of the air underneath is greater than the push of the air from the top, so the kite is held in the air. An airplane is held in the air in much the same way, except that it must keep moving rapidly to make the pressure above and below its wings different. The wind does this for the kite. In a steady airstream, a kite doesn't move backward or forward. It seems to be unaffected by gravity. This is possible because the lifting force of the wind overcomes the downward force of gravity.

If you have ever ridden a bicycle into a strong wind, you may have felt some of the forces of aerodynamics. If you held your hand out to your side, you could feel the air stream flowing around your hand. With your fingers pointed into the wind and your hand held level, there is little lift or drag. But if you raised your fingers slightly, the wind lifted your hand upwards. Raising your hand higher increases the drag and decreases the lift. Your hand is pushed downward. A kite flying in the sky is subject to these same forces.

Directions: Answer these questions about aerodynamics.

1. What is aerodynamics? _____

   _____

2. What three forces are at work to hold a kite in the air?

   1) _____ 2) _____ 3) _____

3. An airplane is held in the air in much the same way, except that it must keep moving rapidly to keep the air above and below its wings different.

   True   False

Comprehension: Getting Your Kite to Fly

There are some basic things to know about kite flying that can help you enjoy the sport more. Here are a few of the most important ones.

First, if you have ever seen someone flying a kite in a movie, you probably saw him or her get the kite off the ground by running into the wind. However, this is not the way to launch a kite. Most beginners will find a "high-start" launch to be the easiest. For a high-start launch, have a friend stand about 100 feet away, facing into the wind. Your friend should face you and hold the kite gently. Place some tension on the flying line by pulling gently on it. With a steady breeze behind you, tug gently on the line, and the kite will rise. If your kite begins to dive, don't panic or pull on the line. Dropping the reel will cause it to spin out of control and could cause someone to be hurt. Simply let the line go slack. This usually will right the kite in midair.

For a kite that is pulling hard away from you, have a friend stand behind you and take up the slack line as you bring it in. Hand over hand, pull down the kite. It is very important to have gloves on to do this, or you may burn or cut your hands. It is recommended that you always wear gloves while kite flying.

When two kite lines get crossed, pulling may cause enough friction to cut one or both of the lines. Instead of pulling, both fliers should walk toward one another until their lines uncross as they pass.

Directions: Circle **True** or **False** for these statements about kite flying.

1. To launch a kite, run into the wind holding the kite behind you.   True   False

2. In a high-start launch, a friend stands about 100 feet away from you, holding the kite.   True   False

3. If your kite begins to dive from the sky, immediately drop the reel.   True   False

4. It is recommended that you always wear gloves when kite flying.   True   False

Recalling Details: Kite Safety Rules

Because kite flying is a relaxed, easy-going sport, it is easy to have the mistaken belief that there are no dangers involved. However, like any sport, kite flying must be approached with care. Here are some important safety rules you should always follow while kite flying:

- **Don't** fly a kite in wet or stormy weather or use wet flying line.
- **Don't** fly a kite near electrical power lines, transmission towers or antennae. If your kite does get caught in one of these, walk away and leave it! If you must get the kite back, contact your local electric company.
- **Don't** use wire for flying line.
- **Don't** use metal for any part of the kite.
- **Don't** fly a kite near a street or in crowded areas.
- **Don't** fly a kite in a field or other area that has rocks or other objects you could trip over.
- **Don't** walk backwards without looking behind you.
- **Don't** fly a kite around trees. (If your kite does happen to get caught in a tree, let the line go slack. Sometimes the wind can work it free.)
- **Don't** fly a kite using unfamiliar equipment. A reel spinning out of control can be quite dangerous.
- **Don't** fly a kite near an airport.
- **Don't** fly a very large kite without proper guidance.
- **Do** wear protective gloves to avoid burns on your hands from rapidly unwinding line.
- **Do** use flying line that has been tested for the type and size of kite you are using.

Directions: Answer these questions about kite safety.

1. List three things you should never fly a kite around.

   1) _____   2) _____   3) _____

2. What should you do if your kite gets caught in a tree? _____

   _____

3. What material should you never use in any part of your kite? _____

Recalling Details: Aviation Pioneer

Lawrence Hargrave was born in Middlesex, England, in 1850. When he was a teenager, his family moved to Australia. There Hargrave went to work for the Australian Stream and Navigation Company, where he spent 5 years gaining practical experience in engineering. He soon became interested in artificial flight.

Hargrave wanted to develop a stable lifting surface that could be used for flying. This goal led to his invention of the box kite, one of the seven basic models. In 1894, he carried out kite experiments along the beaches near his home. One day, in front of onlookers, he was lifted above the beach and out over the sea by four of his box kites. These experiments were very important to the development of air travel, although Hargrave has received little credit for it. In fact, because of his modesty, Hargrave failed to get a patent on his box kite. He spent more than 30 years studying flying, offering many inventions, including a rotary engine.

In 1906, Hargrave began looking for a home for his collection of nearly 200 models of kites and flying machines. After being rejected by several governments, his collection was accepted at a technological museum in Munich, Germany. Unfortunately, many of these models were destroyed during World War I.

Directions: Answer these questions about Lawrence Hargrave.

1. For what kite design was Lawrence Hargrave known? _____

2. What was Hargrave trying to create when he made this kite?

   _____

3. What was one of the inventions Hargrave contributed to aviation? _____

   _____

4. Where was Hargrave's collection of kites and flying machines finally housed?

   _____

Main Idea/Recalling Details: A Kite in History

In June 1752, Benjamin Franklin proved that lightning was a type of electricity by flying a kite with a key tied to the bottom of the line during a thunderstorm. Before his experiment, many people thought that lightning was a supernatural power.

After the success of his experiment, Franklin figured that if lightning could be drawn to a kite in a storm, it could be safely redirected into the ground by a metal rod attached to a house. His idea was met with much doubt, but lightning rods were soon seen on buildings in many of the colonies and later in Europe. During the years between 1683 and 1789, studying the universe and laws of nature was of tremendous importance. It was during this Age of Reason, as it was known, that Franklin's kite experiment gained him international fame and respect. He was elected to the Royal Society of London and the French Academy of Sciences, among other honors.

More than 20 years after his bold experiment, American patriots were enduring many hardships in their struggles for freedom from England. The colonial troops had shortages of guns, gun powder and food. France was sending supplies but not as much as was needed. Benjamin Franklin was chosen to go to France to persuade the French to aid the American cause. Franklin's reputation as a brilliant scientist earned him a hero's welcome there. The French people were so impressed by him that they wanted to help the colonies, even during a time when they could barely afford it. The supplies sent by the French were instrumental to the colonists in winning the war. And it all started with a kite.

Directions: Answer these questions about Ben Franklin and his historical kite.

1. The main idea is:

☐ A kite played a role in the American Revolution and gained a spot in history books.

☐ Benjamin Franklin proved that lightning was a type of electricity by flying a kite with a key tied to the bottom of the line during a storm.

2. From his kite and key experiment, what did Franklin invent? _____

3. What was the era between 1683 and 1789 known as? _____

4. Why was Franklin sent to France in 1776? _____

_____

Name: _____

Summarizing: Pioneers

Directions: Think about the lives and accomplishments of Ben Franklin and Lawrence Hargrave. Write one paragraph about each, summarizing what you have learned about these two men.

Ben Franklin

_____

_____

_____

_____

Lawrence Hargrave

_____

_____

_____

_____

Writing Checklist

Reread your paragraphs carefully.

- [ ] My paragraphs make sense.
- [ ] I used correct spelling.
- [ ] I used correct punctuation.
- [ ] My paragraphs are well-organized.
- [ ] I have a good opening and ending.
- [ ] My paragraphs are interesting.

Review

Directions: Number in order the steps for how to launch a kite.

_____ With a steady breeze behind you, gently pull on the line.

_____ Have your friend face you and gently hold the kite.

_____ Your kite will rise.

_____ Have your friend face into the wind.

_____ Place some tension on the flying line by pulling on it.

_____ Have a friend stand about 100 feet away from you.

Directions: Write **True** or **False** for these statements about kite safety.

_____ 1. You should not use wire for flying line.

_____ 2. Fly any size kite you wish as long as you have the right flying line.

_____ 3. If your kite gets caught in a tree, let the line go slack.

_____ 4. It's okay to fly a kite in the rain.

_____ 5. You should not fly a kite in crowded areas.

_____ 6. You can use metal on your kite as long as it's not the flying line itself.

_____ 7. You don't need to wear gloves unless you're flying a very large kite.

_____ 8. You should not fly a kite around an airport.

_____ 9. If your kite gets caught in power lines, just tug the line gently until it works free.

_____ 10. The best place to fly a kite is in a large field.

Comprehension: Colonists Come to America

After Christopher Columbus discovered America in 1492, many people wanted to come live in the new land. During the 17th and 18th centuries, a great many Europeans, especially the English, left their countries and settled along the Atlantic Coast of North America between Florida and Canada. Some came to make a better life for themselves. Others, particularly the Pilgrims, the Puritans and the Quakers, came for religious freedom.

A group of men who wanted gold and other riches from the new land formed the London Company. They asked the king of England for land in America and for permission to found a colony. They founded Jamestown, the first permanent English settlement in America, in 1607. They purchased ships and supplies, and located people who wanted to settle in America.

The voyage to America took about eight weeks and was very dangerous. Often, fierce winds blew the wooden ships off course. Many were wrecked. The ships were crowded and dirty. Frequently, passengers became ill, and some died. Once in America, the early settlers faced even more hardships.

Directions: Answer these questions about the colonists coming to America.

1. How long did it take colonists to travel from England to America? _____

2. Name three groups that came to America to find religious freedom.

   1) _____   2) _____   3) _____

3. Why was the London Company formed? _____

   _____

4. What was Jamestown? _____

   _____

5. Why was the voyage to America dangerous? _____

   _____

Recalling Details: Early Colonial Homes

When the first colonists landed in America, they had to find shelter quickly. Their first homes were crude bark and mud huts, log cabins or dugouts, which were simply caves dug into the hillsides. As soon as possible, the settlers sought to replace these temporary shelters with comfortable houses.

Until the late 17th century, most of the colonial homes were simple in style. Almost all of the New England colonists—those settling in the northern areas of Massachusetts, Connecticut, Rhode Island and New Hampshire—used wood in building their permanent homes. Some of the buildings had thatched roofs. However, they caught fire easily, and so were replaced by wooden shingles. The outside walls also were covered with wooden shingles to make the homes warmer and less drafty.

In the middle colonies—New York, Pennsylvania, New Jersey and Delaware—the Dutch and German colonists often made brick or stone homes that were two-and-a-half or three-and-a-half stories high. Many southern colonists—those living in Virginia, Maryland, North Carolina, South Carolina and Georgia—lived on large farms called plantations. Their homes were usually made of brick.

In the 18th century, some colonists became wealthy enough to replace their simple homes with mansions, often like those being built by the wealthy class in England. They were called Georgian houses because they were popular during the years that Kings George I, George II and George III ruled England. Most were made of brick. They usually featured columns, ornately carved doors and elaborate gardens.

Directions: Answer these questions about early colonial homes.

1. What were the earliest homes of the colonists?

   _____

2. What were the advantages of using wooden shingles?

   _____

3. What did Dutch and German colonists use to build their homes?

   _____

4. What were Georgian homes?

   _____

Recalling Details: The Colonial Kitchen

The most important room in the home of a colonial family was the kitchen. Sometimes it was the only room in the home. The most important element of the kitchen was the fireplace. Fire was essential to the colonists, and they were careful to keep one burning at all times. Before the man of the house went to bed, he would make sure that the fire was carefully banked so it would burn all night. In the morning, he would blow the glowing embers into flame again with a bellows. If the fire went out, one of the children would be sent to a neighbor's for hot coals. Because there were no matches, it would sometimes take a half hour to light a new fire, using flint, steel and tinder.

The colonial kitchen, quite naturally, was centered around the fireplace. One or two large iron broilers hung over the hot coals for cooking the family meals. Above the fireplace, a large musket and powder horn were kept for protection in the event of an attack and to hunt deer and other game. Also likely to be found near the fireplace was a butter churn, where cream from the family's cow was beaten until yellow flakes of butter appeared.

The furniture in the kitchen—usually benches, a table and chairs—were made by the man or men in the family. It was very heavy and not very comfortable. The colonial family owned few eating utensils—no forks and only a few spoons, also made by members of the family. The dishes included pewter plates, "trenchers"—wooden bowls with handles—and wooden mugs.

Directions: Answer these questions about the colonial kitchen.

1. What was the most important element of the colonial kitchen? _____

2. In colonial days, why was it important to keep a fire burning in the fireplace?

   _____

3. Name two uses of the musket.

   1) _____ 2) _____

4. Who made most of the furniture in the early colonial home?

   _____

Sequencing: Spinning

Most of the colonists could not afford to buy clothes sent over from Europe. Instead, the women and girls, particularly in the New England colonies, spent much time spinning thread and weaving cloth to make their own clothing. They raised sheep for wool and grew flax for linen.

In August, the flax was ready to be harvested and made into linen thread. The plants were pulled up and allowed to dry. Then the men pulled the seed pods from the stalks, bundled the stalks and soaked them in a stream for about five days. The flax next had to be taken out, cleaned and dried. To get the linen fibers from the tough bark and heavy wooden core, the stalks had to be pounded and crushed. Finally, the fibers were pulled through the teeth of a brush called a "hatchel" to comb out the short and broken fibers. The long fibers were spun into linen thread on a spinning wheel.

The spinning wheel was low, so a woman sat down to spin. First, she put flax in the hollow end of a slender stick, called the spindle, at one end of the spinning wheel. It was connected by a belt to a big wheel at the other end. The woman turned the wheel by stepping on a pedal. As it turned, the spindle also turned, twisting the flax into thread. The woman constantly dipped her fingers into water to moisten the flax and keep it from breaking. The linen thread came out through a hole in the side of the spindle. It was bleached and put away to be woven into pieces of cloth.

Directions: Number in order the steps to make linen thread from flax.

_____ The woman sat at the spinning wheel and put flax in the spindle.

_____ Seed pods were pulled from the stalks; stalks were bundled and soaked.

_____ In August, the flax was ready to be harvested and made into thread.

_____ The stalks were pounded and crushed to get the linen fibers.

_____ The thread was bleached and put away to be woven into cloth.

_____ The short fibers were separated out with a "hatchel."

_____ The woman dipped her fingers into water to moisten the flax.

_____ The long fibers were spun into linen thread on a spinning wheel.

_____ The woman turned the wheel by stepping on a pedal, twisting the flax into thread.

_____ The plants were pulled up and allowed to dry.

_____ The linen thread came out through a hole in the side of the spindle.

Recalling Details: Clothing in Colonial Times

The clothing of the colonists varied from the north to the south, accounting for the differences not only in climate, but also in the religions and ancestries of the settlers. The clothes seen most often in the early New England colonies where the Puritans settled were very plain and simple. The materials—wool and linen—were warm and sturdy.

The Puritans had strict rules about clothing. There were no bright colors, jewelry, ruffles or lace. A Puritan woman wore a long-sleeved gray dress with a big white color, cuffs, apron and cap. A Puritan man wore long woolen stockings and baggy leather "breeches," which were knee-length trousers. Adults and children dressed in the same style of clothing.

In the middle colonies, the clothing ranged from the simple clothing of the Quakers to the colorful, loose-fitting outfits of the Dutch colonists. Dutch women wore more colorful outfits than Puritan women, with many petticoats and fur trim. The men had silver buckles on their shoes and wore big hats decked with curling feathers.

In the southern colonies, where there were no religious restrictions against fancy clothes, wealthy men wore brightly colored breeches and coats of velvet and satin sent from England. The women's gowns also were made of rich materials and were decorated with ruffles, ribbons and lace. The poorer people wore clothes similar to the simple dress of the New England Puritans.

Directions: Answer these questions about clothing in colonial times.

1. Why did the clothing of the colonists vary from the north to the south?

   _____

2. Why did the Puritans wear very plain clothing?

   _____

3. What was the nationality of many settlers in the middle colonies?

   _____

4. From what country did wealthy southern colonists obtain their clothing?

   _____

Name: _____

Recalling Details: Venn Diagrams

A **Venn diagram** is used to chart information that shows similarities and differences between two things. The outer part of each circle shows the differences. The intersecting part of the circles shows the similarities.

Example:

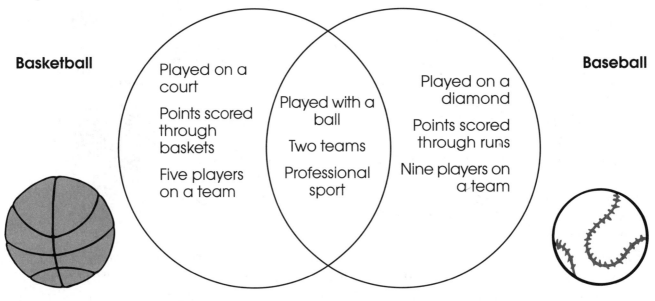

Basketball

Played on a court

Points scored through baskets

Five players on a team

Played with a ball

Two teams

Professional sport

Played on a diamond

Points scored through runs

Nine players on a team

Baseball

Directions: Complete the Venn diagram below. Think of at least three things to write in the outer part of each circle (differences) and at least three things to write in the intersecting part (similarities).

Colonial Kitchen   **Your Kitchen**

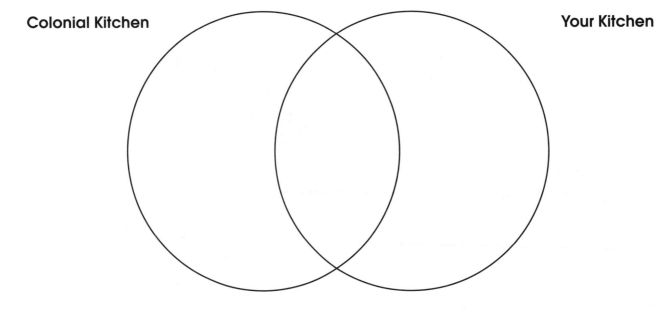

Comprehension: Colonial Schools

In early colonial days, there were no schools or teachers. Children learned what they could at home from their parents, but often their parents couldn't read or write either. Later, some women in the New England colonies began teaching in their homes. These first schools were known as "dame schools." Often the books used in these schools were not books at all, but rather "hornbooks"—flat, paddle-shaped wooden boards with the alphabet or Lord's Prayer on the front.

In 1647, a law was passed in the New England colonies requiring every town of 50 or more families to establish an elementary school. By the 1700s, one-room log schoolhouses were common. Children of all ages studied together under one strict schoolmaster. They attended school six days a week, from 7:00 or 8:00 in the morning until 4:00 or 5:00 in the afternoon. Their only textbooks were the Bible and the *New England Primer*, which contained the alphabet, spelling words, poems and questions about the Bible.

Like the New England colonies, the middle colonies also established schools. However, there were few schools in the southern colonies, where most of the people lived on widely separated farms. Wealthy plantation owners hired private teachers from England to teach their children, but the children of poor families received no education.

Directions: Answer these questions about colonial schools.

1. What was a "hornbook"? _____

_____

2. What was required by the law passed in the New England colonies in 1647?

_____

_____

3. During the 1700s, what textbooks were used in the New England schools?

_____

4. Why was it hard to establish schools in the southern colonies?

_____

Compare/Contrast: Schools

Directions: Think about the differences and similarities between colonial and modern schools. Use the chart below to help organize your ideas. Then, write a paragraph discussing the similarities and a paragraph discussing the differences. The topic sentences have been written for you.

Similarities	Differences

There are several similarities between colonial schools and schools today.

_____

_____

_____

_____

_____

Although there are similarities between colonial schools and modern schools, there are also many differences.

_____

_____

_____

_____

_____

Comprehension: Religion in New England

Many New England colonists had come to America for religious freedom. Religion was very important to them. One of the first buildings erected in any new settlement was a church, or meetinghouse. They were generally in the center of town and were used for public meetings of all kinds. These early meetinghouses were plain, unpainted wood buildings. Later churches were larger and more elaborate. They were usually painted white and had tall, graceful bell towers rising from the roof.

Although they came to America to have freedom of worship, the Puritans thought that everyone in the colonies should worship the same way they did. Because there were so many of them, the Puritans controlled the government in much of New England. They were the only ones allowed to vote, and they passed very strict laws. Lawbreakers received harsh punishments. For example, someone caught lying might be forced to stand in the town square for hours locked in a pillory—wooden boards with holes cut in them for the head and hands. For other minor offenses, the offender was tied to a whipping post and given several lashes with a whip.

Except in cases of extreme illness, everyone in the New England colonies had to attend church on Sunday. The minister stood in a pulpit high above the pews to deliver his sermon, which could last four or five hours. The people sat on hard, straight-backed pews. In the winter, there was no heat, so church members brought foot warmers from home to use during the long services. In many churches, a "tithingman" walked up and down the aisles carrying a long stick. On one end there were feathers attached; the other end had a knob. If anyone dozed off, the tithingman would tickle him or her with the feathers. If this did not rouse the offender, he would thump them soundly with the knob.

Directions: Answer these questions about religion in the colonies.

1. The main idea is:

   ☐ Many New England colonists had come to America for religious freedom, and religion was very important to them.

   ☐ One of the first buildings erected in any new settlement was a church.

2. Which religious group exercised a lot of power in the New England colonies?

   _____

3. What was a pillory? _____

4. What was the only acceptable excuse for missing Sunday church services in the New England colonies? _____

5. What was the job of the tithingman? _____

Writing: Problem and Solution

Directions: Follow the instructions below.

1. Think of a problem the Colonial Americans may have encountered. Write a paragraph about this problem. In the paragraph, be sure to state the problem, then discuss why it would have been a problem for the colonists.

_____

_____

_____

_____

_____

_____

2. Think about a solution to the problem above. Write a paragraph outlining your ideas for the solution. Remember to state the solution to the problem and then your ideas to solve the problem.

_____

_____

_____

_____

_____

_____

Review

Many great colonists made an impact on American history. Among them was Benjamin Franklin, who left his mark as a printer, author, inventor, scientist and statesman. He has been called "the wisest American."

Franklin was born in Boston in 1706, one of 13 children in a very religious Puritan household. Although he had less than two years of formal education, his tremendous appetite for books served him well. At age 12, he became an apprentice printer at *The New England Courant* and soon began writing articles that poked fun at Boston society.

In 1723, Franklin ran away to Philadelphia, where he started his own newspaper. He was very active in the Philadelphia community. He operated a bookstore and was named postmaster. He also helped to establish a library, a fire company, a college, an insurance company and a hospital. His well-known *Poor Richard's Almanac* was first printed in 1732.

Over the years, Franklin maintained an interest in science and mechanics, leading to such inventions as a fireplace stove and bifocal lenses. In 1752, he gained world fame with his kite-and-key experiment, which proved that lightning was a form of electricity.

Franklin was an active supporter of the colonies throughout the Revolutionary War. He helped to write and was a signer of the Declaration of Independence in 1776. In his later years, he skillfully represented America in Europe, helping to work out a peace treaty with Great Britain.

Directions: Answer these questions about Benjamin Franklin.

1. The main idea is:

   ☐ Many great colonists made an impact on American history.

   ☐ Benjamin Franklin was a great colonist who left his mark as a printer, author, inventor, scientist and statesman.

2. How did Benjamin Franklin gain world fame? _____

3. What did Franklin sign and help to write? _____

4. Number in order the following accomplishments of Benjamin Franklin.

   _____ Served as representative of America in Europe

   _____ Began printing *Poor Richard's Almanac*

   _____ Experimented with electricity

   _____ Started his own newspaper

   _____ Helped to write and sign the Declaration of Independence

   _____ Served as apprentice printer on *The New England Courant*

Review

Directions: Match each item with its description. If necessary, review the section on colonial times.

a. hornbooks

b. 1647

c. pillory

d. Ben Franklin

e. plantations

f. 1776

g. tithingman

h. spinning wheel

i. hatchel

j. 1492

k. trenchers

l. flax

m. dame schools

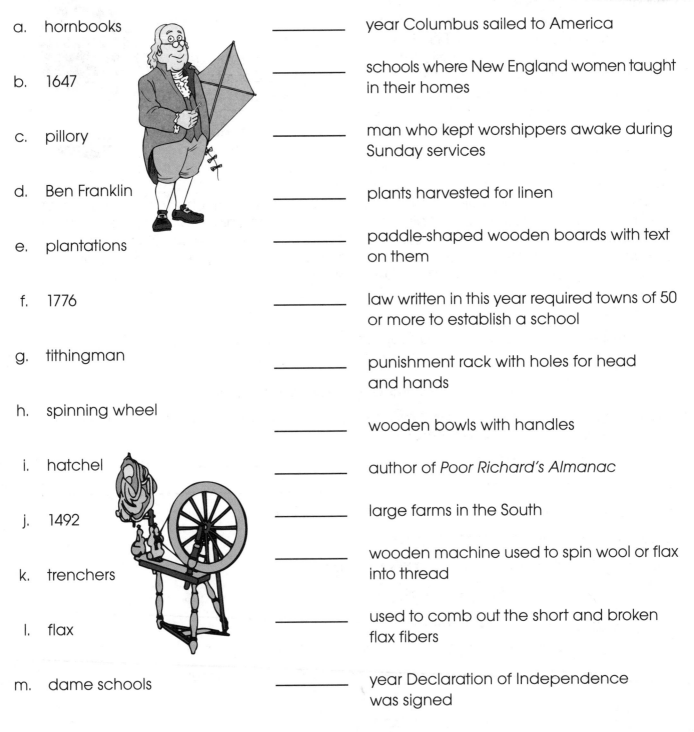

_____ year Columbus sailed to America

_____ schools where New England women taught in their homes

_____ man who kept worshippers awake during Sunday services

_____ plants harvested for linen

_____ paddle-shaped wooden boards with text on them

_____ law written in this year required towns of 50 or more to establish a school

_____ punishment rack with holes for head and hands

_____ wooden bowls with handles

_____ author of *Poor Richard's Almanac*

_____ large farms in the South

_____ wooden machine used to spin wool or flax into thread

_____ used to comb out the short and broken flax fibers

_____ year Declaration of Independence was signed

Using Prior Knowledge:
Abraham Lincoln and the Civil War

Directions: Before reading about Abraham Lincoln and the Civil War in the following section, answer these questions.

1. The Civil War began because _____

_____

_____

2. Abraham Lincoln is famous today because _____

_____

_____

_____

3. What brought about the end of slavery in the United States? _____

_____

_____

4. The *Gettysburg Address* begins with the famous line: "Four score and seven years ago. . . . " What does this mean?

_____

_____

5. How did Abraham Lincoln die? _____

_____

_____

_____

Main Idea: The Gettysburg Address

On November 19, 1863, President Abraham Lincoln gave a short speech to dedicate a cemetery for Civil War soldiers in Gettysburg, Pennsylvania, where a famous battle was fought. He wrote five drafts of the *Gettysburg Address*, one of the most stirring speeches of all time. The war ended in 1865.

Four score and seven years ago, our fathers brought forth on this continent a new nation, conceived in liberty, and dedicated to the proposition that all men are created equal.

Now we are engaged in a great civil war, testing whether that nation, or any nation so conceived and so dedicated, can long endure. We are met on a great battlefield of that war. We have come to dedicate a portion of that field as a final resting place for those who here gave their lives that this nation might live. It is altogether fitting and proper that we should do this.

But, in a larger sense, we cannot dedicate—we cannot consecrate—we cannot hallow—this ground. The brave men, living and dead, who struggled here have consecrated it far above our poor power to add or detract. The world will little note nor long remember what we say here, but it can never forget what they did here. It is for us the living, rather, to be dedicated to the unfinished work which they who fought here have thus far so nobly advanced. It is rather for us to be here dedicated to the great task remaining before us—that from these honored dead we take increased devotion to that cause for which they gave their last full measure of devotion—that we here highly resolve that these dead shall not have died in vain—that this nation, under God, shall have a new birth of freedom—and that government of the people, by the people, for the people shall not perish from this earth.

Directions: Answer the questions about the *Gettysburg Address*.

1. Circle the main idea:

This speech will be long remembered as a tribute to the dead who died fighting in the Civil War.

This speech is to honor the dead soldiers who gave their lives so that the nation could have freedom for all citizens.

2. What happened on the ground where the cemetery stood? _____

_____

Comprehension: The Gettysburg Address

Directions: Use context clues or a dictionary to answer these questions about the *Gettysburg Address*.

1. What is the correct definition of **conceived**? _____

_____

2. What is the correct definition of **consecrate**? _____

_____

3. What is the correct definition of **hallow**? _____

_____

4. What is the correct definition of **devotion**? _____

_____

5. What is the correct definition of **resolve**? _____

_____

6. What is the correct definition of **vain**? _____

_____

7. What is the correct definition of **perish**? _____

_____

8. What is the correct definition of **civil**? _____

_____

9. In your own words, what point was President Lincoln trying to make? _____

_____

_____

Comprehension:
The Emancipation Proclamation

On September 22, 1862, a year before delivering the *Gettysburg Address*, President Lincoln delivered the *Emancipation Proclamation*, which stated that all slaves in Confederate states should be set free. Since the Confederate states had already seceded (withdrawn) from the Union, they ignored the proclamation. However, the proclamation did strengthen the North's war effort. About 200,000 Black men—mostly former slaves—enlisted in the Union Army. Two years later, the 13th Amendment to the Constitution ended slavery in all parts of the United States.

I, Abraham Lincoln, do order and declare that all persons held as slaves within said designated States and parts of States are, and henceforward shall be, free; and that the Executive Government of the United States, including military and naval authorities thereof, shall recognize and maintain the freedom of said persons.

And I hereby enjoin upon the people so declared to be free to abstain from all violence, unless in necessary self-defense; and I recommend to them that, in all cases where allowed, they labor faithfully for reasonable wages.

And I further declare and make known that such persons of suitable condition will be received into the armed forces of the United States to garrison forts, positions, stations, and other places, and to man vessels of all sorts in said service.

(This is not the full text of the *Emancipation Proclamation*.)

Directions: Answer the questions about the *Emancipation Proclamation*.

1. How did the *Emancipation Proclamation* strengthen the North's war effort?

_____

2. Which came first, the *Emancipation Proclamation* or the *Gettysburg Address*?

_____

3. Which amendment to the Constitution grew out of the *Emancipation Proclamation*?

_____

4. **Secede** means to ☐ quit.   ☐ fight.   ☐ withdraw.

Comprehension:
The Emancipation Proclamation

Directions: Use context clues or a dictionary to answer these questions about the *Emancipation Proclamation*.

1. What is the correct definition of **designated**? _____

_____

2. What is the correct definition of **military**? _____

_____

3. What is the correct definition of **naval**? _____

_____

4. What is the correct definition of **abstain**? _____

_____

5. What is the correct definition of **suitable**? _____

_____

6. What is the correct definition of **garrison**? _____

_____

7. What is the correct definition of **vessels**? _____

_____

8. In your own words, what did the *Emancipation Proclamation* accomplish?

_____

_____

_____

Comprehension: Lincoln and the South

Many people think that Abraham Lincoln publicly came out against slavery from the beginning of his term as president. This is not the case. Whatever his private feelings, he did not criticize slavery publicly. Fearful that the southern states would secede, or leave, the Union, he pledged to respect the southern states' rights to own slaves. He also pledged that the government would respect the southern states' runaway slave laws. These laws required all citizens to return runaway slaves to their masters.

Clearly, Lincoln did not want the country torn apart by a civil war. In the following statement, written in 1861 shortly after he became president, he made it clear that the federal government would do its best to avoid conflict with the southern states.

I hold that, in contemplation of the universal law and the Constitution, the Union of these states is perpetual. . . . No state, upon its own mere motion, can lawfully get out of the Union. . . . I shall take care, as the Constitution itself expressly enjoins upon me, that the laws of the Union be faithfully executed in all the states. . . . The power confided to me will be used to hold, occupy, and possess the property and places belonging to the government, and to collect the duties and imposts. . . .

In your hands, my dissatisfied fellow-countrymen, and not in mine, is the momentous issue of civil war. The government will not assail you. You can have no conflict without yourselves being the aggressors. You have no oath registered in heaven to destroy the government, while I shall have the most solemn one to "preserve, protect and defend" it.

Directions: Use context clues for these definitions.

1. What is the correct definition of **assail**? _____

2. What is the correct definition of **enjoin**? _____

3. What is the correct definition of **contemplation**? _____

_____

Directions: Answer these questions about Lincoln and the southern states.

4. Lincoln is telling the southern states that the government

☐ does want a war.   ☐ doesn't want a war.   ☐ will stop a war.

5. As president, Lincoln pledged to "preserve, protect and defend"

☐ slavery.   ☐ the northern states.   ☐ the Union.

Comprehension: Away Down South in Dixie

Although many southerners disapproved of slavery, the pressure to go along with the majority who supported slavery was very strong. Many of those who thought slavery was wrong did not talk about their opinions. It was dangerous to do so!

The main reason the southern states seceded from the Union in 1861 was because they wanted to protect their right to own slaves. They also wanted to increase the number of slaves so they could increase production of cotton and other crops that slaves tended. Many Civil War monuments in the South are dedicated to a war that was described as "just and holy."

"Dixie," a song written in 1859 that is still popular in the South, sums up the attitude of many southerners. As the song lyrics show, southerners' loyalties lay not with the Union representing all the states, but with the South and the southern way of life.

Dixie
I wish I was in Dixie, Hoo-ray! Hoo-ray!
In Dixie land I'll take my stand
To live and die in Dixie.
Away, away, away down south in Dixie!
Away, away, away down south in Dixie!
(This is not the full text of the song.)

Directions: Answer these questions about southerners and "Dixie."

1. Why did southerners who disapproved of slavery keep their opinions to themselves?

_____

_____

2. Why did southerners want more slaves? _____

_____

3. What are the words on some southern Civil War monuments? _____

_____

4. What "stand" is referred to in "Dixie"?

☐ stand for slavery   ☐ stand against slavery   ☐ stand for cotton

Name: _____

Fact and Opinion

Directions: Read each sentence. Then draw an **X** in the box to tell whether it is a fact or opinion.

1. "Dixie" is a beautiful song! ☐ Fact ☐ Opinion

2. It was written in 1859 by a man named Daniel Emmett, who died in 1904. ☐ Fact ☐ Opinion

3. The song became a rallying cry for southerners, because it showed where their loyalties were. ☐ Fact ☐ Opinion

4. I think their loyalty to slavery was absolutely wrong! ☐ Fact ☐ Opinion

5. These four states where people owned slaves did not secede from the Union: Delaware, Maryland, Kentucky and Missouri. ☐ Fact ☐ Opinion

6. The people in these states certainly made the right moral choice. ☐ Fact ☐ Opinion

7. The ownership of one human being by another is absolutely and totally wrong under any circumstances. ☐ Fact ☐ Opinion

8. In the states that did not secede from the Union, some people fought for the Union and others fought for the Confederacy of Southern States. ☐ Fact ☐ Opinion

9. Sometimes brothers fought against brothers on opposite sides of the war. ☐ Fact ☐ Opinion

10. What a horrible situation to be in! ☐ Fact ☐ Opinion

Recalling Details: The Civil War

Although they were outnumbered, most southerners were convinced they could win the Civil War. The white population of the southern states that had seceded from the Union was 5.5 million. The population was 18.9 million in the 19 states that stayed with the Union. Despite these odds, southerners felt history was on their side.

After all, the colonists had been the underdogs against the British and had won the War of Independence. Europeans also felt that Lincoln could not force the South to rejoin the Union. The United Netherlands had successfully seceded from Spain. Greece had seceded from Turkey. Europeans were laying odds that two countries would take the place of what had once been the United States.

Directions: Answer these questions and complete the puzzle about the Civil War.

1. What was the difference in population between the Union and the Confederate states?

_____

2. Circle the main idea:

Although they were outnumbered, many people here and abroad felt the South would win the Civil War.

Because they were outnumbered, the South knew winning the Civil War was a long shot.

Across:
3. They won the War of Independence against England.
5. Did Europeans believe the South would win the war?
6. ____teen states belonged to the Union.

Down:
1. Slave owners lived in this area of the country.
2. The president during the Civil War
4. To withdraw from the Union

Recalling Details: Abraham Lincoln

Directions: Complete the following exercises.

1. Describe two accomplishments of Abraham Lincoln. _____

_____

_____

2. Complete the time line by writing and illustrating the events.

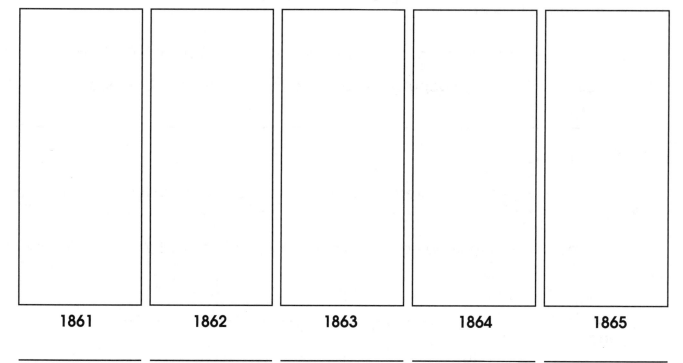

| 1861 | 1862 | 1863 | 1864 | 1865 |

_____ _____ _____ _____ _____

_____ _____ _____ _____ _____

3. In your opinion, what could Lincoln have done differently to end the Civil War sooner?

_____

_____

_____

_____

Fact and Opinion

Directions: Read each sentence. Then draw an **X** in the box to tell whether it is a fact or an opinion.

1. Lincoln warned the southern states that they could not legally leave the Union.

   ☐ Fact   ☐ Opinion

2. I believe Lincoln thought the northern states were the best because they did not have slaves.

   ☐ Fact   ☐ Opinion

3. I think Lincoln did the right thing, don't you?

   ☐ Fact   ☐ Opinion

4. The issues that sparked the Civil War were complicated and difficult ones.

   ☐ Fact   ☐ Opinion

5. It would take a historian to really understand them!

   ☐ Fact   ☐ Opinion

6. The "dissatisfied fellow-countrymen" Lincoln refers to in his statement lived in the southern states.

   ☐ Fact   ☐ Opinion

7. As president, Lincoln took an oath to "preserve, protect and defend" the Union, which included all the states.

   ☐ Fact   ☐ Opinion

8. Lincoln did his personal best to hold the country together, but it didn't do one bit of good.

   ☐ Fact   ☐ Opinion

9. The Confederate States of America had already been organized in February, 1861, a month before Lincoln was sworn in as president.

   ☐ Fact   ☐ Opinion

10. Poor Abraham Lincoln—what a crummy start to his presidency!

    ☐ Fact   ☐ Opinion

Name: _____

Using Prior Knowledge: Anthems and Songs

Directions: Before reading about anthems and songs in the following section, answer these questions.

1. How do national anthems help pull a country together? _____

_____

_____

_____

_____

2. Describe what you know about how and why "The Star-Spangled Banner" was written.

_____

_____

_____

_____

3. What is your favorite anthem or song? _____

4. What images do the words of your favorite anthem or song bring to mind? Why do you like it?

_____

_____

_____

_____

_____

_____

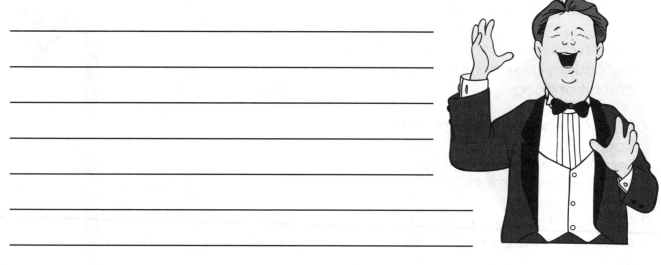

Comprehension: Our National Anthem

Written in 1814 by Francis Scott Key, our American national anthem is stirring, beautiful and difficult to sing. Key wrote the song while aboard a ship off the coast of Maryland, where one long night he watched the gunfire from a British attack on America's Fort McHenry. The following morning, he wrote "The Star-Spangled Banner" when, to his great joy, he saw the American flag still flying over the fort—a sign that the Americans had not lost the battle.

The Star-Spangled Banner
Oh say, can you see, by the dawn's early light,
What so proudly we hail'd at the twilight's last gleaming?
Whose broad stripes and bright stars, thro' the perilous fight,
O'er the ramparts we watch'd were so gallantly streaming?
And the rockets' red glare, the bombs bursting in air,
Gave proof thro' the night that our flag was still there.
Oh say, does that star-spangled banner yet wave
O'er the land of the free and the home of the brave?

Oh, the shore dimly seen thro' the mists of the deep,
Where the foe's haughty host in dread silence reposes,
What is that which the breeze, o'er the towering steep,
As it fitfully blows, half conceals, half discloses?
Now it catches the gleam of the morning's first beam,
In full glory reflected, now shines on the stream:
'Tis the star-spangled banner: O, long may it wave
O'er the land of the free and the home of the brave!

Directions: Answer these questions about the first two verses of "The Star-Spangled Banner."

1. Who wrote "The Star-Spangled Banner"? _____

2. What is "The Star-Spangled Banner"? _____

3. In what year was the song written? _____

4. At what time of day was the song written? _____

5. Tell what is meant by the lines " . . . the rockets' red glare, the bombs bursting in air/Gave proof through the night that our flag was still there."

_____

_____

Comprehension: "The Star-Spangled Banner"

Directions: Use context clues or a dictionary to answer these questions about "The Star-Spangled Banner."

1. What is the correct definition of **spangled**? _____

_____

2. What is the correct definition of **twilight**? _____

_____

3. What is the correct definition of **ramparts**? _____

_____

4. What is the correct definition of **gallantly**? _____

_____

5. What is the correct definition of **haughty**? _____

_____

6. What is the correct definition of **reposes**? _____

_____

7. Why do you think United States citizens only sing the first verse of "The Star-Spangled Banner"?

_____

8. What war was being fought when this song was written?

_____

9. Have you ever heard the second verse of "The Star-Spangled Banner"? Knowing the tune, can you sing the second verse?

_____

Comprehension: "America the Beautiful"

Written in 1895 by Katherine Lee Bates, "America the Beautiful" is another very popular patriotic song. It is so popular, in fact, that some people would like to see it replace "The Star-Spangled Banner" as the United States' national anthem. Ms. Bates was inspired to write the song while visiting Colorado, where she was struck by the splendor of the mountains. Today, "America the Beautiful" remains a tribute to our country's natural beauty.

America the Beautiful
Oh beautiful for spacious skies,
For amber waves of grain,
For purple mountains majesties
Above the fruited plain!
America! America!
God shed His grace on thee,
And crown thy good
With brotherhood
From sea to shining sea!

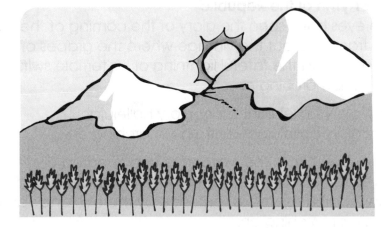

Directions: Use context clues or a dictionary to answer these questions about "America the Beautiful."

1. What is the correct definition of **tribute**? _____

2. What is the correct definition of **amber**? _____

   What other word might you use for **amber** in the song? _____

3. What is the singular form of **majesties**? What does it mean in the song? _____

   _____

4. "From sea to shining sea" means the oceans to the east and west of the United States. What are their names?

   _____   _____

5. Do you think "America the Beautiful" should be our national anthem? Why or why not?

   _____

   _____

Comprehension: Civil War Marching Song

When soldiers march, they sometimes sing a song to help them keep in step. One of the most famous marching songs of the Civil War was the "Battle Hymn of the Republic," written in 1861 by Julia Ward Howe. Mrs. Howe wrote the song after visiting a Union army camp in the North. The words are about how God is on the side of the soldiers.

Battle Hymn of the Republic
Mine eyes have seen the glory of the coming of the Lord,
He is trampling out the vintage where the grapes of wrath are stored,
He has loosed the fateful lightning of his terrible swift sword,
His truth is marching on.

Glory, glory hallelujah! Glory, glory hallelujah!
Glory, glory hallelujah! His truth is marching on.

I have seen him in the watchfires of a hundred circling camps,
I have builded him an altar in the evening dews and damps,
I can read his righteous sentence by the dim and flaring lamps,
His day is marching on.

Glory, glory hallelujah! Glory, glory hallelujah!
Glory, glory hallelujah! His truth is marching on.

Directions: Answer these questions about the "Battle Hymn of the Republic."

1. Who wrote the "Battle Hymn of the Republic"? _____

2. When was the song written? _____

3. What war was in progress at the time? _____

4. Why did soldiers sing while they marched? _____

_____

5. What marches on along with the soldiers? _____

6. What did the soldiers sing about building in the evening?

_____

Review

National anthems, work songs and marching songs share some common characteristics. Perhaps the most important characteristic is that the words strike an emotional response in singers and listeners alike.

Have you ever sung "The Star-Spangled Banner" at a baseball game or other large public event? The next time you do, look around as you sing. You will see that Americans from all walks of life and all races sing the song proudly. The words to the national anthem help create a feeling of unity among people who may not have anything else in common. The same is true of the national anthems of France, England and other countries.

Another characteristic of these types of songs is that the words are simple, the message is clear and the tune should be easy to carry. This is not always true, of course. Many people's voices crack during the high notes of "The Star-Spangled Banner." But attempts to change the national anthem to "America the Beautiful" or another song with a simpler tune have always met with dismal failure. It may be hard to sing, but most Americans wouldn't trade it for any other tune. It's a long-held American tradition and nearly everyone knows the words. Americans love what this song stands for. They are proud to live in a country that is the "land of the free."

Directions: Answer these questions about the characteristics of national anthems, work songs and marching songs.

1. Explain what goes into writing a good national anthem. _____

_____

_____

2. What does our national anthem help do? _____

_____

3. What happens each time someone tries to change the national anthem to "America the Beautiful" or another song?

_____

4. Why do people stick with "The Star-Spangled Banner" as our national anthem?

_____

_____

Recalling Details: The Island Continent

Australia is the only country that fills an entire continent. It is the smallest continent in the world but the sixth largest country. Australia, called the island continent, is totally surrounded by water—the Indian Ocean on the west and south, the Pacific Ocean on the east and the Arafura Sea, which is formed by these two oceans coming together, to the north.

The island continent is, in large part, a very dry, flat land. Yet it supports a magnificent and unusual collection of wildlife. Because of its remoteness, Australia is home to plants and animals that are not found anywhere else in the world. Besides the well-known kangaroo and koala, the strange animals of the continent include the wombat, dingo, kookaburra, emu and, perhaps the strangest of all, the duckbill platypus.

There are many physical features of Australia that also are unique, including the central part of the country known as the "Outback," which consists of three main deserts—the Great Sandy, the Gibson and the Great Victoria. Because much of the country is desert, more than half of all Australians live in large, modern cities along the coast. There are also many people living in the small towns on the edge of the Outback, where there is plenty of grass for raising sheep and cattle. Australia rates first in the world for sheep raising. In fact, there are more than 10 times as many sheep in Australia as there are people!

Directions: Answer these questions about Australia.

1. What are the three large bodies of water that surround Australia?

   1) _____ 2) _____ 3) _____

2. Besides the kangaroo and the koala, name three other unusual animals found only in Australia.

   1) _____ 2) _____ 3) _____

3. What three deserts make up the "Outback?"

   1) _____ 2) _____ 3) _____

Comprehension: The Aborigines

The native, or earliest known, people of Australia are the Aborigines (ab-ur-IJ-uh-neez). They arrived on the continent from Asia more than 20,000 years ago. Before the Europeans began settling in Australia during the early 1800s, there were about 300,000 Aborigines. But the new settlers brought diseases that killed many of these native people. Today there are only about 125,000 Aborigines living in Australia, many of whom now live in the cities.

The way of life of the Aborigines, who still live like their ancestors, is closely related to nature. They live as hunters and gatherers and do not produce crops or raise livestock. The Aborigines have no permanent settlements, only small camps near watering places. Because they live off the land, they must frequently move about in search of food. They have few belongings and little or no clothing.

Some tribes of Aborigines, especially those that live in the desert, may move 100 times in a year. They might move more than 1,000 miles on foot during that time. These tribes set up temporary homes, such as tents made of bark and igloo-like structures made of grass.

The Aborigines have no written language, but they have developed a system of hand signals. These are used during hunting when silence is necessary and during their elaborate religious ceremonies when talking is forbidden.

Directions: Circle **True** or **False** for these statements about Aborigines.

1. The Aborigines came from Europe to settle in Australia.   True   False

2. The Aborigines live as hunters and gatherers rather than as farmers.   True   False

3. The tribes move about often to find jobs.   True   False

4. The people move often to help them raise their livestock.   True   False

5. Aborigine tribes always move 200 times a year.   True   False

Main Idea/Comprehension: The Boomerang

The Aborigines have developed a few tools and weapons, including spears, flint knives and the boomerang. The boomerang comes in different shapes and has many uses. This curved throwing stick is used for hunting, playing, digging, cutting and even making music.

You may have seen a boomerang that, when thrown, returns to the thrower. This type of boomerang is sometimes used in duck hunting, but it is most often used as a toy and for sporting contests. It is lightweight—about three-fourths of a pound—and has a big curve in it. However, the boomerang used by the Aborigines for hunting is much heavier and is nearly straight. It does not return to its thrower.

Because of its sharp edges, the boomerang makes a good knife for skinning animals. The Aborigines also use boomerangs as digging sticks, to sharpen stone blades, to start fires and as swords and clubs in fighting. Boomerangs sometimes are used to make music—two clapped together provide rhythmic background for dances. Some make musical sounds when they are pulled across one another.

To throw a boomerang, the thrower grasps it at one end and holds it behind his head. He throws it overhanded, adding a sharp flick of the wrist at the last moment. It is thrown into the wind to make it come back. A skillful thrower can do many tricks with his boomerang. He can make it spin in several circles, or make a figure eight in the air. He can even make it bounce on the ground several times before it soars into the air and returns.

Directions: Answer these questions about boomerangs.

1. The main idea is:

   ☐ The Aborigines have developed a few tools and weapons, including spears, flint knives and the boomerang.

   ☐ The boomerang comes in different shapes and has many uses.

2. To make it return, the thrower tosses the boomerang

   ☐ into the wind.   ☐ against the wind.

3. List three uses for the boomerang.

   1) _____

   2) _____

   3) _____

Comprehension: The Kangaroo

Many animals found in Australia are not found anywhere else in the world. Because the island continent was separated from the rest of the world for many years, these animals developed in different ways. Many of the animals in Australia are marsupials. Marsupials are animals whose babies are born underdeveloped and are then carried in a pouch on the mother's body until they are able to care for themselves. The kangaroo is perhaps the best known of the marsupials.

There are 45 kinds of kangaroos, and they come in a variety of sizes. The smallest is the musky rat kangaroo, which is about a foot long, including its hairless tail. It weighs only a pound. The largest is the gray kangaroo, which is more than 9 feet long, counting its tail, and can weigh 200 pounds. When moving quickly, a kangaroo can leap 25 feet and move at 30 miles an hour!

A baby kangaroo, called a joey, is totally helpless at birth. It is only three-quarters of an inch long and weighs but a fraction of an ounce. The newly born joey immediately crawls into its mother's pouch and remains there until it is old enough to be independent—which can be as long as eight months.

Kangaroos eat grasses and plants. They can cause problems for farmers and ranchers in Australia because they compete with cattle for pastures. During a drought, kangaroos may invade ranches and even airports looking for food.

Directions: Answer these questions about kangaroos.

1. What are marsupials? _____

   _____

2. What is the smallest kangaroo? _____

3. What is a baby kangaroo called? _____

4. Why did Australian animals develop differently from other animals? _____

   _____

Comprehension: The Koala

The koala lives in eastern Australia in the eucalyptus (you-ca-LIP-tes) forests. These slow, gentle animals hide by day, usually sleeping in the trees. They come out at night to eat. Koalas eat only certain types of eucalyptus leaves. Their entire way of life centers on this unique diet. The koala's digestive system is specially adapted for eating eucalyptus leaves. In fact, to other animals, these leaves are poisonous!

The wooly, round-eared koala looks like a cuddly teddy bear, but it is not related to any bear. It is a marsupial like the kangaroo. And, like the joey, a baby koala requires a lot of care. It will remain constantly in its mother's pouch until it is six months old. After that, a baby koala will ride piggyback on its mother for another month or two, even though it is nearly as big as she is. Koalas have few babies—only one every other year. While in her pouch, the baby koala lives on its mother's milk. After it is big enough to be on its own, the koala will almost never drink anything again.

Oddly, the mother koala's pouch is backwards—the opening is at the bottom. This leads scientists to believe that the koala once lived on the ground and walked on all fours. But at some point, the koala became a tree dweller. This makes an upside-down pouch very awkward! The babies keep from falling to the ground by holding on tightly with their mouths. The mother koala has developed strong muscles around the rim of her pouch that also help to hold the baby in.

Directions: Answer these questions about koalas.

1. What is the correct definition for **eucalyptus**?

   ☐ enormous ☐ a type of tree ☐ rain

2. What is the correct definition for **digestive**?

   ☐ the process in which food is absorbed in the body
   ☐ the process of finding food
   ☐ the process of tasting

3. What is the correct definition for **dweller**?

   ☐ one who climbs ☐ one who eats ☐ one who lives in

Comprehension: The Wombat

Another animal unique to Australia is the wombat. The wombat has characteristics in common with other animals. Like the koala, the wombat is also a marsupial with a backwards pouch. The pouch is more practical for the wombat, which lives on the ground rather than in trees. The wombat walks on all fours so the baby is in less danger of falling out.

The wombat resembles a beaver without a tail. With its strong claws, it is an expert digger. It makes long tunnels beneath cliffs and boulders in which it sleeps all day. At night, it comes out to look for food. It has strong, beaver-like teeth to chew through the various plant roots it eats. A wombat's teeth have no roots, like a rodent's. Its teeth keep growing from the inside as they are worn down from the outside.

The wombat, which can be up to 4 feet long and weighs 60 pounds when full grown, eats only grass, plants and roots. It is a shy, quiet and gentle animal that would never attack. But when angered, it has a strong bite and very sharp teeth! And, while wombats don't eat or attack other animals, the many deep burrows they dig to sleep in are often dangerous to the other animals living nearby.

Directions: Answer these questions about the wombat.

1. How is the wombat similar to the koala? _____

_____

2. How is the wombat similar to the beaver? _____

_____

3. How is the wombat similar to a rodent? _____

_____

_____

Comprehension: The Duckbill Platypus

Australia's duckbill platypus is a most unusual animal. It is very strange-looking and has caused a lot of confusion for people studying it. For many years, even scientists did not know how to classify it. The platypus has webbed feet and a bill like a duck. But it doesn't have wings, has fur instead of feathers and has four legs instead of two. The baby platypus gets milk from its mother, like a mammal, but it is hatched from a tough-skinned egg, like a reptile. A platypus also has a poisonous spur on each of its back legs that is like the tip of a viper's fangs. Scientists have put the platypus—along with another strange animal from Australia called the spiny anteater—in a special class of mammal called "monotremes."

The platypus has an amazing appetite! It has been estimated that a full-grown platypus eats about 1,200 earthworms, 50 crayfish and numerous tadpoles and insects every day. The platypus is an excellent swimmer and diver. It dives under the water of a stream and searches the muddy bottom for food.

A mother platypus lays one or two eggs, which are very small—only about an inch long—and leathery in appearance. During the seven to 14 days it takes for the eggs to hatch, the mother never leaves them, not even to eat. The tiny platypus, which is only a half-inch long, cuts its way out of the shell with a sharp point on its bill. This point is known as an "egg tooth," and it will fall off soon after birth. (Many reptiles and birds have egg teeth, but they are unknown in other mammals.) By the time it is 4 months old, the baby platypus is about a foot long—half its adult size—and is learning how to swim and hunt.

Directions: Answer these questions about the duckbill platypus.

1. In what way is a duckbill platypus like other mammals? _____

_____

2. In what way is it like a reptile? _____

3. What other animal is in the class of mammal called "monotremes"?

_____

4. What makes up the diet of a platypus? _____

5. On what other animals would you see an "egg tooth"? _____

Recalling Details: Animals of Australia

Directions: Complete the chart with information from the selection on Australian animals.

	Gray Kangaroo	Koala	Wombat	Platypus
What are the animal's physical characteristics?				
What is the animal's habitat?				
What does the animal eat?				

Main Idea/Recalling Details: Land Down Under

Australia and New Zealand are often referred to as the "land down under." The name, made popular by American soldiers stationed there during World War II, grew out of the idea that these two countries are opposite or below Europe on the globe. While Australia and New Zealand are often linked, they are individual countries, separated by more than 1,000 miles of ocean.

Their landscapes are quite different. New Zealand is made up of two main islands, North and South Island, which are nearly covered by snowy mountains. One of the most unusual and beautiful areas of New Zealand is the volcanic region around Lake Taupo on North Island. There you will see boiling springs, pools of steaming mud, hot-water geysers, small lakes with beds of brightly colored rocks and waterfalls. While most of the people of New Zealand live and work in the industrialized cities, dairy farming is most important to the country's economy. The New Zealanders eat more meat and butter than people anywhere else in the world, and they sell huge amounts to other countries.

As in Australia, many of the customs in New Zealand would be familiar to a traveler from America because the two countries were settled by British settlers hundreds of years ago. However, the native islanders have descended from Asian ancestors, so the remnants of ancient Eastern practices exist alongside the European way of life.

Directions: Answer these questions about New Zealand and Australia.

1. The main idea is:

   ☐ Australia and New Zealand are often referred to as the "land down under."

   ☐ While Australia and New Zealand are often linked, they are individual countries.

2. What is the correct definition for **landscape**?

   ☐ natural scenery and features   ☐ mountainsides   ☐ natural resources

3. What is the correct definition for **economy**?

   ☐ thrifty   ☐ money management   ☐ countryside

4. What is the nickname for Australia and New Zealand? _____

5. What business is most important to the New Zealand economy? _____

Venn Diagrams: Australia and New Zealand

Directions: Although Australia and New Zealand are close geographically to each other, they have many differences. After reading the selection, "Land Down Under," complete the following Venn diagram.

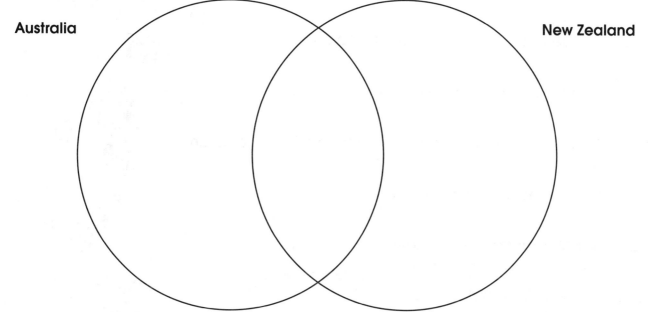

Australia   New Zealand

Directions: Using your knowledge of the United States and Australia, complete the following Venn diagram.

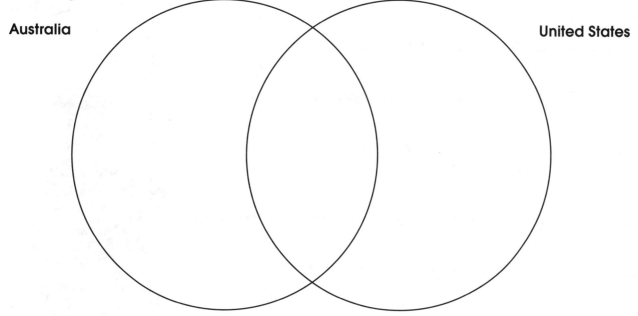

Australia   United States

Name: _____

Review

Directions: Write **T** for true and **F** for false.

_____ 1. Australia and New Zealand are similar in landscape.

_____ 2. Australia is home to the duckbill platypus.

_____ 3. The wombat resembles a beaver without a tail.

_____ 4. The platypus is a special mammal called a monotreme.

_____ 5. A kangaroo is a marsupial.

_____ 6. Baby kangaroos are independent at birth.

_____ 7. Koalas are related to bears.

_____ 8. Female koalas and kangaroos both have pouches.

_____ 9. Koalas eat all types of leaves.

_____ 10. There are over 40 kinds of kangaroos.

_____ 11. The Australian Outback is located in the central part of the country.

_____ 12. Australia raises more sheep than any other country.

_____ 13. Aborigines arrived in Australia over 20,000 years ago.

_____ 14. Aborigines live in one central place.

Using Prior Knowledge: World Cities

Directions: Before reading about world cities in the following section, write one or two sentences telling what you know about each city below.

London, England _____

_____

_____

Berlin, Germany _____

_____

_____

Sydney, Australia _____

_____

_____

Cairo, Egypt _____

_____

_____

Washington, D.C., United States _____

_____

_____

Ottawa, Canada _____

_____

_____

Creative Writing: London

- London is the capital of England.
- Over 6.5 million people live in London.
- Over 60 percent of the people who live in London are employed in service industries. About 10 percent are employed in manufacturing and engineering.
- London is one of Europe's largest seaports.
- London has many historic sites, including Westminster Abbey, Houses of Parliament, Big Ben and Buckingham Palace.
- Buckingham Palace is the residence of the queen of England, Queen Elizabeth II.

Directions: Using the above information, create a tourist article describing London. Do some research and add other interesting information.

_____

_____

_____

_____

_____

_____

_____

When you think of England, what comes to mind?_____

_____

_____

Would you like to visit London? Why or why not? _____

_____

_____

Creative Writing: Berlin

- Berlin is the capital of Germany.
- The population of Berlin is over 3.5 million people.
- Berlin's Inland Harbor is connected to the Baltic Sea.
- This country was once divided into East and West Germany after World War II. East Germany was Communist and West Germany was a Democracy.
- The majority of people living in Berlin are employed in manufacturing.
- Interesting sites in Berlin include the Brandenburg Gate, the State Opera House, Tiergarten Park and the Philharmonic Concert Hall.

Directions: Using the above information, create a tourist article describing Berlin. Do some research and add other interesting information.

_____

_____

_____

_____

_____

_____

When you think of Germany, what comes to mind? _____

_____

_____

Would you like to visit Berlin? Why or why not? _____

_____

_____

Making Inferences: Sydney

- Sydney is the capital of New South Wales, Australia.
- Manufacturing is a strong industry in Sydney. The city is also the headquarters of many large companies.
- Sydney is the major port of southeastern Australia.
- Sydney is Australia's largest city.
- The discovery of gold in 1851 increased Sydney's population. The population today is over 3 million people.
- Interesting sites in Sydney include the Sydney Opera House, the Sydney Harbour Bridge and the Australia Square Tower, which is the country's largest skyscraper.

Directions: Answer these questions about Sydney.

1. Why is manufacturing a strong industry in Sydney, as well as other major cities?

_____

_____

2. Gold was discovered in Australia in what year? _____

3. What two states in the United States were overrun by gold diggers at about the same time?

_____

4. When you think of Australia, what comes to mind? _____

_____

_____

_____

5. Would you like to visit Sydney? Why or why not? _____

_____

_____

Making Inferences: Cairo

- Cairo is the capital of Egypt.
- Cairo is the largest city of not only Egypt but all of Africa and the Middle East.
- The population of Cairo is almost 7 million people.
- Cairo is the cultural center for the Islamic religion.
- Cairo is a major industrial site for Egypt.
- Cairo is a port on the Nile River near the head of the Nile delta.
- Interesting sites include the Egyptian Museum, the Sphinx, the pyramids and the City of the Dead.

Directions: Answer these questions about Cairo.

1. All the major cities discussed so far, including Cairo, have a seaport. Historically speaking, what is the importance of having access to the sea?

_____

_____

_____

2. Cairo has a population of almost 7 million people. What are three problems which could arise from having such a large population?

1) _____

2) _____

3) _____

3. Would you like to visit Cairo? Why or why not? _____

_____

_____

_____

Creative Writing: Washington, D.C.

- Washington, D.C. is the capital of the United States.
- The population of Washington, D.C. is over 600,000 people in the city itself. Many people who work in Washington, D.C. reside in suburbs of the city in Virginia and Maryland.
- One-third of the people employed in Washington, D.C. work for the federal government.
- The Potomac and Anacostia Rivers join in Washington, D.C.
- Interesting sites include the White House, the Vietnam Veterans Memorial, the Lincoln Memorial, the Washington Monument and the United States Capitol Building.

Directions: Using the above information, create a tourist article describing Washington, D.C. Do some research and add other interesting information.

_____

_____

_____

_____

_____

_____

_____

When you think of Washington, D.C., what comes to mind? _____

_____

_____

Would you like to visit Washington, D.C.? Why or why not? _____

_____

_____

Making Inferences: Ottawa

- Ottawa is the capital of Canada and is located in Ontario.
- The federal government employs most people in the city. Manufacturing is another large employer.
- The Rideau Canal connects Ottawa to Lake Ontario.
- The population of Ottawa is over 300,000 people.
- Points of interest include the Peace Tower, Parliament Buildings, the Royal Canadian Mint and the Canadian Museum of Nature.

Directions: Answer these questions about Ottawa.

1. Who employs the most people in Ottawa, Canada? _____

2. What body of water connects Ottawa to Lake Ontario? _____

3. In order from largest to smallest, list the six cities you have read about and their populations.

_____   _____

_____   _____

_____   _____

_____   _____

_____   _____

4. Canada is the United States' neighbor to the north. What problems could arise due to a shared border?

_____

_____

_____

_____

_____

Compare/Contrast: Venn Diagram

A **Venn diagram** is used to chart information that shows similarities and differences between two things. You can use a Venn diagram as an organizational tool before writing a compare/contrast essay.

Directions: Review the completed Venn diagram and the compare/contrast essay below.

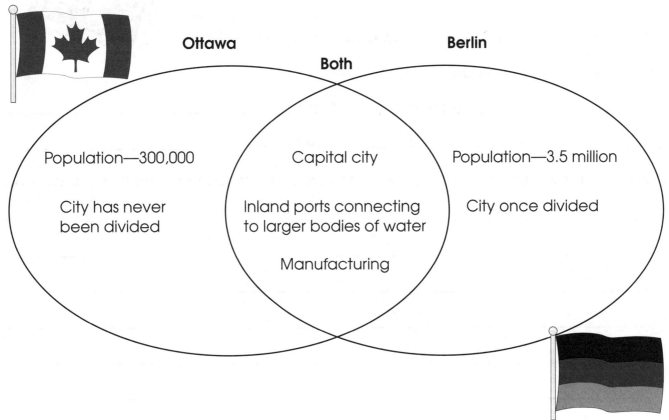

Ottawa

Both

Berlin

Population—300,000

City has never been divided

Capital city

Inland ports connecting to larger bodies of water

Manufacturing

Population—3.5 million

City once divided

Compare/Contrast Essay

Ottawa, Canada and Berlin, Germany share important characteristics. Ottawa and Berlin are both capital cities in their countries. This means that both cities house the country's federal government. Ottawa has access to Lake Ontario through the Rideau Canal. Inland Harbor in Berlin provides that city's access to the Baltic Sea. Finally, both Ottawa and Berlin are sites for major manufacturing industries that help the economy.

Although Ottawa and Berlin are alike in some ways, in other ways, they are very different. The most obvious difference is in population. Ottawa has a mere 300,000 people, while over 3 million reside in Berlin. Also, Berlin was once divided into East and West sections after World War II, with separate governments and facilities. Ottawa has never been divided.

Review

Directions: Using page 162 as a guide, complete the Venn diagram comparing Washington, D.C. and London, England. Then write a two-paragraph compare/contrast essay.

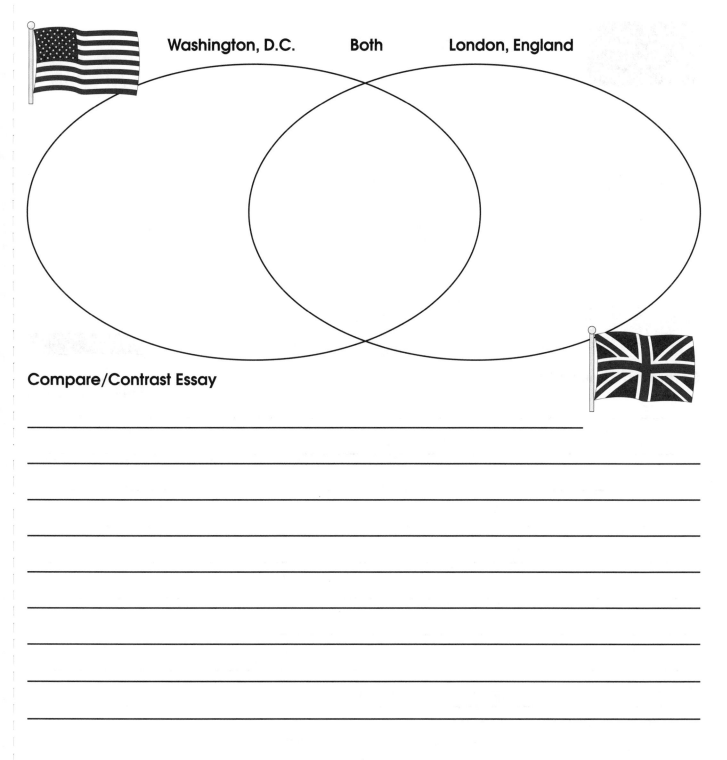

Washington, D.C.   Both   London, England

Compare/Contrast Essay

_____

_____

_____

_____

_____

_____

_____

_____

_____

_____

Name: _____

Review

Directions: Using page 162 as a guide, complete the Venn diagram comparing Sydney, Australia and Cairo, Egypt. Then write a two-paragraph compare/contrast essay.

Sydney, Australia   **Both**   **Cairo, Egypt**

Compare/Contrast Essay

_____

_____

_____

_____

_____

_____

_____

_____

_____

Using Prior Knowledge: Dinosaurs

Everyone is intrigued by dinosaurs. Their size, ferocity and sudden disappearance have fueled scientific investigations for well over a century.

Directions: Before reading about dinosaurs in the following section, answer these questions.

1. Describe what you know about meat-eating dinosaurs. _____

_____

_____

_____

_____

_____

2. Describe what you know about plant-eating dinosaurs. _____

_____

_____

_____

_____

_____

3. Which dinosaur most intrigues you? Why? _____

_____

_____

_____

_____

_____

Main Idea: Small Dinosaurs

When most people think of dinosaurs, they visualize enormous creatures. Actually, there were many species of small dinosaurs—some were only the size of chickens.

Like the larger dinosaurs, the Latin names of the smaller ones usually describe the creature. A small but fast species of dinosaur was Saltopus, which means "leaping foot." An adult Saltopus weighed only about 2 pounds and grew to be approximately 2 feet long. Fossils of this dinosaur, which lived about 200 million years ago, have been found only in Scotland.

Another small dinosaur with an interesting name was Compsognathus, which means "pretty jaw." About the same length as the Saltopus, the Compsognathus weighed about three times more. It's unlikely that these two species knew one another, since Compsognathus remains have been found only in France and Germany.

A small dinosaur whose remains have been found in southern Africa is Lesothosaurus, which means "Lesotho lizard." This lizard-like dinosaur was named only partly for its appearance. The first half of its name is based on the place its remains were found—Lesotho, in southern Africa.

Directions: Answer these questions about small dinosaurs.

1. Circle the main idea:

   People who think dinosaurs were big are completely wrong.

   There are several species of small dinosaurs, some weighing only 2 pounds.

2. How much did Saltopus weigh? _____

3. Which dinosaur's name means "pretty jaw"? _____

Comprehension: Dinosaur History

Dinosaurs are so popular today that it's hard to imagine this not always being the case. The fact is, no one had any idea that dinosaurs ever existed until about 150 years ago.

In 1841, a British scientist named Richard Owen coined the term **Dinosauria** to describe several sets of recently discovered large fossil bones. **Dinosauria** is Latin for "terrible lizards," and even though some dinosaurs were similar to lizards, modern science now also links dinosaurs to birds. Today's birds are thought to be the closest relatives to the dinosaurs.

Like birds, most dinosaurs had fairly long legs that extended straight down from beneath their bodies. Because of their long legs, many dinosaurs were able to move fast. They were also able to balance themselves well. Long-legged dinosaurs, such as the Iguanodon, needed balance to walk upright.

The Iguanodon walked on its long hind legs and used its stubby front legs as arms. On the end of its arms were five hoof-like fingers, one of which functioned as a thumb. Because it had no front teeth for tearing meat, scientists believe the Iguanodon was a plant eater. Its large, flat back teeth were useful for grinding tender plants before swallowing them.

Directions: Answer these questions about the history of dinosaurs.

1. How were dinosaurs like today's birds? _____

_____

_____

2. This man coined the term **Dinosauria**.

☐ Owen Richards   ☐ Richard Owens   ☐ Richard Owen

3. Which of these did the Iguanodon not have?

☐ short front legs   ☐ front teeth   ☐ back teeth

4. List other ways you can think of that dinosaurs and birds are alike. _____

_____

_____

_____

_____

Recalling Details: Dinosaur Puzzler

Directions: Use the facts you have learned about dinosaurs to complete the puzzle.

Across:

5. This dinosaur had five hoof-like fingers on its short front legs.

6. Dinosaurs with flat back teeth were ____ eaters.

9. Because of where their legs were positioned, dinosaurs had good ____.

Down:

1. Most dinosaurs had ____ legs.

2. The word **Dinosauria** means terrible ____.

3. A bone that has been preserved for many years

4. Dinosaurs were not always as ____ as they are now.

7. Iguanodons walked on their ____ legs.

8. Richard ____ coined the term **Dinosauria**.

9. Dinosaurs are closely related to today's ____.

Comprehension: Tyrannosaurus Rex

The largest meat-eating animal ever to roam Earth was Tyrannosaurus Rex. "Rex" is Latin for "king," and because of its size, Tyrannosaurus certainly was at the top of the dinosaur heap. With a length of 46 feet and a weight of 7 tons, there's no doubt this dinosaur commanded respect!

Unlike smaller dinosaurs, Tyrannosaurus wasn't tremendously fast on its huge feet. It could stroll along at a walking speed of 2 to 3 miles an hour. Not bad, considering Tyrannosaurus was pulling along a body that weighed 14,000 pounds! Like other dinosaurs, Tyrannosaurus walked upright, probably balancing its 16-foot-long head by lifting its massive tail.

Compared to the rest of its body, Tyrannosaurus' front claws were tiny. Scientists aren't really sure what the claws were for, although it seems likely that they may have been used for holding food. In that case, Tyrannosaurus would have had to lower its massive head down to its short claws to take anything in its mouth. Maybe it just used the claws to scratch nearby itches!

Because of their low metabolism, dinosaurs did not require a lot of food for survival. Scientists speculate that Tyrannosaurus ate off the same huge piece of meat—usually the carcass of another dinosaur—for several weeks. What do you suppose Tyrannosaurus did the rest of the time?

Directions: Answer these questions about Tyrannosaurus Rex.

1. Why was this dinosaur called "Rex"? _____

_____

2. For what might Tyrannosaurus Rex have used its claws? _____

_____

3. How long was Tyrannosaurus Rex? _____

4. Tyrannosaurus weighed

   ☐ 10,000 lbs.   ☐ 12,000 lbs.   ☐ 14,000 lbs.

5. Tyrannosaurus ate

   ☐ plants.   ☐ other dinosaurs.   ☐ birds.

Name: _____

Generalization: Dinosaur Characteristics

Directions: Read each passage and circle the valid generalization.

1. Not surprisingly, Tyrannosaurus had huge teeth in its mammoth head. They were 6 inches long! Because it was a meat eater, Tyrannosaurus' teeth were sharp. They looked like spikes! In comparison, the long-necked, plant-eating Mamenchisaurus had a tiny head and small, flat teeth.

   a. Scientists can't figure out why some dinosaurs had huge teeth.

   b. Tyrannosaurus was probably scarier looking than Mamenchisaurus.

   c. Sharp teeth would have helped Mamenchisaurus chew better.

2. Dinosaurs' names often reflect their size or some other physical trait. For example, Compsognathus means "pretty jaw." Saltopus means "leaping foot." Lesothosaurus means "lizard from Lesotho."

   a. Of the three species, Lesothosaurus was probably the fastest.

   b. Of the three species, Compsognathus was probably the fastest.

   c. Of the three species, Saltopus was probably the fastest.

3. Edmontosaurus, a huge 3-ton dinosaur, had 1,000 teeth! The teeth were cemented into chewing pads in the back of Edmontosaurus' mouth. Unlike the sharp teeth of the meat-eating Tyrannosaurus, this dinosaur's teeth were flat.

   a. Edmontosaurus did not eat meat.

   b. Edmontosaurus did not eat plants.

   c. Edmontosaurus moved very fast.

Comprehension: Dinosaur Fossils

Imagine putting together the world's largest jigsaw puzzle. That is what scientists who reassemble the fossil bones of dinosaurs must do to find out what the creatures looked like. Fossilized bones are imbedded, or stuck, in solid rock, so scientists must first get the bones out of the rocks without breaking or otherwise damaging them. This task requires enormous patience.

In addition to hammers, drills and chisels, sound waves are used to break up the rock. The drills, which are similar to high-speed dentist drills, cut through the rock very quickly. As the bones are removed, scientists begin trying to figure out how they attach to one another. Sometimes the dinosaur's skeleton was preserved just as it was when it died. This, of course, shows scientists exactly how to reassemble it. Other times, parts of bone are missing. It then becomes a guessing game to decide what goes where.

When scientists discover dinosaur fossils, it is called a "find." A particularly exciting find in 1978 occurred in Montana when, for the first time, fossilized dinosaur eggs, babies and several nests were found. The species of dinosaur in this exciting find was Maiasaura, which means "good mother lizard." From the size of the nest, which was 23 feet, scientists speculated that the adult female Maiasaura was about the same size.

Unlike birds' nests, dinosaur nests were not made of sticks and straw. Instead, since they were land animals, nests were made of dirt hollowed out into a bowl shape. The Maiasaura's nest was 3 feet deep and held about 20 eggs.

Directions: Answer these questions about dinosaur fossils.

1. Name four tools used to remove dinosaur bones from rock. _____

_____

_____

2. What do scientists do with the bones they remove? _____

_____

3. The type of dinosaur fossils found in Montana in 1978 were

☐ Mayiasaura.   ☐ Masaura.   ☐ Maiasaura.

4. When scientists discover dinosaur fossils, it is called a

☐ found.   ☐ find.   ☐ nest.

Generalization: Plant-Eating Dinosaurs

Directions: Read each passage and circle the valid generalization.

1. Many of the plant-eating dinosaurs belonged to a common species called Sauropods. Most Sauropods were very large. They had peg-shaped teeth and they formed herds to search for food. They used their long necks to reach the top branches of trees, where the most tender leaves grew.

   a. Their size, teeth and long necks made Sauropods perfectly suited to their environment.

   b. The Sauropods' peg-like teeth were not well suited to eating meat.

   c. Vegetarian dinosaurs needed short necks and sharp teeth to survive.

2. Sauropods were not the only dinosaurs that traveled in herds. Sets of different-sized fossilized dinosaur footprints discovered in Texas show that other types of dinosaurs also traveled together. The footprints—23 sets of them—were of another plant-eating dinosaur, the Apatosaurus.

   a. All dinosaurs traveled in herds because they needed companionship.

   b. It appears that some plant-eating dinosaurs traveled in herds.

   c. Traveling in herds offered dinosaurs protection and friendship.

3. Not all plant-eating dinosaurs were huge. The Hypsilophodon was only about $6\frac{1}{2}$ feet tall. It stood on its two back legs and, because of its smaller size, probably ran away from danger.

   a. The Hypsilophodon didn't stand a chance against bigger dinosaurs.

   b. The Hypsilophodon could not eat from the tops of tall trees.

   c. The Hypsilophodon was cowardly and always ran from danger.

Comprehension: Dinosaur Tracks

Some scientists refer to dinosaurs' fossilized tracks as "footprints in time." The tracks that survived in Texas for 120 million years had been made in sand or mud. These large footprints were of the Apatosaurus. The footprints were more than 3 feet across!

Although Apatosaurus had a long, heavy tail, there is no sign that the tail hit the ground along with the feet. Scientists speculate that the place where the tracks were found was once a riverbed, and that Apatosaurus' tail floated in the water and thus left no tracks. Another theory is that the dinosaur always carried its tail out behind it. This second theory is not as popular, because scientists say it's unlikely the dinosaur would consistently carry its long, heavy tail off the ground. When Apatosaurus rested, for example, the tail would have left its mark.

Besides Texas, fossilized tracks have been found in England, Canada, Australia and Brazil. Some tracks have also been found in New England. The tracks discovered in Canada were quite a find! They showed a pattern made by 10 species of dinosaurs. In all, about 1,700 fossilized footprints were discovered. Maybe the scientists uncovered what millions of years ago was a dinosaur playground!

Directions: Answer these questions about dinosaur tracks.

1. Circle the main idea:

   Fossilized dinosaur tracks provide scientists with information from which to draw conclusions about dinosaur size and behavior.

   Fossilized dinosaur tracks are not very useful because so few have been found in the United States.

2. Explain how a dinosaur might have crossed a river without its tail leaving a track.

   _____

3. Name five countries where dinosaur tracks have been found. _____

   _____

4. Circle the valid generalization about dinosaur tracks.

   a. The fact that 10 species of tracks were found together proves dinosaurs were friends with others outside their groups.

   b. The fact that 10 species of tracks were found together means the dinosaurs probably gathered in that spot for water or food.

Review

Directions: Reread the following selections. Then write the main idea of each.

Small Dinosaurs _____

_____

_____

_____

Dinosaur History _____

_____

_____

_____

Tyrannosaurus Rex _____

_____

_____

_____

Dinosaur Fossils _____

_____

_____

_____

Dinosaur Tracks _____

_____

_____

_____

Name: _____

The Solar System

This section is about our solar system. It includes the Sun, comparisons among the planets, each planet's physical characteristics and each planet's moons. Before beginning this section, try to answer the following questions.

1. Name the nine planets of the solar system in order beginning with the planet closest to the Sun.

   a. _____   b. _____   c. _____

   d. _____   e. _____   f. _____

   g. _____   h. _____   i. _____

2. Write a distinguishing characteristic for each planet listed below.

   Earth _____

   Jupiter _____

   Saturn _____

   Pluto _____

3. The study of the solar system, stars and outer space is called

   _____ .

4. The _____ is the center of the solar system and is a star.

5. Which planet is similar in size to the Earth? _____

6. Humans have landed on which outer space object? _____

7. Have humans landed on any planets? Why or why not? _____

   _____

   _____

The Sun

Directions: Read the selection. Then answer the questions.

The Sun is the center of our solar system. It is a star that seems massive to those on Earth but is dwarfed in comparison to other giant stars farther out in the universe. It rotates on its axis just like the Earth. The Sun is made up of heated gases, and it releases heat and light energy. The part of the Sun we see is called the photosphere. The chromosphere is the colored ring of gases surrounding the Sun. Solar flares often shoot out from the Sun's surface for thousands of miles. Without the Sun's warmth, life on Earth would cease to exist.

1. Define the following words.

    axis: _____

    _____

    universe: _____

    dwarfed: _____

    cease: _____

2. What effect could a solar flare have on Earth?

    _____

    _____

3. Does the Sun revolve or rotate? _____

4. Why isn't the Sun visible at night? _____

5. Why is it important never to look directly at the Sun?

    _____

    _____

Mercury

Directions: Read the selection. Then answer the questions.

The planet Mercury is named for the Roman god Mercury who was the messenger of the gods. Ancient Greek astronomers named the heavenly bodies "planets," which means "wanderers." Mercury is the planet closest to the Sun and also the smallest of the inner planets. Because of its proximity to the Sun (nearly 36 million miles), its surface is extraordinarily hot. Mercury's solid surface is covered with craters. It rotates on its axis once every 59 days. One year on Mercury lasts 88 Earth days. Mercury has no moons or rings and has virtually no atmosphere.

1. Define the following words:

   astronomer: _____

   _____

   proximity: _____

   atmosphere: _____

   crater: _____

2. Could life survive on Mercury? Why or why not?

   _____

   _____

3. Write a 3 sentence summary of the selection above.

   _____

   _____

4. Mercury's period of revolution is 88 days. How many months would that be?

   _____

Venus

Directions: Read the selection. Then answer the questions.

Located over 67 million miles from the Sun, Venus is an incredibly hot planet. Venus is named for the Roman goddess of love and beauty. Temperatures can reach 470 degrees Celsius. Venus is close in size to the Earth and is often referred to as Earth's twin. Space probes and unmanned crafts have landed on Venus and found Venus to be dust-covered and very windy. Because Venus is very bright, it is often thought of as a star. Venus has no moons or rings. Its period of rotation is 243 days, and it revolves once around the Sun in 225 days.

1. Create a Venn diagram comparing Mercury and Venus.

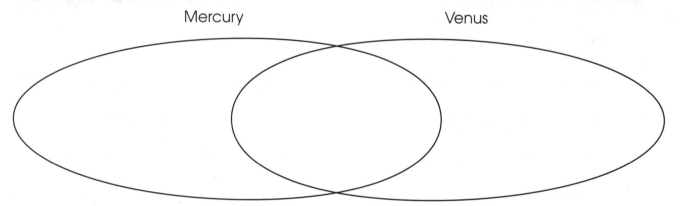

Mercury   Venus

2. Write a 3-sentence summary about Venus.

_____

_____

_____

3. Approximately how far is Venus from Mercury? _____

4. If you were to design a spacecraft capable of landing on Venus, what might it require?

_____

_____

_____

Earth

Directions: Read the selection. Then answer the questions.

Earth is the only planet with known life forms. It revolves around the Sun every 365 1/4 days. One rotation takes 24 hours to complete. Earth has seasons due to the tilt of its axis and its revolution. Rotation causes night and day. The Earth is almost 93 million miles away from the Sun. Its surface is three-fourths water and one-fourth land mass. The Earth is surrounded by gases called the atmosphere, which allows life to survive. The Earth has one moon that has been explored many times.

1. Define the following word.

   mass: _____

   _____

2. Approximately how far is the Earth from Venus?

   _____

3. Approximately how far is Earth from Mercury?

   _____

4. What factors allow life to exist on Earth?

   _____

   _____

5. What causes the seasons?

   _____

6. What differences are there between Earth and the planets Mercury and Venus?

   _____

   _____

   _____

Mars

Directions: Read the selection. Then answer the questions.

Mars is named for the god of war. It is the fourth of the inner planets. Mars is called the Red Planet and has polar caps, craters and evidence of ancient volcanoes. Recently, space probes have landed there and given scientists information about its surface. The red color is produced by the reaction of iron-rich minerals to soil and water, which scientists believe happened long ago. Mars rotates on its axis every 24 hours, 37 minutes and is 142 million miles from the Sun. Its period of revolution is 687 days. Mars has two moons, Phobos and Deimos. Mars' identifying feature is the volcano Olympus Mons. Its temperature varies, but averages –50 degrees Celsius.

1. Define the following words.

    polar: _____

    mineral: _____

2. Name two distinguishing characteristics of Mars.

    _____

    _____

3. Could life survive on Mars? Why or why not?

    _____

    _____

    _____

4. For years, people have been interested in the possibility of Martian life. What special characteristics would life on Mars have?

    _____

    _____

    _____

    _____

Jupiter

Directions: Read the selection. Then answer the questions.

The planet Jupiter is the largest planet of our solar system and is named for the king of the gods. Its distinguishing feature is the Great Red Spot, which changes occasionally in both color and brightness. Jupiter has a thin ring and at least 16 moons. Jupiter is the first of the outer planets, separated from the inner planets by an asteroid belt. It is almost 500 million miles from the Sun and takes nearly 12 years to complete a revolution around the Sun. It rotates on its axis in approximately 10 hours. Jupiter does not have a solid surface but rather a surface of gaseous clouds.

1. Define the following words.

   asteroid: _____

   gaseous: _____

2. Approximately how far is Jupiter from Earth?

   _____

3. Name three characteristics of Jupiter.

   _____

   _____

4. Write a 3-sentence summary about Jupiter.

   _____

   _____

   _____

5. What separates the inner and outer planets?

   _____

6. Why do you think ancient astronomers chose to name Jupiter after the king of the gods?

   _____

Saturn

Directions: Read the selection. Then answer the questions.

Saturn's rings were first discovered in 1610. Scientists now know that Saturn has over 1000 rings of varying color. Not only do the rings rotate at different speeds but also in varying patterns. Saturn has at least 18 moons. It is almost 900 million miles from the Sun and is the second largest planet of our solar system. Saturn rotates on its axis once in just under 11 hours. Saturn is named for the god of agriculture and harvest.

1. Define the following words:

   varying: _____

   agriculture: _____

2. Name two distinguishing characteristics of Saturn.

   _____

   _____

3. Approximately how far is Saturn from Jupiter?

   _____

4. Create a Venn diagram showing the similarities and differences between Saturn and Jupiter.

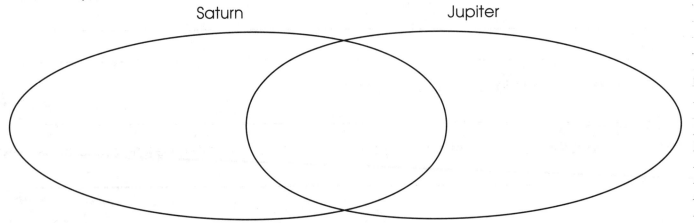

Saturn   Jupiter

Uranus, Neptune, and Pluto

Directions: Read the selection. Then answer the questions.

Because of the immense distance from Earth, it is difficult to study Uranus, Neptune, and Pluto. These planets are named for the god of the skies, the god of the sea and the god of the underworld, respectively.

Uranus rotates on its side, thus making its rings spin vertically rather than horizontally. It has 15 moons and is almost 2 billion miles from the Sun. It rotates on its axis once every 17.25 hours and revolves around the Sun every 84 years.

Neptune is similar in size and color to Uranus. It is almost 3 billion miles from the Sun and takes approximately 164 years to orbit it. Neptune has 8 moons and also has rings. It takes a little over 16 hours to make one rotation on its axis.

Pluto is usually the most distant and smallest planet of our solar system. (It rotated inside Neptune's orbit from January 1979 through February 1999.) It was discovered in 1930. It is approximately 7 billion miles from the Sun and therefore the coldest at -230 degrees Celsius. Pluto takes over 6 days to complete one rotation on its axis and 247 Earth years to complete one revolution around the sun. Pluto has one moon.

1. List the similarities among Uranus, Neptune, and Pluto.

_____

_____

_____

2. What differences are there among Uranus, Neptune, and Pluto?

_____

_____

_____

Uranus, Neptune, and Pluto

Directions: Use the lists you created on page 183 to create a Venn diagram showing the similarities and differences among Uranus, Neptune, and Pluto.

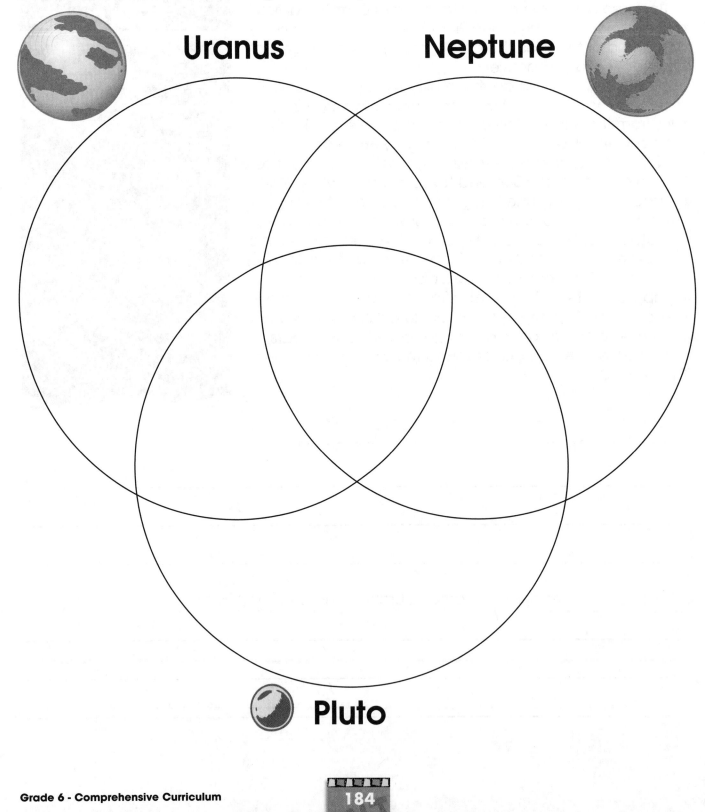

Uranus

Neptune

Pluto

Review

Directions: Follow the instructions for each question.

1. List the four inner planets.

   _____ _____ _____ _____

2. List the five outer planets.

   _____   _____   _____

   _____   _____

3. What separates the inner and outer planets?

   _____

4. Name a distinguishing feature of each planet.

   Mercury: _____

   Venus: _____

   Earth: _____

   Mars: _____

   Jupiter: _____

   Saturn: _____

   Uranus: _____

   Neptune: _____

   Pluto: _____

5. List the planets in order from most moons to least.

   a) _____   f) _____

   b) _____   g) _____

   c) _____   h) _____

   d) _____   i) _____

   e) _____

Review

6. Which planets have rings?

   _____

7. If you were in charge of the space program, what would your priorities be? Why?

   _____

   _____

   _____

   _____

8. Draw a diagram of the planets and the Sun. Be sure to depict color and the following diameter sizes.

   Mercury — 3,031 mi.   Venus — 7,521 mi.   Earth — 7,926 mi.

   Mars — 4,217 mi.   Jupiter — 88,730 mi.   Saturn — 74,900 mi.

   Uranus — 31,763 mi.   Neptune — 30,775 mi.   Pluto — 1,430 mi.

Recalling Details: The Earth's Atmosphere

The most important reason that life can exist on Earth is its atmosphere—the air around us. Without it, plant and animal life could not have developed. There would be no clouds, weather or even sounds, only a deathlike stillness and an endlessly black sky. Without the protection of the atmosphere, the sun's rays would roast the Earth by day. At night, with no blanketing atmosphere, the stored heat would escape into space, dropping the temperature of the planet hundreds of degrees.

Held captive by Earth's gravity, the atmosphere surrounds the planet to a depth of hundreds of miles. However, all but 1 percent of the atmosphere is in a layer about 20 miles deep just above the surface of the Earth. It is made up of a mixture of gases and dusts. About 78 percent of it is a gas called nitrogen, which is very important as food for plants. Most of the remaining gas, 21 percent, is oxygen, which all people and animals depend on for life. The remaining 1 percent is made up of a blend of other gases—including carbon dioxide, argon, ozone and helium—and tiny dust particles. These particles come from ocean salt crystals, bits of rocks and sand, plant pollen, volcanic ash and even meteor dust.

You may not think of air as matter, as something that can be weighed. In fact, the Earth's air weighs billions and billions of tons. Near the surface of the planet, this "air pressure" is greatest. Right now, about 10 tons of air is pressing in on you. Yet, like the fish living near the floor of the ocean, you don't notice this tremendous weight because your body is built to withstand it.

Directions: Answer these questions about the Earth's atmosphere.

1. What is the atmosphere? _____

2. Of what is the atmosphere made? _____

3. What is the most abundant gas in the atmosphere? _____

4. Which of the atmosphere's gases is most important to humans and animals?

   _____

5. What is air pressure? _____

Comprehension: Causes/Effects of Weather

The behavior of the atmosphere, which we experience as weather and climate, affects our lives in many important ways. It is the reason no one lives on the South Pole. It controls when a farmer plants the food we will eat, which crops will be planted and also whether those crops will grow. The weather tells you what clothes to wear and how you will play after school. Weather is the sum of all the conditions of the air that may affect the Earth's surface and its living things. These conditions include the temperature, air pressure, wind and moisture. Climate refers to these conditions but generally applies to larger areas and longer periods of time, such as the annual climate of South America rather than today's weather in Oklahoma City.

Climate is influenced by many factors. It depends first and foremost on latitude. Areas nearest the equator are warm and wet, while the poles are cold and relatively dry. The poles also have extreme seasonal changes, while the areas at the middle latitudes have more moderate climates, neither as cold as the poles nor as hot as the equator. Other circumstances may alter this pattern, however. Land near the oceans, for instance, is generally warmer than inland areas.

Elevation also plays a role in climate. For example, despite the fact that Africa's highest mountain, Kilimanjaro, is just south of the equator, its summit is perpetually covered by snow. In general, high land is cooler and wetter than nearby low land.

Directions: Check the answers to these questions about the causes and effects of weather.

1. What is the correct definition for **atmosphere**?

    ☐ the clouds   ☐ the sky   ☐ where weather occurs

2. What is the correct definition for **foremost**?

    ☐ most important   ☐ highest number   ☐ in the front

3. What is the correct definition for **circumstances**?

    ☐ temperatures   ☐ seasons   ☐ conditions

4. What is the correct definition for **elevation**?

    ☐ height above Earth ☐ nearness to equator ☐ snow covering

5. What is the correct definition for **perpetually**?

    ☐ occasionally   ☐ rarely   ☐ always

Main Idea/Recalling Details: Weather

People have always searched the sky for clues about upcoming weather. Throughout the ages, farmers and sailors have looked to the winds and clouds for signs of approaching storms. But no real understanding of the weather could be achieved without a scientific study of the atmosphere. Such a study depends on being able to measure certain conditions, including pressure, temperature and moisture levels.

A true scientific examination of weather, therefore, was not possible until the development of accurate measuring instruments, beginning in the 17th century. Meteorology—the science of studying the atmosphere—was born in 1643 with the invention of the barometer, which measures atmospheric pressure. The liquid-in-glass thermometer, the hygrometer to measure humidity—the amount of moisture in the air—and the weather map also were invented during the 1600s.

With the measurement of these basic elements, scientists began to work out the relationships between these and other atmospheric conditions, such as wind, clouds and rainfall. Still, their observations failed to show an overall picture of the weather. Such complete weather reporting had to wait two centuries for the rapid transfer of information made possible by the invention of the telegraph during the 1840s.

Today, the forecasts of meteorologists are an international effort. There are thousands of weather stations around the world, both at land and at sea. Upper-level observations are also made by weather balloons and satellites, which continuously send photographs back to earth. All of this information is relayed to national weather bureaus, where meteorologists plot it on graphs and analyze it. The information is then given to the public through newspapers and television and radio stations.

Directions: Answer these questions about studying the weather.

1. The main idea is:

☐ People have always searched the sky for clues about upcoming weather.
☐ A real understanding of weather depends on measuring conditions such as pressure, temperature and moisture levels.

2. List three kinds of instruments used to measure atmospheric conditions, and tell what conditions they measure.

1) _____ _____

2) _____ _____

3) _____ _____

3. During what century were many of these measuring instruments invented? _____

4. Name two things used for upper-level observations.

1) _____ 2) _____

Comprehension: Hurricanes

The characteristics of a hurricane are powerful winds, driving rain and raging seas. Although a storm must have winds blowing at least 74 miles an hour to be classified as a hurricane, it is not unusual to have winds above 150 miles per hour. The entire storm system can be 500 miles in diameter, with lines of clouds that spiral toward a center called the "eye." Within the eye itself, which is about 15 miles across, the air is actually calm and cloudless. But this eye is enclosed by a towering wall of thick clouds where the storm's heaviest rains and highest winds are found.

All hurricanes begin in the warm seas and moist winds of the tropics. They form in either of two narrow bands to the north and south of the equator. For weeks, the blistering sun beats down on the ocean water. Slowly, the air above the sea becomes heated and begins to swirl. More hot, moist air is pulled skyward. Gradually, this circle grows larger and spins faster. As the hot, moist air at the top is cooled, great rain clouds are formed. The storm's fury builds until it moves over land or a cold area of the ocean where its supply of heat and moisture is finally cut off.

Hurricanes that strike North America usually form over the Atlantic Ocean. West coast storms are less dangerous because they tend to head out over the Pacific Ocean rather than toward land. The greatest damage usually comes from the hurricanes that begin in the western Pacific, because they often batter heavily populated regions.

Directions: Answer these questions about hurricanes.

1. What is necessary for a storm to be classified as a hurricane? _____

   _____

2. What is the "eye" of the hurricane? _____

3. Where do hurricanes come from? _____

4. How does a hurricane finally die down? _____

   _____

5. Why do hurricanes formed in the western Pacific cause the most damage?

   _____

Comprehension: Tornadoes

Tornadoes, which are also called twisters, occur more frequently than hurricanes, but they are smaller storms. The zigzag path of a tornado averages about 16 miles in length and only about a quarter of a mile wide. But the tornado is, pound for pound, the more severe storm. When one touches the ground, it leaves a trail of total destruction.

The winds in a tornado average about 200 miles per hour. At the center of the funnel-shaped cloud of a tornado is a partial vacuum. In combination with the high winds, this is what makes the storm so destructive. Its force is so great that a tornado can drive a piece of straw into a tree. The extremely low atmospheric pressure that accompanies the storm can cause a building to actually explode.

Unlike hurricanes, tornadoes are formed over land. They are most likely to occur over the central plains of the United States, especially in the spring and early summer months. Conditions for a tornado arise when warm, moist air from the south becomes trapped under colder, heavier air from the north. When the surfaces of the two air masses touch, rain clouds form and a thunderstorm begins. At first, only a rounded bulge hangs from the bottom of the cloud. It gradually gets longer until it forms a column reaching toward the ground. The tornado is white from the moisture when it first forms, but turns black as it sucks up dirt and trash.

Directions: Circle **True** or **False** for these statements about tornadoes.

1. The tornado is a stronger storm than the hurricane.   True   False

2. The path of a tornado usually covers hundreds of miles.   True   False

3. Like the eye of a hurricane, the center of a tornado is calm.   True   False

4. Tornadoes are most likely to occur in the central plains of the
   United States during the spring and early summer months.   True   False

5. High atmospheric pressure usually accompanies a tornado.   True   False

Comprehension: Thunderstorms

With warm weather comes the threat of thunderstorms. The rapid growth of the majestic thunderhead cloud and the damp, cool winds that warn of an approaching storm are familiar in most regions of the world. In fact, it has been estimated that at any given time 1,800 such storms are in progress around the globe.

As with hurricanes and tornadoes, thunderstorms are formed when a warm, moist air mass meets with a cold air mass. Before long, bolts of lightning streak across the sky, and thunder booms. It is not entirely understood how lightning is formed. It is known that a positive electrical charge builds near the top of the cloud, and a negative charge forms at the bottom. When enough force builds up, a powerful current of electricity zigzags down an electrically charged pathway between the two, causing the flash of lightning.

The clap of thunder you hear after a lightning flash is created by rapidly heated air that expands as the lightning passes through it. The distant rumbling is caused by the thunder's sound waves bouncing back and forth within clouds or between mountains. When thunderstorms rumble through an area, many people begin to worry about tornadoes. But they need to be just as fearful of thunderstorms. In fact, lightning kills more people than any other severe weather condition. In 1988, lightning killed 68 people in the United States, while tornadoes killed 32.

Directions: Answer these questions about thunderstorms.

1. How many thunderstorms are estimated to be occurring at any given time around the world?

   _____

2. When are thunderstorms formed?

   _____

3. What causes thunder?

   _____

4. On average, which causes more deaths, lightning or tornadoes?

   _____

Name: _____

Venn Diagram: Storms

Directions: Complete the Venn diagram below. Think of at least three things to write in the outer parts of each circle and at least three things to write in the intersecting parts.

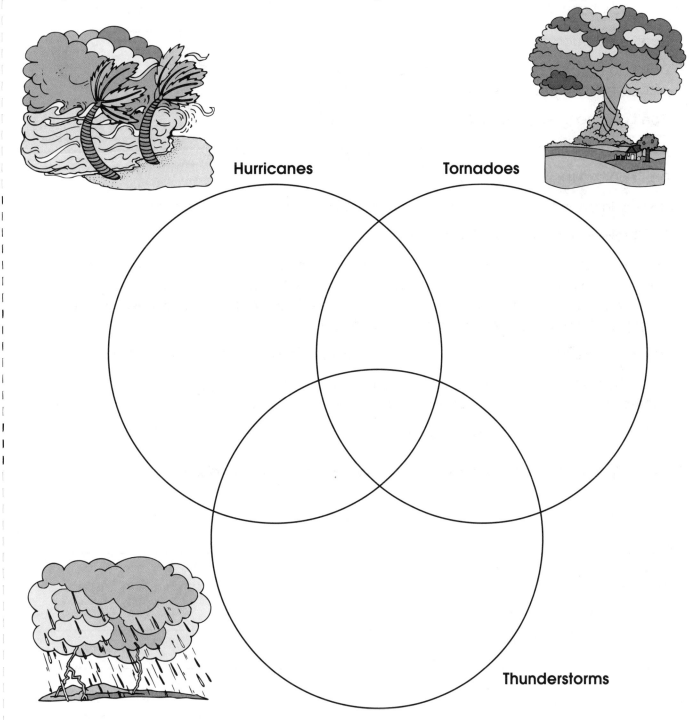

Hurricanes

Tornadoes

Thunderstorms

Grade 6 - Comprehensive Curriculum

Recalling Details: Lightning Safety Rules

Lightning causes more fire damage to forests and property than anything else. More importantly, it kills more people than any other weather event. It is important to know what to do—and what not to do—during a thunderstorm. Here are some important rules to remember:

- **Don't** go outdoors.

- **Don't** go near open doors or windows, fireplaces, radiators, stoves, metal pipes, sinks or plug-in electrical appliances.

- **Don't** use the telephone, as lightning could strike the wires outside.

- **Don't** handle metal objects, such as fishing poles or golf clubs.

- **Don't** go into the water or ride in small boats.

- **Do** stay in an automobile if you are traveling. Cars offer excellent protection.

- **Don't** take laundry off the clothesline.

- **Do** look for shelter if you are outdoors. If there is no shelter, stay away from the highest object in the area. If there are only a few trees nearby, it is best to crouch in the open, away from the trees at a distance greater than the height of the nearest tree. If you are in an area with many trees, avoid the tallest tree. Look for shorter ones.

- **Don't** take shelter near wire fences or clotheslines, exposed sheds or on a hilltop.

- If your hair stands on end or your skin tingles, lightning may be about to strike you. Immediately crouch down, put your feet together and place your hands over your ears.

Directions: Answer these questions about lightning safety rules.

1. Name two things you should avoid if you are looking for shelter outside.

    1) _____

    2) _____

2. What should you do if, during a thunderstorm, your hair stands up or your skin tingles?

    _____

    _____

Main Idea/Comprehension: Rainbows

Although there are some violent, frightening aspects of the weather, there is, of course, considerable beauty, too. The rainbow is one simple, lovely example of nature's atmospheric mysteries.

You usually can see a rainbow when the sun comes out after a rain shower or in the fine spray of a waterfall or fountain. Although sunlight appears to be white, it is actually made up of a mixture of colors—all the colors in the rainbow. We see a rainbow because thousands of tiny raindrops act as mirrors and prisms on the sunlight. Prisms are objects that bend light, splitting it into bands of color.

The bands of color form a perfect semicircle. From the top edge to the bottom, the colors are always in the same order—red, orange, yellow, green, blue, indigo and violet. The brightness and width of each band may vary from one minute to the next. You also may notice that the sky framed by the rainbow is lighter than the sky above. This is because the light that forms the blue and violet bands is more bent and spread out than the light that forms the top red band.

You will always see morning rainbows in the west, with the sun behind you. Afternoon rainbows, likewise, are always in the east. To see a rainbow, the sun can be no higher than 42 degrees—nearly halfway up the sky. Sometimes, if the sunlight is strong and the water droplets are very small, you can see a double rainbow. This happens because the light is reflected twice in the water droplets. The color bands are fainter and in reverse order in the second band.

Directions: Answer these questions about rainbows.

1. Check the statement that is the main idea.

   ☐ Although there are violent, frightening aspects of weather, there is considerable beauty, too.

   ☐ The rainbow is one simple, lovely example of nature's atmospheric mysteries.

2. What is the correct definition for **semicircle**?

   ☐ colored circle   ☐ diameter of a circle   ☐ half circle

3. What is a prism? _____

4. In which direction would you look to see an afternoon rainbow? _____

Comprehension: Cause and Effect

Directions: Complete the chart by listing the cause and effect of each weather phenomenon.

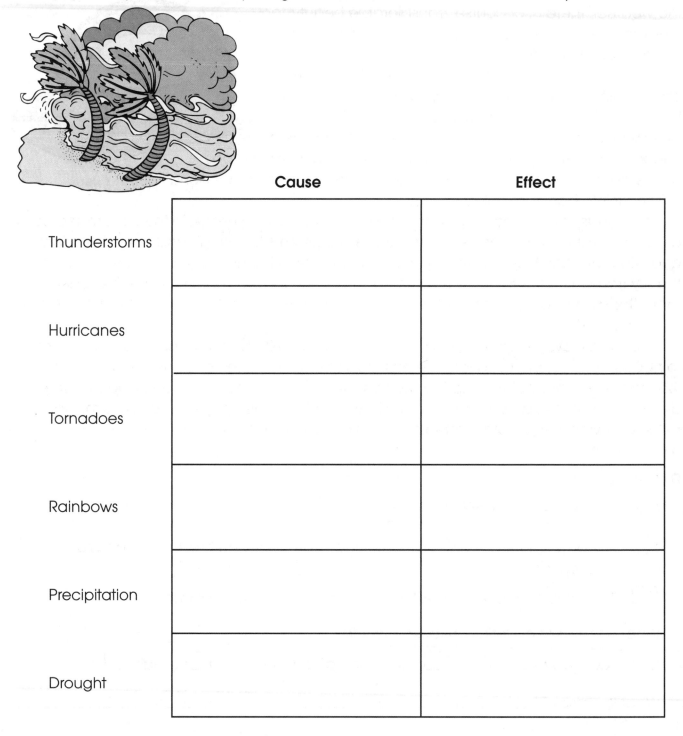

	Cause	Effect
Thunderstorms		
Hurricanes		
Tornadoes		
Rainbows		
Precipitation		
Drought		

Name: _____

Review

Directions: If necessary, review the section on weather to find the answers to the following questions.

1. Describe the earth's atmosphere. _____

_____

2. The science of studying weather is called _____ .

3. Why is it important for weather forecasting to be an international effort?

_____

_____

_____

4. Define **weather**. _____

_____

5. Name three factors that influence climate.

_____ _____ _____

6. Describe the following weather phenomena.

a. hurricane _____

_____

b. tornado _____

_____

c. thunderstorm _____

_____

Using Prior Knowledge: Sports

Directions: Before reading about sports in the following section, write one or two sentences telling what you know about each sport below.

Wrestling _____

_____

Bowling _____

_____

Volleyball _____

_____

Tennis _____

_____

_____

Boxing _____

_____

Football _____

_____

Softball _____

_____

Field Hockey _____

_____

Comprehension: Wrestling Around the World

In many countries, wrestling is an honored sport. In Iceland, wrestling is called "glima"; in Switzerland, it is called "schweitzer schwingen"; and in Ireland, it is called "cumberland." In Japan, a form of wrestling called "sumo" began in 23 B.C.

Sumo wrestling is still popular in Japan today. Wrestlers wear the traditional sumo costume of a loincloth—a piece of cloth draped across the hips and bottom—and nothing else. Sumo wrestlers are big men—their average weight is about 300 pounds. Wrestlers compete in small rings with sand floors. The object of the match is to push the opponent out of the ring.

Even in the wrestling ring, however, the Japanese are astonishingly polite. If one wrestler begins to push the other out of the ring, the other may shout, "Matta!" **Matta** is Japanese for "not yet." At this point, the action stops and the wrestlers step out of the ring to take a break. Some wrestling matches in Japan must take a long, long time to complete!

Directions: Answer these questions about wrestling around the world.

1. What is wrestling called in Switzerland? _____

2. In what country is wrestling called "cumberland"? _____

3. What is wrestling called in Iceland? _____

4. In what country is wrestling called "sumo"? _____

5. How much does an average sumo wrestler weigh? _____

6. What does "matta" mean in Japanese? _____

7. What happens if a wrestler shouts, "Matta"? _____

_____

_____

8. In what year did Sumo wrestling begin? _____

Comprehension: Tennis, Anyone?

Historians say a form of tennis was played outdoors in England in the 16th century. In France, the game had a much, much earlier start. "Court tennis"—named such because royal courts of kings played it—was played indoors about 1000 A.D. Six hundred years later, indoor tennis was still in full swing. Records show there were 2,500 indoor courts in France at that time.

French tennis players and spectators took the game seriously. In 1780, the surgeon general of the French army recommended the game as one good for the lungs and throat. Why? Because of all the loud screaming and shouting that accompanied French games!

The word "tennis" comes from the French term "tenir," which means "take heed" or "watch out." That's what the French yelled out centuries ago when they used huge racquets to whack balls over a sagging net. Later, when the game was adopted in England, "tenir" became "tennis."

Tennis is said to have come to America by way of the island of Bermuda. A young American girl, Mary Outerbridge, played the game when visiting Bermuda in 1873. She brought tennis racquets, balls and a net home to New York with her. The strange equipment puzzled customs officials (government employees who check travelers' bags to make sure they are not smuggling drugs or other substances). They reluctantly permitted Miss Outerbridge to bring the weird game to America, where it has flourished ever since!

Directions: Answer these questions about tennis.

1. In what year were there 2,500 indoor tennis courts in France? _____

2. In 1780, who recommended tennis as good for the lungs and throat?

_____

3. What does the French word "tenir" mean? _____

_____

4. In what state was tennis first played in America? _____

5. The person who brought tennis to America was

☐ Marlene Outbridge.   ☐ Mary Outbridge.   ☐ Mary Outerbridge.

Comprehension: Boxing History

The first known boxers were the ancient Greeks, who "toughened up" young men by making them box with bare fists. Later, a length of leather was wrapped around their hands and forearms to protect them. Although the sport was brutal, in ancient Greece, boxers who killed their opponents received a stiff punishment.

During the Middle Ages—from 500 to 1500 A.D.—boxing fell out of favor. It became popular in England about 100 years later, when the new middle class had the time and money for sports. Boxers would travel to matches held at inns and bars, and their loyal fans would follow. No gloves were used in the early 1600s in England. Instead, like the ancient Greeks, boxers used bare fists and—something new—wrestling holds. Carrier pigeons with messages tied to their bodies were trained to take news of the fights back to the boxers' hometowns.

Because so many people were badly hurt or killed, padded boxing gloves began to be used in the United States around 1880. Boxing became fashionable—and safer. Harvard University offered boxing as an intramural sport in the 1880s. U.S. President Theodore Roosevelt's love of the sport helped to further popularize it. It's said that Roosevelt boxed regularly with a former heavy-weight champion named Mike Donovan.

During World War I, boxing was part of the required training for army recruits. The Golden Gloves championship matches for boys, which began in the 1930s, also helped spread the sport's popularity.

Directions: Answer these questions about boxing history.

1. What people were known as the first boxers? _____

2. During what period did boxing fall out of favor? _____

3. What university offered boxing as a sport in the 1880s? _____

4. Which U.S. president enjoyed boxing? _____

5. In England in the 1600s, news about boxing was sent via

☐ telegrams. ☐ carrier pigeons. ☐ messengers.

6. The Golden Gloves championships were first offered

☐ in the 1930s. ☐ during World War I. ☐ during World War II.

Name: _____

Comprehension: Sports Summaries

Directions: Write a short paragraph summarizing each selection below.

Wrestling Around the World _____

_____

_____

_____

_____

Tennis, Anyone? _____

_____

_____

_____

_____

Boxing History _____

_____

_____

_____

_____

Of the sports listed above, which is your favorite? Why? _____

_____

_____

_____

_____

_____

Name: _____

Main Idea: Bowling Is a Ball

Like tennis and boxing, bowling is also a very old sport. It began in Germany about nine centuries ago. Bowling was first played outdoors with wooden pins and a bowling ball made from a rounded rock.

The first players were church members who bowled with Catholic bishops and priests. Those who bowled a good game were said to be blessed. Those who bowled poorly were believed to be sinners who should improve themselves to improve their games! The name of the game in 11th century Germany was "Kegelspiel."

By the late 19th century, bowling was the most popular sport in Germany. A common expression for a person who had died was that he was "bowled out."

The game was introduced to America by way of Holland, where the Dutch had learned bowling from the Germans. Some Dutch citizens brought the game to Manhattan Island in 1623. The first bowling alley—outdoors, of course—opened in New York City more than 100 years later in 1732. Today, bowling is one of the most popular American sports. People who have never put on boxing gloves or raised a tennis racquet have, at one time or another, lifted and rolled a bowling ball.

Directions: Answer these questions about bowling.

1. Circle the main idea:

   Bowling is a very old and a very popular sport.

   Bad bowlers are sinners who should clean up their acts.

2. Who brought bowling to the United States? _____

3. What was bowling called in Germany? _____

4. What were the first bowling balls made from? _____

5. The first American bowling alley opened in 1732 in what city? _____

6. In 19th century Germany, what was the meaning of the expression "bowled out"?

   _____

Comprehension: Facts About Football

Like tennis courts, football fields are usually laid out in a north–south fashion so the sun doesn't shine directly into one team's eyes. The field is 120 yards long and $53\frac{1}{3}$ yards wide, with a goalpost at each end that is at least 20 feet high.

Regulation-size footballs are 11 inches long and must weigh at least 14 ounces. The object of the game is for one team of 11 to score more points than the opposing team. There are four ways to score points in football.

A touchdown, worth six points, is scored by carrying the ball across the opponent's goal line or by completing a forward pass in the opponent's end zone. When a team makes a touchdown, it gets the chance to make one or two extra points via a play executed from the 3-yard line. A field goal, worth three points, is made by kicking the ball from the field over the crossbar of the opponent's goal. A way to earn two points is through a play called a safety.

Football games are 60 minutes long and are divided into four quarters of 15 minutes each. Because of all the commercials and instant replays, televised games seem much longer. For college games, the halftime shows also take a lot of time.

Traditionally, college football games are played on Saturday afternoons and high school games are played on Friday nights. During the season, professional games are televised several nights a week, as well as on weekend afternoons!

Directions: Answer these questions about football.

1. How long is a regulation football? _____

2. How long is a football field? _____

3. How many players are on a football team? _____

4. A field goal is worth

   ☐ one point. ☐ two points. ☐ three points.

5. A touchdown is worth

   ☐ two points. ☐ three points. ☐ six points.

6. Football games are _____ minutes long

   with four _____ -minute quarters.

Giving Directions: A Perfect Softball Pitch

A good softball pitcher makes the skill look effortless and graceful. In fact, there are very specific things a softball pitcher must do before, during and after he or she throws the ball.

Before throwing, the pitcher must have both feet firmly on the ground and be in contact with the pitcher's plate for at least 1 second. At the beginning of the pitch, the ball must be held in both hands in front of the body. It must be held this way no longer than 20 seconds. While making the pitch, the pitcher must keep one foot on the ground. Until the ball leaves his or her hands, the pitcher cannot take more than one step toward the batter.

A correct softball pitch looks remarkably like the pitch used to throw horseshoes. As with horseshoes, there is a graceful follow-through with the hand and arm once the ball leaves the pitcher's hand.

There are several types of softball pitches. They include the drop, the slow ball and the out-curve. The drop is the fastest pitch. The pitcher's hand is behind the ball in this pitch. For the slow ball, the pitcher grips the ball between his or her thumb and little finger. He or she puts the knuckles of the three middle fingers against the ball. When the out-curve ball is thrown, the pitcher thrusts the thumb back and rotates all his or her fingers out.

Directions: Follow these instructions about softball.

1. Give directions on what to do before pitching a softball. _____

_____

_____

_____

_____

2. Give directions on how to throw a slow ball. _____

_____

_____

3. Give directions on how to throw an out-curve ball. _____

_____

Comprehension: Volleyball

Volleyball began in Italy during the Middle Ages and was introduced to Germany in 1893. Germans called the sport "faustball." Two years later, an American physical education teacher named William Morgan made some changes in faustball and brought the new game to Americans as "mintonette."

In faustball, the ball was permitted to bounce twice before being hit back over the net. In mintonette, as in modern volleyball, no bounces were allowed. Shortly after Morgan introduced the sport, the director of a YMCA convinced him to change the name to something easier to pronounce. To "volley" a ball means to keep it in the air, and that's what volleyball players try to do.

A volleyball court is 60-feet long by 30-feet wide. It's divided in half by an 8-foot-high net. There are six players on each team, standing three by three across on each side of the net; however, the same person may not hit the ball two times in a row. If the serve is not returned, the team that served gets the point.

The most popular serve is the underhand. The server stands with the left foot forward, right knee bent, weight on the right foot. He or she leans slightly forward. The ball is in the partly extended left hand. The server strikes the ball off the left hand with the right hand. (Left-handers use the opposite hands and feet.) The first team to get 15 points wins the game.

Directions: Answer these questions about volleyball.

1. Circle the main idea:

   Volleyball is a sport that requires a lot of strength.

   Volleyball is a simple game with six players on opposing sides.

2. A valid generalization about volleyball is:

   a. It's safe, requires little equipment and can be played by all ages.

   b. It's dangerous, difficult to learn and appeals only to children.

   c. It's dull, slow and takes players a long time to earn 15 points.

3. Give directions on how to deliver an underhand serve. _____

   _____

   _____

Comprehension: Comparing Sports

Directions: Read each paragraph. Then answer the questions comparing field hockey, basketball and softball.

My sister is more interested in sports than I am. Last year, she lettered in field hockey, basketball and softball. I got my exercise walking to school.

1. What sports did the writer play? _____

My sister's favorite sport is field hockey. Because it requires constant running up and down a field, it provides more exercise than basketball and softball. There's also more danger, because every year someone gets her teeth knocked out with a hockey stick. So far at our school, no one has lost any teeth in basketball or softball.

2. Compared to basketball and softball, field hockey provides one benefit and one danger. Name them.

_____   _____

On the other hand, softball players—especially those who play the outfield—can occasionally take some time to daydream. With an ace strikeout pitcher and batters who can't hit far, outfielders' gloves don't get much of a workout.

3. What sports do not allow time for daydreaming? _____

_____

Write a short paragraph telling which sport you like best and why. _____

_____

_____

_____

_____

_____

_____

Famous Athletes

Athletes are heroes in their fields to both young and old alike. Their stories are sometimes about triumph over amazing odds to become one of the best in their sport. Before beginning the section, answer the following questions as a warm-up.

1. What sport most interests you? Why?

_____

_____

2. What sports figure do you most admire? Why?

_____

_____

3. In your opinion, what makes a person a hero?

_____

_____

4. Try to name a sports legend for each of the sports listed below.

Track and Field _____

Swimming _____

Boxing _____

Baseball _____

Speed Skating _____

Tennis _____

Track and Field

Directions: Read the selection. Then answer the questions.

Many people recognize the name "Gail Devers" in the world of track and field. She won a gold medal for the United States at the 1992 Summer Olympics in Barcelona, Spain, in the women's 100-meter dash. However, many people do not know that Gail Devers overcame near insurmountable odds to win that gold medal.

In September, 1990, 24-year-old Gail was diagnosed with Graves' disease, which affects the thyroid gland. She had been fighting this illness for over 2 years before it was finally identified. Graves' disease can cause irregular heartbeat, muscle weakness, nervousness and weight loss. It can also become cancerous. Imagine the difficulties that would create for a person who depends on her muscles in order to compete!

Gail underwent chemotherapy and radiation, which had both good and bad effects on her body. Although the treatments brought her disease under control, the radiation burned her feet so badly that doctors considered amputation.

Amazingly, Gail began her training regimen once again in March, 1991. After competing in several meets and doing well, she went to the United States Olympic Trials and qualified in both the hurdles and the 100-meter dash. Although she came in fifth in the hurdles, the gold medal she claimed in the 100-meter dash represented all her hard work and desire to overcome the odds.

1. Summarize the selection in 3 sentences.

_____

_____

_____

2. Define the following words:

regimen: _____

amputation: _____

thyroid: _____

_____

insurmountable: _____

Name: _____

Speed Skating

Directions: Read the selection. Then answer the questions.

Imagine racing around a rink of glassy ice with only a thin blade of metal supporting you. Now, imagine skating so fast that you set a world record! That's exactly what speed skater Bonnie Blair has done all of her life.

Bonnie started skating before she was walking—on the shoulders of her older brothers and sisters. By the time she was 4, Bonnie was competing. At age 7, Bonnie won the 1971 Illinois state championships and dreamed of becoming an Olympian.

That opportunity soon came. Bonnie competed in the 1988, 1992 and 1994 Olympics. She won a gold medal in the 500 meter race and a bronze medal in the 1,000 meter race in 1988, golds in both the 500 and 1,000 meter races in 1992 and repeated the two golds in 1994. No other U.S. woman has ever won five gold medals in the Olympics in any sport. Bonnie Blair is truly a champion!

1. Define the following words:

   opportunity: _____

   meter: _____

2. Bonnie Blair competed over a period of 6 years in the Olympics. What qualities would be necessary to maintain both physical and mental condition to compete for so long?

   _____

   _____

3. Bonnie Blair participated in long-track skating, in which she raced with one other person against a clock for the best time. Do you think this would be easier or more difficult than racing a group to finish first? Why?

   _____

   _____

4. In your opinion, what makes a good athlete?

   _____

   _____

Baseball

Directions: Read the selection. Then answer the questions.

Babe Ruth was born George Herman Ruth in 1895. His family lived in Baltimore, Maryland and was quite poor. He overcame poverty to become one of the greatest baseball players of all time.

Babe Ruth's baseball career began with the Baltimore Orioles. He was a pitcher but also a tremendous batter. He later played for the Boston Red Sox and started his home run hitting fame with 29 home runs in 1919.

In 1920, while playing for the New York Yankees, Babe Ruth hit 54 home runs. He had become very popular with baseball fans of all ages. Amazingly, by 1925, he was making more money than the president of the United States! His home-run record of 60 home runs in a single season went unshattered until Roger Maris broke it in 1961 with 61 home runs. Then, in 1998, Mark McGwire hit 70 home runs to become the new "home-run king."

Babe Ruth retired from baseball in 1935 with a career total of 714 home runs. He died in 1948 at age 53.

1. Summarize the selection in 3 sentences.

_____

_____

_____

2. In the early 1900s, life expectancy was shorter than it is today. By today's standards, Babe Ruth died at a relatively young age. What factors have contributed to increased life expectancy?

_____

_____

_____

_____

3. Create a time line of Babe Ruth's life beginning with his birth and ending with his death.

Grade 6 - Comprehensive Curriculum

Swimming

Directions: Read the selection. Then answer the questions.

In 1968, 18-year-old Mark Spitz boasted that he would win six gold medals at the Olympics being held in Mexico. He won two golds in team relay events. Having made this claim and then failing to achieve it made Mark Spitz determined to do better in the 1972 Olympics in Munich.

For the next 4 years, Mark Spitz trained ferociously. Indeed, at the 1972 Olympics, Mark Spitz amazed the world by breaking all records and winning seven gold medals in seven different events. While doing so, he set new world record times in each event. Mark Spitz had accomplished his goal.

1. What feelings do you think Mark Spitz had after the 1968 Olympics?

   _____

   _____

   _____

2. What do you think is the moral to this story?

   _____

   _____

   _____

3. Many Olympians are as young as Mark Spitz was, and some participate at even younger ages. Write one paragraph detailing the advantages of being a young Olympian and one paragraph detailing the disadvantages.

   _____

   _____

   _____

   _____

   _____

Boxing

Directions: Read the selection. Then answer the questions.

Muhammad Ali was born Cassius Clay in Louisville, Kentucky in 1942. He won the amateur Golden Gloves championship in 1959 and 1960 and went on to become the heavyweight champion of the 1960 Olympics. Four years later, he was champion of the world.

However, Ali's athletic fame came with its share of difficulties. He converted to the religion of Islam and thus changed his name from Cassius Clay to Muhammad Ali. It was due to his beliefs in Islam that he refused to comply with the military draft for the Vietnam War. Therefore, he was stripped of his world title and banned from boxing from 1967 to 1970.

Ali regained his title in 1974 and won the world championship again in 1978. This accomplishment made Muhammad Ali the first heavyweight boxer to claim the world championship three times. Most notable about Ali's career is his total 56 wins in the ring with 37 knockouts.

1. Define the following words:

   draft: _____

   banned: _____

   amateur: _____

   notable: _____

   comply: _____

2. Why is it necessary for a country to use the military draft?

   _____

   _____

3. Write a 3-sentence summary of the selection.

   _____

   _____

   _____

Tennis

Directions: Read the selection. Then answer the questions.

Martina Navratilova gained fame as the best women's tennis player of the 1980s. She was born in Czechoslovakia in 1956 and moved to the United States at the age of 19. She became a United States citizen in 1981.

Martina Navratilova excelled in the sport of tennis but she enjoyed the Wimbledon championship the most. She won the singles finals in 1978, 1979, 1982, 1983, 1984, 1985, 1986, 1987 and 1990.

In 1982, she became the first woman professional tennis player to earn over one million dollars in a single season.

1. What physical characteristics are necessary to excel in the sport of tennis?

   _____

   _____

   _____

2. In your opinion, why would an athlete from another country desire to come to the U.S.A. to train and compete?

   _____

   _____

   _____

3. Many athletes find it difficult to adjust to their status as "heroes." What are some possible disadvantages to being an athletic superstar?

   _____

   _____

   _____

   _____

   _____

Review

Directions: Follow the instructions for each section.

1. On the line below, create a time line of the years of birth for the six athletes discussed in this section.

```
├────────────────────────────────────────────┤
│                                            │
```

2. What mental and emotional characteristics did all six athletes have in common?

_____

_____

_____

_____

3. On the line below, create a time line of Muhammad Ali's life.

```
├────────────────────────────────────────────┤
│                                            │
```

4. Compare and contrast the sports of tennis and baseball in a two-paragraph essay.

_____

_____

_____

_____

_____

_____

_____

Writing: My Sports Hero

Directions: Write a short essay about a man or woman you admire who has excelled in a sport. Make sure to give details about why you admire this person.

_____

_____

_____

_____

_____

_____

_____

_____

_____

Directions: Interview an adult. Ask him or her about a sports figure he or she admired at your age. Write a short paragraph about this person's sports hero.

_____

_____

_____

_____

_____

_____

_____

_____

Using Prior Knowledge: Poetry

Directions: Before reading about poetry in the following section, answer these questions.

1. Have you ever written a poem? If so, was it difficult to do? Why or why not?

_____

_____

_____

2. Write a poem with rhyming verse.

_____

_____

_____

_____

_____

_____

_____

3. Write a poem with unrhymed verse.

_____

_____

_____

_____

_____

_____

Comprehension: Epitaphs

Epitaphs are verses written on tombstones and were very popular in the past. The following epitaphs were written by unknown authors.

On a Man Named Merideth

Here lies one blown out of breath
Who lived a merry life and died a Merideth.

On a Dentist

Stranger, approach this spot with gravity:
John Brown is filling his last cavity.

On Leslie Moore

Here lies what's left
Of Leslie Moore
No Les
No more

Directions: Answer these questions about the epitaphs.

1. What does the phrase "blown out of breath" mean? _____

_____

2. What does the author mean when he says "and died a Merideth"? _____

_____

3. What cavity is John Brown filling? _____

4. Write an epitaph of your own.

_____

_____

_____

_____

_____

Comprehension: "The Ant and the Cricket"

A silly young cricket, who decided to sing
Through the warm sunny months of summer and spring,
Began to complain when he found that at home
His cupboards were empty and winter had come.

At last by starvation the cricket made bold
To hop through the wintertime snow and the cold.
Away he set off to a miserly ant
To see if to keep him alive he would grant
Shelter from rain, a mouthful of grain.
"I wish only to borrow—I'll repay it tomorrow—
If not, I must die of starvation and sorrow!"

Said the ant to the cricket, "It's true I'm your friend,
But we ants never borrow, we ants never lend;
We ants store up crumbs so when winter arrives
We have just enough food to keep ants alive."

Directions: Use context clues to answer these questions about the poem.

1. What is the correct definition of **cupboards**?

   ☐ where books are stored   ☐ where food is stored   ☐ where shoes are stored

2. What is the correct definition of **miserly**?

   ☐ selfish/stingy   ☐ generous/kind   ☐ mean/ugly

3. What is the correct definition of **grant**?

   ☐ to take away   ☐ to belch   ☐ to give

4. In two sentences, describe what the poet is trying to say with this poem.

   _____

   _____

   _____

   _____

Comprehension: "The Elf and the Dormouse"

Under a toadstool
Crept a wee elf
Out of the rain
To shelter himself.

Under the toadstool
Sound asleep
Sat a big dormouse
All in a heap.

Trembled the wee elf
Frightened, and yet
Fearing to fly away
Lest he got wet.

To the next shelter
Maybe a mile!
Sudden the wee elf
Smiled a wee smile,

Tugged 'til the toadstool
Toppled in two,
Holding it over him
Gaily he flew.

Soon he was safe home,
Dry as could be;
Soon woke the dormouse
"Good gracious me!"

"Where is my toadstool?"
Loud he lamented.
And that's when umbrellas
First were invented.

—Oliver Herford

Directions: Use context clues or a dictionary to answer these questions about the poem.

1. This humorous poem tells about what invention? _____

2. What do you think a **dormouse** is? _____

_____

3. What is the correct definition of **lamented**? _____

_____

4. Write a two-verse poem below describing the invention of a useful object.

_____

_____

_____

_____

Comprehension: "The Eagle"

Personification is a figure of speech in which human characteristics are given to an animal or object.

Example: The trees danced in the wind.

Trees do not dance; therefore, the trees are being personified.

He clasps the crag with crooked hands:
Close to the sun in lonely lands,
Ringed with the azure world, he stands.

The wrinkled sea beneath him crawls;
He watches from his mountain walls,
And like a thunderbolt he falls.

—Alfred, Lord Tennyson

Directions: Answer these questions about the poem.

1. What is the correct definition of **crag**? _____

_____

2. What is the correct definition of **azure**? _____

3. Which phrases in the poem show personification? _____

_____

4. Explain what one of these phrases actually means. _____

_____

_____

5. What is the author trying to say in the last line of the poem? _____

_____

_____

Comprehension: Proverbs

Proverbs are bits of advice for daily life. The following proverbs were written by Benjamin Franklin in 1732. They were published in *Poor Richard's Almanack*.

1. Keep conscience clear,
   Then never fear.

2. Little strokes
   Fell great oaks.

3. From a slip of foot you may soon recover,
   But a slip of the tongue you may never get over.

4. Doing an injury puts you below your enemy;
   Revenging one makes you but even with him;
   Forgiving it sets you above him.

Directions: Explain the meaning of each proverb.

1. _____

   _____

2. _____

   _____

3. _____

   _____

4. _____

   _____

Write a proverb of your own.

_____

_____

_____

_____

Name: _____

Comprehension: Limericks

A **limerick** is a humorous verse consisting of five lines. The first, second and fifth lines rhyme, and the third and fourth lines rhyme.

Old Man From Peru
There was an old man from Peru,
Who dreamed he was eating his shoe.
In the midst of the night
He awoke in a fright
And—good grief!—it was perfectly true.

Old Man From Darjeeling
There was an old man from Darjeeling,
Who boarded a bus bound for Ealing.
He saw on the door:
"Please don't spit on the floor."
So he stood up and spat on the ceiling.

Directions: Answer these questions about these silly limericks.

1. In "Old Man From Peru," what was perfectly true? _____

_____

2. How did the old man from Peru feel when he awoke? _____

3. In "Old Man From Darjeeling," what is Ealing? _____

4. Did the old man from Darjeeling break any rules? _____

Write your own silly limerick below.

_____

_____

_____

_____

_____

Comprehension: "The Tyger"

Imagery is a "picture" that comes into the reader's mind when reading certain words.

Tyger! Tyger! burning bright
In the forests of the night,
What immortal hand or eye
Could frame thy fearful symmetry?

In what distant deeps or skies
Burnt the fire of thine eyes?
On what wings dare he aspire?
What the hand dare seize the fire?

And what shoulder, and what art,
Could twist the sinew of thy heart,
And when thy heart began to beat,
What dread hand? and what dread feet?

What the hammer? what the chain?
In what furnace was thy brain?
What the anvil? what dread grasp
Dare its deadly terrors clasp?

When the stars threw down their spears,
And watered heaven with their tears,
Did he smile his work to see?
Did he who made the lamb make thee?

Tyger! Tyger! burning bright
In the forests of the night,
What immortal hand or eye,
Dare frame thy fearful symmetry?

—*William Blake*

Directions: Use context clues or a dictionary to answer these questions about the poem.

1. What is the correct definition of **symmetry**?

_____

_____

2. What is the correct definition of **immortal**?

_____

_____

3. What is the correct definition of **aspire**?

_____

_____

4. What is the correct definition of **sinew**?

_____

_____

5. What is the correct definition of **anvil**?

_____

_____

6. What is some imagery in this poem?

_____

_____

_____

Comprehension: Old Gaelic Lullaby

A **Gaelic lullaby** is an ancient Irish or Scottish song some parents sing as they rock their babies to sleep.

Hush! The waves are rolling in,
White with foam, white with foam,
Father works amid the din,
But baby sleeps at home.

Hush! The winds roar hoarse and deep—
On they come, on they come!
Brother seeks the wandering sheep,
But baby sleeps at home.

Hush! The rain sweeps over the fields,
Where cattle roam, where cattle roam.
Sister goes to seek the cows,
But baby sleeps at home.

Directions: Answer these questions about the Gaelic lullaby.

1. What is Father doing while baby sleeps? _____

_____

2. What is Brother doing? _____

_____

3. What is Sister doing? _____

_____

4. What do we assume Mother is doing? _____

_____

5. Is it quiet or noisy while Father works? ☐ quiet   ☐ noisy

6. Which is not mentioned in the poem?

☐ wind   ☐ sunshine   ☐ waves   ☐ rain

Name: _____

Comprehension: "The Lark and the Wren"

"Goodnight, Sir Wren!" said the little lark.
"The daylight fades; it will soon be dark.
I've sung my hymn to the parting day.
So now I fly to my quiet glen
In yonder meadow—Goodnight, Wren!"

"Goodnight, poor Lark," said the haughty wren,
With a flick of his wing toward his happy friend.
"I also go to my rest profound
But not to sleep on the cold, damp ground.
The fittest place for a bird like me
Is the topmost bough of a tall pine tree."

Directions: Use context clues for these definitions.

1. What is the correct definition of **hymn**?

   ☐ whisper   ☐ song   ☐ opposite of her

2. What is the correct definition of **yonder**?

   ☐ distant   ☐ mountaintop   ☐ seaside

3. What is the correct definition of **haughty**?

   ☐ happy   ☐ friendly   ☐ pompous

4. What is the correct definition of **profound**?

   ☐ restless   ☐ deep   ☐ uncomfortable

5. What is the correct definition of **bough**?

   ☐ to bend over   ☐ tree roots   ☐ tree branch

6. Write another verse of the poem.

   _____

   _____

   _____

Nouns

A **noun** names a person, place, thing or idea. There are several types of nouns.

Examples:
    proper nouns: Joe, Jefferson Memorial
    common nouns: dog, town
    concrete nouns: book, stove
    abstract nouns: fear, devotion
    collective nouns: audience, flock

A word can be more than one type of noun.

Example: Dog is both a common and a concrete noun.

Directions: Write the type or types of each noun on the lines.

1. desk _____

2. ocean _____

3. love _____

4. cat _____

5. herd _____

6. compassion _____

7. reputation _____

8. eyes _____

9. staff _____

10. day _____

11. Roosevelt Building _____

12. Mr. Timken _____

13. life _____

14. porch _____

15. United States _____

Possessive Nouns

A **possessive** noun owns something. To make a singular noun possessive, add an apostrophe and **s**. **Example:** mayor**'s** campaign.

To make a plural noun possessive when it already ends with **s**, add only an apostrophe. **Example:** dog**s'** tails

To make a plural noun possessive when it doesn't end with **s**, add an apostrophe and **s**. **Example:** men**'s** shirts

Directions: Write the correct form of the word for each sentence in the group. Words may be singular, plural, singular possessive or plural possessive. The first one has been done for you.

teacher
1. How many <u>teachers</u> does your school have?

2. Where is the <u>teacher's</u> coat?

3. All the <u>teachers'</u> mailboxes are in the school office.

reporter
4. Two _____ were assigned to the story.

5. One _____ car broke down on the way to the scene.

6. The other _____ was riding as a passenger.

7. Both _____ notes ended up missing.

child
8. The _____ are hungry.

9. How much spaghetti can one _____ eat?

10. Put this much on each _____ plate.

11. The _____ spaghetti is ready for them.

mouse
12. Some _____ made a nest under those boards.

13. I can see the _____ hole from here.

14. A baby _____ has wandered away from the nest.

15. The _____ mother is coming to get it.

Name: _____

Verbs

A **verb** is a word that tells what something does or that something exists.

There are two types of verbs: **action** and **state of being**.

Examples:
Action: run, read
State of being: feel, sound, taste, stay, look, appear, grow, seem, smell and forms of **be**

Directions: Write **A** if the verb shows action. Write **S** if it shows state of being.

1. _____ He helped his friend.

2. _____ They appear happy and content.

3. _____ Jordi drives to school each day.

4. _____ The snowfall closed schools everywhere.

5. _____ The dog sniffed at its food.

6. _____ The meat tastes funny.

7. _____ Did you taste the ice cream?

8. _____ The young boy smelled the flowers.

9. _____ She looked depressed.

10. _____ The coach announced the dates of the scrimmage.

11. _____ The owner of the store stocks all types of soda.

12. _____ He dribbled the ball down the court.

13. _____ "Everything seems to be in order," said the train conductor.

Name: _____

Verb Tense

Tense is the way a verb is used to express time. To explain what is happening right now, use the **present tense**.

Example: He **is singing** well. He **sings** well.

To explain what has already happened, use the **past tense**.

Example: He **sang** well.

To explain what will happen, use the **future tense**.

Example: He **will sing** well.

Directions: Rewrite each sentence so the verbs are in the same tense. The first one has been done for you.

1. He ran, he jumped, then he is flying.

   <u>He ran, he jumped, then he flew.</u>

2. He was crying, then he will stop.

   _____

3. She feels happy, but she was not sure why.

   _____

4. He is my friend, so was she.

   _____

5. She bit into the cake and says it is good.

   _____

6. He laughs first and then told us the joke.

   _____

Grade 6 - Comprehensive Curriculum

Spelling Different Forms of Verbs

To show that something is happening in the present, we can use a "plain" verb, or we can use **is** or **are** and add **ing** to the verb.

is/are + verb + ing
was/were + verb + ing

Example: We **run**. We **are running**.

To show that something has already happened, we can add **ed** to many verbs, or we can use **was** or **were** and add **ing** to a verb.

Example: The workers **surveyed**. The workers were **surveying**.

If a verb ends in **e**, drop the final **e** before adding an ending that begins with a vowel.

Example: She is **driving**. He **restored** the old car.

If a verb ends in **sh** or **ch**, add **es** instead of **s** to change the form.

Example: He furnish**es**. She watch**es**.

Directions: Complete each sentence with the correct form of the verb given. The first one has been done for you.

1. The florist is (have) a sale this week. _____ *having* _____

2. Last night's tornado (destroy) a barn. _____

3. We are (research) the history of our town. _____

4. My mistake was (use) a plural verb instead of a singular one. _____

5. She (act) quickly in yesterday's emergency. _____

6. Our group is (survey) the parents in our community. _____

7. For our last experiment, we (observe) a plant's growth for 2 weeks. _____

8. A local company already (furnish) all the materials for this project. _____

9. Which dairy (furnish) milk to our cafeteria every day? _____

10. Just (ignore) the mess in here will not help your case. _____

Name: _____

Verb Tense

Directions: Write a sentence using the present tense of each verb.

1. walk _____

   _____

2. dream _____

   _____

3. achieve _____

   _____

Directions: Write a sentence using the past tense of each verb.

4. dance _____

   _____

5. study _____

   _____

6. hike _____

   _____

Directions: Write a sentence using the future tense of each verb.

7. bake _____

   _____

8. write _____

   _____

9. talk _____

   _____

Name: _____

Verb Tense

Verbs can be **present**, **past** or **past participle**.

Add **d** or **ed** to form the past tense.

Past-participle verbs also use a helping verb such as **has** or **have**.

Examples:

Present	Past	Past Participle
help	helped	has or have helped
skip	skipped	has or have skipped

Directions: Write the past and past-participle forms of each present tense verb.

Present	Past	Past Participle
1. paint	painted	has (have) painted
2. dream		
3. play		
4. approach		
5. hop		
6. climb		
7. dance		
8. appear		
9. watch		
10. dive		
11. hurry		
12. discover		
13. decorate		
14. close		
15. jump		

Irregular Verb Forms

The past tense of most verbs is formed by adding **ed**. Verbs that do not follow this format are called **irregular verbs**.

The irregular verb chart shows a few of the many verbs with irregular forms.

Irregular Verb Chart

Present Tense	Past Tense	Past Participle
go	went	has, have or had gone
do	did	has, have or had done
fly	flew	has, have or had flown
grow	grew	has, have or had grown
ride	rode	has, have or had ridden
see	saw	has, have or had seen
sing	sang	has, have or had sung
swim	swam	has, have or had swum
throw	threw	has, have or had thrown

The words **had**, **have** and **has** can be separated from the irregular verb by other words in the sentence.

Directions: Choose the correct verb form from the chart to complete the sentences. The first one has been done for you.

1. The pilot had never before ___**flown**___ that type of plane.

2. She put on her bathing suit and _____ 2 miles.

3. The tall boy had _____ 2 inches over the summer.

4. She insisted she had _____ her homework.

5. He _____ them walking down the street.

6. She _____ the horse around the track.

7. The pitcher has _____ the ball many times.

8. He can _____ safely in the deepest water.

Name: _____

Irregular Verb Forms

Directions: Use the irregular verb chart on the previous page. Write the correct verb form to complete each sentence.

1. Has she ever _____ carrots in her garden?

2. She was so angry she _____ a tantrum.

3. The bird had sometimes _____ from its cage.

4. The cowboy has never _____ that horse before.

5. Will you _____ to the store with me?

6. He said he had often _____ her walking on his street.

7. She insisted she has not _____ taller this year.

8. He _____ briskly across the pool.

9. Have the insects _____ away?

10. Has anyone _____ my sister lately?

11. He hasn't _____ the dishes once this week!

12. Has she been _____ out of the game for cheating?

13. I haven't _____ her yet today.

14. The airplane _____ slowly by the airport.

15. Have you _____ your bike yet this week?

Name: _____

Nouns and Verbs

Some words can be used as both nouns and verbs.

Example:
    The **bait** on his hook was a worm.
    He couldn't **bait** his hook.

In the first sentence, **bait** is used as a **noun** because it names a thing. In the second sentence, **bait** is used as a **verb** because it shows action.

Directions: Write **noun** or **verb** for the word in bold in each sentence. The first one has been done for you.

BAIT!

<u>verb</u>   1. She **piloted** the small plane across the Pacific Ocean.

_____   2. Does she **water** her garden every night?

_____   3. Did you **rebel** against the rules?

_____   4. Dad will pound the fence **post** into the ground.

_____   5. That was good **thinking**!

_____   6. I **object** to your language!

_____   7. He planned to become a **pilot** after graduation.

_____   8. The teacher will **post** the new school calendar.

_____   9. She was **thinking** of a donut.

_____   10. The **object** of the search was forgotten.

_____   11. She was a **rebel** in high school.

_____   12. Would you like fresh **water** for your tea?

Spelling: Plurals

Is **heros** or **heroes** the correct spelling? Many people aren't sure. These rules have exceptions, but they will help you spell the plural forms of most words that end with **o**.

heros or heroes?

- If a word ends with a consonant and **o**, add **es**: hero**es**.
- If a word ends with a vowel and **o**, add **s**: radio**s**.

Here are some other spelling rules for plurals:

- If a word ends with **s**, **ss**, **x**, **ch** or **sh**, add **es**: bus**es**, kiss**es**, tax**es**, peach**es**, wish**es**.
- If a word ends with **f** or **fe**, drop the **f** or **fe** and add **ves**: lea**f**, lea**ves**; wi**fe**, wi**ves**.
- Some plurals don't end with **s** or **es**: **geese**, **deer**, **children**.

Directions: Write the plural forms of the words.

1. Our area doesn't often have (tornado). _____

2. How many (radio) does this store sell every month? _____

3. (Radish) are the same color as apples. _____

4. Does this submarine carry (torpedo)? _____

5. Hawaii has a number of active (volcano). _____

6. Did you pack (knife) in the picnic basket? _____

7. We heard (echo) when we shouted in the canyon. _____

8. Where is the list of (address)? _____

9. What will you do when that plant (reach) the ceiling? _____

10. Sometimes my dad (fix) us milkshakes. _____

11. Every night, my sister (wish) on the first star she sees. _____

12. Who (furnish) the school with pencils and paper? _____

13. The author (research) every detail in her books. _____

Name: _____

Spelling: Plurals

Directions: Write the plural form of each word.

1. mother _____

2. ankle _____

3. journey _____

4. ceiling _____

5. governor _____

6. arch _____

7. carnival _____

8. official _____

9. potato _____

10. vacuum _____

11. stereo _____

12. strategy _____

13. column _____

14. architect _____

15. entry _____

16. summary _____

17. issue _____

18. member _____

19. astronomer _____

20. channel _____

21. harmony _____

22. piece _____

23. chicken _____

24. chemical _____

25. journal _____

26. niece _____

27. mayor _____

28. particle _____

29. entrance _____

30. assistant _____

Simple Subjects

The **simple subject** of a sentence tells who or what the sentence is about. It is a noun or a pronoun.

Example: My **mom** is turning forty this year.
Mom is the simple subject.

Directions: Circle the simple subject in each sentence.

1. The cat ate all its food.

2. They watched the basketball game.

3. Loretta is going to lunch with her friend.

4. José likes strawberry jam on his toast.

5. The reporter interviewed the victim.

6. She turned down the volume.

7. The farm animals waited to be fed.

8. Can you lift weights?

9. The fan did little to cool the hot room.

10. Thomas Jefferson was one of the founding fathers of our country.

11. I have a lot to do tonight.

12. Will you go to the movie with us?

13. We enjoyed the day at the park.

14. Our pet is a dog.

15. She retrieved her homework from the garbage.

Simple Predicates

The **simple predicate** of a sentence tells what the subject does, is doing, did or will do. The simple predicate is always a verb.

Example:
My mom **is turning** forty this year.
"Is turning" is the simple predicate.

Directions: Underline the simple predicate in each sentence. Include all helping verbs.

1. I bought school supplies at the mall.

2. The tiger chased its prey.

3. Mark will be arriving shortly.

4. The hamburgers are cooking now.

5. We will attend my sister's wedding.

6. The dental hygienist cleaned my teeth.

7. My socks are hanging on the clothesline.

8. Where are you going?

9. The dog is running toward its owner.

10. Ramos watched the tornado in fear.

11. Please wash the dishes after dinner.

12. My dad cleaned the garage yesterday.

13. We are going hiking at Yellowstone today.

14. The picture shows our entire family at the family picnic.

15. Our coach will give us a pep talk before the game.

Name: _____

Parallel Structure

Parts of a sentence are **parallel** when they "match" grammatically and structurally.

Faulty parallelism occurs when the parts of a sentence do not match grammatically and structurally.

For sentences to be parallel, all parts of a sentence—including the verbs, nouns and phrases—must match. This means that, in most cases, verbs should be in the same tense.

Examples:
    Correct: She liked running, jumping and swinging outdoors.
    Incorrect: She liked running, jumping and to swing outdoors.

In the correct sentence, all three of the actions the girl liked to do end in **ing**. In the incorrect sentence, they do not.

Directions: Rewrite the sentences so all elements are parallel. The first one has been done for you.

1. Politicians like making speeches and also to shake hands.

   Politicians like making speeches and shaking hands.

2. He liked singing, acting and to perform in general.

   _____

3. The cake had icing, sprinkles and also has small candy hearts.

   _____

4. The drink was cold, frosty and also is a thirst-quencher.

   _____

5. She was asking when we would arrive, and I told her.

   _____

6. Liz felt like shouting, singing and to jump.

   _____

Matching Subjects and Verbs

If the subject of a sentence is singular, the verb must be singular. If the subject is plural, the verb must be plural.

Example:
The **dog** with floppy ears **is eating**.
The **dogs** in the yard **are eating**.

Directions: Write the singular or plural form of the subject in each sentence to match the verb.

1. The (yolk) _____ in this egg is bright yellow.

2. The (child) _____ are putting numbers in columns.

3. Both (coach) _____ are resigning at the end of the year.

4. Those three (class) _____ were assigned to the gym.

5. The (lunch) _____ for the children are ready.

6. (Spaghetti) _____ with meatballs is delicious.

7. Where are the (box) _____ of chalk?

8. The (man) _____ in the truck were collecting broken tree limbs.

9. The (rhythm) _____ of that music is exactly right for dancing.

10. Sliced (tomato) _____ on lettuce are good with salmon.

11. The (announcer) _____ on TV was condemning the dictator.

12. Two (woman) _____ are campaigning for mayor of our town.

13. The (group) _____ of travelers was on its way to three foreign countries.

14. The (choir) _____ of thirty children is singing hymns.

15. In spite of the parade, the (hero) _____ were solemn.

Name: _____

Subject/Verb Agreement

Singular subjects require singular verbs. **Plural subjects** require plural verbs. The subject and verb must agree in a sentence.

Example:
   Singular: My dog runs across the field.
   Plural: My dogs run across the field.

Directions: Circle the correct verb in each sentence.

1. Maria (talk/talks) to me each day at lunch.

2. Mom, Dad and I (is/are) going to the park to play catch.

3. Mr. and Mrs. Ramirez (dance/dances) well together.

4. Astronauts (hope/hopes) for a successful shuttle mission.

5. Trees (prevent/prevents) erosion.

6. The student (is/are) late.

7. She (ask/asks) for directions to the senior high gym.

8. The elephants (plod/plods) across the grassland to the watering hole.

9. My friend's name (is/are) Rebecca.

10. Many people (enjoy/enjoys) orchestra concerts.

11. The pencils (is/are) sharpened.

12. My backpack (hold/holds) a lot of things.

13. The wind (blow/blows) to the south.

14. Sam (collect/collects) butterflies.

15. They (love/loves) cotton candy.

Name: _____

Personal Pronouns

Personal pronouns take the place of nouns. They refer to people or things. **I**, **me**, **we**, **she**, **he**, **him**, **her**, **you**, **they**, **them**, **us** and **it** are personal pronouns.

Directions: Circle the personal pronouns in each sentence.

1. He is a terrific friend.

2. Would you open the door?

3. Jim and I will arrive at ten o'clock.

4. Can you pick me up at the mall after dinner?

5. What did you do yesterday?

6. They are watching the game on television.

7. Jessie's mom took us to the movies.

8. She writes novels.

9. They gave us the refrigerator.

10. Is this the answer she intended to give?

11. What is it?

12. The dog yelped when it saw the cat.

13. I admire him.

14. We parked the bikes by the tree.

15. The ants kept us from enjoying our picnic.

Possessive Pronouns

Possessive pronouns show ownership. **My**, **mine**, **your**, **yours**, **his**, **her**, **hers**, **their**, **theirs**, **our**, **ours** and **its** are possessive pronouns.

Directions: Circle the possessive pronouns in each sentence.

1. My dogs chase cats continually.

2. Jodi put her sunglasses on the dashboard.

3. His mother and mine are the same age.

4. The cat licked its paw.

5. Their anniversary is February 1.

6. This necklace is yours.

7. We will carry our luggage into the airport.

8. Our parents took us to dinner.

9. My brother broke his leg.

10. Her report card was excellent.

11. Raspberry jam is my favorite.

12. Watch your step!

13. The house on the left is mine.

14. My phone number is unlisted.

15. Our garden is growing out of control.

16. Our pumpkins are ten times larger than theirs.

Interrogative Pronouns

An **interrogative pronoun** asks a question. There are three interrogative pronouns: **who**, **what** and **which**.

Use **who** when speaking of persons.
Use **what** when speaking of things.
Use **which** when speaking of persons or things.

Examples:
   Who will go? **What** will you do? **Which** of these is yours?

Who becomes **whom** when it is a direct object or an object of a preposition. The possessive form of **whom** is **whose**.

Examples:
   To **whom** will you write?
   Whose computer is that?

Directions: Write the correct interrogative pronoun.

1. _____ wet raincoat is this?

2. _____ is the president of the United States?

3. _____ is your name?

4. _____ dog made this muddy mess?

5. _____ cat ran away?

6. _____ of you is the culprit?

7. _____ was your grade on the last test?

8. To _____ did you report?

9. _____ do you believe now?

10. _____ is the leader of this English study group?

Personal and Possessive Pronouns

Directions: Write personal or possessive pronouns in the blanks to take the place of the words in bold. The first one has been done for you.

___They___ ___him___ 1. **Maisie and Marni** told **Trent** they would see him later.

_____ 2. **Spencer** told **Nancee and Sandi** good-bye.

_____ 3. **The bike** was parked near **Aaron's** house.

_____ 4. **Maria, Matt and Greg** claimed the car was new.

_____ 5. The dishes were **the property of Cindy and Jake**.

_____ 6. Is this **Carole's**?

_____ 7. **Jon** walked near **Jessica and Esau's** house.

_____ 8. **The dog** barked all night long!

_____ 9. **Dawn** fell and hurt **Dawn's** knee.

_____ 10. **Cory and Devan** gave the dog **the dog's** dinner.

_____ 11. **Tori and I** gave **Brett and Reggie** a ride home.

_____ 12. Do **Josh and Andrea** like cats?

_____ 13. **Sasha and Keesha** gave **Josh and me** a ride home.

_____ 14. Is this sweater **Marni's**?

_____ 15. The cat meowed because **the cat** was hungry.

Pronoun/Antecedent Agreement

Often, a **pronoun** is used in place of a noun to avoid repeating the noun again in the same sentence. The noun that a pronoun refers to is called its **antecedent**. The word "antecedent" means "going before."

If the noun is singular, the pronoun that takes its place must also be singular. If the noun is plural, the pronoun that takes its place must also be plural. This is called *agreement* between the pronoun and its antecedent.

Examples:
> **Mary** (singular noun) said **she** (singular pronoun) would dance.
> The **dogs** (plural noun) took **their** (plural pronoun) dishes outside.

When the noun is singular and the gender unknown, it is correct to use either "his" or "his or her."

Directions: Rewrite the sentences so the pronouns and nouns agree. The first one has been done for you.

1. Every student opened their book.

   Every student opened his book.

   Also correct: Every student opened his or her book.

2. Has anyone lost their wallet lately?

   _____

3. Somebody found the wallet under their desk.

   _____

4. Someone will have to file their report.

   _____

5. Every dog has their day!

   _____

6. I felt Ted had mine best interests at heart.

   _____

Name: _____

Pronoun/Antecedent Agreement

Directions: Write a pronoun that agrees with the antecedent.

1. Donald said _____ would go to the store.

2. My friend discovered _____ wallet had been stolen.

3. The cat licked _____ paw.

4. Did any woman here lose _____ necklace?

5. Someone will have to give _____ report.

6. Jennifer wished _____ had not come.

7. All the children decided _____ would attend.

8. My grandmother hurt _____ back while gardening.

9. Jerry, Marco and I hope _____ win the game.

10. Sandra looked for _____ missing homework.

11. The family had _____ celebration.

12. My dog jumps out of _____ pen.

13. Somebody needs to remove _____ clothes from this chair.

14. Everything has _____ place in Grandma's house.

15. The team will receive _____ uniforms on Monday.

16. Each artist wants _____ painting to win the prize.

Appositives

An **appositive** is a noun or pronoun placed after another noun or pronoun to further identify or rename it. An appositive and the words that go with it are usually set off from the rest of the sentence with commas. Commas are not used if the appositive tells "which one."

Example: Angela's mother, **Ms. Glover**, will visit our school.

Commas are needed because **Ms. Glover** renames Angela's mother.

Example: Angela's neighbor Joan will visit our school.

Commas are not needed because the appositive "Joan" tells **which** neighbor.

Directions: Write the appositive in each sentence in the blank. The first one has been done for you.

__Tina__   1. My friend Tina wants a horse.

_____ 2. She subscribes to the magazine *Horses*.

_____ 3. Her horse is the gelding "Brownie."

_____ 4. We rode in her new car, a convertible.

_____ 5. Her gift was jewelry, a bracelet.

_____ 6. Have you met Ms. Abbott, the senator?

_____ 7. My cousin Karl is very shy.

_____ 8. Do you eat the cereal Oaties?

_____ 9. Kiki's cat, Samantha, will eat only tuna.

_____ 10. My last name, Jones, is very common.

Name: _____

Dangling Modifiers

A **dangling modifier** is a word or group of words that does not modify what it is supposed to modify. To correct dangling modifiers, supply the missing words to which the modifiers refer.

Examples:
   Incorrect: While doing the laundry, the dog barked.
   Correct: While I was doing the laundry, the dog barked.

In the **incorrect** sentence, it sounds as though the dog is doing the laundry. In the **correct** sentence, it's clear that **I** is the subject of the sentence.

Directions: Rewrite the sentences to make the subject of the sentence clear and eliminate dangling modifiers. The first one has been done for you.

1. While eating our hot dogs, the doctor called.

   <u>While we were eating our hot dogs, the doctor called.</u>

2. Living in Cincinnati, the ball park is nearby.

   _____

3. While watching the movie, the TV screen went blank.

   _____

4. While listening to the concert, the lights went out.

   _____

5. Tossed regularly, anyone can make great salad.

   _____

6. While working, something surprised him.

   _____

   _____

Review

Directions: Write **noun** or **verb** to describe the words in bold.

_____ 1. She is one of the fastest **runners** I've seen.

_____ 2. She is **running** very fast!

_____ 3. She **thought** he was handsome.

_____ 4. Please share your **thoughts** with me.

_____ 5. I will **watch** the volleyball game on video.

_____ 6. The sailor fell asleep during his **watch**.

_____ 7. My grandmother believes my purchase was a real **find**.

_____ 8. I hope to **find** my lost books.

Directions: Rewrite the verb in the correct tense.

_____ 9. She **swim** across the lake in 2 hours.

_____ 10. He has **ride** horses for years.

_____ 11. Have you **saw** my sister?

_____ 12. She **fly** on an airplane last week.

_____ 13. My father had **instruct** me in the language.

_____ 14. I **drive** to the store yesterday.

_____ 15. The movie **begin** late.

_____ 16. Where **do** you go yesterday?

Directions: Circle the pronouns.

17. She and I told them to forget it!

18. They all wondered if her dad would drive his new car.

19. We want our parents to believe us.

20. My picture was taken at her home.

Review

Directions: Rewrite the sentences to correct the faulty parallels.

1. The cookies were sweet, crunchy and are delicious.

    _____

2. The town was barren, windswept and is empty.

    _____

3. The dog was black, long-haired and is quite friendly.

    _____

4. My favorite dinners are macaroni and cheese, spaghetti and I loved fish.

    _____

Directions: Rewrite the sentences to make the verb tenses consistent.

5. We laughed, cried and were jumping for joy.

    _____

6. She sang, danced and was doing somersaults.

    _____

7. The class researched, studied and were writing their reports.

    _____

8. Bob and Sue talked about their vacation and share their experiences.

    _____

Directions: Circle the pronouns that agree with their antecedents.

9. She left (her/their) purse at the dance.

10. Each dog wagged (its/their) tail.

11. We walked to (our/he) car.

12. The lion watched (his/its) prey.

Review

Directions: Rewrite the sentences to correct the dangling modifiers.

1. Living nearby, the office was convenient for her.

   _____

2. While doing my homework, the doorbell rang.

   _____

3. Watching over her shoulder, she hurried away.

   _____

4. Drinking from the large mug, he choked.

   _____

Directions: Circle the correct pronouns.

5. She laughed at my brother and (I/me).

6. At dawn, (he and I/him and me) were still talking.

7. Someone left (his or her/their) coat on the floor.

8. Lauren said (her/she) would not be late.

Directions: Circle the appositive.

9. The school nurse, Ms. Franklin, was worried about him.

10. The car, a Volkswagen, was illegally parked.

11. My hero, Babe Ruth, was an outstanding baseball player.

12. Is that car, the plum-colored one, for sale?

13. Will Mr. Zimmer, Todd's father, buy that car?

REVIEW
NOUNS VERBS
SIMPLE SUBJECTS
PERSONAL PRONOUNS
POSSESSIVE PRONOUNS
INTERROGATIVE PRONOUNS
ANT___ENTS
AP___ ___ES
SIMP___ ___DICATES

Adjectives

Adjectives describe nouns.

Examples:
 tall girl
 soft voice
 clean hands

Directions: Circle the adjectives. Underline the nouns they describe. Some sentences may have more than one set of adjectives and nouns.

1. The lonely man sat in the dilapidated house.

2. I hope the large crop of grapes will soon ripen.

3. The white boxes house honeybees.

4. My rambunctious puppy knocked over the valuable flower vase.

5. The "unsinkable" *Titanic* sank after striking a gigantic iceberg.

6. His grades showed his tremendous effort.

7. There are many purple flowers in the large arrangement.

8. These sweet peaches are the best I've tasted.

9. The newsletter describes several educational workshops.

10. The rodeo featured professional riders and funny clowns.

11. My evening pottery class is full of very interesting people.

12. My older brother loves his new pickup truck.

13. Tami's family bought a big-screen TV.

Name: _____

Comparing With Adjectives

When adjectives are used to compare two things, **er** is added at the end of the word for most one-syllable words and some two-syllable words.

Example: It is **colder** today than it was yesterday.

With many two-syllable words and all words with three or more syllables, the word **more** is used with the adjective to show comparison.

Example: Dr. X is **more professional** than Dr. Y.

When adjectives are used to compare three or more things, **est** is added at the end of the word for **most** one-syllable words and some two-syllable words.

Example: Today is the **coldest** day of the year.

With many two-syllable words and all words with three or more syllables, **most** is used with the adjective to show comparison.

Example: Dr. X is the **most professional** doctor in town.

When adding **er** or **est** to one-syllable words, these spelling rules apply.
- Double the last consonant if the word has a short vowel before a final consonant: thinner, fatter.
- If a word ends in **y**, change the **y** to **i** before adding **er** or **est**: earliest, prettiest.
- If a word ends in **e**, drop the final **e** before adding **er** or **est**: simpler, simplest.

Directions: Complete these sentences with the correct form of the adjective.

1. This book is (small) _____ than that one.

2. I want the (small) _____ book in the library.

3. My plan is (practical) _____ than yours.

4. My plan is the (practical) _____ one in the class.

5. I wish the change was (gradual) _____ than it is.

6. My sister is the (childish) _____ girl in her day-care group.

7. There must be a (simple) _____ way to do it than that.

8. This is the (simple) _____ way of the four we thought of.

Name: _____

Adjectives: Positive, Comparative and Superlative

There are three degrees of comparison adjectives: **positive**, **comparative** and **superlative**. The **positive degree** is the adjective itself. The **comparative** and **superlative** degrees are formed by adding **er** and **est**, respectively, to most one-syllable adjectives. The form of the word changes when the adjective is irregular, for example, **good**, **better**, **best**.

Most adjectives of two or more syllables require the words "more" or "most" to form the comparative and superlative degrees.

Examples:

Positive:	big	eager	
Comparative:	bigger	more eager	
Superlative:	biggest	most eager	

Directions: Write the positive, comparative or superlative forms of these adjectives.

Positive	Comparative	Superlative
1. hard	_____	_____
2. _____	happier	_____
3. _____	_____	most difficult
4. cold	_____	_____
5. _____	easier	_____
6. _____	_____	largest
7. little	_____	_____
8. _____	shinier	_____
9. round	_____	_____
10. _____	_____	most beautiful

Adverbs

Adverbs tell when, where or how an action occurred.

Examples:
    I'll go **tomorrow**. (when)
    I sleep **upstairs**. (where)
    I screamed **loudly**. (how)

Directions: Circle the adverb and underline the verb it modifies. Write the question (when, where or how) the adverb answers.

1. I ran quickly toward the finish line.   _____

2. Today, we will receive our report cards.   _____

3. He swam smoothly through the pool.   _____

4. Many explorers searched endlessly for new lands.   _____

5. He looked up into the sky.   _____

6. My friend drove away in her new car.   _____

7. Later, we will search for your missing wallet. _____

8. Most kings rule their kingdoms regally.   _____

9. New plants must be watered daily.   _____

10. The stream near our house is heavily polluted. _____

11. My brother likes to dive backward into our pool.   _____

Adverbs: Positive, Comparative and Superlative

There are also three degrees of comparison adverbs: **positive**, **comparative** and **superlative**. They follow the same rules as adjectives.

Example:

Positive:	rapidly	far
Comparative:	more rapidly	farther
Superlative:	most rapidly	farthest

Directions: Write the positive, comparative or superlative forms of these adverbs.

Positive	Comparative	Superlative
1. easily	_____	_____
2. _____	more quickly	_____
3. _____	_____	most hopefully
4. bravely	_____	_____
5. _____	more strongly	_____
6. near	_____	_____
7. _____	_____	most cleverly
8. _____	more gracefully	_____
9. _____	_____	most humbly
10. excitedly	_____	_____
11. _____	more handsomely	_____
12. slowly	_____	_____

Adjectives and Adverbs

Directions: Write **adjective** or **adverb** in the blanks to describe the words in bold. The first one has been done for you.

adjective   1. Her **old** boots were caked with mud.

_____   2. The baby was **cranky**.

_____   3. He took the test **yesterday**.

_____   4. I heard the **funniest** story last week!

_____   5. She left her wet shoes **outside**.

_____   6. Isn't that the **fluffiest** cat you've ever seen?

_____   7. He ran **around** the track twice.

_____   8. Our elderly neighbor lady seems **lonely**.

_____   9. His **kind** smile lifted my dragging spirits.

_____   10. **Someday** I'll meet the friend of my dreams!

_____   11. His cat never meows **indoors**.

_____   12. Carlos hung his new shirts **back** in the closet.

_____   13. Put that valuable vase **down** immediately!

_____   14. She is the most **joyful** child!

_____   15. Jonathan's wool sweater is totally **moth-eaten**.

Grade 6 - Comprehensive Curriculum

Name: _____

Identifying Sentence Parts

The **subject** tells who or what a sentence is about. Sentences can have more than one subject.

Example: Dogs and **cats** make good pets.

The **predicate** tells what the subject does or that it exists. Predicates can be more than one word. A sentence can have more than one predicate.

Examples: She **was walking**. She **walked** and **ran**.

An **adjective** is a word or group of words that describes the subject or another noun.

Example: The **cheerful yellow** bird with **blue** spots flew across the **flower-covered** meadow.

An **adverb** is a word or group of words that tells how, when, where or how often.

Example: He sat **there** waiting **quietly**.

Directions: Write **S** for subject, **P** for predicate, **ADJ** for adjective or **ADV** for adverb above each underlined word or group of words. The first one has been done for you.

```
     ADJ   S      ADJ            P        ADV
1. A huge  dog  with long teeth  was barking  fiercely.
```

2. My grandmother usually wore a hat with a veil.

3. My niece and her friend are the same height.

4. The lively reindeer danced and pranced briefly on the rooftop.

Directions: Write sentences containing the sentence parts listed. Mark each part even if the verb part gets separated.

1. Write a question with two subjects, two predicates and two adjectives:

_____

2. Write a statement with one subject, two predicates and two adjectives:

_____

Name: _____

Identifying Sentence Parts

Directions: Write **S** for subject, **P** for predicate, **ADJ** for adjective or **ADV** for adverb above the appropriate words in these sentences.

1. The large cat pounced on the mouse ferociously.

2. Did you remember your homework?

3. My mother is traveling to New York tomorrow.

4. I play basketball on Monday and Friday afternoons.

5. The old, decrepit house sat at the end of the street.

6. Several tiny rabbits nibbled at the grass at the edge of the field.

7. The lovely bride wore a white dress with a long train.

8. We packed the clothes for the donation center in a box.

9. The telephone rang incessantly.

10. The lost child cried helplessly.

11. What will we do with these new puppies?

12. Lauren reads several books each week.

13. The picture hung precariously on the wall.

14. I purchased many new school supplies.

15. Computers have changed the business world.

Name: _____

Prepositions

A **preposition** is a word that comes before a noun or pronoun and shows the relationship of that noun or pronoun to some other word in the sentence.

The **object of a preposition** is the noun or pronoun that follows a preposition and adds to its meaning.

A **prepositional phrase** includes the preposition, the object of the preposition and all modifiers.

Example:
She gave him a pat **on his back**.
On is the preposition.
Back is the object of the preposition.
His is a possessive pronoun.

Common Prepositions			
about	down	near	through
above	for	of	to
across	from	off	up
at	in	on	with
behind	into	out	within
by	like	past	without

Directions: Underline the prepositional phrases. Circle the prepositions. Some sentences have more than one prepositional phrase. The first one has been done for you.

1. He claimed he felt (at) home only (on) the West Coast.

2. She went up the street, then down the block.

3. The famous poet was near death.

4. The beautiful birthday card was from her father.

5. He left his wallet at home.

6. Her speech was totally without humor and boring as well.

7. I think he's from New York City.

8. Kari wanted to go with her mother to the mall.

Prepositions

Directions: Complete the sentences by writing objects for the prepositions. The first one has been done for you.

1. He was standing at <u>**the corner of Fifth and Main.**</u> _____

2. She saw her friend across _____

3. Have you ever looked beyond _____

4. His contact lens fell into _____

5. Have you ever gone outside without _____

6. She was anxious for _____

7. Is that dog from _____

8. She was daydreaming and walked past _____

9. The book was hidden behind _____

10. The young couple had fallen in _____

11. She insisted she was through _____

12. He sat down near _____

13. She forgot her umbrella at _____

14. Have you ever thought of _____

15. Henry found his glasses on _____

Object of a Preposition

The **object of a preposition** is the noun or pronoun that follows the preposition and adds to its meaning.

Example:
   Correct: Devan smiled **at** (preposition) **Tori** (noun: object of the preposition) and **me**
      (pronoun: object of the same preposition.)
   Correct: Devan smiled at Tori. Devan smiled at me. Devan smiled at Tori and me.
   Incorrect: Devan smiled at Tori and I.

Tip: If you are unsure of the correct pronoun to use, pair each pronoun with the verb and say the phrase out loud to find out which pronoun is correct.

Directions: Write the correct pronouns on the blanks. The first one has been done for you.

him _____ 1. It sounded like a good idea to Sue and (he/him).

_____ 2. I asked Abby if I could attend with (her/she).

_____ 3. To (we/us), holidays are very important.

_____ 4. Between (we/us), we finished the job quickly.

_____ 5. They gave the award to (he and I/him and me).

_____ 6. The party was for my brother and (I/me).

_____ 7. I studied with (he/him).

_____ 8. Tanya and the others arrived after (we/us).

_____ 9. After the zoo, we stopped at the museum with Bill and (her/she).

_____ 10. The chips for (he/him) are in the bag on top of the refrigerator.

Direct Objects

A **direct object** is a noun or pronoun. It answers the question **whom** or **what** after a verb.

Examples:

My mom baked **bread**.
Bread is the direct object. It tells **what** Mom baked.
We saw **Steve**.
Steve is the direct object. It tells **whom** we saw.

Directions: Write a direct object in each sentence.

1. My dog likes _____. WHAT?

2. My favorite drink is _____. WHAT?

3. I saw _____ today. WHOM?

4. The car struck a _____. WHAT?

5. The fan blew _____ through the room. WHAT?

6. I packed a _____ for lunch. WHAT?

7. We watched _____ play basketball. WHOM?

8. I finished my _____. WHAT?

9. The artist sketched the _____. WHAT?

10. He greets _____ at the door. WHOM?

11. The team attended the victory _____. WHAT?

12. The beautician cut my _____. WHAT?

13. Tamika will write _____. WHAT?

Indirect Objects

An **indirect object** is a noun or pronoun which tells **to whom or what** or **for whom or what** the action is performed. An indirect object usually is found between a verb and a direct object.

Example:
    I gave **Ellen** my address.
    Ellen is the indirect object. It tells **to whom** I gave my address.

Directions: Circle the indirect objects. Underline the direct objects.

1. Joann told Mary the secret.

2. Advertisers promise consumers the world.

3. The dogs showed me their tricks.

4. Aunt Martha gave Rhonda a necklace for her birthday.

5. Ramon brought Mom a bouquet of fresh flowers.

6. I sent my niece a package for Christmas.

7. Mr. Dunbar left his wife a note before leaving.

8. Grandma and Grandpa made their friends dinner.

9. The baby handed her mom a toy.

10. Monica told Stephanie the recipe for meatloaf.

11. We sent Grandma a card.

12. The waiter served us dessert.

13. Mom and Dad sold us the farm.

Joining Sentences

Conjunctions are words that join sentences, words or ideas. When two sentences are joined with **and**, they are more or less equal.

Example: Julio is coming, **and** he is bringing cookies.

When two sentences are joined with **but**, the second sentence contradicts the first one.

Example: Julio is coming, **but** he will be late.

When two sentences are joined with **or**, they name a choice.

Example: Julio might bring cookies, **or** he might bring a cake.

When two sentences are joined with **because**, the second one names the reason for the first one.

Example: I'll bring cookies, too, **because** Julio might forget his.

When two sentences are joined with **so**, the second one names a result of the first one.

Example: Julio is bringing cookies, **so** we will have a snack.

Directions: Complete each sentence. The first one has been done for you.

1. We could watch TV, or _we could play Monopoly.®_____

2. I wanted to seize the opportunity, but _____

3. You had better not deceive me, because _____

4. My neighbor was on vacation, so _____

5. Veins take blood back to your heart, and _____

6. You can't always yield to your impulses, because _____

7. I know that is your belief, but _____

8. It could be reindeer on the roof, or _____

9. Brent was determined to achieve his goal, so _____

10. Brittany was proud of her height, because _____

Name: _____

Conjunctions

The conjunctions **and**, **or**, **but** and **nor** can be used to make a compound subject, a compound predicate or a compound sentence.

Examples:
Compound subject: My friend **and** I will go to the mall.
Compound predicate: We ran **and** jumped in gym class.
Compound sentence: I am a talented violinist,
                       but my father is better.

Directions: Write two sentences of your own in each section.

Compound subject:

1. _____

_____

2. _____

_____

Compound predicate:

1. _____

_____

2. _____

_____

Compound sentence:

1. _____

_____

2. _____

_____

Review

Directions: Write the missing verb tenses.

	Present	Past	Past Participle
1.	catch	_____	_____
2.	_____	stirred	_____
3.	_____	_____	has (have) baked
4.	go	_____	_____
5.	_____	said	_____

Directions: Circle the simple subject and underline the simple predicate in each sentence.

6. Maria got sunburned at the beach.

7. The class watched the program.

8. The tomatoes are ripening.

9. We went grocery shopping.

10. The cross country team practiced all summer.

Directions: Write the missing adjective or adverb forms below.

	Positive	Comparative	Superlative
11.	_____	more friendly	_____
12.	small	_____	_____
13.	_____	_____	most fun
14.	_____	more attractive	_____

Review

Directions: Write **adjective** or **adverb** to describe the words in bold.

_____ 1. My **old** boyfriend lives nearby.

_____ 2. My old boyfriend lives **nearby**.

_____ 3. His hair looked **horrible**.

_____ 4. Have you heard this **silly** joke?

_____ 5. **Suddenly**, the door opened.

_____ 6. The **magnificent** lion raised its head.

_____ 7. I accomplished the task **yesterday**.

_____ 8. This party has **delicious** food.

Directions: Circle the prepositions.

9. He went in the door and up the stairs.

10. Is this lovely gift from you?

11. I was all for it, but the decision was beyond my power.

12. His speech dragged on into the night.

13. My great-grandmother's crystal dish is in the curio cabinet.

14. He received a trophy for his accomplishments on the team.

15. The President of the United States is on vacation.

16. Joel wrote an excellent essay about Christopher Columbus.

Name: _____

Cumulative Review

Directions: Identify the part of speech of the words in bold. The first one has been done for you.

1. The dog ran **across** the field.   _____preposition_____

2. My **parents** allow me to stay up until 10:00 P.M.   _____

3. Our cat **is** long-haired.   _____

4. Matt will wash the **dirty** dishes.   _____

5. Joseph washed the **car** on Saturday.   _____

6. The waterfall crashed **over** the cliff.   _____

7. What will you give **her**?   _____

8. The car **rolled** to a stop.   _____

9. He **slowly** finished his homework.   _____

10. My **nephew** will be 12 years old on Sunday.   _____

11. The news program discussed the **war**.   _____

12. Our **family** portrait was taken in the gazebo.   _____

13. I **would like** to learn to fly a plane.   _____

14. **My** hair needs to be trimmed.   _____

15. **Strawberry** jam is her favorite.   _____

16. The horse **quickly** galloped across the field.   _____

17. **What** will you do next?   _____

18. Please stand **and** introduce yourself.   _____

19. My neighbor takes **great** pride in her garden.   _____

20. She sang **well** tonight.   _____

21. My grandmother is from **Trinidad**.   _____

Name: _____

"Affect" and "Effect"

Affect means to act upon or influence.

Example: Studying will **affect** my test grade.

Effect means to bring about a result or to accomplish something.

Example: The **effect** of her smile was immediate!

Directions: Write **affect** or **effect** in the blanks to complete these sentences correctly. The first one has been done for you.

affects 1. Your behavior (affects/effects) how others feel about you.

_____ 2. His (affect/effect) on her was amazing.

_____ 3. The (affect/effect) of his jacket was striking.

_____ 4. What you say won't (affect/effect) me!

_____ 5. There's a relationship between cause and (affect/effect).

_____ 6. The (affect/effect) of her behavior was positive.

_____ 7. The medicine (affected/effected) my stomach.

_____ 8. What was the (affect/effect) of the punishment?

_____ 9. Did his behavior (affect/effect) her performance?

_____ 10. The cold (affected/effected) her breathing.

_____ 11. The (affect/effect) was instantaneous!

_____ 12. Your attitude will (affect/effect) your posture.

_____ 13. The (affect/effect) on her posture was major.

_____ 14. The (affect/effect) of the colored lights was calming.

_____ 15. She (affected/effected) his behavior.

"Among" and "Between"

Among is a preposition that applies to more than two people or things.

Example: The group divided the cookies **among** themselves.

Between is a preposition that applies to only two people or things.

Example: The cookies were divided **between** Jeremy and Sara.

WE'LL DIVIDE THESE AMONG OURSELVES!

Directions: Write **between** or **among** in the blanks to complete these sentences correctly. The first one has been done for you.

between   1. The secret is (between/among) you and Jon.

_____ 2. (Between/Among) the two of them, whom do you think is nicer?

_____ 3. I must choose (between/among) the cookies, candy and pie.

_____ 4. She threaded her way (between/among) the kids on the playground.

_____ 5. She broke up a fight (between/among) Josh and Sean.

_____ 6. "What's come (between/among) you two?" she asked.

_____ 7. "I'm (between/among) a rock and a hard place," Josh responded.

_____ 8. "He has to choose (between/among) all his friends," Sean added.

_____ 9. "Are you (between/among) his closest friends?" she asked Sean.

_____ 10. "It's (between/among) another boy and me," Sean replied.

_____ 11. "Can't you settle it (between/among) the group?"

_____ 12. "No," said Josh. "This is (between/among) Sean and me."

_____ 13. "I'm not sure he's (between/among) my closest friends."

_____ 14. Sean, Josh and Andy began to argue (between/among) themselves.

_____ 15. I hope Josh won't have to choose (between/among) the two!

Name: _____

"All Together" and "Altogether"

All together is a phrase meaning everyone or everything in the same place.

Example: We put the eggs **all together** in the bowl.

Altogether is an adverb that means entirely, completely or in all.

Example: The teacher gave **altogether** too much homework.

THE EGGS ARE
ALL TOGETHER

Directions: Write **altogether** or **all together** in the blanks to complete these sentences correctly. The first one has been done for you.

___altogether___

1. "You ate (altogether/all together) too much food."

_____ 2. The girls sat (altogether/all together) on the bus.

_____ 3. (Altogether/All together) now: one, two, three!

_____ 4. I am (altogether/all together) out of ideas.

_____ 5. We are (altogether/all together) on this project.

_____ 6. "You have on (altogether/all together) too much makeup!"

_____ 7. They were (altogether/all together) on the same team.

_____ 8. (Altogether/All together), we can help stop

_____   pollution (altogether/all together).

_____ 9. He was not (altogether/all together) happy with his grades.

_____ 10. The kids were (altogether/all together) too loud.

_____ 11. (Altogether/All together), the babies cried gustily.

_____ 12. She was not (altogether/all together) sure what to do.

_____ 13. Let's sing the song (altogether/all together).

_____ 14. He was (altogether/all together) too pushy for her taste.

_____ 15. (Altogether/All together), the boys yelled the school cheer.

"Amount" and "Number"

Amount indicates quantity, bulk or mass.

Example: She carried a large **amount** of money in her purse.

Number indicates units.

Example: What **number** of people volunteered to work?

Directions: Write **amount** or **number** in the blanks to complete these sentences correctly. The first one has been done for you.

____number____   1. She did not (amount/number) him among her closest friends.

_____   2. What (amount/number) of ice cream should we order?

_____   3. The (amount/number) of cookies on her plate was three.

_____   4. His excuses did not (amount/number) to much.

_____   5. Her contribution (amounted/numbered) to half the money raised.

_____   6. The (amount/number) of injured players rose every day.

_____   7. What a huge (amount/number) of cereal!

_____   8. The (amount/number) of calories in the diet was low.

_____   9. I can't tell you the (amount/number) of friends she has!

_____   10. The total (amount/number) of money raised was incredible!

_____   11. The (amount/number) of gadgets for sale was amazing.

_____   12. He was startled by the (amount/number) of people present.

_____   13. He would not do it for any (amount/number) of money.

_____   14. She offered a great (amount/number) of reasons for her actions.

_____   15. Can you guess the (amount/number) of beans in the jar?

Name: _____

"Irritate" and "Aggravate"

Irritate means to cause impatience, to provoke or annoy.

Example: His behavior **irritated** his father.

Aggravate means to make a condition worse.

Example: Her sunburn was **aggravated** by additional exposure to the sun.

Directions: Write **aggravate** or **irritate** in the blanks to complete these sentences correctly. The first one has been done for you.

aggravated 1. The weeds (aggravated/irritated) his hay fever.

_____ 2. Scratching the bite (aggravated/irritated) his condition.

_____ 3. Her father was (aggravated/irritated) about her low grade in math.

_____ 4. It (aggravated/irritated) him when she switched TV channels.

_____ 5. Are you (aggravated/irritated) when the cat screeches?

_____ 6. Don't (aggravate/irritate) me like that again!

_____ 7. He was in a state of (aggravation/irritation).

_____ 8. Picking at the scab (aggravates/irritates) a sore.

_____ 9. Whistling (aggravates/irritates) the old grump.

_____ 10. She was (aggravated/irritated) when she learned about it.

_____ 11. "Please don't (aggravate/irritate) your mother," Dad warned.

_____ 12. His asthma was (aggravated/irritated) by too much stress.

_____ 13. Sneezing is sure to (aggravate/irritate) his allergies.

_____ 14. Did you do that just to (aggravate/irritate) me?

_____ 15. Her singing always (aggravated/irritated) her brother.

"Principal" and "Principle"

Principal means main, leader or chief, or a sum of money that earns interest.

Examples:
    The high school **principal** earned interest on the **principal** in his savings account.
    The **principal** reason for his savings account was to save for retirement.

Principle means a truth, law or a moral outlook that governs the way someone behaves.

Example:
    Einstein discovered some fundamental **principles** of science.
    Stealing is against her **principles**.

Directions: Write **principle** or **principal** in the blanks to complete these sentences correctly. The first one has been done for you.

principle 1. A (principle/principal) of biology is "the survival of the fittest."

_____ 2. She was a person of strong (principles/principals).

_____ 3. The (principles/principals) sat together at the district conference.

_____ 4. How much of the total in my savings account is (principle/principal)?

_____ 5. His hay fever was the (principle/principal) reason for his sneezing.

_____ 6. It's not the facts that upset me, it's the (principles/principals) of the case.

_____ 7. The jury heard only the (principle/principal) facts.

_____ 8. Our school (principle/principal) is strict but fair.

_____ 9. Spend the interest, but don't touch the (principle/principal).

_____ 10. Helping others is a guiding (principle/principal) of the homeless shelter.

_____ 11. In (principle/principal), we agree; on the facts, we do not.

_____ 12. The (principle/principal) course at dinner was leg of lamb.

_____ 13. Some mathematical (principles/principals) are difficult to understand.

_____ 14. The baby was the (principle/principal) reason for his happiness.

"Good" and "Well"

Good is always an adjective. It is used to modify a noun or pronoun.

Examples:
We enjoyed the **good** food.
We had a **good** time yesterday.
It was **good** to see her again.

Well is used to modify verbs, to describe someone's health or to describe how someone is dressed.

Examples:
I feel **well**. He looked **well**.
He was **well**-dressed for the weather.
She sang **well**.

Directions: Write **good** or **well** in the blanks to complete these sentences correctly.

1. She performed _____.

2. You look _____ in that color.

3. These apples are _____.

4. He rides his bike _____.

5. She made a _____ attempt to win the race.

6. The man reported that all was _____ in the coal mine.

7. Jonas said, "I feel _____, thank you."

8. The team played _____.

9. Mom fixed a _____ dinner.

10. The teacher wrote, " _____ work!" on top of my paper.

Name: _____

"Like" and "As"

Like means something is similar, resembles something else or describes how things are similar in manner.

Examples:
    She could sing **like** an angel.
    She looks **like** an angel, too!

As is a conjunction, a joining word, that links two independent clauses in a sentence.

Example: He felt chilly **as** night fell.

Sometimes **as** precedes an independent clause.

Example: As I told you, I will not be at the party.

Directions: Write **like** or **as** in the blanks to complete these sentences correctly. The first one has been done for you.

__as___ 1. He did not behave (like/as) I expected.

_____ 2. She was (like/as) a sister to me.

_____ 3. The puppy acted (like/as) a baby!

_____ 4. (Like/As) I was saying, he will be there at noon.

_____ 5. The storm was 25 miles away, (like/as) he predicted.

_____ 6. He acted exactly (like/as) his father.

_____ 7. The song sounds (like/as) a hit to me!

_____ 8. Grandpa looked (like/as) a much younger man.

_____ 9. (Like/As) I listened to the music, I grew sleepy.

_____ 10. (Like/As) I expected, he showed up late.

_____ 11. She dances (like/as) a ballerina!

_____ 12. (Like/As) she danced, the crowd applauded.

_____ 13. On stage, she looks (like/as) a professional!

_____ 14. (Like/As) I thought, she has taken lessons for years.

Name: _____

Review

Directions: Write the correct word in the blank.

_____ 1. The (affect/effect) of the shot was immediate.

_____ 2. The shot (affected/effected) her allergies.

_____ 3. You have a positive (affect/effect) on me!

_____ 4. I was deeply (affected/effected) by the speech.

_____ 5. The prize was shared (among/between) Art and Lisa.

_____ 6. She was (among/between) the best students in the class.

_____ 7. He felt he was (among/between) friends.

_____ 8. It was hard to choose (among/between) all the gifts.

_____ 9. Does it (irritate/aggravate) you to see people smoke?

_____ 10. Does smoking (irritate/aggravate) his sore throat?

_____ 11. He wondered why she was (irritated/aggravated) at him.

_____ 12. The intensity of his (irritation/aggravation) grew each day.

_____ 13. She had a (principal/principle) part in the play.

_____ 14. Beans were the (principal/principle) food in his diet.

_____ 15. She was a woman of strong (principals/principles).

_____ 16. Mr. Larson was their favorite (principal/principle).

_____ 17. The (amount/number) of ice-cream cones he ate was incredible.

_____ 18. I wouldn't part with it for any (amount/number) of money.

_____ 19. It happened exactly (like/as) I had predicted!

_____ 20. He sounds almost (like/as) his parents.

Review

Directions: Use these words in sentences of your own.

1. affect _____

   _____

2. effect _____

   _____

3. among _____

   _____

4. between _____

   _____

5. irritate _____

   _____

6. aggravate _____

   _____

7. principal _____

   _____

8. principle _____

   _____

9. good _____

   _____

10. well _____

   _____

11. like _____

   _____

12. as _____

   _____

Capitalization

Capitalize . . .
   . . . the first word in a sentence
   . . . the first letter of a person's name
   . . . proper nouns, like the names of planets, oceans and mountain ranges
   . . . titles when used with a person's name, even if abbreviated (Dr., Mr., Lt.)
   . . . days of the week and months of the year
   . . . cities, states and countries

Directions: Write **C** in the blank if the word or phrase is capitalized correctly. Rewrite the word or phrase if it is incorrect.

1. _____ President Abraham Lincoln _____
2. _____ Larry D. Walters _____
3. _____ saturn _____
4. _____ benjamin franklin _____
5. _____ August _____
6. _____ professional _____
7. _____ jupiter _____
8. _____ Pacific Ocean _____
9. _____ white house _____
10. _____ pet _____
11. _____ Congress _____
12. _____ Houston _____
13. _____ federal government _____
14. _____ dr. Samuel White _____
15. _____ milwaukee, Wisconsin _____
16. _____ Appalachian mountains _____
17. _____ lake michigan _____
18. _____ Notre Dame College _____
19. _____ department of the Interior _____
20. _____ monday and Tuesday _____

Name: _____

Capitalization

Words which name places, people, months and landmarks are always capitalized.

Examples:

Abraham Lincoln   Acme Motor Company

White House   Jefferson Memorial

Fifth Avenue   May, June, July

Directions: Rewrite the sentences using correct capitalization.

1. My family and I visited washington, d.c., in july.

_____

2. We saw the washington monument, the capital building and the white house.

_____

3. I was very impressed by our visit to the smithsonian institution.

_____

4. Our taxi driver, from the american cab company, showed us around town.

_____

5. We drove down pennsylvania avenue.

_____

6. We were unable to see the president of the united states.

_____

7. However, we did see the first lady.

_____

8. My parents and I decided to visit arlington national cemetery.

_____

Name: _____

Commas

Use **commas** . . .
   . . . after introductory phrases
   . . . to set off nouns of direct address
   . . . to set off appositives from the words that go with them
   . . . to set off words that interrupt the flow of the sentence
   . . . to separate words or groups of words in a series

Examples:
   Introductory phrase: Of course, I'd be happy to attend.
   Noun of direct address: Ms. Williams, please sit here.
   To set off appositives: Lee, **the club president**, sat beside me.
   Words interrupting flow: My cousin, **who's 13**, will also be there.
   Words in a series: I ate **popcorn**, **peanuts**, **oats** and **barley**.
          or   I ate **popcorn**, **peanuts**, **oats**, and **barley**.

Note: The final comma is optional when punctuating words in a series.

Directions: Identify how the commas are used in each sentence.
          Write: **I** for introductory phrase
                  N for noun of direct address
                  A for appositive
                  WF for words interrupting flow
                  WS for words in a series

_____ 1. Yes, she is my sister.

_____ 2. My teacher, Mr. Hopkins, is very fair.

_____ 3. Her favorite fruits are oranges, plums and grapes.

_____ 4. The city mayor, Carla Ellison, is quite young.

_____ 5. I will buy bread, milk, fruit and ice cream.

_____ 6. Her crying, which was quite loud, soon gave me a headache.

_____ 7. Stephanie, please answer the question.

_____ 8. So, do you know her?

_____ 9. Unfortunately, the item is not returnable.

_____ 10. My sister, my cousin and my friend will accompany me on vacation.

_____ 11. My grandparents, Rose and Bill, are both 57 years old.

Name: _____

Commas

Directions: Use commas to punctuate these sentences correctly.

1. I'll visit her however not until I'm ready.

2. She ordered coats gloves and a hat from the catalog.

3. Eun-Jung the new girl looked ill at ease.

4. Certainly I'll show Eun-Jung around school.

5. Yes I'll be glad to help her.

6. I paid nevertheless I was unhappy with the price.

7. I bought stamps envelopes and plenty of postcards.

8. No I told you I was not going.

9. The date November 12 was not convenient.

10. Her earache which kept her up all night stopped at dawn.

11. My nephew who loves bike riding will go with us.

12. He'll bring hiking boots a tent and food.

13. The cat a Himalayan was beautiful.

14. The tennis player a professional in every sense signed autographs.

15. No you can't stay out past 10:00 P.M.

Commas are important, and you should know when to use them!

COMMAS

Name: _____

Semicolons

A **semicolon** (**;**) signals a reader to pause longer than for a comma, but not as long as for a period. Semicolons are used between closely related independent clauses not joined by **and**, **or**, **nor**, **for**, **yet** or **but**.

An **independent clause** contains a complete idea and can stand alone.

Example: Rena was outgoing; her sister was shy.

Directions: Use semicolons to punctuate these sentences correctly. Some sentences require more than one semicolon.

1. Jeff wanted coffee Sally wanted milk.

2. I thought he was kind she thought he was grouchy.

3. "I came I saw I conquered," wrote Julius Caesar.

4. Jessica read books she also read magazines.

5. I wanted a new coat my old one was too small.

6. The airport was fogged-in the planes could not land.

7. Now, he regrets his comments it's too late to retract them.

8. The girls were thrilled their mothers were not.

Directions: Use a semicolon and an independent clause to complete the sentences.

9. She liked him _____

10. I chose a red shirt _____

11. Andrea sang well _____

12. She jumped for joy _____

13. Dancing is good exercise _____

14. The man was kind _____

15. The tire looked flat _____

16. My bike is missing _____

Name: _____

Colons

Use a **colon** . . .
> . . . after the salutation of a business letter
> . . . between the hour and the minute when showing time
> . . . between the volume and page number of a periodical
> . . . between chapters and verses of the Bible
> . . . before a list of three or more items
> . . . to introduce a long statement or quotation

Examples:
Salutation: Dear Madame:
Hour and minute: 8:45 P.M.
Periodical volume and page number: *Newsweek* 11:32
Bible chapter and verse: John 3:16
Before a list of three or more items: Buy these: fruit, cereal, cheese
To introduce a long statement or quotation: Author Willa Cather said this about experiencing life: "There are only two or three human stories, and they go on repeating themselves as fiercely as if they had never happened before."

Dear Mr. Miller:

I would like to place an order for five of your 1 ton scales. Please contact me, concerning price and delivery date.

Sincerely,
Ms. Jones

Directions: Use colons to punctuate these sentences correctly. Some sentences require more than one colon.

1. At 12 45 the president said this "Where's my lunch?"

2. Look in Proverbs 1 12 for the answer.

3. Don't forget to order these items boots, socks, shoes and leggings.

4. Ask the librarian for *Weekly Reader* 3 14.

5. Dear Sir Please send me two copies of your report.

6. Avoid these at all costs bad jokes, bad company, bad manners.

7. The statement is in either Genesis 1 6 or Exodus 3 2.

8. At 9 15 P.M., she checked in, and at 6 45 A.M., she checked out.

9. I felt all these things at once joy, anger and sadness.

10. Here's a phrase President Bush liked "A thousand points of light."

Name: _____

Dashes

Dashes (—) are used to indicate sudden changes of thought.

Examples:
I want milk—no, make that soda—with my lunch.
Wear your old clothes—new ones would get spoiled.

Directions: If the dash is used correctly in the sentence, write **C** in the blank. If the dash is missing or used incorrectly, draw an **X** in the blank. The first one has been done for you.

___C___ 1. No one—not even my dad—knows about the surprise.

_____ 2. Ask—him—no I will to come to the party.

_____ 3. I'll tell you the answer oh, the phone just rang!

_____ 4. Everyone thought—even her brother—that she looked pretty.

_____ 5. Can you please—oh, forget it!

_____ 6. Just stop it I really mean it!

_____ 7. Tell her that I'll—never mind—I'll tell her myself!

_____ 8. Everyone especially Anna is overwhelmed.

_____ 9. I wish everyone could—forgive me—I'm sorry!

_____ 10. The kids—all six of them—piled into the backseat.

Directions: Write two sentences of your own that include dashes.

11. _____

_____

12. _____

_____

Grade 6 - Comprehensive Curriculum

Quotation Marks

Quotation marks are used to enclose a speaker's exact words. Use commas to set off a direct quotation from other words in the sentence.

Examples:

Kira smiled and said, "Quotation marks come in handy."

"Yes," Josh said, "I'll take two."

Directions: If quotation marks and commas are used correctly, write **C** in the blank. If they are used incorrectly, write an **X** in the blank. The first one has been done for you.

___*C*___ 1. "I suppose," Elizabeth remarked, "that you'll be there on time."

_____ 2. "Please let me help! insisted Mark.

_____ 3. I'll be ready in 2 minutes!" her father said.

_____ 4. "Just breathe slowly," the nurse said, "and calm down."

_____ 5. "No one understands me" William whined.

_____ 6. "Would you like more milk?" Jasmine asked politely.

_____ 7. "No thanks, her grandpa replied, "I have plenty."

_____ 8. "What a beautiful morning!" Jessica yelled.

_____ 9. "Yes, it certainly is" her mother agreed.

_____ 10. "Whose purse is this?" asked Andrea.

_____ 11. It's mine" said Stephanie. "Thank you."

_____ 12. "Can you play the piano?" asked Heather.

_____ 13. "Music is my hobby." Jonathan replied.

_____ 14. Great!" yelled Harry. Let's play some tunes."

_____ 15. "I practice a lot," said Jayne proudly.

"This is exactly what I'm saying! You can tell by my quotation marks!"

Name: _____

Quotation Marks

Directions: Use quotation marks and commas to punctuate these sentences correctly.

1. No Ms. Elliot replied you may not go.

2. Watch out! yelled the coach.

3. Please bring my coat called Renee.

4. After thinking for a moment, Paul said I don't believe you.

5. Dad said Remember to be home by 9:00 P.M.

6. Finish your projects said the art instructor.

7. Go back instructed Mom and comb your hair.

8. I won't be needing my winter coat anymore replied Mei-ling.

9. He said How did you do that?

10. I stood and said My name is Rosalita.

11. No said Misha I will not attend.

12. Don't forget to put your name on your paper said the teacher.

13. Pay attention class said our history teacher.

14. As I came into the house, Mom called Dinner is almost ready!

15. Jake, come when I call you said Mother.

16. How was your trip to France Mrs. Shaw? asked Deborah.

"Remember: quotation marks are used to enclose a speaker's exact words."

Name: _____

Apostrophes

Use an **apostrophe** (') in a contraction to show that letters have been left out. A **contraction** is a shortened form of two words, usually a pronoun and a verb.

Add an **apostrophe** and **s** to form the **possessive** of singular nouns. **Plural possessives** are formed two ways. If the noun ends in **s**, simply add an apostrophe at the end of the word. If the noun does not end in **s**, add an apostrophe and **s**.

Examples:
  Contraction: He **can't** button his sleeves.
  Singular possessive: The **boy's** sleeves are too short.
  Plural noun ending in s: The **ladies'** voices were pleasant.
  Plural noun not ending in s: The **children's** song was long.

Directions: Use apostrophes to punctuate the sentences correctly. The first one has been done for you.

1. I can't understand that child's game.

2. The farmers wagons were lined up in a row.

3. She didnt like the chairs covers.

4. Our parents beliefs are often our own.

5. Sandys mothers aunt isnt going to visit.

6. Two ladies from work didnt show up.

7. The citizens group wasnt very happy.

8. The colonists demands werent unreasonable.

9. The mothers babies cried at the same time.

10. Our parents generation enjoys music.

Directions: Write two sentences of your own that include apostrophes.

11. _____

_____

12. _____

_____

Name: _____

Contractions

Examples:

he will = **he'll**
she is = **she's**
they are = **they're**
can not = **can't**

Contraction Chart

Pronoun		Verb		Contraction
I	+	am	=	I'm
we, you, they	+	are	=	we're, you're, they're
he, she, it	+	is	=	he's, she's, it's
I, we, you, they	+	have	=	I've, we've, you've, they've
I, you, we, she, he, they	+	would	=	I'd, you'd, we'd, she'd, he'd, they'd
I, you, we, she, he, they	+	will	=	I'll, you'll, we'll, she'll, he'll, they'll

---

Directions: Write a sentence using a contraction. The first one has been done for you.

1. I will   <u>I'll see you tomorrow!</u>

2. they are   _____

3. we have   _____

4. she would   _____

5. you are   _____

6. they will   _____

7. she is   _____

8. he would   _____

9. they are   _____

10. I am   _____

Name: _____

Singular Possessives

Directions: Write the singular possessive form of each word. Then, add a noun to show possession. The first one has been done for you.

1. spider <u>spider's web</u>

2. clock _____

3. car _____

4. book _____

5. Mom _____

6. boat _____

7. table _____

8. baby _____

9. woman _____

10. writer _____

11. mouse _____

12. fan _____

13. lamp _____

14. dog _____

15. boy _____

16. house _____

Name: _____

Plural Possessives

Directions: Write the plural possessive form of each word. Then add a noun to show possession. The first one has been done for you.

1. kid ___kids' skates___

2. man _____

3. aunt _____

4. lion _____

5. giraffe _____

6. necklace _____

7. mouse _____

8. team _____

9. clown _____

10. desk _____

11. woman _____

12. worker _____

Directions: Write three sentences of your own that include plural possessives.

13. _____

_____

14. _____

_____

15. _____

_____

Italics

Use **italics** or **underlining** for titles of books, newspapers, plays, magazines and movies.

Examples:
 Book: Have you read *Gone with the Wind*?
 Movie: Did you see *The Muppet Movie*?
 Newspaper: I like to read *The New York Times*.
 Magazine: Some children read *Sports Illustrated*.
 Play: *A Doll's House* is a play by Henrik Ibsen.

Since we cannot write in italics, we underline words that should be in italics.

Directions: Underline the words that should be in italics. The first one has been done for you.

1. I read about a play titled <u>Cats</u> in <u>The Cleveland Plain Dealer</u>.

2. You can find The New York Times in most libraries.

3. Audrey Wood wrote Elbert's Bad Word.

4. Parents and Newsweek are both popular magazines.

5. The original Miracle on 34th Street was filmed long ago.

6. Cricket and Ranger Rick are magazines for children.

7. Bon Appetit means "good appetite" and is a cooking magazine.

8. Harper's, The New Yorker and Vanity Fair are magazines.

9. David Copperfield was written by Charles Dickens.

10. Harriet Beecher Stowe wrote Uncle Tom's Cabin.

11. Paul Newman was in a movie called The Sting.

12. Have you read Ramona the Pest by Beverly Cleary?

13. The Louisville Courier Journal is a Kentucky newspaper.

14. Teen and Boy's Life are magazines for young readers.

15. Have you seen Jimmy Stewart in It's a Wonderful Life?

Name: _____

Complete Sentences

A **complete sentence** has both a simple subject and a simple predicate. It is a complete thought. Sentences which are not complete are called **fragments**.

Example:
    Complete sentence: The wolf howled at the moon.
    Sentence fragment: Howled at the moon.

Directions: Write **C** on the line if the sentence is complete. Write **F** if it is a fragment.

1. _____ The machine is running.

2. _____ What will we do today?

3. _____ Knowing what I do.

4. _____ That statement is true.

5. _____ My parents drove to town.

6. _____ Watching television all afternoon.

7. _____ The storm devastated the town.

8. _____ Our friends can go with us.

9. _____ The palm trees bent in the wind.

10. _____ Spraying the fire all night.

Directions: Rewrite the sentence fragments from above to make them complete sentences.

_____

_____

_____

_____

Name: _____

Run-On Sentences

A **run-on sentence** occurs when two or more sentences are joined together without punctuation or a joining word. Run-on sentences should be divided into two or more separate sentences.

Example:
   Run-on sentence: My parents, sister, brother and I went to the park we saw many animals we had fun.
   Correct: My parents, sister, brother and I went to the park. We saw many animals and had fun.

Directions: Rewrite the run-on sentences correctly.

1. The dog energetically chased the ball I kept throwing him the ball for a half hour.

_____

_____

_____

2. The restaurant served scrambled eggs and bacon for breakfast I had some and they were delicious.

_____

_____

_____

3. The lightning struck close to our house it scared my little brother and my grandmother called to see if we were safe.

_____

_____

_____

_____

_____

Finding Spelling Errors

Directions: One word in each sentence below is misspelled. Write the word correctly on the line.

1. Jeff felt discoraged at the comparison between

   him and his older brother. _____

2. I got inpatient as my curiosity grew. _____

3. She confided that she had not finished the asignment. _____

4. They made the selection after a brief conferrence. _____

5. Obviusly, it's impolite to sneeze on someone. _____

6. This skin cream is practicaly invisible. _____

7. What would prevent you from taking on addtional work? _____

8. I can resite the words to that hymn. _____

9. In a previous columm, the newspaper explained the situation. _____

10. He decieved me so many times that now I distrust him. _____

11. Please have the curtesy to observe the "No Eating" signs. _____

12. The advertisement is so small that it's nearly invisble. _____

13. The best way to communicate is in a face-to-face conservation.

    _____

14. In a cost comparson, salmon is more expensive than tuna. _____

15. Poplarity among friends shouldn't depend on your accomplishments.

    _____

16. Her campaign was quite an acheivement. _____

17. He condemmed it as a poor imitation. _____

Name: _____

Finding Spelling Errors

Directions: Circle all misspelled words. Write the words correctly on the lines at the end of each paragraph. If you need help, consult a dictionary.

Sabrina wanted to aquire a saltwater acquarum. She was worried about the expence, though, so first she did some reseach. She wanted to learn the exxact care saltwater fish need, not just to exsist but to florish. One sorce said she needed to put water in the aquarium and wait 6 weeks before she added the fish. "Good greif!" Sabrina thought. She got a kitten from her nieghbor instead.

_____

_____

_____

One stormy day, Marcel was babysitting his neice. He happened to obsurve that the sky looked darker than norml. At first he ignored it, but then he noticed a black cloud exxpand and grow in hieght. Then a tail dropped down from the twisting cloud and siezed a tree! "It's a tornado!" Marcel shouted. "Maybe two tornados! This is an emergensy!" For a breef moment Marcel wished he hadn't shouted, because his niece looked at him with a very frightened expresion. Just then, the cieling began to sag as if it had a heavy wieght on it. "This is an excelent time to visit the basement," he told the little girl as calmy as possible.

_____

_____

_____

Just before Mother's Day, Bethany went to a flourist to buy some flowers for her mother. "Well, what is your reqest?" the clerk asked. "I don't have much money," Bethany told him. "So make up your mind," he said impatiently. "Do you want quality or quanity?" Bethany wondered if he was giving her a quizz. She tried not to sqwirm as he stared down at her. Finally she said, "I want cortesy," as she headed for the exxit.

_____

_____

_____

Name: _____

Spelling: Correcting Errors

Directions: Find six errors in each paragraph. Write the words correctly on the lines after each paragraph. Use a dictionary if you need help.

My brother Jim took a math coarse at the high school that was too hard for hymn. My father didn't want him to take it, but Jim said, "Oh, you're just too critcal, Dad. Oviously, you don't think I can do it." Jim ingored Dad. That's norm at our house.

_____

_____

Well, the first day Jim went to the course, he came home with a solem expreion on his face, like a condemed man. "That teacher assined us five pages of homework!" he said. "And two addtional problems that we have to reserch!"

_____

_____

"He sounds like an excelent, profesional teacher," my dad said. "We need more teachers of that qwalitu in our schools." Jim squirmed in his seat. Then he gradualy started to smile. "Dad, I need some help with a personl problem," he said. "Five pages of problems, right?" Dad asked. Jim smiled and handed Dad his math book. That's tipical at our house, too.

_____

_____

One day, we had a meddical emergensy at home. My sisters' hand got stuck in a basket with a narrow opening, and she couldn't pull it out. I thought she would have to wear the basket on her hand permanentally! First, I tried to stretch and exxpand the baskets opening, but that didn't work.

_____

_____

Then I smeared a quanity of butter on my sisters hand, and she pulled it right out. I thought she would have the curtesy to thank me, but she just stomped away, still mad. How childsh! Sometimes she seems to think I exxist just to serve her. There are more importanter things in the world than her happiness!

_____

_____

Name: _____

Writing: Four Types of Sentences

There are four main types of sentences: A **statement** tells something. It ends in a period. A **question** asks something. It ends in a question mark. A **command** tells someone to do something. It ends in a period or an exclamation mark. An **exclamation** shows strong feeling or excitement. It ends in an exclamation mark.

Boy, what a cute cat!

Directions: Write what you would say in each situation. Then tell whether the sentence you wrote was a statement, question, exclamation or command. The first one has been done for you.

Write what you might say to:

1. A friend who has a new cat:
   When did you get the new cat? (question)
   or Boy, what a cute cat! (exclamation)

2. A friend who studied all night for the math test:

   _____

   _____

3. Your teacher about yesterday's homework:

   _____

   _____

4. A child you're watching who won't sit still for a second:

   _____

   _____

5. Your sister, who's been on the phone too long:

   _____

   _____

Name: _____

Organizing Paragraphs

A **topic sentence** states the main idea of a paragraph and is usually the first sentence. **Support sentences** follow, providing details about the topic. All sentences in a paragraph should relate to the topic sentence. A paragraph ends with a **conclusion sentence**.

Directions: Rearrange each group of sentences into a paragraph, beginning with the topic sentence. Cross out the sentence in each group that is not related to the topic sentence. Write the new paragraph.

Now, chalk drawings are considered art by themselves. The earliest chalk drawings were found on the walls of caves. Chalk is also used in cement, fertilizer, toothpaste and makeup. Chalk once was used just to make quick sketches. Chalk has been used for drawing for thousands of years. Then the artist would paint pictures from the sketches.

_____

_____

_____

_____

Dams also keep young salmon from swimming downriver to the ocean. Most salmon live in the ocean but return to fresh water to lay their eggs and breed. Dams prevent salmon from swimming upriver to their spawning grounds. Pacific salmon die after they spawn the first time. One kind of fish pass is a series of pools of water that lead the salmon over the dams. Dams are threatening salmon by interfering with their spawning. To help with this problem, some dams have special "fish passes" to allow salmon to swim over the dam.

_____

_____

_____

_____

_____

_____

Building Paragraphs

Directions: Read each group of questions and the topic sentence. On another sheet of paper, write support sentences that answer each question. Number your support sentences in order. Make any necessary changes so the sentences fit together in one paragraph. Then write your paragraph after the topic sentence.

Questions: Why did Jimmy feel sad?
What happened to change how he felt?
How does he feel when he comes to school now?

Jimmy used to look so solemn when he came to school. _____

_____

_____

_____

Questions: Why did Jennifer want to go to another country?
Why couldn't she go?
Does she have any plans to change that?

Jennifer always wanted to visit a foreign country. _____

_____

_____

_____

Questions: What was Paulo's "new way to fix spaghetti"?
Did anyone else like it?
Did Paulo like it himself?

Paulo thought of a new way to fix spaghetti. _____

_____

_____

_____

_____

Name: _____

Explaining With Examples

Some paragraphs paint word pictures using adjectives, adverbs, similes and metaphors. Other paragraphs explain by naming examples.

Example:

Babysitting is not an easy way to earn money. For example, the little girl you're watching may be very cranky and cry until her parents come home. Or maybe the family didn't leave any snacks and you have to starve all night. Even worse, the child could fall and get hurt. Then you have to decide whether you can take care of her yourself or if you need to call for help. No, babysitting isn't easy.

Directions: Write examples for each topic sentence on another sheet of paper. Number them in order to put them in paragraph form. Make any necessary changes so the sentences fit together in one paragraph. Then write your paragraphs below after the topic sentences.

1. Sometimes dreams can be scary. _____

_____

_____

_____

_____

_____

_____

2. You can learn a lot by living in a foreign country. _____

_____

_____

_____

_____

_____

_____

Creating Word Pictures

Painters create pictures with colors. Writers create pictures with words. Adding adjectives and adverbs, using specific nouns, verbs, similes and metaphors in sentences help create word pictures.

Notice how much more interesting and informative these two rewritten sentences are.

Original Sentence
The animal ate its food.

Rewritten sentences
Like a hungry lion, the starving cocker spaniel wolfed down the entire bowl of food in seconds.

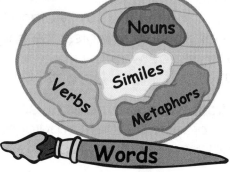

The raccoon delicately washed the berries in the stream before nibbling them slowly, one by one.

Directions: Rewrite each sentence twice, creating two different word pictures.

1. The person built something.

_____

_____

2. The weather was bad.

_____

_____

3. The boy went down the street.

_____

_____

4. The children helped.

_____

_____

Name: _____

Describing People

Often, a writer can show how someone feels by describing how that person looks or what he or she is doing rather than by using emotion words, like angry or happy. This is another way to create word pictures.

Directions: Read the phrases below. Write words to describe how you think that person feels.

1. like a tornado, yelling, raised fists _____

2. slumped, walking slowly, head down _____

3. trembling, breathing quickly, like a cornered animal _____

Directions: Write one or two sentences for each phrase without using emotion words.

4. a runner who has just won a race for his or her school _____

_____

_____

5. a sixth grader on the first day in a new school _____

_____

_____

6. a teenager walking down the street and spotting a house on fire _____

_____

_____

7. a scientist who has just discovered a cure for lung cancer _____

_____

_____

8. a kindergarten child being ignored by his or her best friend _____

_____

_____

Describing Events in Order

When we write to explain what happened, we need to describe the events in the same order they occurred. Words and phrases such as **at first**, **then**, **after that** and **finally** help us relate the order of events.

Directions: Rewrite the paragraph below, putting the topic sentence first and arranging the events in order.

I got dressed, but I didn't really feel like eating breakfast. By the time I got to school, my head felt hot, so I went to the nurse. This day was terrible from the very beginning. Finally, I ended up where I started—back in my own bed. Then she sent me home again! I just had some toast and left for school. When I first woke up in the morning, my stomach hurt.

_____

_____

_____

_____

_____

_____

Directions: Follow these steps to write a paragraph about what happened the last time you tried to cook something or the last time you tried to fix something that was broken.

1. Write your first draft on another sheet of paper. Start with a topic sentence.
2. Add support sentences to explain what happened. Include phrases to keep things in order: **at first**, **then**, **after that**, **finally**, **in the middle of it**, **at last**.
3. Read your paragraph out loud to see if it reads smoothly. Make sure the events are in the correct order.
4. Make any needed changes, then write your paragraph below.

_____

_____

_____

_____

Name: _____

Explaining What Happened

Directions: These pictures tell a story, but they're out of order. Follow these steps to write what happened.

1. On another sheet of paper, write a sentence explaining what is happening in each picture.
2. Put your sentences in order and write a topic sentence.
3. Read the whole paragraph to yourself. Add words to show the order in which things happened.
4. Include adjectives and adverbs and maybe even a simile or metaphor to make your story more interesting.
5. Write your paragraph below. Be sure to give it a title.

_____

_____

_____

_____

_____

_____

_____

_____

_____

_____

Grade 6 - Comprehensive Curriculum

Writing Directions

Directions must be written clearly. They are easiest to follow when they are in numbered steps. Each step should begin with a verb.

How to Peel a Banana:
1. Hold the banana by the stem end.
2. Find a loose edge of peel at the top.
3. Pull the peeling down.
4. Peel the other sections of the banana in the same way.

Directions: Rewrite these directions, number the steps in order and begin with verbs.

How to Feed a Dog

Finally, call the dog to come and eat. Then you carry the filled dish to the place where the dog eats. The can or bag should be opened by you. First, clean the dog's food dish with soap and water. Then get the dog food out of the cupboard. Put the correct amount of food in the dish.

_____

_____

_____

_____

_____

_____

Directions: Follow these steps to write your own directions.

1. On another sheet of paper, draw two symbols, such as a square with a star in one corner or a triangle inside a circle. Don't show your drawing to anyone.
2. On a second sheet of paper, write instructions to make the same drawing. Your directions need to be clear, in order and numbered. Each step needs to begin with a verb.
3. Trade directions (but not pictures) with a partner. See if you can follow each other's directions to make the drawings.
4. Show your partner the drawing you made in step one. Does it look like the one he or she made following your directions? Could you follow your partner's directions? Share what was clear—or not so clear—about each other's instructions.

Review

Directions: Write paragraphs to match the descriptions given. Begin with a topic sentence and add support sentences that tell the events in order. Write the first draft of your paragraph on another sheet of paper. Read it to yourself, make any necessary changes, then write it below.

1. Write a short paragraph to explain something that might happen on your way to school.

_____

_____

_____

_____

_____

2. Write a paragraph that tells what you usually do during the first hour after you get up on a school day.

_____

_____

_____

_____

_____

Directions: Write directions explaining how to brush your teeth. Include at least four steps. Make them as clear as possible. Begin each step with a verb. Write a rough draft on another sheet of paper first.

1. _____

2. _____

3. _____

4. _____

Writing: Stronger Sentences

Sometimes the noun form of a word is not the best way to express an idea. Compare these two sentences:

They made preparations for the party.
They prepared for the party.

The second sentence, using **prepared** as a verb, is shorter and stronger.

Directions: Write one word to replace a whole phrase. Cross out the words you don't need. The first one has been done for you.

1. She ~~made a suggestion~~ **suggested** that we go on Monday.

2. They arranged decorations around the room.

3. Let's make a combination of the two ideas.

4. I have great appreciation for what you did.

5. The buses are acting as transportation for the classes.

6. The group made an exploration of the Arctic Circle.

7. Please make a selection of one quickly.

8. The lake is making a reflection of the trees.

9. The family had a celebration of the holiday.

10. Would you please provide a solution for this problem?

11. Don made an imitation of his cat.

12. Please give a definition of that word.

13. I made an examination of the broken bike.

14. Dexter made an invitation for us to join him.

> Write one word to replace a whole phrase.

Name: _____

Writing: Descriptive Sentences

Descriptive sentences make writing more interesting to the reader. This is done by using adjectives, adverbs, prepositional phrases, similes and metaphors.

Example:
The dog ran down the hill.
The black and white beagle bounded down the steep embankment as though being chased by an invisible dragon.

Directions: Rewrite these sentences so they are more descriptive.

1. Bill likes collecting stamps.

_____

2. Martina drove into town.

_____

3. I enjoy working on the computer.

_____

4. Riverside won the game.

_____

5. Dinner was great.

_____

6. My mom collects antiques.

_____

7. The teacher likes my essay.

_____

8. My brother received a scholarship for college.

_____

Grade 6 - Comprehensive Curriculum

Name: _____

Writing: Different Points of View

A **fact** is a statement that can be proved. An **opinion** is what someone thinks or believes.

Directions: Write **F** if the statement is a fact or **O** if it is an opinion.

1. _____ The amusement park near our town just opened last summer.

2. _____ It's the best one in our state.

3. _____ It has a roller coaster that's 300 feet high.

4. _____ You're a chicken if you don't go on it.

Directions: Think about the last movie or TV show you saw. Write one fact and one opinion about it.

Fact: _____

Opinion: _____

In a story, a **point of view** is how one character feels about an event and reacts to it. Different points of view show how characters feel about the same situation.

What if you were at the mall with a friend and saw a CD you really wanted on sale? You didn't bring enough money, so you borrowed five dollars from your friend to buy the CD. Then you lost the money in the store!

Directions: Write a sentence describing what happened from the point of view of each person named below. Explain how each person felt.

Yourself _____

_____

Your friend _____

_____

The store clerk who watched you look for the money _____

_____

The person who found the money _____

_____

Reading Skills: It's Your Opinion

Your opinion is how you feel or think about something. Although other people may have the same opinion, their reasons could not be exactly the same because of their individuality.

When writing an opinion paragraph, it is important to first state your opinion. Then, in at least three sentences, support your opinion. Finally, end your paragraph by restating your opinion in different words.

Example:

 I believe dogs are excellent pets. For thousands of years, dogs have guarded and protected their owners. Dogs are faithful and have been known to save the lives of those they love. Dogs offer unconditional love as well as company for the quiet times in our lives. For these reasons, I feel that dogs make wonderful pets.

Directions: Write an opinion paragraph on whether you would or would not like to have lived in Colonial America. Be sure to support your opinion with at least three reasons.

_____

_____

_____

_____

_____

_____

_____

Writing Checklist

Reread your paragraph carefully.

☐ My paragraph makes sense. ☐ I have a good opening and ending.

☐ There are no jumps in ideas. ☐ I used correct spelling.

☐ I used correct punctuation. ☐ My paragraph is well-organized.

☐ My paragraph is interesting.

Persuasive Writing

examples / facts / reasons

To **persuade** means to convince someone that your opinion is correct. "Because I said so," isn't a very convincing reason. Instead, you need to offer reasons, facts and examples to support your opinion.

Directions: Write two reasons or facts and two examples to persuade someone.

1. Riding a bicycle "no-handed" on a busy street is a bad idea.

   Reasons/Facts: _____

   _____

   Examples: _____

   _____

   _____

2. Taking medicine prescribed by a doctor for someone else is dangerous.

   Reasons/Facts: _____

   _____

   Examples: _____

   _____

   _____

3. Learning to read well will help you in every other subject in school.

   Reasons/Facts: _____

   _____

   Examples: _____

   _____

   _____

Persuasive Writing

When trying to persuade someone, it helps to look at both sides of the issue. If you can understand both sides, you will have a better idea how to convince someone of your point of view.

Directions: Follow these steps to write two persuasive paragraphs about which form of transportation is better: airplanes or cars.

1. On another sheet of paper, list three or four reasons why planes are better and three or four reasons why cars are better.
2. Put each list of reasons in order. Often, persuasive writing is strongest when the best reason is placed last. Readers tend to remember the last reason best.
3. Write topic sentences for each paragraph.
4. Read each paragraph and make any necessary changes so one sentence leads smoothly to the next.
5. Write your paragraphs below.

Airplanes Are Better Transportation Than Cars _____

_____

_____

_____

_____

_____

Cars Are Better Transportation Than Planes _____

_____

_____

_____

_____

_____

6. Write two more paragraphs on another sheet of paper. Select any topic. Write from both points of view.

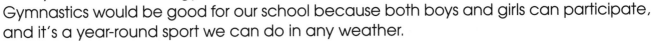

Persuasive Writing

Writing is usually more persuasive if written from the reader's point of view.

If you made cookies to sell at a school fair, which of these sentences would you write on your sign?
I spent a lot of time making these cookies.
These cookies taste delicious!

If you were writing to ask your school board to start a gymnastics program, which sentence would be more persuasive?
I really am interested in gymnastics.
Gymnastics would be good for our school because both boys and girls can participate, and it's a year-round sport we can do in any weather.

In both situations, the second sentence is more persuasive because it is written from the reader's point of view. People care how the cookies taste, not how long it took you to make them. The school board wants to provide activities for all the students, not just you.

Directions: Write **R** if the statement is written from the reader's point of view or **W** if it's written from the writer's point of view.

_____ 1. If you come swimming with me, you'll be able to cool off.

_____ 2. Come swimming with me. I don't want to go alone.

_____ 3. Please write me a letter. I really like to get mail.

_____ 4. Please write me a letter. I want to hear from you.

Directions: Follow these steps to write an "invitation" on another sheet of paper to persuade people to move to your town or city.

1. Think about reasons someone would want to live in your town. Make a list of all the good things there, like the schools, parks, annual parades, historic buildings, businesses where parents could work, scout groups, Little League, and so on. You might also describe your town's population, transportation, restaurants, celebrations or even holiday decorations.
2. Now, select three or four items from your list. Write a sentence (or two) about each one from the reader's point of view. For example, instead of writing "Our Little League team won the championship again last year," you could tell the reader, "You could help our Little League team win the championship again this year."
3. Write a topic sentence to begin your invitation, and put your support sentences in order after it.
4. Read your invitation out loud to another person. Make any needed changes, and copy the invitation onto a clean sheet of paper.

Name: _____

Review

Directions: Read the questions. Then write one or two sentences about the situation from both points of view.

What if your neighbor had a dog that barked all night and kept you awake?

Your point of view: _____

_____

Your neighbor's point of view: _____

_____

What if the school board wanted to begin holding classes every Saturday during the school year?

For Saturday classes: _____

_____

Against Saturday classes: _____

_____

Directions: Rewrite these sentence so they make a stronger statement:

Jacob made a decision to take the test today. _____

_____

Kisha had a dream about the test results. _____

_____

Directions: Write two facts and two opinions about your math class.

Facts: _____

_____

Opinions: _____

_____

Review

Directions: Write a persuasive essay convincing your town that a park is needed for older kids with equipment such as basketball courts, soccer and football fields and a track. Be sure to end with a convincing statement.

_____

_____

_____

_____

_____

_____

Directions: Write a descriptive paragraph about these topics.

My Pet _____

_____

_____

_____

_____

My Mom _____

_____

_____

_____

_____

Describing Characters

When you write a story, your characters must seem like real people. You need to let your reader know not only how they look but how they act, what they look like and how they feel. You could just tell the reader that a character is friendly, scared or angry, but your story will be more interesting if you show these feelings by the characters' actions.

Example:
Character: A frightened child
Adjectives and adverbs: red-haired, freckled, scared, lost, worried
Simile: as frightened as a mouse cornered by a cat
Action: He peeked between his fingers, but his mother was nowhere in sight.

Directions: Write adjectives, adverbs, similes and/or metaphors that tell how each character feels. Then write a sentence that shows how the character feels.

1. an angry woman
   Adjectives and adverbs: _____

   Metaphor or simile: _____

   Sentence: _____

2. a disappointed man
   Adjectives and adverbs: _____

   Metaphor or simile: _____

   Sentence: _____

3. a hungry child
   Adjectives and adverbs: _____

   Metaphor or simile: _____

   Sentence: _____

4. a tired boy
   Adjectives and adverbs: _____

   Metaphor or simile: _____

   Sentence: _____

Setting the Scene

Where and when a story takes place is called the **setting**. As with characters, you can tell about a setting—or you can show what the setting is like. Compare these two pairs of sentences:

The sun was shining.   The bus was crowded.
The glaring sun made my eyes burn.   Paige shouldered her way down the aisle,
                                        searching for an empty seat on the crowded bus.

If you give your readers a clear picture of your story's setting, they'll feel as if they're standing beside your characters. Include words that describe the sights, sounds, smells, feel and even taste if appropriate.

Directions: Write at least two sentences for each setting, clearly describing it for your readers.

1. an empty kitchen early in the morning _____

_____

_____

2. a locker room after a basketball game _____

_____

_____

3. a dark living room during a scary TV movie _____

_____

_____

4. a classroom on the first day of school _____

_____

_____

5. a quiet place in the woods _____

_____

_____

Creating a Plot

When you're writing a story, the **plot** is the problem your characters face and how they solve it. It's helpful to write a plot outline or summary before beginning a story.

In the beginning of a story, introduce the characters, setting and problem.

Example: Scott and Cindy have never met their mother who lives in another state. They decide they would like very much to meet her. They live with their grandmother and father. On the way home from school, they talk about how they can find and contact her.

In the middle, characters try different ways to solve the problem, usually failing at first.

Example: Scott and Cindy hurry home to ask their grandmother if she can help them find their mother. Their grandmother seems nervous and tells Scott and Cindy to discuss the matter with their father when he gets home from work. When Scott and Cindy's father comes home, they tell him about their plan. Their father is very quiet for several minutes. He says he needs some time to think about it and asks if he can let them know tomorrow. Scott and Cindy can hardly sleep that night. Getting through school the next day is tough as well. After school, Scott and Cindy wait by the window for their father's car to pull in the driveway.

In the end, the characters find a way to solve the problem. Not all stories have happy endings. Sometimes, the characters decide they can live with the situation the way it is.

Example: When their father pulls into the driveway, Scott and Cindy rush out to meet him. Their father hands them airplane tickets. Scott and Cindy hug each other. Then they hug their father.

Directions: How do you think this story ends? Write a summary for the ending of this story.

_____

_____

_____

_____

_____

_____

_____

Creating a Plot

As you plan your stories, consider these questions.

- Who are the main characters?
- What do they look like?
- Where do they live?
- When do they live?
- What is the problem?
- Why is there a problem?
- How do they solve it?
- How do they feel at first?
- How do they feel at the end?
- Did I leave any loose ends?
- Do I want a surprise ending?

Directions: Write the plot for a story of your own on another sheet of paper. Follow these steps.

1. Select two characters and a setting. Write some descriptive words and phrases you could use.

2. What kinds of problems might the characters face? Jot down your ideas.

3. Select a problem and think of ways the characters might try to solve it. Number the alternatives in order, with the solution you will use last.

4. Add more details. Then write a plot outline or summary.

5. Finally, write out the whole story. You can change your plot outline if you think of a better idea. Make your story exciting!

6. Read your story out loud to yourself. Is what happened clear? Make any needed changes and rewrite your story neatly or type it on the computer and print it out. Be certain your story has a title.

7. Add illustrations or computer graphics to your story if you wish.

Writing Dialogue

Stories are more interesting when characters talk to each other. Conversations help show the characters' feelings and personalities. Compare these two scenes from a story:

Chad asked Angela to help him with his homework. She said she wouldn't, because she was mad at him for flirting with Nicole.

"Angela, would you be a real friend and help me with this math problem?" Chad asked with a big smile.

"I'm awfully busy, Chad," Angela answered without looking up. "Maybe you should ask Nicole, since you enjoy talking to her so much."

In the second version, we know Angela is angry, even though the writer didn't use that word. You can show how your characters feel by what they say and how they say it.

When you write dialogue, try to make the words sound natural, the way people really talk. Remember to start a new paragraph every time a different person speaks. Put quotation marks around the words the person says. Commas and periods at the ends of sentences go inside the quotation marks.

Directions: Write dialogue for what each character might say to a classmate in this situation. Show how the character feels without using the word for the feeling. Also write the reply from the classmate. Use another sheet of paper for your writing.

The teacher explains a new assignment the class will do in groups. The bell rings and everyone heads for the lunchroom.

1. A discouraged girl who isn't sure she can do the project.

2. A self-confident boy who got an A on the last project.

3. An impatient girl who has an idea and wants to get started.

4. An angry boy who dislikes group projects.

5. A bored girl who doesn't care about the project.

6. A boy who is worried about a different problem in his life.

7. A student who is afraid no one will want him or her for a partner on the project.

Writing Dialogue

When it was Megan's turn to present her book report to the class, she dropped all her notecards! Her face turned red, and she wished she was invisible, but all she could do was stand there and say what she could remember without her cards. It was awful!

Directions: Rewrite each paragraph below. Explain the same scenes and feelings using dialogue.

After class, Megan told her friend Sara she had never been so embarrassed in her life. She saw everyone staring at her, and the teacher looked impatient, but there wasn't anything she could do. Sara assured Megan that no one disliked her because of what had happened.

_____

_____

_____

When Megan got home, she told her mother about her book report. By then, she felt like crying. Her mother said not to get discouraged. In a couple of days, she would be able to laugh about dropping the cards.

_____

_____

_____

When Megan's older brother Jed came home, he asked her what was wrong. She briefly told him and said she never was going back to school. He started laughing. Megan got mad because she thought he was laughing at her. Then Jed explained that he had done almost the same thing when he was in sixth grade. He was really embarrassed, too, but not for long.

_____

_____

_____

_____

Writing: Paraphrasing

Paraphrasing means to restate something in your own words.

Directions: Write the following sentences in your own words. The first one has been done for you.

1. He sat alone and watched movies throughout the cold, rainy night.

   <u>All through the damp, chilly evening, the boy watched television by himself.</u>

2. Many animals such as elephants, zebras and tigers live in the grasslands.

   _____

   _____

3. In art class, Sarah worked diligently on a clay pitcher, molding and shaping it on the pottery wheel.

   _____

   _____

4. The scientists frantically searched for a cure for the new disease that threatened the entire world population.

   _____

   _____

5. Quietly, the detective crept around the abandoned building, hoping to find the missing man.

   _____

   _____

6. The windmill turned lazily in the afternoon breeze.

   _____

   _____

Writing: Paraphrasing

Directions: Using synonyms and different word order, paraphrase the following paragraphs. The first one has been done for you.

Some of the Earth's resources, such as oil and coal, can be used only once. We should always, therefore, be careful how we use them. Some materials that are made from natural resources, including metal, glass and paper, can be reused. This is called recycling.

Many natural resources, including coal and oil, can be used only one time. For this reason, it is necessary to use them wisely. There are other materials made from resources of the Earth that can be recycled, or used again. Materials that can be recycled include metal, glass and paper.

Recycling helps to conserve the limited resources of our land. For example, there are only small amounts of gold and silver ores in the earth. If we can recycle these metals, less of the ores need to be mined. While there is much more aluminum ore in the earth, recycling is still important. It takes less fuel energy to recycle aluminum than it does to make the metal from ore. Therefore, recycling aluminum helps to conserve fuel.

_____

_____

_____

_____

It is impossible to get minerals and fossil fuels from the earth without causing damage to its surface. In the past, people did not think much about making these kinds of changes to the Earth. They did not think about how these actions might affect the future. As a result, much of the land around mines was left useless and ugly. This is not necessary, because such land can be restored to its former beauty.

_____

_____

_____

_____

Name: _____

Writing: Summarizing

A **summary** is a brief retelling of the main ideas of a reading selection. To summarize, write the author's most important points in your own words.

Directions: Write a two-sentence summary for each paragraph.

The boll weevil is a small beetle that is native to Mexico. It feeds inside the seed pods, or bolls, of cotton plants. The boll weevil crossed into Texas in the late 1800s. It has since spread into most of the cotton-growing areas of the United States. The boll weevil causes hundreds of millions of dollars worth of damage to cotton crops each year.

Summary: _____

_____

_____

Each spring, female boll weevils open the buds of young cotton plants with their snouts. They lay eggs inside the buds, and the eggs soon hatch into wormlike grubs. The grubs feed inside the buds, causing the buds to fall from the plant. They eat their way from one bud to another. Several generations of boll weevils may be produced in a single season.

Summary: _____

_____

_____

The coming of the boll weevil to the United States caused tremendous damage to cotton crops. Yet, there were some good results, too. Farmers were forced to plant other crops. In areas where a variety of crops were raised, the land is in better condition than it would have been if only cotton had been grown.

Summary: _____

_____

_____

Writing: Summarizing a Personal Narrative

Directions: Read the following narrative, then follow the directions.

My Greatest Fear

I am scared of spiders. I realize this is not a logical fear, but I cannot help myself. I have been frightened by spiders since I was very young. For the following three reasons, spiders will never be pets of mine.

The first reason that I am scared of spiders is their appearance. I do not like their eight wispy, creepy legs. Spiders are never easily seen, but rather dark and unattractive. They are often hairy, and the mere thought of multiple eyeballs gives me shivers.

Spiders are not well-behaved. They are sly and always ready to sneak up on innocent victims. Spiders have habits of scurrying across floors, dropping from ceilings, and dangling from cobwebs. One never knows what to expect from a spider.

Finally, I am scared of spiders due to a "spider experience" as a child. Having just climbed into bed, I noticed a particularly nasty-looking spider on the ceiling over my bed. My father came into dispose of it, and it fell into bed with me. The thought of it crawling over me drove me from the bed shrieking. After that, I checked the ceiling nightly before getting into bed.

Many people love spiders. They are good for the environment and are certainly needed on our planet. However, because of my fear, irrational though it may be, I'd rather just avoid contact with arachnids.

Directions: Write a four-sentence summary of the narrative.

_____

_____

_____

_____

_____

_____

Writing: Summarizing a Personal Narrative

Write the main idea of the second paragraph.

_____

_____

Write the main idea of the third paragraph.

_____

_____

Write the main idea of the fourth paragraph.

_____

_____

Everyone has a fear of something. On another sheet of paper, write a five-paragraph personal narrative about a fear of your own. Use the following guide to help you organize your narrative.

Paragraph 1. State your fear.

Provide background information about fear.

Paragraph 2. State your first reason for fear.

Support this statement with at least three sentences.

Paragraph 3. State your second reason for fear.

Support this statement with at least three sentences.

Paragraph 4. State your third reason for fear.

Support this statement with at least three sentences.

Paragraph 5. Provide a summary of your narrative.

Restate your fear in different words from the opening sentence.

Writing: Outlining

An **outline** is a skeletal description of the main ideas and important details of a reading selection. Making an outline is a good study aid. It is particularly useful when you must write a paper.

Directions: Read the paragraphs, and then complete the outline below.

Weather has a lot to do with where animals live. Cold-blooded animals have body temperatures that change with the temperature of the environment. Cold-blooded animals include snakes, frogs and lizards. They cannot live anywhere the temperatures stay below freezing for long periods of time. The body temperatures of warm-blooded animals do not depend on the environment.

Any animal with hair or fur—including dogs, elephants and whales—is warm-blooded. Warm-blooded animals can live anywhere in the world where there is enough food to sustain them.

Some warm-blooded animals live where snow covers the ground all winter. These animals have different ways to survive the cold weather. Certain animals store up food to last throughout the snowy season. For example, the tree squirrel may gather nuts to hide in his home. Other animals hibernate in the winter. The ground squirrel, for example, stays in its burrow all winter long, living off the fat reserves in its body.

Title: _____

Main Topic: I. _____

   Subtopic: A. Cold-blooded animals' temperatures change with environment.

   Detail: 1. _____

   Subtopic: B. _____

   Detail: 1. They can live anywhere there is food.

Main Topic: II. _____

   Subtopic: A. Animals have different ways to survive the cold.

   Details: 1. _____

           2. _____

Review

Directions: Read the paragraph, then follow the directions.

According to one estimate, 75 percent of all fresh water on the Earth is in the form of ice. The polar regions of the Earth are almost completely covered by ice. In some places, the ice is more than 8,000 feet thick. If all of this ice were spread out evenly, the Earth would be covered with a 100-foot-thick layer of ice. Although ice is not an important source of fresh water today, it could be in the future. Some people have proposed towing large, floating masses of ice to cities to help keep up with the demand for fresh water.

1. Complete the outline of the paragraph.

Title: _____

Main Topic: I. 75 percent of fresh water on Earth is ice.

Subtopics: A. _____

B. _____

2. Check the most appropriate generalization:

☐ Ice is the most plentiful source of fresh water.

☐ Ice is important to the future.

3. Paraphrase the first sentence by restating it in your own words.

_____

4. Is the author's purpose to inform, entertain or persuade?

_____

5. Where would you look to find information on the polar ice caps?

_____

Review

Directions: Read the paragraph, then follow the directions.

The Constellation Orion

Constellations are groups of stars that have been given names. They often represent an animal, person or object. One of the easiest constellations to identify is the Big Dipper, which is shaped like a spoon. Once the Big Dipper is located, it is easy to see Cassiopeia (a W), the Little Dipper (an upside-down spoon) and the North Star. The North Star's scientific name is Polaris, and it is the last star in the handle of the Little Dipper. Other constellations include Orion the hunter, Gemini the twins, Canis Major the dog and Pegasus the winged horse. Many ancient cultures, including the Greeks and Native Americans, used the position of the stars to guide them. They also planned daily life activities, such as planting, hunting and harvesting, by the path the constellations made through the sky. For thousands of years, humans have gazed at the sky, fascinated by the millions of stars and imagining pictures in the night.

1. Complete the outline of the paragraph.

Title: _____

Main Topic: I. _____

Subtopics: A. _____

B. _____

_____

2. In three sentences, summarize the paragraph.

_____

_____

_____

3. What is the author's purpose? _____

4. Under which topics would you look to find more information on constellations?

_____   _____   _____

Review

Directions: Imagine you are making a speech about one of your hobbies. Complete an outline of the speech.

Title: _____

Main Topic: I. _____

Subtopics: A. _____

B. _____

Who is your audience? _____

Is it appropriately written for that audience? _____

Are you trying to inform, entertain or persuade? _____

In the space below, write your speech in at least 100 words.

_____

_____

_____

_____

_____

_____

_____

_____

_____

Using the Right Resources

Directions: Decide where you would look to find information on the following topics. After each question, write one or more of the following references:

- **almanac** — contains tables and charts of statistics and information
- **atlas** — collection of maps
- **card/computer catalog** — library resource showing available books by topic, title or author
- **dictionary** — contains alphabetical listing of words with their meanings, pronunciations and origins
- **encyclopedia** — set of books or CD-ROM with general information on many subjects
- **Readers' Guide to Periodical Literature** — an index of articles in magazines and newspapers
- **thesaurus** — contains synonyms and antonyms of words

1. What is the capital of The Netherlands? _____

2. What form of government is practiced there? _____

3. What languages are spoken there? _____

4. What is the meaning of the word **indigenous**? _____

5. Where would you find information on conservation? _____

   _____

6. What is a synonym for **catastrophe**? _____

7. Where would you find a review of the play *Cats*? _____

   _____

8. Where would you find statistics on the annual rainfall in the Sahara Desert?

   _____

9. What is the origin of the word **plentiful**? _____

10. What are antonyms for the word **plentiful**? _____

11. Where would you find statistics for the number of automobiles manufactured in the United States last year? _____

Name: _____

Making Inferences: Reference Books

Directions: In the box are four different kinds of reference books. On the line next to each question, write which book you would use to find the information. Some information can be found in more than one reference.

encyclopedia	almanac	dictionary	thesaurus

1. A list of words that mean the same as "strong"   _____

2. How much rain fell in Iowa in the year 1992   _____

3. What part of speech the word "porch" is   _____

4. How many different types of hummingbirds there are   _____

5. Weather patterns in Texas for the last 2 years   _____

6. A list of words that mean the opposite of "cold"   _____

7. Who invented the telescope   _____

8. How to pronounce the word "barometer"

_____

9. How many syllables the word "elephant" has

_____

10. What the difference is between African and Asian elephants

_____

11. The population changes in New York between 1935 and 1995

_____

12. How fast a cheetah can run

_____

Grade 6 - Comprehensive Curriculum

Name: _____

Making Inferences: Encyclopedias

Directions: Read each question. Then check the answer for where you would find the information in an encyclopedia.

1. If you wanted to grow avocado pits on a windowsill, under which topic should you look?

   ☐ window   ☐ avocado   ☐ food

2. To find information about the Cuban revolution of 1959, which topic should you look up?

   ☐ Cuba   ☐ revolution   ☐ 1959

3. Information about Rudolph Diesel, the inventor of the Diesel engine, would be found under which topic?

   ☐ engine   ☐ Diesel   ☐ inventor

4. If you wanted to find out if the giant panda of China was really a bear or a raccoon, what should you look up?

   ☐ bear   ☐ China   ☐ panda

5. Under which topic should you look for information on how to plant a vegetable garden?

   ☐ plant   ☐ vegetable   ☐ gardening

6. If you wanted to write a report on both wild and pet gerbils, under which topic should you look for information?

   ☐ animal   ☐ gerbil   ☐ pet

7. To find out if World War I was fought only on European soil, which topic should you look up?

   ☐ Europe   ☐ World War I   ☐ war

8. Under which topic should you look for information on how bats guide themselves in the dark?

   ☐ guide   ☐ flying   ☐ bat

9. The distance of all the planets from the sun might be found under which topic?

   ☐ planets   ☐ sky   ☐ distance

Name: _____

Review

Directions: Check the best answer for where to find information in an encyclopedia.

1. If you wanted to find out who invented the television, under which topic would you look?

☐ television   ☐ television history   ☐ inventions

2. If you wanted to find out about the Battle of Gettysburg, under which topic would you look?

☐ Civil War   ☐ famous battles   ☐ Gettysburg

3. If you were curious about where most dinosaur fossils have been found, under which topic would you look?

☐ dinosaurs   ☐ finds   ☐ fossils

4. If you wanted to learn about Greek mythology, under which topic would you look?

☐ Greece   ☐ folktales   ☐ mythology

5. If you wanted to learn about different kinds of wild cats, under which topic would you look?

☐ cats   ☐ wild animals   ☐ big cats

Directions: Check the resource book you would use to find the following information.

1. How to play checkers   ☐ almanac   ☐ dictionary   ☐ encyclopedia

2. An example sentence using the word "breathe"

☐ encyclopedia ☐ thesaurus   ☐ dictionary

3. How many inches of snow fell in the Colorado Rockies last year

☐ encyclopedia ☐ almanac   ☐ thesaurus

4. How many syllables are in the word "justification"

☐ almanac   ☐ thesaurus   ☐ dictionary

5. Who won the Civil War

☐ encyclopedia ☐ dictionary   ☐ thesaurus

Name: _____

Table of Contents

The **table of contents**, located in the front of books or magazines, tells a lot about what is inside.

A table of contents in books lists the headings and page numbers for each chapter. **Chapters** are the parts into which books are divided. Also listed are chapter numbers and the sections and subsections, if any. Look at the sample table of contents below:

Directions: Using the table of contents above, answer the following questions.

1. How many chapters are in this book?   _____

2. What chapter contains information about things to plant?   _____

3. On what page does information about fences begin?   _____

4. What chapter tells you what you can use to help your garden grow better?   _____

5. What page tells you how to use fertilizer?   _____

6. What page tells you how far apart to plant pumpkin seeds?   _____

7. What is on page 11? _____

8. What is on page 4? _____

Table of Contents

The table of contents below is divided into units and sections. **Units** are parts into which a book is divided. **Sections** are segments of each unit.

Table of Contents

Directions: Using the table of contents above, answer the following questions.

1. How many units are in this book? _____

2. Where would you find information about life on Mars? _____

3. Where would you find information about the Sun's heat and brightness? _____

4. What is on page 27? _____

5. The Milky Way is a large group of stars, or a galaxy. Where would you find information about it? _____

6. What is on page 101? _____

7. Where would you find information about the moons of Jupiter? _____

8. How many pages in this book are about Earth? _____

9. How many pages in this book are about Polaris? _____

10. Where would you read about the Big Dipper? _____

Name: _____

Table of Contents

In some magazines, the table of contents lists articles in numerical order. Other magazines' tables of contents are organized by subjects, by columns and by features. **Subjects** are the topics covered in the articles. A **feature** is a specific kind of article, such as an article about sports or cooking. "Feature" also has another meaning. A regular feature is something that appears in every issue, such as letters to the editor, movie reviews and sports statistics. Some magazines also call regular features "departments."

Columns are another kind of regular feature published in every issue. Columns are often written by the same person each time. A person who writes a column is called a **columnist**.

Most magazines' tables of contents will also give you an idea of what a story is about. Look at the sample below.

Articles

Kids' Life

10	Skateboarding in the U.S.A.		
	Read about kids from across the country and how they make the best of their boards.		
12	Summer Camp		
	Believe it or not, camp is fun!		
20	Battle of Gettysburg		
	It was a decisive one in the American Civil War.		
25	Snacks in a Flash		
	Look at these treats you can make yourself.		
29	Martin Luther King, Jr.		
	The man who made people think twice.		

Comics

6	Little People
14	Skating Sam
30	Double Trouble

Columns

7	Videos
32	The Great Outdoors
39	Fun and Famous

Departments

34	Your Health
36	Sports
38	Letters to the Editor

Directions: Answer these questions about *Kids' Life* magazine.

1. On what page does the story about summer camp begin? _____

2. List the titles of the departments in this magazine:

   a) _____   b) _____   c) _____

3. Can you tell what the Battle of Gettysburg is by reading the table of contents?

   _____

4. Is there any information in this magazine about in-line skating? _____

Table of Contents

The articles in this magazine are grouped according to subjects.

LIVING
Table of Contents

Exercise	Ride for a while with these experienced cyclists.	13
Discoveries	Walk with a man through the ditches where he discovered dinosaur bones.	27
Happenings	Earth Day becomes important once again.	5
Science	Find out why astronauts like their jobs.	45
Music	Tunes that are sung in the mountains.	33
People	Read about Al Gore and how he got to be Vice President.	20
	Learn about Jim Henson, the man behind the Muppets.	28
Sports	Why the Cleveland Indians might win the title.	42
History	A look at the lives of soldiers who were at Valley Forge.	39

Departments

Living Well	6	Letters to the Editor	9
Comedy	12	Books	16
Movies	24	Snacks	36

Directions: Answer these questions about *LIVING* magazine.

1. How many departments are in this issue of the magazine? _____

2. Circle the topics that are regular features in *LIVING*.

Books	Dinosaurs	Cleveland Indians	Vice Presidents
Comedy	Living Well	Snacks	Earth Day

3. What page would you look at if you wanted to see what was playing at the

   movie theaters? _____

4. Is there any information in this magazine about football? _____

5. Who are the two people featured in this issue? _____

6. Is there anything in this issue about cycling? _____

7. Under what heading is it listed? _____

Name: _____

Indexes

An **index** is an alphabetical listing of names, topics and important words and is found in the back of a book. An index lists every page on which these items appear. For example, in a book about music, dulcimer might be listed this way: Dulcimer 2, 13, 26, 38. Page numbers may also be listed like this: Guitars 18–21. That means that information about guitars begins on page 18 and continues through page 21. **Subject** is the name of the item in an index. **Sub-entry** is a smaller division of the subject. For example, "apples" would be listed under fruit.

Index

N
Neptune 27
NGC 5128 (galaxy) 39
Novas 32

O
Observatories. *See* El Caracol
Orbits of planets 10
Orion rocket 43

P
Planetoids. *See* Asteroids.
Planet rings
   Jupiter 23
   Saturn 9, 25
   Uranus 26
Planets
   discovered by Greeks 7
   outside the solar system 40
   visible with the naked eye 9

See also planet names.
Pleiades 32
Pluto 12, 27
Polaris 35, 36
Pole star. *See* Polaris.
Project Ozma 41

R
Rings. *See* Planet rings.

S
Sagittarius 37
Satellites
   Jupiter 24
   Neptune 27
   Pluto 27
   Saturn 25
   Uranus 26
   See also Galilean satellites
Saturn 25

Directions: Answer the questions about the index from this book about the solar system.

1. On what pages is there information about Pluto? _____

2. On what pages is information about Saturn's first ring found? _____

3. What is on page 41? _____

4. Where is there information about the pole star? _____

5. What is on page 43? _____

6. On what page would you find information about planets that are visible to the eye? _____

7. On what page would you find information about Jupiter's satellites? _____

Name: _____

Indexes

Some magazines use indexes to guide their readers to information they contain.

Appetizers
Bacon-Wrapped Halibut 92
Scallops With Sorrel and Tomato 116
Shrimp and Basil Beignets 116
Shrimp and Vegetable Spring Rolls With Hoisin and Mustard Sauces 85
Sweet Potato Ribbon Chips 136

Soups
Lemongrass Soup, Hot, With Radishes and Chives 84
Roasted Garlic Soup 22
Vegetable Soup With Creamy Asparagus Flan 154

Salads, Salad Dressings
Arugula Salad With Roasted Beets, Walnuts and Daikon 158
Chicken, Fennel, Orange and Olive Salad 24
Jicama Salad 81
Tomato, Onion and Zucchini Salad 152
Walnut Vinaigrette 158

Directions: Answer the questions about the index from *Bon Appetit* magazine.

1. How many kinds of salad are
   listed in this issue?   _____

2. What is the recipe that contains radishes? _____

3. Name the recipe found on page 24.   _____

4. On what page would you find an
   appetizer that includes scallops?   _____

   What is the name of this recipe?   _____

5. Can you find any listings that
   contain halibut?   _____

6. On what page is a recipe made
   from sweet potatoes?   _____

   What is the name of this recipe?   _____

   For what part of a meal would
   it be served?   _____

Review

FARMING
Table of Contents

Directions: Answer the questions about the table of contents from *Farming* magazine.

1. Is there any information about fashion in this magazine?   _____

2. Is there any information about computers in this magazine? _____

3. Information about children on farms is probably included
   in which feature?   _____

4. Are there any features about animals in this magazine?   _____

Directions: Answer the questions about the index from this book about the world.

1. On what pages would you find information about
   the Baltic Sea?   _____

2. What is listed on pages 2–3? _____

3. Where are the two Colorado Rivers? _____

Review

Directions: Follow the instructions for each section.

1. In your own words, explain why a table of contents is helpful.

   _____

   _____

2. A table of contents is often divided into units and sections.

   What is a unit? _____

   What is a section? _____

3. What is the purpose of breaking a table of contents down into units and sections?

   _____

   _____

4. What is an index?

   _____

   _____

5. What are the differences between a table of contents and an index?

   _____

   _____

   _____

6. Look at the table of contents in the front of this book. How many pages does the unit on Famous Athletes span?

   _____

Name: _____

Biographical Research

A **biography** is a written history of a person's life. Often, information for a biography can be obtained from an encyclopedia, especially if a person is famous. Of course, not everyone is listed in a main article in an encyclopedia. Use the encyclopedia's index, which is the last book in the set, to find which volume contains the information you need. Look at this listing taken from an encyclopedia index for Henry Moore, an English artist:

Moore, Henry English sculptor,
1898–1986

    main article Moore 12:106b, illus.
    references in Sculpture 15:290a, illus.

Notice that the listing includes Henry Moore's dates of birth and death and illustrations (illus.). It also includes a short description of his accomplishments: He was an English sculptor. Look below at part of the index from the *Children's Britannica* encyclopedias.

Lincoln, Abraham president of US,
1809–1865
    main article Lincoln 11:49a, illus.
    references in
        Assassination 2:64b
        Caricature, illus. 4:87
        Civil War, American 4:296a fol.
        Confederate States of America 5:113b fol.
        Democracy 6:17a
        Gettysburg, Battle of 8:144a
        Illinois 9:259b
        Thanksgiving Day 17:199a
        United States of America, history of 18:137a fol.
        Westward Movement 19:49a
Lincoln, Benjamin army officer,
1733–1810
    references in American Revolution 1:204b

Lind, Jenny Swedish singer, 1820–87
operatic soprano admired for vocal purity and control; made debut 1838 in Stockholm and sang in Paris and London, becoming known as the "Swedish Nightingale"; toured US with P.T. Barnum 1850; last concert 1883.
    references in Barnum 2:235a
Lindbergh, Anne US author and aviator, b. 1906
    references in Lindbergh 11:53a, illus.
Lindbergh, Charles Augustus US aviator,
1902–1974
    main article Lindbergh 11:53a, illus.
    references in
        Aviation, history of 2:140b, illus.
        Medals and decorations, 11:266b
        Saint Louis, 15:215b
Linde, Karl Von German engineer,
1842–1934
    references in Refrigeration 15:32b

Directions: Answer these questions from the index above.

1. Where is the main article for Abraham Lincoln? _____

2. In addition to the main article, how many other

   places are there references to Abraham Lincoln? _____

3. In which encyclopedia volume is there information about Anne Lindbergh?

_____

Biographical Indexes

If a person has been in the news recently, check the *National Newspaper Index* or an index for the local newspaper to find articles on that person. The *National Newspaper Index* contains the names of articles published by five major newspapers within the last three years. *NewsBank*, a news digest containing information from nearly 200 newspapers throughout the country, should also be checked.

Also check the *Obituary Index* to *The New York Times* or the *Obituary Index* to the (London, England) *Times*. Obituaries are notices of deaths. They usually include a brief biography of the person.

Reader's Guide to Periodical Literature alphabetically lists subjects of articles printed in most major magazines. A *Reader's Guide* entry lists the magazine in which an article appeared, the date of the publication and the page number where the article starts.

Biography Index lists biographical articles published since 1946.

Almanacs also contain information about individuals. For example, *The Kid's World Almanac of Records and Facts* lists the United States presidents and their major accomplishments. It also has information about athletes, composers and others.

Directions: Use the encyclopedias and one or more of the resources listed above to research one of the following people. Begin writing your biographical report in the space provided. (If you need more room, use a separate sheet of paper.)

Research Topics:	
Richard M. Nixon	Jesse Jackson
Mother Theresa	Lech Walesa
Margaret Thatcher	Mikhail Gorbachev

_____

_____

_____

_____

_____

_____

_____

_____

_____

Name: _____

Biographical Dictionaries

Biographical dictionaries, such as *Who's Who*, contain histories of people's lives. In addition to *Who's Who*, there are many other biographical dictionaries. BDs, as they are called, can include books such as the *Biographical Dictionary of English Architects* or *Who's Who in Art Materials*. Some biographical dictionaries list only people who lived during certain eras, such as *Women Artists: 1550–1950*.

Because there are so many biographical dictionaries, master indexes are published to guide researchers. Up to 500 books are listed in some biographical master indexes. A master index may list several biographical dictionaries in which information about a person can be obtained. Here are a few:

1. *The Biography and Genealogy Master Index* contains 11 books and is a good place to begin research. Parts of this index, such as *Children's Authors and Illustrators*, are in separate volumes.

2. *An Analytical Bibliography of Universal Collected Biography* contains information from more than 3,000 biographical dictionaries published before 1933.

3. *In Black and White: A Guide to Magazine Articles, Newspaper Articles and Books Concerning More than 15,000 Black Individuals and Groups* is the title of a large biographical master index.

4. *Marquis Who's Who Publications: Index to All Books* lists names from at least 15 *Who's Who* books published by Marquis each year.

Directions: Complete each sentence about biographical dictionaries.

1. Biographical dictionaries contain

   _____

2. When beginning research in biographical dictionaries, first use a

   _____

3. The _____ has 11 books in its set.

4. *Children's Authors and Illustrators* is a separate volume of the

   _____

5. Information from at least 15 *Who's Who* publications each year is contained in the

   _____

Name: _____

Doing Biographical Research

Directions: Use biographical dictionaries to research a person listed below. Remember to begin with one or more biographical master indexes. There may be more than one biographical dictionary that contains information about the person. Write a report about that person's life in the space provided. Use additional paper, if necessary.

Monica Seles   Steven Spielberg   Elizabeth Dole
John Glenn   Andrew Lloyd Weber   Jodie Foster

_____

_____

_____

_____

_____

_____

_____

_____

_____

_____

_____

_____

_____

_____

_____

_____

Other Biographical Resources

Information about people who belong to clubs, trade unions or other organizations can sometimes be found in libraries or from an organization's main office. If these people work or have worked for corporations, information can be obtained by contacting the public relations office of that company.

Unpublished materials, such as diaries or letters, are usually donated to a library or a historical society when a person dies. Clues that such materials exist may be found when reading other books or articles about a person.

Personal interviews can also provide information about subjects. Following are a few points to remember when conducting an interview:

1. Cover the five main points that you need to know for any story: who, what, when, where and why.
2. Write accurate notes while doing the interview.
3. Use the notes to write the article.
4. If your notes are unclear, check them with the person interviewed.
5. Double-check other facts that you are not sure about. Be sure to check the spelling of the person's name, and check important dates that were mentioned during the interview.
6. Only write things that you are sure the person said.

Directions: Use the tips listed above to conduct an interview with a friend or classmate. Write a brief biography using what you learned during the interview.

_____

_____

_____

_____

_____

_____

_____

_____

_____

Name: _____

CD-ROM's

There are many CD-ROM's which can now assist with biographical research. Often, CD-ROM's not only have written information about an individual's life, but the entry might also include video clips or still-frame pictures. Look for CD-ROM's which are encyclopedias, historical references or famous person indexes.

It is important to correctly type in the person's name when using a CD-ROM. It is also possible to locate a person by typing in an event in which he/she was involved.

Example: Martin Luther King — Civil Rights

Directions: For the following people, write an event in which he/she was involved or another category where you might look for additional information.

1. John F. Kennedy _____

2. Rosa Parks _____

3. John Glenn _____

4. Al Gore _____

5. George Burns _____

6. Benjamin Franklin _____

7. Beverly Cleary _____

8. Michael Jordan _____

9. Margaret Thatcher _____

10. Sally Ride _____

11. Thomas Edison _____

12. Marie Curie _____

13. Jonas Salk _____

14. Tiger Woods _____

15. Tara Lipinski _____

16. Alexander Graham Bell _____

Review

Directions: Write **T** or **F** on the line beside each statement.

_____ 1. Do not use a biographical master index before checking *Who's Who in American Education.*

_____ 2. A biographical dictionary lists people and their histories.

_____ 3. A biographical master index includes listings from only one biographical dictionary.

Directions: Choose the correct word from the box to complete each sentence.

| articles | index | contents | atlases | resource | almanacs |

1. Before finding a listing in an encyclopedia, you should use the

   encyclopedia _____ .

2. The *Reader's Guide to Periodical Literature* lists _____ published in most major magazines.

3. *Biography Index* is a _____ that lists articles published about people since 1946.

4. _____ list odd bits of information about people.

Directions: Write **book** or **article** on the line to tell whether the index named would list books or articles.

1. *Biography Index*   _____

2. *Reader's Guide to Periodical Literature*   _____

3. *Books in Print*   _____

Directions: Fill in the blanks to complete the sentences.

1. A person's original writings would include his or her diary or _____ .

2. If a person works or has worked for a corporation, you could gain information about him

   or her by contacting that firm's _____ office.

Name: _____

Poetry

Format:
Line 1: Name
Line 2: Name is a (metaphor)
Line 3: He/she is like (simile)
Line 4: He/she (three action words)
Line 5: He/she (relationship)
Line 6: Name

Example:
Jessica
Jessica is a joy.
She is like a playful puppy.
She tumbles, runs and laughs.
She's my baby sister!
Jessica

Directions: Build a poem that describes a friend or relative by using similes, metaphors and other words of your choice. Follow the form of the example poem.

Grade 6 - Comprehensive Curriculum

Poetry: Haiku

Haiku is a type of unrhymed Japanese poetry with three lines. The first line has five syllables. The second line has seven syllables. The third line has five syllables.

Example:

Katie

Katie is my dog.
She likes to bark and chase balls.
Katie is my friend.

Directions: Write a haiku about a pet and another about a hobby you enjoy. Be sure to write a title on the first line.

Pet   _____

_____

_____

_____

_____

Hobby   _____

_____

_____

_____

Name: _____

Poetry: Diamanté

A **diamanté** is a poem in the shape of a diamond. Diamantés have seven lines with this format:

Line 1: one-word noun, opposite of word in line 7
Line 2: two adjectives describing line 1
Line 3: three **ing** or **ed** words about line 1
Line 4: two nouns about line 1 and two nouns about line 7
Line 5: three **ing** or **ed** words about line 7
Line 6: two adjectives describing line 7
Line 7: one word noun, opposite of word in line 1

Example:

child
happy, playful
running, singing, laughing
toys, games, job, family
working, driving, nurturing
responsible, busy
adult

Directions: Write a diamanté of your own.

_____

_____

_____

_____

_____

_____

_____

Grade 6 - Comprehensive Curriculum

Writing: Free Verse

Poems that do not rhyme and do not have a regular rhythm are called **free verse**. They often use adjectives, adverbs, similes and metaphors to create word pictures.

My Old Cat
Curled on my bed at night,
Quietly happy to see me,
Soft, sleepy, relaxed,
A calm island in my life.

Directions: Write your own free verse. Use the guidelines for each poem.

1. Write a two-line free verse poem about a feeling. Compare it to some kind of food. For example, anger could be a tangle of spaghetti. Give your poem a title.

_____

_____

_____

2. Think of how someone you know is like a color, happy like yellow, for example. Write a two-line free verse poem on this topic without naming the person. Don't forget a title.

_____

_____

_____

3. Write a four-line free verse poem, like "My Old Cat," that creates a word picture of a day at school

_____

_____

_____

_____

_____

Writing: Limericks

A **limerick** is a short, humorous poem. Limericks are five lines long and follow a specific rhyme pattern. Lines 1, 2 and 5 rhyme, and lines 3 and 4 rhyme.

Example:

There once was a young fellow named Fred
Whose big muscles went right to his head.
"I'll make the girls sigh,
'Cause I'm quite a guy!"
But the girls all liked Ted more than Fred!

Directions: Complete the limericks.

1. There was a young lady from Kent

   Whose drawings were quite excellent.

   _____

   _____

   So to the big city she went.

2. I have a pet squirrel named Sonny

   _____

   He ran up a tree

   As far as could be

   _____

3. There once was a boy who yelled, "Fire!"

   _____

   He just did not see

   _____

   _____

Writing: Acrostics

An **acrostic** is a poem that uses the letters of a word to begin each line. Read down, the first letter of each line spells the word. The poem tells something about the word that is spelled out.

Example:

> **I**n the grass or underground,
> **N**ow and then they fly around.
> **S**lugs and worms and butterflies,
> **E**ach has its own shape and size.
> **C**aterpillars, gnats, a bee,
> **T**ake them all away from me!

Directions: Write acrostic poems for the words shoes and phone. Your poems can rhyme or be free verse.

S _____

H _____

O _____

E _____

S _____

P _____

H _____

O _____

N _____

E _____

Directions: Write an acrostic poem for your name or a word of your choice on another sheet of paper. Draw a picture for your poem.

Friendly Letters

Directions: Study the format for writing a letter to a friend. Then answer the questions.

your return address	123 Waverly Road Cincinnati, Ohio 45241
date	June 23, 1999
greeting	Dear Josh,
body	How is your summer going? I am enjoying mine so far. I have been swimming twice already this week, and it's only Wednesday! I am glad there is a pool near our house. My parents said that you can stay overnight when your family comes for the 4th of July picnic. Do you want to? We can pitch a tent in the back yard and camp out. It will be a lot of fun! Please write back to let me know if you can stay over on the 4th. I will see you then!
closing **signature**	Your friend, Michael

your return address	Michael Delaney 123 Waverly Road Cincinnati, Ohio 45241
main address	Josh Sommers 2250 West First Ave. Columbus, OH 43212

1. What words are in the greeting? _____

2. What words are in the closing?_____

3. On what street does the writer live? _____

Name: _____

Friendly Letters

Directions: Follow the format for writing a letter to a friend. Don't forget to address the envelope!

MATH

Name: _____

Place Value

Place value is the position of a digit in a number. A digit's place in a number shows its value. Numbers left of the decimal point represent **whole numbers**. Numbers right of the decimal point represent a part, or fraction, of a whole number. These parts are broken down into tenths, hundredths, thousandths, and so on.

Example:

3,443,221.621

millions	hundred thousands	ten thousands	thousands	hundreds	tens	ones	tenths	hundredths	thousandths
3	4	4	3	2	2	1	6	2	1

← ———————— Whole Numbers ———————— → ← —— Fractions —— →

Directions: Write the following number words as numbers.

1. Three million, forty-four thousand, six hundred twenty-one _____

2. One million, seventy-seven _____

3. Nine million, six hundred thousand, one hundred two _____

4. Twenty-nine million, one hundred three thousand and nine tenths

_____

5. One million, one hundred thousand, one hundred seventy-one and

   thirteen hundredths _____

Directions: In each box, write the corresponding number for each place value.

1. 4,822,000.00 ☐ hundreds

2. 55,907,003.00 ☐ thousands

3. 190,641,225.07 ☐ hundred thousands

4. 247,308,211.59 ☐ tenths

5. 7,594,097.33 ☐ millions

6. 201,480,110.01 ☐ hundred thousands

7. 42,367,109,074.25 ☐ hundredths

10.25

Name: _____

Place Value

The chart below shows the place value of each number.

trillions			billions			millions			thousands			ones		
h	t	o	h	t	o	h	t	o	h	t	o	h	t	o
		2	1	4	0	9	0	0	6	8	0	3	5	0

Word form: two trillion, one hundred forty billion, nine hundred million, six hundred eighty thousand, three hundred fifty

Directions: Draw a line to the correct value of each underlined digit. The first one is done for you.

6<u>4</u>3,000	2 hundred million
<u>1</u>3,294,125	9 billion
<u>6</u>78,446	40 thousand
389,<u>2</u>76	2 thousand
1<u>9</u>,000,089,965	2 billion
78,<u>7</u>64	1 hundred thousand
61<u>2</u>,689	9 thousand
<u>2</u>98,154,370	70 thousand
8<u>9</u>,256	10 million
1,<u>3</u>70	30 million
853,6<u>7</u>2,175	7 hundred
<u>2</u>,842,751,360	3 hundred
<u>1</u>63,456	2 hundred
4<u>3</u>8,276,587	6 hundred thousand

Expanded Notation

Expanded notation is writing out the value of each digit in a number.

> **Example:**
> 8,920,077 = 8,000,000 + 900,000 + 20,000 + 70 + 7
> **Word form:** Eight million, nine hundred twenty thousand, seventy-seven

Directions: Write the following numbers using expanded notation.

1. 20,769,033 _____

_____

2. 1,183,541,029 _____

_____

3. 776,003,091 _____

_____

4. 5,920,100,808 _____

_____

5. 14,141,543,760 _____

_____

Directions: Write the following numbers.

1. 700,000 + 900 + 60 + 7 _____

2. 35,000,000 + 600,000 + 400 + 40 + 2 _____

3. 12,000,000 + 700,000 + 60,000 + 4,000 + 10 + 4 _____

4. 80,000,000,000 + 8,000,000,000 + 400,000,000 + 80,000,000 + 10,000 + 400 + 30

_____

5. 4,000,000,000 + 16,000,000 + 30 + 2 _____

Addition and Place Value

Directions: Add the problems below in which the digits with the same place value are lined up correctly. Then cross out the problems in which the digits are not lined up correctly.

Find each answer in the diagram and color that section.

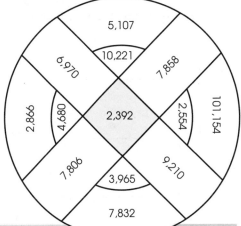

yellow	blue	green	red
638 1,289 + 465 2,392	~~98 324 + 9,756~~	4,326 82 + 699	589 95 + 8,526
579 125 + 244	296 2,183 + 75	93,287 36 + 7,831	51 315 + 7,492
83 1,298 + 62	938 3,297 + 445	1,849 964 + 53	198 72 + 68
987 934 + 3,163	46 390 + 9,785	856 642 + 7,462	591 6,352 + 27
57 7,520 + 463	773 3,118 + 74	64 7,430 + 338	919 52 + 6,835

Addition

Directions: Add the following numbers in your head without writing them out.

1. 17 + 33 = _____

2. 35 + 15 = _____

3. 75 + 25 = _____

4. 41 + 25 = _____

5. 27 + 23 = _____

6. 30 + 20 = _____

7. 12 + 18 = _____

8. 43 + 22 = _____

9. 16 + 34 = _____

10. 9 + 11 + 30 = _____

11. 29 + 21 + 40 = _____

12. 14 + 16 + 20 = _____

13. 37 + 13 + 25 = _____

14. 12 + 22 + 36 = _____

15. 19 + 21 + 57 = _____

16. 21 + 24 + 25 = _____

17. 63 + 14 + 11 = _____

18. 33 + 15 + 42 = _____

19. 25 + 15 + 60 = _____

20. 30 + 20 + 10 = _____

Name: _____

Addition Word Problems

Directions: Solve the following addition word problems.

1. 100 students participated in a sports card show in the school gym. Brad brought his entire collection of 2,000 cards to show his friends. He had 700 football cards and 400 basketball cards. If the rest of his cards were baseball cards, how many baseball cards did he bring with him?

   _____

2. Refreshments were set up in one area of the gym. Hot dogs were a dollar, soda was 50 cents, chips were 35 cents and cookies were a quarter. If you purchased two of each item, how much money would you need?

   _____

3. It took each student 30 minutes to set up for the card show and twice as long to put everything away. The show was open for 3 hours. How much time did each student spend on this event?

   _____

4. 450 people attended the card show. 55 were mothers of students, 67 were fathers, 23 were grandparents, 8 were aunts and uncles and the rest were kids. How many kids attended?

   _____

5. Of the 100 students who set up displays, most of them sold or traded some of their cards. Bruce sold 75 cards, traded 15 cards and collected $225. Kevin only sold 15 cards, traded 81 cards and collected $100. Missi traded 200 cards, sold 10 and earned $35. Of those listed, how many cards were sold, how many were traded and how much money was earned?

   sold _____   traded _____   earned $ _____

Grade 6 - Comprehensive Curriculum

Name: _____

Subtraction

Directions: Subtract the following numbers. When subtracting, begin on the right, especially if you need to regroup and borrow.

549 − 162	823 − 417	370 − 244	648 − 79
700 − 343	475 − 299	603 − 425	354 − 265
1,841 − 952	2,597 − 608	6,832 − 1,774	9,005 − 3,458
23,342 − 9,093	53,790 − 40,813	29,644 − 19,780	35,726 − 16,959
109,432 − 79,145	350,907 − 14,185	217,523 − 44,197	537,411 − 406,514

Name: _____

Subtraction Word Problems

Directions: Solve the following subtraction word problems.

1. Last year, 28,945 people lived in Mike's town. This year there are 31,889. How many people have moved in?

   _____

2. Brad earned $227 mowing lawns. He spent $168 on tapes by his favorite rock group. How much money does he have left?

   _____

3. The school year has 180 days. Carrie has gone to 32 school days so far. How many more days does she have left?

   _____

4. Craig wants a skateboard that costs $128. He has saved $47. How much more does he need?

   _____

5. To get to school, Jennifer walks 1,275 steps and Carolyn walks 2,618 steps. How many more steps does Carolyn walk than Jennifer?

   _____

6. Amy has placed 91 of the 389 pieces in a new puzzle she purchased. How many more does she have left to finish?

   _____

7. From New York, it's 2,823 miles to Los Angeles and 1,327 miles to Miami. How much farther away is Los Angeles?

   _____

8. Sheila read that a piece of carrot cake has 236 calories, but a piece of apple pie has 427 calories. How many calories will she save by eating the cake instead of the pie?

   _____

9. Tim's summer camp costs $223, while Sam's costs $149. How much more does Tim's camp cost?

   _____

10. Last year, the nation's budget was $45,000,000,000, but the nation spent $52,569,342,000. How much more than its budget did the nation spend?

    _____

Name: _____

Multiplication

Directions: Multiply the following numbers. Be sure to keep the numbers aligned, and place a 0 in the ones place when multiplying by the tens digit.

Example:	Correct	Incorrect
	55	55
	x 15	x 15
	275	275
	550	55
	825	330

55   15

1. 12
    x 6

2. 44
    x 9

3. 27
    x 7

4. 92
    x 6

5. 85
    x 9

6. 78
    x 24

7. 32
    x 17

8. 19
    x 46

9. 63
    x 12

10. 38
     x 77

11. 125
     x   6

12. 641
     x 25

13. 713
     x 47

14. 586
     x 45

15. 294
     x 79

16. 20 x 4 x 7 = _____

17. 9 x 5 x 11 = _____

18. 16 x 2 x 2 = _____

19. 7 x 6 x 3 = _____

20. 33 x 11 x 3 = _____

21. 2 x 8 x 10 = _____

Multiplying With Zeros

Directions: Multiply the following numbers. If a number ends with zero, you can eliminate it while calculating the rest of the answer. Then count how many zeros you took off and add them to your answer.

Example:	55~~0~~	Take off 2 zeros	5~~00~~	Take off 2 zeros
	x 5~~0~~		x 5	
	27,5<u>00</u>	Add on 2 zeros	2,5<u>00</u>	Add on 2 zeros

1.	300	2.	400	3.	620	4.	290
	x 6		x 7		x 5		x 7

5.	142	6.	505	7.	340	8.	600
	x 20		x 50		x 70		x 60

9.	550	10.	290	11.	2,040	12.	8,800
	x 380		x 150		x 360		x 200

13. Bruce traveled 600 miles each day of a 10-day trip. How far did he go during the entire trip?   _____

14. 30 children each sold 20 items for the school fund-raiser. Each child earned $100 for the school. How much money did the school collect?   _____

15. 10 x 40 x 2 = _____

16. 30 x 30 x 10 = _____

17. 100 x 60 x 10 = _____

18. 500 x 11 x 2 = _____

19. 9 x 10 x 10 = _____

20. 7,000 x 20 x 10 = _____

Name: _____

Division

In a division problem, the **dividend** is the number to be divided, the **divisor** is the number used to divide and the **quotient** is the answer. To check your work, multiply your answer times the divisor and you should get the dividend.

Example:

$$
\begin{array}{r}
130 \leftarrow \text{quotient} \\
\text{divisor} \rightarrow 4\overline{)520} \leftarrow \text{dividend} \\
\underline{4} \\
12 \\
\underline{12} \\
00
\end{array}
$$

Check:

$$
\begin{array}{r}
130 \leftarrow \text{quotient} \\
\times 4 \leftarrow \text{divisor} \\
\hline
520 \leftarrow \text{dividend}
\end{array}
$$

Directions: Solve the following division problems.

1. $3\overline{)546}$ 2. $5\overline{)720}$ 3. $2\overline{)458}$ 4. $4\overline{)796}$ 5. $7\overline{)896}$

6. $4\overline{)128}$ 7. $4\overline{)376}$ 8. $5\overline{)225}$ 9. $3\overline{)684}$ 10. $6\overline{)924}$

11. $25\overline{)475}$ 12. $16\overline{)768}$ 13. $14\overline{)840}$ 14. $22\overline{)418}$ 15. $21\overline{)693}$

Directions: Solve these division problems in your head. Challenge yourself for speed and accuracy.

1. $22 \div 2 =$ _____   2. $15 \div 3 =$ _____   3. $72 \div 9 =$ _____

4. $36 \div 4 =$ _____   5. $27 \div 9 =$ _____   6. $56 \div 8 =$ _____

7. $81 \div 9 =$ _____   8. $42 \div 6 =$ _____   9. $63 \div 9 =$ _____

10. $60 \div 5 =$ _____   11. $70 \div 10 =$ _____   12. $98 \div 7 =$ _____

13. $55 \div 5 =$ _____   14. $64 \div 8 =$ _____   15. $84 \div 3 =$ _____

Division Word Problems

In the example below, 368 is being divided by 4. 4 won't divide into 3, so move over one position and divide 4 into 36. 4 goes into 36 nine times. Then multiply 4 x 9 to get 36. Subtract 36 from 36. The answer is 0, less than the divisor, so 9 is the right number. Now bring down the 8, divide 4 into it and repeat the process.

Example:

$$\begin{array}{r} 9 \\ 4\overline{\smash{)}368} \\ \underline{36} \\ 0 \end{array} \qquad \begin{array}{r} 92 \\ 4\overline{\smash{)}368} \\ \underline{36} \\ 08 \\ \underline{8} \\ 0 \end{array}$$

To check your division, multiply 4 x 92 = 368.

Directions: Solve the following division problems. (For some problems, you will also need to add or subtract.)

1. Kristy helped the kindergarten teacher put a total of 192 crayons into 8 boxes. How many crayons did they put into each box?

   _____

2. The scout troop has to finish a 12-mile hike in 3 hours. How many miles an hour will they have to walk?

   _____

3. At her slumber party, Shelly had 4 friends and 25 pieces of candy. If she kept 5 pieces and divided the rest among her friends, how many pieces did each friend get?

   _____

4. Kenny's book has 147 pages. He wants to read the same number of pages each day and finish reading the book in 7 days. How many pages should he read each day?

   _____

5. Brian and 2 friends are going to share 27 marbles. How many will each person get?

   _____

6. To help the school, 5 parents agreed to sell 485 tickets for a raffle. How many tickets will each person have to sell to do his/her part?

   _____

7. Tim is going to weed his neighbor's garden for $3 an hour. How many hours does he have to work to make $72?

   _____

Name: _____

Equations

In an **equation**, the value on the left of the equal sign must equal the value on the right. Remember the order of operations: solve from left to right, multiply or divide numbers before adding or subtracting and do the operation inside parentheses first.

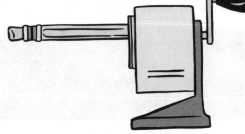

Example:
$$6 + 4 - 2 = 4 \times 2$$
$$10 - 2 \ = \ 8$$
$$8 \ = \ 8$$

Directions: Write the correct operation signs in the blanks to make accurate equations.

1. (25 _____ 25) _____ 2 = 100 _____ 75

2. (76 _____ 24) _____ 3 = 150 _____ 2

3. 140 _____ 2 _____ 10 = 500 _____ 50 _____ 150

4. 2,100 _____ 2,000 _____ 60 = 80 _____ 2

5. 80 _____ 8 _____ 4 = 160 _____ 160 _____ 160

6. (55 _____ 100) _____ 11 = (1,000 _____ 2) _____ 4

7. 137 _____ 81 _____ 52 = 3 _____ 90

8. 3,000 _____ 10 _____ 10 = (600 _____ 300) _____ 30

9. (720 _____ 20) _____ 4 = 37 _____ 5

10. (457 _____ 43) _____ 500 = (21 _____ 40) x 0

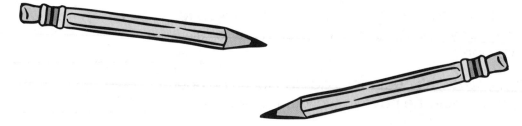

Name: _____

Equations

Directions: Write the correct operation signs in the blanks to make accurate equations.

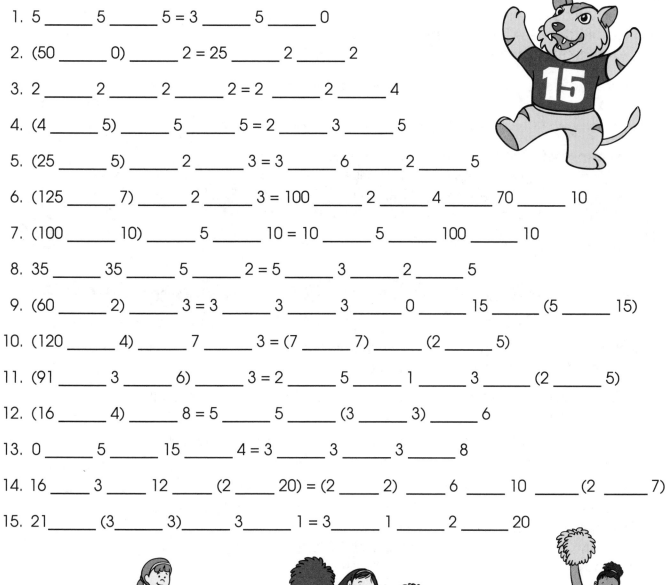

1. 5 _____ 5 _____ 5 = 3 _____ 5 _____ 0

2. (50 _____ 0) _____ 2 = 25 _____ 2 _____ 2

3. 2 _____ 2 _____ 2 _____ 2 = 2 _____ 2 _____ 4

4. (4 _____ 5) _____ 5 _____ 5 = 2 _____ 3 _____ 5

5. (25 _____ 5) _____ 2 _____ 3 = 3 _____ 6 _____ 2 _____ 5

6. (125 _____ 7) _____ 2 _____ 3 = 100 _____ 2 _____ 4 _____ 70 _____ 10

7. (100 _____ 10) _____ 5 _____ 10 = 10 _____ 5 _____ 100 _____ 10

8. 35 _____ 35 _____ 5 _____ 2 = 5 _____ 3 _____ 2 _____ 5

9. (60 _____ 2) _____ 3 = 3 _____ 3 _____ 3 _____ 0 _____ 15 _____ (5 _____ 15)

10. (120 _____ 4) _____ 7 _____ 3 = (7 _____ 7) _____ (2 _____ 5)

11. (91 _____ 3 _____ 6) _____ 3 = 2 _____ 5 _____ 1 _____ 3 _____ (2 _____ 5)

12. (16 _____ 4) _____ 8 = 5 _____ 5 _____ (3 _____ 3) _____ 6

13. 0 _____ 5 _____ 15 _____ 4 = 3 _____ 3 _____ 3 _____ 8

14. 16 _____ 3 _____ 12 _____ (2 _____ 20) = (2 _____ 2) _____ 6 _____ 10 _____ (2 _____ 7)

15. 21 _____ (3 _____ 3) _____ 3 _____ 1 = 3 _____ 1 _____ 2 _____ 20

Grade 6 - Comprehensive Curriculum

Rounding and Estimating

Rounding is expressing a number to the nearest whole number, ten, thousand or other value. **Estimating** is using an approximate number instead of an exact one. When rounding a number, we say a country has 98,000,000 citizens instead of 98,347,425. We can round off numbers to the nearest whole number, the nearest hundred or the nearest million—whatever is appropriate.

Here are the steps: 1) Decide where you want to round off the number. 2) If the digit to the right is less than 5, leave the digit at the rounding place unchanged. 3) If the digit to the right is 5 or more, increase the digit at the rounding place by 1.

> **Examples:** 587 rounded to the nearest hundred is 600.
> 535 rounded to the nearest hundred is 500.
> 21,897 rounded to the nearest thousand is 22,000.
> 21,356 rounded to the nearest thousand is 21,000.
>
> When we estimate numbers, we use rounded, approximate numbers instead of exact ones.
>
> **Example:** A hamburger that costs $1.49 and a drink that costs $0.79 total about $2.30 ($1.50 plus $0.80).

Directions: Use rounding and estimating to find the answers to these questions. You may have to add, subtract, multiply or divide.

1. Debbi is having a party and wants to fill 11 cups from a 67-ounce bottle of pop. About how many ounces should she pour into each cup? _____

2. Tracy studied 28 minutes every day for 4 days. About how long did she study in all? _____

3. About how much does this lunch cost? $1.19 $ 0.39 $ 0.49 _____

4. The numbers below show how long Frank spent studying last week. Estimate how many minutes he studied for the whole week.
Monday: 23 minutes Tuesday: 37 minutes Wednesday: 38 minutes
Thursday: 12 minutes _____

5. One elephant at the zoo weighs 1,417 pounds and another one weighs 1,789 pounds. About how much heavier is the second elephant? _____

6. If Tim studied a total of 122 minutes over 4 days, about how long did he study each day? _____

7. It's 549 miles to Dover and 345 miles to Albany. About how much closer is Albany? _____

Rounding

Directions: Round off each number, then estimate the answer. You can use a calculator to find the exact answer.

Round to the nearest ten. | **Estimate** | **Actual Answer**

1. $86 \div 9 =$ _____ _____

2. $237 + 488 =$ _____ _____

3. $49 \times 11 =$ _____ _____

4. $309 + 412 =$ _____ _____

5. $625 - 218 =$ _____ _____

Round to the nearest hundred.

6. $790 - 70 =$ _____ _____

7. $690 \div 70 =$ _____ _____

8. $2,177 - 955 =$ _____ _____

9. $4,792 + 3,305 =$ _____ _____

10. $5,210 \times 90 =$ _____ _____

Round to the nearest thousand.

11. $4,078 + 2,093 =$ _____ _____

12. $5,525 - 3,065 =$ _____ _____

13. $6,047 \div 2,991 =$ _____ _____

14. $1,913 \times 4,216 =$ _____ _____

15. $7,227 + 8,449 =$ _____ _____

Decimals

A **decimal** is a number that includes a period called a **decimal point**. The digits to the right of the decimal point are a value less than one.

one whole **one tenth** **one hundredth**

The place value chart below helps explain decimals.

hundreds	tens	ones	tenths	hundredths	thousandths
6	3	2 .	4		
	4	7 .	0	5	
		8 .	0	0	9

A decimal point is read as "and." The first number, 632.4, is read as "six hundred thirty-two and four tenths." The second number, 47.05, is read as "forty-seven and five hundredths." The third number, 8.009, is read as "eight and nine thousandths."

Directions: Write the decimals shown below. Two have been done for you.

1. __1.4__   2. _____   3. _____

4. six and five tenths   __6.5__

5. twenty-two and nine tenths   _____

6. thirty-six and fourteen hundredths   _____

7. forty-seven hundredths   _____

8. one hundred six and four tenths   _____

9. seven and three hundredths   _____

10. one tenth less than 0.6   _____

11. one hundredth less than 0.34   _____

12. one tenth more than 0.2   _____

Name: _____

Adding and Subtracting Decimals

When adding or subtracting decimals, place the decimal points under each other. That way, you add tenths to tenths, for example, not tenths to hundredths. Add or subtract beginning on the right, as usual. Carry or borrow numbers in the same way. Adding 0 to the end of decimals does not change their value, but sometimes makes them easier to add and subtract.

Examples:	39.40	0.064	3.56	6.83
	+ 6.81	+ 0.470	− .09	− 2.14
	46.21	0.534	3.47	4.69

Directions: Solve the following problems.

1. Write each set of numbers in a column and add them.

    a. 2.56 + 0.6 + 76 =   _____

    b. 93.5 + 23.06 + 1.45 =   _____

    c. 3.23 + 91.34 + 0.85 =   _____

2. Write each pair of numbers in a column and subtract them.

    A. 7.89 − 0.56 = _____   B. 34.56 − 6.04 = _____   C. 7.6 − 3.24 = _____

3. In a relay race, Alice ran her part in 23.6 seconds, Cindy did hers in 24.7 seconds and Erin took 20.09 seconds. How many seconds did they take altogether?   _____

4. Although Erin ran her part in 20.09 seconds today, yesterday it took her 21.55 seconds. How much faster was she today?   _____

5. Add this grocery bill:
   potatoes—$3.49; milk—$2.09; bread—$0.99; apples—$2.30   _____

6. A yellow coat cost $47.59, and a blue coat cost $36.79. How much more did the yellow coat cost?   _____

7. A box of Oat Boats cereal has 14.6 ounces. A box of Sugar Circles has 17.85 ounces. How much more cereal is in the Sugar Circles box?   _____

8. The Oat Boats cereal has 4.03 ounces of sugar in it. Sugar Circles cereal has only 3.76 ounces. How much more sugar is in a box of Oats Boats?   _____

Name: _____

Mulitplying Decimals by Two-Digit Numbers

To multiply by a 2-digit number, just repeat the same steps. In the example below, first multiply 4 times 9, 4 times 5 and 4 times 3. Then multiply 2 times 9, 2 times 5 and 2 times 3. You may want to place a 0 in the ones place to make sure this answer, 718, is one digit to the left. Now add 1,436 + 7,180 to get the final answer.

Example:	359	359	359	359	359	359
	x 24	x 24	x 24	x 24	x 24	x 24
	6	36	1,436	1,436	1,436	1,436
				80	180	7,180
						8,616

When one or both numbers in a multiplication problem have decimals, check to see how many digits are right of the decimal. Then place the decimal point the same number of places to the left in the answer. Here's how the example above would change if it included decimals:

$$\begin{array}{r} 35.9 \\ \times\ 0.24 \\ \hline 8.616 \end{array} \qquad \begin{array}{r} 3.59 \\ \times\ 24 \\ \hline 86.16 \end{array}$$

The first example has one digit to the right of the decimal in 35.9 and two more in 0.24, so the decimal point is placed three digits to the left in the answer: 8.616. The second example has two digits to the right of the decimal in 3.59 and none in 24, so the decimal point is placed two digits to the left in the answer: 86.16. (Notice that you do not have to line up the decimals in a multiplication problem.)

Directions: Solve the following problems.

1. Jennie wants to buy 3 T-shirts that cost $15.99 each. How much will they cost altogether? _____

2. Steve is making $3.75 an hour packing groceries. How much will he make in 8 hours? _____

3. Justin made 36 cookies and sold them all at the school carnival for $0.75 each. How much money did he make? _____

4. Last year, the carnival made $467. This year it made 2.3 times as much. How much money did the carnival make this year? _____

5. Troy's car will go 21.8 miles on a gallon of gasoline. His motorcycle will go 1.7 times as far. How far will his motorcycle travel on one gallon of gas? _____

Multiplying Decimals

In some problems, you may need to add zeros in order to place the decimal point correctly.

Examples:

0.34	0.0067	0.046
x 0.08	x 4	x 0.07
0.0272	0.0268	0.00322

Directions: Solve the following problems.

1.   0.15
   x 0.02

2.   0.67
   x 0.08

3.   7.3
   x 0.06

4.   3.59
   x 0.08

5.   0.061
   x 0.014

6.   7.10
   x 0.042

7.   5.05
   x 0.08

8.   8.75
   x 0.067

9. 0.0647
   x   0.3

10.   3.62
   x 0.003

11.   1.07
   x 0.05

12.   3.03
   x 0.07

13.   0.02
   x 0.02

14. 0.501
   x 0.03

15.   0.321
   x 0.09

16. The players and coaches gathered around for refreshments after the soccer game. Of the 30 people there, 0.50 of them had fruit drinks, 0.20 of them had fruit juice and 0.30 of them had soft drinks. How many people had each type of drink?

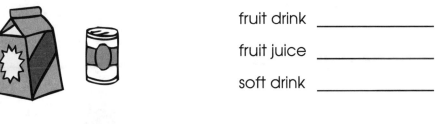

fruit drink _____

fruit juice _____

soft drink _____

Dividing Decimals by Two-Digit Numbers

Dividing by a 2-digit divisor (34 in the example below) is very similar to dividing by a 1-digit divisor. In this example, 34 will divide into 78 twice. Then multiply 34 x 2 to get 68. Subtract 68 from 78. The answer is 10, which is smaller than the divisor, so 2 was the right number. Now bring down the next 8. 34 goes into 108 three times. Continue dividing as with a 1-digit divisor.

Example:

$$
\begin{array}{r} 2 \\ 34\overline{)7,888} \\ 68 \\ \hline 10 \end{array}
\qquad
\begin{array}{r} 23 \\ 34\overline{)7,888} \\ 68 \\ \hline 108 \\ 102 \\ \hline 6 \end{array}
\qquad
\begin{array}{r} 232 \\ 34\overline{)7,888} \\ 68 \\ \hline 108 \\ 102 \\ \hline 68 \\ 68 \\ \hline 0 \end{array}
$$

To check your division, multiply: 34 x 232 = 7,888.

When the dividend has a decimal, place the decimal point for the answer directly above the decimal point in the dividend.

Examples:

$$
\begin{array}{r} 3.6 \\ 14\overline{)50.4} \end{array}
\qquad
\begin{array}{r} 8.92 \\ 34\overline{)303.28} \end{array}
$$

Directions: Solve the following problems.

1. $56\overline{)7.28}$ 2. $23\overline{)18.63}$ 3. $62\overline{)255.44}$ 4. $71\overline{)82.36}$ 5. $4\overline{)8.580}$

6. If socks cost $8.97 for 3 pairs, how much does one pair cost? _____

7. If candy bars are 6 for $2.58, how much is one candy bar? _____

8. You buy a bike for $152.25 and agree to make 21 equal payments. How much will each payment be? _____

9. You and two friends agree to spend several hours loading a truck. The truck driver gives you $36.75 to share. How much will each person get? _____

10. You buy 14 hamburgers and the bill comes to $32.06. How much did each hamburger cost? _____

Dividing With Zeros

Sometimes you have a remainder in division problems. You can add a decimal point and zeros to the dividend and keep dividing until you have the answer.

Example:

$$
\begin{array}{r}
49 \\
25\overline{)1{,}241} \\
1\,00 \\
\hline
241 \\
225 \\
\hline
16
\end{array}
$$

$$
\begin{array}{r}
49.64 \\
25\overline{)1{,}241.00} \\
1\,00 \\
\hline
241 \\
225 \\
\hline
160 \\
150 \\
\hline
100 \\
100 \\
\hline
0
\end{array}
$$

Directions: Solve the following problems.

1. $2\overline{)2.5}$ 2. $4\overline{)115}$ 3. $12\overline{)738}$ 4. $8\overline{)586}$ 5. $25\overline{)3{,}415}$

6. Susie's grandparents sent her a check for $130 to share with her 7 brothers and sisters. How much will each of the 8 children get if the money is divided evenly?   _____

7. A vendor had 396 balloons to sell and 16 workers. How many balloons should each worker sell in order to sell out?   _____

8. Eight of the workers turned in a total of $753. How much did each worker collect if he/she sold the same number of items?   _____

9. A total of 744 tickets were collected from 15 amusement ride operators on the first day of the fair. If each ride required one ticket per person, and they each collected the same number of tickets, how many people rode each ride?   _____

   Do you think that was possible? Why? _____

   _____

10. Five people were hired to clean up the area after the fair closed. They turned in a bill for 26 hours of labor. How many hours did each person work?   _____

Grade 6 - Comprehensive Curriculum

Dividing Decimals by Decimals

When a divisor has a decimal, eliminate it before dividing. If there is one digit right of the decimal in the divisor, multiply the divisor and dividend by 10. If there are two digits right of the decimal in the divisor, multiply the divisor and dividend by 100.

Multiply the divisor and dividend by the same number whether or not the dividend has a decimal. The goal is to have a divisor with no decimal.

Examples: $2.3\overline{)89} \times 10 = 23\overline{)890}$ $4.11\overline{)67.7} \times 100 = 411\overline{)6,770}$

$4.9\overline{)35.67} \times 10 = 49\overline{)356.7}$ $0.34\overline{)789} \times 100 = 34\overline{)78,900}$

After removing the decimal from the divisor, work the problem in the usual way.

Directions: Solve the following problems.

1. $3.5\overline{)10.15}$ 2. $6.7\overline{)415.4}$ 3. $0.21\overline{)924}$ 4. $73\overline{)50.37}$

5. The body can burn only 0.00015 of an ounce of alcohol an hour. If an average-sized person has 1 drink, his/her blood alcohol concentration (BAC) is 0.0003. How many hours will it take his/her body to remove that much alcohol from the blood? _____

6. If the same person has 2 drinks in 1 hour, his/her blood alcohol concentration increases to 0.0006. Burning 0.00015 ounce of alcohol an hour, how many hours will it take that person's body to burn off 2 drinks? _____

7. If someone has 3 drinks in 1 hour, the blood alcohol concentration rises to 0.0009. At 0.00015 an hour, how many hours will it take to burn off 3 drinks? _____

8. After a drunk driving conviction, the driver's car insurance can increase by as much as $2,000. Still, this is only 0.57 of the total cost of the conviction. What is the total cost, in round numbers? _____

9. In Ohio in 1986, about 335 fatal car crashes were alcohol related. That was 0.47 of the total number of fatal car crashes. About how many crashes were there altogether, in round numbers? _____

Decimals and Fractions

A **fraction** is a number that names part of something. The top number in a fraction is called the **numerator**. The bottom number is called the **denominator**. Since a decimal also names part of a whole number, every decimal can also be written as a fraction. For example, 0.1 is read as "one tenth" and can also be written $\frac{1}{10}$. The decimal 0.56 is read as "fifty-six hundredths" and can also be written $\frac{56}{100}$.

Examples:

$$0.7 = \frac{7}{10} \quad 0.34 = \frac{34}{100} \quad 0.761 = \frac{761}{1,000} \quad \frac{5}{10} = 0.5 \quad \frac{58}{100} = 0.58 \quad \frac{729}{1,000} = 0.729$$

Even a fraction that doesn't have 10, 100 or 1,000 as the denominator can be written as a decimal. Sometimes you can multiply both the numerator and denominator by a certain number so the denominator is 10, 100 or 1,000. (You can't just multiply the denominator. That would change the amount of the fraction.)

Examples:

$$\frac{3 \times 2}{5 \times 2} = \frac{6}{10} = 0.6 \qquad \frac{4 \times 4}{25 \times 4} = \frac{16}{100} = 0.16$$

Other times, divide the numerator by the denominator.

Examples:

$$\frac{3}{4} = 4\overline{)3.00} \; \frac{0.75}{} = 0.75 \qquad \frac{5}{8} = 8\overline{)5.000} \; \frac{0.625}{} = 0.625$$

Directions: Follow the instructions below.

1. For each square, write a decimal and a fraction to show the part that is colored. The first one has been done for you.

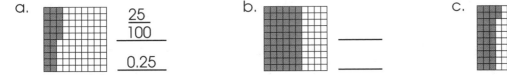

   a. $\frac{25}{100}$ b.   _____   c.   _____

                         0.25

2. Change these decimals to fractions.

   a. 0.6 =   b. 0.54 =   c. 0.751 =   d. 0.73 =   e. 0.592 =   f. 0.2 =

3. Change these fractions to decimals. If necessary, round off the decimals to the nearest hundredth.

   a. $\frac{3}{10} =$ b. $\frac{89}{100} =$ c. $\frac{473}{1,000} =$ d. $\frac{4}{5} =$ e. $\frac{35}{50} =$

   f. $\frac{7}{9} =$ g. $\frac{1}{3} =$ h. $\frac{23}{77} =$ i. $\frac{12}{63} =$ j. $\frac{4}{16} =$

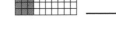

Equivalent Fractions and the Lowest Term

Equivalent fractions name the same amount. For example, $\frac{1}{2}$, $\frac{5}{10}$, and $\frac{50}{100}$ are exactly the same amount. They all mean half of something. (And they are all written as the same decimal: 0.5.) To find an equivalent fraction, multiply the numerator and denominator of any fraction by the same number.

Examples: $\frac{3 \times 3 = 9 \times 4 = 36}{4 \times 3 = 12 \times 4 = 48}$ Thus, $\frac{3}{4}$, $\frac{9}{12}$ and $\frac{36}{48}$ are all equivalent fractions.

Most of the time, we want fractions in their lowest terms. It's easier to work with $\frac{3}{4}$ than $\frac{36}{48}$. To find a fraction's lowest term, instead of multiplying both parts of a fraction by the same number, divide.

Examples: $\frac{36 \div 12 = 3}{48 \div 12 = 4}$ The lowest term for $\frac{36}{48}$ is $\frac{3}{4}$.

If the numerator and denominator in a fraction can't be divided by any number, the fraction is in its lowest term. The fractions below are in their lowest terms.

Examples: $\frac{34}{61}$ $\frac{3}{5}$ $\frac{7}{9}$ $\frac{53}{90}$ $\frac{78}{83}$ $\frac{3}{8}$

Directions: Follow the instructions below.

1. Write two equivalent fractions for each fraction. Make sure you multiply the numerator and denominator by the same number. The first one is done for you.

   a. $\frac{1 \times 3 = 3}{2 \times 3 = 6}$ $\frac{1 \times 4 = 4}{2 \times 4 = 8}$ b. $\frac{2 \times \underline{\quad} = \underline{\quad}}{3 \times \underline{\quad} = \underline{\quad}}$ $\frac{2 \times \underline{\quad} = \underline{\quad}}{3 \times \underline{\quad} = \underline{\quad}}$

   c. $\frac{3 \times \underline{\quad} = \underline{\quad}}{5 \times \underline{\quad} = \underline{\quad}}$ $\frac{3 \times \underline{\quad} = \underline{\quad}}{5 \times \underline{\quad} = \underline{\quad}}$ d. $\frac{8 \times \underline{\quad} = \underline{\quad}}{9 \times \underline{\quad} = \underline{\quad}}$ $\frac{8 \times \underline{\quad} = \underline{\quad}}{9 \times \underline{\quad} = \underline{\quad}}$

2. Find the lowest terms for each fraction. Make sure your answers can't be divided by any other numbers. The first one has been done for you.

   a. $\frac{2 \div 2 = 1}{36 \div 2 = 18}$ b. $\frac{12 \div \underline{\quad} = \underline{\quad}}{25 \div \underline{\quad} = \underline{\quad}}$ c. $\frac{12 \div \underline{\quad} = \underline{\quad}}{16 \div \underline{\quad} = \underline{\quad}}$

   d. $\frac{3 \div \underline{\quad} = \underline{\quad}}{9 \div \underline{\quad} = \underline{\quad}}$ e. $\frac{25 \div \underline{\quad} = \underline{\quad}}{45 \div \underline{\quad} = \underline{\quad}}$ f. $\frac{11 \div \underline{\quad} = \underline{\quad}}{44 \div \underline{\quad} = \underline{\quad}}$

Name: _____

Greatest Common Factor

The **greatest common factor (GCF)** is the largest number that will divide evenly into a set of numbers. In the example, both numbers can be divided evenly by 2 and 4; therefore, 4 is the greatest common factor.

Example: 12 and 20   2, 4 (can be divided evenly into both numbers)
                          4 (greatest common factor)

Directions: Circle the greatest common factor for each pair of numbers.

1. 56 and 72	6	10	8	2
2. 45 and 81	7	5	9	3
3. 28 and 49	7	11	4	6
4. 10 and 35	3	5	9	7
5. 42 and 30	4	2	5	6
6. 121 and 33	12	9	4	11
7. 96 and 48	48	15	6	3
8. 12 and 132	2	10	12	9
9. 108 and 27	14	9	3	27
10. 44 and 32	4	6	8	10
11. 16 and 88	12	2	8	5
12. 72 and 144	9	11	7	72

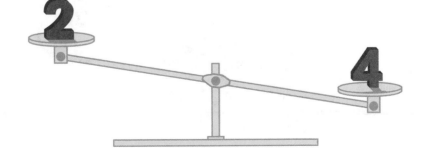

Grade 6 - Comprehensive Curriculum

Name: _____

Least Common Multiple

The **least common multiple (LCM)** is the lowest possible multiple any pair of numbers have in common.

Examples: 2 and 4
> The lowest common multiple is 4, because 4 is a multiple for each number and it is the lowest possible.
>
> 6 and 7
> Multiples of 6 are 6, 12, 18, 24, 30, 36, 42.
> Multiples of 7 are 7, 14, 21, 28, 35, 42.
> 42 is the lowest multiple that 6 and 7 have in common.

Directions: Find the least common multiple for each pair of numbers.

1. 7 and 8 = _____

2. 2 and 3 = _____

3. 11 and 4 = _____

4. 5 and 3 = _____

5. 7 and 2 = _____

6. 9 and 4 = _____

7. 2 and 6 = _____

8. 10 and 3 = _____

9. 7 and 5 = _____

10. 9 and 6 = _____

11. 12 and 8 = _____

12. 15 and 3 = _____

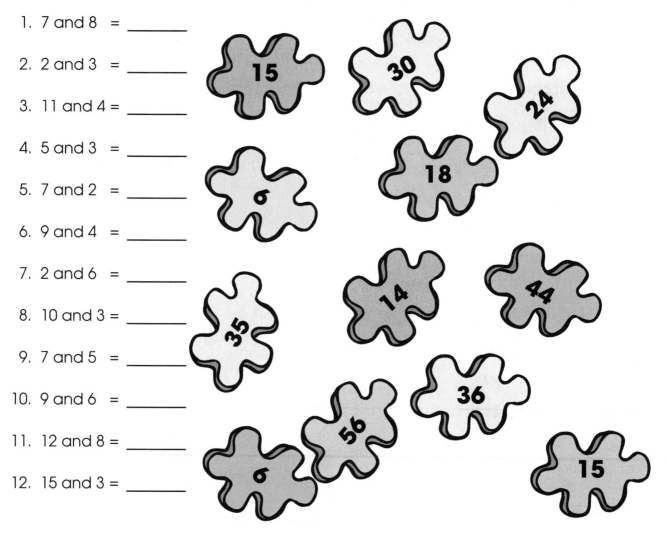

Name: _____

Comparing Decimals and Fractions

The symbol **>** means greater than. The number on its left is greater than that on its right. The symbol **<** means less than. The number on its left is less than that on its right. An equal sign, **=**, shows the same value on each side.

Directions: Use the sign >, = or < to make each statement true.

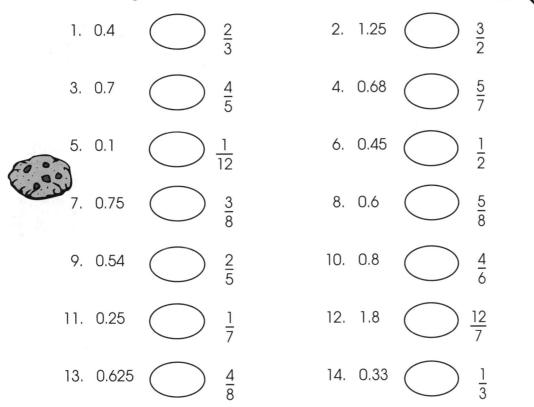

1. 0.4 $\bigcirc$ $\frac{2}{3}$

2. 1.25 $\bigcirc$ $\frac{3}{2}$

3. 0.7 $\bigcirc$ $\frac{4}{5}$

4. 0.68 $\bigcirc$ $\frac{5}{7}$

5. 0.1 $\bigcirc$ $\frac{1}{12}$

6. 0.45 $\bigcirc$ $\frac{1}{2}$

7. 0.75 $\bigcirc$ $\frac{3}{8}$

8. 0.6 $\bigcirc$ $\frac{5}{8}$

9. 0.54 $\bigcirc$ $\frac{2}{5}$

10. 0.8 $\bigcirc$ $\frac{4}{6}$

11. 0.25 $\bigcirc$ $\frac{1}{7}$

12. 1.8 $\bigcirc$ $\frac{12}{7}$

13. 0.625 $\bigcirc$ $\frac{4}{8}$

14. 0.33 $\bigcirc$ $\frac{1}{3}$

15. Jenna looked carefully at the labels on two different types of cookies. The chocolate ones had $\frac{3}{4}$ pound in the package. The package of vanilla cookies claimed it had 0.67 pound of cookies inside. Were the chocolate cookies <, > or = to the vanilla cookies? _____

Mixed Numbers and Improper Fractions

A **mixed number** is a whole number and a fraction, such as $1\frac{3}{4}$. An **improper fraction** has a numerator that is larger than its denominator, such as $\frac{16}{3}$. To write an improper fraction as a mixed number, divide the numerator by the denominator. The quotient becomes the whole number and the remainder becomes the fraction.

Examples:

$$\frac{16}{3} = 3\overline{)16} = 5\frac{1}{3}$$

$$\frac{28}{5} = 5\overline{)28} = 5\frac{3}{5}$$

To change a mixed number into an improper fraction, multiply the whole number by the denominator and add the numerator.

Examples:

$$4\frac{1}{3} = 4 \times 3 = 12 + 1 = 13 \quad \frac{13}{3}$$

$$8\frac{4}{7} = 8 \times 7 = 56 + 4 = 60 \quad \frac{60}{7}$$

Directions: Follow the instructions below.

1. Change the improper fractions to mixed numbers and reduce to lowest terms. Use another sheet of paper if necessary. The first one has been done for you.

a. $\frac{34}{6} = 6\overline{)34} = 5\frac{4}{6} = 5\frac{2}{3}$

b. $\frac{65}{4} =$ c. $\frac{23}{8} =$ d. $\frac{89}{3} =$

e. $\frac{45}{9} =$ f. $\frac{32}{5} =$ g. $\frac{13}{7} =$

h. $\frac{24}{9} =$ i. $\frac{31}{2} =$ j. $\frac{84}{23} =$

2. Change these mixed numbers into improper fractions. The first one has been done for you.

a. $4\frac{6}{7} = 4 \times 7 = 28 + 6 = \frac{34}{7}$ b. $2\frac{1}{9} =$ c. $5\frac{4}{5} =$ d. $12\frac{1}{4} =$

e. $6\frac{7}{8} =$ f. $3\frac{9}{11} =$ g. $8\frac{3}{12} =$ h. $1\frac{6}{14} =$ i. $4\frac{2}{3} =$ j. $9\frac{4}{15} =$

Name: _____

Adding Fractions

When adding fractions, if the denominators are the same, simply add the numerators. When the result is an improper fraction, change it to a mixed number.

Examples: $\frac{3}{5} + \frac{1}{5} = \frac{4}{5}$ $\qquad$ $\frac{3}{9} + \frac{7}{9} = \frac{10}{9} = 1\frac{1}{9}$

If the denominators of fractions are different, change them so they are the same. To do this, find equivalent fractions. In the first example below, $\frac{1}{4}$ and $\frac{3}{8}$ have different denominators, so change $\frac{1}{4}$ to the equivalent fraction $\frac{2}{8}$. Then add the numerators. In the second example, $\frac{5}{7}$ and $\frac{2}{3}$ also have different denominators. Find a denominator both 7 and 3 divide into. The lowest number they both divide into is 21. Multiply the numerator and denominator of $\frac{5}{7}$ by 3 to get the equivalent fraction $\frac{15}{21}$. Then multiply the numerator and denominator of $\frac{2}{3}$ by 7 to get the equivalent fraction $\frac{14}{21}$.

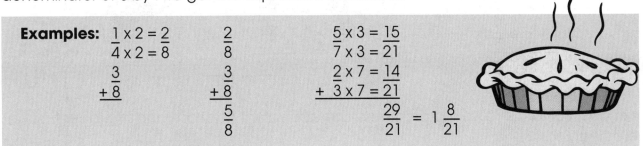

Examples:

$$\begin{array}{ll} \dfrac{1 \times 2 = 2}{4 \times 2 = 8} \\ \dfrac{3}{+\ 8} \end{array} \qquad \begin{array}{l} \dfrac{2}{8} \\ \dfrac{3}{+\ 8} \\ \hline \dfrac{5}{8} \end{array} \qquad \begin{array}{l} \dfrac{5 \times 3 = 15}{7 \times 3 = 21} \\ \dfrac{2 \times 7 = 14}{+\ 3 \times 7 = 21} \\ \hline \dfrac{29}{21} = 1\dfrac{8}{21} \end{array}$$

Directions: Solve the following problems. Find equivalent fractions when necessary.

1. $\begin{array}{r} \frac{3}{5} \\ \frac{1}{5} \\ + \\ \hline \end{array}$ $\qquad$ 2. $\begin{array}{r} \frac{7}{8} \\ \frac{2}{16} \\ + \\ \hline \end{array}$ $\qquad$ 3. $\begin{array}{r} \frac{1}{9} \\ \frac{2}{3} \\ + \\ \hline \end{array}$ $\qquad$ 4. $\begin{array}{r} \frac{2}{6} \\ \frac{2}{3} \\ + \\ \hline \end{array}$ $\qquad$ 5. $\begin{array}{r} \frac{2}{15} \\ \frac{1}{5} \\ + \\ \hline \end{array}$

6. Cora is making a cake. She needs $\frac{1}{2}$ cup butter for the cake and $\frac{1}{4}$ cup butter for the frosting. How much butter does she need altogether? _____

7. Henry is painting a wall. Yesterday he painted $\frac{1}{3}$ of it. Today he painted $\frac{1}{4}$ of it. How much has he painted altogether? _____

8. Nancy ate $\frac{1}{6}$ of a pie. Her father ate $\frac{1}{4}$ of it. How much did they eat altogether? _____

Name: _____

Subtracting Fractions

Subtracting fractions is very similar to adding them in that the denominators must be the same. If the denominators are different, use equivalent fractions.

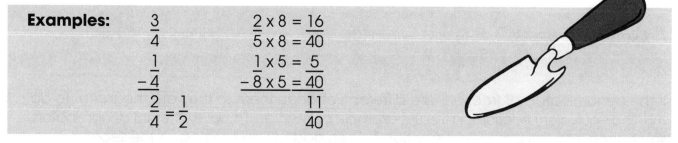

Adding and subtracting mixed numbers are also similar. Often, though, change the mixed numbers to improper fractions. If the denominators are different, use equivalent fractions.

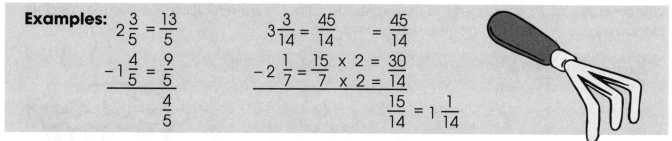

Directions: Solve the following problems. Use equivalent fractions and improper fractions where necessary.

1.
$$\frac{6}{7}$$
$$-\frac{5}{7}$$

2.
$$1\frac{2}{9}$$
$$-\frac{4}{9}$$

3.
$$2\frac{3}{6}$$
$$-\frac{4}{5}$$

4.
$$\frac{3}{4}$$
$$-\frac{1}{2}$$

5.
$$2\frac{1}{3}$$
$$-\frac{3}{4}$$

6. Carol promised to weed the flower garden for $1\frac{1}{2}$ hours this morning. So far she has pulled two weeds for $\frac{3}{4}$ of an hour. How much longer does she have to work? _____

7. Dil started out with $1\frac{1}{4}$ gallons of paint. He used $\frac{3}{8}$ gallon of the paint on his boat. How much paint is left? _____

8. A certain movie lasts $2\frac{1}{2}$ hours. Susan has already watched it for $1\frac{2}{3}$ hours. How much longer is the movie? _____

9. Bert didn't finish $\frac{1}{8}$ of the math problems on a test. He made mistakes on $\frac{1}{6}$ of the problems. The rest he answered correctly. What fraction of the problems did he answer correctly? _____

Multiplying Fractions

To multiply two fractions, multiply the numerators and then multiply the denominators. If necessary, change the answer to its lowest term.

Examples: $\frac{3}{4} \times \frac{2}{3} = \frac{6}{12} = \frac{1}{2}$ $\frac{1}{8} \times \frac{4}{5} = \frac{4}{40} = \frac{1}{10}$

To multiply a whole number by a fraction, first write the whole number as a fraction (with 1 as the denominator). Then multiply as above. You may need to change an improper fraction to a mixed number.

Examples: $\frac{2}{3} \times \frac{4}{1} = \frac{8}{3} = 2\frac{2}{3}$ $\frac{3}{7} \times \frac{6}{1} = \frac{18}{7} = 2\frac{4}{7}$

Directions: Solve the following problems, writing answers in their lowest terms.

1. $\frac{1}{5} \times \frac{2}{3} =$

2. $\frac{1}{3} \times \frac{4}{7} =$

3. $\frac{2}{8} \times 3 =$

4. $\frac{2}{6} \times \frac{1}{2} =$

5. Tim lost $\frac{1}{8}$ of his marbles. If he had 56 marbles, how many did he lose? _____

6. Jeff is making $\frac{2}{3}$ of a recipe for spaghetti sauce. How much will he need of each ingredient below? _____

   $1\frac{1}{4}$ cups water = _____   2 cups tomato paste = _____

   $\frac{3}{4}$ teaspoon oregano = _____ $4\frac{1}{2}$ teaspoons salt = _____

7. Carrie bought 2 dozen donuts and asked for $\frac{3}{4}$ of them to be chocolate. How many were chocolate? _____

8. Christy let her hair grow 14 inches long and then had $\frac{1}{4}$ of it cut off. How much was cut off? _____

9. Kurt has finished $\frac{7}{8}$ of 40 math problems. How many has he done? _____

10. If Sherryl's cat eats $\frac{2}{3}$ can of cat food every day, how many cans should Sherryl buy for a week? _____

Dividing Fractions

Reciprocals are two fractions that, when multiplied together, make 1. To divide a fraction by a fraction, turn one of the fractions upside down and multiply. The upside-down fraction is a reciprocal of its original fraction. If you multiply a fraction by its reciprocal, you always get 1.

Examples of reciprocals: $\frac{2}{3} \times \frac{3}{2} = \frac{6}{6} = 1$ $\frac{9}{11} \times \frac{11}{9} = \frac{99}{99} = 1$

Examples of dividing by fractions: $\frac{1}{2} \div \frac{2}{3} = \frac{1}{2} \times \frac{3}{2} = \frac{3}{4}$ $\frac{2}{5} \div \frac{2}{7} = \frac{2}{5} \times \frac{7}{2} = \frac{14}{10} = \frac{7}{5} = 1\frac{2}{5}$

To divide a whole number by a fraction, first write the whole number as a fraction (with a denominator of 1). (Write a mixed number as an improper fraction.) Then finish the problem as explained above.

Examples: $4 \div \frac{2}{6} = \frac{4}{1} \times \frac{6}{2} = \frac{24}{2} = 12$ $3\frac{1}{2} \div \frac{2}{5} = \frac{7}{2} \times \frac{5}{2} = \frac{35}{4} = 8\frac{3}{4}$

Directions: Solve the following problems, writing answers in their lowest terms. Change any improper fractions to mixed numbers.

1. $\frac{1}{3} \div \frac{2}{5} =$

2. $\frac{6}{7} \div \frac{1}{3} =$

3. $3 \div \frac{3}{4} =$

4. $\frac{1}{4} \div \frac{2}{3} =$

5. Judy has 8 candy bars. She wants to give $\frac{1}{3}$ of a candy bar to everyone in her class. Does she have enough for all 24 students? _____

6. A big jar of glue holds $3\frac{1}{2}$ cups. How many little containers that hold $\frac{1}{4}$ cup each can you fill? _____

7. A container holds 27 ounces of ice cream. How many $4\frac{1}{2}$-ounce servings is that? _____

8. It takes $2\frac{1}{2}$ teaspoons of powdered mix to make 1 cup of hot chocolate. How many cups can you make with 45 teaspoons of mix? _____

9. Each cup of hot chocolate also takes $\frac{2}{3}$ cup of milk. How many cups of hot chocolate can you make with 12 cups of milk? _____

Review

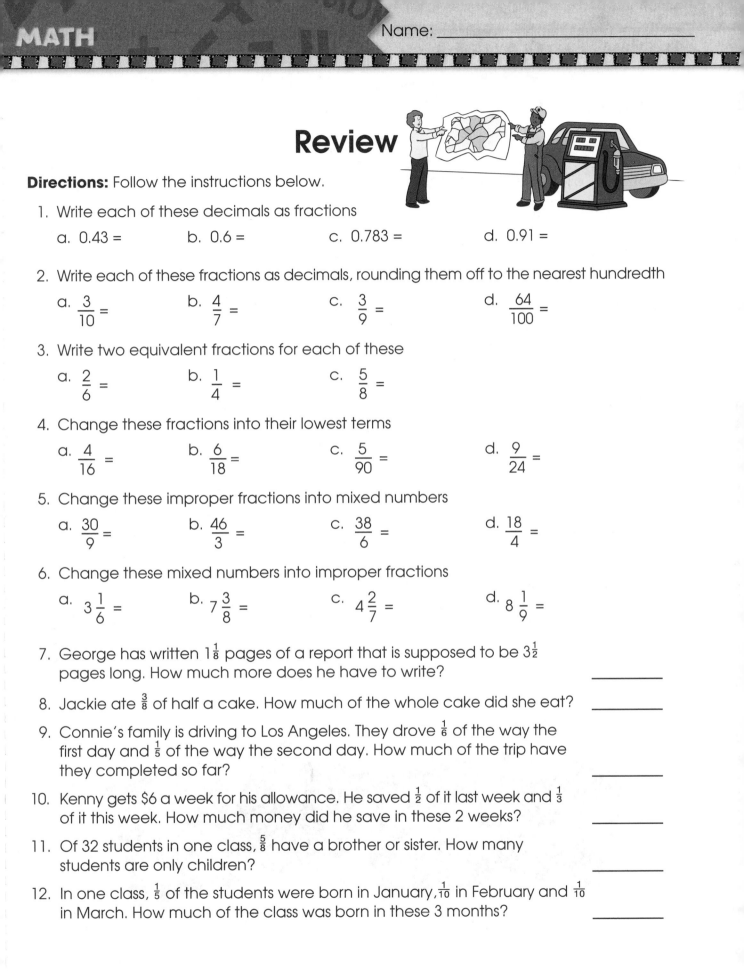

Directions: Follow the instructions below.

1. Write each of these decimals as fractions

   a. 0.43 =   b. 0.6 =   c. 0.783 =   d. 0.91 =

2. Write each of these fractions as decimals, rounding them off to the nearest hundredth

   a. $\dfrac{3}{10}$ =   b. $\dfrac{4}{7}$ =   c. $\dfrac{3}{9}$ =   d. $\dfrac{64}{100}$ =

3. Write two equivalent fractions for each of these

   a. $\dfrac{2}{6}$ =   b. $\dfrac{1}{4}$ =   c. $\dfrac{5}{8}$ =

4. Change these fractions into their lowest terms

   a. $\dfrac{4}{16}$ =   b. $\dfrac{6}{18}$ =   c. $\dfrac{5}{90}$ =   d. $\dfrac{9}{24}$ =

5. Change these improper fractions into mixed numbers

   a. $\dfrac{30}{9}$ =   b. $\dfrac{46}{3}$ =   c. $\dfrac{38}{6}$ =   d. $\dfrac{18}{4}$ =

6. Change these mixed numbers into improper fractions

   a. $3\dfrac{1}{6}$ =   b. $7\dfrac{3}{8}$ =   c. $4\dfrac{2}{7}$ =   d. $8\dfrac{1}{9}$ =

7. George has written $1\dfrac{1}{8}$ pages of a report that is supposed to be $3\dfrac{1}{2}$ pages long. How much more does he have to write? _____

8. Jackie ate $\dfrac{3}{8}$ of half a cake. How much of the whole cake did she eat? _____

9. Connie's family is driving to Los Angeles. They drove $\dfrac{1}{6}$ of the way the first day and $\dfrac{1}{5}$ of the way the second day. How much of the trip have they completed so far? _____

10. Kenny gets $6 a week for his allowance. He saved $\dfrac{1}{2}$ of it last week and $\dfrac{1}{3}$ of it this week. How much money did he save in these 2 weeks? _____

11. Of 32 students in one class, $\dfrac{5}{8}$ have a brother or sister. How many students are only children? _____

12. In one class, $\dfrac{1}{5}$ of the students were born in January, $\dfrac{1}{10}$ in February and $\dfrac{1}{10}$ in March. How much of the class was born in these 3 months? _____

Name: _____

Review

Directions: Follow the instructions below.

Add.

1. $\dfrac{4}{16} + \dfrac{5}{8} =$ 2. $\dfrac{1}{6} + \dfrac{1}{3} =$ 3. $\dfrac{2}{10} + \dfrac{4}{5} =$ 4. $\dfrac{3}{5} + \dfrac{9}{10} =$

Subtract.

1. $\dfrac{15}{9} - \dfrac{2}{3} =$ 2. $\dfrac{3}{4} - \dfrac{3}{8} =$ 3. $\dfrac{4}{7} - \dfrac{2}{14} =$ 4. $\dfrac{3}{5} - \dfrac{1}{10} =$

Multiply.

1. $\dfrac{1}{2} \times \dfrac{4}{16} =$ 2. $\dfrac{1}{3} \times \dfrac{4}{9} =$ 3. $\dfrac{5}{12} \times \dfrac{1}{4} =$ 4. $\dfrac{3}{16} \times \dfrac{3}{4} =$

Divide.

1. $\dfrac{3}{5} \div \dfrac{1}{3} =$ 2. $4 \div \dfrac{1}{2} =$ 3. $\dfrac{1}{4} \div \dfrac{1}{3} =$ 4. $3\dfrac{3}{4} \div \dfrac{1}{3} =$

Write >, < or = to make the statements true.

1. $0.5 \bigcirc \dfrac{5}{8}$ 2. $0.8 \bigcirc \dfrac{4}{5}$ 3. $0.35 \bigcirc \dfrac{2}{5}$ 4. $1.3 \bigcirc \dfrac{7}{8}$

Trial and Error

Often, the quickest way to solve a problem is to make a logical guess and test it to see if it works. The first guess, or trial, will probably not be the correct answer—but it should help figure out a better, more reasonable guess.

Directions: Use trial and error to find the solutions to these problems.

1. Mr. McFerrson is between 30 and 50 years old. The sum of the digits in his age is 11. His age is an even number. How old is Mr. McFerrson?

_____

_____

2. The key for number 5 does not work on Rusty's calculator. How can he use his broken calculator to subtract 108 from 351?

_____

_____

3. Tasha likes to swim a certain number of miles each day for 3 days straight. Then, she increases her mileage by 1 for the next 3 days, and so on. Over a nine day period, Tasha swims a total of 27 miles. She swims equal mileage Monday, Tuesday and Wednesday. She swims another amount on Thursday, Friday and Saturday. She swims yet a third amount on Sunday, Monday and Tuesday. How many miles does Tasha swim each day?

_____ Monday   _____ Tuesday   _____ Wednesday

_____ Thursday   _____ Friday   _____ Saturday

_____ Sunday   _____ Monday   _____ Tuesday

Name: _____

Trial and Error

Directions: Use trial and error to complete each diagram so all the equations work.

Example:

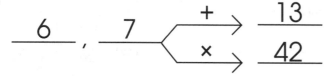

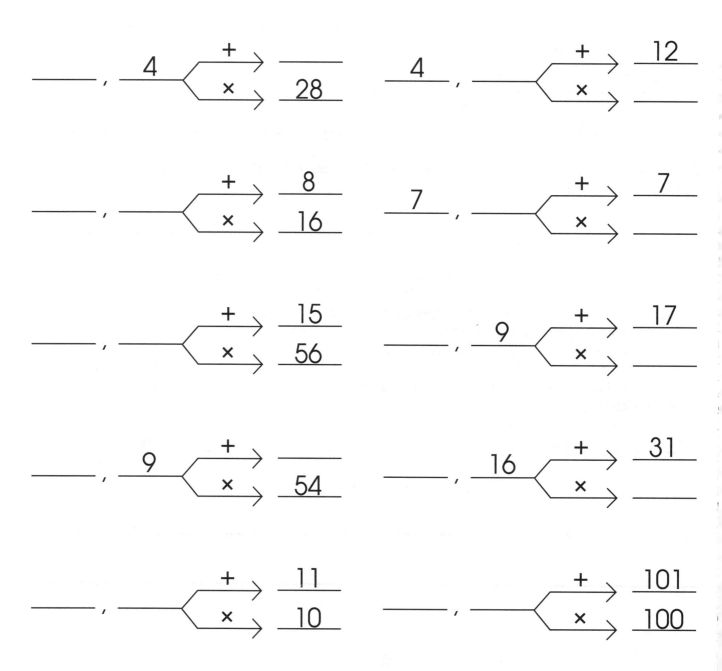

Name: _____

Choosing a Method

This table explains different methods of computation that can be used to solve a problem.

Method		
Mental Math	– Calculating in your head.	– Use with small numbers, memorized facts and multiples of tens, hundreds, thousands, and so on.
Objects/Diagram	– Drawing or using an object to represent the problem.	– Use to model the situation.
Pencil and Paper	– Calculating the answer on paper.	– Use when a calculator is not available and the problem is too difficult to solve mentally.
Calculator	– Using a calculator or computer to find the solution.	– Use with large numbers or for a quick answer.
Trial and Error	– Making a guess at the answer and trying to see if it works.	– Use when unsure what to do or if none of the methods above work.

Directions: Circle the method of computation that seems best for solving each problem. Then solve the problem.

1. The School Days Fun Fair has 38 booths and 23 games. How many booths and games total are in the fair?

   • Paper and Pencil   Answer: _____

   • Objects/Diagram

2. The lemonade stand was stocked with 230 cups. On the first day, 147 drinks were sold. How many cups were left?

   • Objects/Diagram   Answer: _____

   • Paper and Pencil

3. There are 3 cars in the tram to transport people from the parking lot to the fair. Each car can seat 9 people. How many people can ride the tram at one time?

   • Objects/Diagram   Answer: _____

   • Trial and Error

Choosing a Method

Directions: Write what method you will use for each problem. Then find the answer.

1. Jenna receives an allowance of $3.50 a week. This week, her mother pays her in nickels, dimes and quarters. She received more dimes than quarters. How many of each coin did her mom use to pay her?

   Method: _____

   Answer: _____

2. You are buying your lunch at school. There are 4 people in front of you and 7 people behind you. How many people are standing in line? (Hint: it's not 11 people.)

   Method: _____

   Answer: _____

3. A runner can run 1 mile in 12 minutes. He ran for 30 minutes today. How far did he run?

   Method: _____

   Answer: _____

4. A family of four goes out to dinner. They decide to order a 16-cut pizza. Each person likes something different on his/her pizza, but each will eat equal amounts. Maria likes pepperoni and sausage, Tony likes ham and pineapple, Mom likes cheese only and Dad likes mushrooms. Maria is allergic to mushrooms, so her slices can't be next to Dad's. Mom detests pineapple, so her slices can't be next to Tony's. How will the restaurant arrange their pizza?

   Method: _____

   Answer: _____

5. The Petting Zoo has 72 animals in aquariums, 32 animals in cages and 57 animals fenced in. How many animals does the Petting Zoo have?

   Method: _____

   Answer: _____

Name: _____

Multi-Step Problems

Some problems take more than one step to solve. First, plan each step needed to find the solution. Then solve each part to find the answer.

Example: Tickets for a bargain matinee cost $4 for adults and $3 for children. How much would tickets cost for a family of 2 adults and 3 children?

Step 1: Find the cost of the adults' tickets.

Step 2: Find the cost of the children's tickets.

Step 3: Add to find the sum of the tickets.

2 adults	x	$4 each ticket	=	$8 total
3 children	x	$3 each ticket	=	$9 total
$8 adults	+	$9 children	=	$17 total

The tickets cost $17 total.

Directions: Write the operations you will use to solve each problem. Then find the answer.

1. Arden and her father are riding their bikes 57 miles to Arden's grandma's house. They ride 13 miles, then take a water break. Then they ride 15 miles to a rest area for a picnic lunch. How many miles do Arden and her father have left to ride after lunch?

   Operations: _____

   Answer: _____

2. A triathlete bikes 15 miles at 20 miles per hour, runs 5 miles at 6 miles per hour and swims 1 mile at 4 miles per hour. How long does the triathlon take her to complete?

   Operations: _____

   Answer: _____

3. Ray bought strawberries for $1.99, blueberries for $1.40 and 2 pints of raspberries for $1.25 per pint. How much did Ray spend on berries?

   Operations: _____

   Answer: _____

Hidden Questions

When solving a story problem, you may find that some information you want is not stated in the problem. You must ask yourself what information you need and decide how you can use the data in the problem to find this information. The problem contains a hidden question to find before you can solve it.

Example: Chris and his mother are building a birdhouse. He buys 4 pieces of wood for $2.20 each. How much change should he get back from $10?

Step 1: Find the hidden question:
What is the total cost of the wood? $2.20 x 4 = $8.80

Step 2: Use your answer to the hidden
question to solve the problem. $10.00 − $8.80 = $1.20

Directions: Write the hidden questions. Then solve the problems.

1. Chris used 3 nails to attach each board to the frame. After nailing 6 boards, he had 1 nail left. How many nails did Chris have before he started?

   Hidden Question: _____

   Answer: _____

2. Chris sawed a 72-inch post into 3 pieces. Two of the pieces were each 20 inches long. How long was the third piece?

   Hidden Question: _____

   Answer: _____

3. It took Chris and his mom 15 hours to make a birdhouse. They thought it would take 3 days. How many hours early did they complete the job?

   Hidden Question: _____

   Answer: _____

4. It takes Chris 15 hours to make a birdhouse and 9 hours to make a birdfeeder. He worked for 42 hours and made 1 birdhouse and some birdfeeders. How many birdfeeders did Chris make?

   Hidden Question: _____

   Answer: _____

Logic Problems

Directions: Use the clues below to figure out this logic problem.

Three friends all enjoy sports. Each of their favorite sports involves a ball. Two of these sports are played on courts, and one is played on a field.

- Rachel likes to run, and doesn't have to be a good catcher.

- Melinda is a good jumper.

- Betsy is also a good jumper, but she is a good ball handler.

Which sport does each girl play?

Melinda _____

Betsy _____

Rachel _____

Name: _____

A Cool Logic Problem

A family with five children went to the ice-cream shop. The children all ordered different flavors.

Directions: Use the clues and the chart to help you write which child ate which flavor of ice cream. Write a dot in the chart for the correct answer. Cross out all the other boxes in that row and column.

- No person had ice cream with the same first initial as his/her name.

- Neither of the twins, Corey and Cody, like peanut butter. Corey thinks vanilla is boring.

- The children are the twins, Vicki, the brother who got chocolate and the sister who ate peanut butter.

	Rocky Road	Chocolate Chip	Vanilla	Chocolate	Peanut Butter
Corey					
Cody					
Randa					
Vicki					
Paul					

Who ate which flavor?

Corey _____

Cody _____

Randa _____

Vicki _____

Paul _____

Perimeter

The **perimeter** is the distance around a shape formed by straight lines, such as a square or triangle. To find the perimeter of a shape, add the lengths of its sides.

Examples:

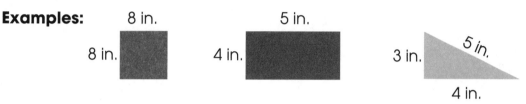

For the square, add 8 + 8 + 8 + 8 = 32. Or, write a formula using **P** for **perimeter** and **s** for the **sides**: $P = 4 \times s$
$P = 4 \times 8$
$P = 32$ inches

For the rectangle, add 4 + 5 + 4 + 5 = 18. Or, use a different formula, using **l** for **length** and **w** for **width**. In formulas with parentheses, first do the adding, multiplying, and so on, in the parentheses:

$$P = (2 \times l) + (2 \times w)$$
$$P = (2 \times 5) + (2 \times 4)$$
$$P = 10 + 8$$
$$P = 18$$

For the triangle, the sides are all different lengths, so the formula doesn't help. Instead, add the sides: 3 + 4 + 5 = 12 inches.

Directions: Find the perimeter of each shape below. Use the formula whenever possible.

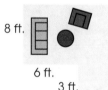

1. Find the perimeter of the room pictured at left.   P = _____

2. Brandy plans to frame a picture with a sheet of construction paper. Her picture is 8 in. wide and 13 in. long. She wants the frame to extend 1 in. beyond the picture on all sides. How wide and long should the frame be? What is the perimeter of her picture and of the frame?

Length and width of frame: _____

Perimeter of picture: _____

Perimeter of frame: _____

3. A square has a perimeter of 120 feet. How long is each side?   _____

4. A triangle with equal sides has a perimeter of 96 inches.
   How long is each side?   _____

5. A rectangle has two sides that are each 14 feet long and a
   perimeter of 50 feet. How wide is it?   _____

Perimeter

Directions: Find the perimeter of each shape below.

1.

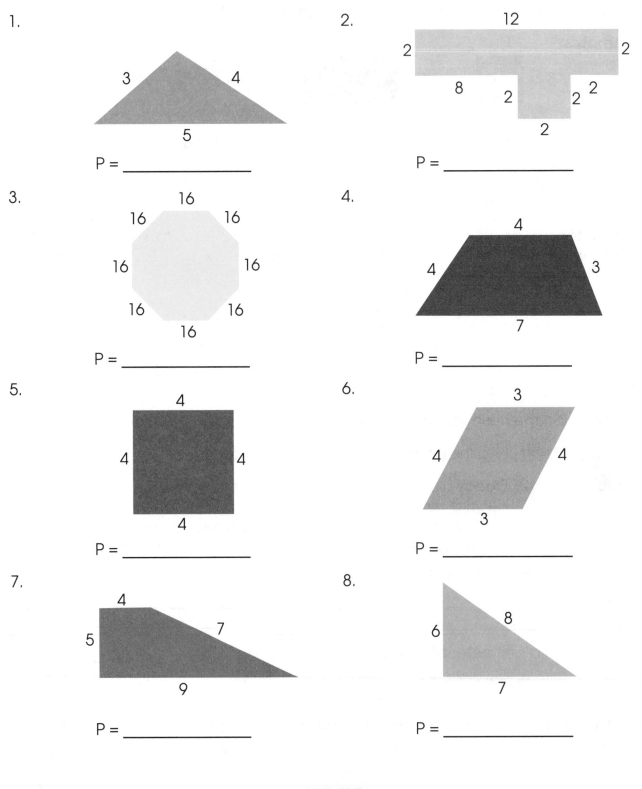

3   4

5

P = _____

2.

12

2   2

8   2   2 2

2

P = _____

3.

16

16   16

16   16

16   16

16

P = _____

4.

4

4   3

7

P = _____

5.

4

4   4

4

P = _____

6.

3

4   4

3

P = _____

7.

4

5   7

9

P = _____

8.

8

6

7

P = _____

Area: Squares and Rectangles

The **area** is the number of square units that covers a certain space. To find the area, multiply the length by the width. The answer is in square units, shown by adding a superscript 2 (^{2}) to the number.

Examples:

 3 in.

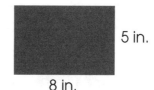 5 in.

8 in.

For the rectangle, use this formula: **A = l x w**
$$A = 8 \times 5$$
$$A = 40 \text{ in.}^2$$

For the square formula, **s** stands for side: **A = s x s** (or s^2)
$$A = 3 \times 3 \text{ (or } 3^2)$$
$$A = 9 \text{ in.}^2$$

Directions: Find the area of each shape below.

7 ft.

12 ft.

1. Find the area of a room which is 12 feet long and 7 feet wide.   A = _____

2. A farmer's field is 32 feet on each side. How many square feet does he have to plow?   _____

3. Steve's bedroom is 10 feet by 12 feet. How many square feet of carpeting would cover the floor?   _____

4. Two of Steve's walls are 7.5 feet high and 12 feet long. The other two are the same height and 10 feet long. How many square feet of wallpaper would cover all four walls?
Square feet for 12-foot wall = _____ x 2 = _____
Square feet for 10-foot wall = _____ x 2 = _____

5. A clothes shop moved from a store that was 35 by 22 feet to a new location that was 53 by 32 feet. How many more square feet does the store have now?
Square feet for first location = _____
Square feet for new location = _____ Difference = _____

6. A school wanted to purchase a climber for the playground. The one they selected would need 98 square feet of space. The only space available on the playground was 12 feet long and 8 feet wide. Will there be enough space for the climber? _____

Area: Triangles

Finding the area of a triangle requires knowing the size of the base and the height. For the triangle formula, use **b** for **base** and **h** for **height**. Multiply $\frac{1}{2}$ times the size of the base and then multiply by the height. The answer will be in square units.

Example:

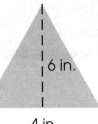

6 in.

4 in.

$A = \frac{1}{2} \times b \times h$

$A = \frac{1}{2} \times 4 \times 6$

$A = 12$ in.^{2}

Directions: Apply the formula to find the area of each triangle below.

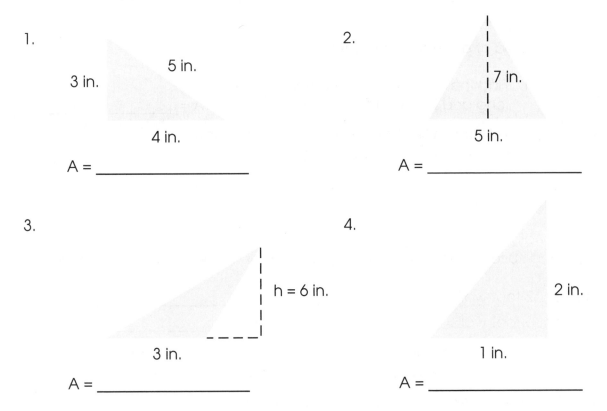

1.

5 in.

3 in.

4 in.

A = _____

2.

7 in.

5 in.

A = _____

3.

h = 6 in.

3 in.

A = _____

4.

2 in.

1 in.

A = _____

5. Diane wanted to make a sail for her new boat. The base of the triangular sail would be 7 feet and the height would be 6 feet. Find the area.

A = _____

Name: _____

Area Challenge

When finding the area of an unusual shape, first try to divide it into squares, rectangles or triangles. Find the area of each of those parts, then add your answers together to find the total area of the object.

Directions: Find the area of each shape below.

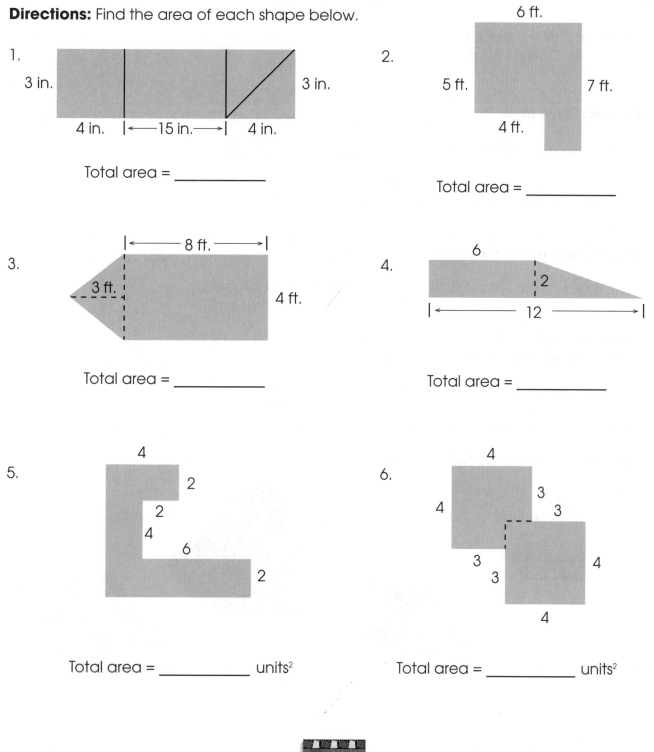

1.

3 in.   3 in.

4 in. |←—15 in.—→| 4 in.

Total area = _____

2.

6 ft.

5 ft.   7 ft.

4 ft.

Total area = _____

3.

|←——— 8 ft. ———→|

3 ft.   4 ft.

Total area = _____

4.

6

2

|←——— 12 ———→|

Total area = _____

5.

4

2

2

4

6

2

Total area = _____ units²

6.

4

3

4   3

3

3   4

3

4

Total area = _____ units²

Volume

Volume is the number of cubic units that fills a space. A **cubic unit** has 6 equal sides, like a child's block. To find the volume (**V**) of something, multiply the length (**l**) by the width (**w**) by the height (**h**), or **V = l x w x h**. The answer will be in cubic units (^{3}). Sometimes it's easier to understand volume if you imagine a figure is made of small cubes.

Example: **V = l x w x h**
V = 4 x 6 x 5
V = 120 in.^{3}

Directions: Solve the following problems.

1. What is the volume of a cube that is 7 inches on each side? _____

2. How many cubic inches of cereal are in a box that is 10 inches long, 6 inches wide and 4.5 inches high? _____

3. Jeremy made a tower of five blocks that are each 2.5 inches square. How many cubic inches are in his tower? _____

4. How many cubic feet of gravel are in the back of a full dump truck that measures 7 feet wide by 4 feet tall by 16 feet long? _____

5. Will 1,000 cubic inches of dirt fill a flower box that is 32 inches long, 7 inches wide and 7 inches tall? _____

6. A mouse needs 100 cubic inches of air to live for an hour. Will your pet mouse be okay for an hour in an airtight box that's 4.5 inches wide by 8.25 inches long by 2.5 inches high? _____

7. Find the volume of the figures below. 1 cube = 1 inch^3

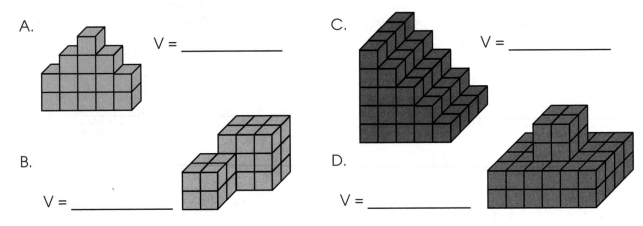

A. V = _____

B. V = _____

C. V = _____

D. V = _____

Name: _____

Geometric Patterns

Geometric patterns can be described in several ways. **Similar shapes** have the same shape but in differing sizes. **Congruent shapes** have the same geometric pattern but may be facing in different directions. **Symmetrical shapes** are identical when divided in half.

Directions: Use the terms **similar**, **congruent** or **symmetrical** to describe the following patterns.

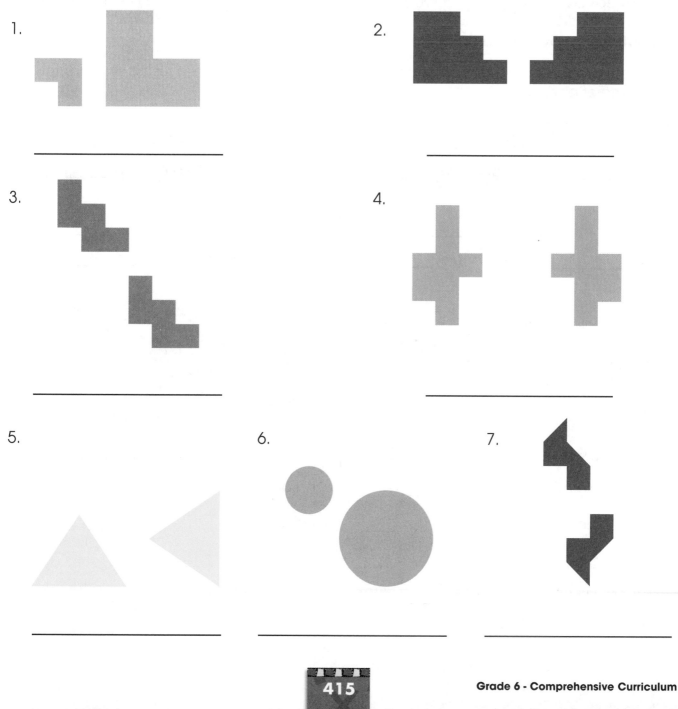

1. _____

2. _____

3. _____

4. _____

5. _____

6. _____

7. _____

Angles

Angles are named according to the number of degrees between the lines. The degrees are measured with a protractor.

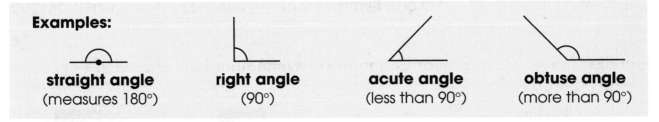

Examples:

| **straight angle** | **right angle** | **acute angle** | **obtuse angle** |
| (measures 180°) | (90°) | (less than 90°) | (more than 90°) |

Directions: Study the examples. Then follow the instructions below.

1. Use a protractor to measure each angle below. Then write whether it is straight, right, acute or obtuse.

A.

Degrees: _____

Kind of angle: _____

C.

Degrees: _____

Kind of angle: _____

B.

Degrees: _____

_____   Kind of angle: _____

D.

Degrees: _____

Kind of angle: _____

2. The angles in this figure are named by letters. Write the number of degrees in each angle and whether it is straight, right, acute or obtuse.

a. Angle AFB   Degrees: _____   Kind of angle: _____

b. Angle AFC   Degrees: _____   Kind of angle: _____

c. Angle AFD   Degrees: _____   Kind of angle: _____

d. Angle AFE   Degrees: _____   Kind of angle: _____

e. Angle BFD   Degrees: _____   Kind of angle: _____

Types of Triangles

The sum of angles in all triangles is 180°. However, triangles come in different shapes. They are categorized by the length of their sides and by their types of angles.

Equilateral:

Three equal sides

Acute:

Three acute angles

Isosceles:

Two equal sides

Right:

One right angle

Scalene:

Zero equal sides

Obtuse:

One obtuse angle

One triangle can be a combination of types, such as isosceles and obtuse.

Directions: Study the examples. Then complete the exercises below.

1. Read these directions and color in the correct triangles.

   Color the right scalene triangle blue.
   Color the obtuse scalene triangle red.
   Color the equilateral triangle yellow.
   Color the right isosceles triangle green.
   Color the acute isosceles triangle black.

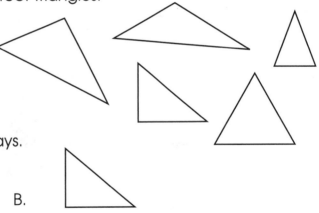

2. Describe each of these triangles in two ways.

   A.   B.

   _____ _____   _____ _____

3. In the space below, draw the following triangles.

   scalene triangle   equilateral triangle   obtuse triangle

Name: _____

Finding Angles

All triangles have three angles. The sum of these angles is 180°. Therefore, if we know the number of degrees in two of the angles, we can add them together, then subtract from 180 to find the size of the third angle.

Directions: Follow the instructions below.

1. Circle the number that shows the third angle of triangles A through F. Then describe each triangle two ways. The first one has been done for you.

   A. 60°, 60°   45° 50° (60°)   _____equilateral, acute_____

   B. 35°, 55°   27° 90° 132°   _____

   C. 30°, 120°   30° 74° 112°   _____

   D. 15°, 78°   65° 87° 98°   _____

   E. 28°, 93°   61° 59° 70°   _____

   F. 12°, 114°   60° 50° 54°   _____

2. Find the number of degrees in the third angle of each triangle below.

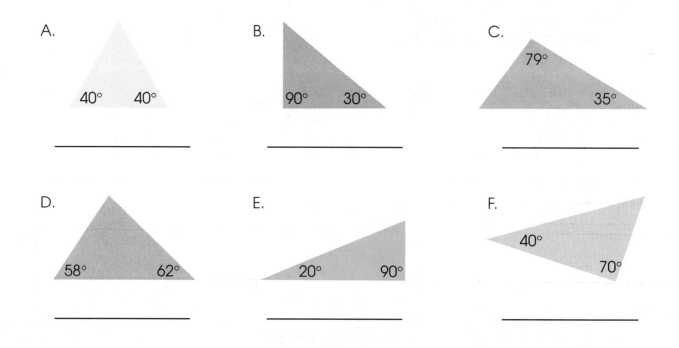

A.

40°   40°

_____

B.

90°   30°

_____

C.

79°

35°

_____

D.

58°   62°

_____

E.

20°   90°

_____

F.

40°

70°

_____

Types of Quadrilaterals

A **quadrilateral** is a shape with four sides and four angles. The sum of angles in all quadrilaterals is 360°. Like triangles, quadrilaterals come in different shapes and are categorized by their sides and their angles.

A **square** has four parallel sides of equal length and four 90° angles.

A **rectangle** has four parallel sides, but only its opposite sides are equal length; it has four 90° angles.

A **parallelogram** has four parallel sides, with the opposite sides of equal length.

A **trapezoid** has two opposite sides that are parallel; its sides may or may not be equal length; its angles may include none, one or two that are 90°.

Directions: Study the examples. Then complete the exercises below.

1. Color in the correct quadrilaterals.

Color two squares blue.
Color two parallelograms yellow.

Color two rectangles red.
Color two trapezoids green.

2. Circle the number that shows the missing angle for each quadrilateral. Then name the possible quadrilaterals that could have those angles.

A. 90°, 90°, 90°	45°	90°	180°	_____
B. 65°, 115°, 65°	65°	90°	115°	_____
C. 90°, 110°, 90°	45°	70°	125°	_____
D. 100°, 80°, 80°	40°	80°	100°	_____
E. 90°, 120°, 50°	50°	75°	100°	_____

Length in Customary Units

The **customary system** of measurement is the most widely used in the United States. It measures length in inches, feet, yards and miles.

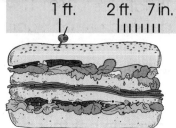

Examples:

12 inches (in.) = 1 foot (ft.)
3 ft. (36 in.) = 1 yard (yd.)
5,280 ft. (1,760 yds.) = 1 mile (mi.)

To change to a larger unit, divide. To change to a smaller unit, multiply.

Examples:
To change inches to feet, divide by 12.	24 in. = 2 ft.	27 in. = 2 ft. 3 in.
To change feet to inches, multiply by 12.	3 ft. = 36 in.	4 ft = 48 in.
To change inches to yards, divide by 36.	108 in. = 3 yd.	80 in. = 2 yd. 8 in.
To change feet to yards, divide by 3.	12 ft. = 4 yd.	11 ft. = 3 yd. 2 ft.

Sometimes in subtraction you have to borrow units.

Examples:

3 ft. 4 in.	=	2 ft. 16 in.		3 yd.	=	2 yd. 3 ft.
− 1 ft. 11 in.		− 1 ft. 11 in.		− 1 yd. 2 ft.		− 1 yd. 2 ft.
		1 ft. 5 in.				1 yd. 1 ft.

Directions: Solve the following problems.

1. 108 in. = _____ ft.

2. 68 in. = _____ ft. _____ in.

3. 8 ft. = _____ yd. _____ ft.

4. 3,520 yd. = _____ mi.

5. What form of measurement (inches, feet, yards or miles) would you use for each item below?

   a. pencil _____   b. vacation trip _____

   c. playground _____   d. wall _____

6. One side of a square box is 2 ft. 4 in. What is the perimeter of the box? _____

7. Jason is 59 in. tall. Kent is 5 ft. 1 in. tall. Who is taller and by how much? _____

8. Karen bought a doll 2 ft. 8 in. tall for her little sister. She found a box that is 29 in. long. Will the doll fit in that box? _____

9. Dan's dog likes to go out in the backyard, which is 85 ft. wide. The dog's chain is 17 ft. 6 in. long. If Dan attaches one end of the chain to a pole in the middle of the yard, will his dog be able to leave the yard? _____

Length in Metric Units

The **metric system** measures length in meters, centimeters, millimeters, and kilometers.

Examples:
  A **meter (m)** is about 40 inches or 3.3 feet.
  A **centimeter (cm)** is $\frac{1}{100}$ of a meter or 0.4 inches.
  A **millimeter (mm)** is $\frac{1}{1000}$ of a meter or 0.04 inches.
  A **kilometer (km)** is 1,000 meters or 0.6 miles.

As before, divide to find a larger unit and multiply to find a smaller unit.

Examples:
  To change cm to mm, multiply by 10.
  To change cm to meters, divide by 100.
  To change mm to meters, divide by 1,000.
  To change km to meters, multiply by 1,000.

Directions: Solve the following problems.

1. 600 cm = _____ m   2. 12 cm = _____ mm   3. 47 m = _____ cm   4. 3 km = _____ m

5. In the sentences below, write the missing unit: m, cm, mm or km.

    a. A fingernail is about 1 _____ thick.

    b. An average car is about 5 _____ long.

    c. Someone could walk 1 _____ in 10 minutes.

    d. A finger is about 7 _____ long.

    e. A street could be 3 _____ long.

    f. The Earth is about 40,000 _____ around at the equator.

    g. A pencil is about 17 _____ long.

    h. A noodle is about 4 _____ wide.

    i. A teacher's desk is about 1 _____ wide.

6. A nickel is about 1 mm thick. How many nickels would be in a stack 1 cm high?   _____

7. Is something 25 cm long closer to 10 inches or 10 feet?   _____

8. Is something 18 mm wide closer to 0.7 inch or 7 inches?   _____

9. Would you get more exercise running 4 km or 500 m?   _____

10. Which is taller, something 40 m or 350 cm?   _____

Weight in Customary Units

Here are the main ways to measure weight in customary units:

16 ounces (oz.) = 1 pound (lb.)
2,000 lb. = 1 ton (tn.)
To change ounces to pounds, divide by 16.
To change pounds to ounces, multiply by 16.

As with measurements of length, you may have to borrow units in subtraction.

BRIDGE UNSAFE FOR TRUCKS OVER 2 TONS

Example:	4 lb. 5 oz.	=	3 lb. 21 oz.
	– 2 lb. 10 oz.		– 2 lb. 10 oz.
			1 lb. 11 oz.

Directions: Solve the following problems.

1. 48 oz. = _____ lb.   2. 39 oz. = _____ lb.   3. 4 lb. = _____ oz.   4. 1.25 tn. = _____ lb.

5. What form of measurement would you use for each of these: ounces, pounds or tons?

   a. pencil _____   b. elephant _____   c. person _____

6. Which is heavier, 0.25 ton or 750 pounds?   _____

7. Twenty-two people, each weighing an average of 150 lb., want to get on an elevator that can carry up to 1.5 tons. How many of them should wait for the next elevator?   _____

8. A one ton truck is carrying 14 boxes that weigh 125 lb. each. It comes to a small bridge with a sign that says, "Bridge unsafe for trucks over 2 tons." Is it safe for the truck and the boxes to cross the bridge?   _____

9. A large box of Oat Boats contains 2 lb. 3 oz. of cereal, while a box of Honey Hunks contains 1 lb. 14 oz. How many more ounces are in the box of Oat Boats?   _____

10. A can of Peter's Powdered Drink Mix weighs 2 lb. 5 oz. A can of Petunia's Powdered Drink Mix weighs 40 oz. Which one is heavier?   _____

11. A can of Peter's Drink Mix is 12 cents an ounce. How much does it cost?   _____

12. How many 5-oz. servings could you get from a fish that weighs 3 lb. 12 oz.?   _____

Name: _____

Weight in Metric Units

A **gram** (**g**) is about 0.035 oz.
A **milligram** (**mg**) is $\frac{1}{1000}$ g or about 0.000035 oz.
A **kilogram** (**kg**) is 1,000 g or about 2.2 lb.
A **metric ton** (**t**) is 1,000 kg or about 1.1 tn.

To change g to mg, multiply by 1,000.
To change g to kg, divide by 1,000.
To change kg to g, multiply by 1,000.
To change t to kg, multiply by 1,000.

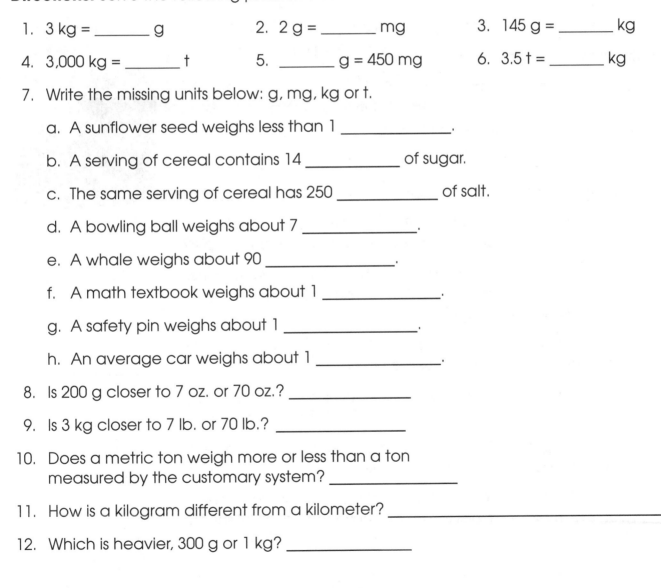

Directions: Solve the following problems.

1. 3 kg = _____ g

2. 2 g = _____ mg

3. 145 g = _____ kg

4. 3,000 kg = _____ t

5. _____ g = 450 mg

6. 3.5 t = _____ kg

7. Write the missing units below: g, mg, kg or t.

   a. A sunflower seed weighs less than 1 _____.

   b. A serving of cereal contains 14 _____ of sugar.

   c. The same serving of cereal has 250 _____ of salt.

   d. A bowling ball weighs about 7 _____.

   e. A whale weighs about 90 _____.

   f. A math textbook weighs about 1 _____.

   g. A safety pin weighs about 1 _____.

   h. An average car weighs about 1 _____.

8. Is 200 g closer to 7 oz. or 70 oz.? _____

9. Is 3 kg closer to 7 lb. or 70 lb.? _____

10. Does a metric ton weigh more or less than a ton measured by the customary system? _____

11. How is a kilogram different from a kilometer? _____

12. Which is heavier, 300 g or 1 kg? _____

Name: _____

Capacity in Customary Units

Here are the main ways to measure capacity (how much something will hold) in customary units:

8 fluid ounces (fl. oz.) = 1 cup (c.)
2 c. = 1 pint (pt.)
2 pt. = 1 quart (qt.)
4 qt. = 1 gallon (gal.)

To change ounces to cups, divide by 8.
To change cups to ounces, multiply by 8.
To change cups to pints or quarts, divide by 2.
To change pints to cups or quarts to pints, multiply by 2.

As with measurements of length and weight, you may have to borrow units in subtraction.

Example: 3 gal. 2 qt. =   2 gal. 6 qt.
                – 1 gal. 3 qt.   – 1 gal. 3 qt.
                                 1 gal. 3 qt.

Directions: Solve the following problems.

1. 32 fl. oz. = _____ pt.   2. 4 gal. = _____ pt.   3. _____ c. = 24 fl. oz.

4. 5 pt. = _____ qt.   5. 16 pt. = _____ gal.   6. 3 pt. = _____ fl. oz.

7. A large can of soup contains 19 fl. oz. A serving is about 8 oz.
   How many cans should you buy if you want to serve 7 people?   _____

8. A container of strawberry ice cream holds 36 fl. oz. A container
   of chocolate ice cream holds 2 pt. Which one has more ice
   cream? How much more?   _____

9. A day-care worker wants to give 15 children each 6 fl. oz. of milk.
   How many quarts of milk does she need?   _____

10. This morning, the day-care supervisor bought 3 gal. of milk.
    The kids drank 2 gal. 3 c. How much milk is left for tomorrow?   _____

11. Harriet bought 3 gal. 2 qt. of paint for her living room. She used
    2 gal. 3 qt. How much paint is left over?   _____

12. Jason's favorite punch takes a pint of raspberry sherbet. If he
    wants to make $1\frac{1}{2}$ times the recipe, how many fl. oz. of sherbet
    does he need?   _____

Capacity in Metric Units

A **liter** (**L**) is a little over 1 quart.
A **milliliter** (**mL**) is $\frac{1}{1000}$ of a liter or about 0.03 oz.
A **kiloliter** (**kL**) is 1,000 liters or about 250 gallons.

Directions: Solve the following problems.

1. 5,000 mL = _____ L

2. 2,000 L = _____ kL

3. 3 L = _____ mL

4. Write the missing unit: L, mL or kL.

   a. A swimming pool holds about 100 _____ of water.

   b. An eyedropper is marked for 1 and 2 _____.

   c. A pitcher could hold 1 or 2 _____ of juice.

   d. A teaspoon holds about 5 _____ of medicine.

   e. A birdbath might hold 5 _____ of water.

   f. A tablespoon holds about 15 _____ of salt.

   g. A bowl holds about 250 _____ of soup.

   h. We drank about 4 _____ of punch at the party.

5. Which is more, 3 L or a gallon? _____

6. Which is more, 400 mL or 40 oz.? _____

7. Which is more, 1 kL or 500 L? _____

8. Is 4 L closer to a quart or a gallon? _____

9. Is 480 mL closer to 2 cups or 2 pints? _____

10. Is a mL closer to 4 drops or 4 teaspoonsful? _____

11. How many glasses of juice containing 250 mL each could you pour from a 1-L jug? _____

12. How much water would you need to water an average-sized lawn, 1 kL or 1 L? _____

Temperature in Customary and Metric Units

The customary system measures temperature in Fahrenheit (F°) degrees.

220 — 212° boiling
200
180
160
140
120
100
80
60
40 — 32° freezing
20
0
−20

The metric system uses Celsius (C°) degrees.

110
100 — 100° boiling
90
80
60
40
30
20
10
0 — 0° freezing
−10
−20

Directions: Study the thermometers and answer these questions.

1. Write in the temperature from both systems:

	Fahrenheit	**Celsius**
a. freezing	_____	_____
b. boiling	_____	_____
c. comfortable room temperature	_____	_____
d. normal body temperature	_____	_____

2. Underline the most appropriate temperature for both systems.

   a. a reasonably hot day   34°   54°   84°   10°   20°   35°

   b. a cup of hot chocolate   95°   120°   190°   60°   90°   120°

   c. comfortable water to swim in   55°   75°   95°   10°   25°   40°

3. If the temperature is 35°C is it summer or winter?   _____

4. Would ice cream stay frozen at 35°F?   _____

5. Which is colder, −10°C or −10°F?   _____

6. Which is warmer, 60°C or 60°F?   _____

Name: _____

Review

Directions: Complete the following exercises.

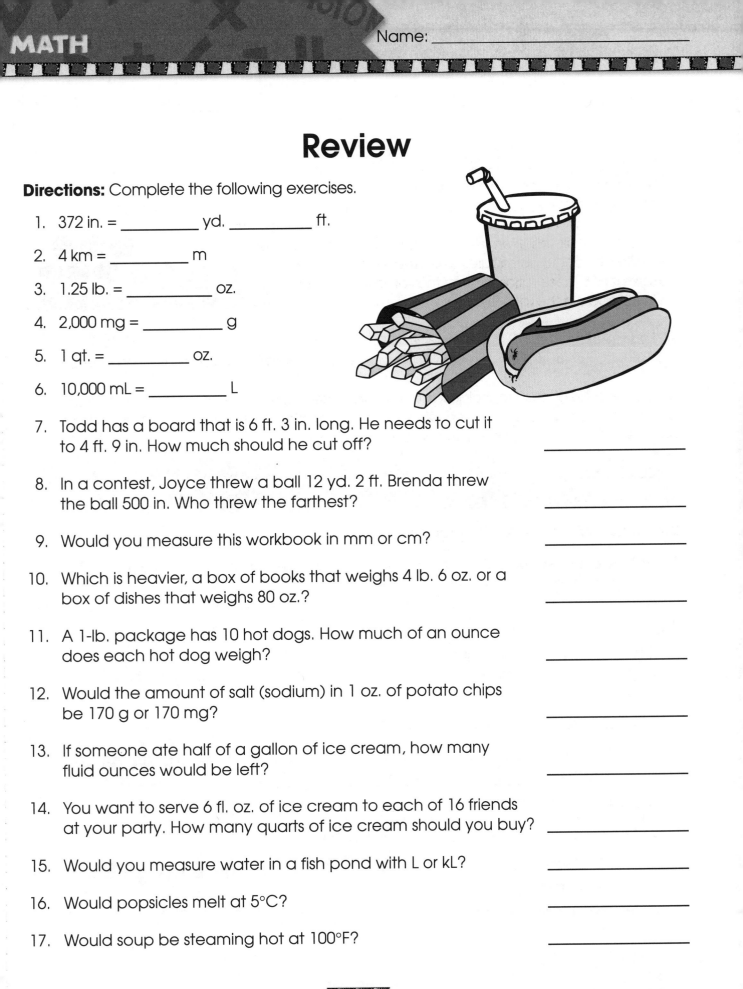

1. 372 in. = _____ yd. _____ ft.

2. 4 km = _____ m

3. 1.25 lb. = _____ oz.

4. 2,000 mg = _____ g

5. 1 qt. = _____ oz.

6. 10,000 mL = _____ L

7. Todd has a board that is 6 ft. 3 in. long. He needs to cut it to 4 ft. 9 in. How much should he cut off?   _____

8. In a contest, Joyce threw a ball 12 yd. 2 ft. Brenda threw the ball 500 in. Who threw the farthest?   _____

9. Would you measure this workbook in mm or cm?   _____

10. Which is heavier, a box of books that weighs 4 lb. 6 oz. or a box of dishes that weighs 80 oz.?   _____

11. A 1-lb. package has 10 hot dogs. How much of an ounce does each hot dog weigh?   _____

12. Would the amount of salt (sodium) in 1 oz. of potato chips be 170 g or 170 mg?   _____

13. If someone ate half of a gallon of ice cream, how many fluid ounces would be left?   _____

14. You want to serve 6 fl. oz. of ice cream to each of 16 friends at your party. How many quarts of ice cream should you buy?   _____

15. Would you measure water in a fish pond with L or kL?   _____

16. Would popsicles melt at 5°C?   _____

17. Would soup be steaming hot at 100°F?   _____

Ratios

A **ratio** is a comparison of two quantities. For example, a wall is 96 in. high; a pencil is 8 in. long. By dividing 8 into 96, you find it would take 12 pencils to equal the height of the wall. The ratio, or comparison, of the wall to the pencil can be written three ways: 1 to 12; 1:12; $\frac{1}{12}$. In this example, the ratio of triangles to circles is 4:6. The ratio of triangles to squares is 4:9. The ratio of circles to squares is 6:9. These ratios will stay the same if we divide both numbers in the ratio by the same number.

Examples: $\dfrac{4 \div 2 = 2}{6 \div 2 = 3}$ $\dfrac{6 \div 3 = 2}{9 \div 3 = 3}$ (There is no number that will divide into both 4 and 9.)

By reducing 4:6 and 6:9 to their lowest terms, they are the same—2:3. This means that 2:3, 4:6 and 6:9 are all equal ratios. You can also find equal ratios for all three by multiplying both numbers of the ratio by the same number.

Examples: $\dfrac{4 \times 3 = 12}{6 \times 3 = 18}$ $\dfrac{6 \times 5 = 30}{9 \times 5 = 45}$ $\dfrac{4 \times 4 = 16}{9 \times 4 = 36}$

Directions: Solve the following problems.

1. Write two more equal ratios for each of the following by multiplying or dividing both numbers in the ratio by the same number.

    a. $\dfrac{1}{2}$ $\dfrac{2}{4}$ $\dfrac{3}{6}$ _____ _____

    b. $\dfrac{1}{4}$ $\dfrac{2}{8}$ $\dfrac{4}{16}$ _____ _____

    c. $\dfrac{8}{24}$ $\dfrac{1}{3}$ $\dfrac{3}{9}$ _____ _____

2. Circle the ratios that are equal.

    a. $\dfrac{1}{6}$ $\dfrac{3}{6}$ b. $\dfrac{15}{25}$ $\dfrac{3}{5}$ c. $\dfrac{2}{7}$ $\dfrac{10}{35}$ d. $\dfrac{2}{3}$ $\dfrac{6}{10}$

3. Write each ratio three ways.

    a. stars to crosses _____

    b. crosses to trees _____

    c. stars to all other shapes _____

4. Write two equal ratios (multiplying or dividing) for:

    a. stars to crosses _____

    b. crosses to trees _____

    c. stars to all other shapes _____

Name: _____

Missing Numbers in Ratios

You can find a missing number (n) in an equal ratio. First, figure out which number has already been multiplied to get the number you know. (In the first example, 3 is multiplied by 3 to get 9; in the second example, 2 is multiplied by 6 to get 12.) Then multiply the other number in the ratio by the same number (3 and 6 in the examples).

Examples: $\frac{3}{4} = \frac{9}{n}$ $\quad \frac{3}{4} \times \frac{3}{3} = \frac{9}{12}$ $\quad n = 12$ $\qquad \frac{1}{2} = \frac{n}{12}$ $\quad \frac{1}{2} \times \frac{6}{6} = \frac{6}{12}$ $\quad n = 6$

Directions: Solve the following problems.

1. Find each missing number.

   a. $\frac{1}{2} = \frac{n}{12}$ $\quad n =$ _____

   b. $\frac{1}{5} = \frac{n}{15}$ $\quad n =$ _____

   c. $\frac{3}{2} = \frac{18}{n}$ $\quad n =$ _____

   d. $\frac{5}{8} = \frac{n}{32}$ $\quad n =$ _____

   e. $\frac{8}{3} = \frac{16}{n}$ $\quad n =$ _____

   f. $\frac{n}{14} = \frac{5}{7}$ $\quad n =$ _____

2. If a basketball player makes 9 baskets in 12 tries, what is her ratio of baskets to tries, in lowest terms?

   _____

3. At the next game, the player has the same ratio of baskets to tries. If she tries 20 times, how many baskets should she make?

   _____

4. At the third game, she still has the same ratio of baskets to tries. This time she makes 12 baskets. How many times did she probably try?

   _____

5. If a driver travels 40 miles in an hour, what is his ratio of miles to minutes, in lowest terms?

   _____

6. At the same speed, how far would the driver travel in 30 minutes?

   _____

7. At the same speed, how long would it take him to travel 60 miles?

   _____

Name: _____

Proportions

A **proportion** is a statement that two ratios are equal. To make sure ratios are equal, called a proportion, we multiply the cross products.

Examples of proportions: $\frac{1}{5} = \frac{2}{10}$ $\frac{1}{2} \times \frac{10}{5} = \frac{10}{10}$ $\frac{3}{7} = \frac{15}{35}$ $\frac{3}{7} \times \frac{35}{15} = \frac{105}{105}$

These two ratios are not a proportion: $\frac{4}{3} = \frac{5}{6}$ $\frac{4}{3} \times \frac{6}{5} = \frac{24}{15}$

To find a missing number (*n*) in a proportion, multiply the cross products and divide.

Examples:

$$\frac{n}{30} = \frac{1}{6}$$

$n \times 6 = 1 \times 30$ $n \times 6 = 30$

$n = \frac{30}{6}$

$n = 5$

Directions: Solve the following problems.

1. Write = between the ratios if they are a proportion. Write ≠ if they are not a proportion. The first one has been done for you.

   a. $\frac{1}{2}$ ⬭= $\frac{6}{12}$ b. $\frac{13}{18}$ ◯ $\frac{20}{22}$ c. $\frac{2}{6}$ ◯ $\frac{5}{15}$ d. $\frac{5}{6}$ ◯ $\frac{20}{24}$

2. Find the missing numbers in these proportions.

   a. $\frac{2}{5} = \frac{n}{15}$ *n* = _____   b. $\frac{3}{8} = \frac{9}{n}$ *n* = _____   c. $\frac{n}{18} = \frac{4}{12}$ *n* = _____

3. One issue of a magazine costs $2.99, but if you buy a subscription, 12 issues cost $35.88. Is the price at the same proportion?   _____

4. A cookie recipe calls for 3 cups of flour to make 36 cookies. How much flour is needed for 48 cookies?   _____

5. The same recipe requires 4 teaspoons of cinnamon for 36 cookies. How many teaspoons is needed to make 48 cookies? (Answer will include a fraction.)   _____

6. The recipe also calls for 2 cups of sugar for 36 cookies. How much sugar should you use for 48 cookies? (Answer will include a fraction.)   _____

7. If 2 kids can eat 12 cookies, how many can 8 kids eat?   _____

Name: _____

Percents

Percent means "per 100." A percent is a ratio that compares a number with 100. The same number can be written as a decimal and a percent. To change a decimal to a percent, move the decimal point two places to the right and add the % sign. To change a percent to a decimal, drop the % sign and place a decimal point two places to the left.

Examples: 0.25 = 25%   0.1 = 10%   1.456 = 145.6%
               32% = 0.32   99% = 0.99   203% = 2.03

A percent or decimal can also be written as a ratio or fraction.

Example: $0.25 = 25\% = \dfrac{25}{100} = \dfrac{1}{4} = 1{:}4$

To change a fraction or ratio to a percent, first change it to a decimal. Divide the numerator by the denominator.

Examples: $\dfrac{1}{3} = 3\overline{)1.00}$ $0.33\tfrac{1}{3} = 33\tfrac{1}{3}\%$ $\dfrac{2}{5} = 5\overline{)2.0}$ $0.4 = 40\%$

Directions: Solve the following problems.

1. Change the percents to decimals.

   a. 3% = _____   b. 75% = _____   c. 14% = _____   d. 115% = _____

2. Change the decimals and fractions to percents.

   a. 0.56 = _____ %   b. 0.03 = _____ %   c. $\dfrac{3}{4}$ = _____ %   d. $\dfrac{1}{5}$ = _____ %

3. Change the percents to ratios in their lowest terms. The first one has been done for you.

   a. 75% = _____ $\dfrac{75}{100} = \dfrac{3}{4} = 3{:}4$ _____   b. 40% = _____

   c. 35% = _____   d. 70% = _____

4. The class was 45% girls. What percent was boys?   _____

5. Half the shoes in one store were on sale. What percent
   of the shoes were their ordinary price?   _____

6. Kim read 84 pages of a 100-page book. What percent
   of the book did she read?   _____

Percents

To find the percent of a number, change the percent to a decimal and multiply.

Examples: 45% of $20 = 0.45 x $20 = $9.00
125% of 30 = 1.25 x 30 = 37.50

Directions: Solve the following problems. Round off the answers to the nearest hundredth where necessary.

1. Find the percent of each number.

    a. 26% of 40 = _____   b. 12% of 329 = _____

    c. 73% of 19 = _____   d. 2% of 24 = _____

2. One family spends 35% of its weekly budget of $150 on food. How much do they spend?   _____

3. A shirt in a store usually costs $15.99, but today it's on sale for 25% off. The clerk says you will save $4.50. Is that true?   _____

4. A book that usually costs $12 is on sale for 25% off. How much will it cost?   _____

5. After you answer 60% of 150 math problems, how many do you have left to do?   _____

6. A pet store's shipment of tropical fish was delayed. Nearly 40% of the 1,350 fish died. About how many lived?   _____

7. The shipment had 230 angelfish, which died in the same proportion as the other kinds of fish. About how many angelfish died?   _____

8. A church youth group was collecting cans of food. Their goal was 1,200 cans, but they exceeded their goal by 25%. How many cans did they collect?   _____

Name: _____

Probability

Probability is the ratio of favorable outcomes to possible outcomes in an experiment. You can use probability (P) to figure out how likely something is to happen. For example, six picture cards are turned facedown—3 cards have stars, 2 have triangles and 1 has a circle. What is the probability of picking the circle? Using the formula below, you have a 1 in 6 probability of picking the circle, a 2 in 6 probability of picking a triangle and a 3 in 6 probability of picking a star.

Example: $\underline{P = \dfrac{\text{number of favorable outcomes}}{\text{number of trials}}}$ $P = \dfrac{1}{6} = 1{:}6$

Directions: Solve the following problems.

1. A class has 14 girls and 15 boys. If all of their names are put on separate slips in a hat, what is the probability of each person's name being chosen?   _____

2. In the same class, what is the probability that a girl's name will be chosen?   _____

3. In this class, 3 boys are named Mike. What is the probability that a slip with "Mike" written on it will be chosen?   _____

4. A spinner on a board game has the numbers 1–8. What is the probability of spinning and getting a 4?   _____

5. A paper bag holds these colors of wooden beads: 4 blue, 5 red and 6 yellow. If you select a bead without looking, do you have an equal probability of getting each color?   _____

6. Using the same bag of beads, what is the probability of reaching in and drawing out a red bead (in lowest terms)?   _____

7. In the same bag, what is the probability of not getting a blue bead?   _____

8. In a carnival game, plastic ducks have spots. The probability of picking a duck with a yellow spot is 2:15. There is twice as much probability of picking a duck with a red spot. What is the probability of picking a duck with a red spot?   _____

9. In this game, all the other ducks have green spots. What is the probability of picking a duck with a green spot (in lowest terms)?   _____

Possible Combinations

Today the cafeteria is offering 4 kinds of sandwiches, 3 kinds of drinks and 2 kinds of cookies. How many possible combinations could you make? To find out, multiply the number of choices together.

Example: 4 x 3 x 2 = 24 possible combinations

Directions: Solve the following problems.

1. If Juan has 3 shirts and 4 pairs of shorts, how many combinations can he make? _____

2. Janice can borrow 1 book and 1 magazine at a time from her classroom library. The library has 45 books and 16 magazines. How many combinations are possible? _____

3. Kerry's mother is redecorating the living room. She has narrowed her choices to 6 kinds of wallpaper, 3 shades of paint and 4 colors of carpeting that all match. How many possible combinations are there? _____

4. Pam has 6 sweaters that she can combine with pants to make 24 outfits. How many pairs of pants does she have? _____

5. Kenny can get to school by walking, taking a bus, riding his bike or asking his parents for a ride. He can get home the same ways, except his parents aren't available then. How many combinations can he make of ways to get to school and get home? _____

6. Sue's middle school offers 3 different language classes, 3 art classes and 2 music classes. If she takes one class in each area, how many possible combinations are there? _____

7. Bart's school offers 4 language classes, 3 art classes and some music classes. If Bart can make 36 possible combinations, how many music classes are there? _____

8. AAA Airlines schedules 12 flights a day from Chicago to Atlanta. Four of those flights go on to Orlando. From the Orlando airport you can take a bus, ride in a taxi or rent a car to get to Disneyworld. How many different ways are there to get from Chicago to Disneyworld if you make part of your trip on AAA Airlines? _____

Name: _____

Review

Directions: Solve the following problems. Round answers to the nearest hundredth where necessary.

1. Write an equal ratio for each of these:

   a. $\dfrac{1}{7}$ = _____   b. $\dfrac{5}{8}$ = _____   c. $\dfrac{15}{3}$ = _____   d. $\dfrac{6}{24}$ = _____

2. State the ratios below in lowest terms.

   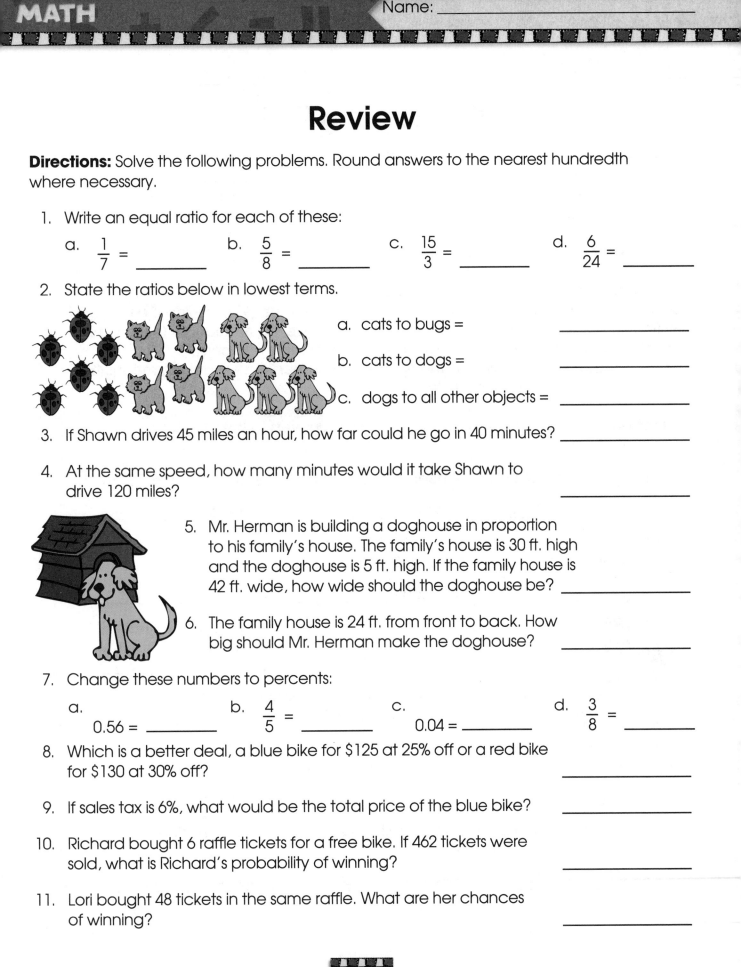

   a. cats to bugs = _____

   b. cats to dogs = _____

   c. dogs to all other objects = _____

3. If Shawn drives 45 miles an hour, how far could he go in 40 minutes? _____

4. At the same speed, how many minutes would it take Shawn to drive 120 miles? _____

5. Mr. Herman is building a doghouse in proportion to his family's house. The family's house is 30 ft. high and the doghouse is 5 ft. high. If the family house is 42 ft. wide, how wide should the doghouse be? _____

6. The family house is 24 ft. from front to back. How big should Mr. Herman make the doghouse? _____

7. Change these numbers to percents:

   a. 0.56 = _____   b. $\dfrac{4}{5}$ = _____   c. 0.04 = _____   d. $\dfrac{3}{8}$ = _____

8. Which is a better deal, a blue bike for $125 at 25% off or a red bike for $130 at 30% off? _____

9. If sales tax is 6%, what would be the total price of the blue bike? _____

10. Richard bought 6 raffle tickets for a free bike. If 462 tickets were sold, what is Richard's probability of winning? _____

11. Lori bought 48 tickets in the same raffle. What are her chances of winning? _____

Name: _____

Comparing Data

Data (**datum**—singular) are gathered information. The **range** is the difference between the highest and lowest number in a group of numbers. The **median** is the number in the middle when numbers are listed in order. The **mean** is the average of the numbers. We can compare numbers or data by finding the range, median and mean.

Example: 16, 43, 34, 78, 8, 91, 26

To compare these numbers, we first need to put them in order: 8 16 26 34 43 78 91. By subtracting the lowest number (8) from the highest one (91), we find the range: 83. By finding the number that falls in the middle, we have the median: 34 (If no number fell exactly in the middle, we would average the two middle numbers.) By adding them and dividing by the number of numbers (7), we get the mean: 42.29 (rounded to the nearest hundredth).

Directions: Solve the following problems. Round answers to the nearest hundredth where necessary.

1. Find the range, median and mean of these numbers: 19, 5, 84, 27, 106, 38, 75.

   Range: _____   Median: _____   Mean: _____

2. Find the range, median and mean finishing times for 6 runners in a race. Here are their times in seconds: 14.2, 12.9, 13.5, 10.3, 14.8, 14.7.

   Range: _____   Median: _____   Mean: _____

3. If the runner who won the race in 10.3 seconds had run even faster and finished in 7 seconds, would the mean time be higher or lower? _____

4. If that runner had finished in 7 seconds, what would be the median time? _____

5. Here are the high temperatures in one city for a week: 65, 72, 68, 74, 81, 68, 85. Find the range, median and mean temperatures.

   Range: _____   Median: _____   Mean: _____

6. Find the range, median and mean test scores for this group of students: 41, 32, 45, 36, 48, 38, 37, 42, 39, 36.

   Range: _____   Median: _____   Mean: _____

Tables

Organizing data into tables makes it easier to compare numbers. As evident in the example, putting many numbers in a paragraph is confusing. When the same numbers are organized in a table, you can compare numbers in a glance. Tables can be arranged several ways and still be easy to read and understand.

Example: Money spent on groceries:
Family A: week 1 — $68.50; week 2 — $72.25; week 3 — $67.00; week 4 — $74.50.
Family B: week 1 — $42.25; week 2 — $47.50; week 3 — $50.25; week 4 — $53.50.

	Week 1	**Week 2**	**Week 3**	**Week 4**
Family A	$68.50	$72.25	$67.00	$74.50
Family B	$42.25	$47.50	$50.25	$53.50

Directions: Complete the following exercises.

1. Finish the table below, then answer the questions.
   Data: Steve weighs 230 lb. and is 6 ft. 2 in. tall. George weighs 218 lb. and is 6 ft. 3 in. tall. Chuck weighs 225 lb. and is 6 ft. 1 in. tall. Henry weighs 205 lb. and is 6 ft. tall.

	Henry	**George**	**Chuck**	**Steve**
Weight				
Height				

   a. Who is tallest?_____   b. Who weighs the least?_____

2. On another sheet of paper, prepare 2 tables comparing the amount of money made by 3 booths at the school carnival this year and last year. In the first table, write the names of the games in the left-hand column (like **Family A** and **Family B** in the example). In the second table (using the same data), write the years in the left-hand column. Here is the data: fish pond—this year $15.60, last year $13.50; bean-bag toss—this year $13.45, last year $10.25; ring toss—this year $23.80, last year $18.80. After you complete both tables, answer the following questions.

   a. Which booth made the most money this year?   _____

   b. Which booth made the biggest improvement from last year to this year?_____

Bar Graphs

Another way to organize information is a **bar graph**. The bar graph in the example compares the number of students in 4 elementary schools. Each bar stands for 1 school. You can easily see that School A has the most students and School C has the least. The numbers along the left show how many students attend each school.

Example:

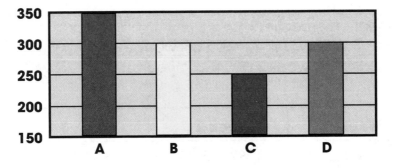

Directions: Complete the following exercises.

1. This bar graph will show how many calories are in 1 serving of 4 kinds of cereal. Draw the bars the correct height and label each with the name of the cereal. After completing the bar graph, answer the questions. Data: Korn Kernals—150 calories; Oat Floats—160 calories; Rite Rice—110 calories; Sugar Shapes—200 calories.

    A. Which cereal is the best to eat if you're trying to lose weight?   _____

    B. Which cereal has nearly the same number of calories as Oat Floats? _____

2. On another sheet of paper, draw your own graph, showing the number of TV commercials in 1 week for each of the 4 cereals in the graph above. After completing the graph, answer the questions. Data: Oat Boats—27 commercials; Rite Rice—15; Sugar Shapes—35; Korn Kernals—28.

    A. Which cereal is most heavily advertised?   _____

    B. What similarities do you notice between the graph of calories and the graph of TV commercials? _____

Name: _____

Picture Graphs

Newspapers and textbooks often use pictures in graphs instead of bars. Each picture stands for a certain number of objects. Half a picture means half the number. The picture graph in the example indicates the number of games each team won. The Astros won 7 games, so they have $3\frac{1}{2}$ balls.

Example:

	Games Won
Astros	⚾ ⚾ ⚾ ◖
Orioles	⚾ ⚾
Bluebirds	⚾ ⚾ ⚾ ⚾
Sluggers	⚾

(1 ball = 2 games)

Directions: Complete the following exercises.

Finish this picture graph, showing the number of students who have dogs in 4 sixth-grade classes. Draw simple dogs in the graph, letting each drawing stand for 2 dogs.
Data: Class 1—12 dogs; Class 2—16 dogs; Class 3—22 dogs; Class 4—12 dogs.
After completing the graph, answer the questions.

	Dogs Owned by Students
Class 1	
Class 2	
Class 3	
Class 4	

(One dog drawing = 2 students' dogs)

1. Why do you think newspapers use picture graphs?_____
   _____

2. Would picture graphs be appropriate to show exact number of dogs living in America? Why or why not?_____
   _____

Name: _____

Line Graphs

Still another way to display information is a line graph. The same data can often be shown in both a bar graph and a line graph. Nevertheless, line graphs are especially useful in showing changes over a period of time.

The line graph in the example shows changes in the number of students enrolled in a school over a 5-year period. Enrollment was highest in 1988 and has decreased gradually each year since then. Notice how labeling the years and enrollment numbers make the graph easy to understand.

Example:

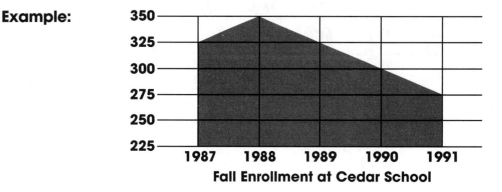

Fall Enrollment at Cedar School

Directions: Complete the following exercises.

1. On another sheet of paper, draw a line graph that displays the growth of a corn plant over a 6-week period. Mark the correct points, using the data below, and connect them with a line. After completing the graph, answer the questions. Data: week 1—3.5 in.; week 2—4.5 in.; week 3—5 in.; week 4—5.5 in.; week 5—5.75 in.; week 6—6 in.

   a. Between which weeks was the growth fastest? _____

   b. Between which weeks was the growth slowest? _____

2. On another sheet of paper draw a line graph to show how the high temperature varied during one week. Then answer the questions. Data: Sunday—high of 53 degrees; Monday—51; Tuesday—56; Wednesday—60; Thursday—58; Friday—67; Saturday—73. Don't forget to label the numbers.

   a. In general, did the days get warmer or cooler? _____

   b. Do you think this data would have been as clear in a bar graph? _____
      Explain your answer.

      _____

      _____

Name: _____

Circle Graphs

Circle graphs are useful in showing how something is divided into parts. The circle graph in the example shows how Carly spent her $10 allowance. Each section is a fraction of her whole allowance. For example, the movie tickets section is $\frac{1}{2}$ of the circle, showing that she spent $\frac{1}{2}$ of her allowance, $5, on movie tickets.

Directions: Complete the following exercises.

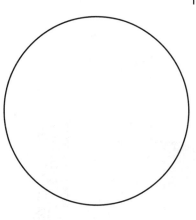

1. When the middle school opened last fall, $\frac{1}{2}$ of the students came from East Elementary, $\frac{1}{4}$ came from West Elementary, $\frac{1}{8}$ came from North Elementary and the remaining students moved into the town from other cities. Make a circle graph showing these proportions. Label each section. Then answer the questions.

   a. What fraction of students at the new school moved into the area from other cities? _____

   b. If the new middle school has 450 students enrolled, how many used to go to East Elementary? _____

2. This circle graph will show the hair color of 24 students in one class. Divide the circle into 4 sections to show this data: black hair—8 students; brown hair—10 students; blonde hair—4 students; red hair—2 students. (Hint: 8 students are $\frac{8}{24}$ or $\frac{1}{3}$ of the class.) Be sure to label each section by hair color. Then answer the questions.

   a. Looking at your graph, what fraction of the class is the combined group of blonde- and red-haired students? _____

   b. Which two fractions of hair color combine to total half the class? _____

Comparing Presentation Methods

Tables and different kinds of graphs have different purposes. Some are more helpful for certain kinds of information. The table and three graphs below all show basically the same information—the amount of money Mike and Margaret made in their lawn-mowing business over a 4-month period.

Combined Income per Month

	Mike	Margaret
June	$34	$36
July	41	35
August	27	28
Sept.	36	40
Totals	$138	$139

Combined Income per Month

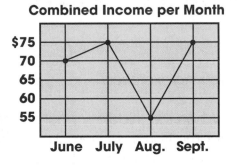

Combined Income per Month

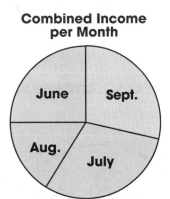

Combined Income per Month

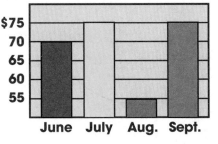

Directions: Study the graphs and table. Then circle the one that answers each question below.

1. Which one shows the fraction of the total income that Mike and Margaret made in August?

   table   line graph   bar graph   circle graph

2. Which one compares Mike's earnings with Margaret's?

   table   line graph   bar graph   circle graph

3. Which one has the most exact numbers?

   table   line graph   bar graph   circle graph

4. Which one has no numbers?

   table   line graph   bar graph   circle graph

5. Which two best show how Mike and Margaret's income changed from month to month?

   table   line graph   bar graph   circle graph

Graphing Data

Directions: Complete the following exercises.

1. Use the following information to create a bar graph.

Cities	Population (in 1,000's)
Dover	20
Newton Falls	12
Springdale	25
Hampton	17
Riverside	5

2. Study the data and create a line graph showing the number of baskets Jonah scored during the season.

Game 1 — 10
Game 2 — 7
Game 3 — 11
Game 4 — 10
Game 5 — 9
Game 6 — 5
Game 7 — 9

Fill in the blanks.

a. High game: _____

b. Low game: _____

c. Average baskets per game: _____

3. Study the graph, then answer the questions.

a. Which flavor is the most popular? _____

b. Which flavor sold the least? _____

c. What decimal represents the two highest sellers? _____

d. Which flavor had $\frac{1}{10}$ of the sales? _____

Ice-Cream Sales

Name: _____

Integers

An **integer** is a whole number above or below 0: –2, –1, 0, +1, +2, and so on. **Opposite integers** are two integers the same distance from 0, but in different directions, such as –2 and +2.

Think of the water level in the picture as 0. The part of the iceberg sticking out of the water is positive. The iceberg has +3 feet above water. The part of the iceberg below the water is negative. The iceberg extends – 9 feet under water.

Numbers greater than 0 are **positive** numbers. Numbers less than 0 are **negative** numbers. Pairs of positive and negative numbers are called **opposite integers**.

3 feet

water level

9 feet

Examples of opposite integers:
  –5 and +5
  losing 3 pounds and gaining 3 pounds
  earning $12 and spending $12

Directions: Complete the following exercises.

1. Write each of these as an integer. The first one is done for you.

    a. positive 6 = **+6**   b. losing $5 = _____

    c. 5 degrees below 0 = _____   d. receiving $12 = _____

2. Write the **opposite** integer of each of these. The first one is done for you.

    a. negative 4 = **+4**   b. positive 10 = _____

    c. 2 floors below ground level = _____   d. winning a card game by 6 points = _____

3. Write integers to show each idea.

    a. A train that arrives 2 hours after it was scheduled: _____

    b. A package that has 3 fewer cups than it should: _____

    c. A board that's 3 inches too short: _____   d. A golf score 5 over par: _____

    e. A paycheck that doesn't cover $35 of a family's expenses: _____

    f. 30 seconds before a missile launch: _____

    g. A team that won 6 games and lost 2: _____

Comparing Integers

Comparing two integers can be confusing unless you think of them as being on a number line, as shown below. Remember that the integer farther to the right is greater. Thus, +2 is greater than –3, 0 is greater than –4 and –2 is greater than –5.

```
┬   ┬   ┬   ┬   ┬   ┬   ┬   ┬   ┬   ┬   ┬
–5  –4  –3  –2  –1   0  +1  +2  +3  +4  +5
```

Directions: Study the number line. Then complete the following exercises.

1. Write in integers to complete the number line.

```
┬   ┬   ┬   ┬   ┬   ┬   ┬   ┬   ┬   ┬   ┬
–5 ___ –3  –2  ___  0  +1 ___ ___ +4  +5
```

2. Write < for "less than" or > for "greater than" to compare the integers. The first one is done for you.

   a. –5 __<__ +5   b. +3 _____ –3   c. +2 _____ –4

   d. –4 _____ –3   e. –1 _____ +3   f. –1 _____ –5

3. Write **T** for true or **F** for false. (All degrees are in Fahrenheit.)

   a. +7 degrees is colder than –3 degrees.   _____

   b. –14 degrees is colder than –7 degrees.   _____

   c. +23 degrees is colder than –44 degrees.   _____

   d. –5 degrees is colder than +4 degrees.   _____

4. Draw an **X** by the series of integers that are in order from least to greatest.

   _____ +2, +3, –4

   _____ –3, 0, +1

   _____ –7, –4, –1

   _____ –3, –4, –5

Grade 6 - Comprehensive Curriculum

Adding Integers

The sum of two positive integers is a positive integer.
    Thus, +4 + +1 = +5.
The sum of two negative integers is a negative integer.
    Thus, –5 + –2 = –7.
The sum of a positive and a negative integer has the
sign of the integer that is farther from 0.
    Thus, –6 + +3 = –3.
The sum of opposite integers is 0.
    Thus, +2 + –2 = 0

Directions: Complete the following exercises.

1. Add these integers.

    a. +2 + +7 = _____   b. –4 + –2 = _____   c. +5 + –3 = _____   d. +4 + –4 = _____

    e. –10 + –2 = _____   f.   +6 + –1 = _____   g. +45 + –30 = _____   h. –39 + +26 = _____

2. Write the problems as integers. The first one has been done for you.

    a. One cold morning, the temperature was –14 degrees.
        The afternoon high was 20 degrees warmer. What was the
        high temperature that day?   –14 + +20 = +6

    b. Another day, the high temperature was 26 degrees,
        but the temperature dropped 35 degrees during the
        night. What was the low that night?   _____

    c. Sherri's allowance was $7. She paid $4 for a movie ticket.
        How much money did she have left?   _____

    d. The temperature in a meat freezer was –10 degrees, but
        the power went off and the temperature rose 6 degrees.
        How cold was the freezer then?   _____

    e. The school carnival took in $235, but it had expenses of $185.
        How much money did the carnival make after paying
        its expenses?   _____

Name: _____

Subtracting Integers

To subtract an integer, change its sign to the opposite and add it. If you are subtracting a negative integer, make it positive and add it: +4 − −6 = +4 + +6 = +10. If you are subtracting a positive integer, make it negative and add it: +8 − +2 = +8 + −2 = +6.

More examples: −5 − −8 = −5 + +8 = +3
                     +3 − +7 = +3 + −7 = −4

Directions: Complete the following exercises.

1. Before subtracting these integers, rewrite each problem. The first one has been done for you.

   −6 − −8 = ____−6 + +8 = +2____   +3 − −4 = _____

   +9 − +3 = _____   −1 − −7 = _____

   +7 − −5 = _____   −4 − +3 = _____

2. Write these problems as integers. The first one is done for you.

   a. The high temperature in the Arctic Circle one day was
      −42 degrees. The low was −67 degrees. What
      was the difference between the two?   ____−42 − −67 = −42 + +67 = +25____

   b. At the equator one day, the high temperature was
      +106 degrees. The low was +85 degrees. What
      was the difference between the two?   _____

   c. At George's house one morning, the thermometer showed it was
      +7 degrees. The radio announcer said it was −2 degrees. What is the
      difference between the two temperatures?   _____

   d. What is the difference between a temperature of +11 degrees
      and a wind-chill factor of −15 degrees?   _____

   e. During a dry spell, the level of a river dropped from 3 feet above
      normal to 13 feet below normal. How many
      feet did it drop?   _____

   f. Here are the average temperatures in a meat freezer for four days:
      −12, −11, −14 and −9 degrees. What is the difference between
      the highest and lowest temperature?   _____

Plotting Graphs

A graph with horizontal and vertical number lines can show the location of certain points. The horizontal number line is called the **x axis**, and the vertical number line is called the **y axis**. Two numbers, called the **x coordinate** and the **y coordinate**, show where a point is on the graph.

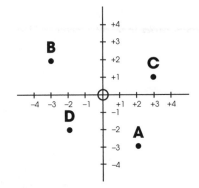

The first coordinate, x, tells how many units to the right or left of 0 the point is located. On the example graph, point A is +2, two units to the right of 0.

The second coordinate, y, tells how many units above or below 0 the point is located. On the example, point A is –3, three units below 0.

Thus, the coordinates of A are +2, –3. The coordinates of B are –3, +2. (Notice the order of the coordinates.) The coordinates of C are +3, +1; and D, –2, –2.

Directions: Study the example. Then answer these questions about the graph below.

1. What towns are at these coordinates?

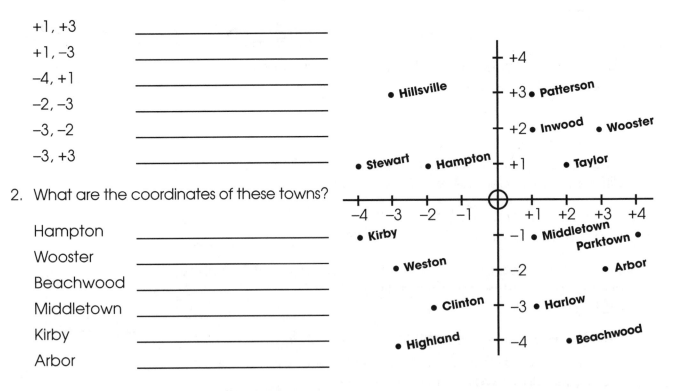

+1, +3 _____

+1, –3 _____

–4, +1 _____

–2, –3 _____

–3, –2 _____

–3, +3 _____

2. What are the coordinates of these towns?

Hampton _____

Wooster _____

Beachwood _____

Middletown _____

Kirby _____

Arbor _____

Ordered Pairs

Ordered pairs is another term used to describe pairs of integers used to locate points on a graph.

Directions: Complete the following exercises.

1. Place the following points on the graph, using the ordered pairs as data.

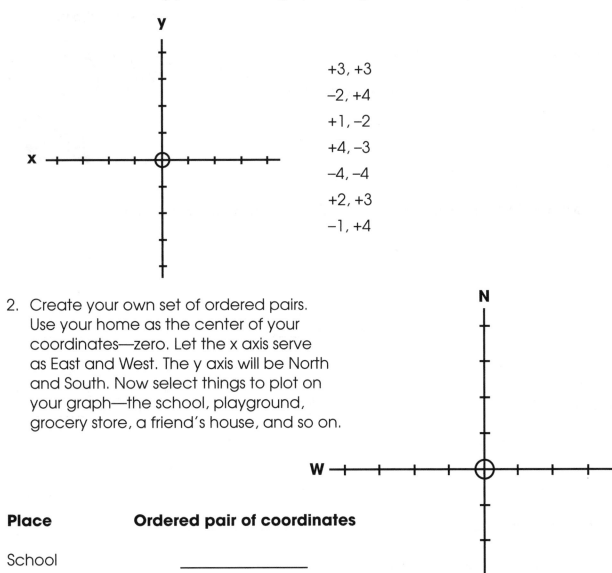

+3, +3

−2, +4

+1, −2

+4, −3

−4, −4

+2, +3

−1, +4

2. Create your own set of ordered pairs. Use your home as the center of your coordinates—zero. Let the x axis serve as East and West. The y axis will be North and South. Now select things to plot on your graph—the school, playground, grocery store, a friend's house, and so on.

Place   **Ordered pair of coordinates**

School   _____

Grocery store   _____

Playground   _____

Friend's house _____

Review

Directions: Complete the following exercises.

1. Write the **opposite** integers of the following:

    a. 14 degrees above 0 _____

    b. Spending $21 _____

2. Write integers to show these ideas.

    a. 4 seconds after the launch of the space shuttle _____

    b. A lake 3 feet below its usual level _____

    c. 2 days before your birthday _____

3. Write < for "less than" or > for "greater than" to compare these integers.

    −2 _____ −4   +2 _____ −3   −1 _____ +1

4. Add the integers.

    −14 **+** −11 = _____   −6 **+** +5 = _____   −7 **+** +7 = _____

5. Subtract the integers.

    −4 **−** −5 = _____   +3 **−** −6 = _____   +7 **−** +2 = _____

6. Write **T** for true or **F** for false.

    a. The x coordinate is on the horizontal number line.   _____

    b. Add the x and y coordinates to find the location of a point.   _____

    c. Always state the x coordinate first.   _____

    d. A y coordinate of +2 would be above the horizontal number line.   _____

    e. An x coordinate of +2 would be to the right of the vertical number line. _____

CERTIFICATE

Congratulations to

_____
(Your Name)

for finishing this workbook!

_____
(Date)

Acrostic: A poem that uses the letters of a word to begin each line. Read down, the first letter of each line spells the word.

Acute Angle: An angle of less than 90 degrees.

Adjective: A word that describes a noun.

Adverb: A word that tells something about a verb, adjective or another adverb. It answers the questions when, where or how.

Analogy: A comparison showing how two things relate to each other. Example: Nose is to smell as tongue is to taste (nose : smell :: tongue : taste).

Angle: The amount of space where two lines meet.

Antecedent: The noun or nouns to which a pronoun refers.

Antonym: A word that means the opposite of another word.

Appositive: A noun or pronoun placed after another noun or pronoun to further identify it.

Area: The number of square units that covers a certain space.

Author's Purpose: The reason why an author writes a particular story or book.

Average: A value that lies within a range of values.

Biographical Dictionary: A book containing histories of people's lives.

Biography: A written history of a person's life.

Cause: The reason something happens.

Chapter: Parts into which some books are divided.

Character: A person in a story.

Classifying: Placing similar things into categories.

Column: A regular feature in a magazine or newspaper, often written by the same person, which states an opinion.

Columnist: A person who writes a column.

Combining Form: A word or word base used in forming words. Example: tele in telephone.

Command: A sentence telling someone to do something. It ends in a period or exclamation mark.

Comparative Adjectives: Compare two persons, places, things or ideas.

Comparison: A way to show how things are alike or different.

Complete Sentence: A sentence that has both a simple subject and a simple predicate.

Comprehension: Understanding what is seen, read or heard.

Conclusion Sentences: End a paragraph. They often restate the main idea.

Congruent Shapes: Identical geometric shapes. They can face in different directions.

Conjunction: A word that joins two or more sentences, words or ideas.

Connotation: The meaning of a word, including all the emotions associated with it.

Contraction: A shortened form of two words. An apostrophe (') is used to show where some letters have been left out.

Cubic Unit: A unit with six equal sides, like a child's block.

Customary System: Measures length in inches and feet, capacity in cups and pints, weight in ounces and pounds, and temperature in Fahrenheit.

Dangling Modifier: A word, or words, that does not modify what it is meant to modify.

Data: Gathered information (datum—singular).

Decimal: A number that includes a period called a decimal point. The digits to the right of the decimal point are a value less than one.

Denominator: The bottom number in a fraction.

Denotation: The literal or dictionary definition of a word.

Dialogue: The words spoken by characters in a story.

Diamanté: A seven-line poem in the shape of a diamond.

Digit: A numeral.

Direct Object: A noun or pronoun which answers "what" or "whom" after the verb.

Dividend: The number to be divided in a division problem.

Divisor: The number used to divide another number.

Effect: What happens as a result of the cause.

Entertain: To hold the attention of or to amuse someone.

Epitaph: A verse written on a tombstone, very popular in the past.

Equation: A number sentence in which the value on the left of the equal sign must equal the value on the right of the equal sign.

Equilateral Triangle: A triangle with three equal sides.

Equivalent Fractions: Fractions that name the same amount, such as $\frac{1}{2}$ and $\frac{5}{10}$.

Estimating: Using an approximate number instead of an exact one.

Exclamation: A sentence that shows strong feeling or excitement. It ends with an exclamation mark.

Expanded Notation: Writing out the value of each digit in a number.

Fact: Information that can be proven to be true. Example: Hawaii is a state.

Faulty Parallelism: When parts of a sentence do not match grammatically or structurally.

Feature: A specific type of article in a magazine or newspaper.

Fraction: A number that names part of something.

Free Verse: Poems that do not rhyme and do not have a regular rhythm.

Future Tense: Explains what will happen.

Gaelic Lullaby: An ancient Irish or Scottish song some parents sing as they rock their babies to sleep.

Generalization: A statement or rule that applies to many situations or examples.

Geometry: The study of lines and angles, the shapes they create and how they relate to one another.

Giving Directions: Providing clear information explaining how to do or create something.

Greatest Common Factor (GCF): The largest number that will divide evenly into a set of numbers.

Haiku: A Japanese verse of three lines having five, seven and five syllables each.

Homographs: Words that have the same spelling but different meanings.

Homophones: Words that sound alike but have different spellings and meanings.

Idiom: A phrase that says one thing but actually means something quite different.

Imagery: A "picture" that comes into the reader's mind when reading certain words.

Improper Fraction: A fraction that has a larger numerator than its denominator.

Independent Clause: Part of a sentence that contains a complete idea. It can stand alone.

Index: An alphabetical listing of names, topics and important words that is found in the back of a book.

Indirect Object: A noun or pronoun that tells "to whom" or "what" or "for whom" or "what" the action is performed.

Inform: To give factual information.

Integers: Numbers above or below zero: –2, –1, 0, +1, +2, and so on.

Interrogative Pronoun: A pronoun used to ask a question. "Who," "what" and "which" are interrogative pronouns.

Irregular Verb: A verb whose past tense is not formed by adding "ed."

Isosceles Triangle: A triangle with two equal sides.

Least Common Multiple (LCM): The lowest possible multiple any pair of numbers have in common.

Limerick: A humorous verse consisting of five lines with the first, second, and fifth lines rhyming, and the third and fourth lines rhyming.

Main Idea: The most important idea, or main points, in a sentence, paragraph or story.

Making Inferences: Being able to come to conclusions based on what is suggested in the text.

Magazine: A periodical, regularly printed, containing articles, photographs, advertisements, etc.

Mean: The average of a group of numbers.

Median: The number in the middle when numbers are listed in order.

Metaphor: A figure of speech that directly compares one thing to another. Example: The grass is a velvet carpet.

Metric System: Measures length in meters, capacity in liters, mass in grams and temperature in Celsius.

Mixed Number: A whole number and a fraction, such as $1\frac{1}{2}$.

Negative Numbers: Numbers less than zero.

Noun: A word that names a person, place, thing or idea.

Numerator: The top number in a fraction.

Object of a Preposition: The noun or pronoun that follows a preposition and adds to its meaning.

Obtuse Angle: An angle of more than 90 degrees.

Opinion: A statement that expresses how someone feels or what he/she thinks about something. It cannot be proven.

Opposite Integers: Two integers the same distance from 0 but in different directions, such as –2 and +2.

Ordered Pairs: Another term used to describe two integers used to locate points on a graph.

Outline: A skeletal description of the main ideas and important details of a reading selection.

Paragraph: A group of sentences that tells about one main idea.

Parallel: Parts of a sentence which match grammatically and structurally.

Parallelogram: Has four parallel sides, with the opposite sides of equal length.

Paraphrase: To restate something in your own words.

Past Tense: Explains what has already happened.

Percent: A kind of ratio that compares a number with 100.

Perimeter: The distance around a shape formed by straight lines, such as a square.

Personal Pronoun: A word that takes the place of a noun. It refers to a person or a thing.

Personification: A figure of speech in which human characteristics are given to an animal or object.

Persuade: To convince someone to believe what is being stated.

Place Value: The position of a digit in a number.

Plot: The problem characters in a story face and how they solve it.

Plural: A word that refers to more than one thing.

Point of View: How a person or character in a story feels about an event and reacts to it.

Positive Adjectives: The adjectives themselves.

Positive Numbers: Numbers greater than zero.

Possessive Noun: A noun that shows ownership. Examples: Jill's book or the women's hair.

Possessive Pronoun: A pronoun that shows ownership. Examples: mine, his, hers, yours, its, ours, theirs.

Predicate: A word, or several words, that tells what the subject does or that it exists.

Prefix: A syllable added to the beginning of a word that changes its meaning.

Preposition: A word that comes before a noun or pronoun and shows the relationship of that noun or pronoun to some other word in the sentence.

Prepositional Phrase: A group of words that includes a preposition, the object of the preposition and all modifiers.

Present Tense: Explains what is happening now.

Probability: The ratio of favorable outcomes to possible outcomes in an experiment.

Pronoun: A word that takes the place of a noun. Examples: I, he, she, we, it, you and them.

Proportion: A statement that two ratios are equal.

Proverb: A bit of advice for daily life.

Quadrilateral: A shape with four sides and four angles.

Question: A sentence that asks something. It ends with a question mark.

Quotient: The answer in a division problem.

Range: The difference between the highest and lowest number in a group of numbers.

Ratio: A comparison of two quantities.

Recalling Details: Being able to pick out and remember the who, what, when, where, why, and how of what is read.

Reciprocals: Two fractions that, when multiplied together, make 1, such as $\frac{2}{7}$ and $\frac{7}{2}$.

Rectangle: Has four parallel sides, but only its opposite sides are equal lengths; it has four 90-degree angles.

Right Angle: An angle of 90 degrees.

Root Word: A word that is the common stem from which related words get their meanings.

Rounding: Expressing a number to the nearest whole number, ten, thousand or other value.

Run-On Sentence: Two or more sentences joined together without punctuation or a joining word.

Scalene Triangle: A triangle with no equal sides.

Scan: To look for certain words in a reading selection to locate facts or answer questions.

Sections: Segments of each unit in a book.

Sentence Fragment: A phrase, not a complete sentence.

Sequencing: Placing items or events in logical order.

Setting: Where and when an event or story takes place.

Similar Shapes: The same geometric shape in differing sizes.

Simile: A figure of speech comparing two things, using the words "like" or "as." Example: She was as quiet as a mouse.

Simple Predicate: A verb in a sentence telling what the subject does, is doing, did or will do.

Simple Subject: A noun or pronoun that tells who or what the sentence is about.

Singular: A word that refers to only one thing.

Skim: To read quickly to get a general idea of what a reading selection is about.

Square: Has four parallel sides of equal length and four 90-degree angles.

Statement: A sentence that tells something. It ends with a period.

Straight Angle: An angle of 180 degrees.

Subentry: A smaller division of a subject.

Subject: 1. A word, or several words, that tells who or what a sentence is about; 2. The topic covered or the name of an item in an index; 3. the person in a biography.

Suffix: A syllable added to the end of a word that changes its meaning.

Summary: A brief retelling of the main ideas in a reading selection.

Superlative Adjectives: Compare more than two persons, places, things or ideas.

Support Sentences: Provide details about the topic.

Syllable: A word or part of a word with only one vowel sound.

Symbolism: The use of something to stand for (symbolize) something else.

Symmetrical Shapes: Shapes that, when divided in half, are identical.

Synonym: A word that means the same or nearly the same as another word.

Table of Contents: A listing of headings and page numbers for chapters or articles located in the front of a book or magazine.

Tense: The way a verb is used to express time.

Topic Sentence: A sentence which states the main idea of a paragraph and is usually the first sentence.

Trapezoid: Has two opposite sides that are parallel; its sides may or may not be of equal lengths.

Units: Parts into which a book is divided.

Using Prior Knowledge: Being able to use what one already knows to find an answer or get information.

Venn Diagram: A diagram used to chart information that shows similarities and differences between two things; used to compare and contrast two things.

Verb: A word in a sentence that tells what something does or that something exists.

Verb Tense: The way a verb expresses time.

Volume: The number of cubic units that fills a space.

X Axis: The horizontal number line in a plotting graph.

X Coordinate/Y Coordinate: Show where a point is on a plotting graph.

Y Axis: The vertical number line in a plotting graph.

Page 6

Spelling: Words With ă

Directions: Write a sentence for each word. Use a dictionary if you are unsure of the meaning of a word.

1. favorite
2. gable
3. dangerous
4. patient
5. lakefront
6. statement
7. nation
8. negotiate
9. operate
10. decade

Answers will vary.

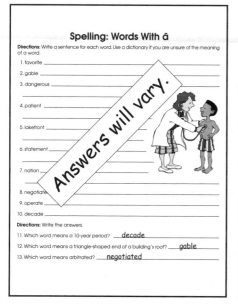

Directions: Write the answers.

11. Which word means a 10-year period? __decade__
12. Which word means a triangle-shaped end of a building's roof? __gable__
13. Which word means arbitrated? __negotiated__

Page 7

Spelling: Words With ē

Directions: Write a sentence for each word. Use a dictionary if you are unsure of the meaning of a word.

1. niece
2. meaningful
3. conceited
4. baleen
5. field
6. disease
7. reactivate
8. peony
9. seafaring
10. theme

Answers will vary.

Directions: Write the answers.

11. Which word is a summer-blooming flower? __peony__
12. Which word is a type of whale? __baleen__
13. Which word means an illness? __disease__

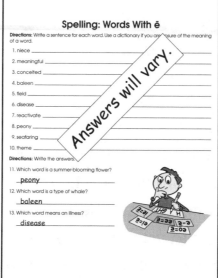

Page 8

Spelling: Words With Ī

Directions: Write a sentence for each word. Use a dictionary if you are unsure of the meaning of a word.

1. bisect
2. identify
3. frightened
4. glider
5. idol
6. library
7. pipeline
8. hieroglyphic
9. rhinoceros
10. silent

Answers will vary.

Directions: Write the answers.

11. Which word means to be scared? __frightened__
12. Which word means to divide into two sections? __bisect__
13. Which word is an animal? __rhinoceros__
14. Which word is a type of ancient writing? __hieroglyphic__

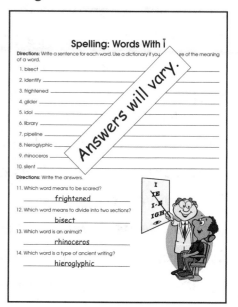

Page 9

Spelling: Words With ō

Directions: Write a sentence for each word. Use a dictionary if you are unsure of the meaning of a word.

1. clothing
2. slogan
3. total
4. stethoscope
5. voltage
6. stereo
7. protein
8. negotiate
9. locust
10. locomotive

Answers will vary.

Directions: Write the answers.

11. Which word is an insect? __locust__
12. Which word means a train? __locomotive__
13. Which word means a listening device to hear the heart? __stethoscope__
14. Which word means to bargain? __negotiate__

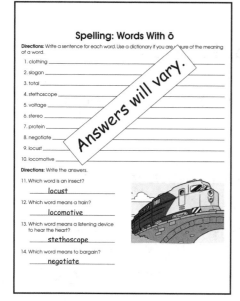

Page 10

Spelling: Words With ū

Directions: Write a sentence for each word. Use a dictionary if you are unsure of the meaning of a word.

1. universe
2. cruise
3. absolute
4. influence
5. unanimous
6. vacuum
7. putrid
8. incubate
9. peruse
10. numerous

Answers will vary.

Directions: Write the answers.

11. Which word means to read carefully? __peruse__
12. Which word means that everyone is in agreement? __unanimous__
13. Which word means a sea voyage taken for pleasure? __cruise__
14. Which word means to keep eggs warm until they hatch? __incubate__

Page 11

Spelling: I Before E, Except After C

Use an **i** before **e**, except after **c** or when **e** and **i** together sound like long **a**.

Examples:
relieve
deceive
neighbor

Exceptions: weird, foreign, height, seize

Directions: Write **C** in the blank if the word in bold is spelled correctly. Draw an **X** in the blank if it is spelled incorrectly. The first one has been done for you.

_C_ 1. They stopped at the crossing for the **freight** train.
_X_ 2. How much does that **wiegh**?
_C_ 3. Did you **believe** his story?
_X_ 4. He **recieved** an A on his paper!
_X_ 5. She said it was the **nieghborly** thing to do.
_C_ 6. The guards **seized** the package.
_X_ 7. That movie was **wierd**!
_X_ 8. Her **hieght** is five feet, six inches.
_C_ 9. It's not right to **deceive** others.
_X_ 10. Your answers should be **breif**.
_C_ 11. She felt a lot of **grief** when her dog died.
_X_ 12. He is still **greiving** about his loss.
_C_ 13. Did the police catch the **thief**?
_X_ 14. She was their **cheif** source of information.
_C_ 15. Can you speak a **foreign** language?

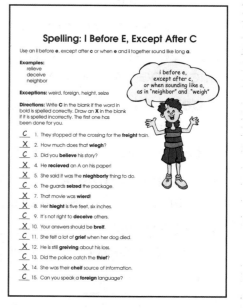

Page 12

Spelling: Words With ie and ei

Many people have trouble remembering when to use **ie** and when to use **ei**. The following rules have many exceptions, but they may be helpful to you.
Rule 1: If the two letters are pronounced like **ē** and are preceded by an **s** sound, use **ei**, as in receive.
Rule 2: If the two letters are pronounced like **ē**, but are not preceded by an **s** sound, use **ie** in believe.
Rule 3: If the two letters are pronounced like **ā**, use **ei** in as **eight** and **vein**.
Rule 4: If the two letters are pronounced like **ī**, use **ei** as in height.

The sound **s** could be produced by the letter **s** as in **single** or the letter **c** as in **cease**.

Directions: Write the words from the box on the lines after the spelling rule that applies.

veil	brief	deceive	belief	niece
reindeer	yield	achieve	height	neighbor
grief	ceiling	weight	vein	seize

Rule 1: __ceiling, deceive, seize__
Rule 2: __grief, brief, yield, achieve, belief, niece__
Rule 3: __veil, reindeer, weight, vein, neighbor__
Rule 4: __height__

Directions: Complete the sentences with words that have the vowel sound shown. Use each word from the box only once.
1. My next-door (ā) __neighbor__ wore a long (ā) __veil__ at her wedding.
2. Will the roof hold the (ā) __weight__ of Santa's (ā) __reindeer__ ?
3. My nephew and (ē) __niece__ work hard to (ē) __achieve__ their goals.
4. I have a strong (ē) __belief__ they would never (ē) __deceive__ me.
5. For a (ē) __brief__ moment, I thought Will would (ē) __yield__ the game to me.
6. The blood rushed through my (ā) __veins__ .
7. What is the (ī) __height__ of this (ē) __ceiling__ ?

Page 13

Spelling: Words With ûr and ôr

The difference between **ûr** and **ôr** is clear in the words **fur** and **for**. The **ûr** sound can be spelled **ur** as in **fur**, **our** as in **journal**, **er** as in **her** and **ear** as in **search**.

The **ôr** sound can be spelled **or** as in **for**, **our** as in **four**, **oar** as in **soar** and **ore** as in **more**.

Directions: Write the words from the box on the lines to match the sounds.

florist	plural	ignore	courtesy	observe
survey	research	furnish	normal	emergency
tornado	coarse	flourish	source	restore

ûr __survey, plural, research, furnish, flourish, courtesy, observe, emergency__
ôr __florist, tornado, coarse, ignore, normal, source, restore__

Directions: Complete the sentences with words that have the sound shown. Use each word only once.
1. We all get along better when we remember to use (ûr) __courtesy__ .
2. My brother likes flowers and wants to be a (ôr) __florist__ .
3. What was the (ôr) __source__ of the (ûr) __research__ for your report?
4. He waved at her, but she continued to (ôr) __ignore__ him.
5. For a plural subject, use a (ûr) __plural__ verb.
6. Beneath the dark clouds a (ôr) __tornado__ formed!
7. Firefighters are used to handling an (ûr) __emergency__ .
8. When will they be able to (ôr) __restore__ our electricity?
9. How are you going to (ûr) __furnish__ your apartment?

Page 14

Spelling: Words Beginning With sh and th

Directions: Write a definition for each word. Use a dictionary if you are unsure of the meaning of a word.

1. shallow: _____
2. thimble: _____
3. shear: _____
4. sheriff: _____
5. thermal: _____
6. throttle: _____
7. shingle: _____
8. shot put: _____
9. thrifty: _____
10. shoreline: _____
11. threaten: _____
12. thyroid: _____

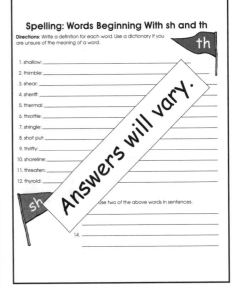

Use two of the above words in sentences.
13. _____
14. _____

Answers will vary.

Page 15

Spelling: Words Beginning With ch

Directions: Write a definition for each word. Use a dictionary if you are unsure of the meaning of a word.

1. chimney: _____
2. china: _____
3. cheetah: _____
4. charity: _____
5. channel: _____
6. chandelier: _____
7. challenge: _____
8. _____
9. _____
10. _____
11. ch_____
12. chisel: _____

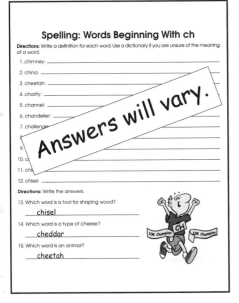

Directions: Write the answers.
13. Which word is a tool for shaping wood?
__chisel__
14. Which word is a type of cheese?
__cheddar__
15. Which word is an animal?
__cheetah__

Answers will vary.

Page 16

Spelling: The Letter Q

In English words, the letter **q** is always followed by the letter **u**.

Examples:
question
square
quick

Directions: Write the correct spelling of each word in the blank. The first one has been done for you.

1. qill — __quill__
2. eqality — __equality__
3. qarrel — __quarrel__
4. qarter — __quarter__
5. qart — __quart__
6. qibble — __quibble__
7. qench — __quench__
8. qeen — __queen__
9. qip — __quip__
10. qiz — __quiz__
11. eqipment — __equipment__
12. qiet — __quiet__
13. qite — __quite__
14. eqity — __equity__
15. eqator — __equator__
16. eqivalent — __equivalent__
17. eqitable — __equitable__
18. eqestrian — __equestrian__
19. eqation — __equation__
20. qantity — __quantity__

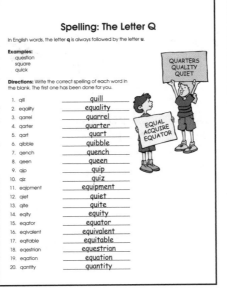

QUARTERS
QUALITY
QUIET

EQUAL
ACQUIRE
EQUATOR

Page 17

Spelling: Words With kw, ks and gz

The consonant **q** is always followed by **u** in words and is pronounced **kw**. The letter **x** can be pronounced **ks** as in **mix**. When **x** is followed by a vowel, it is usually pronounced **gz** as in **example**.

Directions: Write the words from the box on the lines to match the sounds shown.

expense	exist	aquarium	acquire	request	exact
expand	exit	quality	excellent	quantity	quiz
exhibit	squirm	expression			

kw __squirm, aquarium, quality, acquire, request, quality, quiz__
ks __expense, expand, expression, excellent__
gz __exhibit, exist, exit, exact__

Directions: Complete the sentences with words that have the sound shown. Use words from the box only once.
1. We went to the zoo to see the fish (gz) __exhibit__ .
2. I didn't know its (gz) __exact__ location, so we followed the map.
3. The zoo plans to (kw) __acquire__ some sharks for its (kw) __aquarium__ .
4. Taking care of sharks is a big (ks) __expense__ , but a number of people have asked the zoo to (ks) __expand__ its display of fish.
5. These people want a better (kw) __quality__ of fish, not a bigger (kw) __quantity__ of them.
6. I think the zoo already has an (ks) __excellent__ display.
7. Some of its rare fish no longer (gz) __exist__ in the ocean.

ANSWER KEY

Page 18

Spelling: Words With Silent Letters

Some letters in words are not pronounced, like the **b** in **crumb**, the **l** in **yolk**, the **n** in **autumn**, the **g** in **design** and the **h** in **hour**.

Directions: Write the words from the box on the lines to match the silent letters. Use a dictionary if you are unsure of the meaning or pronunciation of a word.

condemn	yolk	campaign	assign	salmon
hymn	limb	chalk	tomb	foreign
resign	column	spaghetti	rhythm	solemn

n __condemn, hymn, column, solemn__

l __yolk, chalk, salmon__

g __resign, campaign, assign, foreign__

b __limb, tomb__

h __spaghetti, rhythm__

Directions: Write words from the box to complete these sentences.

1. What did the teacher (g) __assign__ for homework?
2. She put words in a (n) __column__ on the board.
3. When she finished writing, her hands were white with (l) __chalk__.
4. The church choir clapped in (h) __rhythm__ with the (n) __hymn__.
5. While I was cracking an egg, the (l) __yolk__ slipped onto the floor.
6. Did the explorers find anything in the ancient (b) __tomb__?
7. My favorite dinner of all is (h) __spaghetti__ and meatballs.
8. Do not (n) __condemn__ me for making one little mistake.

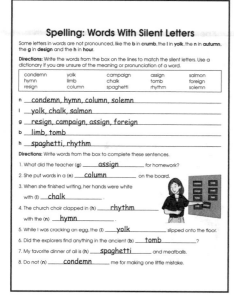

Page 19

Spelling: Words With ph or kn

The letters **ph** produce the same sound as the letter **f**. When the letters **kn** are together, the **k** is silent.

Directions: Write a definition for each word. Use a dictionary if you are unsure of the meaning of a word.

1. photographer: _____
2. knowledge: _____
3. knee: _____
4. telephone: _____
5. knock: _____
6. phonics: _____
7. physician: _____
8. knife: _____
9. pharmacy: _____
10. knight: _____
11. knit: _____
12. pheasant: _____

Answers will vary.

Directions: Write the answers.

13. Which word is a place to buy medicine?
__pharmacy__
14. Which word is a synonym for doctor?
__physician__
15. Which word names a bird?
__pheasant__

Page 20

Spelling: Words With gh or gn

Directions: Use the clues and the words in the box to complete the crossword puzzle.

recognize	drought
lightning	night
straight	throughout
assign	fought

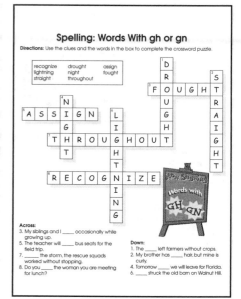

(Crossword answers: FOUGHT, ASSIGN, THROUGHOUT, RECOGNIZE, DROUGHT, STRAIGHT, LIGHTNING, NIGHT)

Words with GH GN

Across:
3. My siblings and I _____ occasionally while growing up.
5. The teacher will _____ bus seats for the field trip.
7. _____ the storm, the rescue squads worked without stopping.
8. Do you _____ the woman you are meeting for lunch?

Down:
1. The _____ left farmers without crops.
2. My brother has _____ hair, but mine is curly.
4. Tomorrow _____ we will leave for Florida.
6. _____ struck the old barn on Walnut Street.

Page 21

Root Words

A **root word** is the common stem that gives related words their basic meanings.

Example: Separate is the root word for **separately, separation, inseparable** and **separator**.

Directions: Identify the root word in each group of words. Look up the meaning of the root word in the dictionary and write its definition. The first one has been done for you.

1. colorless, colorful, discolor, coloration
Root word: __color__
Definition: __any coloring matter, dye, pigment or paint__

2. creator, creation, creating, creative, recreate
Root word: __create__
Definition: __to bring into being__

3. remove, movement, movable, immovable, removable
Root word: __move__
Definition: __to change the place or position of__

4. contentment, malcontent, discontent, discontentment
Root word: __content__
Definition: __happy with what one has__

5. pleasure, displeasure, pleasing, pleasant, unpleasant
Root word: __please__
Definition: __to be agreeable to__

6. successor, unsuccessful, successful
Root word: __success__
Definition: __a favorable outcome__

Page 22

Greek and Latin Roots

Many word patterns in the English language are combinations of Greek or Latin words. When you know what part of a word means, you may be able to figure out the meaning of the rest of the word. For example, if **cycle** means "circle or wheel" and **bi** means "two," then you can figure out that **bicycle** means "two wheels." **Root words** are the words that longer words are based on. For example, duct, which means "to lead," is the root of **conduct** or **induct**. Look at the chart below. It has several root words and their meanings on it.

Root	Meaning	Example	Definition
act	to do	interact	to act with others
aqua	water	aquatint	dyed water
auto	self	automobile	to move oneself
centi	a hundred	centennial	one hundred years

Directions: Look at each word equation below. The meaning of one part is shown in parentheses. Consult the chart of root words to find the meaning of the other part. Write the meaning in the blank. Combine the _____ dictionary definition in the space provided.

Answers may vary.

1. react re (again) + act __to do__ = __again to do__
Dictionary definition: To act or do again

2. automatic auto __self__ + matic (having a mind) = self having a mind
Dictionary definition: __self-acting or self-moving__

3. transact trans (across) + act __to do__ = __to do across__
Dictionary definition: __to carry on or conduct to a settlement__

4. centimeter centi __a hundred__ + meter (meter) = __a hundred meters__
Dictionary definition: __one hundredth of a meter__

5. aquanaut aqua __water__ + naut (sailor) = __water sailor__
Dictionary definition: __an underwater explorer__

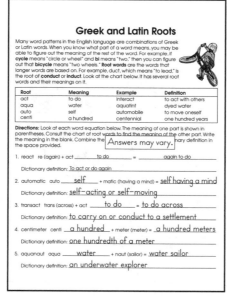

Page 23

Root Words

Root	Meaning	Example	Definition
cede	to go	supercede	to go beyond
cept	seize	intercept	to seize during
duce	lead	deduce	to find the lead
fer	carry	interfere	to carry into
port	carry	transport	to carry across
spect	to look	inspect	to look in
tain	to hold	obtain	to gain by action
vene	to come	conv...	...start

Directions: Complete the exercises below. *Answers may vary.*

1. precede pre (before) + cede __to go__ = __before to go__
Dictionary definition: __to be, go or come before__

2. report re (again) + port __carry__ = __carry again__
Dictionary definition: __to carry and repeat, as in a message__

3. intervene inter (between) + vene __to come__ = __to come between__
Dictionary definition: __to come between__

4. induce in (in) + duce __lead__ = __lead in__
Dictionary definition: __to lead by persuasion__

5. retrospect retro (backward) + spect __to look__ = __to look backward__
Dictionary definition: __to look back on past events__

6. refer re (again) + fer __carry__ = __carry again__
Dictionary definition: __to hand over for consideration__

7. retain re (again) + tain __to hold__ = __to hold again__
Dictionary definition: __to keep possession of__

8. concept con (with) + cept __seize__ = __seized with__
Dictionary definition: __a general notion or idea__

Page 24

Prefixes

A **prefix** is a syllable added to the beginning of a word to change its meaning. The prefix **re** means "back" or "again," as in **return**. **Pre** means "before," as in **prepare**. **Dis** means "do the opposite," as in **disappear**. **In** and **im** both mean "not," as in **impossible**. (These two prefixes also have other meanings.) **Com** and **con** both mean "with," as in **companion** and **concert**. Use **im** and **com** with words that start with **p, b** or **m**. Use **in** and **con** with words that begin with a vowel or other consonants.

Directions: Match each word from the box to its definition.

disbelieve	recite	connotation	impolite	preview
impatient	distrust	configuration	prevision	incomplete
invisible	dislike	confederate	recover	compassion

1. share another's feelings — **compassion**
2. not finished — **incomplete**
3. another meaning — **connotation**
4. become normal again — **recover**
5. take away confidence — **distrust**
6. look to the future — **prevision**
7. arrangement of parts — **configuration**
8. say from memory — **recite**
9. ally — **confederate**
10. hate — **dislike**
11. look at — **preview**
12. rude — **impolite**
13. in a hurry — **impatient**
14. doubt — **disbelieve**
15. not seen — **invisible**

Directions: Add the rest of the word to each prefix in these sentences. Use words from the box only once. Be sure to use the correct form of the word.

16. When he re **covered** from his cold, Jeff was im **patient** to get back to work.
17. Jonah stared at the ghostly figure with dis **belief** and dis **trust**.
18. I'd like to re **cite** that poem, but my memory of it is in **complete**.
19. She was very im **polite** during the movie pre **view**.

Page 25

Prefixes

A **prefix** is a syllable added to the beginning of a word that changes its meaning. The prefixes **in, il, ir** and **im** all mean **not**.

Directions: Create new words by adding **in, il, ir** or **im** to these root words. Use a dictionary to check that the new words are correct. The first one has been done for you.

	Prefix		Root Word		New Word
1.	il	+	logical	=	illogical
2.	il	+	literate	=	illiterate
3.	im	+	patient	=	impatient
4.	im	+	probable	=	improbable
5.	ir	+	reversible	=	irreversible
6.	ir	+	responsible	=	irresponsible
7.	in	+	active	=	inactive
8.	im	+	moral	=	immoral
9.	ir	+	removable	=	irremovable
10.	il	+	legible	=	illegible
11.	im	+	mature	=	immature
12.	im	+	perfect	=	imperfect

Page 26

Prefixes

The prefixes **un** and **non** also mean **not**.

Examples:
Unhappy means not happy.
Nonproductive means not productive.

Directions: Divide each word into its prefix and root word. The first one has been done for you.

		Prefix	Root Word
1.	unappreciated	un	appreciate
2.	unlikely	un	like
3.	unkempt	un	keep
4.	untimely	un	time
5.	nonstop	non	stop
6.	nonsense	non	sense
7.	nonprofit	non	profit
8.	nonresident	non	reside

Directions: Use the clues in the first sentence to complete the second sentence with one of the words from the box. The first one has been done for you.

9. She didn't reside at school. She was a **nonresident.**
10. He couldn't stop talking. He talked **nonstop.**
11. The company did not make a profit. It was a **nonprofit** company.
12. She was not talking sense. She was talking **nonsense.**
13. He visited at a bad time. His visit was **untimely.**
14. No one appreciated his efforts. He felt **unappreciated.**
15. He did not "keep up" his hair. His hair was **unkempt.**
16. She was not likely to come. Her coming was **unlikely.**

Page 27

Prefixes

The prefixes **co, col, com, con** and **cor** mean "with" or "together." The prefixes **anti, contra** and **ob** mean "against."

Directions: Write each word's prefix and root word in the space provided.

Word	Prefix	Root Word
coexist	co	exist
concurrent	con	current
correlate	cor	relate
codependent	co	depend
antigravity	anti	gravity
contraband	contra	band

Directions: Use the words from the chart above to complete the sentences.

1. When airplanes fly very high and then quickly drop down, they cause an **antigravity** affect.
2. Materials that are illegal are called **contraband**.
3. A dog and a cat can **coexist** in the same house if they get along well.
4. Events that happen at the same time are **concurrent**.
5. When two people rely on each other, they are said to be **codependent**.
6. The textbook will **correlate** with the teacher's lectures.

Page 28

Prefixes

The prefixes **epi, hyper, over** and **super** mean "above" or "over." The prefixes **under** and **sub** mean "under."

Directions: Write each word's prefix and root word in the space provided.

Word	Prefix	Root Word
hyperactive	hyper	active
overanxious	over	anxious
superimpose	super	impose
epilogue	epi	logue
underestimate	under	estimate
subordinate	sub	ordinate

Directions: Use the words above to complete the following sentences.

1. A photographer could **superimpose** one image on top of another.
2. The **epilogue** of the book may tell additional information about the story.
3. All the other children settled down for the night except the boy who was **hyperactive**.
4. He could not sleep because he was **overanxious** about the upcoming trip.
5. The company's president told his **subordinate** to take over some of the responsibilities.
6. Just because you think you are weak, don't **underestimate** how strong you could be.

Page 29

Numerical Prefixes

Some prefixes are related to numbers. For example, in Latin **uni** means "one." The prefix **mono** means "one" in Greek. The chart below lists prefixes for numbers one through ten from both the Latin and Greek languages.

Number	Latin	Example	Greek	Example
1	uni	university	mon, mono	monopoly
2	du	duplex	di	digress
3	tri	tricycle	tri	trio
4	quad	quadrant	tetro	tetrameter
5	quin	quintuplets	penta	pentagon
6	sex	sexennial	hex	hexagon
7	sept	septuagenarian	hept	heptagon
8	oct	octopus	oct	octagon
9	nov	novena	enne	ennead (group of nine)
10	dec	decade	dec	

Answers may vary.

Directions: Complete the exercises below.

1. unicycle uni **one** + cycle (wheel) = **one wheel**
   Dictionary definition: **one-wheeled vehicle**
2. monogram mono **one** + gram (writing) = **one writing**
   Dictionary definition: **interlaced initials of a name**
3. sextet sex **six** + tet (group) = **six group**
   Dictionary definition: **a group of six**
4. quadrant quad **four** + rant (part) = **four part**
   Dictionary definition: **one of four parts**
5. decigram dec **ten** + gram (gram) = **ten grams**
   Dictionary definition: **one tenth of a gram**

Grade 6 - Comprehensive Curriculum

Page 30

Review

Roots	Meanings	Prefixes	Meanings
fer	carry	dis	separate
graph	write	epi	upon, above
rupt	break	ex	out
tend	stretch	in	in
vade	go	trans	across

Answers may vary.

Directions: Complete the exercises below.

1. invade   in   in   + vade   go   go   =   go in
   Dictionary definition: to intrude upon

2. disrupt dis   separate   + rupt   break   =   separate break
   Dictionary definition: to interrupt or disturb

3. transfer trans   across   + fer   carry   =   carry across
   Dictionary definition: to carry or remove from one place to another

4. extend ex   out   + tend   stretch   =   stretch out
   Dictionary definition: to stretch or draw out

5. epigraph epi   upon   + graph   write   =   upon write
   Dictionary definition: an inscription

Directions: The prefixes **mono** and **uni** both mean one. Write each word's prefix and root in the space provided.

Word	Prefix	Root
monorhyme	mono	rhyme
monosyllable	mono	syllable
unilingual	uni	lingual
uniparental	uni	parent
unilateral	uni	lateral

Page 31

Suffixes

A **suffix** is a syllable added to the end of a root word that changes its meaning.

When a word ends in silent **e**, keep the **e** before adding a suffix beginning with a consonant.

Example: amuse + ment = amusement

Exception: argue + ment = argument

When a word ends in silent **e**, drop the **e** before adding a suffix beginning with a vowel.

Example: amuse = amusing

Exceptions: hoeing, shoeing, canoeing

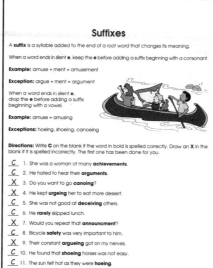

Directions: Write **C** on the blank if the word in bold is spelled correctly. Draw an **X** in the blank if it is spelled incorrectly. The first one has been done for you.

- C 1. She was a woman of many **achievements**.
- C 2. He hated to hear their **arguments**.
- X 3. Do you want to go **canoing**?
- X 4. He kept **urging** her to eat more dessert.
- C 5. She was not good at **deceiving** others.
- C 6. He rarely skipped lunch.
- X 7. Would you repeat that **announcment**?
- C 8. Bicycle **safety** was very important to him.
- X 9. Their constant **argueing** got on my nerves.
- C 10. He found that **shoeing** horses was not easy.
- C 11. The sun felt hot as they were **hoeing**.
- X 12. She was so **relieved** that she laughed.

Page 32

Suffixes: Words Ending in Y

If a word ends in a vowel and **y**, keep the **y** when you add a suffix.

Example:
bray + ed = brayed
bray + ing = braying

Exception: lay + ed = laid

If a word ends in a consonant and **y**, change the **y** to **i** when you add a suffix unless the suffix begins with **i**.

Example:
baby + ed = babied
baby + ing = babying

Directions: Write **C** in the blank if the word in bold is spelled correctly. Draw an **X** if it is spelled incorrectly. The first one has been done for you.

- C 1. She was a good student who did well at her **studies**.
- X 2. Will you please stop **babing** him?
- X 3. She **layed** her purse on the couch.
- X 4. Both the **ferrys** left on schedule.
- C 5. Could you repeat what he was **saying**?
- X 6. He was **tring** to do his best.
- C 7. How many **cherries** are in this pie?
- C 8. The cat **stayed** away for two weeks.
- X 9. He is **saveing** all his money.
- C 10. The lake was **muddier** than I remembered.
- X 11. It was the **muddyest** lake I've ever seen!
- C 12. Her mother **babied** her when she was sick.

Page 33

Suffixes: Doubling Final Consonants

If a one-syllable word ends in one vowel and consonant, double the last consonant when you add a suffix that begins with a vowel.

Examples: big + er = bigger

Directions: Add the suffixes shown to the root words, doubling the final consonants when appropriate. The first one has been done for you.

1. brim + ing = brimming
2. big + est = biggest
3. hop + ing = hopping
4. swim + er = swimmer
5. thin + er = thinner
6. spin + ing = spinning
7. smack + ing = smacking
8. sink + ing = sinking
9. win + er = winner
10. thin + est = thinnest
11. slim + er = slimmer
12. slim + ing = slimming
13. thread + ing = threading
14. thread + er = threader
15. win + ing = winning
16. sing + ing = singing
17. stop + ing = stopping
18. thrill + ing = thrilling
19. drop + ed = dropped
20. mop + ing = mopping

Page 34

Suffixes: Doubling Final Consonants

When two-syllable words have the accent on the second syllable and end in a consonant preceded by a vowel, double the final consonant to add a suffix that begins with a vowel.

Examples: occur + ing = occurring   occur + ed = occurred

If the accent shifts to the first syllable when the suffix is added to the two-syllable root word, the final consonant is not doubled.

Example: refer + ence = reference

Directions: Say the words listed to hear where the accent falls when the suffix is added. Then add the suffix to the root word, doubling the final consonant when appropriate. The first one has been done for you.

1. excel + ence = excellence
2. infer + ing = inferring
3. regret + able = regrettable
4. control + able = controllable
5. submit + ing = submitting
6. confer + ing = conferring
7. refer + al = referral
8. differ + ing = differing
9. compel + ing = compelling
10. commit + ed = committed
11. regret + ing = regretting
12. depend + able = dependable
13. upset + ing = upsetting
14. propel + ing = propelling
15. repel + ed = repelled
16. prefer + ing = preferring
17. prefer + ence = preference
18. differ + ence = difference
19. refer + ing = referring
20. control + ing = controlling

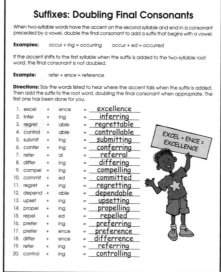

EXCEL + ENCE = EXCELLENCE

Page 35

Suffixes

A **suffix** is a syllable added to the end of a word that changes its meaning. Some suffixes change nouns into adjectives.

Examples: fool — **foolish** nation — **national**

Other suffixes change adjectives into adverbs.

Examples: foolish — **foolishly** national — **nationally**

Directions: Match the root words with words from the box.

personal	stylish	obviously	professional
typical	childish	practical	medical
permanently	ticklish	additional	critical
gradually	physical	musical	

1. tickle **ticklish**   6. grade **gradually**   11. type **typical**
2. critic **critical**   7. practice **practical**   12. music **musical**
3. add **additional**   8. physician **physical**   13. style **stylish**
4. person **personal**   9. permanent **permanently**   14. obvious **obviously**
5. child **childish**   10. medic **medical**   15. profess **professional**

Directions: Circle the word or words in each sentence that are a synonym for a word from the box. Write the word from the box on the line. The first one has been done for you.

16. Knowing how to cook is a (useful) skill.   **practical**
17. The lake (slowly) warmed up.   **gradually**
18. (Clearly) I should have stayed on the path.   **Obviously**
19. That is a (fashionable) outfit.   **stylish**
20. Wanting your own way all the time is (for little kids).   **childish**
21. Getting lost is (common) for me.   **typical**
22. My grades are (a private matter).   **personal**

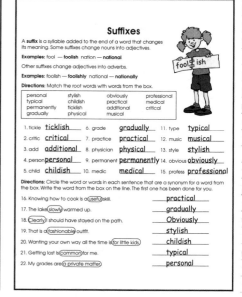

fool-ish

Page 36

Suffixes: "ion," "tion" and "ation"

The suffixes **ion, tion** and **ation** change verbs into nouns.

Examples: imitate + **ion** = imitation   combine + **ation** = combination

Directions: Match each word from the box with its definition.

celebration	solution	imitation	exploration	selection
reflection	conversation	population	invitation	suggestion
combination	decoration	appreciation	definition	transportation

1. a copy   imitation
2. talking   conversation
3. a request   invitation
4. the meaning   definition
5. a search   exploration
6. mirror image reflection
7. cars, trucks transportation
8. ornament   decoration

9. choice   selection
10. a party   celebration
11. the answer   solution
12. people   population
13. a joining   combination
14. new idea   suggestion
15. thankfulness appreciation

Directions: Write the correct forms of the words in the sentences. The first one has been done for you.

16. **transport** How are we _transporting_ our project to school?
    Did anyone arrange _transportation_ ?
17. **decorate** Today, we are _decorating_ the classroom.
    We brought the _decorations_ from home.
18. **solve** Have you _solved_ the problem yet?
    We need a _solution_ by the end of the day.

Page 37

Suffixes: "ment" and "ity"

The suffixes **ment** and **ity** change verbs and some adjectives to nouns.

Examples: treat — treatment   able — ability

Directions: Circle the word or words in each sentence that are synonyms for words from the box. Write the word from the box on the line. The first one has been done for you.

equipment	responsibility	activity		
accomplishment	adjustment	ability	treatment	
assignment	personality	achievement	appointment	
popularity	astonishment	advertisement	curiosity	

1. The workers are bringing in their (machines).   equipment
2. Whose (duty) is it to take out the trash?   responsibility
3. Do you know our (homework) for tonight?   assignment
4. I could see the (surprise) in his face.   astonishment
5. Ken is happy with his new (position).   appointment
6. I was filled with (wondering).   curiosity
7. She lists one (achievement) in particular.   accomplishment
8. Look at the (exercise) on page 16.   activity
9. The way you get along with others is part of your (character).   personality
10. I heard that (commercial) a hundred times.   advertisement
11. Amy has a strong athletic (skill).   ability
12. Jason's kindness led to his (acceptance by his friends).   popularity
13. I need to make a (change) in my schedule.   adjustment
14. That is quite an (accomplishment).   achievement
15. The doctor is trying another (way) to help my allergies.   treatment

Page 38

Suffixes

The suffix **less** means **lacking** or **without**. The suffix **some** means **full of** or **like**.

Examples:
Hopeless means without hope.
Awesome means filled with awe.

Directions: Create new words by adding **some** or **less** to these root words. Use a dictionary to check that the new words are correct. The first one has been done for you.

	Root Word		Suffix		New Word
1.	heart	+	less	=	heartless
2.	trouble	+	some	=	troublesome
3.	home	+	less	=	homeless
4.	humor	+	less	=	humorless
5.	awe	+	some	=	awesome
6.	child	+	less	=	childless
7.	win	+	some	=	winsome

Directions: Use the clues in the first sentence to complete the second sentence with one of the words from the box. The first one has been done for you.

8. Her smile was winning and delightful. She had a _winsome_ smile.
9. The mean man seemed to have no heart. He was _heartless._
10. She never smiled or laughed. She appeared to be _humorless._
11. The solar system fills me with awe. It is _awesome._
12. The couple had no children. They were _childless._
13. He had no place to live. He was _homeless._
14. The pet caused the family trouble. It was _troublesome._

Page 39

Suffixes: "ship," "ful" and "ist"

Directions: Write the meaning of each word on the line. Use a dictionary if you are unsure of the meaning of a word.

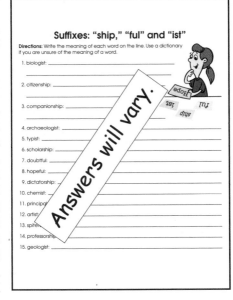

1. biologist: _____
2. citizenship: _____
3. companionship: _____
4. archaeologist: _____
5. typist: _____
6. scholarship: _____
7. doubtful: _____
8. hopeful: _____
9. dictatorship: _____
10. chemist: _____
11. principal: _____
12. artist: _____
13. spiteful: _____
14. professorship: _____
15. geologist: _____

Answers will vary.

Page 40

Suffixes: "ance" and "ence"

Directions: Write words from the box to complete the sentences. Use a dictionary if you are unsure of the meaning of a word.

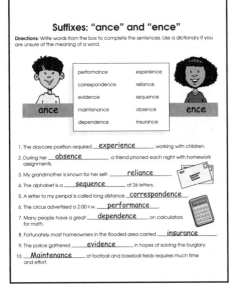

ance / **ence**

performance	experience
correspondence	reliance
evidence	sequence
maintenance	absence
dependence	insurance

1. The daycare position required _experience_ working with children.
2. During her _absence_ , a friend phoned each night with homework assignments.
3. My grandmother is known for her self-_reliance_.
4. The alphabet is a _sequence_ of 26 letters.
5. A letter to my penpal is called long distance _correspondence_.
6. The circus advertised a 2:00 P.M. _performance_.
7. Many people have a great _dependence_ on calculators for math.
8. Fortunately, most homeowners in the flooded area carried _insurance_.
9. The police gathered _evidence_ in hopes of solving the burglary.
10. _Maintenance_ of football and baseball fields requires much time and effort.

Page 41

Suffixes

The suffix **ment** means the **act of** or **state of**. The suffixes **ible** and **able** mean **able to**.

Directions: Create new words by adding **ment** or **able** to these root words. Use a dictionary to check that the new words are correct. The first one has been done for you.

	Root Word		Suffix		New Word
1.	rely	+	able	=	reliable
2.	retire	+	ment	=	retirement
3.	sense	+	ible	=	sensible
4.	commit	+	ment	=	commitment
5.	repair	+	able	=	repairable
6.	love	+	able	=	loveable (also lovable)
7.	quote	+	able	=	quotable
8.	honor	+	able	=	honorable

Directions: Use the clues in the first sentence to complete the second sentence with one of the words from the box. The first one has been done for you.

9. Everyone loved her. She was _loveable (also lovable)._
10. He had a lot of sense. He was _sensible._
11. She committed time to the project. She made a _commitment._
12. He always did the right thing. His behavior was _honorable._
13. The fire could not be fixed. It was not _repairable._
14. They would not buy the car. The car was not _reliable._
15. He gave the reporter good comments. His comments were _quotable._
16. She was ready to retire. She looked forward to _retirement._

Page 42

Review

Directions: Add one of the prefixes, suffixes or combining forms to a word in the box to complete each sentence. Use the definition in parentheses as a clue.

ian	ous	ship	an	ist	extra	trans	pre	micro	super

friend	music	geology	sensory	America
paid	wave	market	atlantic	danger

1. The __supermarket__ has a huge selection of fruits and vegetables. (large food store)
2. The first __transatlantic__ flight was a remarkable feat in the history of aviation. (across the Atlantic Ocean)
3. The woman claimed that she knew the future because of her __extrasensory__ capabilities. (beyond the normal senses)
4. When mailing your payment, please use the __prepaid__ envelope. (paid in advance)
5. Mrs. Johnson studied the violin for many years to become the accomplished __musician__ she is today. (person skilled in music)
6. The __microwave__ oven is a modern-day convenience. (operating with extremely small electromagnetic waves)
7. Lightning is the most __dangerous__ part of a storm. (characterized by danger)
8. They raised the __American__ flag over their campground in a gesture of patriotism. (belonging to America)
9. The Native Americans would often smoke a peace pipe as a sign of __friendship__. (the state of being friends)
10. Dr. Stokes is the finest __geologist__ at the university. (one who is skilled at geology, the study of the earth's crust)

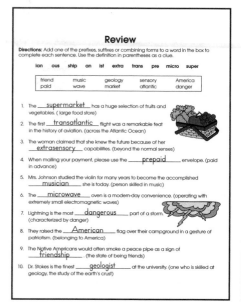

Page 43

Review

Directions: Add suffixes to change these nouns into adjectives.

1. person_al_   music_al_   child _ish_

Directions: Add suffixes to change these adjectives into adverbs.

2. permanent_ly_   obvious_ly_   gradual_ly_

Directions: Add the prefix **pre**, **un**, **in**, **re** or **con** to each word and use the word in a sentence.

3. search __research__
4. join __conjoin__
5. compatible __incompatible__
6. wrap __unwrap__
7. school __preschool__

Sentences will vary.

Directions: Add the suffix **ish**, **ment**, **ion**, **ship** or **ful** to each word and use the word in a sentence.

8. square __squarish__
9. invent __invention__
10. force __forceful__
11. replace __replacement__
12. chairman __chairmanship__

Sentences will vary.

Directions: Add suffixes to make the noun forms of these verbs.

13. select __selection__   16. imitate __imitation__
14. decorate __decoration__   17. reflect __reflection__
15. invite __invitation__

Page 44

Review

Directions: Spell these silent **e** words correctly.

1. achievments __achievements__
2. canoing __canoeing__
3. amuseing __amusing__
4. urgeing __urging__

Directions: Add the suffixes to these words ending in **y** and spell them correctly.

5. baby + ies = __babies__
6. stay + ed = __stayed__

Directions: Add the suffixes and spell these one-syllable words correctly.

7. hope + ing = __hoping__
8. stop + ing = __stopping__

Directions: Add the suffixes and spell these two-syllable words correctly.

9. recur + ing = __recurring__
10. defer + ence = __deference__

Directions: Spell these words correctly by inserting **ie** or **ei**.

11. h_e__i_ght
12. ch_i__e_f

Directions: Circle the **q** words in each row that are spelled correctly.

13. (quip)   qeen   qick   (quit)
14. qestion   (equator)   (quiet)   qart
15. (squirrel)   sqare   (squirm)   sqeak

Page 45

Analyzing Words and Their Parts

A **syllable** is a word or part of a word with only one vowel sound.

Directions: Fill in the missing syllables. Use words from the box. Write the number of syllables after each word. The first one has been done for you.

expense	exist	aquarium	acquire	request
exact	expand	exit	quality	excellent
quiz	quantity	expression	exhibit	squirm

1. ex _c_ _e_ l lent (3)   6. ac**quire** (2)   11. __re__ quest (2)
2. __—__ squirm (1)   7. quali**ty** (3)   12. ex **hib** it (3)
3. __ex__ act (2)   8. __ex__ it (2)   13. __ex__ pense (2)
4. __—__ quiz (1)   9. ex **pres** sion (3)   14. __ex__ pand (2)
5. aquar _i_ um (4)   10. __ex__ ist (2)   15. quan __ti__ ty (3)

Directions: Write words that rhyme. Use words in the box.

16. fizz __quiz__   21. It's been sent __excellent__   26. fire __acquire__
17. resist __exist__   22. this is it __exhibit__   27. best __request__
18. fact __exact__   23. made for me __quality__   28. fit __exit__
19. fence __expense__   24. reflection __expression__
20. sand __expand__   25. worm __squirm__

A **root word** is a common stem which gives related words their basic meaning.

Directions: Write the root word for the bold word in each sentence.

29. I know **exactly** what I want. __exact__
30. Those shoes look **expensive**. __expense__
31. She didn't like my **expression** when I frowned. __express__
32. We went to the train **exhibition** at the park. __exhibit__

Page 46

Dividing Words Into Syllables

Directions: Divide these words into syllables by putting a hyphen (-) between each syllable. The first one has been done for you.

1. multiplication
   __mul-ti-pli-ca-tion__
2. discover
   __dis-cov-er__
3. ultimate
   __ul-ti-mate__
4. transfer
   __trans-fer__
5. continent
   __con-ti-nent__
6. follow
   __fol-low__
7. British
   __Brit-ish__
8. American
   __A-mer-i-can__
9. president
   __pres-i-dent__
10. discrimination
    __dis-crim-i-na-tion__
11. spectacular
    __spec-tac-u-lar__
12. commercial
    __com-mer-cial__
13. probability
    __prob-a-bil-i-ty__
14. country
    __coun-try__
15. casual
    __ca-su-al__
16. political
    __po-lit-i-cal__
17. wrestle
    __wres-tle__
18. basketball
    __bas-ket-ball__
19. particular
    __par-tic-u-lar__
20. cereal
    __ce-re-al__
21. picture
    __pic-ture__
22. plumber
    __plumb-er__
23. personal
    __per-son-al__
24. sentence
    __sen-tence__

Page 47

Synonyms

A **synonym** is a word that means the same or nearly the same as another word. **Example:** mean and cruel.

Directions: Circle the word or group of words in each sentence that is a synonym for a word in the box. Write the synonym from the box on the line. The first one has been done for you.

florist	courtesy	research	emergency	flourish
plural	observe	furnish	tornado	source
ignored	survey	normally	coarse	restore

1. The children seemed to (thrive) in their new school. __flourish__
2. Her (politeness) made me feel welcome. __courtesy__
3. The principal came to (watch) our class. __observe__
4. Are you going to (fix up) that old house? __restore__
5. Six weeks after the (disaster) the neighborhood looked as it usually did. __emergency__
6. What was the (origin) of that rumor? __source__
7. The (cyclone) destroyed two houses. __tornado__
8. She (neglected) her homework. __ignored__
9. The material had a (rough) feel to it. __coarse__
10. Did you fill out the (questionnaire) yet? __survey__

Directions: Select three words from the box below. Write a sentence for each word that shows you understand the meaning of the word.

plural	flourish	source	restore	observe	furnish	research

Answers will vary.

Page 48

Antonyms

An **antonym** is a word which means the opposite of another word.

Example: hopeful and discouraged

Directions: Circle the word or group of words in each sentence that is an antonym for a word in the box. Write the antonym from the box on the line.

nuisance	considerate
delicate	frivolous
entrance	shiny
divide	parallel
success	valley

1. It seemed as though we'd never make it to the top of the (butte). — **valley**
2. Rosa thought the woman was (rude) to the store clerk. — **considerate**
3. The two streets run (perpendicular) to each other. — **parallel**
4. The school carnival was a total (failure) due to the stormy weather. — **success**
5. Be sure to wash this (sturdy) sweater with other heavy items. — **delicate**
6. The third grade class worked hard learning to (multiply). — **divide**
7. The (exit) was blocked by a table. — **entrance**
8. The purchase of the coat was quite (practical). — **frivolous**
9. The teacher wrote that Colin was a (joy) to have in class. — **nuisance**
10. The stone in her ring was (dull and cloudy). — **shiny**

Page 49

Spelling: Homophones

Homophones are words that sound the same, but have different spellings and different meanings.

Examples: night and knight, fair and fare, not and knot

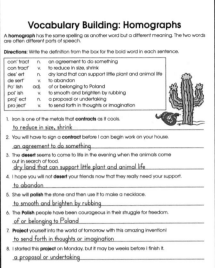

Directions: Complete each sentence with the correct homophone. Then write a sentence using the other homophone. Use a dictionary if you don't know the meaning of a word. The first one has been done for you.

1. eight / ate — I **ate** two cookies.
   Joanie had eight cookies!
2. vein / vain — Since the newspaper printed his picture, Keith has been self-centered and **vain**.
   Sentences will vary.
3. weight / wait — We had to **wait** a long time for the show to start.
4. weigh / way — He always insists that we do everything his **way**.
5. seize / seas — The explorers charted the **seas**.
6. straight / strait — It is sometimes difficult to draw perfectly **straight** lines freehand.
7. principle / principal — The **principal** summoned the student body to the auditorium for a special program.
8. their / they're — I'm sure **they're** meeting us at the park rather than at home.

Page 50

Vocabulary Building: Homographs

A **homograph** has the same spelling as another word but a different meaning. The two words are often different parts of speech.

Directions: Write the definition from the box for the bold word in each sentence.

con' tract	n.	an agreement to do something
con tract'	v.	to reduce in size, shrink
des' ert	n.	dry land that can support little plant and animal life
de sert'	v.	to abandon
Po' lish	adj.	of or belonging to Poland
pol' ish	v.	to smooth and brighten by rubbing
proj' ect	n.	a proposal or undertaking
pro ject'	v.	to send forth in thoughts or imagination

1. Iron is one of the metals that **contracts** as it cools.
   to reduce in size, shrink
2. You will have to sign a **contract** before I can begin work on your house.
   an agreement to do something
3. The **desert** seems to come to life in the evening when the animals come out in search of food.
   dry land that can support little plant and animal life
4. I hope you will not **desert** your friends now that they really need your support.
   to abandon
5. She will **polish** the stone and then use it to make a necklace.
   to smooth and brighten by rubbing
6. The **Polish** people have been courageous in their struggle for freedom.
   of or belonging to Poland
7. **Project** yourself into the world of tomorrow with this amazing invention!
   to send forth in thoughts or imagination
8. I started this **project** on Monday, but it may be weeks before I finish it.
   a proposal or undertaking

Page 51

Vocabulary Building: Homographs

Directions: After each sentence, write the meaning of the bold word. Write another sentence using a homograph for the word.

1. The owner of the pet store tied a bright red **bow** around the puppies' necks.
   Meaning: a knot tied with a ribbon
   Sentence:
2. Today, fewer pipes are made from **lead**.
   Meaning: a metal
   Sentence:

   Sentences will vary.

3. Marcia's new house is very **close** to ours.
   Meaning: near
   Sentence:
4. Please **record** the time and day that we finished the project.
   Meaning: write down
   Sentence:
5. It takes only a **minute** to fasten your seatbelt, but it can save your life.
   Meaning: 60 seconds
   Sentence:
6. I cannot **subject** the animal to that kind of treatment.
   Meaning: expose
   Sentence:

Page 52

Multiple Meanings

Directions: Use a dictionary to write the meaning of the bold word in each sentence. Be sure the meaning fits the context of the sentence and the part of speech. The first one has been done for you.

Sample Answers:

1. Rosa will **graduate** summa cum laude.
   to receive an academic degree
2. The **graduate** looked for suitable employment.
   one who has graduated
3. The woman balanced her purse on the **counter**.
   a flat surface
4. The boss **countered** the employee's request for a large raise.
   to oppose
5. Julio Mentarre will **conduct** the orchestra tonight.
   to direct or guide
6. Metal **conducts** electricity.
   to convey or transmit
7. His **conduct** was questionable in that situation.
   action or behavior
8. Please **file** these reports today.
   to put in a useful order
9. The principal asked the students to leave in single **file**.
   a row or line
10. "Please hand me a **file**," said the woodworker to his daughter.
   a tool used for smoothing rough surfaces

Page 53

Vocabulary Building: Multiple Meanings

Directions: Use a dictionary to choose the correct definition for each bold word. The first one has been done for you.

1. My grandfather always has his **spectacles** perched on his nose.
   Meaning: lenses worn in front of the eyes to aid vision
2. The Fourth of July fireworks display was an amazing **spectacle**.
   Meaning: dramatic public display
3. We enjoy a rugged vacation, staying in a hunting **lodge** rather than a hotel.
   Meaning: large rustic cabin for vacationers
4. Don't let the baby have hard candy, because it could **lodge** in his throat.
   Meaning: get stuck
5. Termites will **bore** through the rotten wood in our basement if we don't have it replaced.
   Meaning: to make a hole by digging
6. That television show could **bore** even a small child!
   Meaning: to weary by being dull
7. Don't **resort** to lies just to get what you want!
   Meaning: to go back to habitually
8. The **resort** is packed with tourists from May to September each year.
   Meaning: place providing recreation and entertainment

Page 54

Vocabulary Building: Multiple Meanings

Directions: Read each sentence, then write another sentence using a different meaning for the bold word.

1. The prince will **succeed** his mother as ruler of the country.

2. All through the National Anthem, Johnny was singing in the wrong **key**.

3. There has been only a **trace** of rain this month.

4. I can't get involved in a **cause** which I don't really believe.

5. It is very impor... *Answers will vary.*

6. A police officer can **issue** a warning to those disturbing the peace.

7. There is a mayoral candidate from each of the major political **parties**.

8. You can take that **stack** of newspapers to be recycled.

9. The judge will likely **sentence** the offender to a year in prison.

10. The lawyer made a **motion** to have the charges dropped.

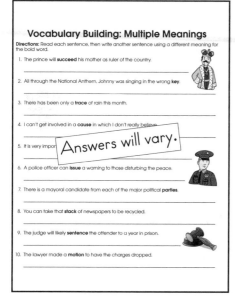

Page 55

Reading Skills: Classifying

Classifying is placing similar things into categories.

Example: January, May and October can be classified as months.

Directions: Write a category name for each group of words.

1. accordion   clarinet   trumpet   __musical instruments__
2. wasp   bumblebee   mosquito   __insects__
3. antique   elderly   prehistoric   __words for "old"__
4. chemist   astronomer   geologist   __scientists__
5. nest   cocoon   burrow   __animal homes__

Directions: In each row, draw an **X** through the word that does not belong. Then write a sentence telling why it does not belong.

1. encyclopedia   atlas   no~~v~~el   dictionary
   __A novel is not a reference book.__
2. bass   o~~t~~ter   tuna   trout
   __An otter is not a fish.__
3. sister   grandmother   niece   un~~c~~le
   __An uncle is not a female relative.__
4. b~~a~~rk   beech   dogwood   spruce
   __Bark is not a type of tree.__
5. pebble   gravel   boulder   ce~~m~~ent
   __Cement is not a form of rock.__
6. spaniel   Sia~~m~~ese   collie   Doberman
   __A Siamese is not a type of dog.__

Page 56

Reading Skills: Classifying

Directions: In each row, draw an **X** through the word that does not belong. Then write a word that belongs.

Sample answers:

1. monkey   ele~~p~~hant   do~~g~~   __giraffe__
2. daisies   roses   violets   fe~~r~~ns   pansies   __tulips__
3. paper   p~~e~~n   pencil   eraser   stapler   __pen__
4. sister   cousin   father   aunt   fri~~e~~nd   __mother__
5. hand   mouth   sh~~i~~rt   foot   elbow   __leg__
6. shy   c~~a~~t   happy   angry   sad   __grumpy__
7. puppy   do~~g~~   kitten   cub   lamb   __chick__
8. red   blue   c~~o~~lor   yellow   purple   __green__
9. Earth   Jupiter   Saturn   Pluto   S~~u~~n   __Mars__
10. si~~n~~k   bed   desk   dresser   lamp   __chair__

Directions: Name each category above.

1. __African animals__   6. __feelings__
2. __flowers__   7. __baby animals__
3. __school supplies__   8. __colors__
4. __relatives__   9. __planets__
5. __body parts__   10. __bedroom furniture__

Page 57

Reading Skills: Classifying

Directions: Write three things that would belong in each category below. The first one has been done for you.

Sample answers:

1. mammals
   __whale__   __horse__   __elephant__
2. rainforest animals
   __toucan__   __tree frog__   __snake__
3. capital cities
   __Sacramento__   __Portland__   __Seattle__
4. oceans
   __Pacific__   __Atlantic__   __Indian__
5. occupations
   __editor__   __lawyer__   __teacher__
6. Native American tribes
   __Blackfoot__   __Cherokee__   __Pawnee__
7. wars
   __WWII__   __Korean War__   __Vietnam War__
8. planets
   __Venus__   __Mars__   __Earth__
9. track and field sports
   __hurdles__   __discus__   __high jump__
10. famous Americans
   __George Washington__   __Rosa Parks__   __Martin Luther King, Jr.__

Page 58

Types of Analogies

An **analogy** shows similarities, or things in common, between a pair of words. The relationships between the words in analogies usually fall into these categories:

1. **Purpose** — One word in the pair shows the **purpose** of the other word (scissors: cut).
2. **Antonyms** — The words are **opposites** (light: dark).
3. **Part/whole** — One word in the pair is a **part**; the other is a **whole** (leg: body).
4. **Action/object** — One word in the pair involves an **action** with or to an **object** (fly: airplane).
5. **Association** — One word in the pair is what you think of or **associate** when you see the other (cow: milk).
6. **Object/location** — One word in the pair tells the **location** of where the other word, an **object**, is found (car: garage).
7. **Cause/effect** — One word in the pair tells the **cause**; the other word shows the **effect** (practice: improvement).
8. **Synonyms** — The words are **synonyms** (small: tiny).

Directions: Write the relationship between the words in each pair. The first two have been done for you.

1. cow: farm   __object/location__
2. toe: foot   __part/whole__
3. watch: TV   __action/object__
4. bank: money   __association__
5. happy: unhappy   __antonyms__
6. listen: radio   __action/object__
7. inning: ballgame   __part/whole__
8. knife: cut   __action/object__
9. safe: dangerous   __antonyms__
10. carrots: soup   __part/whole__

Page 59

Writing Analogies

Once you have determined the relationship between the words in the first pair, the next step is to find a similar relationship between another pair of words.

Examples:
Scissors is to **cut** as **broom** is to **sweep**.
Black is to **white** as **up** is to **down**.

Scissors cut. Brooms sweep. The first analogy shows the **purpose** of scissors and brooms. In the second example, up and down are **antonyms**, as are black and white.

Directions: Choose the correct word to complete each analogy. The first one has been done for you.

1. **Sky** is to **blue** as **grass** is to
   A. earth   B. green   C. lawn   D. yard   __green__
2. **Snow** is to **winter** as **rain** is to
   A. umbrella   B. wet   C. slicker   D. spring   __spring__
3. **Sun** is to **day** as **moon** is to
   A. dark   B. night   C. stars   D. blackness   __night__
4. **5** is to **10** as **15** is to
   A. 50   B. 25   C. 30   D. 40   __30__
5. **Collie** is to **dog** as **Siamese** is to
   A. pet   B. kitten   C. baby   D. cat   __cat__
6. **Letter** is to **word** as **note** is to
   A. tuba   B. music   C. instruments   D. singer   __music__
7. **100** is to **10** as **1,000** is to
   A. 10   B. 200   C. 100   D. 10,000   __100__
8. **Back** is to **rear** as **pit** is to
   A. peach   B. hole   C. dark   D. punishment   __hole__

Page 60

Analogies of Purpose

Directions: Choose the correct word to complete each analogy of purpose. The first one has been done for you.

1. **Knife** is to **cut** as **copy machine** is to

   A. duplicate   B. paper   C. copies   D. office   _duplicate_

2. **Bicycle** is to **ride** as **glass** is to

   A. dishes   B. dinner   C. drink   D. break   _drink_

3. **Hat** is to **cover** as **eraser** is to

   A. chalkboard   B. pencil   C. mistake   D. erase   _erase_

4. **Mystery** is to **clue** as **door** is to

   A. house   B. key   C. window   D. open   _key_

5. **Television** is to **see** as **CD** is to

   A. sound   B. hear   C. play   D. dance   _hear_

6. **Clock** is to **time** as **ruler** is to

   A. height   B. length   C. measure   D. inches   _measure_

7. **Fry** is to **pan** as **bake** is to

   A. cookies   B. dinner   C. oven   D. baker   _oven_

8. **Bowl** is to **fruit** as **wrapper** is to

   A. present   B. candy   C. paper   D. ribbon   _candy_

Page 61

Antonym Analogies

Directions: Write antonyms for these words.   Answers will vary but may include:

1. run: _walk_
2. start: _stop_
3. laugh: _cry_
4. dependent: _independent_
5. young: _old_
6. North: _South_
7. sink: _float_
8. success: _failure_
9. combine: _separate_
10. laugh: _cry_
11. polluted: _clean_
12. leader: _follower_
13. fascinate: _bore_
14. man: _woman_

15. awake: _asleep_
16. begin: _end_
17. increase: _decrease_
18. reverse: _forward_
19. enlarge: _shrink_
20. East: _West_
21. rural: _urban_
22. amateur: _professional_
23. patient: _impatient_
24. rich: _poor_
25. empty: _full_
26. fancy: _plain_
27. introduction: _conclusion_
28. modern: _old-fashion_

Directions: Write two antonym analogies of your own.

29. _Answers will vary._

30.

Page 62

Part/Whole Analogies

Directions: Determine whether each analogy is whole to part or part to whole by studying the relationship between the first pair of words. Then choose the correct word to complete each analogy. The first one has been done for you.

1. **Shoestring** is to **shoe** as **brim** is to

   A. cup   B. shade   C. hat   D. scarf   _hat_

2. **Egg** is to **yolk** as **suit** is to

   A. clothes   B. shoes   C. business   D. jacket   _jacket_

3. **Stanza** is to **poem** as **verse** is to

   A. rhyme   B. singing   C. song   D. music   _song_

4. **Wave** is to **ocean** as **branch** is to

   A. stream   B. lawn   C. office   D. tree   _tree_

5. **Chicken** is to **farm** as **giraffe** is to

   A. animal   B. zoo   C. tall   D. stripes   _zoo_

6. **Finger** is to **nail** as **leg** is to

   A. arm   B. torso   C. knee   D. walk   _knee_

7. **Player** is to **team** as **inch** is to

   A. worm   B. measure   C. foot   D. short   _foot_

8. **Peak** is to **mountain** as **crest** is to

   A. wave   B. ocean   C. beach   D. water   _wave_

Page 63

Action/Object Analogies

Directions: Determine whether each analogy is action/object or object/action by studying the relationship between the first pair of words. Then choose the correct word to complete each analogy. The first one has been done for you.

1. **Mow** is to **grass** as **shear** is to

   A. cut   B. fleece   C. sheep   D. barber   _sheep_

2. **Rod** is to **fishing** as **gun** is to

   A. police   B. crime   C. shoot   D. hunting   _hunting_

3. **Ship** is to **captain** as **airplane** is to

   A. fly   B. airport   C. pilot   D. passenger   _pilot_

4. **Car** is to **mechanic** as **body** is to

   A. patient   B. doctor   C. torso   D. hospital   _doctor_

5. **Cheat** is to **exam** as **swindle** is to

   A. criminal   B. business   C. crook   D. crime   _business_

6. **Actor** is to **stage** as **surgeon** is to

   A. patient   B. hospital   C. operating room   D. knife   _operating room_

7. **Ball** is to **throw** as **knife** is to

   A. cut   B. spoon   C. dinner   D. silverware   _cut_

8. **Lawyer** is to **trial** as **surgeon** is to

   A. patient   B. hospital   C. operation   D. operating room   _operation_

Page 64

Analogies of Association

Directions: Choose the correct word to complete each analogy. The first one has been done for you.

1. **Flowers** are to **spring** as **leaves** are to

   A. rakes   B. trees   C. fall   D. green   _fall_

2. **Ham** is to **eggs** as **butter** is to

   A. fat   B. toast   C. breakfast   D. spread   _toast_

3. **Bat** is to **swing** as **ball** is to

   A. throw   B. dance   C. base   D. soft   _throw_

4. **Chicken** is to **egg** as **cow** is to

   A. barn   B. calf   C. milk   D. beef   _milk_

5. **Bed** is to **sleep** as **chair** is to

   A. sit   B. couch   C. relax   D. table   _sit_

6. **Cube** is to **square** as **sphere** is to

   A. circle   B. triangle   C. hemisphere   D. spear   _circle_

7. **Kindness** is to **friend** as **cruelty** is to

   A. meanness   B. enemy   C. war   D. unkindness   _enemy_

8. **Pumpkin** is to **pie** as **chocolate** is to

   A. cake   B. dark   C. taste   D. dessert   _cake_

Page 65

Object/Location Analogies

Directions: Write a location word for each object.   Answers will vary but may include:

1. shirt: _closet_
2. milk: _carton_
3. vase: _table_
4. screwdriver: _toolbox_
5. cow: _barn_
6. chalkboard: _classroom_
7. shower: _bathroom_
8. cucumbers: _garden_
9. silverware: _drawer_
10. car: _garage_
11. pages: _book_
12. bees: _beehive_
13. money: _bank_
14. salt water: _sea_

15. dress: _dress shop_
16. ice cream: _freezer_
17. table: _dining room_
18. medicine: _pharmacy_
19. dog: _doghouse_
20. basketball: _hoop_
21. bed: _bedroom_
22. roses: _vase_
23. dishwasher: _kitchen_
24. toys: _toy box_
25. cookies: _cookie jar_
26. bird: _birdhouse_
27. seashells: _beach_
28. asteroids: _sky_

Page 66

Cause/Effect Analogies

Directions: Determine whether the analogy is cause/effect or effect/cause by studying the relationship between the first pair of words. Then choose the correct word to complete each analogy. The first one has been done for you.

You caused this...and now look at the effect!

1. **Ashes** are to **flame** as **darkness** is to
   A. light   B. daylight   C. eclipse   D. sun   **eclipse**

2. **Strong** is to **exercising** as **elected** is to
   A. office   B. senator   C. politician   D. campaigning   **campaigning**

3. **Fall** is to **pain** as **disobedience** is to
   A. punishment   B. morals   C. behavior   D. carelessness   **punishment**

4. **Crying** is to **sorrow** as **smiling** is to
   A. teeth   B. mouth   C. joy   D. friends   **joy**

5. **Germ** is to **disease** as **war** is to
   A. soldiers   B. enemies   C. destruction   D. tanks   **destruction**

6. **Distracting** is to **noise** as **soothing** is to
   A. balm   B. warmth   C. hugs   D. music   **music**

7. **Food** is to **nutrition** as **light** is to
   A. vision   B. darkness   C. sunshine   D. bulb   **vision**

8. **Clouds** are to **rain** as **winds** are to
   A. springtime   B. hurricanes   C. clouds   D. March   **hurricanes**

Page 67

Synonym Analogies

Directions: Write synonyms for these words.

Answers will vary but may include:

1. miniature: **tiny**
2. wind: **gale**
3. picture: **photo**
4. quiet: **silent**
5. run: **jog**
6. cloth: **material**
7. mean: **nasty**
8. cup: **mug**
9. sweet: **tasty**
10. difficult: **hard**
11. obey: **do**
12. plenty: **lots**
13. scent: **smell**
14. sudden: **quick**
15. gigantic: **huge**
16. rain: **shower**
17. cabinet: **cupboard**
18. loud: **noisy**
19. leap: **jump**
20. jeans: **pants**
21. kind: **nice**
22. dish: **plate**
23. feline: **cat**
24. simple: **easy**
25. beautiful: **pretty**
26. scorch: **burn**
27. story: **tale**
28. thaw: **unfreeze**

Directions: Write two synonym analogies of your own.

29. _____

30. _____ *Answers will vary.*

Page 68

Reading Skills: Fact or Opinion?

A **fact** is information that can be proved. An **opinion** is information that tells how someone feels or what he/she thinks about something.

Directions: For each sentence, write **F** for fact or **O** for opinion. The first one has been done for you.

F 1. Each of the countries in South America has its own capital.

O 2. All South Americans are good swimmers.

O 3. People like the climate in Peru better than in Brazil.

F 4. The continent of South America is almost completely surrounded by water.

F 5. The only connection with another continent is a narrow strip of land, called the Isthmus of Panama, which links it to North America.

F 6. The Andes Mountains run all the way down the western edge of the continent.

F 7. The Andes are the longest continuous mountain barrier in the world.

O 8. The Andes are the most beautiful mountain range.

F 9. The Amazon River is the second longest river in the world—about 4,000 miles long.

F 10. Half of the people in South America are Brazilians.

O 11. Life in Brazil is better than life in other South American countries.

O 12. Brazil is the best place for South Americans to live.

F 13. Cape Horn is at the southern tip of South America.

F 14. The largest land animal in South America is the tapir, which reaches a length of 6 to 8 feet.

Page 69

Reading Skills: Fact or Opinion?

Directions: Read the paragraphs below. For each numbered sentence, write **F** for fact or **O** for opinion. Write the reason for your answer. The first one has been done for you.

(1) The two greatest poems in the history of the world are the *Iliad* and the *Odyssey*. (2) The *Iliad* is the story of the Trojan War; the *Odyssey* tells about the wanderings of the Greek hero Ulysses after the war. (3) These poems are so long that they each fill an entire book.

(4) The author of the poems, according to Greek legend, was a blind poet named Homer. (5) Almost nothing is known about Homer. (6) This indicates to me that it is possible that Homer never existed. (7) Maybe Homer existed but didn't write the *Iliad* and the *Odyssey*.

(8) Whether or not there was a Homer does not really matter. We have these wonderful poems, written more than 2,500 years after they were written.

Sample answers:

1. **O** Reason: This cannot be proven. People have different opinions about which are the greatest poems.

2. **F** Reason: explains what the poems are about

3. **F** Reason: tells how long the poems are

4. **F** Reason: tells a fact about a Greek legend

5. **F** Reason: tells that not much is known about Homer

6. **O** Reason: not everyone thinks Homer did not exist

7. **O** Reason: some people may believe this and some may not

8. **O** Reason: some people may not agree with this

Page 70

Chilies

Directions: Read about chilies. Find the one opinion in each passage and write it on the lines.

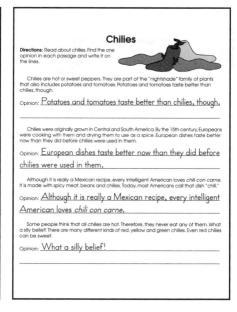

Chilies are hot or sweet peppers. They are part of the "nightshade" family of plants that also includes potatoes and tomatoes. Potatoes and tomatoes taste better than chilies, though.

Opinion: **Potatoes and tomatoes taste better than chilies, though.**

Chilies were originally grown in Central and South America. By the 15th century, Europeans were cooking with them and drying them to use as a spice. European dishes taste better now than they did before chilies were used in them.

Opinion: **European dishes taste better now than they did before chilies were used in them.**

Although it is really a Mexican recipe, every intelligent American loves chili con carne. It is made with spicy meat, beans and chilies. Today, most Americans call that dish "chili."

Opinion: **Although it is really a Mexican recipe, every intelligent American loves *chili con carne.***

Some people think that all chilies are hot. Therefore, they never eat any of them. What a silly belief! There are many different kinds of red, yellow and green chilies. Even red chilies can be sweet.

Opinion: **What a silly belief!**

Page 71

Carol's Country Restaurant

Directions: Write in the corresponding numbered blank below whether each numbered sentence gives a fact or an opinion.

(1) I have visited Carol's Country Restaurant seven times in the past 2 weeks. (2) The meals there are excellent. (3) They often feature country dishes such as meatloaf, ham with scalloped potatoes and fried chicken.

(4) Owner Carol Murphy makes wonderful vegetable soup that includes all home-grown vegetables. (5) It's simmered with egg noodles. (6) Another of my favorite dishes is Carol's chili. (7) I'm sure it is the spiciest chili this side of the Mississippi River. (8) Carol says she uses secret ingredients in all her dishes.

(9) Whether ordering a main dish or a dessert, you can't go wrong at Carol's. (10) Everything is superb.

(11) Carol's Country Restaurant is on Twig Street in Freeport. (12) Prices for main entrees range from $5.95 to $12.95.

1. **fact**
2. **opinion**
3. **fact**
4. **opinion**
5. **fact**
6. **fact**
7. **opinion**
8. **fact**
9. **opinion**
10. **opinion**
11. **fact**
12. **fact**

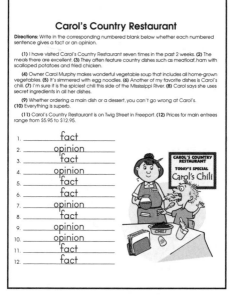

CAROL'S COUNTRY RESTAURANT — TODAY'S SPECIAL — Carol's Chili

Page 72

Review

Directions: Write 5 sentences that are facts and 5 that are opinions.

Facts:

1. _____
2. _____
3. _____
4. _____
5. _____

Opinions:

Answers will vary.

6. _____
7. _____
8. _____
9. _____
10. _____

Page 73

Reading Skills: Cause and Effect

A **cause** is the reason something happens. The **effect** is what happens as the result of the cause.

Directions: Read the paragraphs below. For each numbered sentence, circle the cause or causes and underline the effect or effects. The first one has been done for you.

(1) *All living things in the ocean are endangered* by (humans polluting the water.) Pollution occurs in several ways. One way is the dumping of certain waste materials, such as garbage and sewage, into the ocean. (2) (The decaying bacteria that feed on the garbage use up much of the oxygen in the surrounding water,) so *other creatures in the area often don't get enough.*

Other substances, such as radioactive waste material, can also cause pollution. These materials are often placed in the water in securely sealed containers. (3) But (after years of being exposed to the ocean water,) *the containers may begin to leak.*

Oil is another major source of concern. (4) *Oil is spilled into the ocean when* (tankers run aground and sink or when oil wells in the ocean cannot be capped.) (5) The (oil covers the gills of fish) and *causes them to smother.* (6) (Diving birds get the oil on their wings) and are *unable to fly.* (7) (When they clean themselves,) *they are often poisoned by the oil.*

Rivers also can contribute to the pollution of oceans. Many rivers receive the runoff water from farmlands. (8) (Fertilizers used on the farms may be carried to the ocean,) where they *cause a great increase in the amount of certain plants.* Too much of some plants can actually be poisonous to fish.

Worse yet are the pesticides carried to the ocean. These chemicals slowly build up in shellfish and other small animals. These animals then pass the pesticides on to the larger animals that feed on them. (9) (The buildup of these chemicals in the animals) can make *them ill or cause their babies to be born dead or deformed.*

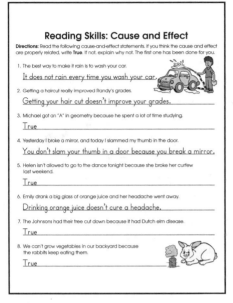

Page 74

Reading Skills: Cause and Effect

Directions: Read the following cause-and-effect statements. If you think the cause and effect are properly related, write **True**. If not, explain why not. The first one has been done for you.

1. The best way to make it rain is to wash your car.

   It does not rain every time you wash your car.

2. Getting a haircut really improved Randy's grades.

   Getting your hair cut doesn't improve your grades.

3. Michael got an "A" in geometry because he spent a lot of time studying.

   True

4. Yesterday I broke a mirror, and today I slammed my thumb in the door.

   You don't slam your thumb in a door because you break a mirror.

5. Helen isn't allowed to go to the dance tonight because she broke her curfew last weekend.

   True

6. Emily drank a big glass of orange juice and her headache went away.

   Drinking orange juice doesn't cure a headache.

7. The Johnsons had their tree cut down because it had Dutch elm disease.

   True

8. We can't grow vegetables in our backyard because the rabbits keep eating them.

   True

Page 75

Review

Directions: Write **Fact** or **Opinion** to describe each sentence.

Fact 1. Hurricanes are also known as typhoons.

Opinion 2. Hurricanes are the worst natural disasters.

Fact 3. All hurricanes begin over the ocean near the equator.

Opinion 4. All people are concerned about pollution.

Opinion 5. Pesticides should never be used.

Fact 6. Many colonists died due to lack of food and sickness.

Opinion 7. Kites are the best gift to give a child.

Fact 8. The names of Columbus' three ships were the *Niña*, the *Pinta* and the *Santa Maria*.

Directions: If the sentence demonstrates a logical cause and effect relationship, write **Yes** on the line. If the sentence is illogical, write **No**.

No 1. I ate fish and got sick, so all fish will make me sick.

Yes 2. The farmer began practicing crop rotation, and his crop yield improved.

No 3. I know how to swim, so I cannot possibly drown.

Yes 4. While learning to ski, Jim broke his leg.

Yes 5. The river overflowed its banks and caused much damage.

No 6. The Cincinnati Reds won 100 games last year, so they probably will win this year.

No 7. Because I started using a new toothpaste, I will make more friends.

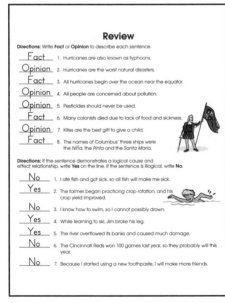

Page 76

Reading Skills: Personification

When an author gives an object or animal human characteristics, it is called **personification**.

Example: The dragon quickly *thought* out its next move in the attack on the village.

Thought is a human process and not associated with mythical creatures, therefore, the dragon is personified in that sentence.

Directions: In the following sentences, underline the personification.

1. The cave's gaping mouth led to internal passageways.

2. The tractor sprang to life with a turn of the key.

3. The lights blinked twice and then died.

4. Crops struggled to survive in the blistering heat, hoping for rainfall.

5. The engine of the car coughed and sputtered as if it wanted to breathe but couldn't.

6. The arrow flew through the air, eyeing its target.

7. Snowmen smile from the safety of their yards.

8. Four-year-old Stephanie's doll sipped tea delicately.

Directions: Write a sentence that personifies the following objects.

1. flower _____

2. stuffed animal _____

3. car _____

Answers will vary.

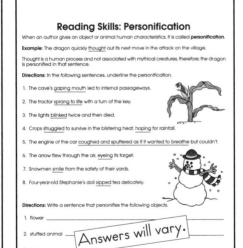

Page 77

Reading Skills: Symbolism

Symbolism is the use of something to stand for (symbolize) something else.

Example:

The elderly woman held the pearl necklace in her wrinkled hand and thought back on her life. Many years had gone by since her husband had given her the necklace, as many years as there were pearls. Some of the pearls, she noticed, were darker than others, just as some years in her life had been darker than other years.

The pearl necklace symbolizes the life of the elderly woman. Each pearl stands for a year in her life, and the necklace represents the many years that have passed.

Directions: Write [Sample answers:] ...ed in the paragraph on the lines below.

The refugees boarded the small ship with high hopes. They had to believe that their destiny was to find the New World and seek shelter there. A few dared to dream of the riches to be found. For them, the boat itself looked like a treasure chest waiting to be discovered.

The boat symbolizes a treasure chest as something that holds riches and excitement for a great future.

For 12-year-old Sam, the basketball court was the best place to be. In Sam's neighborhood, crime ran rampant, and it was the one safe place for kids like Sam to play. Sam spent most nights at the court, practicing lay-ups, jump shots and three-point shots. Sam worked hard because for him it wasn't just a sport, it was a golden key.

Basketball symbolizes a golden key, because if Sam becomes good enough at it, it could be the "key" to getting him into a good school and giving him a good future.

Page 78

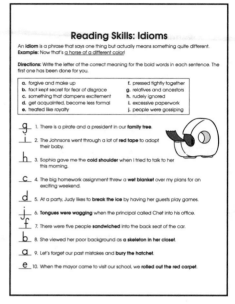

Reading Skills: Idioms

An **idiom** is a phrase that says one thing but actually means something quite different.
Example: Now that's *a horse of a different color*!

Directions: Write the letter of the correct meaning for the bold words in each sentence. The first one has been done for you.

a. forgive and make up	**f.** pressed tightly together
b. fact kept secret for fear of disgrace	**g.** relatives and ancestors
c. something that dampens excitement	**h.** rudely ignored
d. get acquainted, become less formal	**i.** excessive paperwork
e. treated like royalty	**j.** people were gossiping

g 1. There is a pirate and a president in our **family tree**.

i 2. The Johnsons went through a lot of **red tape** to adopt their baby.

h 3. Sophia gave me the **cold shoulder** when I tried to talk to her this morning.

c 4. The big homework assignment threw a **wet blanket** over my plans for an exciting weekend.

d 5. At a party, Judy likes to **break the ice** by having her guests play games.

j 6. **Tongues were wagging** when the principal called Chet into his office.

f 7. There were five people **sandwiched** into the back seat of the car.

b 8. She viewed her poor background as a **skeleton in her closet**.

a 9. Let's forget our past mistakes and **bury the hatchet**.

e 10. When the mayor came to visit our school, we **rolled out the red carpet**.

Page 79

Reading Skills: Idioms

Directions: Use the following idioms in a sentence of your own. Then tell what the phrase means in your own words.

Sentences will vary.

1. raining cats and dogs

a. _____
b. raining very hard

2. going to the dogs

a. _____
b. getting run down, deteriorating

3. barking up the wrong tree

a. _____
b. asking the wrong person, searching in the wrong place

4. hit the nail on the head

a. _____
b. got the exact right idea

5. went out on a limb

a. _____
b. took a chance

6. all in the same boat

a. _____
b. all in the same situation

7. keep up with the Joneses

a. _____
b. keep up with the people around you

Page 80

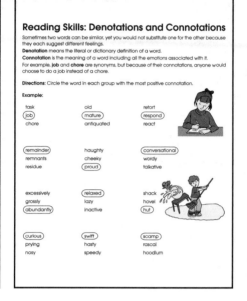

Reading Skills: Denotations and Connotations

Sometimes two words can be similar, yet you would not substitute one for the other because they each suggest different feelings.
Denotation means the literal or dictionary definition of a word.
Connotation is the meaning of a word including all the emotions associated with it. For example, **job** and **chore** are synonyms, but because of their connotations, anyone would choose to do a job **instead** of a chore.

Directions: Circle the word in each group with the most positive connotation.

Example:

task	old	retort
(job)	(mature)	(respond)
chore	antiquated	react

(remainder)	haughty	(conversational)
remnants	cheeky	wordy
residue	(proud)	talkative

excessively	(relaxed)	shack
grossly	lazy	hovel
(abundantly)	inactive	(hut)

(curious)	(swift)	(scamp)
prying	hasty	rascal
nosy	speedy	hoodlum

Page 81

Reading Skills: Denotations and Connotations

Directions: Replace the bold word in each sentence with a word that has a more positive connotation.

Sample answers:

Example:
shut
He **slammed** the door when he left.

The dog's energy was **uncontrollable**. bountiful

We hoped to settle our **fight** peacefully. disagreement

The mother **reprimanded** the children when people began to look at them. scolded

The children **gossiped** at lunchtime. talked

The girl **scribbled** a hasty note to leave behind. wrote

Our conversation ended **abruptly** when the phone rang. suddenly

The principal was a **severe** man. serious

The boy **snatched** the toy from his baby brother. took

The couple **rejected** their offer of help. refused

Dad reminded me to clean my **disastrous** room. messy

Page 82

Similes and Metaphors

A **simile** compares two unlike things using the word **like** or **as**.
Example: The fog was **like** a blanket around us. The fog was **as** thick **as** a blanket.
A **metaphor** compares two unlike things without using the word **like** or **as**.
Example: The fog was a blanket around us.

"The fog was thick," is not a simile or a metaphor. **Thick** is an adjective. Similes and metaphors compare two unlike things that are both nouns.

Directions: Underline the two things being compared in each sentence. Then write **S** for simile or **M** for metaphor on the lines.

M 1. The florist's <u>shop</u> was <u>a summer garden.</u>

S 2. The <u>towels</u> were <u>as rough as sandpaper.</u>

M 3. The <u>survey</u> was <u>a fountain</u> of information.

S 4. Her <u>courtesy</u> was <u>as welcome as a cool breeze on a hot day.</u>

S 5. The <u>room</u> was <u>like a furnace.</u>

Directions: Use similes to complete these sentences.

6. The tornado was as dark as _____

7. His voice was like _____

8. The emergency was as unexpected as _____

9. The kittens were like _____

Directions: Use metaphors to complete the sentences.

10. To me, research was _____

11. The flourishing plants were _____

12. My observation at the hospital was _____

Answers will vary.

Metaphor

Simile
Like
As

Page 83

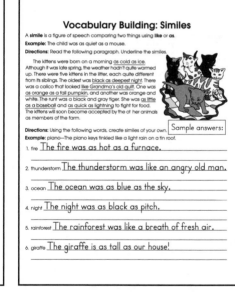

Vocabulary Building: Similes

A **simile** is a figure of speech comparing two things using **like** or **as**.
Example: The child was as quiet as a mouse.
Directions: Read the following paragraph. Underline the similes.

The kittens were born on a morning <u>as cold as ice</u>. Although it was late spring, the weather hadn't quite warmed up. There were five kittens in the litter, each quite different from its siblings. The oldest was <u>black as deepest night</u>. There was a calico that looked <u>like Grandma's old quilt</u>. One was <u>as orange as a fall pumpkin</u>, and another was orange and white. The runt was a black and gray tiger. She was <u>as little as a baseball</u> and as <u>quick as lightning</u> to fight for food. The kittens will soon become accepted by the other animals as members of the farm.

Directions: Using the following words, create similes of your own. Sample answers:
Example: piano—The piano keys tinkled like a light rain on a tin roof.

1. fire The fire was as hot as a furnace.

2. thunderstorm The thunderstorm was like an angry old man.

3. ocean The ocean was as blue as the sky.

4. night The night was as black as pitch.

5. rainforest The rainforest was like a breath of fresh air.

6. giraffe The giraffe is as tall as our house!

ANSWER KEY

Page 84

Vocabulary Building: Metaphors

A **metaphor** is a figure of speech that directly compares one thing with another.

Example: As it set, the sun was a glowing orange ball of fire.

The sun is being compared to a glowing orange ball of fire.

<u>sun</u>   <u>glowing orange ball of fire</u>

Directions: Underline the metaphor in each sentence.
Then write the two things that are being compared on the lines.

1. The ocean, a swirling mass of anger, released its fury on the shore.

<u>ocean</u>   <u>swirling mass of anger</u>

2. He was a top spinning out of control.

<u>He</u>   <u>top spinning out of control</u>

3. The heat covered the crowd, a blanket smothering them all.

<u>heat</u>   <u>blanket smothering them all</u>

4. I fed my dog a steak, and it was a banquet for her senses.

<u>steak</u>   <u>banquet for her senses</u>

5. The flowers in the garden were a stained glass window.

<u>flowers</u>   <u>stained glass window</u>

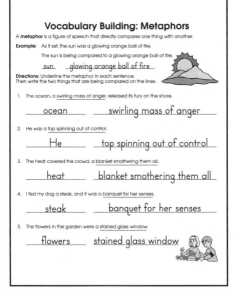

Page 85

Vocabulary Building: Metaphors and Similes

Directions: Underline the metaphors in the following sentences. Then rewrite each sentence using a simile.

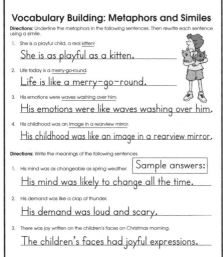

1. She is a playful child, a real kitten!

She is as playful as a kitten.

2. Life today is a merry-go-round.

Life is like a merry-go-round.

3. His emotions were waves washing over him.

His emotions were like waves washing over him.

4. His childhood was an image in a rearview mirror.

His childhood was like an image in a rearview mirror.

Directions: Write the meanings of the following sentences.

1. His mind was as changeable as spring weather.   [Sample answers:]

His mind was likely to change all the time.

2. His demand was like a clap of thunder.

His demand was loud and scary.

3. There was joy written on the children's faces on Christmas morning.

The children's faces had joyful expressions.

Page 86

Reading Skills: Generalizations

A **generalization** is a statement or rule that applies to many situations or examples.

Example: All children get into trouble at one time or another.

Directions: Read each paragraph, then circle the generalization that best describes the information given.

Although many people think of reptiles as slimy, snakes and other reptiles are covered with scales that are dry to the touch. Scales are outgrowths of the animal's skin. Although in some species they are nearly invisible, in most they form a tile-like covering. The turtle's shell is made up of hardened scales that are fused together. The crocodile has a tough but more flexible covering.

- (Every reptile has scales.)
- The scales of all reptiles are alike.
- There are many different kinds of scales.

The reptile's scales help to protect it from its enemies and conserve moisture in its body. Some kinds of lizards have fan-shaped scales that they can raise up to scare away other animals. The scales also can be used to court a mate. A reptile called a gecko can hang from a ceiling because of specialized scales on its feet. Some desert lizards have other kinds of scales on their feet that allow them to run over the loose sand.

- (Scales have many functions.)
- Scales scare away other animals.
- Scales help reptiles adapt to their environments.

A snake will periodically shed its skin, leaving behind a thin impression of its body—scales and all. A lizard sheds its skin too, but it tears off in smaller pieces rather than in one big piece. Before a snake begins this process, which is called molting, its eyes cloud over. The snake will go into hiding until they clear. When it comes out again, it brushes against rough surfaces to pull off the old skin.

- Snakes go into hiding before they molt.
- (Reptiles periodically shed their skin.)
- A lizard's skin molts in smaller pieces.

Page 87

Reading Skills: Generalizations

Directions: Identify which statements below are generalizations and which are specific. Write G for generalization and S for specific.

- G 1. We want to have lots of good food for the party.
- S 2. Jenna gave me three pink shirts and two pairs of jeans.
- G 3. Americans are generous and friendly.
- S 4. There are ten more female teachers than male teachers at our school.
- S 5. She wants me to buy watermelon at the grocery store.
- G 6. She will never believe anything I say.
- S 7. I got poison ivy because I didn't watch out for the foliage on our hike.
- G 8. My mom is the best mom in the world.
- G 9. I get depressed every time the weather turns bad.
- S 10. The team is so good because they work out and practice every day.
- G 11. Cats are so bad-tempered.
- S 12. My dog has a good temperment because he's had lots of training.
- G 13. Our football team is the best this county has ever seen.
- S 14. I love the feel of rain on my skin, because it's cool.
- G 15. That classroom is always out of control.

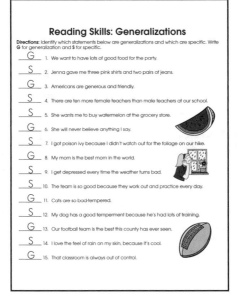

Page 88

Reading Skills: Skimming and Scanning

Skimming is reading quickly to get a general idea of what a reading selection is about. When skimming, look for headings and key words to give you an overall idea of what you are reading.

Scanning is looking for certain words to find facts or answer questions. When scanning, r or think of questions first.

Directions: Scan the paragraphs below to find the answers to the questions. Then look for specific words that will help you locate the answers. For example, in the second question, scan for the word **smallest**.

There are many different units to measure time. Probably the smallest unit that you use is the second, and the longest unit is the year. While 100 years seems like a very long time to us, in the history of the Earth, it is a smaller amount of time than one second is in a person's entire lifetime.

To describe the history of the Earth, scientists use geologic time. Even a million years is a fairly short period in geologic time. Much of the history of our Earth can only be speculated by scientists before it was written down. Some scientists believe that our planet is about 4,600 million years old. Since a thousand million is a billion, the Earth is believed to be 4.6 billion years old.

1. What kind of time is used to describe the history of the Earth?

geologic time

2. For the average person, what is the smallest unit of time used?

the second

3. In millions of years, how old do some scientists believe the Earth is?

4,600 million years

4. How would you express that in billions of years?

4.6 billion years

Page 89

The Author's Purpose

Authors write to entertain, inform or persuade. To entertain means to hold the attention of or to amuse someone. A fiction book about outer space entertains its reader, as does a joke book.

To inform means to give factual information. A cookbook informs the reader of new recipes. A newspaper tells what is happening in the world.

To persuade means to convince them. Newspaper editorial writers try to persuade readers to accept their opinions. Doctors write health columns to persuade readers to eat nutritious foods.

Directions: Read each of the passages below. Tell whether they entertain, inform or persuade. (They may do more than one.) Give the reasons why.

George Washington was b_____ _____ _____ __ ___ P_tomac River in Virginia on Feb. 11, 1732. When he was 11 [Answers may include:] his half-brother, Lawrence, at Mount Vernon.

Author's Purpose: Inform

Reason: The passage contains only facts about George Washington.

When George Washington was a child, he always measured and counted things. Maybe that is why he became a surveyor when he grew up. Surveyors like to measure and count things, too.

Author's Purpose: Persuade and inform

Reason: The passage gives the author's opinion, as well as some facts.

George Washington was the best president America has ever had. He led a new nation to independence. He made all the states feel as if they were part of the United States. All presidents should be as involved with the country as George Washington was.

Author's Purpose: Persuade

Reason: Most of the information in this passage is opinion. The author tries to persuade the reader to agree with his point of view.

Grade 6 - Comprehensive Curriculum

Page 90

Llamas

Directions: Read each paragraph. Tell whether it informs, entertains or persuades. One paragraph does more than one. Then write your reason on the line below.

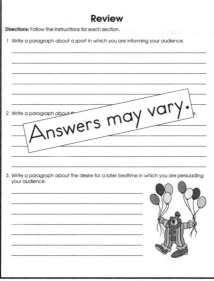

A llama (LAH'MAH) is a South American animal that is related to the camel. It is raised for its wool. Also, it can carry heavy loads. Some people who live near mountains in the United States train llamas to go on mountains ~~Answers may include:~~ because they have two long to~~es~~

Author's Purpose: inform

Reason: All information is factual.

Llamas are the best animals to have if you're planning to backpack in the mountains. They can climb easily and carry your supplies. No one should ever go for a long hiking trip in the mountains without a llama.

Author's Purpose: persuade/inform

Reason: The paragraph contains some opinion and some fact.

Llamas can be stubborn animals. Sometimes they suddenly stop walking for no reason. People have to push them to get them moving again. Stubborn llamas can be frustrating when hiking up a steep mountain.

Author's Purpose: inform

Reason: All information is factual.

Greg is an 11-year-old boy who raises llamas to climb mountains. One of his llamas is named Dallas. Although there are special saddles for llamas, Greg likes to ride bareback.

Author's Purpose: entertain

Reason: This information is presented to interest the reader. It tells a story.

Now use a separate sheet of paper to inform readers about llamas.

Page 91

Roller Coasters

Directions: Read each paragraph and determine the author's purpose. Then write down your reason on the line below.

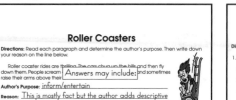

Roller coaster rides are thrilling. The cars chug up the hills and then fly down them. People scream ~~Answers may include:~~ and sometimes raise their arms above their~~heads~~

Author's Purpose: inform/entertain

Reason: This is mostly fact but the author adds descriptive words.

The first roller coasters were giant slides made of ice in Russia. That was more than 300 years ago! The slides were about 70 feet high, and people had to climb steep ladders to reach their tops. Riders got into carts and slid down very fast. Then they climbed the ladders again. Early roller coasters were more work than fun.

Author's Purpose: inform

Reason: These are facts about the first roller coasters.

The first roller coaster in America was built in 1884. It cost only a nickel to ride the "Switchback Gravity Pleasure Railway" at Coney Island in New York. Roller coasters did not become very popular until the late 1920s.

Author's Purpose: inform

Reason: These are facts about early roller coasters.

Have you ever ridden a giant roller coaster? Some of the most famous ones in the world include the "Mamba" at Worlds of Fun in Kansas City, Missouri; the "Ultra Twister" at Six Flags Astroworld in Houston, Texas; and the "Magnum" at Cedar Point in Sandusky, Ohio. Roller coasters are fun because they have thrilling twists and turns. Some go very high and some turn upside down. Everyone should go on a roller coaster at least once in his or her life.

Author's Purpose: entertain/inform/persuade

Reason: There are facts here but the author is trying to persuade the reader to join in his entertainment about roller coasters.

Now use a separate sheet of paper to persuade people to ride roller coasters.

Page 92

Review

Directions: Follow the instructions for each section.

1. Write a paragraph about a sport in which you are informing your audience.

2. Write a paragraph about the

Answers may vary.

3. Write a paragraph about the desire for a later bedtime in which you are persuading your audience.

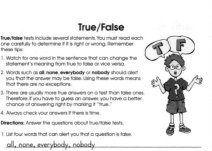

Page 93

Multiple Choice

Multiple choice questions are frequently asked on tests. Such questions include three or four possible answers. When answering a multiple choice question, first read the question carefully. Then read all the answers that are offered. If you do not know the correct answer, eliminate some of the ones you know are wrong until you have only one left. Remember these points when taking multiple choice tests:

1. Answers that contain phrases such as **all people, no one** or **everybody** are probably not correct. For example, a statement such as "all children like candy" is probably not correct because it allows for no exceptions. If there is one child who does not like candy, the statement is not correct. However, if you know that more than one answer is correct and the last choice in the group is "all of the above," then that phrase is probably the correct answer.

2. Answers that contain words you have never seen before probably are not correct. Teachers don't expect you to know material you haven't studied.

3. Answers that are silly usually aren't correct.

4. When two of the answers provided look nearly the same, one of them is probably correct.

5. Always check your answers if there is time.

Directions: Answer the questions about multiple choice tests.

1. The first thing you should do during a multiple choice test is read the question carefully.

2. When you are reading the possible answers to a multiple choice question and you know the first one is right, should you immediately mark it without reading the other answers? No

Why or why not? There may be more than 1 right answer.

3. Write three phrases that might tell you that an answer is probably not correct.

Answers may include: all people   always
no one   never
everybody

Page 94

True/False

True/false tests include several statements. You must read each one carefully to determine if it is right or wrong. Remember these tips:

1. Watch for one word in the sentence that can change the statement's meaning from true to false or vice versa.

2. Words such as **all, none, everybody** or **nobody** should alert you that the answer may be false. Using these words means that there are no exceptions.

3. There are usually more true answers on a test than false ones. Therefore, if you have to guess an answer, you have a better chance of answering right by marking it "true."

4. Always check your answers if there is time.

Directions: Answer the questions about true/false tests.

1. List four words that can alert you that a question is false.

all, none, everybody, nobody

2. One word in a sentence can change the statement's meaning from true to false.

3. If you must guess an answer, is it wiser to guess true or false? true

4. True/false tests are made up of several statements.

5. Can you do well on a true/false test by only skimming each statement? no

6. If the word "everybody" is in the statement, is the answer probably true or false? false

7. When the word "all" appears in the statement, is the answer probably true or false? false

8. What should you do last when taking a true/false test? Check your answers.

Page 95

Fill-In-the-Blank

Fill-in-the-blank tests are more difficult than true/false or multiple choice tests. However, there may be clues in each sentence that help determine the answer. Look at this example:

The _____ of the United States serves a _____ -year term.

Can you tell that the first blank needs a person? (The answer is "president.") The second blank needs a number because it refers to years. ("Four" is the answer.) Think about these other tips for taking fill-in-the-blank tests:

1. Always plan your time wisely. Don't waste too much time on one question. Check the clock or your watch periodically when taking a test.

2. First read through the entire test. Then go back to the beginning and answer the questions that you know. Put a small mark beside the questions you are not sure about.

3. Go back to the questions you were not sure of or that you didn't know. Carefully read each one. Think about possible answers. If you think it could be more than one answer, try to eliminate some of the possible answers.

4. Save the most difficult questions to answer last. Don't waste time worrying if you don't know the answer to a question.

5. Sometimes you should guess at an answer because it may be right. There are some tests, though, that deduct points if your answer is wrong, but not if it is left blank. Make sure you know how the test will be scored.

6. Review your test. Make sure you have correctly read the directions and each question. Check your answers.

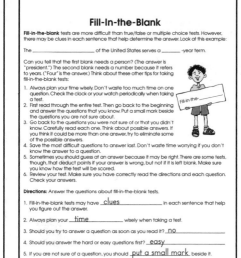

Directions: Answer the questions about fill-in-the-blank tests.

1. Fill-in-the-blank tests may have clues in each sentence that help you figure out the answer.

2. Always plan your time wisely when taking a test.

3. Should you try to answer a question as soon as you read it? no

4. Should you answer the hard or easy questions first? easy

5. If you are not sure of a question, you should put a small mark beside it.

Page 96

Matching

Matching tests have two columns of information. A word or fact from one column matches information in the other. Read these tips to help with matching tests:

1. Look at one question at a time. Start with the first word or phrase in one of the columns. Then look at the possible answers in the other column until you find the correct one. Then go to the next word or phrase in the first column. If you don't know the answer to one question, skip it and go back to it later.
2. If there are several words in one column and several definitions in the other column, it is often easier to read the definition first and then find the word that goes with it.
3. Carefully read the directions. Sometimes one column on a matching test is longer than the other. Find out if there is one answer that won't be used or if an answer in the opposite column can be used twice.
4. Check your answers if there is time.

Directions: Answer the questions about matching tests.

1. Matching tests have how many columns of information? __two__

2. If one column has words in it and the other column has definitions in it, which one should you look at first to make the test easier? __definitions__

3. To eliminate confusion, you should look at __one__ question at a time.

4. Do the columns on a matching test always have the same number of things in them? __no__

5. Are there ever items left unmatched on a matching test? __yes__

6. Does it matter if you look at the right or left column of a matching test first? __no__

Page 97

Essays

Essay questions give you a chance to demonstrate what you have learned. They also provide the opportunity to express your opinion. Although many students think essay questions are the most difficult, they can be the most fun. Remember these tips when writing the answer to an essay question:

1. Think about the answer before you write it. Take time to organize your thoughts so that you can better express yourself.
2. Write a few notes or an outline on a piece of scrap paper or on the back of the test. This helps remind you what you want to write.
3. State your answer clearly. Don't forget to use complete sentences.
4. Review the answer before time runs out. Sometimes words are left out. It doesn't take much time to read through your essay to make sure it says what you want it to say.

Directions: Use these essay-writing tips to answer the following question in the space provided.

What is your favorite type of test? Give several reasons why.

Answers will vary.

Page 98

Review

Directions: Complete each question about tests.

1. Four steps for writing an answer for an essay test include:
   1) __Think about your answer before you write it.__
   2) __Write a few notes on a scrap paper or on the back of the test.__
   3) __State your answer clearly using complete sentences.__
   4) __Review the answers before time runs out. Proofread it.__

2. In a matching test, it is sometimes easier to read the __definition__ and then match it with a word from the opposite column.

3. One column on a __matching test__ may be longer than the other.

4. Tests that require you to fill in the blanks may provide __clues__ in each statement.

5. Always __check your__ answers if there is time.

6. Certain words such as **none** and **all** should alert you that an answer may be __false__.

7. There are usually, but not always, more __true__ statements on a true/false test.

8. If **everybody** or **everything** is used in one of the answers for a __multiple choice test (or true/false)__, it is likely that that answer is not right.

9. If two possible answers for a multiple-choice question sound nearly the __same__, one of them is probably correct.

10. If two answers to a multiple choice question appear to be correct, the answer could be one that says __all of the above__.

Page 100

Comprehension: Fun With Photography

The word "photography" means "writing with light." "Photo" is from the Greek word "photos," which means "light." "Graphy" is from the Greek word "graphic," which means "writing." Cameras don't literally write pictures, of course. Instead, they imprint an image onto a piece of film.

Even the most sophisticated camera is basically a box with a piece of light-sensitive film inside. The box has a hole at the opposite end from the film. The light enters the box through the hole—the camera's lens—and shines on the surface of the film to create a picture. The picture that's created on the film is the image the camera's lens is pointed toward.

A lens is a circle of glass that is thinner at the edges and thicker in the center. The outer edges of the lens collect the light rays and draw them together at the center of the lens.

The shutter helps control the amount of light that enters the lens. Too much light will make the picture too light. Too little light will result in a dark picture. Electronic flash—either built into the camera or attached to the top of it—provides light when needed.

Cameras with automatic electronic flashes provide the additional light automatically. Electronic flashes—or simply "flashes," as they are often called—require batteries. If your flash quits working, a dead battery is probably the cause.

Directions: Answer these questions about photography.

1. From what language is the word "photography" derived? __Greek__

2. Where is the camera lens thickest? __in the center__

3. What do the outer edges of the lens do? __collect the light rays and draw them together to the center of the lens__

4. When is a flash needed? __when there isn't enough light__

5. What does the shutter do? __It helps control the amount of light that enters the lens.__

Page 101

Comprehension: Photography Terms

Like other good professionals, photographers make their craft look easy. Their skill—like that of the graceful ice skater—comes from years of practice. Where skaters develop a sense of balance, photographers develop an "eye" for pictures. They can make important technical decisions about photographing, or "shooting," a particular scene in the twinkling of an eye.

It's interesting to know some of the technical language that professional photographers use. "Angle of view" refers to the angle from which a photograph is taken. "Depth of field" is the distance between the nearest point and the farthest point that is in focus in a photo.

"Filling the frame" refers to the amount of space the object being photographed takes up in the picture. A close-up picture of a dog, flower or person would fill the frame. A far-away picture would not.

"ASA" refers to the speed of different types of films. "Speed" means the film's sensitivity to light. The letters **ASA** stand for the American Standards Association. Film manufacturers give their films ratings of 200ASA, 400ASA, and so on to indicate film speed. The higher the number on the film, the higher its sensitivity to light, and the faster its speed. The faster its speed, the better it will be at clearly capturing sports images and other action shots.

Directions: Answer these question about photography terms.

1. Name another term for photographing. __"shooting"__

2. This is the distance between the nearest point and the farthest point that is in focus in a photo. __depth of field__

3. This refers to the speed of different types of film. __ASA__

4. A close-up picture of someone's face would
   ☐ provide depth of field.   ☐ create an ASA.   ☒ fill the frame.

5. To photograph a swimming child, which film speed is better?
   ☐ 200ASA   ☒ 400ASA

Page 102

Comprehension: Photographing Animals

Animals are a favorite subject of many young photographers. Cats, dogs, hamsters and other pets top the list, followed by zoo animals and the occasional lizard.

Because it's hard to get them to sit still and "perform on command," some professional photographers refuse to photograph pets. There are ways around the problem of short attention spans, however.

One way to get an appealing portrait of a cat or dog is to hold a biscuit or treat above the camera. The animal's longing look toward the food will be captured by the camera as a soulful gaze. Because it's above the camera—out of the camera's range—the treat won't appear in the picture. When you show the picture to your friends afterwards, they will be impressed by your pet's loving expression.

If you are using fast film, you can take some good, quick shots of a pet by simply snapping a picture right after calling its name. You'll get a different expression from your pet using this technique. Depending on your pet's disposition, the picture will capture an inquisitive expression or possibly a look of annoyance, especially if you've awakened Rover from a nap!

Taking pictures of zoo animals requires a little more patience. After all, you can't wake up a lion! You may have to wait for a while until the animal does something interesting or moves into a position for you to get a good shot. When photographing zoo animals, don't get too close to the cages, and never tap on the glass or throw things between the bars of a cage! Concentrate on shooting some good pictures, and always respect the animals you are photographing.

Directions: Answer these questions about photographing animals.

1. Why do some professionals dislike photographing animals? __because it's difficult to get them to sit still__

2. What speed of film should you use to photograph quick-moving pets? __fast__

3. To capture a pet's loving expression, hold this out of camera range. __a treat__

4. Compared to taking pictures of pets, what does photographing zoo animals require? __more patience__

Page 103

Generalization: Taking Pictures

A **generalization** is a statement that applies to many different situations.

Directions: Read each passage and circle the valid generalization.

1. Most people can quickly be taught to use a simple camera. However, it takes time, talent and a good eye to learn to take professional quality photographs. Patience is another quality that good photographers must possess. Those who photograph nature often will wait hours to get just the right light or shadow in their pictures.

   a. Anyone can learn to use a camera. *(circled)*

   b. Any patient person can become a good photographer.

   c. Good photographers have a good eye for pictures.

2. Photographers such as Diane Arbus, who photograph strange or odd people, also must wait for just the right picture. Many "people photographers" stake out a busy city sidewalk and study faces in the crowd. Then they must leap up quickly and ask to take a picture or sneakily take one without being observed. Either way, it's not an easy task!

   a. Staking out a busy sidewalk is a boring task.

   b. "People photographers" must be patient people and good observers. *(circled)*

   c. Sneak photography is not a nice thing to do to strangers.

3. Whether the subject is nature or humans, many photographers insist that dawn is the best time to take pictures. The light is clear at this early hour, and mist may still be in the air. The mist gives these early morning photos a haunting, "other world" quality that is very appealing.

   a. Morning mist gives an unusual quality to most outdoor photographs. *(circled)*

   b. Photographers all agree that dawn is the best time to take pictures.

   c. Misty light is always important in taking pictures.

Page 104

Generalization: Camera Care

Directions: Read each passage and circle the valid generalization.

1. Professional photographers know it's important to keep their cameras clean and in good working order. Amateur photographers should make sure theirs are, too. However, to take good care of your camera, you must first understand the equipment. Camera shop owners say at least half the "defective" cameras people bring in simply need to have the battery changed!

   a. Cameras are delicate and require constant care so they will work properly.

   b. Many problems amateurs have are caused by lack of familiarity with their equipment. *(circled)*

   c. Amateur photographers don't know how their cameras work.

2. Once a year, some people take their cameras to a shop to be cleaned. Most never have them cleaned at all. Those who know how can clean their cameras themselves. To avoid scratching the lens, they should use the special cloths and tissues professionals rely on. Amateurs are warned never to loosen screws, bolts or nuts inside the camera.

   a. The majority of amateur photographers never bother to have their cameras cleaned. *(circled)*

   b. Cleaning a camera can be tricky and should be left to professionals.

   c. It's hard to find the special cleaning cloths professionals use.

3. Another simple tip from professionals is to make sure your camera works before you take it on vacation. They suggest taking an entire roll of film and having it developed before your trip. That way, if necessary, you'll have time to have the lens cleaned or other repairs made.

   a. Check out your camera before you travel to make sure it's in good working order. *(circled)*

   b. Vacation pictures are often disappointing because the camera needs to be repaired.

   c. Take at least one roll of film along on every vacation.

Page 105

Generalization: Using a Darkroom

The room where photographs are developed is called a "darkroom." Can you guess why? The room must be dark so that light does not get on the film as it is being developed. Specially colored lights allow photographers to see without damaging the film. Because of the darkness and the chemicals used in the developing process, it's important to follow certain darkroom safety procedures.

To avoid shocks while in the darkroom, never touch light switches with wet hands. To avoid touching chemicals, use tongs to transfer prints from one chemical solution to another. When finished with the chemicals, put them back in their bottles. Never leave chemicals out in trays once the developing process is complete.

To avoid skin irritation from chemicals, wipe down all countertops and surfaces when you are finished. Another sensible precaution—make sure you have everything you need before exposing the film to begin the developing process. Any light that enters the darkroom can ruin the pictures being developed.

Directions: Answer these questions about using a darkroom.

1. Which generalization is correct?

   a. Developing pictures is a time-consuming and difficult process.

   b. It's dangerous to develop pictures in a darkroom.

   c. Sensible safety procedures are important for darkroom work. *(circled)*

2. Write directions for working with photography chemicals. **Use tongs to transfer prints from one chemical solution to another. Put chemicals away when finished. Clean surfaces when you finish.**

3. What is the most important precaution to take to make sure pictures aren't ruined in the darkroom? **The room must be kept dark while developing photographs.**

Page 106

Review

Directions: Circle the missing word for each sentence.

1. The Greek word _____ means writing.

   a. photos

   b. amateur

   c. graphic *(circled)*

2. The distance between the nearest point and the farthest point in a photo is called the _____.

   a. graphic

   b. shooting

   c. depth of field *(circled)*

3. _____ refers to the angle from which a photograph is taken.

   a. Photos

   b. Angle of view *(circled)*

   c. Lens

4. The _____ of the film is its sensitivity to light.

   a. tripod

   b. amateur

   c. speed *(circled)*

5. The speed of different types of film is called _____.

   a. professional

   b. amateur

   c. ASA *(circled)*

6. The _____ of the camera collects the light rays and draws them together at the center.

   a. shutter

   b. lens *(circled)*

   c. ASA

7. Taking a picture is often referred to as _____.

   a. shooting *(circled)*

   b. graphic

   c. speed

Page 107

Main Idea/Recalling Details: Kites

Kites are a familiar sight on breezy fall days. They come in a great variety of sizes, colors and designs. It is not known who invented kites, but kites have been flown since the beginning of recorded history. While today children and adults use them for recreation, throughout history kites have had other uses.

In the United States, kites have been used in weather and other scientific research experiments. Before airplanes and weather balloons, the National Weather Service had kites carry weather instruments as high as 4 miles above the earth. In addition, the United States military used kites for observing the enemy and sending messages between troops.

In other countries, kites had cultural and religious importance. The ancient Chinese flew kites over their homes to drive out evil spirits. The Chinese still enjoy kites so much that one day each year they celebrate Kites' Day.

On some Pacific islands, kites were thought to have spiritual qualities. They were believed to symbolize both sides of nature—life and death. On some Polynesian islands, kites were used as protection against evil. These kites were often shaped like birds and used as soaring messengers to the heavens. In Hawaii, kites were also used to establish land ownership. A kite was released in the air, and a claim was given for the area where it came down.

Directions: Answer these questions about kites.

1. The main idea is:

   ☐ Kites come in a great variety of sizes, color and designs.

   ☒ While today kites are used for recreation, throughout history they have had other uses.

2. Besides recreation, name two ways kites have been used in the United States.

   1) **for weather and other scientific research**

   2) **The military used them for observation and to send messages.**

3. What country celebrates a holiday called Kites' Day? **China**

4. How did Hawaiians use kites to decide land ownership? **A kite was released into the air, and a claim was given for the area where it came down.**

Page 108

Comprehension: Aerodynamics

Kites are able to fly because of the principle of aerodynamics. This big word simply means the study of forces that are put into action by moving air. Three main forces work to keep a heavier-than-air kite flying—lift, gravity and drag.

This is how it works: The flying lines, or strings, are attached to the kite to hold it at a slant. The wind pushes against the underside of the kite. At the same time, the wind rushes around the edges of the kite and "drags" some of the air from the upper side. This creates a partial vacuum there. The push of the air underneath is greater than the push of the air from the top, so the kite is held in the air. An airplane is held in the air in much the same way, except that it must keep moving rapidly to make the pressure above and below its wings different. The wind does this for the kite. In a steady airstream, a kite doesn't move backward or forward. It seems to be unaffected by gravity. This is possible because the lifting force of the wind overcomes the downward force of gravity.

If you have ever ridden a bicycle into a strong wind, you may have felt some of the forces of aerodynamics. If you held your hand out to your side, you could feel the air stream flowing around your hand. With your fingers pointed into the wind and your hand held level, there is little lift or drag. But if you raised your fingers slightly, the wind lifted your hand upwards. Raising your hand higher increases the drag and decreases the lift. Your hand is pushed downward. A kite flying in the sky is subject to these same forces.

Directions: Answer these questions about aerodynamics.

1. What is aerodynamics? **the study of forces that are put into action by moving air**

2. What three forces are at work to hold a kite in the air?

   1) **lift**   2) **gravity**   3) **drag**

3. An airplane is held in the air in much the same way, except that it must keep moving rapidly to keep the kite above and below its wings different.

   True *(circled)*   False

ANSWER KEY

Page 109

Comprehension: Getting Your Kite to Fly

There are some basic things to know about kite flying that can help you enjoy the sport more. Here are a few of the most important ones.

First, if you have ever seen someone flying a kite in a movie, you probably saw him or her get the kite off the ground by running into the wind. However, this is not the way to launch a kite. Most beginners will find a "high-start" launch to be the easiest. For a high-start launch, have a friend stand about 100 feet away, facing into the wind. Your friend should face you and hold the kite gently. Place some tension on the flying line by pulling gently on it. With a steady breeze behind you, tug gently on the line, and the kite will rise. If your kite begins to dive, don't panic or pull on the line. Dropping the reel will cause it to spin out of control and could cause someone to be hurt. Simply let the line go slack. This usually will right the kite in midair.

For a kite that is pulling hard away from you, have a friend stand behind you and take up the slack line as you bring it in. Hand over hand, pull down the line. It is very important to wear gloves on to do this, or you may burn or cut your hands. It is recommended that you always wear gloves while kite flying.

When two kite lines get crossed, pulling may cause enough friction to cut one or both of the lines. Instead of pulling, both fliers should walk toward one another until their lines uncross as they pass.

Directions: Circle **True** or **False** for these statements about kite flying.

1. To launch a kite, run into the wind holding the kite behind you. True (False)
2. In a high-start launch, a friend stands about 100 feet away from you, holding the kite. (True) False
3. If your kite begins to dive from the sky, immediately drop the reel. True (False)
4. It is recommended that you always wear gloves when kite flying. (True) False

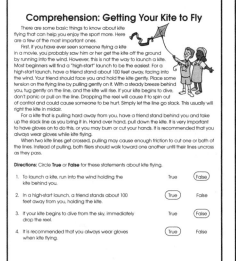

Page 110

Recalling Details: Kite Safety Rules

Because kite flying is a relaxed, easy-going sport, it is easy to have the mistaken belief that there are no dangers involved. However, like any sport, kite flying must be approached with care. Here are some important safety rules you should always follow while kite flying:

- **Don't** fly a kite in wet or stormy weather or use wet flying line.
- **Don't** fly a kite near electrical power lines, transmission towers or antennae. If your kite does get caught in one of these, walk away and leave it! If you must get the kite back, contact your local electric company.
- **Don't** use wire for flying line.
- **Don't** use metal for any part of the kite.
- **Don't** fly a kite near a street or in crowded areas.
- **Don't** fly a kite in a field or other area that has rocks or other objects you could trip over.
- **Don't** walk backwards without looking behind you.
- **Don't** fly a kite around trees. (If your kite does happen to get caught in a tree, let the line go slack. Sometimes the wind can work it free.)
- **Don't** fly a kite using unfamiliar equipment. A reel spinning out of control can be quite dangerous.
- **Don't** fly a kite near an airport.
- **Don't** fly a very large kite without proper guidance.
- **Do** wear protective gloves to avoid burns on your hands from rapidly unwinding line.
- **Do** use flying line that has been tested for the type and size of kite you are using.

Directions: Answer these questions about kite safety. | Answers may include: |

1. List three things you should never fly a kite around.
   1) _trees_ 2) _airport_ 3) _electrical power lines_
2. What should you do if your kite gets caught in a tree? _Let the line go slack, and the wind may work it free._
3. What material should you never use in any part of your kite? _metal_

Page 111

Recalling Details: Aviation Pioneer

Lawrence Hargrave was born in Middlesex, England, in 1850. When he was a teenager, his family moved to Australia. There Hargrave went to work for the Australian Stream and Navigation Company, where he spent 5 years gaining practical experience in engineering. He soon became interested in artificial flight.

Hargrave wanted to develop a stable lifting surface that could be used for flying. This goal led to his invention of the box kite, one of the seven basic models. In 1894, he carried out kite experiments along the beaches near his home. One day, in front of onlookers, he was lifted above the beach and out over the sea by four of his box kites. These experiments were very important to the development of air travel, although Hargrave has received little credit for it. In fact, because of his modesty, Hargrave failed to get a patent on his box kite. He spent more than 30 years studying flying, offering many inventions, including a rotary engine.

In 1906, Hargrave began looking for a home for his collection of nearly 200 models of kites and flying machines. After being rejected by several governments, his collection was accepted at a technological museum in Munich, Germany. Unfortunately, many of these models were destroyed during World War I.

Directions: Answer these questions about Lawrence Hargrave.

1. For what kite design was Lawrence Hargrave known? _box kite_
2. What was Hargrave trying to create when he made this kite? _a stable lifting surface that could be used for flying_
3. What was one of the inventions Hargrave contributed to aviation? _the rotary engine_
4. Where was Hargrave's collection of kites and flying machines finally housed? _a technological museum in Munich, Germany_

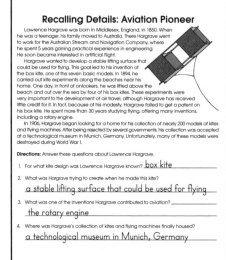

Page 112

Main Idea/Recalling Details: A Kite in History

In June 1752, Benjamin Franklin proved that lightning was a type of electricity by flying a kite with a key tied to the bottom of the line during a thunderstorm. Before his experiment, many people thought that lightning was a supernatural power.

After the success of his experiment, Franklin figured that if lightning could be drawn to a kite in a storm, it could be safely redirected into the ground by a metal rod attached to a house. His idea was met with much doubt, but lightning rods were soon seen on buildings in many of the colonies and later in Europe. During the years between 1683 and 1789, studying the universe and laws of nature was of tremendous importance. It was during this Age of Reason, as it was known, that Franklin's kite experiment gained him international fame and respect. He was elected to the Royal Society of London and the French Academy of Sciences, among other honors.

More than 20 years after his bold experiment, American patriots were enduring many hardships in their struggles for freedom from England. The colonial troops had shortages of guns, gun powder and food. France was sending supplies but not as much as was needed. Benjamin Franklin was chosen to go to France to persuade the French to aid the American cause. Franklin's reputation as a brilliant scientist earned him a hero's welcome there. The French people were so impressed by him that they wanted to help the colonies, even during a time when they could barely afford it. The supplies sent by the French were instrumental to the colonists in winning the war. And it all started with a kite.

Directions: Answer these questions about Ben Franklin and his historical kite.

1. The main idea is:
   [X] A kite played a role in the American Revolution and gained a spot in history books.
   [ ] Benjamin Franklin proved that lightning was a type of electricity by flying a kite with a key tied to the bottom of the line during a storm.
2. From his kite and key experiment, what did Franklin invent? _lightning rod_
3. What was the era between 1683 and 1789 known as? _Age of Reason_
4. Why was Franklin sent to France in 1776? _to persuade the French to aid the American struggle for freedom from England_

Page 113

Summarizing: Pioneers

Directions: Think about the lives and accomplishments of Ben Franklin and Lawrence Hargrave. Write one paragraph about each, summarizing what you have learned about these two men.

| Answers should include: | **Ben Franklin** |
1752 kite-and-key experiment
studied universe and laws of nature
ambassador to France
born in Boston in 1706
apprentice printer

| Answers should include: | **Lawrence Hargrave** |
born in Middlesex, England, in 1850
engineer
invented box kite
used four box kites to lift himself
studied flying for 30 years, creating many inventions

Writing Checklist
Reread your paragraphs carefully.
- [ ] My paragraphs make sense.
- [ ] I used correct punctuation.
- [ ] I have a good opening and ending.
- [ ] I used correct spelling.
- [ ] My paragraphs are well-organized.
- [ ] My paragraphs are interesting.

Page 114

Review

Directions: Number in order the steps for how to launch a kite.
_5_ With a steady breeze behind you, gently pull on the line.
_3_ Have your friend face you and gently hold the kite.
_6_ Your kite will rise.
_2_ Have your friend face into the wind.
_4_ Place some tension on the flying line by pulling on it.
_1_ Have a friend stand about 100 feet away from you.

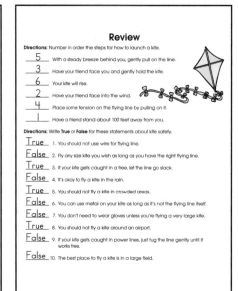

Directions: Write True or False for these statements about kite safety.
True 1. You should not use wire for flying line.
False 2. Fly any size kite you wish as long as you have the right flying line.
True 3. If your kite gets caught in a tree, let the line go slack.
False 4. It's okay to fly a kite in the rain.
True 5. You should not fly a kite in crowded areas.
False 6. You can use metal on your kite as long as it's not the flying line itself.
False 7. You don't need to wear gloves unless you're flying a very large kite.
True 8. You should not fly a kite around an airport.
False 9. If your kite gets caught in power lines, just tug the line gently until it works free.
False 10. The best place to fly a kite is in a large field.

Page 115

Comprehension: Colonists Come to America

After Christopher Columbus discovered America in 1492, many people wanted to come live in the new land. During the 17th and 18th centuries, a great many Europeans, especially the English, left their countries and settled along the Atlantic Coast of North America between Florida and Canada. Some came to make a better life for themselves. Others, particularly the Pilgrims, the Puritans and the Quakers, came for religious freedom.

A group of men who wanted gold and other riches from the new land formed the London Company. They asked the king of England for land in America and for permission to found a colony. They founded Jamestown, the first permanent English settlement in America, in 1607. They purchased ships and supplies, and located people who wanted to settle in America.

The voyage to America took about eight weeks and was very dangerous. Often, fierce winds blew the wooden ships off course. Many were wrecked. The ships were crowded and dirty. Frequently, passengers became ill, and some died. Once in America, the early settlers faced even more hardships.

Directions: Answer these questions about the colonists coming to America.

1. How long did it take colonists to travel from England to America? __8 weeks__

2. Name three groups that came to America to find religious freedom.

   1) __Pilgrims__ 2) __Puritans__ 3) __Quakers__

3. Why was the London Company formed? __to ask the king of England if they could found a colony in America__

4. What was Jamestown? __the first permanent English settlement in America__

5. Why was the voyage to America dangerous? __Many ships wrecked. They were crowded and dirty, and passengers became ill.__

Page 116

Recalling Details: Early Colonial Homes

When the first colonists landed in America, they had to find shelter quickly. Their first homes were crude bark and mud huts, log cabins or dugouts, which were simply caves dug into the hillsides. As soon as possible, the settlers sought to replace these temporary shelters with comfortable houses.

Until the late 17th century, most of the colonial homes were simple in style. Almost all of the New England colonists—those settling in the northern areas of Massachusetts, Connecticut, Rhode Island and New Hampshire—used wood in building their permanent homes. Some of the buildings had thatched roofs. However, they caught fire easily, and so were replaced by wooden shingles. The outside walls also were covered with wooden shingles to make the homes warmer and less drafty.

In the middle colonies—New York, Pennsylvania, New Jersey and Delaware—the Dutch and German colonists often made brick or stone homes that were two-and-a-half or three-and-a-half stories high. Many southern colonists—those living in Virginia, Maryland, North Carolina, South Carolina and Georgia—lived on large farms called plantations. Their homes were usually made of brick.

In the 18th century, some colonists became wealthy enough to replace their simple homes with mansions, often like those being built by the wealthy class in England. They were called Georgian houses because they were popular during the years that Kings George I, George II and George III ruled England. Most were made of brick. They usually featured columns, ornately carved doors and elaborate gardens.

Directions: Answer these questions about early colonial homes.

1. What were the earliest homes of the colonists? __bark and mud huts, log cabins, dugouts__

2. What were the advantages of using wooden shingles? __They didn't catch fire as easily as thatched roofs.__

3. What did Dutch and German colonists use to build their homes? __brick and stone__

4. What were Georgian homes? __mansions with columns, ornate doors and elaborate gardens__

Page 117

Recalling Details: The Colonial Kitchen

The most important room in the home of a colonial family was the kitchen. Sometimes it was the only room in the home. The most important element of the kitchen was the fireplace. Fire was essential to the colonists, and they were careful to keep one burning at all times. Before the man of the house went to bed, he would make sure that the fire was carefully banked so it would burn all night. In the morning, he would blow the glowing embers into flame again with a bellows. If the fire went out, one of the children would be sent to a neighbor's for hot coals. Because there were no matches, it would sometimes take a half hour to light a new fire, using flint, steel and tinder.

The colonial kitchen, quite naturally, was centered around the fireplace. One or two large iron broilers hung over the hot coals for cooking the family meals. Above the fireplace, a large musket and powder horn were kept for protection in the event of an attack and to hunt deer and other game. Also likely to be found near the fireplace was a butter churn, where cream from the family's cow was beaten until yellow flakes of butter appeared.

The furniture in the kitchen—usually benches, a table and chairs—were made by the man or men in the family. It was very heavy and not very comfortable. The colonial family owned few eating utensils—no forks and only a few spoons, also made by members of the family. The dishes included pewter plates, "trenchers"—wooden bowls with handles—and wooden mugs.

Directions: Answer these questions about the colonial kitchen.

1. What was the most important element of the colonial kitchen? __fireplace__

2. In colonial days, why was it important to keep a fire burning in the fireplace? __There were no matches, and fires were hard to start.__

3. Name two uses of the musket.

   1) __hunting__ 2) __protection__

4. Who made most of the furniture in the early colonial home? __men in the family__

Page 118

Sequencing: Spinning

Most of the colonists could not afford to buy clothes sent over from Europe. Instead, the women and girls, particularly in the New England colonies, spent much time spinning thread and weaving cloth to make their own clothing. They raised sheep for wool and grew flax for linen.

In August, the flax was ready to be harvested and made into linen thread. The plants were pulled up and allowed to dry. Then the men pulled the seed pods from the stalks, bundled the stalks and soaked them in a stream for about five days. The flax next had to be taken out, cleaned and dried. To get the linen fibers from the tough bark and heavy wooden core, the stalks had to be pounded and crushed. Finally, the fibers were pulled through the teeth of a brush called a "hatchel" to comb out the short and broken fibers. The long fibers were spun into linen thread on a spinning wheel.

The spinning wheel was low, so a woman sat down to spin. First, she put flax in the hollow end of a slender stick, called the spindle, at one end of the spinning wheel. It was connected by a belt to a big wheel at the other end. The woman turned the wheel by stepping on a pedal. As it turned, the spindle also turned, twisting the flax into thread. The woman constantly dipped her fingers into water to moisten the flax and keep it from breaking. The linen thread came out through a hole in the side of the spindle. It was bleached and put away to be woven into pieces of cloth.

Directions: Number in order the steps to make linen thread from flax.

__7__ The woman sat at the spinning wheel and put flax in the spindle.
__3__ Seed pods were pulled from the stalks; stalks were bundled and soaked.
__1__ In August, the flax was ready to be harvested and made into thread.
__4__ The stalks were pounded and crushed to get the linen fibers.
__11__ The thread was bleached and put away to be woven into cloth.
__5__ The short fibers were separated out with a "hatchel."
__9__ The woman dipped her fingers into water to moisten the flax.
__6__ The long fibers were spun into linen thread on a spinning wheel.
__8__ The woman turned the wheel by stepping on a pedal, twisting the flax into thread.
__2__ The plants were pulled up and allowed to dry.
__10__ The linen thread came out through a hole in the side of the spindle.

Page 119

Recalling Details: Clothing in Colonial Times

The clothing of the colonists varied from the north to the south, accounting for the differences not only in climate, but also in the religions and ancestries of the settlers. The clothes seen most often in the early New England colonies where the Puritans settled were very plain and simple. The materials—wool and linen—were warm and sturdy.

The Puritans had strict rules about clothing. There were no bright colors, jewelry, ruffles or lace. A Puritan woman wore a long-sleeved gray dress with a big white collar, cuffs, apron and cap. A Puritan man wore long woolen stockings and baggy leather "breeches," which were knee-length trousers. Adults and children dressed in the same style of clothing.

In the middle colonies, the clothing ranged from the simple clothing of the Quakers to the colorful, loose-fitting outfits of the Dutch colonists. Dutch women wore more colorful outfits than Puritan women, with many petticoats and fur trim. The men had silver buckles on their shoes and wore big hats decked with curling feathers.

In the southern colonies, where there were no religious restrictions against fancy clothes, wealthy men wore brightly colored breeches and coats of velvet and satin sent from England. The women's gowns also were made of rich materials and were decorated with ruffles, ribbons and lace. The poorer people wore clothes similar to the simple dress of the New England Puritans.

Directions: Answer these questions about clothing in colonial times.

1. Why did the clothing of the colonists vary from the north to the south? __differences in climate, religions and ancestries__

2. Why did the Puritans wear very plain clothing? __They had very strict rules and religious restrictions.__

3. What was the nationality of many settlers in the middle colonies? __Dutch__

4. From what country did wealthy southern colonists obtain their clothing? __England__

Page 120

Recalling Details: Venn Diagrams

A **Venn diagram** is used to chart information that shows similarities and differences between two things. The outer part of each circle shows the differences. The intersecting part of the circles shows the similarities.

Example:

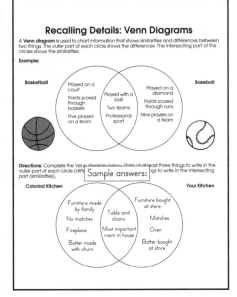

Basketball — Played on a court; Points scored through baskets; Five players on a team
(intersecting) Played with a ball; Two teams; Professional sport
Baseball — Played on a diamond; Points scored through runs; Nine players on a team

Directions: Complete the Venn diagram below. Think of at least three things to write in the outer part of each circle (diff...) ...ngs to write in the intersecting part (similarities).

Sample answers:

Colonial Kitchen — Furniture made by family; No matches; Fireplace; Butter made with churn
(intersecting) Table and chairs; Most important room in house
Your Kitchen — Furniture bought at store; Matches; Oven; Butter bought at store

Page 121

Comprehension: Colonial Schools

In early colonial days, there were no schools or teachers. Children learned what they could at home from their parents, but often their parents couldn't read or write either. Later, some women in the New England colonies began teaching in their homes. These first schools were known as "dame schools." Often the books used in these schools were not books at all, but rather "hornbooks"—flat, paddle-shaped wooden boards with the alphabet or Lord's Prayer on the front.

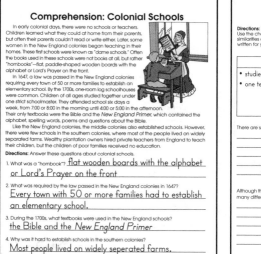

In 1647, a law was passed in the New England colonies requiring every town of 50 or more families to establish an elementary school. By the 1700s, one-room log schoolhouses were common. Children of all ages studied together under one strict schoolmaster. They attended school six days a week, from 7:00 or 8:00 in the morning until 4:00 or 5:00 in the afternoon. Their only textbooks were the Bible and the *New England Primer*, which contained the alphabet, spelling, poems and questions about the Bible.

Like the New England colonies, the middle colonies also established schools. However, there were few schools in the southern colonies, where most of the people lived on widely separated farms. Wealthy plantation owners hired private teachers from England to teach their children, but the children of poor families received no education.

Directions: Answer these questions about colonial schools.

1. What was a "hornbook"? **flat wooden boards with the alphabet or Lord's Prayer on the front**

2. What was required by the law passed in the New England colonies in 1647? **Every town with 50 or more families had to establish an elementary school.**

3. During the 1700s, what textbooks were used in the New England schools? **the Bible and the *New England Primer***

4. Why was it hard to establish schools in the southern colonies? **Most people lived on widely seperated farms.**

Page 122

Compare/Contrast: Schools

Directions: Think about the differences and similarities between colonial and modern schools. Use the chart below to help organize your ideas. Then, write a paragraph discussing the similarities and a paragraph discussing the differences. The topic sentences have been written for you.

Sample answers:

Similarities	Differences
• studied alphabet, spelling, poems	• one-room log schoolhouses
• one teacher in the room	• six-day school week
	• 8–9 hour school day
	• only two textbooks

There are several similarities between colonial schools and schools today.

Answers will vary.

Although there are _____ and modern schools, there are also many differences.

Page 123

Comprehension: Religion in New England

Many New England colonists had come to America for religious freedom. Religion was very important to them. One of the first buildings erected in any new settlement was a church, or meetinghouse. They were generally in the center of town and were used for public meetings of all kinds. These early meetinghouses were plain, unpainted wood buildings. Later churches were larger and more elaborate. They were usually painted white and had tall, graceful bell towers rising from the roof.

Although they came to America to have freedom of worship, the Puritans thought that everyone in the colonies should worship the same way they did. Because there were so many of them, the Puritans controlled the government in much of New England. They were the only ones allowed to vote, and they passed very strict laws. Lawbreakers received harsh punishments. For example, someone caught lying might be forced to stand in the town square for hours locked in a pillory—wooden boards with holes cut in them for the head and hands. For other minor offenses, the offender was tied to a whipping post and given several lashes with a whip.

Except in cases of extreme illness, everyone in the New England colonies had to attend church on Sunday. The minister stood in a pulpit high above the pews to deliver his sermon, which could last four or five hours. The people sat on hard, straight-backed pews. In the winter, there was no heat, so church members brought foot warmers from home to use during the long services. In many churches, a "tithingman" walked up and down the aisles carrying a long stick. On one end were feathers attached; the other end had a knob. If anyone dozed off, the tithingman would tickle him or her with the feathers. If this did not rouse the offender, he would thump them soundly with the knob.

Directions: Answer these questions about religion in the colonies.

1. The main idea is:
   ☒ Many New England colonists had come to America for religious freedom, and religion was very important to them.
   ☐ One of the first buildings erected in any new settlement was a church.

2. Which religious group exercised a lot of power in the New England colonies? **Puritans**

3. What was a pillory? **wooden boards with holes cut for the head and hands**

4. What was the only acceptable excuse for missing Sunday church services in the New England colonies? **extreme illness**

5. What was the job of the tithingman? **to keep people awake in church**

Page 124

Writing: Problem and Solution

Directions: Follow the instructions below.

1. Think of a problem the Colonial Americans may have encountered. Write a paragraph about this problem. In the paragraph, be sure to state the problem, then discuss why it would have been a problem for the colonists.

Answers will vary.

2. Think about a solution to the problem above. Write a paragraph outlining your ideas for the solution. Remember to state the solution to the problem and then your ideas to solve the problem.

Page 125

Review

Many great colonists made an impact on American history. Among them was Benjamin Franklin, who left his mark as a printer, author, inventor, scientist and statesman. He has been called "the wisest American."

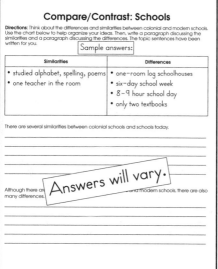

Franklin was born in Boston in 1706, one of 13 children in a very religious Puritan household. Although he had less than two years of formal education, his tremendous appetite for books served him well. At age 12, he became an apprentice printer at *The New England Courant* and soon began writing articles that poked fun at Boston society.

In 1723, Franklin ran away to Philadelphia, where he started his own newspaper. He was very active in the Philadelphia community. He operated a bookstore and was named postmaster. He also helped to establish a library, a fire company, a college, an insurance company and a hospital. His well-known *Poor Richard's Almanac* was first printed in 1732.

Over the years, Franklin maintained an interest in science and mechanics, leading to such inventions as a fireplace stove and bifocal lenses. In 1752, he gained world fame with his kite-and-key experiment, which proved that lightning was a form of electricity.

Franklin was an active supporter of the colonies throughout the Revolutionary War. He helped to write and was a signer of the Declaration of Independence in 1776. In his later years, he skillfully represented America in Europe, helping to work out a peace treaty with Great Britain.

Directions: Answer these questions about Benjamin Franklin.

1. The main idea is:
   ☐ Many great colonists made an impact on American history.
   ☒ Benjamin Franklin was a great colonist who left his mark as a printer, author, inventor, scientist and statesman.

2. How did Benjamin Franklin gain world fame? **his kite-and-key experiment**

3. What did Franklin sign and help to write? **Declaration of Independence**

4. Number in order the following accomplishments of Benjamin Franklin.
   6 Served as representative of America in Europe
   3 Began printing *Poor Richard's Almanac*
   4 Experimented with electricity
   2 Started his own newspaper
   5 Helped to write and sign the Declaration of Independence
   1 Served as apprentice printer on *The New England Courant*

Page 126

Review

Directions: Match each item with its description. If necessary, review the section on colonial times.

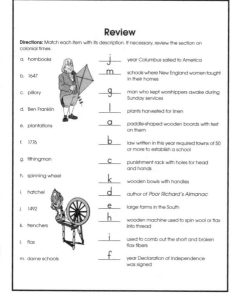

a. hornbooks	**j**	year Columbus sailed to America
b. 1647	**m**	schools where New England women taught in their homes
c. pillory	**g**	man who kept worshippers awake during Sunday services
d. Ben Franklin	**l**	plants harvested for linen
e. plantations	**a**	paddle-shaped wooden boards with text on them
f. 1776	**b**	law written in this year required towns of 50 or more to establish a school
g. tithingman	**c**	punishment rack with holes for head and hands
h. spinning wheel	**k**	wooden bowls with handles
i. hatchel	**d**	author of *Poor Richard's Almanac*
j. 1492	**e**	large farms in the South
k. trenchers	**h**	wooden machine used to spin wool or flax into thread
l. flax	**i**	used to comb out the short and broken flax fibers
m. dame schools	**f**	year Declaration of Independence was signed

Page 127

Using Prior Knowledge: Abraham Lincoln and the Civil War

Directions: Before reading about Abraham Lincoln and the Civil War in the following section, answer these questions.

1. The Civil War began because _____

2. Abraham Lincoln is famous today because _____

3. What brought about the end of slavery? _____

4. The *Gettysburg Address* _____ famous line: "Four score and seven years ago. . . ." What does _____

5. How did Abra _____

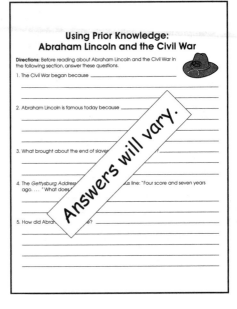
Answers will vary.

Page 128

Main Idea: The Gettysburg Address

On November 19, 1863, President Abraham Lincoln gave a short speech to dedicate a cemetery for Civil War soldiers in Gettysburg, Pennsylvania, where a famous battle was fought. He wrote five drafts of the *Gettysburg Address*, one of the most stirring speeches of all time. The war ended in 1865.

Four score and seven years ago, our fathers brought forth on this continent a new nation, conceived in liberty, and dedicated to the proposition that all men are created equal. Now we are engaged in a great civil war, testing whether that nation, or any nation so conceived and so dedicated, can long endure. We are met on a great battlefield of that war. We have come to dedicate a portion of that field as a final resting place for those who here gave their lives that this nation might live. It is altogether fitting and proper that we should do this.

But, in a larger sense, we cannot dedicate—we cannot consecrate—we cannot hallow—this ground. The brave men, living and dead, who struggled here have consecrated it far above our poor power to add or detract. The world will little note nor long remember what we say here, but it can never forget what they did here. It is for us the living, rather, to be dedicated here to the unfinished work which they who fought here have thus far so nobly advanced. It is rather for us to be here dedicated to the great task remaining before us—that from these honored dead we take increased devotion to that cause for which they gave their last full measure of devotion—that we here highly resolve that these dead shall not have died in vain—that this nation, under God, shall have a new birth of freedom—and that government of the people, by the people, for the people shall not perish from this earth.

Directions: Answer the questions about the *Gettysburg Address*.

1. Circle the main idea:

This speech will be long remembered as a tribute to the dead who died fighting in the Civil War.

(This speech is to honor the dead soldiers who gave their lives so that the nation could have freedom for all citizens.)

2. What happened on the ground where the cemetery stood? __A great battle was fought and many lives were lost.__

Page 129

Comprehension: The Gettysburg Address

Directions: Use context clues or a dictionary to answer these questions about the *Gettysburg Address*.

1. What is the correct definition of **conceived**? __to form an idea__

2. What is the correct definition of **consecrate**? __bless__

3. What is the correct definition of **hallow**? __to revere as holy__

4. What is the correct definition of **devotion**? __dedication to__

5. What is the correct definition of **resolve**? __end, finish, to find a solution__

6. What is the correct definition of **vain**? __without cause or reason__

7. What is the correct definition of **perish**? __to die__

8. What is the correct definition of **civil**? __pertaining to a community, country or civilians__

9. In your own words, what point was President Lincoln trying to make? __Answers will vary.__

Page 130

Comprehension: The Emancipation Proclamation

On September 22, 1862, a year before delivering the *Gettysburg Address*, President Lincoln delivered the *Emancipation Proclamation*, which stated that all slaves in Confederate states should be set free. Since the Confederate states had already seceded (withdrawn) from the Union, they ignored the proclamation. However, the proclamation did strengthen the North's war effort. About 200,000 Black men—mostly former slaves—enlisted in the Union Army. Two years later, the 13th Amendment to the Constitution ended slavery in all parts of the United States.

I, Abraham Lincoln, do order and declare that all persons held as slaves within said designated States and parts of States are, and henceforward shall be, free; and that the Executive Government of the United States, including military and naval authorities thereof, shall recognize and maintain the freedom of said persons.

And I hereby enjoin upon the people so declared to be free to abstain from all violence, unless in necessary self-defense; and I recommend to them that, in all cases where allowed, they labor faithfully for reasonable wages.

And I further declare and make known that such persons of suitable condition will be received into the armed forces of the United States to garrison forts, positions, stations, and other places, and to man vessels of all sorts in said service.

(This is not the full text of the *Emancipation Proclamation*.)

Directions: Answer the questions about the *Emancipation Proclamation*.

1. How did the *Emancipation Proclamation* strengthen the North's war effort? __About 200,000 Black men enlisted in the Union army.__

2. Which came first, the *Emancipation Proclamation* or the *Gettysburg Address*? __The *Emancipation Proclamation*__

3. Which amendment to the Constitution grew out of the *Emancipation Proclamation*? __13th__

4. **Secede** means to ☐ quit. ☐ fight. ☒ withdraw.

Page 131

Comprehension: The Emancipation Proclamation

Directions: Use context clues or a dictionary to answer these questions about the *Emancipation Proclamation*.

1. What is the correct definition of **designated**? __appointed__

2. What is the correct definition of **military**? __an army__

3. What is the correct definition of **naval**? __related to warships__

4. What is the correct definition of **abstain**? __keep away from, refrain from__

5. What is the correct definition of **suitable**? __appropriate__

6. What is the correct definition of **garrison**? __a fort__

7. What is the correct definition of **vessels**? __ships__

8. In your own words, what did the *Emancipation Proclamation* accomplish? __Answers will vary.__

Page 132

Comprehension: Lincoln and the South

Many people think that Abraham Lincoln publicly came out against slavery from the beginning of his term as president. This is not the case. Whatever his private feelings, he did not criticize slavery publicly. Fearful that the southern states would secede, or leave, the Union, he pledged to respect the southern states' rights to own slaves. He also pledged that the government would respect the southern states' runaway slave laws. These laws required all citizens to return runaway slaves to their masters. Lincoln did not come out against slavery. In the following statement, written in 1861 shortly after he became president, he made it clear that the federal government would do its best to avoid conflict with the southern states.

I hold that, in contemplation of the universal law and the Constitution, the Union of these states is perpetual. . . . No state, upon its own mere motion, can lawfully get out of the Union. . . . I shall take care, as the Constitution itself expressly enjoins upon me, that the laws of the Union be faithfully executed in all the states. . . . The power confided to me will be used to hold, occupy, and possess the property and places belonging to the government, and to collect the duties and imposts. . . .

In your hands, my dissatisfied fellow-countrymen, and not in mine, is the momentous issue of civil war. The government will not assail you. You can have no conflict without yourselves being the aggressors. You have no oath registered in heaven to destroy the government, while I shall have the most solemn one to "preserve, protect and defend" it.

Directions: Use context clues for these definitions.

1. What is the correct definition of **assail**? __to attack, to confront__

2. What is the correct definition of **enjoin**? __to impose a rule or law__

3. What is the correct definition of **contemplation**? __meditation, considering before making a decision__

Directions: Answer these questions about Lincoln and the southern states.

4. Lincoln is telling the southern states that the government

☐ does want a war. ☒ doesn't want a war. ☐ will stop a war.

5. As president, Lincoln pledged to "preserve, protect and defend"

☐ slavery. ☐ the northern states. ☒ the Union.

Page 133

Comprehension: Away Down South in Dixie

Although many southerners disapproved of slavery, the pressure to go along with the majority who supported slavery was very strong. Many of those who thought slavery was wrong did not talk about their opinions. It was dangerous to do so!

The main reason the southern states seceded from the Union in 1861 was because they wanted to protect their right to own slaves. They also wanted to increase the number of slaves so they could increase production of cotton and other crops that slaves tended. Many Civil War monuments in the South are dedicated to a war that was described as "just and holy."

"Dixie," a song written in 1859 that is still popular in the South, sums up the attitude of many southerners. As the song lyrics show, southerners' loyalties lay not with the Union representing all the states, but with the South and the southern way of life.

Dixie
I wish I was in Dixie, Hoo-ray! Hoo-ray!
In Dixie land I'll take my stand
To live and die in Dixie.
Away, away, away down south in Dixie!
Away, away, away down south in Dixie!
(This is not the full text of the song.)

Directions: Answer these questions about southerners and "Dixie."

1. Why did southerners who disapproved of slavery keep their opinions to themselves?
   <u>It was dangerous to express their opinions.</u>

2. Why did southerners want more slaves? <u>to increase production of</u> <u>cotton and other crops</u>

3. What are the words on some southern Civil War monuments? <u>"just and holy"</u>

4. What "stand" is referred to in "Dixie"?
   [X] stand for slavery   [ ] stand against slavery   [ ] stand for cotton

Page 134

Fact and Opinion

Directions: Read each sentence. Then draw an **X** in the box to tell whether it is a fact or opinion.

1. "Dixie" is a beautiful song! [ ] Fact [X] Opinion
2. It was written in 1859 by a man named Daniel Emmett, who died in 1904. [X] Fact [ ] Opinion
3. The song became a rallying cry for southerners, because it showed where their loyalties were. [X] Fact [ ] Opinion
4. I think their loyalty to slavery was absolutely wrong! [ ] Fact [X] Opinion
5. These four states where people owned slaves did not secede from the Union: Delaware, Maryland, Kentucky and Missouri. [X] Fact [ ] Opinion
6. The people in these states certainly made the right moral choice. [ ] Fact [X] Opinion
7. The ownership of one human being by another is absolutely and totally wrong under any circumstances. [ ] Fact [X] Opinion
8. In the states that did not secede from the Union, some people fought for the Union and others fought for the Confederacy of Southern States. [X] Fact [ ] Opinion
9. Sometimes brothers fought against brothers on opposite sides of the war. [X] Fact [ ] Opinion
10. What a horrible situation to be in! [ ] Fact [X] Opinion

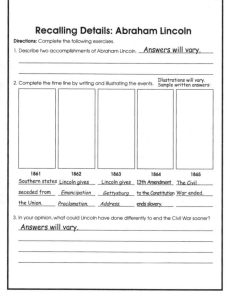

Page 135

Recalling Details: The Civil War

Although they were outnumbered, most southerners were convinced they could win the Civil War. The white population of the southern states that had seceded from the Union was 5.5 million. The population was 18.9 million in the 19 states that stayed with the Union. Despite these odds, southerners felt history was on their side.

After all, the colonists had been the underdogs against the British and had won the War of Independence. Europeans also felt that Lincoln could not force the South to rejoin the Union. The United Netherlands had successfully seceded from Spain. Greece had seceded from Turkey. Europeans were laying odds that two countries would take the place of what had once been the United States.

Directions: Answer these questions and complete the puzzle about the Civil War.

1. What was the difference in population between the Union and the Confederate states?
   <u>13.4 million</u>

2. Circle the main idea:
   (Although they were outnumbered, many people here and abroad felt the South would win the Civil War.)

   Because they were outnumbered, the South knew winning the Civil War was a long shot.

Across:
3. They won the War of Independence against England.
5. Did Europeans believe the South would win the war?
6. ____ teen states belonged to the Union.

Down:
1. Slave owners lived in this area of the country.
2. The president during the Civil War
4. To withdraw from the Union

Crossword:
COLONISTS
YES
NINE
(SOUTH, LINCOLN)

Page 136

Recalling Details: Abraham Lincoln

Directions: Complete the following exercises.

1. Describe two accomplishments of Abraham Lincoln. <u>Answers will vary.</u>

2. Complete the time line by writing and illustrating the events. *Illustrations will vary. Sample written answers:*

1861	1862	1863	1864	1865
Southern states seceded from the Union.	Lincoln gives Emancipation Proclamation.	Lincoln gives Gettysburg Address.	13th Amendment to the Constitution ends slavery.	The Civil War ended.

3. In your opinion, what could Lincoln have done differently to end the Civil War sooner?
   <u>Answers will vary.</u>

Page 137

Fact and Opinion

Directions: Read each sentence. Then draw an **X** in the box to tell whether it is a fact or an opinion.

1. Lincoln warned the southern states that they could not legally leave the Union. [X] Fact [ ] Opinion
2. I believe Lincoln thought the northern states were the best because they did not have slaves. [ ] Fact [X] Opinion
3. I think Lincoln did the right thing, don't you? [ ] Fact [X] Opinion
4. The issues that sparked the Civil War were complicated and difficult ones. [X] Fact [ ] Opinion
5. It would take a historian to really understand them! [ ] Fact [X] Opinion
6. The "dissatisfied fellow-countrymen" Lincoln refers to in his statement lived in the southern states. [X] Fact [ ] Opinion
7. As president, Lincoln took an oath to "preserve, protect and defend" the Union, which included all the states. [X] Fact [ ] Opinion
8. Lincoln did his personal best to hold the country together, but it didn't do one bit of good. [ ] Fact [X] Opinion
9. The Confederate States of America had already been organized in February, 1861, a month before Lincoln was sworn in as president. [X] Fact [ ] Opinion
10. Poor Abraham Lincoln—what a crummy start to his presidency! [ ] Fact [X] Opinion

Page 138

Using Prior Knowledge: Anthems and Songs

Directions: Before reading about anthems and songs in the following section, answer these questions.

1. How do national anthems help pull a country together? _____

2. Describe what you know about how and why "_____" was written.

3. What is your favorite _____

4. What images do the _____ anthem or song bring to mind? Why do you like it?

<u>Answers will vary.</u>

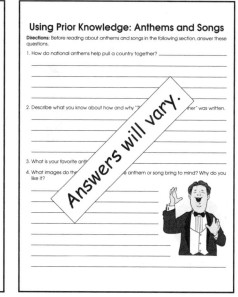

Page 139

Comprehension: Our National Anthem

Written in 1814 by Francis Scott Key, our American national anthem is stirring, beautiful and difficult to sing. Key wrote the song while aboard a ship off the coast of Maryland, where one night he watched the gunfire from a British attack on America's Fort McHenry. The following morning, he wrote "The Star-Spangled Banner" when, to his great joy, he saw the American flag still flying over the fort—a sign that the Americans had not lost the battle.

The Star-Spangled Banner
Oh say, can you see, by the dawn's early light,
What so proudly we hail'd at the twilight's last gleaming?
Whose broad stripes and bright stars, thro' the perilous fight,
O'er the ramparts we watch'd were so gallantly streaming?
And the rockets' red glare, the bombs bursting in air,
Gave proof thro' the night that our flag was still there.
Oh say, does that star-spangled banner yet wave
O'er the land of the free and the home of the brave?

Oh, the shore dimly seen thro' the mists of the deep,
Where the foe's haughty host in dread silence reposes,
What is that which the breeze, o'er the towering steep,
As it fitfully blows, half conceals, half discloses?
Now it catches the gleam of the morning's first beam,
In full glory reflected, now shines on the stream:
'Tis the star-spangled banner: O, long may it wave
O'er the land of the free and the home of the brave!

Directions: Answer these questions about the first two verses of "The Star-Spangled Banner."

1. Who wrote "The Star-Spangled Banner"? __Francis Scott Key__
2. What is "The Star-Spangled Banner"? __the American national anthem__
3. In what year was the song written? __1814__
4. At what time of day was the song written? __morning__
5. Tell what is meant by the lines ". . . the rockets' red glare, the bombs bursting in air/Gave proof through the night that our flag was still there."
__He would see the U.S. flag flying by the light of the__
__rockets and bombs.__

Page 140

Comprehension: "The Star-Spangled Banner"

Directions: Use context clues or a dictionary to answer these questions about "The Star-Spangled Banner."

1. What is the correct definition of **spangled**? __glittering material__

2. What is the correct definition of **twilight**? __early evening, dusk__

3. What is the correct definition of **ramparts**? __walls of a fort__

4. What is the correct definition of **gallantly**? __bravely, proudly__

5. What is the correct definition of **haughty**? __proud__

6. What is the correct definition of **reposes**? __rests, sleeps__

7. Why do you think United States citizens only sing the first verse of "The Star-Spangled Banner"?
__Answers will vary.__

8. What war was being fought when this song was written?
__The War of 1812__

9. Have you ever heard the second verse of "The Star-Spangled Banner"? Knowing the tune, can you sing the second verse?
__Answers will vary.__

Page 141

Comprehension: "America the Beautiful"

Written in 1895 by Katherine Lee Bates, "America the Beautiful" is another very popular patriotic song. It is so popular, in fact, that some people would like to see it replace "The Star-Spangled Banner" as the United States' national anthem. Ms. Bates was inspired to write the song while visiting Colorado, where she was struck by the splendor of the mountains. Today, "America the Beautiful" remains a tribute to our country's natural beauty.

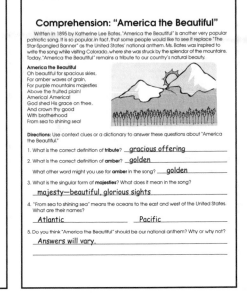

America the Beautiful
Oh beautiful for spacious skies,
For amber waves of grain,
For purple mountains majesties
Above the fruited plain!
America! America!
God shed His grace on thee,
And crown thy good
With brotherhood
From sea to shining sea!

Directions: Use context clues or a dictionary to answer these questions about "America the Beautiful."

1. What is the correct definition of **tribute**? __gracious offering__
2. What is the correct definition of **amber**? __golden__
   What other word might you use for **amber** in the song? __golden__
3. What is the singular form of **majesties**? What does it mean in the song?
   __majesty—beautiful, glorious sights__
4. "From sea to shining sea" means the oceans to the east and west of the United States. What are their names?
   __Atlantic__   __Pacific__
5. Do you think "America the Beautiful" should be our national anthem? Why or why not?
   __Answers will vary.__

Page 142

Comprehension: Civil War Marching Song

When soldiers march, they sometimes sing a song to help them keep in step. One of the most famous marching songs of the Civil War was the "Battle Hymn of the Republic," written in 1861 by Julia Ward Howe. Mrs. Howe wrote the song after visiting a Union army camp in the North. The words are about how God is on the side of the soldiers.

Battle Hymn of the Republic
Mine eyes have seen the glory of the coming of the Lord,
He is trampling out the vintage where the grapes of wrath are stored.
He has loosed the fateful lightning of his terrible swift sword,
His truth is marching on.

Glory, glory hallelujah! Glory, glory hallelujah!
Glory, glory hallelujah! His truth is marching on.

I have seen him in the watchfires of a hundred circling camps,
I have builded him an altar in the evening dews and damps,
I can read his righteous sentence by the dim and flaring lamps,
His day is marching on.

Glory, glory hallelujah! Glory, glory hallelujah!
Glory, glory hallelujah! His truth is marching on.

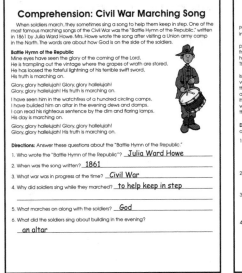

Directions: Answer these questions about the "Battle Hymn of the Republic."

1. Who wrote the "Battle Hymn of the Republic"? __Julia Ward Howe__
2. When was the song written? __1861__
3. What war was in progress at the time? __Civil War__
4. Why did soldiers sing while they marched? __to help keep in step__
5. What marches on along with the soldiers? __God__
6. What did the soldiers sing about building in the evening?
   __an altar__

Page 143

Review

National anthems, work songs and marching songs share some common characteristics. Perhaps the most important characteristic is that the words strike an emotional response in singers and listeners alike.

Have you ever sung "The Star-Spangled Banner" at a baseball game or other large public event? The next time you do, look around as you sing. You will see that Americans from all walks of life and all races sing the song proudly. The words to the national anthem help create a feeling of unity among people who may not have anything else in common. The same is true of the national anthems of France, England and other countries.

Another characteristic of these types of songs is that the words are simple, the message is clear and the tune should be easy to carry. This is not always true, of course. Many people's voices crack during the high notes of "The Star-Spangled Banner." But attempts to change the national anthem to "America the Beautiful" or another song with a simpler tune have always met with dismal failure. It may be hard to sing, but most Americans wouldn't trade it for any other tune. It's a long-held American tradition and nearly everyone knows the words. Americans love what this song stands for. They are proud to live in a country that is the "land of the free."

Directions: Answer these questions about the characteristics of national anthems, work songs and marching songs.

1. Explain what goes into writing a good national anthem. __They must strike__
   __an emotional response, create a feeling of unity, have__
   __simple words and melody.__
2. What does our national anthem help do? __It helps create a feeling__
   __of unity among people.__
3. What happens each time someone tries to change the national anthem to "America the Beautiful" or another song?
   __met with failure__
4. Why do people stick with "The Star-Spangled Banner" as our national anthem?
   __It's traditional and most people know the words.__

Page 144

Recalling Details: The Island Continent

Australia is the only country that fills an entire continent. It is the smallest continent in the world but the sixth largest country. Australia, called the island continent, is totally surrounded by water—the Indian Ocean on the west and south, the Pacific Ocean on the east and the Arafura Sea, which is formed by these two oceans coming together, to the north.

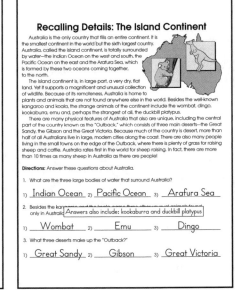

The island continent is, in large part, a very dry, flat land. Yet it supports a magnificent and unusual collection of wildlife. Because of its remoteness, Australia is home to plants and animals that are not found anywhere else in the world. Besides the well-known kangaroo and koala, the strange animals of the continent include the wombat, dingo, kookaburra, emu and, perhaps the strangest of all, the duckbill platypus.

There are many physical features of Australia that also are unique, including the central part of the country known as the "Outback," which consists of three main deserts—the Great Sandy, the Gibson and the Great Victoria. Because much of the country is desert, more than half of all Australians live in large, modern cities along the coast. There are also many people living in the small towns on the edge of the Outback, where there is plenty of grass for raising sheep and cattle. Australia rates first in the world for sheep raising. In fact, there are more than 10 times as many sheep in Australia as there are people!

Directions: Answer these questions about Australia.

1. What are the three large bodies of water that surround Australia?
   1) __Indian Ocean__ 2) __Pacific Ocean__ 3) __Arafura Sea__
2. Besides the kangaroo and the koala, name three other unusual animals found only in Australia. Answers also include: kookaburra and duckbill platypus
   1) __Wombat__ 2) __Emu__ 3) __Dingo__
3. What three deserts make up the "Outback"?
   1) __Great Sandy__ 2) __Gibson__ 3) __Great Victoria__

Page 145

Comprehension: The Aborigines

The native, or earliest known, people of Australia are the Aborigines (ab-ur-IJ-uh-neez). They arrived on the continent from Asia more than 20,000 years ago. Before the Europeans began settling in Australia during the early 1800s, there were about 300,000 Aborigines. But the new settlers brought diseases that killed many of these native people. Today there are only about 125,000 Aborigines living in Australia, many of whom now live in the cities.

The way of life of the Aborigines, who still live like their ancestors, is closely related to nature. They live as hunters and gatherers and do not produce crops or raise livestock. The Aborigines have no permanent settlements, only small camps near watering places. Because they live off the land, they must frequently move about in search of food. They have few belongings and little or no clothing.

Some tribes of Aborigines, especially those that live in the desert, may move 100 times in a year. They might move more than 1,000 miles on foot during that time. These tribes set up temporary homes, such as tents made of bark and igloo-like structures made of grass.

The Aborigines have no written language, but they have developed a system of hand signals. These are used during hunting when silence is necessary and during their elaborate religious ceremonies when talking is forbidden.

Directions: Circle **True** or **False** for these statements about Aborigines.

1. The Aborigines came from Europe to settle in Australia.   True (False)
2. The Aborigines live as hunters and gatherers rather than as farmers.   (True) False
3. The tribes move about often to find jobs.   True (False)
4. The people move often to help them raise their livestock.   True (False)
5. Aborigine tribes always move 200 times a year.   True (False)

Page 146

Main Idea/Comprehension: The Boomerang

The Aborigines have developed a few tools and weapons, including spears, flint knives and the boomerang. The boomerang comes in different shapes and has many uses. This curved throwing stick is used for hunting, playing, digging, cutting and even making music.

You may have seen a boomerang that, when thrown, returns to the thrower. This type of boomerang is sometimes used in duck hunting, but it is most often used as a toy and for sporting contests. It is lightweight—about three-fourths of a pound—and has a big curve in it. However, the boomerang used by the Aborigines for hunting is much heavier and is nearly straight. It does not return to its thrower.

Because of its sharp edges, the boomerang makes a good knife for skinning animals. The Aborigines also use boomerangs as digging sticks, to sharpen stone blades, to start fires and as swords and clubs in fighting. Boomerangs sometimes are used to make music—two clapped together provide rhythmic background for dances. Some make musical sounds when they are pulled across one another.

To throw a boomerang, the thrower grasps it at one end and holds it behind his head. He throws it overhanded, adding a sharp flick of the wrist at the last moment. It is thrown into the wind to make it come back. A skillful thrower can do many tricks with his boomerang. He can make it spin in several circles, or make a figure eight in the air. He can even make it bounce on the ground several times before it soars into the air and returns.

Directions: Answer these questions about boomerangs.

1. The main idea is:
   - [ ] The Aborigines have developed a few tools and weapons, including spears, flint knives and the boomerang.
   - [X] The boomerang comes in different shapes and has many uses.
2. To make it return, the thrower tosses the boomerang
   - [X] into the wind.   [ ] against the wind.
3. List three uses for the boomerang. | Sample answers: |
   1) hunting
   2) playing
   3) digging

Page 147

Comprehension: The Kangaroo

Many animals found in Australia are not found anywhere else in the world. Because the island continent was separated from the rest of the world for many years, these animals developed in different ways. Many of the animals in Australia are marsupials. Marsupials are animals whose babies are born underdeveloped and are then carried in a pouch on the mother's body until they are able to care for themselves. The kangaroo is perhaps the best known of the marsupials.

There are 45 kinds of kangaroos, and they come in a variety of sizes. The smallest is the musky rat kangaroo, which is about a foot long, including its hairless tail. It weighs only a pound. The largest is the gray kangaroo, which is more than 9 feet long, counting its tail, and can weigh 200 pounds. When moving quickly, a kangaroo can leap 25 feet and move at 30 miles an hour!

A baby kangaroo, called a joey, is totally helpless at birth. It is only three-quarters of an inch long and weighs but a fraction of an ounce. The newly born joey immediately crawls into its mother's pouch and remains there until it is old enough to be independent—which can be as long as eight months.

Kangaroos eat grasses and plants. They can cause problems for farmers and ranchers in Australia because they compete with cattle for pastures. During a drought, kangaroos may invade ranches and even airports looking for food.

Directions: Answer these questions about kangaroos.

1. What are marsupials? animals whose babies are born underdeveloped and are carried in a pouch on the mother until they can care for themselves
2. What is the smallest kangaroo? musky rat kangaroo
3. What is a baby kangaroo called? joey
4. Why did Australian animals develop differently from other animals? The island continent was separated from the rest of the world for many years.

Page 148

Comprehension: The Koala

The koala lives in eastern Australia in the eucalyptus (you-ca-LIP-tes) forests. These slow, gentle animals hide by day, usually sleeping in the trees. They come out at night to eat. Koalas eat only certain types of eucalyptus leaves. Their entire way of life centers on this unique diet. The koala's digestive system is specially adapted for eating eucalyptus leaves. In fact, to other animals, these leaves are poisonous!

The wooly, round-eared koala looks like a cuddly teddy bear, but it is not related to any bear. It is a marsupial like the kangaroo. And, like the joey, a baby koala requires a lot of care. It will remain constantly in its mother's pouch until it is six months old. After that, a baby koala will ride piggyback on its mother for another month or two, even though it is nearly as big as she is. Koalas have few babies—only one every other year. While in her pouch, the baby koala lives on its mother's milk. After it is big enough to be on its own, the koala will almost never drink anything again.

Oddly, the mother koala's pouch is backwards—the opening is at the bottom. This leads scientists to believe that the koala once lived on the ground and walked on all fours. But at some point, the koala became a tree dweller. This makes an upside-down pouch very awkward! The babies keep from falling to the ground by holding on tightly with their mouths. The mother koala has developed strong muscles around the rim of her pouch that also help to hold the baby in.

Directions: Answer these questions about koalas.

1. What is the correct definition for **eucalyptus**?
   - [ ] enormous   [X] a type of tree   [ ] rain
2. What is the correct definition for **digestive**?
   - [X] the process in which food is absorbed in the body
   - [ ] the process of finding food
   - [ ] the process of tasting
3. What is the correct definition for **dweller**?
   - [ ] one who climbs   [ ] one who eats   [X] one who lives in

Page 149

Comprehension: The Wombat

Another animal unique to Australia is the wombat. The wombat has characteristics in common with other animals. Like the koala, the wombat is also a marsupial with a backwards pouch. The pouch is more practical for the wombat, which lives on the ground rather than in trees. The wombat walks on all fours so the baby is in less danger of falling out.

The wombat resembles a beaver without a tail. With its strong claws, it is an expert digger. It makes long tunnels beneath cliffs and boulders in which it sleeps all day. At night, it comes out to look for food. It has strong, beaver-like teeth to chew through the various plant roots it eats. A wombat's teeth have no roots, like a rodent's. Its teeth keep growing from the inside as they are worn down from the outside.

The wombat, which can be up to 4 feet long and weighs 60 pounds when full grown, eats only grass, plants and roots. It is a shy, quiet and gentle animal that would never attack. But when angered, it has a strong bite and very sharp teeth! And, while wombats don't eat or attack other animals, the many deep burrows they dig to sleep in are often dangerous to the other animals living nearby.

Directions: Answer these questions about the wombat.

1. How is the wombat similar to the koala? It is a marsupial with a backwards pouch.
2. How is the wombat similar to the beaver? It has strong claws to dig and strong teeth to chew through plants.
3. How is the wombat similar to a rodent? Its teeth have no roots but keep growing from the inside as they are worn down from the outside.

Page 150

Comprehension: The Duckbill Platypus

Australia's duckbill platypus is a most unusual animal. It is very strange-looking and has caused a lot of confusion for people studying it. For many years, even scientists did not know how to classify it. The platypus has webbed feet and a bill like a duck. But it doesn't have wings, has fur instead of feathers and has four legs instead of two. The baby platypus gets milk from its mother, like a mammal, but it is hatched from a tough-skinned egg, like a reptile. A platypus also has a poisonous spur on each of its back legs that is like the tip of a viper's fangs. Scientists have put the platypus—along with another strange animal from Australia called the spiny anteater—in a special class of mammal called "monotremes."

The platypus has an amazing appetite. It has been estimated that a full-grown platypus eats about 1,200 earthworms, 50 crayfish and numerous tadpoles and insects every day. The platypus is an excellent swimmer and diver. It dives under the water of a stream and searches the muddy bottom for food.

A mother platypus lays one or two eggs, which are very small—only about an inch long—and leathery in appearance. During the seven to 14 days it takes for the eggs to hatch, the mother never leaves them, not even to eat. The tiny platypus, which is only a half-inch long, cuts its way out of the shell with a sharp point on its bill. This point is known as an "egg tooth," and it will fall off soon after birth. (Many reptiles and birds have egg teeth, but they are unknown in other mammals.) By the time it is 4 months old, the baby platypus is about a foot long—half its adult size—and is learning how to swim and hunt.

Directions: Answer these questions about the duckbill platypus.

1. In what way is a duckbill platypus like other mammals? It gets milk from its mother.
2. In what way is it like a reptile? It hatches from a tough-skinned egg.
3. What other animal is in the class of mammal called "monotremes"? the spiny anteater
4. What makes up the diet of a platypus? earthworms, crayfish, tadpoles and insects
5. On what other animals would you see an "egg tooth"? many reptiles and birds

Page 151

Recalling Details: Animals of Australia

Directions: Complete the chart with information from the selection on Australian animals.

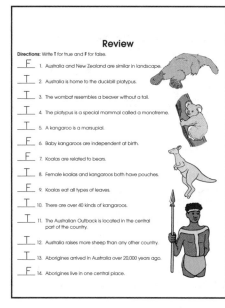

	Gray Kangaroo	Koala	Wombat	Platypus
What are the animal's physical characteristics?	9 feet long 200 pounds marsupial good leaper fast mover	wooly round-eared marsupial good climber	marsupial walks on all fours strong claws and teeth up to 4 feet long 60 pounds	webbed feet duck-like bill fur, four legs hatches from egg poisonous spur 2 feet long good swimmer
What is the animal's habitat?	farmland of Australia	eucalyptus forests of eastern Australia	tunnels beneath cliffs and boulders	streams with muddy bottoms
What does the animal eat?	grasses, plants	eucalyptus leaves	grass, plants, roots	earthworms, crayfish, tadpoles, insects

Page 152

Main Idea/Recalling Details: Land Down Under

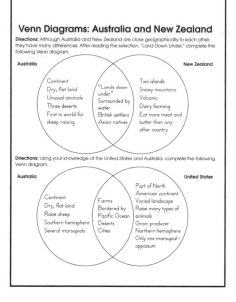

Australia and New Zealand are often referred to as the "land down under." The name, made popular by American soldiers stationed there during World War II, grew out of the idea that these two countries are opposite or below Europe on the globe. While Australia and New Zealand are often linked, they are individual countries, separated by more than 1,000 miles of ocean.

Their landscapes are quite different. New Zealand is made up of two main islands, North and South Island, which are nearly covered by snowy mountains. One of the most unusual and beautiful areas of New Zealand is the volcanic region around Lake Taupo on North Island. There you will see boiling springs, pools of steaming mud, hot-water geysers, small lakes with beds of brightly colored rocks and waterfalls. While most of the people of New Zealand live and work in the industrialized cities, dairy farming is most important to the country's economy. The New Zealanders eat more meat and butter than people anywhere else in the world, and they sell huge amounts to other countries.

As in Australia, many of the customs in New Zealand would be familiar to a traveler from America because the two countries were settled by British settlers hundreds of years ago. However, the native islanders have descended from Asian ancestors, so the remnants of ancient Eastern practices exist alongside the European way of life.

Directions: Answer these questions about New Zealand and Australia.

1. The main idea is:
   - ☐ Australia and New Zealand are often referred to as the "land down under."
   - ☒ While Australia and New Zealand are often linked, they are individual countries.
2. What is the correct definition for **landscape**?
   - ☒ natural scenery and features ☐ mountainsides ☐ natural resources
3. What is the correct definition for **economy**?
   - ☐ thrifty ☒ money management ☐ countryside
4. What is the nickname for Australia and New Zealand? <u>land down under</u>
5. What business is most important to the New Zealand economy? <u>dairy farming</u>

Page 153

Venn Diagrams: Australia and New Zealand

Directions: Although Australia and New Zealand are close geographically to each other, they have many differences. After reading the selection, "Land Down Under," complete the following Venn diagram.

Australia — New Zealand

Australia: Continent; Dry, flat land; Unusual animals; Three deserts; First in world for sheep raising

Both: "Lands down under"; Surrounded by water; British settlers; Asian natives

New Zealand: Two islands; Snowy mountains; Volcanic; Dairy farming; Eat more meat and butter than any other country

Directions: Using your knowledge of the United States and Australia, complete the following Venn diagram.

Australia — United States

Australia: Continent; Dry, flat land; Raise sheep; Southern hemisphere; Several marsupials

Both: Farms; Bordered by Pacific Ocean; Deserts; Cities

United States: Part of North American continent; Varied landscape; Raise many types of animals; Grain producer; Northern hemisphere; Only one marsupial—oppossum

Page 154

Review

Directions: Write **T** for true and **F** for false.

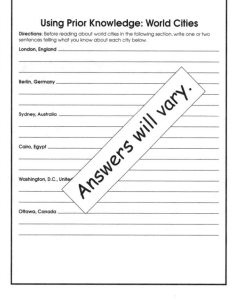

- F 1. Australia and New Zealand are similar in landscape.
- T 2. Australia is home to the duckbill platypus.
- T 3. The wombat resembles a beaver without a tail.
- T 4. The platypus is a special mammal called a monotreme.
- T 5. A kangaroo is a marsupial.
- F 6. Baby kangaroos are independent at birth.
- F 7. Koalas are related to bears.
- T 8. Female koalas and kangaroos both have pouches.
- F 9. Koalas eat all types of leaves.
- T 10. There are over 40 kinds of kangaroos.
- T 11. The Australian Outback is located in the central part of the country.
- T 12. Australia raises more sheep than any other country.
- T 13. Aborigines arrived in Australia over 20,000 years ago.
- F 14. Aborigines live in one central place.

Page 155

Using Prior Knowledge: World Cities

Directions: Before reading about world cities in the following section, write one or two sentences telling what you know about each city below.

London, England

Berlin, Germany

Sydney, Australia

Cairo, Egypt

Washington, D.C., United

Ottawa, Canada

Answers will vary.

Page 156

Creative Writing: London

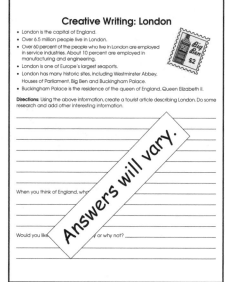

- London is the capital of England.
- Over 6.5 million people live in London.
- Over 60 percent of the people who live in London are employed in service industries. About 10 percent are employed in manufacturing and engineering.
- London is one of Europe's largest seaports.
- London has many historic sites, including Westminster Abbey, Houses of Parliament, Big Ben and Buckingham Palace.
- Buckingham Palace is the residence of the queen of England, Queen Elizabeth II.

Directions: Using the above information, create a tourist article describing London. Do some research and add other interesting information.

When you think of England, who

Would you like... or why not?

Answers will vary.

ANSWER KEY

Page 157

Creative Writing: Berlin

- Berlin is the capital of Germany.
- The population of Berlin is over 3.5 million people.
- Berlin's Inland Harbor is connected to the Baltic Sea.
- This country was once divided into East and West Germany after World War II. East Germany was Communist and West Germany was a Democracy.
- The majority of people living in Berlin are employed in manufacturing.
- Interesting sites in Berlin include the Brandenburg Gate, the State Opera House, Tiergarten Park and the Philharmonic Concert Hall.

Directions: Using the above information, create a tourist article describing Berlin. Do some research and add other interesting information.

When you think of Germany, wh...

Would you like t... why not?

Answers will vary.

Page 158

Making Inferences: Sydney

- Sydney is the capital of New South Wales, Australia.
- Manufacturing is a strong industry in Sydney. The city is also the headquarters of many large companies.
- Sydney is the major port of southeastern Australia.
- Sydney is Australia's largest city.
- The discovery of gold in 1851 increased Sydney's population. The population today is over 3 million people.
- Interesting sites in Sydney include the Sydney Opera House, the Sydney Harbour Bridge and the Australia Square Tower, which is the country's largest skyscraper.

Directions: Answer these questions about Sydney.

1. Why is manufacturing a strong industry in Sydney, as well as other major cities?

   It is the headquarters of many large companies, a major port and the largest city.

2. Gold was discovered in Australia in what year? 1851

3. What two states in the United States were overrun by gold diggers at about the same time?

   California and Alaska

4. When you think of Australia, what comes to mind?

5. Would you like to visit Sydney? Why or...

Answers will vary.

Page 159

Making Inferences: Cairo

- Cairo is the capital of Egypt.
- Cairo is the largest city of not only Egypt but all of Africa and the Middle East.
- The population of Cairo is almost 7 million people.
- Cairo is the cultural center for the Islamic religion.
- Cairo is a major industrial site for Egypt.
- Cairo is a port on the Nile River near the head of the Nile delta.
- Interesting sites include the Egyptian Museum, the Sphinx, the pyramids and the City of the Dead.

Directions: Answer these questions about Cairo.

1. All the major cities discussed so far, including Cairo, have a se... Historically speaking, what is the importance of having access to the sea?

2. Cairo has a population of almost 7 millio... ... problems which could arise from having such a large popula...

   1)
   2)
   3)

3. Would you like to vi... ...hot?

Answers will vary.

Page 160

Creative Writing: Washington, D.C.

- Washington, D.C. is the capital of the United States.
- The population of Washington, D.C. is over 600,000 people in the city itself. Many people who work in Washington, D.C. reside in suburbs of the city in Virginia and Maryland.
- One-third of the people employed in Washington, D.C. work for the federal government.
- The Potomac and Anacostia Rivers join in Washington, D.C.
- Interesting sites include the White House, the Vietnam Veterans Memorial, the Lincoln Memorial, the Washington Monument and the United States Capitol Building.

Directions: Using the above information, create a tourist article describing Washington, D.C. Do some research and add other interesting information.

When you think of Washington... ...mind?

Would you lik... ...D.C.? Why or why not?

Answers will vary.

Page 161

Making Inferences: Ottawa

- Ottawa is the capital of Canada and is located in Ontario.
- The federal government employs most people in the city. Manufacturing is another large employer.
- The Rideau Canal connects Ottawa to Lake Ontario.
- The population of Ottawa is over 300,000 people.
- Points of interest include the Peace Tower, Parliament Buildings, the Royal Canadian Mint and the Canadian Museum of Nature.

Directions: Answer these questions about Ottawa.

1. Who employs the most people in Ottawa, Canada? the federal government

2. What body of water connects Ottawa to Lake Ontario? Rideau Canal

3. In order from largest to smallest, list the six cities you have read about and their populations.

Cairo	7 million
London	6.5 million
Berlin	3.5 million
Sydney	3 million
Washington, D.C.	600,000
Ottawa	300,000

4. Canada is the United States' neighbor to the north. What problems could arise due to a shared border?

   Answers will vary.

Page 162

Compare/Contrast: Venn Diagram

A **Venn diagram** is used to chart information that shows similarities and differences between two things. You can use a Venn diagram as an organizational tool before writing a compare/contrast essay.

Directions: Review the completed Venn diagram and the compare/contrast essay below.

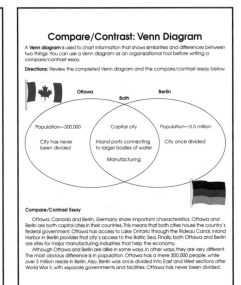

Ottawa | Both | Berlin

Population—300,000

City has never been divided

Capital city

Inland ports connecting to larger bodies of water

Manufacturing

Population—3.5 million

City once divided

Compare/Contrast Essay

   Ottawa, Canada and Berlin, Germany share important characteristics. Ottawa and Berlin are both capital cities in their countries. This means that both cities house the country's federal government. Ottawa has access to Lake Ontario through the Rideau Canal. Inland Harbor in Berlin provides that city's access to the Baltic Sea. Finally, both Ottawa and Berlin are sites for major manufacturing industries that help the economy.

   Although Ottawa and Berlin are alike in some ways, in other ways, they are very different. The most obvious difference is in population. Ottawa has a mere 300,000 people, while over 3 million reside in Berlin. Also, Berlin was once divided into East and West sections after World War II, with separate governments and facilities. Ottawa has never been divided.

Grade 6 - Comprehensive Curriculum

Page 163

Review

Directions: Using page 162 as a guide, complete the Venn diagram comparing Washington, D.C. and London, England. Then write a two-paragraph compare/contrast essay.

Washington, D.C.   Both   London, England

Answers will vary.

Compare/Contrast Essay

Essays will vary.

Page 164

Review

Directions: Using page 162 as a guide, complete the Venn diagram comparing Sydney, Australia and Cairo, Egypt. Then write a two-paragraph compare/contrast essay.

Sydney, Australia   Both   Cairo, Egypt

Answers will vary.

Compare/Contrast Essay

Essays will vary.

Page 165

Using Prior Knowledge: Dinosaurs

Everyone is intrigued by dinosaurs. Their size, ferocity and sudden disappearance have fueled scientific investigations for well over a century.

Directions: Before reading about dinosaurs in the following section, answer these questions.

1. Describe what you know about meat-eating dinosaurs. _____

2. Describe what you know about plant-eating _____

Answers will vary.

3. Which dinosaur _____ Why? _____

Page 166

Main Idea: Small Dinosaurs

When most people think of dinosaurs, they visualize enormous creatures. Actually, there were many species of small dinosaurs—some were only the size of chickens.

Like the larger dinosaurs, the Latin names of the smaller ones usually describe the creature. A small but fast species of dinosaur was Saltopus, which means "leaping foot." An adult Saltopus weighed only about 2 pounds and grew to be approximately 2 feet long. Fossils of this dinosaur, which lived about 200 million years ago, have been found only in Scotland.

Another small dinosaur with an interesting name was Compsognathus, which means "pretty jaw." About the same length as the Saltopus, the Compsognathus weighed about three times more. It's unlikely that these two species knew one another, since Compsognathus remains have been found only in France and Germany.

A small dinosaur whose remains have been found in southern Africa is Lesothosaurus, which means "Lesotho lizard." This lizard-like dinosaur was named only partly for its appearance. The first half of its name is based on the place its remains were found—Lesotho, in southern Africa.

Directions: Answer these questions about small dinosaurs.

1. Circle the main idea:

People who think dinosaurs were big are completely wrong.

(There are several species of small dinosaurs, some weighing only 2 pounds.)

2. How much did Saltopus weigh? __about 2 pounds__

3. Which dinosaur's name means "pretty jaw"? __Compsognathus__

Page 167

Comprehension: Dinosaur History

Dinosaurs are so popular today that it's hard to imagine this not always being the case. The fact is, no one had any idea that dinosaurs ever existed until about 150 years ago.

In 1841, a British scientist named Richard Owen coined the term **Dinosauria** to describe several sets of recently discovered large fossil bones. **Dinosauria** is Latin for "terrible lizards," and even though some dinosaurs were similar to lizards, modern science now also links dinosaurs to birds. Today's birds are thought to be the closest relatives to the dinosaurs.

Like birds, most dinosaurs had fairly long legs that extended straight down from beneath their bodies. Because of their long legs, many dinosaurs were able to move fast. They were also able to balance themselves well. Long-legged dinosaurs, such as the Iguanodon, needed balance to walk upright.

The Iguanodon walked on its long hind legs and used its stubby front legs as arms. On the end of its arms were five hoof-like fingers, one of which functioned as a thumb. Because it had no front teeth for tearing meat, scientists believe the Iguanodon was a plant eater. Its large, flat back teeth were useful for grinding tender plants before swallowing them.

Directions: Answer these questions about the history of dinosaurs.

1. How were dinosaurs like today's birds? __most had fairly long, straight legs that extended straight down beneath their bodies__

2. This man coined the term **Dinosauria**.

☐ Owen Richards ☐ Richard Owens ☒ Richard Owen

3. Which of these did the Iguanodon not have?

☐ short front legs ☒ front teeth ☐ back teeth

4. List other ways you can think of that dinosaurs and birds are alike.

__Answers will vary.__

Page 168

Recalling Details: Dinosaur Puzzler

Directions: Use the facts you have learned about dinosaurs to complete the puzzle.

Across:
5. This dinosaur had five hoof-like fingers on its short front legs.
6. Dinosaurs with flat back teeth were ____ eaters.
9. Because of where their legs were positioned, dinosaurs had good ____.

Down:
1. Most dinosaurs had ____ legs.
2. The word **Dinosauria** means terrible ____.
3. A bone that has been preserved for many years
4. Dinosaurs were not always as ____ as they are now.
7. Iguanodons walked on their ____ legs.
8. Richard ____ coined the term **Dinosauria**.
9. Dinosaurs are closely related to today's ____.

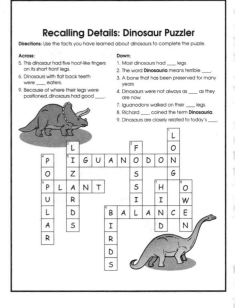

Page 169

Comprehension: Tyrannosaurus Rex

The largest meat-eating animal ever to roam Earth was Tyrannosaurus Rex. "Rex" is Latin for "king," and because of its size, Tyrannosaurus certainly was at the top of the dinosaur heap. With a length of 46 feet and a weight of 7 tons, there's no doubt this dinosaur commanded respect!

Unlike smaller dinosaurs, Tyrannosaurus wasn't tremendously fast on its huge feet. It could stroll along at a walking speed of 2 to 3 miles an hour. Not bad, considering Tyrannosaurus was pulling along a body that weighed 14,000 pounds! Like other dinosaurs, Tyrannosaurus walked upright, probably balancing its 16-foot-long head by lifting its massive tail.

Compared to the rest of its body, Tyrannosaurus' front claws were tiny. Scientists aren't really sure what the claws were for, although it seems likely that they may have been used for holding food. In that case, Tyrannosaurus would have had to lower its massive head down to its short claws to take anything in its mouth. Maybe it just used the claws to scratch nearby itches!

Because of their low metabolism, dinosaurs did not require a lot of food for survival. Scientists speculate that Tyrannosaurus ate off the same huge piece of meat—usually the carcass of another dinosaur—for several weeks. What do you suppose Tyrannosaurus did the rest of the time?

Directions: Answer these questions about Tyrannosaurus Rex.

1. Why was this dinosaur called "Rex"? __It means king.__
_____

2. For what might Tyrannosaurus Rex have used its claws? __to hold food__

3. How long was Tyrannosaurus Rex? __about 46 feet__
4. Tyrannosaurus weighed
☐ 10,000 lbs.   ☐ 12,000 lbs.   ☒ 14,000 lbs.
5. Tyrannosaurus ate
☐ plants.   ☒ other dinosaurs.   ☐ birds.

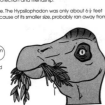

Page 170

Generalization: Dinosaur Characteristics

Directions: Read each passage and circle the valid generalization.

1. Not surprisingly, Tyrannosaurus had huge teeth in its mammoth head. They were 6 inches long! Because it was a meat eater, Tyrannosaurus' teeth were sharp. They looked like spikes! In comparison, the long-necked, plant-eating Mamenchisaurus had a tiny head and small, flat teeth.

a. Scientists can't figure out why some dinosaurs had huge teeth.

b. Tyrannosaurus was probably scarier looking than Mamenchisaurus.

c.(Sharp teeth would have helped Mamenchisaurus chew better.)

2. Dinosaurs' names often reflect their size or some other physical trait. For example, Compsognathus means "pretty jaw." Saltopus means "leaping foot." Lesothosaurus means "lizard from Lesotho."

a. Of the three species, Lesothosaurus was probably the fastest.

b. Of the three species, Compsognathus was probably the fastest.

c.(Of the three species, Saltopus was probably the fastest.)

3. Edmontosaurus, a huge 3-ton dinosaur, had 1,000 teeth! The teeth were cemented into chewing pads in the back of Edmontosaurus' mouth. Unlike the sharp teeth of the meat-eating Tyrannosaurus, this dinosaur's teeth were flat.

a.(Edmontosaurus did not eat meat.)

b. Edmontosaurus did not eat plants.

c. Edmontosaurus moved very fast.

Page 171

Comprehension: Dinosaur Fossils

Imagine putting together the world's largest jigsaw puzzle. That is what scientists who reassemble the fossil bones of dinosaurs must do to find out what the creatures looked like. Fossilized bones are imbedded, or stuck, in solid rock, so scientists must first get the bones out of the rocks without breaking or otherwise damaging them. This task requires enormous patience.

In addition to hammers, drills and chisels, sound waves are used to break up the rock. The drills, which are similar to high-speed dentist drills, cut through the rock very quickly. As the bones are removed, scientists begin trying to figure out how they attach to one another. Sometimes the dinosaur's skeleton was preserved just as it was when it died. This, of course, shows scientists exactly how to reassemble it. Other times, parts of bone are missing. It then becomes a guessing game to decide what goes where.

When scientists discover dinosaur fossils, it is called a "find." A particularly exciting find in 1978 occurred in Montana when, for the first time, fossilized dinosaur eggs, babies and several nests were found. The species of dinosaur in this exciting find was Maiasaura, which means "good mother lizard." From the size of the nest, which was 23 feet, scientists speculated that the adult female Maiasaura was about the same size.

Unlike birds' nests, dinosaur nests were not made of sticks and straw. Instead, since they were land animals, nests were made of dirt hollowed out into a bowl shape. The Maiasaura's nest was 3 feet deep and held about 20 eggs.

Directions: Answer these questions about dinosaur fossils.

1. Name four tools used to remove dinosaur bones from rock. __hammers, drills,__
__chisels, sound waves__

2. What do scientists do with the bones they remove? __They try to reassemble__
__them.__

3. The type of dinosaur fossils found in Montana in 1978 were
☐ Mayiasaura.   ☐ Masaura.   ☒ Maiasaura.
4. When scientists discover dinosaur fossils, it is called a
☐ found.   ☒ find.   ☐ nest.

Page 172

Generalization: Plant-Eating Dinosaurs

Directions: Read each passage and circle the valid generalization.

1. Many of the plant-eating dinosaurs belonged to a common species called Sauropods. Most Sauropods were very large. They had peg-shaped teeth and they formed herds to search for food. They used their long necks to reach the top branches of trees, where the most tender leaves grew.

a.(Their size, teeth and long necks made Sauropods perfectly suited to their environment.)

b. The Sauropods' peg-like teeth were not well suited to eating meat.

c. Vegetarian dinosaurs needed short necks and sharp teeth to survive.

2. Sauropods were not the only dinosaurs that traveled in herds. Sets of different-sized fossilized dinosaur footprints discovered in Texas show that other types of dinosaurs also traveled together. The footprints—23 sets of them—were of another plant-eating dinosaur, the Apatosaurus.

a. All dinosaurs traveled in herds because they needed companionship.

b.(It appears that some plant-eating dinosaurs traveled in herds.)

c. Traveling in herds offered dinosaurs protection and friendship.

3. Not all plant-eating dinosaurs were huge. The Hypsilophodon was only about 6½ feet tall. It stood on its two back legs and, because of its smaller size, probably ran away from danger.

a. The Hypsilophodon didn't stand a chance against bigger dinosaurs.

b.(The Hypsilophodon could not eat from the tops of tall trees.)

c. The Hypsilophodon was cowardly and always ran from danger.

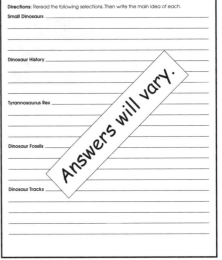

Page 173

Comprehension: Dinosaur Tracks

Some scientists refer to dinosaurs' fossilized tracks as "footprints in time." The tracks that survived in Texas for 120 million years had been made in sand or mud. These large footprints were of the Apatosaurus. The footprints were more than 3 feet across!

Although Apatosaurus had a long, heavy tail, there is no sign that the tail hit the ground along with the feet. Scientists speculate that the place where the tracks were found was once a riverbed, and that Apatosaurus' tail floated in the water and thus left no tracks. Another theory is that the dinosaur always carried its tail out behind it. This second theory is not as popular, because scientists say it's unlikely the dinosaur would consistently carry its long, heavy tail off the ground. When Apatosaurus rested, for example, the tail would have left its mark.

Besides Texas, fossilized tracks have been found in England, Canada, Australia and Brazil. Some tracks have also been found in New England. The tracks discovered in Canada were quite a find! They showed a pattern made by 10 species of dinosaurs. In all, about 1,700 fossilized footprints were discovered. Maybe the scientists uncovered what millions of years ago was a dinosaur playground!

Directions: Answer these questions about dinosaur tracks.

1. Circle the main idea:

(Fossilized dinosaur tracks provide scientists with information from which to draw conclusions about dinosaur size and behavior.)

Fossilized dinosaur tracks are not very useful because so few have been found in the United States.

2. Explain how a dinosaur might have crossed a river without its tail leaving a track.
__It may have floated.__

3. Name five countries where dinosaur tracks have been found. __England,__
__Canada, Australia, Brazil and U.S.__

4. Circle the valid generalization about dinosaur tracks.

a. The fact that 10 species of tracks were found together proves dinosaurs were friends with others outside their groups.

b.(The fact that 10 species of tracks were found together means the dinosaurs probably gathered in that spot for water or food.)

Page 174

Review

Directions: Reread the following selections. Then write the main idea of each.

Small Dinosaurs _____

Dinosaur History _____

Tyrannosaurus Rex _____

Dinosaur Fossils _____

Dinosaur Tracks _____

Answers will vary.

ANSWER KEY

Page 175

The Solar System

This section is about our solar system. It includes the Sun, comparisons among the planets, each planet's physical characteristics and each planet's moons. Before beginning this section, try to answer the following questions.

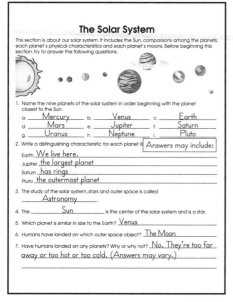

1. Name the nine planets of the solar system in order beginning with the planet closest to the Sun.
   a. <u>Mercury</u>   b. <u>Venus</u>   c. <u>Earth</u>
   d. <u>Mars</u>   e. <u>Jupiter</u>   f. <u>Saturn</u>
   g. <u>Uranus</u>   h. <u>Neptune</u>   i. <u>Pluto</u>

2. Write a distinguishing characteristic for each planet li [Answers may include:]
   Earth <u>We live here.</u>
   Jupiter <u>the largest planet</u>
   Saturn <u>has rings</u>
   Pluto <u>the outermost planet</u>

3. The study of the solar system, stars and outer space is called <u>Astronomy</u>

4. The <u>Sun</u> is the center of the solar system and is a star.

5. Which planet is similar in size to the Earth? <u>Venus</u>

6. Humans have landed on which outer space object? <u>The Moon</u>

7. Have humans landed on any planets? Why or why not? <u>No. They're too far away or too hot or too cold. (Answers may vary.)</u>

Page 176

The Sun

Directions: Read the selection. Then answer the questions.

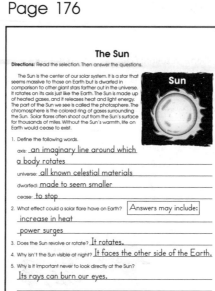

The Sun is the center of our solar system. It is a star that seems massive to those on Earth but is dwarfed in comparison to other giant stars farther out in the universe. It rotates on its axis just like the Earth. The Sun is made up of heated gases, and it releases heat and light energy. The part of the Sun we see is called the photosphere. The chromosphere is the colored ring of gases surrounding the Sun. Solar flares often shoot out from the Sun's surface for thousands of miles. Without the Sun's warmth, life on Earth would cease to exist.

1. Define the following words.
   axis: <u>an imaginary line around which a body rotates</u>
   universe: <u>all known celestial materials</u>
   dwarfed: <u>made to seem smaller</u>
   cease: <u>to stop</u>

2. What effect could a solar flare have on Earth? [Answers may include:]
   <u>increase in heat</u>
   <u>power surges</u>

3. Does the Sun revolve or rotate? <u>It rotates.</u>

4. Why isn't the Sun visible at night? <u>It faces the other side of the Earth.</u>

5. Why is it important never to look directly at the Sun? <u>Its rays can burn our eyes.</u>

Page 177

Mercury

Directions: Read the selection. Then answer the questions.

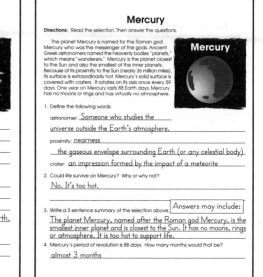

The planet Mercury is named for the Roman god Mercury who was the messenger of the gods. Ancient Greek astronomers named the heavenly bodies "planets," which means "wanderers." Mercury is the planet closest to the Sun and also the smallest of the inner planets. Because of its proximity to the Sun (nearly 36 million miles), its surface is extraordinarily hot. Mercury's solid surface is covered with craters. It rotates on its axis once every 59 days. One year on Mercury lasts 88 Earth days. Mercury has no moons or rings and has virtually no atmosphere.

1. Define the following words.
   astronomer: <u>Someone who studies the universe outside the Earth's atmosphere.</u>
   proximity: <u>nearness</u>
   <u>the gaseous envelope surrounding Earth (or any celestial body)</u>
   crater: <u>an impression formed by the impact of a meteorite</u>

2. Could life survive on Mercury? Why or why not? <u>No. It's too hot.</u>

3. Write a 3 sentence summary of the selection above. [Answers may include:]
   <u>The planet Mercury, named after the Roman god Mercury, is the smallest inner planet and is closest to the Sun. It has no moons, rings or atmosphere. It is too hot to support life.</u>

4. Mercury's period of revolution is 88 days. How many months would that be? <u>almost 3 months</u>

Page 178

Venus

Directions: Read the selection. Then answer the questions.

Located over 67 million miles from the Sun, Venus is an incredibly hot planet. Venus is named for the Roman goddess of love and beauty. Temperatures can reach 470 degrees Celsius. Venus is close in size to the Earth and is often referred to as Earth's twin. Space probes and unmanned crafts have landed on Venus and found Venus to be dust-covered and very windy. Because Venus is very bright, it is often thought of as a star. Venus has no moons or rings. Its period of rotation is 243 days, and it revolves once around the Sun in 225 days.

1. Create a Venn diagram co[mparing] [Answers may include:]enus

   Merc[ury]
   Rotates every 59 days / Revolves around the Sun every 88 days / Many craters
   Has no moons or rings / Very hot
   Earth's "twin" / Rotates every 243 days / Revolves around the Sun every 225 days / Very windy and dusty / Venus is next to Earth

2. Write a 3-sentence summary about Venus. [Answers may vary.]

3. Approximately how far is Venus from Mercury? <u>31 million miles.</u>

4. If you were to design a spacecraft capable of landing on Venus, what might it require? [Answers will vary.]

Page 179

Earth

Directions: Read the selection. Then answer the questions.

Earth is the only planet with known life forms. It revolves around the Sun every 365 1/4 days. One rotation takes 24 hours to complete. Earth has seasons due to the tilt of its axis and its revolution. Rotation causes night and day. The Earth is almost 93 million miles away from the Sun. Its surface is three-fourths water and one-fourth land mass. The Earth is surrounded by gases called the atmosphere, which allows life to survive. The Earth has one moon that has been explored many times.

1. Define the following word.
   mass: <u>how dense something is; the matter a body possesses</u>

2. Approximately how far is the Earth from Venus? <u>about 26 million miles</u>

3. Approximately how far is Earth from Mercury? <u>57,000 million miles</u>

4. What factors allow life to exist on Earth? <u>Its atmosphere and its distance from the Sun (which helps temperatures)</u>

5. What causes the seasons? <u>The tilt of Earth's axis and its revolution cause the seasons.</u>

6. What differences are there be[tween pla]nets Mercury and Venus? [Answers may include:] <u>Earth's atmosphere and cooler surface will support life, Mercury and Venus are much hotter. Earth has a moon while Mercury and Venus do not.</u>

Page 180

Mars

Directions: Read the selection. Then answer the questions.

Mars is named for the god of war. It is the fourth of the inner planets. Mars is called the Red Planet and has polar caps, craters and evidence of ancient volcanoes. Recently, space probes have landed there and given scientists information about its surface. The red color is produced by the reaction of iron-rich minerals to soil and water, which scientists believe happened long ago. Mars rotates on its axis every 24 hours, 37 minutes and is 142 million miles from the Sun. Its period of revolution is 687 days. Mars has two moons, Phobos and Deimos. Mars' identifying feature is the volcano Olympus Mons. Its temperature varies, but averages –50 degrees Celsius.

1. Define the following words.
   polar: <u>the ends of a planet's axis</u>
   mineral: <u>an inorganic substance occurring in nature</u>

2. Name two distinguishing characteristics of Mars. <u>Mars is red and it has a volcano named Olympus Mons.</u>

3. Could life survive on Mars? Why or why not?

4. For years, pe[ople]... characteristic... [Answers will vary.] ...at special

---

Grade 6 - Comprehensive Curriculum

486

Page 181

Jupiter

Directions: Read the selection. Then answer the questions.

The planet Jupiter is the largest planet of our solar system and is named for the king of the gods. Its distinguishing feature is the Great Red Spot, which changes occasionally in both color and brightness. Jupiter has a thin ring and at least 16 moons. Jupiter is the first of the outer planets, separated from the inner planets by an asteroid belt. It is almost 500 million miles from the Sun and takes nearly 12 years to complete a revolution around the Sun. It rotates on its axis in approximately 10 hours. Jupiter does not have a solid surface but rather a surface of gaseous clouds.

Jupiter

1. Define the following words.

asteroid: any small body that revolves around the Sun in orbit.

gaseous: containing gas

2. Approximately how far is Jupiter from Earth?
About 407 million miles

3. Name three characteristics of Jupiter. | Answers may include: |
Jupiter is the largest planet in our solar system. Its distinguishing feature is the Great Red Spot. It also has a thin ring and 16 moons.

4. Write a 3-sentence summary about Jupiter.

| Answers will vary. |

5. What separates the inner and outer planets? | Answers may include: |
an asteroid belt

6. Why do you think ancient astronomers chose to name Jupiter after the king of the gods?
because it is the largest planet

Page 182

Saturn

Directions: Read the selection. Then answer the questions.

Saturn's rings were first discovered in 1610. Scientists now know that Saturn has over 1000 rings of varying color. Not only do the rings rotate at different speeds but also in varying patterns. Saturn has at least 18 moons. It is almost 900 million miles from the Sun and is the second largest planet of our solar system. Saturn rotates on its axis once in just under 11 hours. Saturn is named for the god of agriculture and harvest.

Saturn

1. Define the following words:

varying: differing

agriculture: farming/harvest

2. Name two distinguishing characteristics of Saturn.

its rings

It is the second largest planet.

3. Approximately how far is Saturn from Jupiter?
It's about 400 million miles from Jupiter.

| Answers may include: |

18 moons

900 million miles from Sun

has one or more rings

is one of the outer planets

rotates on its axis every 11 hours

16 moons

500 million miles from Sun

Great Red Spot

takes 12 years to revolve around Sun

rotates every 10 hours

Page 183

Uranus, Neptune, and Pluto

Directions: Read the selection. Then answer the questions.

Because of the immense distance from Earth, it is difficult to study Uranus, Neptune, and Pluto. These planets are named for the god of the skies, the god of the sea and the god of the underworld, respectively.

Uranus rotates on its side, thus making its rings spin vertically rather than horizontally. It has 15 moons and is almost 2 billion miles from the Sun. It rotates on its axis once every 17.25 hours and revolves around the Sun every 84 years.

Neptune is similar in size and color to Uranus. It is almost 3 billion miles from the Sun and takes approximately 164 years to orbit it. Neptune has 8 moons and also has rings. It takes a little over 16 hours to make one rotation on its axis.

Pluto is usually the most distant and smallest planet of our solar system (it rotated inside Neptune's orbit from January 1979 through February 1999.) It was discovered in 1930. It is approximately 7 billion miles from the Sun and therefore the coldest at -230 degrees Celsius. Pluto takes over 6 days to complete one rotation on its axis and 247 Earth years to complete one revolution around the sun. Pluto has one moon.

Uranus
Neptune
Pluto

| Answers may include: |

1. List the similarities among Uranus, Neptune, and Pluto.
They are the three outermost planets.
They are all named after mythological gods.
They all take many years to revolve around the sun.

2. What differences are there among Uranus, Neptune, and Pluto? | Answers may include: |
Uranus, Neptune are large and similar in size: Pluto is the smallest planet. Uranus rotates on its side, so its ring spins vertically. They have different number of moons.

Page 184

Uranus, Neptune and Pluto

Directions: Use the lists you created on page 183 to create a Venn diagram showing the similarities and differences a... | Answers may include: |

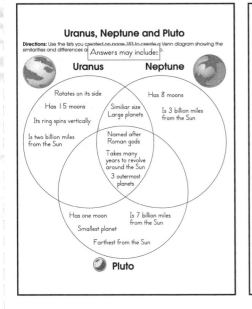

Uranus
- Rotates on its side
- Has 15 moons
- Its ring spins vertically
- Is two billion miles from the Sun

Neptune
- Has 8 moons
- Is 3 billion miles from the Sun

Similar size
Large planets

Named after Roman gods

Takes many years to revolve around the Sun

3 outermost planets

- Has one moon
- Smallest planet
- Farthest from the Sun

Is 7 billion miles from the Sun

Pluto

Page 185

Review

Directions: Follow the instructions for each question.

1. List the four inner planets.
Mercury   Venus   Earth   Mars

2. List the five outer planets.
Jupiter   Saturn   Uranus   Neptune   Pluto

3. What separates the inner and outer planets?
An asteroid belt

4. Name a distinguishing feature of each planet. | Sample answers: |
Mercury: the closest planet to the Sun
Venus: Earth's "twin" in the solar system
Earth: We live here.
Mars: the red planet
Jupiter: owner of the Great Red Spot
Saturn: has over 1,000 rings
Uranus: rotates on its side
Neptune: 2nd to last planet
Pluto: farthest from the Sun and smallest planet

5. List the planets in order from most moons to least.
a) Saturn (18 moons)   f) Pluto (1 moon)
b) Jupiter (16 moons)   g) Earth (1 moon)
c) Uranus (15 moons)   h) Venus (0 moons)
d) Neptune (8 moons)   i) Mercury (0 moons)
e) Mars (2 moons)

Page 186

Review

6. Which planets have rings?
Jupiter, Saturn, Uranus, Neptune

7. If you were in charge of the space program, what would your priorities be? Why?

| Answers will vary. |

8. Draw a diagram of the planets and the Sun. Be sure to depict color and the following diameter sizes.

Mercury — 3,031 mi.   Venus — 7,521 mi.   Earth — 7,926 mi.
Mars — 4,217 mi.   Jupiter — 88,730 mi.   Saturn — 74,900 mi.
Uranus — 31,763 mi.   Neptune — 30,775 mi.   Pluto — 1,430 mi.

Answer: Diagram of Solar System.

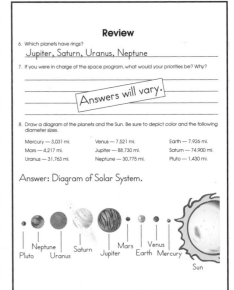

Pluto Neptune Uranus Saturn Jupiter Mars Earth Venus Mercury Sun

Page 187

Recalling Details: The Earth's Atmosphere

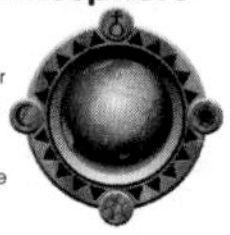

The most important reason that life can exist on Earth is its atmosphere—the air around us. Without it, plant and animal life could not have developed. There would be no clouds, weather or even sounds, only a deathlike stillness and an endlessly black sky. Without the protection of the atmosphere, the sun's rays would roast the Earth by day. At night, with no blanketing atmosphere, the stored heat would escape into space, dropping the temperature of the planet hundreds of degrees.

Held captive by Earth's gravity, the atmosphere surrounds the planet to a depth of hundreds of miles. However, all but 1 percent of the atmosphere is in a layer about 20 miles deep just above the surface of the Earth. It is made up of a mixture of gases and dusts. About 78 percent of it is a gas called nitrogen, which is very important as food for plants. Most of the remaining gas, 21 percent, is oxygen, which all people and animals depend on for life. The remaining 1 percent is made up of a blend of other gases—including carbon dioxide, argon, ozone and helium—and tiny dust particles. These particles come from ocean salt crystals, bits of rocks and sand, plant pollen, volcanic ash and even meteor dust.

You may not think of air as matter, as something that can be weighed. In fact, the Earth's air weighs billions and billions of tons. Near the surface of the planet, this "air pressure" is greatest. Right now, about 10 tons of air is pressing in on you. Yet, like the fish living near the floor of the ocean, you don't notice this tremendous weight because your body is built to withstand it.

Directions: Answer these questions about the Earth's atmosphere.

1. What is the atmosphere? the air around us
2. Of what is the atmosphere made? a mixture of gases and dusts
3. What is the most abundant gas in the atmosphere? nitrogen
4. Which of the atmosphere's gases is most important to humans and animals? oxygen
5. What is air pressure? the weight of the air on Earth

Page 188

Comprehension: Causes/Effects of Weather

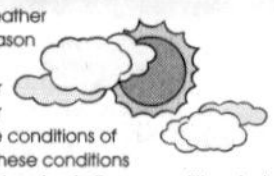

The behavior of the atmosphere, which we experience as weather and climate, affects our lives in many important ways. It is the reason no one lives on the South Pole. It controls when a farmer plants the food we will eat, which crops will be planted and also whether those crops will grow. The weather tells you what clothes to wear and how you will play after school. Weather is the sum of all the conditions of the air that may affect the Earth's surface and its living things. These conditions include the temperature, air pressure, wind and moisture. Climate refers to these conditions but generally applies to larger areas and longer periods of time, such as the annual climate of South America rather than today's weather in Oklahoma City.

Climate is influenced by many factors. It depends first and foremost on latitude. Areas nearest the equator are warm and wet, while the poles are cold and relatively dry. The poles also have extreme seasonal changes, while the areas at the middle latitudes have more moderate climates, neither as cold as the poles nor as hot as the equator. Other circumstances may alter this pattern, however. Land near the oceans, for instance, is generally warmer than inland areas.

Elevation also plays a role in climate. For example, despite the fact that Africa's highest mountain, Kilimanjaro, is just south of the equator, its summit is perpetually covered by snow. In general, high land is cooler and wetter than nearby low land.

Directions: Check the answers to these questions about the causes and effects of weather.

1. What is the correct definition for **atmosphere**?
   - ☐ the clouds ☐ the sky ☒ where weather occurs
2. What is the correct definition for **foremost**?
   - ☒ most important ☐ highest number ☐ in the front
3. What is the correct definition for **circumstances**?
   - ☐ temperatures ☐ seasons ☒ conditions
4. What is the correct definition for **elevation**?
   - ☒ height above Earth ☐ nearness to equator ☐ snow covering
5. What is the correct definition for **perpetually**?
   - ☐ occasionally ☐ rarely ☒ always

Page 189

Main Idea/Recalling Details: Weather

People have always searched the sky for clues about upcoming weather. Throughout the ages, farmers and sailors have looked to the winds and clouds for signs of approaching storms. But no real understanding of the weather could be achieved without a scientific study of the atmosphere. Such a study depends on being able to measure certain conditions, including pressure, temperature and moisture levels.

A true scientific examination of weather, therefore, was not possible until the development of accurate measuring instruments, beginning in the 17th century. Meteorology—the science of studying the atmosphere—was born in 1643 with the invention of the barometer, which measures atmospheric pressure. The liquid-in-glass thermometer, the hygrometer to measure humidity—the as amount of moisture in the air—and the weather map also were invented during the 1600s.

With the measurement of these basic elements, scientists began to work out the relationships between these and other atmospheric conditions, such as wind, clouds and rainfall. Still, their observations failed to show an overall picture of the weather. Such complete weather reporting had to wait two centuries for the rapid transfer of information made possible by the invention of the telegraph during the 1840s.

Today, the forecasts of meteorologists are an international effort. There are thousands of weather stations around the world, both at land and at sea. Upper-level observations are also made by weather balloons and satellites, which continuously send photographs back to earth. All of this information is relayed to national weather bureaus, where meteorologists plot it on graphs and analyze it. The information is then given to the public through newspapers and television and radio stations.

Directions: Answer these questions about studying the weather.

1. The main idea is:
   - ☐ People have always searched the sky for clues about upcoming weather.
   - ☒ A real understanding of weather depends on measuring conditions such as pressure, temperature and moisture levels.
2. List three kinds of instruments used to measure atmospheric conditions, and tell what conditions they measure.
   1) barometer — atmospheric pressure
   2) hygrometer — humidity
   3) liquid-in-glass thermometer — temperature
3. During what century were many of these measuring instruments invented? 17th
4. Name two things used for upper-level observations.
   1) weather balloon 2) satellite

Page 190

Comprehension: Hurricanes

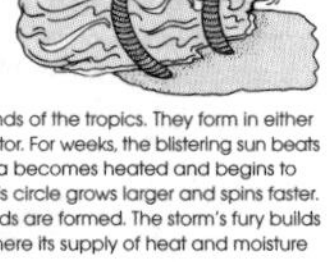

The characteristics of a hurricane are powerful winds, driving rain and raging seas. Although a storm must have winds blowing at least 74 miles an hour to be classified as a hurricane, it is not unusual to have winds above 150 miles per hour. The entire storm system can be 500 miles in diameter, with lines of clouds that spiral toward a center called the "eye." Within the eye itself, which is about 15 miles across, the air is actually calm and cloudless. But this eye is enclosed by a towering wall of thick clouds where the storm's heaviest rains and highest winds are found.

All hurricanes begin in the warm seas and moist winds of the tropics. They form in either of two narrow bands to the north and south of the equator. For weeks, the blistering sun beats down on the ocean water. Slowly, the air above the sea becomes heated and begins to swirl. More hot, moist air is pulled skyward. Gradually, this circle grows larger and spins faster. As the hot, moist air at the top is cooled, great rain clouds are formed. The storm's fury builds until it moves over land or a cold area of the ocean where its supply of heat and moisture is finally cut off.

Hurricanes that strike North America usually form over the Atlantic Ocean. West coast storms are less dangerous because they tend to head out over the Pacific Ocean rather than toward land. The greatest damage usually comes from the hurricanes that begin in the western Pacific, because they often batter heavily populated regions.

Directions: Answer these questions about hurricanes.

1. What is necessary for a storm to be classified as a hurricane? winds blowing at least 74 miles an hour
2. What is the "eye" of the hurricane? lines of clouds that spiral toward the center
3. Where do hurricanes come from? warm seas and moist winds of the tropics
4. How does a hurricane finally die down? It moves over land or a cold area of the ocean where its supply of heat and moisture is cut off.
5. Why do hurricanes formed in the western Pacific cause the most damage? They often batter heavily populated areas.

Page 191

Comprehension: Tornadoes

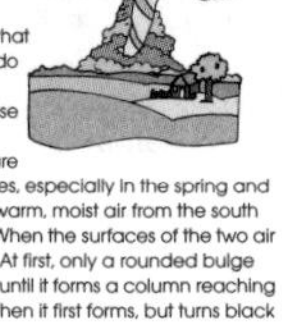

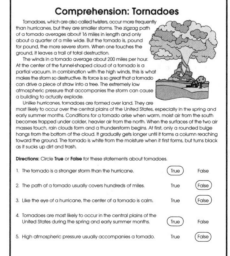

Tornadoes, which are also called twisters, occur more frequently than hurricanes, but they are smaller storms. The zigzag path of a tornado averages about 16 miles in length and only about a quarter of a mile wide. But the tornado is, pound for pound, the more severe storm. When one touches the ground, it leaves a trail of total destruction.

The winds in a tornado average about 200 miles per hour. At the center of the funnel-shaped cloud of a tornado is a partial vacuum. In combination with the high winds, this is what makes the storm so destructive. Its force is so great that a tornado can drive a piece of straw into a tree. The extremely low atmospheric pressure that accompanies the storm can cause a building to actually explode.

Unlike hurricanes, tornadoes are formed over land. They are most likely to occur over the central plains of the United States, especially in the spring and early summer months. Conditions for a tornado arise when warm, moist air from the south becomes trapped under colder, heavier air from the north. When the surfaces of the two air masses touch, rain clouds form and a thunderstorm begins. At first, only a rounded bulge hangs from the bottom of the cloud. It gradually gets longer until it forms a column reaching toward the ground. The tornado is white from the moisture when it first forms, but turns black as it sucks up dirt and trash.

Directions: Circle **True** or **False** for these statements about tornadoes.

1. The tornado is a stronger storm than the hurricane.	(True)	False
2. The path of a tornado usually covers hundreds of miles.	True	(False)
3. Like the eye of a hurricane, the center of a tornado is calm.	True	(False)
4. Tornadoes are most likely to occur in the central plains of the United States during the spring and early summer months.	(True)	False
5. High atmospheric pressure usually accompanies a tornado.	True	(False)

Page 192

Comprehension: Thunderstorms

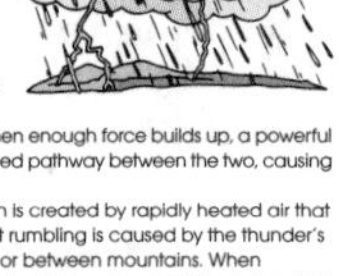

With warm weather comes the threat of thunderstorms. The rapid growth of the majestic thunderhead cloud and the damp, cool winds that warn of an approaching storm are familiar in most regions of the world. In fact, it has been estimated that at any given time 1,800 such storms are in progress around the globe.

As with hurricanes and tornadoes, thunderstorms are formed when a warm, moist air mass meets with a cold air mass. Before long, bolts of lightning streak across the sky, and thunder booms. It is not entirely understood how lightning is formed. It is known that a positive electrical charge builds near the top of the cloud, and a negative charge forms at the bottom. When enough force builds up, a powerful current of electricity zigzags down an electrically charged pathway between the two, causing the flash of lightning.

The clap of thunder you hear after a lightning flash is created by rapidly heated air that expands as the lightning passes through it. The distant rumbling is caused by the thunder's sound waves bouncing back and forth within clouds or between mountains. When thunderstorms rumble through an area, many people begin to worry about tornadoes. But they need to be just as fearful of thunderstorms. In fact, lightning kills more people than any other severe weather condition. In 1988, lightning killed 68 people in the United States, while tornadoes killed 32.

Directions: Answer these questions about thunderstorms.

1. How many thunderstorms are estimated to be occurring at any given time around the world? 1,800
2. When are thunderstorms formed? when a warm, moist air mass meets a cold air mass
3. What causes thunder? rapidly heated air that expands as lightning passes through it
4. On average, which causes more deaths, lightning or tornadoes? lightning

Page 193

Venn Diagram: Storms

Directions: Complete the Venn diagram below. Think of at least three things to write in the outer parts of each circle and at least three things to write in the intersecting parts.

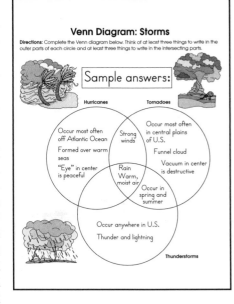

Sample answers:

Hurricanes
- Occur most often off Atlantic Ocean
- Formed over warm seas
- "Eye" in center is peaceful

Tornadoes
- Occur most often in central plains of U.S.
- Funnel cloud
- Vacuum in center is destructive

Thunderstorms
- Occur anywhere in U.S.
- Thunder and lightning

Strong winds

Rain Warm, moist air

Occur in spring and summer

Page 194

Recalling Details: Lightning Safety Rules

Lightning causes fire damage to forests and property than anything else. More importantly, it kills more people than any other weather event. It is important to know what to do—and what not to do—during a thunderstorm. Here are some important rules to remember:

- **Don't** go outdoors.
- **Don't** go near open doors or windows, fireplaces, radiators, stoves, metal pipes, sinks or plug-in electrical appliances.
- **Don't** use the telephone, as lightning could strike the wires outside.
- **Don't** handle metal objects, such as fishing poles or golf clubs.
- **Don't** go into the water or ride in small boats.
- **Do** stay in an automobile if you are traveling. Cars offer excellent protection.
- **Don't** take laundry off the clothesline.
- **Do** look for shelter if you are outdoors. If there is no shelter, stay away from the highest object in the area. If there are only a few trees nearby, it is best to crouch in the open, away from the trees at a distance greater than the height of the nearest tree. If you are in an area with many trees, avoid the tallest tree. Look for shorter ones.
- **Don't** take shelter near wire fences or clotheslines, exposed sheds or on a hilltop.
- If your hair stands on end or your skin tingles, lightning may be about to strike. Immediately crouch down, put your feet together and place your hands over your ears.

Directions: Answer these questions about lightning safety rules.

1. Name two things you should avoid if you are looking for shelter outside.
   1) <u>the highest object in the area</u>
   2) <u>the tallest tree</u>

2. What should you do if, during a thunderstorm, your hair stands up or your skin tingles?
   <u>Immediately crouch down, put your feet together and place your hands over your ears.</u>

Page 195

Main Idea/Comprehension: Rainbows

Although there are some violent, frightening aspects of the weather, there is, of course, considerable beauty, too. The rainbow is one simple, lovely example of nature's atmospheric mysteries.

You usually can see a rainbow when the sun comes out after a rain shower or in the fine spray of a waterfall or fountain. Although sunlight appears to be white, it is actually made up of a mixture of colors—all the colors in the rainbow. We see a rainbow because thousands of tiny raindrops act as mirrors and prisms on the sunlight, splitting it into bands of color. Prisms are objects that bend light.

The bands of color form a perfect semicircle. From the top edge to the bottom, the colors are always in the same order—red, orange, yellow, green, blue, indigo and violet. The brightness and width of each band may vary from one minute to the next. You also may notice that the sky framed by the rainbow is lighter than the sky above. This is because the light that forms the blue and violet bands is more bent and spread out than the light that forms the top red band.

You will always see morning rainbows in the west, with the sun behind you. Afternoon rainbows, likewise, are always in the east. To see a rainbow, the sun can be no higher than 42 degrees—nearly halfway up the sky. Sometimes, if the sunlight is strong and the water droplets are very small, you can see a double rainbow. This happens because the light is reflected twice in the water droplets. The color bands are fainter and in reverse order in the second band.

Directions: Answer these questions about rainbows.

1. Check the statement that is the main idea.
   - [ ] Although there are violent, frightening aspects of weather, there is considerable beauty, too.
   - [X] The rainbow is one simple, lovely example of nature's atmospheric mysteries.

2. What is the correct definition for **semicircle**?
   - [ ] colored circle
   - [ ] diameter of a circle
   - [X] half circle

3. What is a prism? <u>an object that bends light and splits it into bands of color</u>

4. In which direction would you look to see an afternoon rainbow? <u>east</u>

Page 196

Comprehension: Cause and Effect

Directions: Complete the chart by listing the cause and effect of each weather phenomenon.

	Cause	Effect
Thunderstorms	warm, moist air mass collides with cold air mass	lightning, thunder, rain
Hurricanes	air above the sea heats and swirls; hot, moist air is pulled up and spins faster	rain clouds form; spiraling wind
Tornadoes	warm, moist air gets trapped under cold, heavy air	rain clouds form; thunderstorms occur; tornado develops
Rainbows	sun comes out after rain	raindrops reflect sun's light like mirrors and act like prisms, bending light into bands of color
Precipitation	warm, moist air; low pressure system	rain
Drought	lack of rain and dew	dry earth, loss of livestock, dust bowl conditions

Page 197

Review

Directions: If necessary, review the section on weather to find the answers to the following questions.

1. Describe the earth's atmosphere. <u>a mixture of gases and dusts that surrounds Earth at a depth of 100 miles</u>

2. The science of studying weather is called <u>meteorology</u>

3. Why is it important for weather forecasting to be an international effort?
   <u>Answers will vary but may include: As more people travel, knowledge of weather in other countries becomes important. It is also important to track weather systems.</u>

4. Define **weather**. <u>the sum of all the conditions of the air that may affect the Earth's surface and its living things</u>

5. Name three factors that influence climate.
   <u>latitude</u>   <u>elevation</u>   <u>proximity to ocean</u>

6. Describe the following weather phenomena. Sample answers:
   a. hurricane <u>powerful winds, driving rain and raging seas</u>
   b. tornado <u>warm, moist winds trapped under cold, heavy air that results in a funnel cloud</u>
   c. thunderstorm <u>warm, moist air meets a cold air mass which results in rain, thunder and lightning</u>

Page 198

Using Prior Knowledge: Sports

Directions: Before reading about sports in the following section, write one or two sentences telling what you know about each sport below.

Wrestling

Bowling

Volleyball

Tennis

Boxing

Football

Softball

Field Hockey

Answers will vary.

Page 199

Comprehension: Wrestling Around the World

In many countries, wrestling is an honored sport. In Iceland, wrestling is called "glima"; in Switzerland, it is called "schweitzer schwingen"; and in Ireland, it is called "cumberland." In Japan, a form of wrestling called "sumo" began in 23 B.C.

Sumo wrestling is still popular in Japan today. Wrestlers wear the traditional sumo costume of a loincloth—a piece of cloth draped across the hips and bottom—and nothing else. Sumo wrestlers are big men—their average weight is about 300 pounds. Wrestlers compete in small rings with sand floors. The object of the match is to push the opponent out of the ring.

Even in the wrestling ring, however, the Japanese are astonishingly polite. If one wrestler begins to push the other out of the ring, the other may shout, "Matta!" **Matta** is Japanese for "not yet." At this point, the action stops and the wrestlers step out of the ring to take a break. Some wrestling matches in Japan must take a long, long time to complete!

Directions: Answer these questions about wrestling around the world.

1. What is wrestling called in Switzerland? **"schweitzer schwingen"**

2. In what country is wrestling called "cumberland"? **Ireland**

3. What is wrestling called in Iceland? **"glima"**

4. In what country is wrestling called "sumo"? **Japan**

5. How much does an average sumo wrestler weigh? **about 300 pounds**

6. What does "matta" mean in Japanese? **not yet**

7. What happens if a wrestler shouts, "Matta"? **The action stops and the wrestlers step out of the ring to take a break.**

8. In what year did Sumo wrestling begin? **23 B.C.**

Page 200

Comprehension: Tennis, Anyone?

Historians say a form of tennis was played outdoors in England in the 16th century. In France, the game had a much, much earlier start. "Court tennis"—named such because royal courts of kings played it—was played indoors about 1000 A.D. Six hundred years later, indoor tennis was still in full swing. Records show there were 2,500 indoor courts in France at that time.

French tennis players and spectators took the game seriously. In 1780, the surgeon general of the French army recommended the game as one good for the lungs and throat. Why? Because of all the loud screaming and shouting that accompanied French games!

The word "tennis" comes from the French term "tenir," which means "take heed" or "watch out." That's what the French yelled out centuries ago when they used huge racquets to whack balls over a sagging net. Later, when the game was adopted in England, "tenir" became "tennis."

Tennis is said to have come to America by way of the island of Bermuda. A young American girl, Mary Outerbridge, played the game when visiting Bermuda in 1873. She brought tennis racquets, balls and a net home to New York with her. The strange equipment puzzled customs officials (government employees who check travelers' bags to make sure they are not smuggling drugs or other substances). They reluctantly permitted Miss Outerbridge to bring the weird game to America, where it has flourished ever since!

Directions: Answer these questions about tennis.

1. In what year were there 2,500 indoor tennis courts in France? **1600**

2. In 1780, who recommended tennis as good for the lungs and throat?
   the surgeon general of the French army

3. What does the French word "tenir" mean? **take heed**

4. In what state was tennis first played in America? **New York**

5. The person who brought tennis to America was

☐ Marlene Outbridge.   ☐ Mary Outbridge.   ☒ Mary Outerbridge.

Page 201

Comprehension: Boxing History

The first known boxers were the ancient Greeks, who "toughened up" young men by making them box with bare fists. Later, a length of leather was wrapped around their hands and forearms to protect them. Although the sport was brutal, in ancient Greece, boxers who killed their opponents received a stiff punishment.

During the Middle Ages—from 500 to 1500 A.D.—boxing fell out of favor. It became popular in England about 100 years later, when the new middle class had the time and money for sports. Boxers would travel to matches held at inns and bars, and their loyal fans would follow. No gloves were used in the early 1600s in England. Instead, like the ancient Greeks, boxers used bare fists—something new—wrestling holds. Carrier pigeons with messages tied to their bodies were trained to take news of the fights back to the boxers' hometowns.

Because so many people were badly hurt or killed, padded boxing gloves began to be used in the United States around 1880. Boxing became fashionable—and safer. Harvard University offered boxing as an intramural sport in the 1880s. U.S. President Theodore Roosevelt's love of the sport helped to further popularize it. It's said that Roosevelt boxed regularly with a former heavy-weight champion named Mike Donovan.

During World War I, boxing was part of the required training for army recruits. The Golden Gloves championship matches for boys, which began in the 1930s, also helped spread the sport's popularity.

Directions: Answer these questions about boxing history.

1. What people were known as the first boxers? **ancient Greeks**

2. During what period did boxing fall out of favor? **Middle Ages**

3. What university offered boxing as a sport in the 1880s? **Harvard**

4. Which U.S. president enjoyed boxing? **Theodore Roosevelt**

5. In England in the 1600s, news about boxing was sent via

☐ telegrams.   ☒ carrier pigeons.   ☐ messengers.

6. The Golden Gloves championships were first offered

☒ in the 1930s.   ☐ during World War I.   ☐ during World War II.

Page 202

Comprehension: Sports Summaries

Directions: Write a short paragraph summarizing each selection below.

Wrestling Around the World

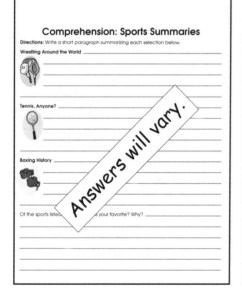

Tennis, Anyone?

Boxing History

Answers will vary.

Of the sports listed, _____ your favorite? Why? _____

Page 203

Main Idea: Bowling Is a Ball

Like tennis and boxing, bowling is also a very old sport. It began in Germany about nine centuries ago. Bowling was first played outdoors with wooden pins and a bowling ball made from a round rock.

The first players were church members who bowled with Catholic bishops and priests. Those who bowled a good game were said to be blessed. Those who bowled poorly were believed to be sinners who should improve themselves to improve their games! The name of the game in 11th century Germany was "Kegelspiel."

By the late 19th century, bowling was the most popular sport in Germany. A common expression for a person who had died was that he was "bowled out."

The game was introduced to America by way of Holland, where the Dutch had learned bowling from the Germans. Some Dutch citizens brought the game to Manhattan Island in 1623. The first bowling alley—outdoors, of course—opened in New York City more than 100 years later in 1732. Today, bowling is one of the most popular American sports. People who have never put on boxing gloves or raised a tennis racquet have, at one time or another, lifted and rolled a bowling ball.

Directions: Answer these questions about bowling.

1. Circle the main idea:
   (Bowling is a very old and a very popular sport.)
   Bad bowlers are sinners who should clean up their acts.

2. Who brought bowling to the United States? **the Dutch**

3. What was bowling called in Germany? **"Kegelspiel"**

4. What were the first bowling balls made from? **round rocks**

5. The first American bowling alley opened in 1732 in what city? **New York City**

6. In 19th century Germany, what was the meaning of the expression "bowled out"?
   It meant someone had died.

Page 204

Comprehension: Facts About Football

Like tennis courts, football fields are usually laid out in a north-south fashion so the sun doesn't shine directly into one team's eyes. The field is 120 yards long and 53⅓ yards wide, with a goalpost at each end that is at least 20 feet high.

Regulation-size footballs are 11 inches long and must weigh at least 14 ounces. The object of the game is for one team of 11 to score more points than the opposing team. There are four ways to score points in football.

A touchdown, worth six points, is scored by carrying the ball across the opponent's goal line or by completing a forward pass in the opponent's end zone. When a team makes a touchdown, it gets the chance to make one or two extra points via a play executed from the 3-yard line. A field goal, worth three points, is made by kicking the ball from the field over the crossbar of the opponent's goal. A way to earn two points is through a play called a safety.

Football games are 60 minutes long and are divided into four quarters of 15 minutes each. Because of all the commercials and instant replays, televised games seem much longer. For college games, the halftime shows also take a lot of time.

Traditionally, college football games are played on Saturday afternoons and high school games are played on Friday nights. During the season, professional games are televised several nights a week, as well as on weekend afternoons!

Directions: Answer these questions about football.

1. How long is a regulation football? **11 inches**

2. How long is a football field? **120 yards**

3. How many players are on a football team? **11**

4. A field goal is worth

☐ one point.   ☐ two points.   ☒ three points.

5. A touchdown is worth

☐ two points.   ☐ three points.   ☒ six points.

6. Football games are **60** minutes long with four **15**-minute quarters.

Page 205

Giving Directions: A Perfect Softball Pitch

A good softball pitcher makes the skill look effortless and graceful. In fact, there are very specific things a softball pitcher must do before, during and after he or she throws the ball.

Before throwing, the pitcher must have both feet firmly on the ground and be in contact with the pitcher's plate for at least 1 second. At the beginning of the pitch, the ball must be held in both hands in front of the body. It must be held this way no longer than 20 seconds. While making the pitch, the pitcher must keep one foot on the ground. Until the ball leaves his or her hands, the pitcher cannot take more than one step toward the batter.

A correct softball pitch looks remarkably like the pitch used to throw horseshoes. As with horseshoes, there is a graceful follow-through with the hand and arm once the ball leaves the pitcher's hand.

There are several types of softball pitches. They include the drop, the slow ball and the out-curve. The drop is the fastest pitch. The pitcher's hand is behind the ball in this pitch. For the slow ball, the pitcher grips the ball between his or her thumb and little finger. He or she puts the knuckles of the three middle fingers against the ball. When the out-curve ball is thrown, the pitcher thrusts the thumb back and rotates all his or her fingers out.

Directions: Follow these instructions about softball.

1. Give directions on what to do before pitching a softball. __Place both feet firmly on the ground. Be in contact with the pitcher's plate for at least 1 second. Hold the ball in both hands for no more than 20 seconds.__

2. Give directions on how to throw a slow ball. __Grip the ball between the thumb and little fingers with the knuckles of the three middle fingers against the ball.__

3. Give directions on how to throw an out-curve ball. __The pitcher thrusts the thumb back and rotates all fingers out.__

Page 206

Comprehension: Volleyball

Volleyball began in Italy during the Middle Ages and was introduced to Germany in 1893. Germans called the sport "faustball." Two years later, an American physical education teacher named William Morgan made some changes in faustball and brought the new game to Americans as "mintonette."

In faustball, the ball was permitted to bounce twice before being hit back over the net. In mintonette, as in modern volleyball, no bounces were allowed. Shortly after Morgan introduced the sport, the director of a YMCA convinced him to change the name to something easier to pronounce. To "volley" a ball means to keep it in the air, and that's what volleyball players try to do.

A volleyball court is 60-feet long by 30-feet wide. It's divided in half by an 8-foot-high net. There are six players on each team, standing three by three across on each side of the net; however, the same person may not hit the ball two times in a row. If the serve is not returned, the team that served gets the point.

The most popular serve is the underhand. The server stands with the left foot forward, right knee bent, weight on the right foot. He or she leans slightly forward. The ball is in the partly extended left hand. The server strikes the ball off the left hand with the right hand. (Left-handers use the opposite hands and feet.) The first team to get 15 points wins the game.

Directions: Answer these questions about volleyball.

1. Circle the main idea:

   Volleyball is a sport that requires a lot of strength.

   (Volleyball is a simple game with six players on opposing sides.)

2. A valid generalization about volleyball is:

   a.(It's safe, requires little equipment and can be played by all ages.)

   b. It's dangerous, difficult to learn and appeals only to children.

   c. It's dull, slow and takes players a long time to earn 15 points.

3. Give directions on how to deliver an underhand serve. __Stand with left front foot forward, right knee bent, weight on right foot. Lean slightly forward. Strike the ball off the left hand with the right hand.__

Page 207

Comprehension: Comparing Sports

Directions: Read each paragraph. Then answer the questions comparing field hockey, basketball and softball.

My sister is more interested in sports than I am. Last year, she lettered in field hockey, basketball and softball. I got my exercise walking to school.

1. What sports did the writer play? __none__

   My sister's favorite sport is field hockey. Because it requires constant running up and down a field, it provides more exercise than basketball and softball. There's also more danger, because every year someone gets her teeth knocked out with a hockey stick. So far at our school, no one has lost any teeth in basketball or softball.

2. Compared to basketball and softball, field hockey provides one benefit and one danger. Name them.

   __more exercise__   __more danger__

   On the other hand, softball players—especially those who play the outfield—can occasionally take some time to daydream. With an ace strikeout pitcher and batters who can't hit far, outfielders' gloves don't get much of a workout.

3. What sports do not allow time for daydreaming? __field hockey and basketball.__

Write a short paragraph telling which sport you like best and why. _____

Answers will vary.

Page 208

Famous Athletes

Athletes are heroes in their fields to both young and old alike. Their stories are sometimes about triumph over amazing odds to become one of the best in their sport. Before beginning the section, answer the following questions as a warm-up.

1. What sport most interests you? Why?

   _____

2. What sports figure do you most admire? Why?

   Answers will vary.

3. In your opinion, what makes a person a hero?

   _____

4. Try to name a sports legend for each of the sports. _Answers may include:_

   Track and Field __Carl Lewis, Gail Devers__

   Swimming __Esther Williams, Mark Spitz__

   Boxing __Muhammad Ali, George Forman__

   Baseball __Babe Ruth, Sammy Sosa__

   Speed Skating __Dan Jansen, Bonnie Blair__

   Tennis __John McEnroe, Martina Navratilova, Chris Everett__

Page 209

Track and Field

Directions: Read the selection. Then answer the questions.

Many people recognize the name "Gail Devers" in the world of track and field. She won a gold medal for the United States at the 1992 Summer Olympics in Barcelona, Spain, in the women's 100-meter dash. However, many people do not know that Gail Devers overcame near insurmountable odds to win that gold medal.

In September, 1990, 24-year-old Gail was diagnosed with Graves' disease, which affects the thyroid gland. She had been fighting this illness for over 2 years before it was finally identified. Graves' disease can cause irregular heartbeat, muscle weakness, nervousness and weight loss. It can also become cancerous. Imagine the difficulties that would create for a person who depends on her muscles in order to compete!

Gail underwent chemotherapy and radiation, which had both good and bad effects on her body. Although the treatments brought her disease under control, the radiation burned her feet so badly that doctors considered amputation.

Amazingly, Gail began her training regimen once again in March, 1991. After competing in several meets and doing well, she went to the United States Olympic Trials and qualified in both the hurdles and the 100-meter dash. Although she came in fifth in the hurdles, the gold medal she claimed in the 100-meter dash represented all her hard work and desire to overcome the odds.

1. Summarize the selection in 3 sentences.

   Answers will vary.

2. Define the following words: _Answers may include:_

   regimen: __a regulated course of treatment or behavior__

   amputation: __cutting off__

   thyroid: __a large gland at the base of the neck which affects growth, development and metabolism.__

   insurmountable: __incapable of being overcome__

Page 210

Speed Skating

Directions: Read the selection. Then answer the questions.

Imagine racing around a rink of glassy ice with only a thin blade of metal supporting you. Now, imagine skating so fast that you set a world record! That's exactly what speed skater Bonnie Blair has done all of her life.

Bonnie started skating before she was walking—on the shoulders of her older brothers and sisters. By the time she was 4, Bonnie was competing. At age 7, Bonnie won the 1971 Illinois state championships and dreamed of becoming an Olympian.

That opportunity soon came. Bonnie competed in the 1988, 1992 and 1994 Olympics. She won a gold medal in the 500 meter race and a bronze medal in the 1,000 meter race in 1988, golds in both the 500 and 1,000 meter races in 1992 and repeated the two golds in 1994. No other U.S. woman has ever won five gold medals in the Olympics in any sport. Bonnie Blair is truly a champion!

1. Define the following words: _Answers may include:_

   opportunity: __a favorable combination of circumstances, time and place.__

   meter: __the basic metric unit of length (equals 39.37 inches)__

2. Bonnie Blair competed over a period of 6 years in the Olympics. What qualities would be necessary to maintain both physical and mental condition to compete for so long?

   _____

   Answers may vary.

3. Bonnie Blair participated in long-track skating... with one other person against a clock for the best time. Do you... easier or more difficult than racing a group to finish first? Why?...

4. In your opin... ...d athlete?

   _____

Page 211

Baseball

Directions: Read the selection. Then answer the questions.

Babe Ruth was born George Herman Ruth in 1895. His family lived in Baltimore, Maryland and was quite poor. He overcame poverty to become one of the greatest baseball players of all time.

Babe Ruth's baseball career began with the Baltimore Orioles. He was a pitcher but also a tremendous batter. He later played for the Boston Red Sox and started his home run hitting fame in 1919.

In 1920, while playing for the New York Yankees, Babe Ruth hit 54 home runs. He had become very popular with baseball fans of all ages. Amazingly, by 1925, he was making more money than the president of the United States! His home-run record of 60 home runs in a single season went unshattered until Roger Maris broke it in 1961 with 61 home runs. Then, in 1998, Mark McGwire hit 70 home runs to become the new "home-run king."

Babe Ruth retired from baseball in 1935 with a career total of 714 home runs. He died in 1948 at age 53.

1. Summarize the selection in 3 sentences.

Answers will vary.

2. In the early 1900s, life ex_____ today's standards. Babe Ruth died at a relatively _Answers may include:_ uted to increased life expectancy?

Better medical care; people are more educated about self-care; the invention of new medicines; better medical facilities.

Babe Ruth born	B.R. hit 29 home runs with Boston Red Sox	B.R. hit 54 home runs in N.Y. Yankees	B.R. retired with 714 home runs	Babe Ruth died
1895	1919	1920	1935	1943

Page 212

Swimming

Directions: Read the selection. Then answer the questions.

In 1968, 18-year-old Mark Spitz boasted that he would win six gold medals at the Olympics being held in Mexico. He won two golds in team relay events. Having made this claim and then failing to achieve it made Mark Spitz determined to do better in the 1972 Olympics in Munich.

For the next 4 years, Mark Spitz trained ferociously. Indeed, at the 1972 Olympics, Mark Spitz amazed the world by breaking all records and winning seven gold medals in seven different events. While doing so, he set new world record times in each event. Mark Spitz had accomplished his goal.

1. What feelings do you think Mark Spitz had after the 1968 Olympics?

2. What do you think is the moral to this story?

Answers may vary.

3. Many Olym_____ ____ Mark Spitz was, and some participate at even younger ages. Write one paragraph detailing the advantages of being a young Olympian and one paragraph detailing the disadvantages.

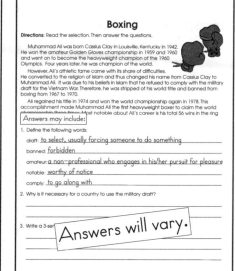

Page 213

Boxing

Directions: Read the selection. Then answer the questions.

Muhammad Ali was born Cassius Clay in Louisville, Kentucky in 1942. He won the amateur Golden Gloves championship in 1959 and 1960 and went on to become the heavyweight champion of the 1960 Olympics. Four years later, he was champion of the world.

However, Ali's athletic fame came with its share of difficulties. He converted to the religion of Islam and thus changed his name from Cassius Clay to Muhammad Ali. It was due to his beliefs in Islam that he refused to comply with the military draft for the Vietnam War. Therefore, he was stripped of his world title and banned from boxing from 1967 to 1970.

Ali regained his title in 1974 and won the world championship again in 1978. This accomplishment made Muhammad Ali the first heavyweight boxer to claim the world championship three times. Most notable about Ali's career is his total 56 wins in the ring

Answers may include:

1. Define the following words:

draft: _to select, usually forcing someone to do something_

banned: _forbidden_

amateur: _a non-professional who engages in his/her pursuit for pleasure_

notable: _worthy of notice_

comply: _to go along with_

2. Why is it necessary for a country to use the military draft?

3. Write a 3-se_____ _Answers will vary._

Page 214

Tennis

Directions: Read the selection. Then answer the questions.

Martina Navratilova gained fame as the best women's tennis player of the 1980s. She was born in Czechoslovakia in 1956 and moved to the United States at the age of 19. She became a United States citizen in 1981.

Martina Navratilova excelled in the sport of tennis but she enjoyed the Wimbledon championship the most. She won the singles finals in 1978, 1979, 1982, 1983, 1984, 1985, 1986, 1987 and 1990.

In 1982, she became the first woman professional tennis player to earn over one million dollars in a single season.

1. What physical characteristics are necessary to excel in the sport of tennis?

2. In your opinion, why would an _____ ____me to the U.S.A. to train_____

Answers will vary.

3. Many athletes find it difficult to adjust to their status as "heroes." What are some possible disadvantages to being an athletic superstar?

Page 215

Review

Directions: Follow the instructions for each section.

1. On the line below, create a time line of the years of birth for the six athletes discussed in this section.

		1950 Mark Spitz		1964 Bonnie Blair
1895 Babe Ruth	1942 Cassius Clay	1956 Martina Navratilova		1966 Gail Devers

2. What mental and emotional characteristics did all six athletes have in common?

Answers will vary.

3. On the line below, create a time line of Muhammad Ali's life.

M.A. won Golden Gloves Championship 1960	Heavyweight champion of the world	1967 1970
1942 1959	M.A. won Olympics 1964	M.A. banned from boxing and stripped of world title

4. Compare and contrast the sports of tennis and baseball in a two-paragraph essay.

Answers will vary.

Page 216

Writing: My Sports Hero

Directions: Write a short essay about a man or woman you admire who has excelled in a sport. Make sure to give details about why you admire this person.

Directions: Interview an adult, _____ sports figure he or she admired at your age. Write a short parag_____ _son's sports hero.

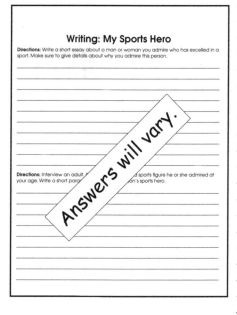

Answers will vary.

Page 217

Using Prior Knowledge: Poetry

Directions: Before reading about poetry in the following section, answer these questions.

1. Have you ever written a poem? If so, was it difficult to do? Why or why not?

2. Write a poem with rhyming verse.

3. Write a poem with u...

Answers will vary.

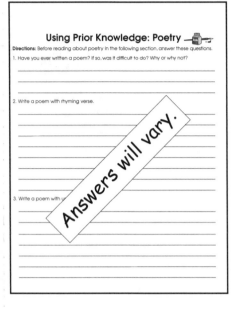

Page 218

Comprehension: Epitaphs

Epitaphs are verses written on tombstones and were very popular in the past. The following epitaphs were written by unknown authors.

On a Man Named Merideth
Here lies one blown out of breath
Who lived a merry life and died a Merideth.

On a Dentist
Stranger, approach this spot with gravity:
John Brown is filling his last cavity.

On Leslie Moore
Here lies what's left
Of Leslie Moore
No Les
No more

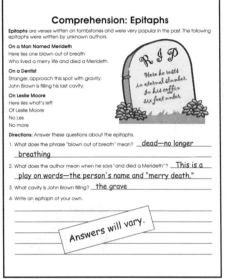

Directions: Answer these questions about the epitaphs.

1. What does the phrase "blown out of breath" mean? __dead—no longer breathing__

2. What does the author mean when he says "and died a Merideth"? __This is a play on words—the person's name and "merry death."__

3. What cavity is John Brown filling? __the grave__

4. Write an epitaph of your own.

Answers will vary.

Page 219

Comprehension: "The Ant and the Cricket"

A silly young cricket, who decided to sing
Through the warm sunny months of summer and spring,
Began to complain when he found that at home
His cupboards were empty and winter had come.

At last by starvation the cricket made bold
To hop through the wintertime snow and the cold.
Away he set off to a miserly ant
To see if to keep him alive he would grant
Shelter from rain, a mouthful of grain.
"I wish only to borrow—I'll repay it tomorrow—
If not, I must die of starvation and sorrow!"

Said the ant to the cricket, "It's true I'm your friend,
But we ants never borrow, we ants never lend;
We ants store up crumbs so when winter arrives
We have just enough food to keep ants alive."

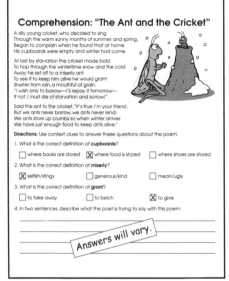

Directions: Use context clues to answer these questions about the poem.

1. What is the correct definition of **cupboards**?
☐ where books are stored ☒ where food is stored ☐ where shoes are stored

2. What is the correct definition of **miserly**?
☒ selfish/stingy ☐ generous/kind ☐ mean/ugly

3. What is the correct definition of **grant**?
☐ to take away ☐ to belch ☒ to give

4. In two sentences, describe what the poet is trying to say with this poem.

Answers will vary.

Page 220

Comprehension: "The Elf and the Dormouse"

Under a toadstool
Crept a wee elf
Out of the rain
To shelter himself.

Under the toadstool
Sound asleep
Sat a big dormouse
All in a heap.

Trembled the wee elf
Frightened, and yet
Fearing to fly away
Lest he got wet.

To the next shelter
Maybe a mile!
Sudden the wee elf
Smiled a wee smile.

Tugged 'til the toadstool
Toppled in two.
Holding it over him
Gaily he flew.

Soon he was safe home,
Dry as could be;
Soon woke the dormouse
"Good gracious me!

"Where is my toadstool?"
Loud he lamented.
And that's when umbrellas
First were invented.

—Oliver Herford

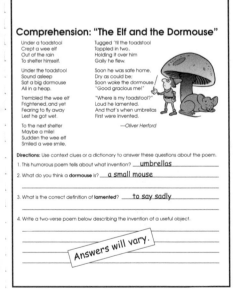

Directions: Use context clues or a dictionary to answer these questions about the poem.

1. This humorous poem tells about what invention? __umbrellas__

2. What do you think a **dormouse** is? __a small mouse__

3. What is the correct definition of **lamented**? __to say sadly__

4. Write a two-verse poem below describing the invention of a useful object.

Answers will vary.

Page 221

Comprehension: "The Eagle"

Personification is a figure of speech in which human characteristics are given to an animal or object.

Example: The trees danced in the wind.

Trees do not dance; therefore, the trees are being personified.

He clasps the crag with crooked hands:
Close to the sun in lonely lands,
Ringed with the azure world, he stands.

The wrinkled sea beneath him crawls;
He watches from his mountain walls,
And like a thunderbolt he falls.

—Alfred, Lord Tennyson

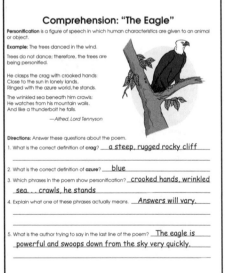

Directions: Answer these questions about the poem.

1. What is the correct definition of **crag**? __a steep, rugged rocky cliff__

2. What is the correct definition of **azure**? __blue__

3. Which phrases in the poem show personification? __crooked hands, wrinkled sea . . . crawls, he stands__

4. Explain what one of these phrases actually means. __Answers will vary.__

5. What is the author trying to say in the last line of the poem? __The eagle is powerful and swoops down from the sky very quickly.__

Page 222

Comprehension: Proverbs

Proverbs are bits of advice for daily life. The following proverbs were written by Benjamin Franklin in 1732. They were published in *Poor Richard's Almanack*.

1. Keep conscience clear.
Then never fear.

2. Little strokes
Fell great oaks.

3. From a slip of foot you may soon recover,
But a slip of the tongue you may never get over.

4. Doing an injury puts you below your enemy;
Revenging one makes you but even with him;
Forgiving it sets you above him.

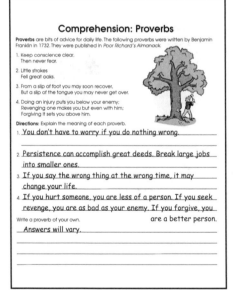

Directions: Explain the meaning of each proverb.

1. __You don't have to worry if you do nothing wrong.__

2. __Persistence can accomplish great deeds. Break large jobs into smaller ones.__

3. __If you say the wrong thing at the wrong time, it may change your life.__

4. __If you hurt someone, you are less of a person. If you seek revenge, you are as bad as your enemy. If you forgive, you are a better person.__

Write a proverb of your own. __Answers will vary.__

Page 223

Comprehension: Limericks

A **limerick** is a humorous verse consisting of five lines. The first, second and fifth lines rhyme, and the third and fourth lines rhyme.

Old Man From Peru
There was an old man from Peru,
Who dreamed he was eating his shoe.
In the midst of the night
He awoke in a fright
And—good grief!—it was perfectly true.

Old Man From Darjeeling
There was an old man from Darjeeling,
Who boarded a bus bound for Ealing.
He saw on the door:
"Please don't spit on the floor."
So he stood up and spat on the ceiling.

Directions: Answer these questions about these silly limericks.

1. In "Old Man From Peru," what was perfectly true? **He was eating his shoe.**

2. How did the old man from Peru feel when he awoke? **frightened**

3. In "Old Man From Darjeeling," what is Ealing? **a city in England**

4. Did the old man from Darjeeling break any rules? **no**

Write your own silly limerick below.

Answers will vary.

Page 224

Comprehension: "The Tyger"

Imagery is a "picture" that comes into the reader's mind when reading certain words.

Tyger! Tyger! burning bright
In the forests of the night,
What immortal hand or eye
Could frame thy fearful symmetry?

In what distant deeps or skies
Burnt the fire of thine eyes?
On what wings dare he aspire?
What the hand dare seize the fire?

And what shoulder, and what art,
Could twist the sinew of thy heart.
And when thy heart began to beat,
What dread hand? and what dread feet?

What the hammer? what the chain?
In what furnace was thy brain?
What the anvil? what dread grasp
Dare its deadly terrors clasp?

When the stars threw down their spears,
And watered heaven with their tears,
Did he smile his work to see?
Did he who made the lamb make thee?

Tyger! Tyger! burning bright
In the forests of the night,
What immortal hand or eye,
Dare frame thy fearful symmetry?
—*William Blake*

Directions: Use context clues or a dictionary to answer these questions about the poem.

1. What is the correct definition of **symmetry**?
in balance—one side the same as the other

2. What is the correct definition of **immortal**?
eternal, undying

3. What is the correct definition of **aspire**?
to be eager to achieve

4. What is the correct definition of **sinew**?
physical strength or tendon

5. What is the correct definition of **anvil**?
an iron blacksmiths use to hammer metal upon

6. What is some imagery in this poem?
Answers will vary.

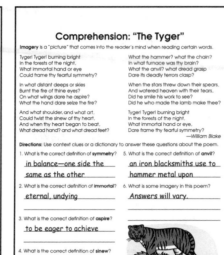

Page 225

Comprehension: Old Gaelic Lullaby

A **Gaelic lullaby** is an ancient Irish or Scottish song some parents sing as they rock their babies to sleep.

Hush! The waves are rolling in,
White with foam, white with foam,
Father works amid the din,
But baby sleeps at home.

Hush! The winds roar hoarse and deep—
On they come, on they come!
Brother seeks the wandering sheep,
But baby sleeps at home.

Hush! The rain sweeps over the fields,
Where cattle roam, where cattle roam,
Sister goes to seek the cows,
But baby sleeps at home.

Directions: Answer these questions about the Gaelic lullaby.

1. What is Father doing while baby sleeps? **Father is working.**

2. What is Brother doing? **Brother is looking for the wandering sheep.**

3. What is Sister doing? **Sister goes to look for the cows.**

4. What do we assume Mother is doing? **Answers will vary.**

5. Is it quiet or noisy while Father works? ☐ quiet ☒ noisy
6. Which is not mentioned in the poem?
☐ wind ☒ sunshine ☐ waves ☐ rain

Page 226

Comprehension: "The Lark and the Wren"

"Goodnight, Sir Wren!" said the little lark.
"The daylight fades; it will soon be dark.
I've sung my hymn to the parting day.
So now I fly to my quiet glen
In yonder meadow—Goodnight, Wren!"

"Goodnight, poor Lark," said the haughty wren,
With a flick of his wing toward his happy friend.
"I also go to my rest profound
But not to sleep on the cold, damp ground.
The fittest place for a bird like me
Is the topmost bough of a tall pine tree."

Directions: Use context clues for these definitions.

1. What is the correct definition of **hymn**?
☐ whisper ☒ song ☐ opposite of her
2. What is the correct definition of **yonder**?
☒ distant ☐ mountaintop ☐ seaside
3. What is the correct definition of **haughty**?
☐ happy ☐ friendly ☒ pompous
4. What is the correct definition of **profound**?
☐ restless ☒ deep ☐ uncomfortable
5. What is the correct definition of **bough**?
☐ to bend over ☐ tree roots ☒ tree branch
6. Write another verse of the poem.
Answers will vary.

Page 228

Nouns

A **noun** names a person, place, thing or idea.
There are several types of nouns.

Examples:
proper nouns: Joe, Jefferson Memorial
common nouns: dog, town
concrete nouns: book, stove
abstract nouns: fear, devotion
collective nouns: audience, flock

A word can be more than one type of noun.

Example: Dog is both a common and a concrete noun.

Directions: Write the type or types of each noun on the lines.

1. desk **common, concrete**
2. ocean **common, concrete**
3. love **common, abstract**
4. cat **common, concrete**
5. herd **common, concrete, collective**
6. compassion **common, abstract**
7. reputation **common, abstract**
8. eyes **common, concrete**
9. staff **common, concrete, collective**
10. day **common, concrete**
11. Roosevelt Building **proper, concrete**
12. Mr. Timken **proper, concrete**
13. life **common, abstract**
14. porch **common, concrete**
15. United States **proper, concrete or abstract**

Page 229

Possessive Nouns

A **possessive** noun owns something. To make a singular noun possessive, add an apostrophe and **s**. **Example:** mayor's campaign.

To make a plural noun possessive when it already ends with **s**, add only an apostrophe. **Example:** dogs' tails

To make a plural noun possessive when it doesn't end with **s**, add an apostrophe and **s**. **Example:** men's shirts

Directions: Write the correct form of the word for each sentence in the group. Words may be singular, plural, singular possessive or plural possessive. The first one has been done for you.

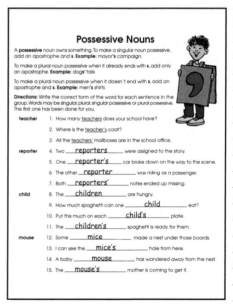

teacher
1. How many **teachers** does your school have?
2. Where is the **teacher's** coat?
3. All the **teachers'** mailboxes are in the school office.

reporter
4. Two **reporters** were assigned to the story.
5. One **reporter's** car broke down on the way to the scene.
6. The other **reporter** was riding as a passenger.
7. Both **reporters'** notes ended up missing.

child
8. The **children** are hungry.
9. How much spaghetti can one **child** eat?
10. Put this much on each **child's** plate.
11. The **children's** spaghetti is ready for them.

mouse
12. Some **mice** made a nest under those boards.
13. I can see the **mice's** hole from here.
14. A baby **mouse** has wandered away from the nest.
15. The **mouse's** mother is coming to get it.

Page 230

Verbs

A **verb** is a word that tells what something does or that something exists.

There are two types of verbs: **action** and **state of being**.

Examples:
Action: run, read
State of being: feel, sound, taste, stay, look, appear, grow, seem, smell and forms of **be**

Directions: Write **A** if the verb shows action. Write **S** if it shows state of being.

1. __A__ He helped his friend.
2. __S__ They appear happy and content.
3. __A__ Jordi drives to school each day.
4. __A__ The snowfall closed schools everywhere.
5. __A__ The dog sniffed at its food.
6. __S__ The meat tastes funny.
7. __A__ Did you taste the ice cream?
8. __A__ The young boy smelled the flowers.
9. __S__ She looked depressed.
10. __A__ The coach announced the dates of the scrimmage.
11. __A__ The owner of the store stocks all types of soda.
12. __A__ He dribbled the ball down the court.
13. __S__ "Everything seems to be in order," said the train conductor.

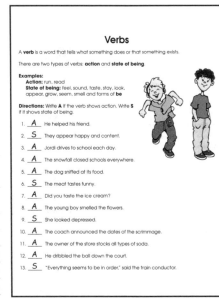

Page 231

Verb Tense

Tense is the way a verb is used to express time. To explain what is happening right now, use the **present tense**.

Example: He **is** singing well. He **sings** well.

To explain what has already happened, use the **past tense**.

Example: He **sang** well.

To explain what will happen, use the **future tense**.

Example: He **will** sing well.

Directions: Rewrite each sentence so the verbs are in the same tense. The first one has been done for you.

1. He ran, he jumped, then he is flying.
   He ran, he jumped, then he flew.
2. He was crying, then he will stop.
   He was crying, then he stopped.
3. She feels happy, but she was not sure why.
   She feels happy, but she is not sure why.
4. He is my friend, so was she.
   He is my friend, and so is she.
5. She bit into the cake and says it is good.
   She bit into the cake and said it was good.
6. He laughs first and then told us the joke.
   He laughed first, then told us the joke.

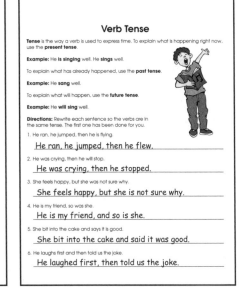

Page 232

Spelling Different Forms of Verbs

To show that something is happening in the present, we can use a "plain" verb, or we can use **is** or **are** and add **ing** to the verb.

is/are + verb + ing
was/were + verb + ing

Example: We run. We are running.

To show that something has already happened, we can add **ed** to many verbs, or we can use **was** or **were** and add **ing** to a verb.

Example: The workers surveyed. The workers were **surveying**.

If a verb ends in **e**, drop the final **e** before adding an ending that begins with a vowel.

Example: She is **driving**. He **restored** the old car.

If a verb ends in **sh** or **ch**, add **es** instead of **s** to change the form.

Example: He **furnishes**. She **watches**.

Directions: Complete each sentence with the correct form of the verb given. The first one has been done for you.

1. The florist is (have) a sale this week. — __having__
2. Last night's tornado (destroy) a barn. — __destroyed__
3. We are (research) the history of our town. — __researching__
4. My mistake was (use) a plural verb instead of a singular one. — __using__
5. She (act) quickly in yesterday's emergency. — __acted__
6. Our group is (survey) the parents in our community. — __surveying__
7. For our last experiment, we (observe) a plant's growth for 2 weeks. — __observed__
8. A local company already (furnish) all the materials for this project. — __furnished__
9. Which dairy (furnish) milk to our cafeteria every day? — __furnishes__
10. Just (ignore) the mess in here will not help your case. — __ignoring__

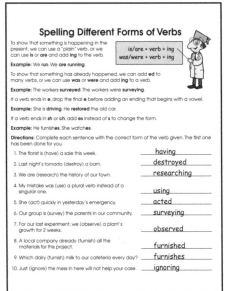

Page 233

Verb Tense

Directions: Write a sentence using the present tense of each verb.

1. walk _____
2. dream _____
3. achieve _____

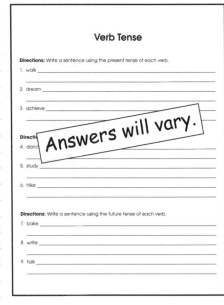

Answers will vary.

Directions:
4. dance _____
5. study _____
6. hike _____

Directions: Write a sentence using the future tense of each verb.

7. bake _____
8. write _____
9. talk _____

Page 234

Verb Tense

Verbs can be **present**, **past** or **past participle**.

Add **d** or **ed** to form the past tense.

Past-participle verbs also use a helping verb such as **has** or **have**.

Examples:
Present	Past	Past Participle
help	helped	has or have helped
skip	skipped	has or have skipped

Directions: Write the past and past-participle forms of each present tense verb.

Present	Past	Past Participle
1. paint	painted	has (have) painted
2. dream	dreamed	has (have) dreamed
3. play	played	has (have) played
4. approach	approached	has (have) approached
5. hop	hopped	has (have) hopped
6. climb	climbed	has (have) climbed
7. dance	danced	has (have) danced
8. appear	appeared	has (have) appeared
9. watch	watched	has (have) watched
10. dive	dove, dived	has (have) dived
11. hurry	hurried	has (have) hurried
12. discover	discovered	has (have) discovered
13. decorate	decorated	has (have) decorated
14. close	closed	has (have) closed
15. jump	jumped	has (have) jumped

Page 235

Irregular Verb Forms

The past tense of most verbs is formed by adding **ed**. Verbs that do not follow this format are called **irregular verbs**.

The irregular verb chart shows a few of the many verbs with irregular forms.

Irregular Verb Chart		
Present Tense	**Past Tense**	**Past Participle**
go	went	has, have or had gone
do	did	has, have or had done
fly	flew	has, have or had flown
grow	grew	has, have or had grown
ride	rode	has, have or had ridden
see	saw	has, have or had seen
sing	sang	has, have or had sung
swim	swam	has, have or had swum
throw	threw	has, have or had thrown

The words **had**, **have** and **has** can be separated from the irregular verb by other words in the sentence.

Directions: Choose the correct verb form from the chart to complete the sentences. The first one has been done for you.

1. The pilot had never before __flown__ that type of plane.
2. She put on her bathing suit and __swam__ 2 miles.
3. The tall boy had __grown__ 2 inches over the summer.
4. She insisted she had __done__ her homework.
5. He __saw__ them walking down the street.
6. She __rode__ the horse around the track.
7. The pitcher has __thrown__ the ball many times.
8. He can __swim__ safely in the deepest water.

ANSWER KEY

Page 236

Irregular Verb Forms

Directions: Use the irregular verb chart on the previous page. Write the correct verb form to complete each sentence.

1. Has she ever _____ **grown** _____ carrots in her garden?
2. She was so angry she _____ **threw** _____ a tantrum.
3. The bird had sometimes _____ **flown** _____ from its cage.
4. The cowboy has never _____ **ridden** _____ that horse before.
5. Will you _____ **go** _____ to the store with me?
6. He said he had often _____ **seen** _____ her walking on his street.
7. She insisted she has not _____ **grown** _____ taller this year.
8. He _____ **swam** _____ briskly across the pool.
9. Have the insects _____ **flown** _____ away?
10. Has anyone _____ **seen** _____ my sister lately?
11. He hasn't _____ **done** _____ the dishes once this week!
12. Has she been _____ **thrown** _____ out of the game for cheating?
13. I haven't _____ **seen** _____ her yet today.
14. The airplane _____ **flew** _____ slowly by the airport.
15. Have you _____ **ridden** _____ your bike yet this week?

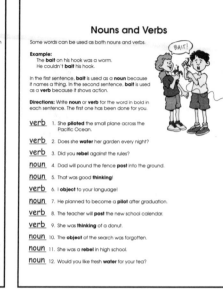

Page 237

Nouns and Verbs

Some words can be used as both nouns and verbs.

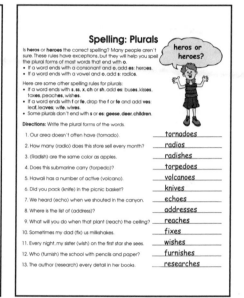

Example:
The **bait** on his hook was a worm.
He couldn't **bait** his hook.

In the first sentence, **bait** is used as a **noun** because it names a thing. In the second sentence, **bait** is used as a **verb** because it shows action.

Directions: Write **noun** or **verb** for the word in bold in each sentence. The first one has been done for you.

verb 1. She **piloted** the small plane across the Pacific Ocean.
verb 2. Does she **water** her garden every night?
verb 3. Did you **rebel** against the rules?
noun 4. Dad will pound the fence **post** into the ground.
noun 5. That was good **thinking**!
verb 6. I **object** to your language!
noun 7. He planned to become a **pilot** after graduation.
verb 8. The teacher will **post** the new school calendar.
verb 9. She was **thinking** of a donut.
noun 10. The **object** of the search was forgotten.
noun 11. She was a **rebel** in high school.
noun 12. Would you like fresh **water** for your tea?

Page 238

Spelling: Plurals

Is **heros** or **heroes** the correct spelling? Many people aren't sure. These rules have exceptions, but they will help you spell the plural forms of most words that end with **o**.
• If a word ends with a consonant and **o**, add **es**: heroes.
• If a word ends with a vowel and **o**, add **s**: radios.

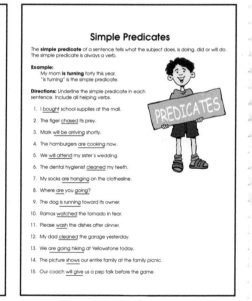
heros or heroes?

Here are some other spelling rules for plurals:
• If a word ends with **s, ss, x, ch** or **sh**, add **es**: buses, kisses, taxes, peaches, wishes.
• If a word ends with **f** or **fe**, drop the **f** or **fe** and add **ves**: leaf, leaves; wife, wives.
• Some plurals don't end with **s** or **es**: **geese, deer, children**.

Directions: Write the plural forms of the words.

1. Our area doesn't often have (tornado). _____ **tornadoes**
2. How many (radio) does this store sell every month? _____ **radios**
3. (Radish) are the same color as apples. _____ **radishes**
4. Does this submarine carry (torpedo)? _____ **torpedoes**
5. Hawaii has a number of active (volcano). _____ **volcanoes**
6. Did you pack (knife) in the picnic basket? _____ **knives**
7. We heard (echo) when we shouted in the canyon. _____ **echoes**
8. Where is the list of (address)? _____ **addresses**
9. What will you do when that plant (reach) the ceiling? _____ **reaches**
10. Every night, my dad (fix) us milkshakes. _____ **fixes**
11. Every night, my sister (wish) on the first star she sees. _____ **wishes**
12. Who (furnish) the school with pencils and paper? _____ **furnishes**
13. The author (research) every detail in her books. _____ **researches**

Page 239

Spelling: Plurals

Directions: Write the plural form of each word.

1. mother — **mothers**
2. ankle — **ankles**
3. journey — **journeys**
4. ceiling — **ceilings**
5. governor — **governors**
6. arch — **arches**
7. carnival — **carnivals**
8. official — **officials**
9. potato — **potatoes**
10. vacuum — **vacuums**
11. stereo — **stereos**
12. strategy — **strategies**
13. column — **columns**
14. architect — **architects**
15. entry — **entries**
16. summary — **summaries**
17. issue — **issues**
18. member — **members**
19. astronomer — **astronomers**
20. channel — **channels**
21. harmony — **harmonies**
22. piece — **pieces**
23. chicken — **chickens**
24. chemical — **chemicals**
25. journal — **journals**
26. niece — **nieces**
27. mayor — **mayors**
28. particle — **particles**
29. entrance — **entrances**
30. assistant — **assistants**

Page 240

Simple Subjects

The **simple subject** of a sentence tells who or what the sentence is about. It is a noun or a pronoun.

Example: My **mom** is turning forty this year.
Mom is the simple subject.

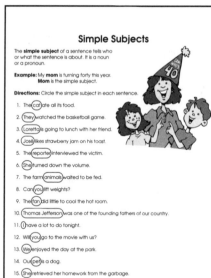

Directions: Circle the simple subject in each sentence.

1. The (cat) ate all its food.
2. (They) watched the basketball game.
3. (Loretta) is going to lunch with her friend.
4. (Jose) likes strawberry jam on his toast.
5. The (reporter) interviewed the victim.
6. (She) turned down the volume.
7. The farm (animals) waited to be fed.
8. Can (you) lift weights?
9. The (fan) did little to cool the hot room.
10. (Thomas Jefferson) was one of the founding fathers of our country.
11. (I) have a lot to do tonight.
12. Will (you) go to the movie with us?
13. (We) enjoyed the day at the park.
14. Our (pet) is a dog.
15. (She) retrieved her homework from the garbage.

Page 241

Simple Predicates

The **simple predicate** of a sentence tells what the subject does, is doing, did or will do. The simple predicate is always a verb.

Example:
My mom **is turning** forty this year.
"Is turning" is the simple predicate.

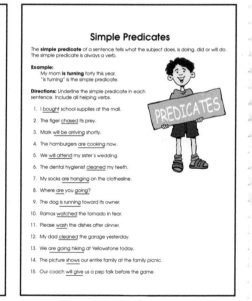

Directions: Underline the simple predicate in each sentence. Include all helping verbs.

1. I <u>bought</u> school supplies at the mall.
2. The tiger <u>chased</u> its prey.
3. Mark <u>will be arriving</u> shortly.
4. The hamburgers <u>are cooking</u> now.
5. We <u>will attend</u> my sister's wedding.
6. The dental hygienist <u>cleaned</u> my teeth.
7. My socks <u>are hanging</u> on the clothesline.
8. Where <u>are</u> you <u>going</u>?
9. The dog <u>is running</u> toward its owner.
10. Ramos <u>watched</u> the tornado in fear.
11. Please <u>wash</u> the dishes after dinner.
12. My dad <u>cleaned</u> the garage yesterday.
13. We <u>are going</u> hiking at Yellowstone today.
14. The picture <u>shows</u> our entire family at the family picnic.
15. Our coach <u>will give</u> us a pep talk before the game.

Grade 6 - Comprehensive Curriculum

Page 242

Parallel Structure

Parts of a sentence are **parallel** when they "match" grammatically and structurally.

Faulty parallelism occurs when the parts of a sentence do not match grammatically and structurally.

For sentences to be parallel, all parts of a sentence—including the verbs, nouns and phrases—must match. This means that, in most cases, verbs should be in the same tense.

Examples:
Correct: She liked running, jumping and swinging outdoors.
Incorrect: She liked running, jumping and to swing outdoors.

In the correct sentence, all three of the actions the girl liked to do end in **ing**. In the incorrect sentence, they do not.

Directions: Rewrite the sentences so all elements are parallel. The first one has been done for you.

1. Politicians like making speeches and also to shake hands.
   Politicians like making speeches and shaking hands.

2. He liked singing, acting and to perform in general.
   He liked singing, acting and performing in general.

3. The cake had icing, sprinkles and also has small candy hearts.
   The cake had icing, sprinkles and small candy hearts.

4. The drink was cold, frosty and also is a thirst-quencher.
   The drink was cold, frosty and a thirst-quencher.

5. She was asking when we would arrive, and I told her.
   She asked when we would arrive, and I told her.

6. Liz felt like shouting, singing and to jump.
   Liz felt like shouting, singing and jumping.

Page 243

Matching Subjects and Verbs

If the subject of a sentence is singular, the verb must be singular. If the subject is plural, the verb must be plural.

Example:
The **dog** with floppy ears **is eating**.
The **dogs** in the yard **are eating**.

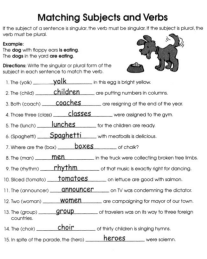

Directions: Write the singular or plural form of the subject in each sentence to match the verb.

1. The (yolk) ___yolk___ in this egg is bright yellow.
2. The (child) ___children___ are putting numbers in columns.
3. Both (coach) ___coaches___ are resigning at the end of the year.
4. Those three (class) ___classes___ were assigned to the gym.
5. The (lunch) ___lunches___ for the children are ready.
6. (Spaghetti) ___Spaghetti___ with meatballs is delicious.
7. Where are the (box) ___boxes___ of chalk?
8. The (man) ___men___ in the truck were collecting broken tree limbs.
9. The (rhythm) ___rhythm___ of that music is exactly right for dancing.
10. Sliced (tomato) ___tomatoes___ on lettuce are good with salmon.
11. The (announcer) ___announcer___ on TV was condemning the dictator.
12. Two (woman) ___women___ are campaigning for mayor of our town.
13. The (group) ___group___ of travelers was on its way to three foreign countries.
14. The (choir) ___choir___ of thirty children is singing hymns.
15. In spite of the parade, the (hero) ___heroes___ were solemn.

Page 244

Subject/Verb Agreement

Singular subjects require singular verbs. **Plural subjects** require plural verbs. The subject and verb must agree in a sentence.

Example:
Singular: My dog runs across the field.
Plural: My dogs run across the field.

Directions: Circle the correct verb in each sentence.

1. Maria (talk/**talks**) to me each day at lunch.
2. Mom, Dad and I (is/**are**) going to the park to play catch.
3. Mr. and Mrs. Ramirez (**dance**/dances) well together.
4. Astronauts (**hope**/hopes) for a successful shuttle mission.
5. Trees (**prevent**/prevents) erosion.
6. The student (is/**are**) late.
7. She (ask/**asks**) for directions to the senior high gym.
8. The elephants (**plod**/plods) across the grassland to the watering hole.
9. My friend's name (**is**/are) Rebecca.
10. Many people (**enjoy**/enjoys) orchestra concerts.
11. The pencils (is/**are**) sharpened.
12. My backpack (hold/**holds**) a lot of things.
13. The wind (blow/**blows**) to the south.
14. Sam (collect/**collects**) butterflies.
15. They (**love**/loves) cotton candy.

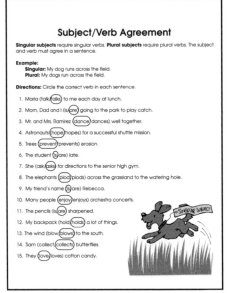

Page 245

Personal Pronouns

Personal pronouns take the place of nouns. They refer to people or things. **I**, **me**, **we**, **she**, **he**, **him**, **her**, **you**, **they**, **them**, **us** and **it** are personal pronouns.

Directions: Circle the personal pronouns in each sentence.

1. (He) is a terrific friend.
2. Would (you) open the door?
3. Jim and (I) will arrive at ten o'clock.
4. Can (you) pick (me) up at the mall after dinner?
5. What did (you) do yesterday?
6. (They) are watching the game on television.
7. Jessie's mom took (us) to the movies.
8. (She) writes novels.
9. (They) gave (us) the refrigerator.
10. Is this the answer (she) intended to give?
11. What is (it)?
12. The dog yelped when (it) saw the cat.
13. (I) admire (him).
14. (We) parked the bikes by the tree.
15. The ants kept (us) from enjoying (our) picnic.

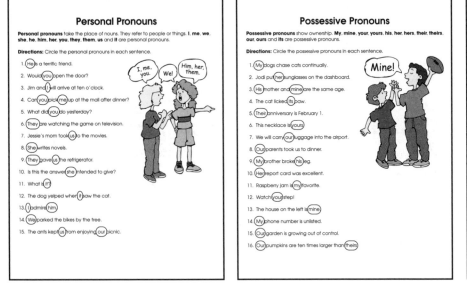

Page 246

Possessive Pronouns

Possessive pronouns show ownership. **My**, **mine**, **your**, **yours**, **his**, **her**, **hers**, **their**, **theirs**, **our**, **ours** and **its** are possessive pronouns.

Directions: Circle the possessive pronouns in each sentence.

1. (My) dogs chase cats continually.
2. Jodi put (her) sunglasses on the dashboard.
3. (His) mother and (mine) are the same age.
4. The cat licked (its) paw.
5. (Their) anniversary is February 1.
6. This necklace is (yours).
7. We will carry (our) luggage into the airport.
8. (Our) parents took us to dinner.
9. (My) brother broke (his) leg.
10. (Her) report card was excellent.
11. Raspberry jam is (my) favorite.
12. Watch (your) step!
13. The house on the left is (mine).
14. (My) phone number is unlisted.
15. (Our) garden is growing out of control.
16. (Our) pumpkins are ten times larger than (theirs).

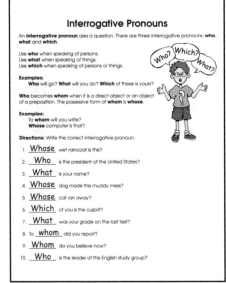

Page 247

Interrogative Pronouns

An **interrogative pronoun** asks a question. There are three interrogative pronouns: **who**, **what** and **which**.

Use **who** when speaking of persons.
Use **what** when speaking of things.
Use **which** when speaking of persons or things.

Examples:
Who will go? **What** will you do? **Which** of these is yours?

Who becomes **whom** when it is a direct object or an object of a preposition. The possessive form of **whom** is **whose**.

Examples:
To **whom** will you write?
Whose computer is that?

Directions: Write the correct interrogative pronoun.

1. ___Whose___ wet raincoat is this?
2. ___Who___ is the president of the United States?
3. ___What___ is your name?
4. ___Whose___ dog made this muddy mess?
5. ___Whose___ cat ran away?
6. ___Which___ of you is the culprit?
7. ___What___ was your grade on the last test?
8. To ___whom___ did you report?
9. ___Whom___ do you believe now?
10. ___Who___ is the leader of this English study group?

Grade 6 - Comprehensive Curriculum

Page 248

Personal and Possessive Pronouns

Directions: Write personal or possessive pronouns in the blanks to take the place of the words in bold. The first one has been done for you.

They him	1.	**Maisie and Marni** told **Trent** they would see him later.
He them	2.	**Spencer** told **Nancee and Sandi** good-bye.
It his	3.	**The bike** was parked near **Aaron's** house.
They	4.	**Maria, Matt and Greg** claimed the car was new.
theirs	5.	The dishes were **the property of Cindy and Jake.**
hers	6.	Is this **Carole's**?
He their	7.	**Jon** walked near **Jessica and Esau's** house.
It	8.	**The dog** barked all night long!
She her	9.	**Dawn** fell and hurt **Dawn's** knee.
They its	10.	**Cory and Devan** gave the dog **the dog's** dinner.
We them	11.	**Tori and I** gave **Brett and Reggie** a ride home.
they	12.	Do **Josh and Andrea** like cats?
They us	13.	**Sasha and Keesha** gave **Josh and me** a ride home.
hers	14.	Is this sweater **Marni's**?
it	15.	The cat meowed because **the cat** was hungry.

Page 249

Pronoun/Antecedent Agreement

Often, a **pronoun** is used in place of a noun to avoid repeating the noun again in the same sentence. The noun that a pronoun refers to is called its **antecedent**. The word "antecedent" means "going before."

If the noun is singular, the pronoun that takes its place must also be singular. If the noun is plural, the pronoun that takes its place must also be plural. This is called *agreement* between the pronoun and its antecedent.

Examples:
Mary (singular noun) said **she** (singular pronoun) would dance.
The **dogs** (plural noun) took **their** (plural pronoun) dishes outside.

When the noun is singular and the gender unknown, it is correct to use either "his" or "his or her."

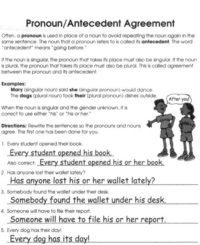

Directions: Rewrite the sentences so the pronouns and nouns agree. The first one has been done for you.

1. Every student opened their book.
   Every student opened his book.
   Also correct: Every student opened his or her book.
2. Has anyone lost their wallet lately?
   Has anyone lost his or her wallet lately?
3. Somebody found the wallet under their desk.
   Somebody found the wallet under his desk.
4. Someone will have to file their report.
   Someone will have to file his or her report.
5. Every dog has their day!
   Every dog has its day!
6. I felt Ted had mine best interests at heart.
   I felt Ted had my best interests at heart.

Page 250

Pronoun/Antecedent Agreement

Directions: Write a pronoun that agrees with the antecedent.

1. Donald said ___he___ would go to the store.
2. My friend discovered ___his (or her)___ wallet had been stolen.
3. The cat licked ___its___ paw.
4. Did any woman here lose ___her___ necklace?
5. Someone will have to give ___his (or her)___ report.
6. Jennifer wished ___she___ had not come.
7. All the children decided ___they___ would attend.
8. My grandmother hurt ___her___ back while gardening.
9. Jerry, Marco and I hope ___we___ win the game.
10. Sandra looked for ___her___ missing homework.
11. The family had ___its___ celebration.
12. My dog jumps out of ___its___ pen.
13. Somebody needs to remove ___his (or her)___ clothes from this chair.
14. Everything has ___its___ place in Grandma's house.
15. The team will receive ___their___ uniforms on Monday.
16. Each artist wants ___his (or her)___ painting to win the prize.

Page 251

Appositives

An **appositive** is a noun or pronoun placed after another noun or pronoun to further identify or rename it. An appositive and the words that go with it are usually set off from the rest of the sentence with commas. Commas are not used if the appositive tells "which one."

Example: Angela's mother, **Ms. Glover**, will visit our school.

Commas are needed because **Ms. Glover** renames Angela's mother.

Example: Angela's neighbor Joan will visit our school.

Commas are not needed because the appositive "Joan" tells **which** neighbor.

Directions: Write the appositive in each sentence in the blank. The first one has been done for you.

Tina	1.	My friend Tina wants a horse.
Horses	2.	She subscribes to the magazine Horses.
"Brownie"	3.	Her horse is the gelding "Brownie."
convertible	4.	We rode in her new car, a convertible.
bracelet	5.	Her gift was jewelry, a bracelet.
senator	6.	Have you met Ms. Abbott, the senator?
Karl	7.	My cousin Karl is very shy.
Oaties	8.	Do you eat the cereal Oaties?
Samantha	9.	Kiki's cat, Samantha, will eat only tuna.
Jones	10.	My last name, Jones, is very common.

Page 252

Dangling Modifiers

A **dangling modifier** is a word or group of words that does not modify what it is supposed to modify. To correct dangling modifiers, supply the missing words to which the modifiers refer.

Examples:
Incorrect: While doing the laundry, the dog barked.
Correct: While I was doing the laundry, the dog barked.

In the **incorrect** sentence, it sounds as though the dog is doing the laundry. In the **correct** sentence, it's clear that **I** is the subject of the sentence.

Directions: Rewrite the sentences to make the subject of the sentence clear and eliminate dangling modifiers. The first one has been done for you.

1. While eating our hot dogs, the doctor called.
   While we were eating our hot dogs, the doctor called.
2. Living in Cincinnati, the ball park is nearby.
   I live in Cincinnati, and the ball park is nearby.
3. While watching the movie, the TV screen went blank.
   While we were watching the movie, the TV screen went blank.
4. While listening to the concert, the lights went out.
   While we were listening to the concert, the lights went out.
5. Tossed regularly, anyone can make great salad.
   Anyone can make a great salad if it's tossed regularly.
6. While working, something surprised him.
   While he was working, something surprised him.

Page 253

Review

Directions: Write **noun** or **verb** to describe the words in bold.

noun	1.	She is one of the fastest **runners** I've seen.
verb	2.	She is **running** very fast!
verb	3.	She **thought** he was handsome.
noun	4.	Please share your **thoughts** with me.
verb	5.	I will **watch** the volleyball game on video.
noun	6.	The sailor fell asleep during his **watch**.
noun	7.	My grandmother believes my purchase was a real **find**.
verb	8.	I hope to **find** my lost books.

Directions: Rewrite the verb in the correct tense.

swam	9.	She **swim** across the lake in 2 hours.
ridden	10.	He has **ride** horses for years.
seen	11.	Have you **saw** my sister?
flew	12.	She **fly** on an airplane last week.
instructed	13.	My father had **instruct** me in the language.
drove	14.	I **drive** to the store yesterday.
began	15.	The movie **begin** late.
did	16.	Where do you go yesterday?

Directions: Circle the pronouns.

17. She and I told them to forget it.
18. They all wondered if her dad would drive his new car.
19. We want our parents to believe us.
20. My picture was taken at her home.

Page 254

Review

Directions: Rewrite the sentences to correct the faulty parallels.

1. The cookies were sweet, crunchy and are delicious.
   The cookies were sweet, crunchy and delicious.

2. The town was barren, windswept and is empty.
   The town was barren, windswept and empty.

3. The dog was black, long-haired and quite friendly.
   The dog was black, long-haired and quite friendly.

4. My favorite dinners are macaroni and cheese, spaghetti and I loved fish.
   My favorite dinners are macaroni and cheese, spaghetti and fish.

Directions: Rewrite the sentences to make the verb tenses consistent.

5. We laughed, cried and were jumping for joy.
   We laughed, cried and jumped for joy.

6. She sang, danced and was doing somersaults.
   She sang, danced and did somersaults.

7. The class researched, studied and were writing their reports.
   The class researched, studied and wrote their reports.

8. Bob and Sue talked about their vacation and share their experiences.
   Bob and Sue talked about their vacation and shared their experiences.

Directions: Circle the pronouns that agree with their antecedents.

9. She left (her/their) purse at the dance.
10. Each dog wagged (its/their) tail.
11. We walked to (our/he) car.
12. The lion watched (his/its) prey.

Page 255

Review Answers may vary.

Directions: Rewrite the sentences to correct the dangling modifiers.

1. Living nearby, the office was convenient for her.
   She lived nearby and the office was convenient for her.

2. While doing my homework, the doorbell rang.
   While I was doing my homework, the doorbell rang.

3. Watching over her shoulder, she hurried away.
   She watched over her shoulder and hurried away.

4. Drinking from the large mug, he choked.
   While he was drinking from the large mug, he choked.

Directions: Circle the correct pronouns.

5. She laughed at my brother and (I/me).
6. At dawn, (he and I/him and me) were still talking.
7. Someone left (his or her/their) coat on the floor.
8. Lauren said (her/she) would not be late.

Directions: Circle the appositive.

9. The school nurse, (Ms. Franklin) was worried about him.
10. The car, (a Volkswagen) was illegally parked.
11. My hero, (Babe Ruth) was an outstanding baseball player.
12. Is that car, (the plum-colored one) for sale?
13. Will Mr. Zimmer, (Todd's father) buy that car?

REVIEW
NOUNS VERBS
SIMPLE SUBJECTS
PERSONAL PRONOUNS
POSSESSIVE PRONOUNS
INTERROGATIVE PRONOUNS
ANTECEDENTS
APPOSITIVES
SIMPLE PREDICATES

Page 256

Adjectives

Adjectives describe nouns.

Examples:
   tall girl
   soft voice
   clean hands

Directions: Circle the adjectives. Underline the nouns they describe. Some sentences may have more than one set of adjectives and nouns.

1. The (lonely) man sat in the (dilapidated) house.
2. I hope the (large) crop of grapes will soon ripen.
3. The (white) boxes house honeybees.
4. My (rambunctious) puppy knocked over the (valuable) (flower) vase.
5. The (unsinkable) Titanic sank after striking a (gigantic) iceberg.
6. His grades showed (his) (tremendous) effort.
7. There are (many) (purple) flowers in the (large) arrangement.
8. (These) (sweet) peaches are the (best) I've tasted.
9. The newsletter describes (several) (educational) workshops.
10. The rodeo featured (professional) riders and (funny) clowns.
11. My (evening) (pottery) class is full of (very) (interesting) people.
12. My (older) brother loves (his) (new) (pickup) truck.
13. (Tami's) family bought a (big-screen) TV.

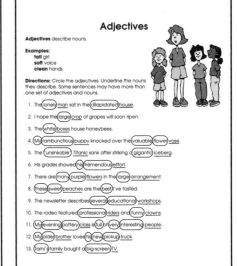

Page 257

Comparing With Adjectives

When adjectives are used to compare two things, **er** is added at the end of the word for most one-syllable words and some two-syllable words.

Example: It is **colder** today than it was yesterday.

With many two-syllable words and all words with three or more syllables, the word **more** is used with the adjective to show comparison.

Example: Dr. X is **more professional** than Dr. Y.

When adjectives are used to compare three or more things, **est** is added at the end of the word for **most** one-syllable words and some two-syllable words.

Example: Today is the **coldest** day of the year.

With many two-syllable words and all words with three or more syllables, **most** is used with the adjective to show comparison.

Example: Dr. X is the **most professional** doctor in town.

When adding **er** or **est** to one-syllable words, these spelling rules apply.
• Double the last consonant if the word has a short vowel before a final consonant: thinner, fatter.
• If a word ends in **y**, change the **y** to **i** before adding **er** or **est**: earliest, prettiest.
• If a word ends in **e**, drop the final **e** before adding **er** or **est**: simpler, simplest.

Directions: Complete these sentences with the correct form of the adjective.

1. This book is (small) **smaller** than that one.
2. I want the (small) **smallest** book in the library.
3. My plan is (practical) **more practical** than yours.
4. My plan is the (practical) **most practical** one in the class.
5. I wish the change was (gradual) **more gradual** than it is.
6. My sister is the (childish) **most childish** girl in her day-care group.
7. There must be a (simple) **simpler** way to do it than that.
8. This is the (simple) **simplest** way of the four we thought of.

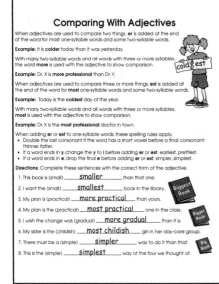

cold est

Page 258

Adjectives: Positive, Comparative and Superlative

There are three degrees of comparison adjectives: **positive, comparative** and **superlative**. The **positive degree** is the adjective itself. The **comparative** and **superlative** degrees are formed by adding **er** and **est**, respectively, to most one-syllable adjectives. The form of the word changes when the adjective is irregular, for example, **good, better, best**.

Most adjectives of two or more syllables require the words "more" or "most" to form the comparative and superlative degrees.

Examples:
Positive:	big	eager
Comparative:	bigger	more eager
Superlative:	biggest	most eager

Directions: Write the positive, comparative or superlative forms of these adjectives.

Positive	Comparative	Superlative
1. hard	harder	hardest
2. happy	happier	happiest
3. difficult	more difficult	most difficult
4. cold	colder	coldest
5. easy	easier	easiest
6. large	larger	largest
7. little	less	least
8. shiny	shinier	shiniest
9. round	rounder	roundest
10. beautiful	more beautiful	most beautiful

Page 259

Adverbs

Adverbs tell when, where or how an action occurred.

Examples:
   I'll go **tomorrow**. (when)
   I sleep **upstairs**. (where)
   I screamed **loudly**. (how)

Directions: Circle the adverb and underline the verb it modifies. Write the question (when, where or how) the adverb answers.

1. I ran (quickly) toward the finish line. — how
2. (Today) we will receive our report cards. — when
3. He swam (smoothly) through the pool. — how
4. Many explorers searched (endlessly) for new lands. — how
5. He looked (up) into the sky. — where
6. My friend drove (away) in her new car. — where
7. (Later) we will search for your missing wallet. — when
8. Most kings rule their kingdoms (regally). — how
9. New plants must be watered (daily). — when
10. The stream near our house is (heavily) polluted. — how
11. My brother likes to dive (backward) into our pool. — how

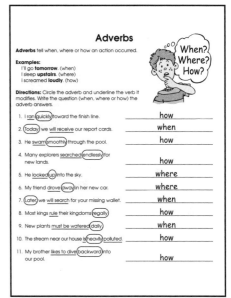

When?
Where?
How?

Page 260

Adverbs: Positive, Comparative and Superlative

There are also three degrees of comparison adverbs: **positive**, **comparative** and **superlative**. They follow the same rules as adjectives.

Example:
Positive:	rapidly	far
Comparative:	more rapidly	farther
Superlative:	most rapidly	farthest

Directions: Write the positive, comparative or superlative forms of these adverbs.

Positive	Comparative	Superlative
1. easily	more easily	most easily
2. quickly	more quickly	most quickly
3. hopefully	more hopefully	most hopefully
4. bravely	more bravely	most bravely
5. strongly	more strongly	most strongly
6. near	nearer	nearest
7. cleverly	more cleverly	most cleverly
8. gracefully	more gracefully	most gracefully
9. humbly	more humbly	most humbly
10. excitedly	more excitedly	most excitedly
11. handsomely	more handsomely	most handsomely
12. slowly	more slowly	most slowly

Page 261

Adjectives and Adverbs

Directions: Write **adjective** or **adverb** in the blanks to describe the words in bold. The first one has been done for you.

1. adjective — Her **old** boots were caked with mud.
2. adjective — The baby was **cranky**.
3. adverb — He took the test **yesterday**.
4. adjective — I heard the **funniest** story last week!
5. adverb — She left her wet shoes **outside**.
6. adjective — Isn't that the **fluffiest** cat you've ever seen?
7. adverb — He ran **around** the track twice.
8. adjective — Our elderly neighbor lady seems **lonely**.
9. adjective — His **kind** smile lifted my dragging spirits.
10. adverb — **Someday** I'll meet the friend of my dreams!
11. adverb — His cat never meows **indoors**.
12. adverb — Carlos hung his new shirts **back** in the closet.
13. adverb — Put that valuable vase **down** immediately!
14. adjective — She is the most **joyful** child!
15. adjective — Jonathan's wool sweater is totally **moth-eaten**.

Page 262

Identifying Sentence Parts

The **subject** tells who or what a sentence is about. Sentences can have more than one subject.

Example: Dogs and cats make good pets.

The **predicate** tells what the subject does or that it exists. Predicates can be more than one word. A sentence can have more than one predicate.

Examples: She was walking. She walked and ran.

An **adjective** is a word or group of words that describes the subject or another noun.

Example: The cheerful yellow bird with blue spots flew across the flower-covered meadow.

An **adverb** is a word or group of words that tells how, when, where or how often.

Example: He sat there waiting quietly.

Directions: Write **S** for subject, **P** for predicate, **ADJ** for adjective or **ADV** for adverb above each underlined word or group of words. The first one has been done for you.

1. A huge dog with long teeth was barking fiercely.
2. My grandmother usually wore a hat with a veil.
3. My niece and her friend are the same height.
4. The lively reindeer danced and pranced briefly on the rooftop.

Directions: Write sentences containing the sentence parts listed. Mark each part even if the verb part gets separated.

1. Write a question with two subjects, two predicates and two adjectives:

2. Write a statement with ~~Answers will vary.~~ cates and two adjectives:

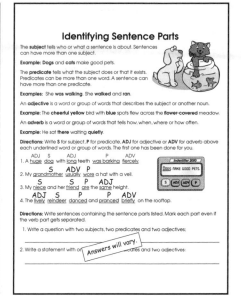

Page 263

Identifying Sentence Parts

Directions: Write **S** for subject, **P** for predicate, **ADJ** for adjective or **ADV** for adverb above the appropriate words in these sentences.

1. The large cat pounced on the mouse ferociously.
2. Did you remember your homework?
3. My mother is traveling to New York tomorrow.
4. I play basketball on Monday and Friday afternoons.
5. The old, decrepit house sat at the end of the street.
6. Several tiny rabbits nibbled at the grass at the edge of the field.
7. The lovely bride wore a white dress with a long train.
8. We packed the clothes for the donation center in a box.
9. The telephone rang incessantly.
10. The lost child cried helplessly.
11. What will we do with these new puppies?
12. Lauren reads several books each week.
13. The picture hung precariously on the wall.
14. I purchased many new school supplies.
15. Computers have changed the business world.

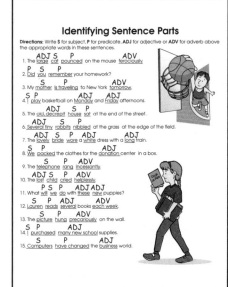

Page 264

Prepositions

A **preposition** is a word that comes before a noun or pronoun and shows the relationship of that noun or pronoun to some other word in the sentence.

The **object of a preposition** is the noun or pronoun that follows a preposition and adds to its meaning.

A **prepositional phrase** includes the preposition, the object of the preposition and all modifiers.

Example:
She gave him a pat on his back.
On is the preposition.
Back is the object of the preposition.
His is a possessive pronoun.

Common Prepositions			
about	down	near	through
above	for	of	to
across	from	off	up
at	in	on	with
behind	into	out	within
by	like	past	without

Directions: Underline the prepositional phrases. Circle the prepositions. Some sentences have more than one prepositional phrase. The first one has been done for you.

1. He claimed he felt at home only on the West Coast.
2. She went up the street, then down the block.
3. The famous poet was near death.
4. The beautiful birthday card was from her father.
5. He left his wallet at home.
6. Her speech was totally without humor and boring as well.
7. I think he's from New York City.
8. Kari wanted to go with her mother to the mall.

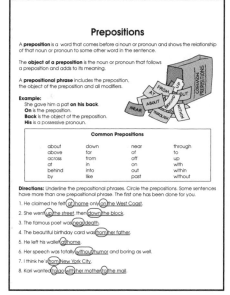

Page 265

Prepositions

Directions: Complete the sentences by writing objects for the prepositions. The first one has been done for you.

1. He was standing at the corner of Fifth and Main.
2. She saw her friend across ___
3. Have you ever looked beyond ___
4. His contact lens fell into ___
5. Have ___
6. She ___
7. Is that ___
8. She was daydreaming and walked past ___
9. The book was hidden behind ___
10. The young couple had fallen in ___
11. She insisted she was through ___
12. He sat down near ___
13. She forgot her umbrella at ___
14. Have you ever thought of ___
15. Henry found his glasses on ___

Answers will vary.

Page 266

Object of a Preposition

The **object of a preposition** is the noun or pronoun that follows the preposition and adds to its meaning.

Example:
   Correct: Devan smiled **at** (preposition) **Tori** (noun: object of the preposition) and **me** (pronoun: object of the same preposition.)
   Correct: Devan smiled at Tori. Devan smiled at me. Devan smiled at Tori and me.
   Incorrect: Devan smiled at Tori and I.

Tip: If you are unsure of the correct pronoun to use, pair each pronoun with the verb and say the phrase out loud to find out which pronoun is correct.

Directions: Write the correct pronouns on the blanks. The first one has been done for you.

him 1. It sounded like a good idea to Sue and (he/him).
her 2. I asked Abby if I could attend with (her/she).
us 3. To (we/us), holidays are very important.
us 4. Between (we/us), we finished the job quickly.
him and me 5. They gave the award to (he and I/him and me).
me 6. The party was for my brother and (I/me).
him 7. I studied with (he/him).
us 8. Tanya and the others arrived after (we/us).
her 9. After the zoo, we stopped at the museum with Bill and (her/she).
him 10. The chips for (he/him) are in the bag on top of the refrigerator.

Page 267

Direct Objects

A **direct object** is a noun or pronoun. It answers the question **whom** or **what** after a verb.

Examples:
   My mom baked **bread**.
   Bread is the direct object. It tells **what** Mom baked.
   We saw **Steve**.
   Steve is the direct object. It tells **whom** we saw.

Directions: Write a direct object in each sentence.

1. My dog likes _____. WHAT?
2. My favorite drink is _____. WHAT?
3. I saw _____.
4. Th_____
5. The _____ through the room. WHAT?
6. I packed a _____ for lunch. WHAT?
7. We watched _____ play basketball. WHOM?
8. I finished my _____. WHAT?
9. The artist sketched the _____. WHAT?
10. He greets _____ at the door. WHOM?
11. The team attended the victory _____. WHAT?
12. The beautician cut my _____. WHAT?
13. Tamika will write _____. WHAT?

Answers will vary.

Page 268

Indirect Objects

An **indirect object** is a noun or pronoun which tells **to whom or what** or **for whom or what** the action is performed. An indirect object usually is found between a verb and a direct object.

Example:
   I gave **Ellen** my address.
   Ellen is the indirect object. It tells **to whom** I gave my address.

Directions: Circle the indirect objects. Underline the direct objects.

1. Joann told (Mary) the secret.
2. Advertisers promise (consumers) the world.
3. The dogs showed (me) their tricks.
4. Aunt Martha gave (Rhonda) a necklace for her birthday.
5. Ramon brought (Mom) a bouquet of fresh flowers.
6. I sent my (niece) a package for Christmas.
7. Mr. Dunbar left his (wife) a note before leaving.
8. Grandma and Grandpa made their (friends) dinner.
9. The baby handed her (mom) a toy.
10. Monica told (Stephanie) the recipe for meatloaf.
11. We sent (Grandma) a card.
12. The waiter served (us) dessert.
13. Mom and Dad sold (us) the farm.

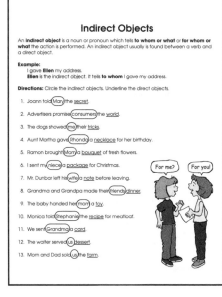

For me?   For you!

Page 271

Review

Directions: Write the missing verb tenses.

Present	Past	Past Participle
1. catch	**caught**	**has (have) caught**
2. **stir**	stirred	**has (have) stirred**
3. **bake**	**baked**	has (have) baked
4. **go**	**went**	**has (have) gone**
5. **say**	said	**has (have) said**

Directions: Circle the simple subject and underline the simple predicate in each sentence.

6. (Maria) got sunburned at the beach.
7. The (class) watched the program.
8. The (tomatoes) are ripening.
9. (We) went grocery shopping.
10. The (cross country team) practiced all summer.

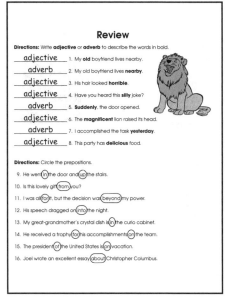

Directions: Write the missing adjective or adverb forms below.

Positive	Comparative	Superlative
11. **friendly**	more friendly	**most friendly**
12. small	**smaller**	**smallest**
13. **fun**	**more fun**	most fun
14. **attractive**	more attractive	**most attractive**

Page 272

Review

Directions: Write **adjective** or **adverb** to describe the words in bold.

adjective 1. My **old** boyfriend lives nearby.
adverb 2. My old boyfriend lives **nearby**.
adjective 3. His hair looked **horrible**.
adjective 4. Have you heard this **silly** joke?
adverb 5. **Suddenly**, the door opened.
adjective 6. The **magnificent** lion raised its head.
adverb 7. I accomplished the task **yesterday**.
adjective 8. This party has **delicious** food.

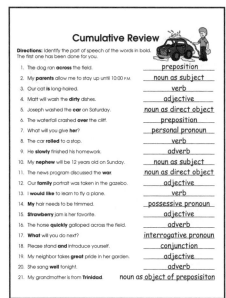

Directions: Circle the prepositions.

9. He went (in) the door and (up) the stairs.
10. Is this lovely gift (from) you?
11. I was all (for) it, but the decision was (beyond) my power.
12. His speech dragged on (into) the night.
13. My great-grandmother's crystal dish is (in) the curio cabinet.
14. He received a trophy (for) his accomplishments (on) the team.
15. The president (of) the United States is (on) vacation.
16. Joel wrote an excellent essay (about) Christopher Columbus.

Page 273

Cumulative Review

Directions: Identify the part of speech of the words in bold. The first one has been done for you.

1. The dog ran **across** the field. — **preposition**
2. My **parents** allow me to stay up until 10:00 P.M. — **noun as subject**
3. Our cat **is** long-haired. — **verb**
4. Matt will wash the **dirty** dishes. — **adjective**
5. Joseph washed the **car** on Saturday. — **noun as direct object**
6. The waterfall crashed **over** the cliff. — **preposition**
7. What will you give **her**? — **personal pronoun**
8. The car **rolled** to a stop. — **verb**
9. He **slowly** finished his homework. — **adverb**
10. My **nephew** will be 12 years old on Sunday. — **noun as subject**
11. The news program discussed the **war**. — **noun as direct object**
12. Our **family** portrait was taken in the gazebo. — **adjective**
13. I **would like** to learn to fly a plane. — **verb**
14. **My** hair needs to be trimmed. — **possessive pronoun**
15. **Strawberry** jam is her favorite. — **adjective**
16. The horse **quickly** galloped across the field. — **adverb**
17. **What** will you do next? — **interrogative pronoun**
18. Please stand **and** introduce yourself. — **conjunction**
19. My neighbor takes **great** pride in her garden. — **adjective**
20. She sang **well** tonight. — **adverb**
21. My grandmother is from **Trinidad**. — **noun as object of preposisiton**

Page 274

"Affect" and "Effect"

Affect means to act upon or influence.

Example: Studying will **affect** my test grade.

Effect means to bring about a result or to accomplish something.

Example: The **effect** of her smile was immediate!

Directions: Write **affect** or **effect** in the blanks to complete these sentences correctly. The first one has been done for you.

affects	1.	Your behavior (affects/effects) how others feel about you.
effect	2.	His (affect/effect) on her was amazing.
effect	3.	The (affect/effect) of his jacket was striking.
affect	4.	What you say won't (affect/effect) me!
effect	5.	There's a relationship between cause and (affect/effect).
effect	6.	The (affect/effect) of her behavior was positive.
affected	7.	The medicine (affected/effected) my stomach.
effect	8.	What was the (affect/effect) of the punishment?
affect	9.	Did his behavior (affect/effect) her performance?
affected	10.	The cold (affected/effected) her breathing.
effect	11.	The (affect/effect) was instantaneous!
affect	12.	Your attitude will (affect/effect) your posture.
effect	13.	The (affect/effect) on her posture was major.
effect	14.	The (affect/effect) of the colored lights was calming.
affected	15.	She (affected/effected) his behavior.

Page 275

"Among" and "Between"

Among is a preposition that applies to more than two people or things.

Example: The group divided the cookies **among** themselves.

Between is a preposition that applies to only two people or things.

Example: The cookies were divided **between** Jeremy and Sara.

Directions: Write **between** or **among** in the blanks to complete these sentences correctly. The first one has been done for you.

between	1.	The secret is (between/among) you and Jon.
Between	2.	(Between/Among) the two of them, whom do you think is nicer?
among	3.	I must choose (between/among) the cookies, candy and pie.
among	4.	She threaded her way (between/among) the kids on the playground.
between	5.	She broke up a fight (between/among) Josh and Sean.
between	6.	"What's come (between/among) you two?" she asked.
between	7.	"I'm (between/among) a rock and a hard place," Josh responded.
among	8.	"He has to choose (between/among) all his friends," Sean added.
among	9.	"Are you (between/among) his closest friends?" she asked Sean.
between	10.	"It's (between/among) another boy and me," Sean replied.
among	11.	"Can't you settle it (between/among) the group?"
between	12.	"No," said Josh. "This is (between/among) Sean and me."
among	13.	"I'm not sure he's (between/among) my closest friends."
among	14.	Sean, Josh and Andy began to argue (between/among) themselves.
between	15.	I hope Josh won't have to choose (between/among) the two!

Page 276

"All Together" and "Altogether"

All together is a phrase meaning everyone or everything in the same place.

Example: We put the eggs **all together** in the bowl.

Altogether is an adverb that means entirely, completely or in all.

Example: The teacher gave **altogether** too much homework.

Directions: Write **altogether** or **all together** in the blanks to complete these sentences correctly. The first one has been done for you.

altogether	1.	"You ate (altogether/all together) too much food."
all together	2.	The girls sat (altogether/all together) on the bus.
All together	3.	(Altogether/All together) now: one, two, three!
altogether	4.	I am (altogether/all together) out of ideas.
all together	5.	We are (altogether/all together) on this project.
altogether	6.	"You have on (altogether/all together) too much makeup!"
all together	7.	They were (altogether/all together) on the same team.
All together	8.	(Altogether/All together), we can help stop pollution.
altogether	9.	He was not (altogether/all together) happy with his grades.
altogether	10.	The kids were (altogether/all together) too loud.
All together	11.	(Altogether/All together), the babies cried gustily.
altogether	12.	She was not (altogether/all together) sure what to do.
all together	13.	Let's sing the song (altogether/all together).
altogether	14.	He was (altogether/all together) too pushy for her taste.
All together	15.	(Altogether/All together), the boys yelled the school cheer.

Page 277

"Amount" and "Number"

Amount indicates quantity, bulk or mass.

Example: She carried a large **amount** of money in her purse.

Number indicates units.

Example: What **number** of people volunteered to work?

Directions: Write **amount** or **number** in the blanks to complete these sentences correctly. The first one has been done for you.

number	1.	She did not (amount/number) him among her closest friends.
amount	2.	What (amount/number) of ice cream should we order?
number	3.	The (amount/number) of cookies on her plate was three.
amount	4.	His excuses did not (amount/number) to much.
amounted	5.	Her contribution (amounted/numbered) to half the money raised.
number	6.	The (amount/number) of injured players rose every day.
amount	7.	What a huge (amount/number) of cereal!
number	8.	The (amount/number) of calories in the diet was low.
number	9.	I can't tell you the (amount/number) of friends she has!
amount	10.	The total (amount/number) of money raised was incredible!
number	11.	The (amount/number) of gadgets for sale was amazing.
number	12.	He was startled by the (amount/number) of people present.
amount	13.	He would not do it for any (amount/number) of money.
number	14.	She offered a great (amount/number) of reasons for her actions.
number	15.	Can you guess the (amount/number) of beans in the jar?

Page 278

"Irritate" and "Aggravate"

Irritate means to cause impatience, to provoke or annoy.

Example: His behavior **irritated** his father.

Aggravate means to make a condition worse.

Example: Her sunburn was **aggravated** by additional exposure to the sun.

Directions: Write **aggravate** or **irritate** in the blanks to complete these sentences correctly. The first one has been done for you.

aggravated	1.	The weeds (aggravated/irritated) his hay fever.
aggravated	2.	Scratching the bite (aggravated/irritated) his condition.
irritated	3.	Her father was (aggravated/irritated) about her low grade in math.
irritated	4.	It (aggravated/irritated) him when she switched TV channels.
irritated	5.	Are you (aggravated/irritated) when the cat screeches?
irritate	6.	Don't (aggravate/irritate) me like that again!
irritation	7.	He was in a state of (aggravation/irritation).
aggravates	8.	Picking at the scab (aggravates/irritates) a sore.
irritates	9.	Whistling (aggravates/irritates) the old grump.
irritated	10.	She was (aggravated/irritated) when she learned about it.
irritate	11.	"Please don't (aggravate/irritate) your mother," Dad warned.
aggravated	12.	His asthma was (aggravated/irritated) by too much stress.
aggravate	13.	Sneezing is sure to (aggravate/irritate) his allergies.
irritate	14.	Did you do that just to (aggravate/irritate) me?
irritated	15.	Her singing always (aggravated/irritated) her brother.

Page 279

"Principal" and "Principle"

Principal means main, leader or chief, or a sum of money that earns interest.

Examples:
The high school **principal** earned interest on the **principal** in his savings account.
The **principal** reason for his savings account was to save for retirement.

Principle means a truth, law or a moral outlook that governs the way someone behaves.

Example:
Einstein discovered some fundamental **principles** of science.
Stealing is against her **principles**.

Directions: Write **principle** or **principal** in the blanks to complete these sentences correctly. The first one has been done for you.

principle	1.	A (principle/principal) of biology is "the survival of the fittest."
principles	2.	She was a person of strong (principles/principals).
principals	3.	The (principles/principals) sat together at the district conference.
principal	4.	How much of the total in my savings account is (principle/principal)?
principal	5.	His hay fever was the (principle/principal) reason for his sneezing.
principles	6.	It's not the facts that upset me, it's the (principles/principals) of the case.
principal	7.	The jury heard only the (principle/principal) facts.
principal	8.	Our school (principle/principal) is strict but fair.
principal	9.	Spend the interest, but don't touch the (principle/principal).
principle	10.	Helping others is a guiding (principle/principal) of the homeless shelter.
principle	11.	In (principle/principal), we agree; on the facts, we do not.
principal	12.	The (principle/principal) course at dinner was leg of lamb.
principles	13.	Some mathematical (principles/principals) are difficult to understand.
principal	14.	The baby was the (principle/principal) reason for his happiness.

Page 280

"Good" and "Well"

Good is always an adjective. It is used to modify a noun or pronoun.

Examples:
We enjoyed the **good** food.
We had a **good** time yesterday.
It was **good** to see her again.

Well is used to modify verbs, to describe someone's health or to describe how someone is dressed.

Examples:
I feel **well**. He looked **well**.
He was **well**-dressed for the weather.
She sang **well**.

Directions: Write **good** or **well** in the blanks to complete these sentences correctly.

1. She performed ___well___.
2. You look ___good___ in that color.
3. These apples are ___good___.
4. He rides his bike ___well___.
5. She made a ___good___ attempt to win the race.
6. The man reported that all was ___well___ in the coal mine.
7. Jonas said, "I feel ___well___, thank you."
8. The team played ___well___.
9. Mom fixed a ___good___ dinner.
10. The teacher wrote, "___Good___ work!" on top of my paper.

Page 281

"Like" and "As"

Like means something is similar, resembles something else or describes how things are similar in manner.

Examples:
She could sing **like** an angel.
She looks **like** an angel, too!

As is a conjunction, a joining word, that links two independent clauses in a sentence.

Example: He felt chilly **as** night fell.

Sometimes **as** precedes an independent clause.

Example: As I told you, I will not be at the party.

Directions: Write **like** or **as** in the blanks to complete these sentences correctly. The first one has been done for you.

1. ___as___ He did not behave (like/as) I expected.
2. ___like___ She was (like/as) a sister to me.
3. ___like___ The puppy acted (like/as) a baby!
4. ___As___ (Like/As) I was saying, he will be there at noon.
5. ___as___ The storm was 25 miles away, (like/as) he predicted.
6. ___like___ He acted exactly (like/as) his father.
7. ___like___ The song sounds (like/as) a hit to me!
8. ___like___ Grandpa looked (like/as) a much younger man.
9. ___As___ (Like/As) I listened to the music, I grew sleepy.
10. ___As___ (Like/As) I expected, he showed up late.
11. ___like___ She dances (like/as) a ballerina!
12. ___As___ (Like/As) she danced, the crowd applauded.
13. ___like___ On stage, she looks (like/as) a professional!
14. ___As___ (Like/As) I thought, she has taken lessons for years.

Page 282

Review

Directions: Write the correct word in the blank.

1. ___effect___ The (affect/effect) of the shot was immediate.
2. ___affected___ The shot (affected/effected) her allergies.
3. ___effect___ You have a positive (affect/effect) on me!
4. ___affected___ I was deeply (affected/effected) by the speech.
5. ___between___ The prize was shared (among/between) Art and Lisa.
6. ___among___ She was (among/between) the best students in the class.
7. ___among___ He felt he was (among/between) friends.
8. ___among___ It was hard to choose (among/between) all the gifts.
9. ___irritate___ Does it (irritate/aggravate) you to see people smoke?
10. ___aggravate___ Does smoking (irritate/aggravate) his sore throat?
11. ___irritated___ He wondered why she was (irritated/aggravated) at him.
12. ___irritation___ The intensity of his (irritation/aggravation) grew each day.
13. ___principal___ She had a (principal/principle) part in the play.
14. ___principal___ Beans were the (principal/principle) food in his diet.
15. ___principles___ She was a woman of strong (principals/principles).
16. ___principal___ Mr. Larson was their favorite (principal/principle).
17. ___number___ The (amount/number) of ice-cream cones he ate was incredible.
18. ___amount___ I wouldn't part with it for any (amount/number) of money.
19. ___as___ It happened exactly (like/as) I had predicted!
20. ___like___ He sounds almost (like/as) his parents.

Page 283

Review

Directions: Use these words in sentences of your own.

1. affect _____
2. effect _____
3. among _____
4. between _____
5. irritate _____
6. aggravate _____
7. principal _____
8. principle _____
9. good _____
10. well _____
11. like _____
12. as _____

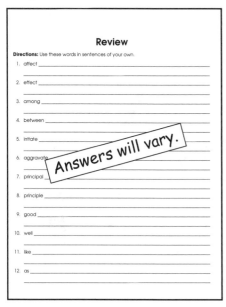

Answers will vary.

Page 285

Capitalization

Capitalize . . .
. . . the first word in a sentence
. . . the first letter of a person's name
. . . proper nouns, like the names of planets, oceans and mountain ranges
. . . titles when used with a person's name, even if abbreviated (Dr., Mr., Lt.)
. . . days of the week and months of the year
. . . cities, states and countries

Directions: Write **C** in the blank if the word or phrase is capitalized correctly. Rewrite the word or phrase if it is incorrect.

1. ___C___ President Abraham Lincoln _____
2. ___C___ Larry D. Walters _____
3. _____ saturn ___Saturn___
4. _____ benjamin franklin ___Benjamin Franklin___
5. ___C___ August _____
6. ___C___ professional _____
7. _____ jupiter ___Jupiter___
8. ___C___ Pacific Ocean _____
9. _____ white house ___White House___
10. ___C___ pet _____
11. ___C___ Congress _____
12. ___C___ Houston _____
13. ___C___ federal government _____
14. _____ dr. Samuel White ___Dr. Samuel White___
15. _____ milwaukee, Wisconsin ___Milwaukee, Wisconsin___
16. _____ Appalachian mountains ___Appalachian Mountains___
17. _____ lake michigan ___Lake Michigan___
18. ___C___ Notre Dame College _____
19. _____ department of the interior ___Department of the Interior___
20. _____ monday and Tuesday ___Monday and Tuesday___

Page 286

Capitalization

Words which name places, people, months and landmarks are always capitalized.

Examples:
Abraham Lincoln   Acme Motor Company
White House   Jefferson Memorial
Fifth Avenue   May, June, July

Directions: Rewrite the sentences using correct capitalization.

1. My family and I visited washington, d.c., in july.
   My family and I visited Washington, D.C. in July.

2. We saw the washington monument, the capital building and the white house.
   We saw the Washington Monument, the Capital Building and the White House.

3. I was very impressed by our visit to the smithsonian institution.
   I was very impressed by our visit to the Smithsonian Institution.

4. Our taxi driver, from the american cab company, showed us around town.
   Our taxi driver, from the American Cab Company, showed us around town.

5. We drove down pennsylvania avenue.
   We drove down Pennsylvania Avenue.

6. We were unable to see the president of the united states.
   We were unable to see the president of the United States.

7. However, we did see the first lady.
   However, we did see the First Lady, Mrs. Clinton.

8. My parents and I decided to visit arlington national cemetery.
   My parents and I decided to visit Arlington National Cemetery.

Page 287

Commas

Use **commas** . . .
. . . after introductory phrases
. . . to set off nouns of direct address
. . . to set off appositives from the words that go with them
. . . to set off words that interrupt the flow of the sentence
. . . to separate words or groups of words in a series

Examples:
Introductory phrase: Of course. I'd be happy to attend.
Noun of direct address: Ms. Williams, please sit here.
To set off appositives: Lee, **the club president,** sat beside me.
Words interrupting flow: My cousin, **who's 13,** will also be there.
or   I ate **popcorn, peanuts, oats** and **barley.**
Words in a series: I ate **popcorn, peanuts, oats,** and **barley.**

Note: The final comma is optional when punctuating words in a series.

Directions: Identify how the commas are used in each sentence.
Write: **I** for introductory phrase
         N for noun of direct address
         A for appositive
         WF for words interrupting flow
         WS for words in a series

__I__ 1. Yes, she is my sister.
__A__ 2. My teacher, Mr. Hopkins, is very fair.
__WS__ 3. Her favorite fruits are oranges, plums and grapes.
__A__ 4. The city mayor, Carla Ellison, is quite young.
__WS__ 5. I will buy bread, milk, fruit and ice cream.
__WF__ 6. Her crying, which was quite loud, soon gave me a headache.
__N__ 7. Stephanie, please answer the question.
__I__ 8. So, do you know her?
__I__ 9. Unfortunately, the item is not returnable.
__WS__ 10. My sister, my cousin and my friend will accompany me on vacation.
__A__ 11. My grandparents, Rose and Bill, are both 57 years old.

Page 288

Commas

Directions: Use commas to punctuate these sentences correctly.

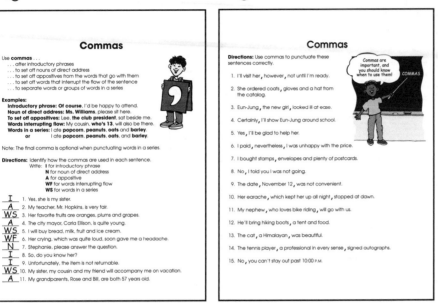
Commas are important, and you should know when to use them!
COMMAS

1. I'll visit her , however , not until I'm ready.
2. She ordered coats , gloves and a hat from the catalog.
3. Eun-Jung , the new girl , looked ill at ease.
4. Certainly , I'll show Eun-Jung around school.
5. Yes , I'll be glad to help her.
6. I paid , nevertheless , I was unhappy with the price.
7. I bought stamps , envelopes and plenty of postcards.
8. No , I told you I was not going.
9. The date , November 12, was not convenient.
10. Her earache , which kept her up all night , stopped at dawn.
11. My nephew , who loves bike riding , will go with us.
12. He'll bring hiking boots , a tent and food.
13. The cat , a Himalayan , was beautiful.
14. The tennis player , a professional in every sense , signed autographs.
15. No , you can't stay out past 10:00 P.M.

Page 289

Semicolons

A **semicolon** (;) signals a reader to pause longer than for a comma, but not as long as for a period. Semicolons are used between closely related independent clauses not joined by **and, or, nor, for, yet** or **but.**

An **independent clause** contains a complete idea and can stand alone.

Example: Rena was outgoing; her sister was shy.

Directions: Use semicolons to punctuate these sentences correctly. Some sentences require more than one semicolon.

1. Jeff wanted coffee; Sally wanted milk.
2. I thought he was kind; she thought he was grouchy.
3. "I came, I saw, I conquered," wrote Julius Caesar.
4. Jessica read books; she also read magazines.
5. I wanted a new coat; my old one was too small.
6. The airport was fogged-in; the planes could not land.
7. Now, he regrets his comments; it's too late to retract them.
8. The girls were thrilled; their mothers were not.

Directions: Use a semicolon and an independent clause to complete the sentences.

9. She liked him _____
10. I chose a red shirt _____
11. Andrea sang well _____
12. She jumped _____
13. Dancing is _____ *Answers will vary.*
14. The man wa _____
15. The tire looked flat _____
16. My bike is missing _____

Page 290

Colons

Use a **colon** . . .
. . . after the salutation of a business letter
. . . between the hour and the minute when showing time
. . . between the volume and page number of a periodical
. . . between chapters and verses of the Bible
. . . before a list of three or more items
. . . to introduce a long statement or quotation

Dear Mr. Miller:
I would like to place an order for five of your 1 ton scales. Please contact me, concerning price and delivery date.
Sincerely,
Ms. Jones

Examples:
Salutation: Dear Madame:
Hour and minute: 8:45 P.M.
Periodical volume and page number: Newsweek 11:32
Bible chapter and verse: John 3:16
Before a list of three or more items: Buy these: fruit, cereal, cheese
To introduce a long statement or quotation: Author Willa Cather said this about experiencing life: "There are only two or three human stories, and they go on repeating themselves as fiercely as if they had never happened before."

Directions: Use colons to punctuate these sentences correctly. Some sentences require more than one colon.

1. At 12:45 the president said this: "Where's my lunch?"
2. Look in Proverbs 1:12 for the answer.
3. Don't forget to order these items: boots, socks, shoes and leggings.
4. Ask the librarian for *Weekly Reader* 3:14.
5. Dear Sir: Please send me two copies of your report.
6. Avoid these at all costs: bad jokes, bad company, bad manners.
7. The statement is in either Genesis 1:6 or Exodus 3:2.
8. At 9:15 P.M., she checked in, and at 6:45 A.M., she checked out.
9. I felt all these things at once: joy, anger and sadness.
10. Here's a phrase President Bush liked: "A thousand points of light."

Page 291

Dashes

Dashes (—) are used to indicate sudden changes of thought.

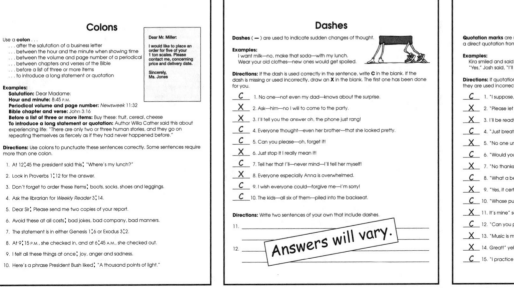

Examples:
I want milk—no, make that soda—with my lunch.
Wear your old clothes—new ones would get spoiled.

Directions: If the dash is used correctly in the sentence, write **C** in the blank. If the dash is missing or used incorrectly, draw an **X** in the blank. The first one has been done for you.

__C__ 1. No one—not even my dad—knows about the surprise.
__X__ 2. Ask—him—no I will to come to the party.
__X__ 3. I'll tell you the answer oh, the phone just rang!
__C__ 4. Everyone thought—even her brother—that she looked pretty.
__C__ 5. Can you please—oh, forget it!
__X__ 6. Just stop it I really mean it!
__C__ 7. Tell her that I'll—never mind—I'll tell her myself!
__X__ 8. Everyone especially Anna is overwhelmed.
__C__ 9. I wish everyone could—forgive me—I'm sorry!
__C__ 10. The kids—all six of them—piled into the backseat.

Directions: Write two sentences of your own that include dashes.

11. _____
12. _____ *Answers will vary.*

Page 292

Quotation Marks

Quotation marks are used to enclose a speaker's exact words. Use commas to set off a direct quotation from other words in the sentence.

Examples:
Kira smiled and said, "Quotation marks come in handy."
"Yes," Josh said, "I'll take two."

Directions: If quotation marks and commas are used correctly, write **C** in the blank. If they are used incorrectly, write an **X** in the blank. The first one has been done for you.

__C__ 1. "I suppose," Elizabeth remarked, "that you'll be there on time."
__X__ 2. "Please let me help! insisted Mark.
__X__ 3. I'll be ready in 2 minutes!" her father said.
__C__ 4. "Just breathe slowly," the nurse said, "and calm down."
__X__ 5. "No one understands me" William whined.
__C__ 6. "Would you like more milk?" Jasmine asked politely.
__X__ 7. "No thanks, her grandpa replied, "I have plenty."
__C__ 8. "What a beautiful morning!" Jessica yelled.
__X__ 9. "Yes, it certainly is" her mother agreed.
__C__ 10. "Whose purse is this?" asked Andrea.
__X__ 11. It's mine" said Stephanie. "Thank you."
__C__ 12. "Can you play the piano?" asked Heather.
__X__ 13. "Music is my hobby," Jonathan replied.
__X__ 14. Great!" yelled Harry. "Let's play some tunes."
__C__ 15. "I practice a lot." said Jayne proudly.

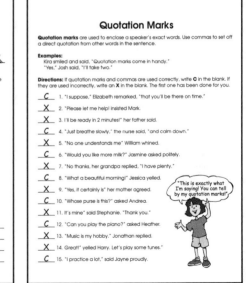
"This is exactly what I'm saying! You can tell by my quotation marks!"

Page 293

Quotation Marks

Directions: Use quotation marks and commas to punctuate these sentences correctly.

"Remember: quotation marks are used to enclose a speaker's exact words."

1. "No," Ms. Elliot replied, "you may not go."
2. "Watch out!" yelled the coach.
3. "Please bring my coat," called Renee.
4. After thinking for a moment, Paul said, "I don't believe you."
5. Dad said, "Remember to be home by 9:00 P.M."
6. "Finish your projects," said the art instructor.
7. "Go back," instructed Mom, "and comb your hair."
8. "I won't be needing my winter coat anymore," replied Mei-ling.
9. He said, "How did you do that?"
10. I stood and said, "My name is Rosalita."
11. "No," said Misha, "I will not attend."
12. "Don't forget to put your name on your paper," said the teacher.
13. "Pay attention, class," said our history teacher.
14. As I came into the house, Mom called, "Dinner is almost ready!"
15. "Jake, come when I call you," said Mother.
16. "How was your trip to France, Mrs. Shaw?" asked Deborah.

Page 294

Apostrophes

Use an **apostrophe** (') in a contraction to show that letters have been left out. A **contraction** is a shortened form of two words, usually a pronoun and a verb.

Add an **apostrophe** and **s** to form the **possessive** of singular nouns. **Plural possessives** are formed two ways. If the noun ends in **s**, simply add an apostrophe at the end of the word. If the noun does not end in **s**, add an apostrophe and **s**.

Examples:
Contraction: He **can't** button his sleeves.
Singular possessive: The **boy's** sleeves are too short.
Plural noun ending in s: The **ladies'** voices were pleasant.
Plural noun not ending in s: The **children's** song was long.

Directions: Use apostrophes to punctuate the sentences correctly. The first one has been done for you.

1. I can't understand that child's game.
2. The farmers' wagons were lined up in a row.
3. She didn't like the chairs' covers.
4. Our parents' beliefs are often our own.
5. Sandy's mother's aunt isn't going to visit.
6. Two ladies from work didn't show up.
7. The citizen's group wasn't very happy.
8. The colonists' demands weren't unreasonable.
9. The mothers' babies cried at the same time.
10. Our parent's generation enjoys music.

Use John's pencil!

I can't. The lead's broken.

Directions: Write two sentences of your own that include apostrophes.

11.
12. *Answers will vary.*

Page 295

Contractions

Examples:
he will = **he'll**
she is = **she's**
they are = **they're**
can not = **can't**

Contraction Chart

Pronoun		Verb		Contraction
I	+	am	=	I'm
we, you, they	+	are	=	we're, you're, they're
he, she, it	+	is	=	he's, she's, it's
I, we, you, they	+	have	=	I've, we've, you've, they've
I, you, we, she, he, they	+	would	=	I'd, you'd, we'd, she'd, he'd, they'd
I, you, she, he, they	+	will	=	I'll, you'll, we'll, she'll, he'll, they'll

Directions: Write a sentence using a contraction. The first one has been done for you.

1. I will   *I'll see you tomorrow!*
2. they are
3. we have
4. she would
5. you are   *Answers will vary.*
6. they have
7. she is
8. he would
9. they are
10. I am

Page 296

Singular Possessives

Directions: Write the singular possessive form of each word. Then, add a noun to show possession. The first one has been done for you.

1. spider   spider's web
2. clock   clock's
3. car   car's
4. book   book's   (Nouns will vary.)
5. Mom   Mom's
6. boat   boat's
7. table   table's
8. baby   baby's
9. woman   woman's
10. writer   writer's
11. mouse   mouse's
12. fan   fan's
13. lamp   lamp's
14. dog   dog's
15. boy   boy's
16. house   house's

Page 297

Plural Possessives

Directions: Write the plural possessive form of each word. Then add a noun to show possession. The first one has been done for you.

1. kid   kids' skates
2. man   men's   (Nouns will vary.)
3. aunt   aunts'
4. lion   lions'
5. giraffe   giraffes'
6. necklace   necklaces'
7. mouse   mice's
8. team   teams'
9. clown   clowns'
10. desk   desks'
11. woman   women's
12. worker   workers'

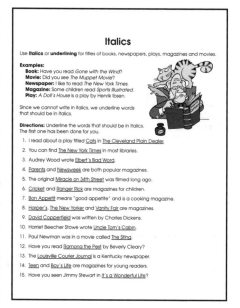

Directions: Write three sentences of your own that include plural possessives.

13.
14. *Answers will vary.*
15.

Page 298

Italics

Use **italics** or **underlining** for titles of books, newspapers, plays, magazines and movies.

Examples:
Book: Have you read *Gone with the Wind*?
Movie: Did you see *The Muppet Movie*?
Newspaper: I like to read *The New York Times*.
Magazine: Some children read *Sports Illustrated*.
Play: *A Doll's House* is a play by Henrik Ibsen.

Since we cannot write in italics, we underline words that should be in italics.

Directions: Underline the words that should be in italics. The first one has been done for you.

1. I read about a play titled <u>Cats</u> in <u>The Cleveland Plain Dealer</u>.
2. You can find <u>The New York Times</u> in most libraries.
3. Audrey Wood wrote <u>Elbert's Bad Word</u>.
4. <u>Parents</u> and <u>Newsweek</u> are both popular magazines.
5. The original <u>Miracle on 34th Street</u> was filmed long ago.
6. <u>Cricket</u> and <u>Ranger Rick</u> are magazines for children.
7. <u>Bon Appetit</u> means "good appetite" and is a cooking magazine.
8. <u>Harper's</u>, <u>The New Yorker</u> and <u>Vanity Fair</u> are magazines.
9. <u>David Copperfield</u> was written by Charles Dickens.
10. Harriet Beecher Stowe wrote <u>Uncle Tom's Cabin</u>.
11. Paul Newman was in a movie called <u>The Sting</u>.
12. Have you read <u>Ramona the Pest</u> by Beverly Cleary?
13. The <u>Louisville Courier Journal</u> is a Kentucky newspaper.
14. <u>Teen</u> and <u>Boy's Life</u> are magazines for young readers.
15. Have you seen Jimmy Stewart in <u>It's a Wonderful Life</u>?

505

Page 299

Complete Sentences

A **complete sentence** has both a simple subject and a simple predicate. It is a complete thought. Sentences which are not complete are called **fragments**.

Example:
   Complete sentence: The wolf howled at the moon.
   Sentence fragment: Howled at the moon.

Directions: Write **C** on the line if the sentence is complete. Write **F** if it is a fragment.

1. **C** The machine is running.
2. **C** What will we do today?
3. **F** Knowing what I do.
4. **C** That statement is true.
5. **C** My parents drove to town.
6. **F** Watching television all afternoon.
7. **C** The storm devastated the town.
8. **C** Our friends can go with us.
9. **C** The palm trees bent in the wind.
10. **F** Spraying the fire all night.

Directions: Rewrite the sentence fragments from above to make them complete sentences.

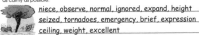

Answers will vary.

Page 300

Run-On Sentences

A **run-on sentence** occurs when two or more sentences are joined together without punctuation or a joining word. Run-on sentences should be divided into two or more separate sentences.

Example:
   Run-on sentence: My parents, sister, brother and I went to the park we saw many animals we had fun.
   Correct: My parents, sister, brother and I went to the park. We saw many animals and had fun.

Directions: Rewrite the run-on sentences correctly.

Sample answers:

1. The dog energetically chased the ball I kept throwing him the ball for a half hour.
   The dog energetically chased the ball. I kept throwing him the ball for a half hour.

2. The restaurant served scrambled eggs and bacon for breakfast I had some and they were delicious.
   The restaurant served bacon and scrambled eggs for breakfast. I had some, and they were delicious.

3. The lightning struck close to our house it scared my little brother and my grandmother called to see if we were safe.
   The lightning struck close to our house. It scared my little brother. My grandmother called to see if we were safe.

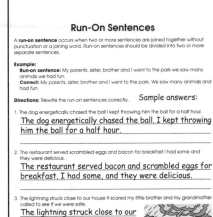

Page 301

Finding Spelling Errors

Directions: One word in each sentence below is misspelled. Write the word correctly on the line.

1. Jeff felt discoraged at the comparison between him and his older brother. **discouraged**
2. I got inpatient as my curiosity grew. **impatient**
3. She confided that she had not finished the assignment. **assignment**
4. They made the selection after a brief conference. **conference**
5. Obvisuly, it's impolite to sneeze on someone. **Obviously**
6. This skin cream is practically invisible. **practically**
7. What would prevent you from taking on addtional work? **additional**
8. I can resite the words to that hymn. **recite**
9. In a previous columm, the newspaper explained the situation. **column**
10. He decievd me so many times that now I distrust him. **deceived**
11. Please have the curtesy to observe the "No Eating" signs. **courtesy**
12. The advertisement is so small that it's nearly invisible. **invisible**
13. The best way to communicate is in a face-to-face conservation. **conversation**
14. In a cost comparison, salmon is more expensive than tuna. **comparison**
15. Popularity among friends shouldn't depend on your accomplishments. **Popularity**
16. Her campaign was quite an acheivement. **achievement**
17. He condemned it as a poor imitation. **condemned**

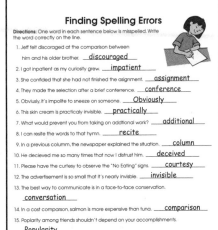

Page 302

Finding Spelling Errors

Directions: Circle all misspelled words. Write the words correctly on the lines at the end of each paragraph. If you need help, consult a dictionary.

Sabrina wanted to aquire a saltwater aquarium She was worried about the expence, though, so first she did some reserch She wanted to learn the exact care saltwater fish need, not just to exsis but to florish One sorce said she needed to put water in the aquarium and wait 6 weeks before she added the fish. "Good greif" Sabrina thought. She got a kitten from her nieghbor instead.

acquire, aquarium, expense, research, exact, exist, flourish, source, grief, neighbor

One day, Marcel was babysitting his neice He happened to obsurve that the sky looked darker than norm At first he ignored it, but then he noticed a black cloud expand and grow in hieght Then he said impatiently down from the twisting cloud and seized a tree! "It's a tornado!" Marcel shouted. "Maybe two tornados This is an emergency" For a breef moment Marcel wished he hadn't shouted, because his niece looked at him with a very frightened expresion Just then, the cieling began to sag as if it had a heavy wieght on it. "This is an excelent time to visit the basement," he told the little girl as calmy as possible.

niece, observe, normal, ignored, expand, height seized, tornados, emergency, brief, expression ceiling, weight, excellent

Just before Mother's Day, Bethany went to a flourist to buy some flowers for her mother. "Well, what is your reqest?" the clerk asked. "I don't have much money." Bethany told him. "So make up your mind," he said impatiently. "Do you want quallity or quanity?" Bethany wondered if he was giving her a quiz She tried not to squrim as she stared down at her feet. Finally she said, "I want cortesy," as she headed for the exsit.

florist, request, quality, quantity, quiz, squirm courtesy, exit

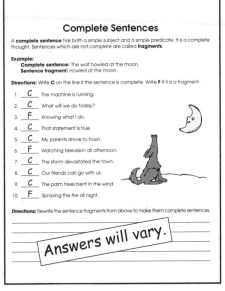

Page 303

Spelling: Correcting Errors

Directions: Find six errors in each paragraph. Write the words correctly on the lines after each paragraph. Use a dictionary if you need help.

My brother Jim took a math coarse at the high school that was too hard for hymn My father didn't want him to take it, but Jim said, "Oh, you're just too critcal Dad. Oviously you don't think I can do it." Jim ignored Dad. That's norm at our house.
course, him, critical, obviously, ignored, normal

Well, the first day Jim went to the course, he came home with a solem expreion on his face, like a condemed man. "That teacher assine us five pages of homework!" he said. "And two additonal problems that we have to reserch!"
solemn, expression, condemned, assigned, additional, research

"He sounds like an excelent profesional teacher," my dad said. "We need more teachers of that quallity in our schools." Jim squirmed in his seat. Then he gradualy started to smile. "Dad, I need some help with a person problem," he said. "Five pages of problems, right?" Dad asked. Jim smiled and handed Dad his math book. That's typical at our house, too.
excellent, professional, quality, gradually, personal, typical

One day, we had a meddical emergensy at home. My sisters hand got stuck in a basket with a narrow opening, and she couldn't pull it out. I thought she would have to wear the basket on her hand permanentally First, I tried to stretch and expand the baskets opening, but that didn't work.
medical, emergency, sister's, permanently, expand, basket's

Then I smeared a quanity of butter on my sisters hand, and she pulled it right out. I thought she would have the curtesy to thank me, but she just stomped away, still mad. How childish Sometimes she seems to think I exsit just to serve her. There are more importante things in the world than her happiness!
quantity, sister's, courtesy, childish, exist, important

Page 304

Writing: Four Types of Sentences

There are four main types of sentences: A **statement** tells something. It ends in a period. A **question** asks something. It ends in a question mark. A **command** tells someone to do something. It ends in a period or an exclamation mark. An **exclamation** shows strong feeling or excitement. It ends in an exclamation mark.

Directions: Write what you would say in each situation. Then tell whether the sentence you wrote was a statement, question, exclamation or command. The first one has been done for you.

Write what you might say to:

1. A friend who has a new cat:
   When did you get the new cat? (question)
   or Boy, what a cute cat! (exclamation)
2. A friend who studied all night for the math test:
3. Your teacher about yesterday's homework:
4. A child you're watching for a second:
5. Your sister on the phone too long:

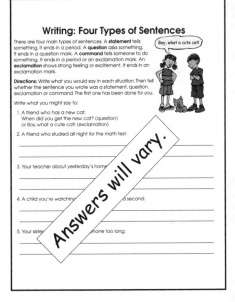

Answers will vary.

Page 305

Organizing Paragraphs

A **topic sentence** states the main idea of a paragraph and is usually the first sentence. **Support sentences** follow, providing details about the topic. All sentences in a paragraph should relate to the topic sentence. A paragraph ends with a **conclusion sentence.**

Directions: Rearrange each group of sentences into a paragraph, beginning with the topic sentence. Cross out the sentence in each group that is not related to the topic sentence. Write the new paragraph.

Now, chalk drawings are considered art by themselves. The earliest chalk drawings were found on the walls of caves. Chalk is also used in cement, fertilizer, toothpaste and makeup. Chalk once was used just to make quick sketches. Then the artist would paint pictures from the sketches. Chalk has been used for drawing for thousands of years.

Chalk has been used for drawing for thousands of years. The earliest chalk drawings were found on the walls of caves. Chalk once was used just to make quick sketches. Then the artist would paint pictures from the sketches. Now, chalk drawings are considered art by themselves.

Dams also keep young salmon from swimming downriver to the ocean. Most salmon live in the ocean but return to fresh water to lay their eggs and breed. Dams prevent salmon from swimming upriver to their spawning grounds. Pacific salmon die after they spawn the first time. One kind of fish pass is a series of pools of water that lead the salmon over the dams. Dams are threatening salmon by interfering with their spawning. To help with this problem, some dams have special "fish passes" to allow salmon to swim over the dam.

Dams are threatening salmon by interfering with their spawning. Most salmon live in the ocean but return to fresh water to lay their eggs and breed. Dams prevent salmon from swimming upriver to their spawning grounds. Dams also keep young salmon from swimming downriver to the ocean. To help with this problem, some dams have special "fish passes" to allow salmon to swim over the dam. One kind of fish pass is a series of pools of water that lead the salmon over the dams.

Page 309

Describing People

Often, a writer can show how someone feels by describing how that person looks or what he or she is doing rather than by using emotion words, like angry or happy. This is another way to create word pictures.

Directions: Read the phrases below. Write words to describe how you think that person feels.

1. like a tornado, yelling, raised fists   angry

2. slumped, walking slowly, head down   depressed, dejected

3. trembling, breathing quickly, like a cornered animal   frightened

Directions: Write one or two sentences for each phrase without using emotion words.

4. a runner who has just won a race for his or her school _____

5. a sixth grader on the first day in a new school _____

6. a teenager walking down the street ... se on fire

7. a scientist who has just ... for lung cancer _____

8. a kindergarten child be... ignored by his or her best friend _____

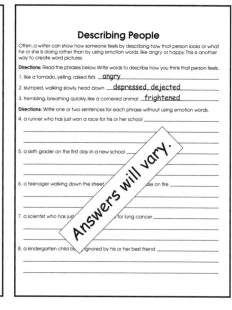
Answers will vary.

Page 310

Describing Events in Order

When we write to explain what happened, we need to describe the events in the same order they occurred. Words and phrases such as **at first, then, after that** and **finally** help us relate the order of events.

Directions: Rewrite the paragraph below, putting the topic sentence first and arranging the events in order.

I got dressed, but I didn't really feel like eating breakfast. By the time I got to school, my head felt hot, so I went to the nurse. This day was terrible from the very beginning. Finally, I ended up where I started—back in my own bed. Then she sent me home again! I just had some toast and left for school. When I first woke up in the morning, my stomach hurt.

This day was terrible from the very beginning. When I first woke up in the morning, my stomach hurt. I got dressed, but I didn't really feel like eating breakfast. I just had some toast and left for school. By the time I got to school, my head felt hot, so I went to the nurse. Then she sent me home again! Finally, I ended up where I started—back in my bed!

Directions: Follow these steps to write a paragraph about what happened the last time you tried to cook something or the last time you tried to fix something that was broken.

1. Write your first draft on another sheet of paper. Start with a topic sentence.
2. Add support sentences to explain what happened. Include phrases to keep things in order: **at first, then, after that, finally, in the middle of it, at last.**
3. Read your paragraph out loud to see if it reads smoothly. Make sure the events are in the correct order.
4. Make any needed changes, then write your paragraph below.

Paragraphs will vary.

Page 311

Explaining What Happened

Directions: These pictures tell a story, but they're out of order. Follow these steps to write what happened.

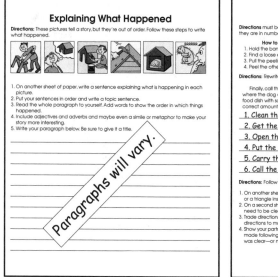

1. On another sheet of paper, write a sentence explaining what is happening in each picture.
2. Put your sentences in order and write a topic sentence.
3. Read the whole paragraph to yourself. Add words to show the order in which things happened.
4. Include adjectives and adverbs and maybe even a simile or metaphor to make your story more interesting.
5. Write your paragraph below. Be sure to give it a title.

Paragraphs will vary.

Page 312

Writing Directions

Directions:

Directions must be written clearly. They are easiest to follow when they are in numbered steps. Each step should begin with a verb.

How to Peel a Banana
1. Hold the banana by the stem end.
2. Find a loose edge of peel at the top.
3. Pull the peeling down.
4. Peel the other sections of the banana in the same way.

Directions: Rewrite these directions, number the steps in order and begin with verbs.

How to Feed a Dog
Finally, call the dog to come and eat. Then you carry the filled dish to the place where the dog eats. The can or bag should be opened by you. First, clean the dog's food dish with soap and water. Then get the dog food out of the cupboard. Put the correct amount of food in the dish.

1. Clean the dog's food dish with soap and water.
2. Get the dog food out of the cupboard.
3. Open the can or bag.
4. Put the correct amount of food in the dish.
5. Carry the filled dish to the place where the dog eats.
6. Call the dog to come and eat.

Directions: Follow these steps to write your own directions.

1. On another sheet of paper, draw two symbols, such as a square with a star in one corner or a triangle inside a circle. Don't show your drawing to anyone.
2. On a second sheet of paper, write instructions to make the same drawing. Your directions need to be clear, in order and numbered. Each step needs to begin with a verb.
3. Trade directions (but not pictures) with a partner. See if you can follow each other's directions to make the drawings.
4. Show your partner the drawing you made in step one. Does it look like the one he or she made following your directions? Could you follow your partner's directions? Share what was clear—or not so clear—about each other's instructions.

Page 313

Review

Directions: Write paragraphs to match the descriptions given. Begin with a topic sentence and add support sentences that tell the events in order. Write the first draft of your paragraph on another sheet of paper. Read it to yourself, make any necessary changes, then write it below.

1. Write a short paragraph to explain something that might happen on your way to school.

2. Write a paragraph that tells what you usually ... ur after you get up on a school day.

Directions: Write... how to brush your teeth. Include at least four steps. Make them as cle... in each step with a verb. Write a rough draft on another sheet of paper first.

1. _____
2. _____
3. _____
4. _____

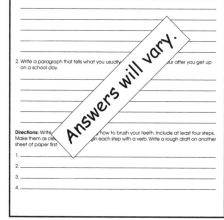
Answers will vary.

Page 314

Writing: Stronger Sentences

Sometimes the noun form of a word is not the best way to express an idea. Compare these two sentences:

They made preparations for the party.
They prepared for the party.

The second sentence, using **prepared** as a verb, is shorter and stronger.

Directions: Write one word to replace a whole phrase. Cross out the words you don't need. The first one has been done for you.

1. She ~~made a suggestion~~ that we go on Monday. *suggested*
2. They ~~arranged decorations around~~ the room. *decorated*
3. Let's ~~make a combination of~~ the two ideas. *combine*
4. I ~~have great appreciation for~~ what you did. *appreciate*
5. The buses ~~are acting as transportation for~~ the classes. *transport*
6. The group ~~made an exploration of~~ the Arctic Circle. *explored*
7. Please ~~make a selection of~~ one quickly. *select*
8. The lake is ~~making a reflection of~~ the trees. *reflects*
9. The family ~~had a celebration of~~ the holiday. *celebrated*
10. Would you please ~~provide a solution for~~ this problem? *solve*
11. Don ~~made an imitation of~~ his cat. *imitated*
12. Please ~~give a definition of~~ that word. *define*
13. I ~~made an examination of~~ the broken bike. *examined*
14. Dexter ~~made an invitation for~~ us to join him. *invited*

Write one word to replace a whole phrase.

Page 315

Writing: Descriptive Sentences

Descriptive sentences make writing more interesting to the reader. This is done by using adjectives, adverbs, prepositional phrases, similes and metaphors.

Example:
The dog ran down the hill.
The black and white beagle bounded down the steep embankment as though being chased by an invisible dragon.

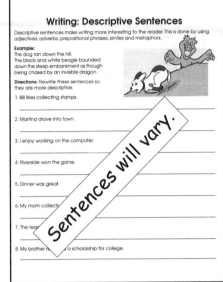

Directions: Rewrite these sentences so they are more descriptive.

1. Bill likes collecting stamps.

2. Martina drove into town.

3. I enjoy working on the computer.

4. Riverside won the game.

5. Dinner was great.

6. My mom collects

7. The tea

8. My brother i   a scholarship for college.

Sentences will vary.

Page 316

Writing: Different Points of View

A **fact** is a statement that can be proved. An **opinion** is what someone thinks or believes.

Directions: Write **F** if the statement is a fact or **O** if it is an opinion.

1. _F_ The amusement park near our town just opened last summer.
2. _O_ It's the best one in our state.
3. _F_ It has a roller coaster that's 300 feet high.
4. _O_ You're a chicken if you don't go in it.

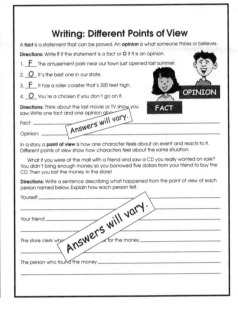

OPINION

FACT

Directions: Think about the last movie or TV show you saw. Write one fact and one opinion ab

Fact: _____

Opinion: _____

Answers will vary.

In a story, a **point of view** is how one character feels about an event and reacts to it. Different points of view show how characters feel about the same situation.

What if you were at the mall with a friend and saw a CD you really wanted on sale? You didn't bring enough money, so you borrowed five dollars from your friend to buy the CD. Then you lost the money in the store!

Directions: Write a sentence describing what happened from the point of view of each person named below. Explain how each person felt.

Yourself _____

Your friend _____

The store clerk who   for the money _____

The person who found the money _____

Answers will vary.

Page 317

Reading Skills: It's Your Opinion

Your opinion is how you feel or think about something. Although other people may have the same opinion, their reasons could not be exactly the same because of their individuality.

When writing an opinion paragraph, it is important to first state your opinion. Then, in at least three sentences, support your opinion. Finally, end your paragraph by restating your opinion in different words.

Example:
I believe dogs are excellent pets. For thousands of years, dogs have guarded and protected their owners. Dogs are faithful and have been known to save the lives of those they love. Dogs offer unconditional love as well as company for the quiet times in our lives. For these reasons, I feel that dogs make wonderful pets.

Directions: Write an opinion paragraph on whether you would or would not like to have lived in Colonial America. Be sure to support your opinion with at least three reasons.

Answers will vary.

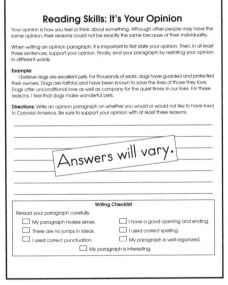

Writing Checklist
Reread your paragraph carefully.

☐ My paragraph makes sense.   ☐ I have a good opening and ending.
☐ There are no jumps in ideas.   ☐ I used correct spelling.
☐ I used correct punctuation.   ☐ My paragraph is well-organized.
                    ☐ My paragraph is interesting.

Page 318

Persuasive Writing

To **persuade** means to convince someone that your opinion is correct. "Because I said so," isn't a very convincing reason. Instead, you need to offer reasons, facts and examples to support your opinion.

Directions: Write two reasons or facts and two examples to persuade someone.

1. Riding a bicycle "no-handed" on a busy street is a bad idea.

Reasons/Facts: _____

Examples: _____

2. Taking medicine prescribed by a docto   dangerous.

Reasons/Facts: _____

Examples: _____

3. Learning to   in every other subject in school.

Reason

Examples: _____

Answers will vary.

Page 319

Persuasive Writing

When trying to persuade someone, it helps to look at both sides of the issue. If you can understand both sides, you will have a better idea how to convince someone of your point of view.

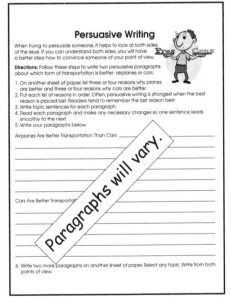

Pros Cons

Directions: Follow these steps to write two persuasive paragraphs about which form of transportation is better: airplanes or cars.

1. On another sheet of paper, list three or four reasons why planes are better and three or four reasons why cars are better.
2. Put each list of reasons in order. Often, persuasive writing is strongest when the best reason is placed last. Readers tend to remember the last reason best.
3. Write topic sentences for each paragraph.
4. Read each paragraph and make any necessary changes so one sentence leads smoothly to the next.
5. Write your paragraphs below.

Airplanes Are Better Transportation Than Cars _____

Cars Are Better Transportat

Paragraphs will vary.

6. Write two more paragraphs on another sheet of paper. Select any topic. Write from both points of view.

Page 320

Persuasive Writing

Writing is usually more persuasive if written from the reader's point of view.

If you made cookies to sell at a school fair, which of these sentences would you write on your sign?
I spent a lot of time making these cookies.
These cookies taste delicious!

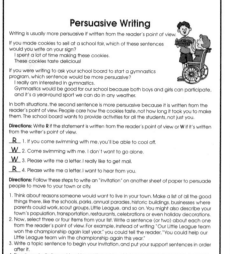

If you were writing to ask your school board to start a gymnastics program, which sentence would be more persuasive?
I really am interested in gymnastics.
Gymnastics would be good for our school because both boys and girls can participate, and it's a year-round sport we can do in any weather.

In both situations, the second sentence is more persuasive because it is written from the reader's point of view. People care how the cookies taste, not how long it took you to make them. The school board wants to provide activities for all the students, not just you.

Directions: Write **R** if the statement is written from the reader's point of view or **W** if it's written from the writer's point of view.

R 1. If you come swimming with me, you'll be able to cool off.

W 2. Come swimming with me. I don't want to go alone.

W 3. Please write me a letter. I really like to get mail.

R 4. Please write me a letter. I want to hear from you.

Directions: Follow these steps to write an "invitation" on another sheet of paper to persuade people to move to your town or city.

1. Think about reasons someone would want to live in your town. Make a list of all the good things there, like the schools, parks, annual parades, historic buildings, businesses where parents could work, scout groups, Little League, and so on. You might also describe your town's population, transportation, restaurants, celebrations or even holiday decorations.
2. Now, select three or four items from your list. Write a sentence (or two) about each one from the reader's point of view. For example, instead of writing "Our Little League team won the championship again last year," you could tell the reader, "You could help our Little League team win the championship again this year."
3. Write a topic sentence to begin your invitation, and put your support sentences in order after it.
4. Read your invitation out loud to another person. Make any needed changes, and copy the invitation onto a clean sheet of paper.

Page 321

Review

Directions: Read the questions. Then write one or two sentences about the situation from both points of view.

What if your neighbor had a dog that barked all night and kept you awake?

Your point of view: _____

Your neighbor's point of view: _____

What if the school board wanted to begin holding classes ___ school year?

For Saturday classes: _____

Against Saturday classes: _____

Directions: Rewrite these sen ___ nger statement:

Jacob made a decision ___

Kisha had a d ___

Directions ___ two opinions about your math class.

Facts: _____

Opinions: _____

Answers will vary.

Page 322

Review

Directions: Write a persuasive essay convincing your town that a park is needed for older kids with equipment such as basketball courts, soccer and football fields and a track. Be sure to end with a convincing statement.

<u>Essays will vary.</u>

Directions: Write a descriptive paragraph about these top ___

My Pet _____

My Mom _____

Paragraphs will vary.

Page 323

Describing Characters

When you write a story, your characters must seem like real people. You need to let your reader know not only how they look but how they act, what they look like and how they feel. You could just tell the reader that a character is friendly, scared or angry, but your story will be more interesting if you show these feelings by the characters' actions.

Example:
Character: A frightened child
Adjectives and adverbs: red-haired, freckled, scared, lost, worried
Simile: as frightened as a mouse cornered by a cat
Action: He peeked between his fingers, but his mother was nowhere in sight.

Directions: Write adjectives, adverbs, similes and/or metaphors that tell how each character feels. Then write a sentence that shows how the character feels.

1. an angry woman
Adjectives and adverbs: _____
Metaphor or simile: _____
Sentence: _____

2. a disappointed man
Adjectives and adverbs: _____
Metaphor or simile: _____
Sentence: _____

3. a hungry child
Adjectives and adverbs: _____
Metaphor or simile: _____
Sentence: _____

4. a tired boy
Adjectives and adverbs: _____
Metaphor or simile: _____
Sentence: _____

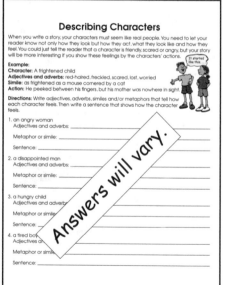

Answers will vary.

Page 324

Setting the Scene

Where and when a story takes place is called the **setting**. As with characters, you can tell about a setting—or you can show what the setting is like. Compare these two pairs of sentences:

The sun was shining.
The glaring sun made my eyes burn.

The bus was crowded.
Paige shouldered her way down the aisle, searching for an empty seat on the crowded bus.

If you give your readers a clear picture of your story's setting, they'll feel as if they're standing beside your characters. Include words that describe the sights, sounds, smells, feel and even taste if appropriate.

Directions: Write at least two sentences for each setting, clearly describing it for your readers.

1. an empty kitchen early in the morning _____

2. a locker room after a basketball game _____

3. a dark living room during a scary TV ___

4. a classroom on the fi ___

5. a quiet place i ___

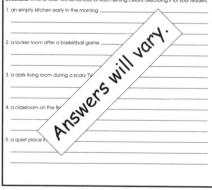

Answers will vary.

Page 325

Creating a Plot

When you're writing a story, the **plot** is the problem your characters face and how they solve it. It's helpful to write a plot outline or summary before beginning a story.

In the beginning of a story, introduce the characters, setting and problem.

Example: Scott and Cindy have never met their mother who lives in another state. They decide they would like very much to meet her. They live with their grandmother and father. On the way home from school, they talk about how they can find and contact her.

In the middle, characters try different ways to solve the problem, usually failing at first.

Example: Scott and Cindy hurry home to ask their grandmother if she can help them find their mother. Their grandmother seems nervous and tells Scott and Cindy to discuss the matter with their father when he gets home from work. When Scott and Cindy's father comes home, they tell him about their plan. Their father is very quiet for several minutes. He says he needs some time to think about it and asks if he can let them know tomorrow. Scott and Cindy can hardly sleep that night. Getting through school the next day is tough as well. After school, Scott and Cindy wait by the window for their father's car to pull in the driveway.

In the end, the characters find a way to solve the problem. Not all stories have happy endings. Sometimes, the characters decide they can live with the situation the way it is.

Example: When their father pulls into the driveway, Scott and Cindy rush out to meet him. Their father hands them airplane tickets. Scott and Cindy hug each other. Then they hug their father.

Directions: How do you think this story ends? Write a summary for the ending of this story.

Answers will vary.

Page 328

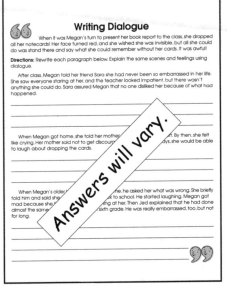

Writing Dialogue

When it was Megan's turn to present her book report to the class, she dropped all her notecards! Her face turned red, and she wished she was invisible, but all she could do was stand there and say what she could remember without her cards. It was awful!

Directions: Rewrite each paragraph below. Explain the same scenes and feelings using dialogue.

After class, Megan told her friend Sara she had never been so embarrassed in her life. She saw everyone staring at her, and the teacher looked impatient, but there wasn't anything she could do. Sara assured Megan that no one disliked her because of what had happened.

When Megan got home, she told her mother ... By then, she felt like crying. Her mother said not to get discour... ays, she would be able to laugh about dropping the cards.

When Megan's older ... he, he asked her what was wrong. She briefly told him and said ... ck to school. He started laughing. Megan got mad because she ... ing at her. Then Jed explained that he had done almost the same ... sixth grade. He was really embarrassed, too, but not for long.

Answers will vary.

Page 329

Writing: Paraphrasing

Paraphrasing means to restate something in your own words.

Directions: Write the following sentences in your own words. The first one has been done for you.

1. He sat alone and watched movies throughout the cold, rainy night.

   All through the damp, chilly evening, the boy watched television by himself.

2. Many animals such as elephants, zebras and tigers live in the grasslands.

3. In art class, Sarah worked diligently on a clay pitcher, molding and shaping it on the pottery wheel.

Answers will vary.

4. The scientists frantically searched for a cure for the new disease that threatened the entire world population.

5. Quietly, the detective crept around the abandoned building, hoping to find the missing man.

6. The windmill turned lazily in the afternoon breeze.

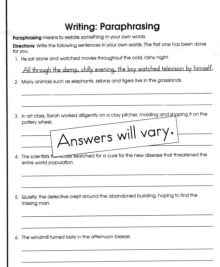

Page 330

Writing: Paraphrasing

Directions: Using synonyms and different word order, paraphrase the following paragraphs. The first one has been done for you.

Some of the Earth's resources, such as oil and coal, can be used only once. We should always, therefore, be careful how we use them. Some materials that are made from natural resources, including metal, glass and paper, can be reused. This is called recycling.

Many natural resources, including coal and oil, can be used only one time. For this reason, it is necessary to use them wisely. There are other materials made from resources of the Earth that can be recycled, or used again. Materials that can be recycled include metal, glass and paper.

Recycling helps to conserve the limited resources of our land. For example, there are only small amounts of gold and silver ores in the earth. If we can recycle these metals, less of the ores need to be mined. While there is much more aluminum ore in the earth, recycling is still important. It takes less fuel energy to recycle aluminum than it does to make the metal from ore. Therefore, recycling aluminum helps to conserve fuel.

Answers will vary.

It is impossible to get minerals and fossil fuels from the earth without causing damage to its surface. In the past, people did not think much about making these kinds of changes to the Earth. They did not think about how these actions might affect the future. As a result, much of the land around mines was left useless and ugly. This is not necessary, because such land can be restored to its former beauty.

Page 331

Writing: Summarizing

A **summary** is a brief retelling of the main ideas of a reading selection. To summarize, write the author's most important points in your own words.

Directions: Write a two-sentence summary for each paragraph.

The boll weevil is a small beetle that is native to Mexico. It feeds inside the seed pods, or bolls, of cotton plants. The boll weevil crossed into Texas in the late 1800s. It has since spread into most of the cotton-growing areas of the United States. The boll weevil causes hundreds of millions of dollars worth of damage to cotton crops each year.

Summary: _____

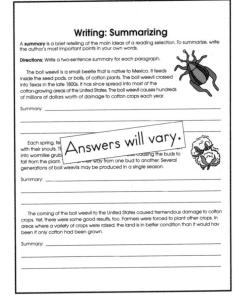

Each spring, fe... with their snouts. T... into wormlike grub... fall from the plant. ... their way from one bud to another. Several generations of boll weevils may be produced in a single season.

Summary: _____

Answers will vary.

The coming of the boll weevil to the United States caused tremendous damage to cotton crops. Yet, there were some good results, too. Farmers were forced to plant other crops. In areas where a variety of crops were raised, the land is in better condition than it would have been if only cotton had been grown.

Summary: _____

Page 332

Writing: Summarizing a Personal Narrative

Directions: Read the following narrative, then follow the directions.

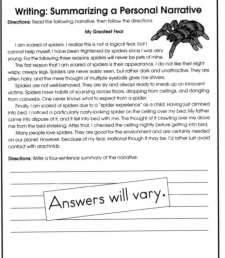

My Greatest Fear

I am scared of spiders. I realize this is not a logical fear, but I cannot help myself. I have been frightened by spiders since I was very young. For the following three reasons, spiders will never be pets of mine.

The first reason that I am scared of spiders is their appearance. I do not like their eight wispy, creepy legs. Spiders are never easily seen, but rather dark and unattractive. They are often hairy, and the mere thought of multiple eyeballs gives me shivers.

Spiders are not well-behaved. They are sly and always ready to sneak up on innocent victims. Spiders have habits of scurrying across floors, dropping from ceilings, and dangling from cobwebs. One never knows what to expect from a spider.

Finally, I am scared of spiders due to a "spider experience" as a child. Having just climbed into bed, I noticed a particularly nasty-looking spider on the ceiling over my bed. My father came into dispose of it, and it fell into bed with me. The thought of it crawling over me drove me from the bed shrieking. After that, I checked the ceiling nightly before getting into bed.

Many people love spiders. They are good for the environment and are certainly needed on our planet. However, because of my fear, irrational though it may be, I'd rather just avoid contact with arachnids.

Directions: Write a four-sentence summary of the narrative.

Answers will vary.

Page 333

Writing: Summarizing a Personal Narrative

Write the main idea of the second paragraph.
The author doesn't like spiders because of their appearance.

Write the main idea of the third paragraph.
The author doesn't like spiders because they are not well-behaved.

Write the main idea of the fourth paragraph.
The author doesn't like spiders because of a bad experience as a child.

Everyone has a fear of something. On another sheet of paper, write a five-paragraph personal narrative about a fear of your own. Use the following guide to help you organize your narrative.

Paragraph 1. State your fear.

Provide background information about fear.

Paragraph 2. State your first reason for fear.

Support this state...

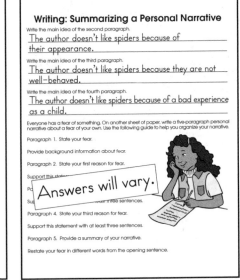

Pa...

Su... ... ee sentences.

Answers will vary.

Paragraph 4. State your third reason for fear.

Support this statement with at least three sentences.

Paragraph 5. Provide a summary of your narrative.

Restate your fear in different words from the opening sentence.

Page 334

Writing: Outlining

An **outline** is a skeletal description of the main ideas and important details of a reading selection. Making an outline is a good study aid. It is particularly useful when you must write a paper.

Directions: Read the paragraphs, and then complete the outline below.

Weather has a lot to do with where animals live. Cold-blooded animals have body temperatures that change with the temperature of the environment. Cold-blooded animals include snakes, frogs and lizards. They cannot live anywhere the temperatures stay below freezing for long periods of time. The body temperatures of warm-blooded animals do not depend on the environment. Any animal with hair or fur—including dogs, elephants and whales—is warm-blooded. Warm-blooded animals can live anywhere in the world where there is enough food to sustain them.

Some warm-blooded animals live where snow covers the ground all winter. These animals have different ways to survive the cold weather. Certain animals store up food to last throughout the snowy season. For example, the tree squirrel may gather nuts to hide in his home. Other animals hibernate in the winter. The ground squirrel, for example, stays in its burrow all winter long, living off the fat reserves in its body.

Sample answers:

Title: Animal Habitats

Main Topic: I. Weather has a lot to do with where animals live.

Subtopic: A. Cold-blooded animals' temperatures change with environment.

Detail: 1. They cannot live anywhere it stays below freezing very long.

Subtopic: B. Warm-blooded animals' temperatures do not depend on the environment.

Detail: 1. They can live anywhere there is food.

Main Topic: II. Some warm-blooded animals can live in the snow all winter.

Subtopic: A. Animals have different ways to survive the cold.

Details: 1. Some animals store food for the winter.

2. Some animals hibernate in the winter.

Page 335

Review

Directions: Read the paragraph, then follow the directions.

According to one estimate, 75 percent of all fresh water on the Earth is in the form of ice. The polar regions of the Earth are almost completely covered by ice. In some places, the ice is more than 8,000 feet thick. If all of this ice were spread out evenly, the Earth would be covered with a 100-foot-thick layer of ice. Although ice is not an important source of fresh water today, it could be in the future. Some people have proposed towing large, floating masses of ice to cities to help keep up with the demand for fresh water.

1. Complete the outline of the paragraph.

Sample answers:

Title: Using Ice for Fresh Water

Main Topic: I. 75 percent of fresh water on Earth is ice.

Subtopics: A. The polar regions have the largest source of ice.

B. Ice could be an important source of fresh water in the future.

2. Check the most appropriate generalization:

[X] Ice is the most plentiful source of fresh water.

[ ] Ice is important to the future.

3. Paraphrase the first sentence by restating it in your own words.

Answer will vary.

4. Is the author's purpose to inform, entertain or persuade?

to inform

5. Where would you look to find information on the polar ice caps?

an encyclopedia and/or an almanac

Page 336

Review

Directions: Read the paragraph, then follow the directions.

Constellations are groups of stars that have been given names. They often represent an animal, person or object. One of the easiest constellations to identify is the Big Dipper, which is shaped like a spoon. Once the Big Dipper is located, it is easy to see Cassiopeia (a W), the Little Dipper (an upside-down spoon) and the North Star. The North Star's scientific name is Polaris, and it is the last star in the handle of the Little Dipper. Other constellations include Orion the hunter, Gemini the twins, Canis Major the dog and Pegasus the winged horse. Many ancient cultures, including the Greeks and Native Americans, used the position of the stars to guide them. They also planned daily life activities, such as planting, hunting and harvesting, by the path the constellations made through the sky. For thousands of years, humans have gazed at the sky, fascinated by the millions of stars and imagining pictures in the night.

The Constellation Orion

1. Complete the outline of the paragraph.

Sample answers:

Title: Constellations

Main Topic: I. Constellations are groups of stars that represent something.

Subtopics: A. How to locate a few of the constellations

B. The meaning of constellations to ancient Greeks and Native Americans

2. In three sentences, summarize the paragraph.

Sentences will vary.

3. What is the author's purpose? to inform

4. Under which topics would you look to find more information on constellations?

astronomy   Greek mythology   Native American star legends

Page 337

Review

Directions: Imagine you are making a speech about one of your hobbies. Complete an outline of the speech.

Title: _____

Main Topic: I. _____

Subtopics: A. _____

B. _____

Who is your audience? _____

Is it appropriately written for that audience? _____

Are you trying to inform, entertain...

Answers will vary.

In the space below...

Page 338

Using the Right Resources

Directions: Decide where you would look to find information on the following topics. After each question, write one or more of the following references:

- **almanac** — contains tables and charts of statistics and information
- **atlas** — collection of maps
- **card/computer catalog** — library resource showing available books by topic, title or author
- **dictionary** — contains alphabetical listing of words with their meanings, pronunciations and origins
- **encyclopedia** — set of books or CD-ROM with general information on many subjects
- **Readers' Guide to Periodical Literature** — an index of articles in magazines and newspapers
- **thesaurus** — contains synonyms and antonyms of words

1. What is the capital of The Netherlands? atlas, encyclopedia

2. What form of government is practiced there? almanac, encyclopedia

3. What languages are spoken there? almanac, encyclopedia

4. What is the meaning of the word **indigenous**? dictionary, thesaurus

5. Where would you find information on conservation? card/computer catalog, encyclopedia, Readers' Guide to Periodical Literature

6. What is a synonym for **catastrophe**? thesaurus

7. Where would you find a review of the play Cats? Readers' Guide to Periodical Literature

8. Where would you find statistics on the annual rainfall in the Sahara Desert? almanac

9. What is the origin of the word **plentiful**? dictionary

10. What are antonyms for the word **plentiful**? thesaurus

11. Where would you find statistics for the number of automobiles manufactured in the United States last year? almanac

Page 339

Making Inferences: Reference Books

Directions: In the box are four different kinds of reference books. On the line next to each question, write which book you would use to find the information. Some information can be found in more than one reference.

| encyclopedia | almanac | dictionary | thesaurus |

1. A list of words that mean the same as "strong" — thesaurus

2. How much rain fell in Iowa in the year 1992 — almanac

3. What part of speech the word "porch" is — dictionary

4. How many different types of hummingbirds there are — encyclopedia

5. Weather patterns in Texas for the last 2 years — almanac

6. A list of words that mean the opposite of "cold" — thesaurus

7. Who invented the telescope — encyclopedia

8. How to pronounce the word "barometer" — dictionary

9. How many syllables the word "elephant" has — dictionary

10. What the difference is between African and Asian elephants — encyclopedia

11. The population changes in New York between 1935 and 1995 — almanac

12. How fast a cheetah can run — encyclopedia

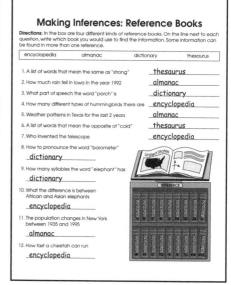

Page 340

Making Inferences: Encyclopedias

Directions: Read each question. Then check the answer for where you would find the information in an encyclopedia.

1. If you wanted to grow avocado pits on a windowsill, under which topic should you look?
☐ window ☒ avocado ☐ food

2. To find information about the Cuban revolution of 1959, which topic should you look up?
☒ Cuba ☐ revolution ☐ 1959

3. Information about Rudolph Diesel, the inventor of the Diesel engine, would be found under which topic?
☐ engine ☒ Diesel ☐ inventor

4. If you wanted to find out if the giant panda of China was really a bear or a raccoon, what should you look up?
☐ bear ☐ China ☒ panda

5. Under which topic should you look for information on how to plant a vegetable garden?
☐ plant ☐ vegetable ☒ gardening

6. If you wanted to write a report on both wild and pet gerbils, under which topic should you look for information?
☐ animal ☒ gerbil ☐ pet

7. To find out if World War I was fought only on European soil, which topic should you look up?
☐ Europe ☒ World War I ☐ war

8. Under which topic should you look for information on how bats guide themselves in the dark?
☐ guide ☐ flying ☒ bat

9. The distance of all the planets from the sun might be found under which topic?
☒ planets ☐ sky ☐ distance

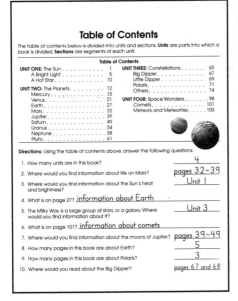

Page 341

Review

Directions: Check the best answer for where to find information in an encyclopedia.

1. If you wanted to find out who invented the television, under which topic would you look?
☐ television ☒ television history ☐ inventions

2. If you wanted to find out about the Battle of Gettysburg, under which topic would you look?
☐ Civil War ☒ famous battles ☐ Gettysburg

3. If you were curious about where most dinosaur fossils have been found, under which topic would you look?
☐ dinosaurs ☐ finds ☒ fossils

4. If you wanted to learn about Greek mythology, under which topic would you look?
☐ Greece ☐ folktales ☒ mythology

5. If you wanted to learn about different kinds of wild cats, under which topic would you look?
☐ cats ☐ wild animals ☒ big cats

Directions: Check the resource book you would use to find the following information.

1. How to play checkers ☐ almanac ☐ dictionary ☒ encyclopedia

2. An example sentence using the word "breathe"
☐ encyclopedia ☐ thesaurus ☒ dictionary

3. How many inches of snow fell in the Colorado Rockies last year
☐ encyclopedia ☒ almanac ☐ thesaurus

4. How many syllables are in the word "justification"
☐ almanac ☐ thesaurus ☒ dictionary

5. Who won the Civil War
☒ encyclopedia ☐ dictionary ☐ thesaurus

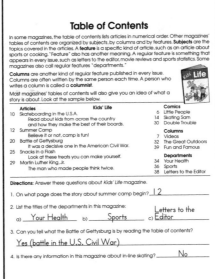

Page 342

Table of Contents

The **table of contents**, located in the front of books or magazines, tells a lot about what is inside.

A table of contents in books lists the headings and page numbers for each chapter. **Chapters** are the parts into which books are divided. Also listed are chapter numbers and the sections and subsections, if any. Look at the sample table of contents below:

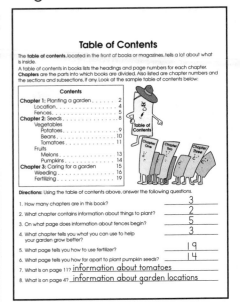

Contents

Directions: Using the table of contents above, answer the following questions.

1. How many chapters are in this book? **3**

2. What chapter contains information about things to plant? **2**

3. On what page does information about fences begin? **5**

4. What chapter tells you what you can use to help your garden grow better? **3**

5. What page tells you how to use fertilizer? **19**

6. What page tells you how far apart to plant pumpkin seeds? **14**

7. What is on page 11? **information about tomatoes**

8. What is on page 4? **information about garden locations**

Page 343

Table of Contents

The table of contents below is divided into units and sections. **Units** are parts into which a book is divided. **Sections** are segments of each unit.

Table of Contents

Directions: Using the table of contents above, answer the following questions.

1. How many units are in this book? **4**

2. Where would you find information about life on Mars? **pages 32–39**

3. Where would you find information about the Sun's heat and brightness? **Unit 1**

4. What is on page 27? **information about Earth**

5. The Milky Way is a large group of stars, or a galaxy. Where would you find information about it? **Unit 3**

6. What is on page 101? **information about comets**

7. Where would you find information about the moons of Jupiter? **pages 39–49**

8. How many pages in this book are about Earth? **5**

9. How many pages in this book are about Polaris? **3**

10. Where would you read about the Big Dipper? **pages 67 and 68**

Page 344

Table of Contents

In some magazines, the table of contents lists articles in numerical order. Other magazines' tables of contents are organized by subjects, by columns and by features. **Subjects** are the topics covered in the articles. A **feature** is a specific kind of article, such as an article about sports or cooking. "Feature" also has another meaning. A regular feature is something that appears in every issue, such as letters to the editor, movie reviews and sports statistics. Some magazines also call regular features "departments."

Columns are another kind of regular feature published in every issue. Columns are often written by the same person each time. A person who writes a column is called a **columnist**.

Most magazines' tables of contents will also give you an idea of what a story is about. Look at the sample below.

Directions: Answer these questions about *Kids' Life* magazine.

1. On what page does the story about summer camp begin? **12**

2. List the titles of the departments in this magazine.
a) **Your Health** b) **Sports** c) **Letters to the Editor**

3. Can you tell what the Battle of Gettysburg is by reading the table of contents?
Yes (battle in the U.S. Civil War)

4. Is there any information in this magazine about in-line skating? **No**

Page 345

Table of Contents

The articles in this magazine are grouped according to subjects.

Directions: Answer these questions about *LIVING* magazine.

1. How many departments are in this issue of the magazine? **6**

2. Circle the topics that are regular features in *LIVING*.
(Books) Dinosaurs Cleveland Indians Vice Presidents
(Comedy) (Living Well) (Snacks) Earth Day

3. What page would you look at if you wanted to see what was playing at the movie theaters? **24**

4. Is there any information in this magazine about football? **No**

5. Who are the two people featured in this issue? **Al Gore and Jim Henson**

6. Is there anything in this issue about cycling? **Yes**

7. Under what heading is it listed? **Exercise**

Page 346

Indexes

An **index** is an alphabetical listing of names, topics and important words and is found in the back of a book. An index lists every page on which these items appear. For example, in a book about music, dulcimer might be listed this way: Dulcimer 2, 13, 26, 38. Page numbers may also be listed like this: Guitars 18-21. That means that information about guitars begins on page 18 and continues through page 21. **Subject** is the name of the item in an index. **Sub-entry** is a smaller division of the subject. For example, "apples" would be listed under fruit.

Index

N		See also planet names.	
Neptune	27	Pleiades	32
NGC 5128 (galaxy)	39	Pluto	12, 27
Novas	32	Polaris	35, 36
		Pole star. See Polaris.	
O		Project Ozma	41
Observatories. See El Caracol.			
Orbits of planets	10	R	
Orion rocket	43	Rings. See Planet rings.	
P		S	
Planetoids. See Asteroids.		Sagittarius	37
Planet rings		Satellites	
Jupiter	23	Jupiter	24
Saturn	9, 25	Neptune	27
Uranus	26	Pluto	27
Planets		Saturn	25
discovered by Greeks	7	Uranus	26
outside the solar system	40	See also Galilean satellites.	
visible with the naked eye	9	Saturn	25

Directions: Answer the questions about the index from this book about the solar system.

1. On what pages is there information about Pluto? **pages 12 and 27**
2. On what pages is information about Saturn's first ring found? **page 9 or 25**
3. What is on page 41? **information about Project Ozma**
4. Where is there information about the pole star? **pages 35 and 36**
5. What is on page 43? **information about the Orion rocket**
6. On what page would you find information about planets that are visible to the eye? **page 9**
7. On what page would you find information about Jupiter's satellites? **page 24**

Page 347

Indexes

Some magazines use indexes to guide their readers to information they contain.

Appetizers

Bacon-Wrapped Halibut	92
Scallops With Sorrel and Tomato	116
Shrimp and Basil Beignets	116
Shrimp and Vegetable Spring Rolls With Hoisin and Mustard Sauces	85
Sweet Potato Ribbon Chips	136

Soups

Lemongrass Soup, Hot, With Radishes and Chives	84
Roasted Garlic Soup	22
Vegetable Soup With Creamy Asparagus Flan	154

Salads, Salad Dressings

Arugula Salad With Roasted Beets, Walnuts and Daikon	158
Chicken, Fennel, Orange and Olive Salad	24
Jicama Salad	81
Tomato, Onion and Zucchini Salad	152
Walnut Vinaigrette	158

Directions: Answer the questions about the index from *Bon Appétit* magazine.

1. **4**
2. **Lemongrass soup**
3. **Chicken, Fennel, Orange and Olive Salad**
4. **116**
5. **Yes. Bacon-wrapped Halibut, page 92**
6. **136**
   Sweet Potato Ribbon Chips
   Appetizer

Page 348

Review

FARMING
Table of Contents

9	Farmers of the Midwest — Read about small farmers still trying to survive in the business.
15	Farmers' Markets — Some farmers take their goods to town and sell them to the city folk.
26	Hay: The Cheapest Way — New technology helps produce bales of hay quicker and cheaper than in the past.
36	The Farm Family — Farming is a way of life, and everybody helps!

Departments

Letters to the Editor	5
Finances	7
High Tech	13
Haymaker	27

INDEX

Africa	6
Alabama	49
Alps	21, 25
Antarctica	10-12
Antarctic Circle	8-10
Arctic	12-14
Arctic Circle	14
Arctic Ocean	15
Asia	37
Athens	33
Atlantic Ocean	11
Baltic Sea	15, 30
Baltimore	51
Black Sea	37
Bombay	39
Brazil	59
British Isles	19
Buffalo	52
Bug River	31
Cadiz	27
California	48
Cambridge	19
Cape of Good Hope	49
China	11, 41
Colorado River, Argentina	61
Colorado River, U.S.A.	62
Continents	2-3
Cuba	55

Directions: Answer the questions about the table of contents from *Farming* magazine.

1. Is there any information about fashion in this magazine? **No**
2. Is there any information about computers in this magazine? **No**
3. Information about children on farms is probably included in which feature? **The Farm Family**
4. Are there any features about animals in this magazine? **No**

Directions: Answer the questions about the index from this book about the world.

1. On what pages would you find information about the Baltic Sea? **15, 30**
2. What is listed on pages 2-3? **Continents**
3. Where are the two Colorado Rivers? **pages 61 and 62**

Page 349

Review

Directions: Follow the instructions for each section.

1. In your own words, explain why a table of contents is helpful.
   Answers will vary.

2. A table of contents is often divided into units and sections.
   What is a unit? **parts into which a book is divided**
   What is a section? **segments of each unit**

3. What is the purpose of breaking a table of contents down into units and sections?
   It helps make the information easier for the reader to find.

4. What is an index?
   An index is an alphabetical listing of names, topics and important words. It is found in the back of a book.

5. What are the differences between a table of contents and an index?
   The information contained in each may differ slightly. Indexes are organized alphabetically, and tables of contents are organized according to subject, column or feature in numerical order. The table of contents is in front, the index, the back.

6. Look at the table of contents in the front of this book. How many pages does the unit on Famous Athletes span?
   8 pages

Page 350

Biographical Research

A **biography** is a written history of a person's life. Often, information for a biography can be obtained from an encyclopedia, especially if a person is famous. Of course, not everyone is listed in a main article in an encyclopedia. Use the encyclopedia's index, which is the last book in the set, to find which volume contains the information you need. Look at this listing taken from an encyclopedia index for Henry Moore, an English artist:

Moore, Henry English sculptor.
1898-1986
main article Moore 12:106b, illus.
references in Sculpture 15:290a, illus.

Notice that the listing includes Henry Moore's dates of birth and death and illustrations (illus.). It also includes a short description of his accomplishments: He was an English sculptor. Look below at part of the index from the *Children's Britannica* encyclopedias.

Lincoln, Abraham president of US.
1809-1865
main article Lincoln 11:49a, illus.
references in
Assassination 2:64b
Caricature, illus. 4:87
Civil War, American 4:296a fol.
Confederate States of America 5:113b fol.
Democracy 6:17a
Gettysburg, Battle of 8:144a
Illinois 9:256b
Thanksgiving Day 17:199a
United States of America, history of 18:137a fol.
Westward Movement 19:49a

Lincoln, Benjamin army officer.
1733-1810
references in American Revolution 1:204b

Lind, Jenny Swedish singer. 1820-87
operatic soprano admired for vocal purity and control; made debut 1838 in Stockholm and sang in Paris and London, becoming known as the "Swedish Nightingale"; toured US with P.T. Barnum 1850; last concert 1883.
references in Barnum 2:235a

Lindbergh, Anne US author and aviator. b. 1906
references in Lindbergh 11:53a, illus.

Lindbergh, Charles Augustus US aviator.
1902-1974
main article Lindbergh 11:53a, illus.
references in
Aviation, history of 2:140b, illus.
Medals and decorations, 11:266b
Saint Louis, 15:215b

Linde, Karl Von German engineer.
1842-1934
references in Refrigeration 15:32b

Directions: Answer these questions from the index above.

1. Where is the main article for Abraham Lincoln? **volume 11, page 49**
2. In addition to the main article, how many other places are there references to Abraham Lincoln? **10**
3. In which encyclopedia volume is there information about Anne Lindbergh? **volume 11**

Page 351

Biographical Indexes

If a person has been in the news recently, check the *National Newspaper Index* or an index for the local newspaper to find articles on that person. The *National Newspaper Index* contains the names of articles published by five major newspapers within the last three years. *NewsBank*, a news digest containing information from nearly 200 newspapers throughout the country, should also be checked.

Also check the *Obituary Index* to *The New York Times* or the *Obituary Index* to the (London, England) *Times*. Obituaries are notices of deaths. They usually include a brief biography of the person.

Reader's Guide to Periodical Literature alphabetically lists subjects of articles printed in most major magazines. A *Reader's Guide* entry lists the magazine in which an article appeared, the date of the publication and the page number where the article starts.

Biography Index lists biographical articles published since 1946.

Almanacs also contain information about individuals. For example, *The Kid's World Almanac of Records and Facts* lists the United States presidents and their major accomplishments. It also has information about athletes, composers and others.

Directions: Use the encyclopedias and one or more of the resources listed above to research one of the following people. Begin writing your biographical report in the space provided. (If you need more room, use a separate sheet of paper.)

Research Topics:

Richard M. Nixon	Jesse Jackson
Mother Theresa	Lech Walesa
Margaret Thatcher	Mikhail Gorbachev

Answers will vary.

Page 352

Biographical Dictionaries

Biographical dictionaries, such as *Who's Who*, contain histories of people's lives. In addition to *Who's Who*, there are many other biographical dictionaries. BDs, as they are called, can include books such as the *Biographical Dictionary of English Architects* or *Who's Who in Art Materials*. Some biographical dictionaries list only people who lived during certain eras, such as *Women Artists: 1550–1950*.

Because there are so many biographical dictionaries, master indexes are published to guide researchers. Up to 500 books are listed in some biographical master indexes. A master index may list several biographical dictionaries in which information about a person can be obtained. Here are a few:

1. *The Biography and Genealogy Master Index* contains 11 books and is a good place to begin research. Parts of this index, such as *Children's Authors*, are in separate volumes.
2. *An Analytical Bibliography of Universal Collected Biography* contains information from more than 3,000 biographical dictionaries published before 1933.
3. *In Black and White: A Guide to Magazine Articles, Newspaper Articles and Books Concerning More than 15,000 Black Individuals and Groups* is the title of a large biographical master index.
4. *Marquis Who's Who Publications: Index to All Books* lists names from at least 15 *Who's Who* books published by Marquis each year.

Directions: Complete each sentence about biographical dictionaries.

1. Biographical dictionaries contain
   __histories of people's lives.__
2. When beginning research in biographical dictionaries, first use a
   __master index.__
3. The __Biography and Geneology Master Index__ has 11 books in its set.
4. *Children's Authors and Illustrators* is a separate volume of the
   __Biography and Geneology Master Index.__
5. Information from at least 15 *Who's Who* publications each year is contained in the
   __Marquis Who's Who Publications: Index to All Books.__

Page 354

Other Biographical Resources

Information about people who belong to clubs, trade unions or other organizations can sometimes be found in libraries or from an organization's main office. If these people work or have worked for corporations, information can be obtained by contacting the public relations office of that company.

Unpublished materials, such as diaries or letters, are usually donated to a library or a historical society when a person dies. Clues that such materials exist may be found when reading other books or articles about a person.

Personal interviews can also provide information about subjects. Following are a few points to remember when conducting an interview:

1. Cover the five main points that you need to know for any story: who, what, when, where and why.
2. Write accurate notes while doing the interview.
3. Use the notes to write the article.
4. If your notes are unclear, check them with the person interviewed.
5. Double-check other facts that you are not sure about. Be sure to check the spelling of the person's name, and check important dates that were mentioned during the interview.
6. Only write things that you are sure the person said.

Directions: Use the tips listed above to conduct an interview with a friend or classmate. Write a brief biography using what you learned during the interview.

__Answers will vary.__

Page 355

CD-ROM's

There are many CD-ROM's which can now assist with biographical research. Often, CD-ROM's not only have written information about an individual's life, but the entry might also include video clips or still-frame pictures. Look for CD-ROM's which are encyclopedias, historical references or famous person indexes.

It is important to correctly type in the person's name when using a CD-ROM. It is also possible to locate a person by typing in an event in which he/she was involved.

Example: Martin Luther King — Civil Rights

Directions: For the following people, [Answers may include:] was involved or another category where you might look for:

1. John F. Kennedy __Presidents__
2. Rosa Parks __Civil Rights__
3. John Glenn __Astronauts__
4. Al Gore __Vice Presidents__
5. George Burns __Entertainers__
6. Benjamin Franklin __Inventors__
7. Beverly Cleary __Writers__
8. Michael Jordan __NBA__
9. Margaret Thatcher __England__
10. Sally Ride __Astronauts__
11. Thomas Edison __Inventors__
12. Marie Curie __Inventors__
13. Jonas Salk __Researchers__
14. Tiger Woods __Golf__
15. Tara Lipinski __Ice Skating__
16. Alexander Graham Bell __Inventors__

Page 356

Review

Directions: Write **T** or **F** on the line beside each statement.

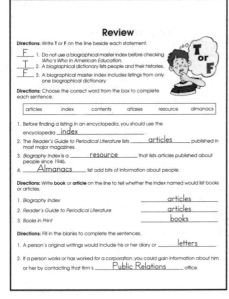

__F__ 1. Do not use a biographical master index before checking *Who's Who in American Education*.
__T__ 2. A biographical dictionary lists people and their histories.
__F__ 3. A biographical master index includes listings from only one biographical dictionary.

Directions: Choose the correct word from the box to complete each sentence.

| articles | index | contents | atlases | resource | almanacs |

1. Before finding a listing in an encyclopedia, you should use the encyclopedia __index__
2. The *Reader's Guide to Periodical Literature* lists __articles__ published in most major magazines.
3. *Biography Index* is a __resource__ that lists articles published about people since 1946.
4. __Almanacs__ list odd bits of information about people.

Directions: Write **book** or **article** on the line to tell whether the index named would list books or articles.

1. *Biography Index* __articles__
2. *Reader's Guide to Periodical Literature* __articles__
3. *Books in Print* __books__

Directions: Fill in the blanks to complete the sentences.

1. A person's original writings would include his or her diary or __letters__.
2. If a person works or has worked for a corporation, you could gain information about him or her by contacting that firm's __Public Relations__ office.

Page 363

Friendly Letters

Directions: Study the format for writing a letter to a friend. Then answer the questions.

your return address — 123 Waverly Road, Cincinnati, Ohio 45241
date — June 23, 1999
greeting — Dear Josh,
body —
How is your summer going? I am enjoying mine so far. I have been swimming twice already this week, and it's only Wednesday! I am glad there is a pool near our house.
My parents said that you can stay overnight when your family comes for the 4th of July picnic. Do you want to? We can pitch a tent in the back yard and camp out. It will be a lot of fun!
Please write back to let me know if you can stay over on the 4th. I will see you then!
closing — Your friend,
signature — Michael

your return address — Michael Delaney, 123 Waverly Road, Cincinnati, Ohio 45241
main address — Josh Sommers, 2250 West First Ave., Columbus, OH 43212

1. What words are in the greeting? __Dear Josh__
2. What words are in the closing? __Your friend__
3. On what street does the writer live? __Waverly Road__

Page 366

Place Value

Place value is the position of a digit in a number. A digit's place in a number shows its value. Numbers left of the decimal point represent **whole numbers**. Numbers right of the decimal point represent a part, or fraction, of a whole number. These parts are broken down into tenths, hundredths, thousandths, and so on.

Example:
3,443,221.621

millions	hundred thousands	ten thousands	thousands	hundreds	tens	ones	tenths	hundredths	thousandths
3	4	4	3	2	2	1	6	2	1

◄—— Whole Numbers ——► | ◄— Fractions —►

Directions: Write the following number words as numbers.

1. Three million, forty-four thousand, six hundred twenty-one __3,044,621__
2. One million, seventy-seven __1,000,077__
3. Nine million, six hundred thousand, one hundred two __9,600,102__
4. Twenty-nine million, one hundred three thousand and nine tenths __29,103,000.9__
5. One million, one hundred thousand, one hundred seventy-one and thirteen hundredths __1,100,171.13__

Directions: In each box, write the corresponding number for each place value.

1. 4,822,000.00 __0__ hundreds
2. 55,907,003.00 __7__ thousands
3. 190,641,225.07 __6__ hundred thousands
4. 247,308,211.59 __5__ tenths
5. 7,594,097.33 __7__ millions
6. 201,480,110.01 __4__ hundred thousands
7. 42,367,109,074.25 __5__ hundredths

Page 367

Place Value

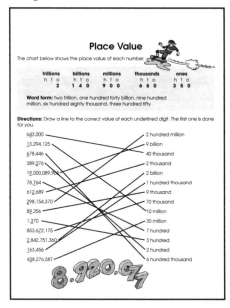

The chart below shows the place value of each number.

trillions	billions	millions	thousands	ones
h t o	h t o	h t o	h t o	h t o
2	1 4 0	9 0 0	6 8 0	3 5 0

Word form: two trillion, one hundred forty billion, nine hundred million, six hundred eighty thousand, three hundred fifty

Directions: Draw a line to the correct value of each underlined digit. The first one is done for you.

643,000 — 2 hundred million
13,294,125 — 9 billion
678,446 — 40 thousand
389,276 — 2 thousand
19,000,089,906 — 2 billion
78,764 — 1 hundred thousand
612,689 — 9 thousand
298,154,370 — 70 thousand
89,256 — 10 million
1,370 — 30 thousand
853,672,175 — 7 hundred
2,842,751,360 — 3 hundred
163,456 — 3 hundred
438,276,587 — 6 hundred thousand

8,920,077

Page 368

Expanded Notation

Expanded notation is writing out the value of each digit in a number.

Example:
8,920,077 = 8,000,000 + 900,000 + 20,000 + 70 + 7
Word form: Eight million, nine hundred twenty thousand, seventy-seven

Directions: Write the following numbers using expanded notation.

1. 20,769,033 20,000,000 + 700,000 + 60,000 + 9,000 + 30 + 3

2. 1,183,541,029 1,000,000,000 + 100,000,000 + 80,000,000 + 3,000,000 + 500,000 + 40,000 + 1,000 + 20 + 9

3. 776,003,091 700,000,000 + 70,000,000 + 6,000,000 + 3,000 + 90 + 1

4. 5,920,100,808 5,000,000,000 + 900,000,000 + 20,000,000 + 100,000 + 800 + 8

5. 14,141,543,760 10,000,000,000 + 4,000,000,000 + 100,000,000 + 40,000,000 + 1,000,000 + 500,000 + 40,000 + 3,000 + 700 + 60

Directions: Write the following numbers.

1. 700,000 + 900 + 60 + 7 700,967

2. 35,000,000 + 600,000 + 400 + 40 + 2 35,600,442

3. 12,000,000 + 700,000 + 60,000 + 4,000 + 10 + 4 12,764,014

4. 80,000,000,000 + 8,000,000,000 + 400,000,000 + 80,000,000 + 10,000 + 400 + 30 88,480,010,430

5. 4,000,000,000 + 16,000,000 + 30 + 2 4,016,000,032

Page 369

Addition and Place Value

Directions: Add the problems below in which the digits with the same place value are lined up correctly. Then cross out the problems in which the digits are not lined up correctly.

Find each answer in the diagram and color that section.

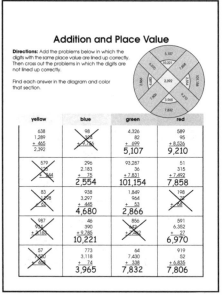

yellow	blue	green	red
638 1,289 + 465 2,392	98 ~~324~~ ~~+ 9,785~~	4,326 82 + 699 5,107	589 95 + 8,526 9,210
~~579~~ ~~725~~ ~~+ 544~~	296 2,183 + 75 2,554	93,287 36 + 7,831 101,154	51 315 + 7,492 7,858
83 1,298 + 52	938 3,297 + 445 4,680	1,849 964 + 53 2,866	~~198~~ ~~+ 68~~
987 ~~934~~ ~~+ 9,105~~	46 390 + 9,785 10,221	856 ~~+ 7,269~~	591 6,352 + 27 6,970
57 ~~3,118~~ ~~+ 74~~	773 3,118 + 74 3,965	64 7,430 + 338 7,832	919 52 + 6,835 7,806

Page 370

Addition

Directions: Add the following numbers in your head without writing them out.

1. 17 + 33 = **50**
2. 35 + 15 = **50**
3. 75 + 25 = **100**
4. 41 + 25 = **66**
5. 27 + 23 = **50**
6. 30 + 20 = **50**
7. 12 + 18 = **30**
8. 43 + 22 = **65**
9. 16 + 34 = **50**
10. 9 + 11 + 30 = **50**
11. 29 + 21 + 40 = **90**
12. 14 + 16 + 20 = **50**
13. 37 + 13 + 25 = **75**
14. 12 + 22 + 36 = **70**
15. 19 + 21 + 57 = **97**
16. 21 + 24 + 25 = **70**
17. 63 + 14 + 11 = **88**
18. 33 + 15 + 42 = **90**
19. 25 + 15 + 60 = **100**
20. 30 + 20 + 10 = **60**

14 + 12 + 7 + 20 + 9 + 18 = ?

Page 371

Addition Word Problems

Directions: Solve the following addition word problems.

1. 100 students participated in a sports card show in the school gym. Brad brought his entire collection of 2,000 cards to show his friends. He had 700 football cards and 400 basketball cards. If the rest of his cards were baseball cards, how many baseball cards did he bring with him?
   900 baseball cards

2. Refreshments were set up in one area of the gym. Hot dogs were a dollar, soda was 50 cents, chips were 35 cents and cookies were a quarter. If you purchased two of each item, how much money would you need?
   $4.20

3. It took each student 30 minutes to set up for the card show and twice as long to put everything away. The show was open for 3 hours. How much time did each student spend on this event?
   4 1/2 hours

4. 450 people attended the card show. 55 were mothers of students, 67 were fathers, 23 were grandparents, 8 were aunts and uncles and the rest were kids. How many kids attended?
   297 kids

5. Of the 100 students who set up displays, most of them sold or traded some of their cards. Bruce sold 75 cards, traded 15 cards and collected $225. Kevin only sold 15 cards, traded 81 cards and collected $100. Missi traded 200 cards, sold 10 and earned $35. Of those listed, how many cards were sold, how many were traded and how much money was earned?
   sold **100**   traded **296**   earned $ **360**

Page 372

Subtraction

Directions: Subtract the following numbers. When subtracting, begin on the right, especially if you need to regroup and borrow.

549 − 162 387	823 − 417 406	370 − 244 126	648 − 79 569
700 − 343 357	475 − 299 176	603 − 425 178	354 − 265 89
1,841 − 952 889	2,597 − 608 1,989	6,832 − 1,774 5,058	9,005 − 3,458 5,547
23,342 − 9,093 14,249	53,790 − 40,813 12,977	29,644 − 19,780 9,864	35,726 − 16,959 18,767
109,432 − 79,145 30,287	350,907 − 14,185 336,722	217,523 − 44,197 173,326	537,411 − 406,514 130,897

Grade 6 - Comprehensive Curriculum

Page 373

Subtraction Word Problems

Directions: Solve the following subtraction word problems.

1. Last year, 28,945 people lived in Mike's town. This year there are 31,889. How many people have moved in? **2,944 people**

2. Brad earned $227 mowing lawns. He spent $168 on tapes by his favorite rock group. How much money does he have left? **$59**

3. The school year has 180 days. Carrie has gone to 32 school days so far. How many more days does she have left? **148 days**

4. Craig wants a skateboard that costs $128. He has saved $47. How much more does he need? **$81**

5. To get to school, Jennifer walks 1,275 steps and Carolyn walks 2,618 steps. How many more steps does Carolyn walk than Jennifer? **1,343 steps**

6. Amy has placed 91 of the 389 pieces in a new puzzle she purchased. How many more does she have left to finish? **298 pieces**

7. From New York, it's 2,823 miles to Los Angeles and 1,327 miles to Miami. How much farther away is Los Angeles? **1,496 miles**

8. Sheila read that a piece of carrot cake has 236 calories, but a piece of apple pie has 427 calories. How many calories will she save by eating the cake instead of the pie? **191 calories**

9. Tim's summer camp costs $223, while Sam's costs $149. How much more does Tim's camp cost? **$74**

10. Last year, the nation's budget was $45,000,000,000, but the nation spent $52,569,342,000. How much more than its budget did the nation spend? **$ 7,569,342,000**

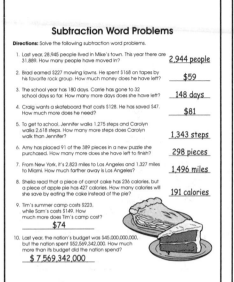

Page 374

Multiplication

Directions: Multiply the following numbers. Be sure to keep the numbers aligned, and place a 0 in the ones place when multiplying by the tens digit.

Example:	Correct	Incorrect
	55	55
	x 15	x 15
	275	275
	550	55
	825	330

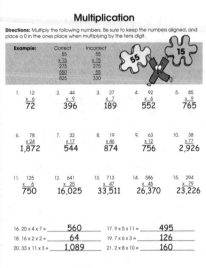

1. 12 x 6 = **72**
2. 44 x 9 = **396**
3. 27 x 7 = **189**
4. 92 x 6 = **552**
5. 85 x 9 = **765**

6. 78 x 24 = **1,872**
7. 32 x 17 = **544**
8. 19 x 46 = **874**
9. 63 x 12 = **756**
10. 38 x 77 = **2,926**

11. 125 x 6 = **750**
12. 641 x 25 = **16,025**
13. 713 x 47 = **33,511**
14. 586 x 45 = **26,370**
15. 294 x 79 = **23,226**

16. 20 x 4 x 7 = **560**
17. 9 x 5 x 11 = **495**
18. 16 x 2 x 2 = **64**
19. 7 x 6 x 3 = **126**
20. 33 x 11 x 3 = **1,089**
21. 2 x 8 x 10 = **160**

Page 375

Multiplying With Zeros

Directions: Multiply the following numbers. If a number ends with zero, you can eliminate it while calculating the rest of the answer. Then count how many zeros you took off and add them to your answer.

Example:	550	Take off 2 zeros	500	Take off 2 zeros
	x 50		x 5	
	27,500	Add on 2 zeros	2,500	Add on 2 zeros

1. 300 x 6 = **1,800**
2. 400 x 7 = **2,800**
3. 620 x 5 = **3,100**
4. 290 x 7 = **2,030**

5. 142 x 20 = **2,840**
6. 505 x 50 = **25,250**
7. 340 x 70 = **23,800**
8. 600 x 60 = **36,000**

9. 550 x 380 = **209,000**
10. 290 x 150 = **43,500**
11. 2,040 x 360 = **734,400**
12. 8,800 x 200 = **1,760,000**

13. Bruce traveled 600 miles each day of a 10-day trip. How far did he go during the entire trip? **6,000 miles**

14. 30 children each sold 20 items for the school fund-raiser. Each child earned $100 for the school. How much money did the school collect? **$2,000**

15. 10 x 40 x 2 = **800**
16. 30 x 30 x 10 = **9,000**
17. 100 x 60 x 10 = **60,000**
18. 500 x 11 x 2 = **11,000**
19. 9 x 10 x 10 = **900**
20. 7,000 x 20 x 10 = **1,400,000**

Page 376

Division

In a division problem, the **dividend** is the number to be divided, the **divisor** is the number used to divide and the **quotient** is the answer. To check your work, multiply your answer times the divisor and you should get the dividend.

Example:	130 ← quotient	Check:	130 ← quotient
divisor→	4)520 ← dividend		x 4 ← divisor
	4		520 ← dividend
	12		
	12		
	00		

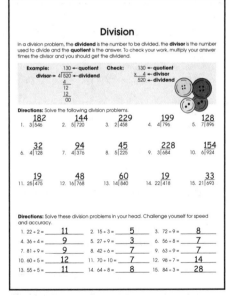

Directions: Solve the following division problems.

1. 3)546 = **182**
2. 5)720 = **144**
3. 2)458 = **229**
4. 4)796 = **199**
5. 7)896 = **128**

6. 4)128 = **32**
7. 4)376 = **94**
8. 5)225 = **45**
9. 3)684 = **228**
10. 6)924 = **154**

11. 25)475 = **19**
12. 16)768 = **48**
13. 14)840 = **60**
14. 22)418 = **19**
15. 21)693 = **33**

Directions: Solve these division problems in your head. Challenge yourself for speed and accuracy.

1. 22 ÷ 2 = **11**
2. 15 ÷ 3 = **5**
3. 72 ÷ 9 = **8**
4. 36 ÷ 4 = **9**
5. 27 ÷ 9 = **3**
6. 56 ÷ 8 = **7**
7. 81 ÷ 9 = **9**
8. 42 ÷ 6 = **7**
9. 63 ÷ 9 = **7**
10. 60 ÷ 5 = **12**
11. 70 ÷ 10 = **7**
12. 98 ÷ 7 = **14**
13. 55 ÷ 5 = **11**
14. 64 ÷ 8 = **8**
15. 84 ÷ 3 = **28**

Page 377

Division Word Problems

In the example below, 368 is being divided by 4. 4 won't divide into 3, so move over one position and divide 4 into 36. 4 goes into 36 nine times. Then multiply 4 x 9 to get 36. Subtract 36 from 36. The answer is 0, less than the divisor, so 9 is the right number. Now bring down the 8, divide 4 into it and repeat the process.

Example:	9		92
	4)368		4)368
	36		36
	0		08
			8
			0

To check your division, multiply 4 x 92 = 368.

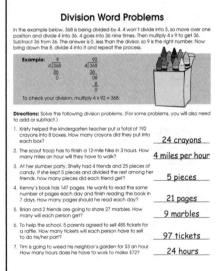

Directions: Solve the following division problems. (For some problems, you will also need to add or subtract.)

1. Kristy helped the kindergarten teacher put a total of 192 crayons into 8 boxes. How many crayons did they put into each box? **24 crayons**

2. The scout troop has to finish a 12-mile hike in 3 hours. How many miles an hour will they have to walk? **4 miles per hour**

3. At her slumber party, Shelly had 4 friends and 25 pieces of candy. If she kept 5 pieces and divided the rest among her friends, how many pieces did each friend get? **5 pieces**

4. Kenny's book has 147 pages. He wants to read the same number of pages each day and finish reading the book in 7 days. How many pages should he read each day? **21 pages**

5. Brian and 2 friends are going to share 27 marbles. How many will each person get? **9 marbles**

6. To help the school, 5 parents agreed to sell 485 tickets for a raffle. How many tickets will each person have to sell to do his/her part? **97 tickets**

7. Tim is going to weed his neighbor's garden for $3 an hour. How many hours does he have to work to make $72? **24 hours**

Page 378

Equations

In an **equation**, the value on the left of the equal sign must equal the value on the right. Remember the order of operations: solve from left to right, multiply or divide numbers before adding or subtracting and do the operation inside parentheses first.

Example:	6 + 4 − 2 = 4 x 2
	10 − 2 = 8
	8 = 8

Directions: Write the correct operation signs in the blanks to make accurate equations.

1. (25 **+** 25) **÷** 2 = 100 **−** 75
2. (76 **+** 24) **X** 3 = 150 **X** 2
3. 140 **÷** 2 **X** 10 = 500 **+** 50 **+** 150
4. 2,100 **−** 2,000 **+** 60 = 80 **X** 2
5. 80 **X** 8 **÷** 4 = 160 **+** 160 **−** 160
6. (55 **X** 100) **÷** 11 = (1,000 **X** 2) **÷** 4
7. 137 **+** 81 **+** 52 = 3 **X** 90
8. 3,000 **÷** 10 **+** 10 = (600 **+** 300) **÷** 30
9. (720 **+** 20) **÷** 4 = 37 **X** 5
10. (457 **+** 43) **−** 500 = (21 **+** 40) x 0

Page 379

Equations

Directions: Write the correct operation signs in the blanks to make accurate equations.

1. 5 **+** 5 **+** 5 = 3 **X** 5 **+** 0
2. (50 **+** 0) **X** 2 = 25 **X** 2 **X** 2
3. 2 **X** 2 **X** 2 **X** 2 = 2 **X** 2 **X** 4
4. (4 **X** 5) **+** 5 **+** 5 = 2 **X** 3 **X** 5
5. (25 **÷** 5) **X** 2 **X** 3 = 3 **X** 6 **X** 2 **X** 5
6. (125 **X** 7) **+** 2 **+** 10 = 100 **X** 2 **X** 4 **+** 70 **+** 10
7. (100 **X** 10) **X** 5 **+** 10 = 10 **X** 5 **X** 100 **+** 10
8. 35 **+** 35 **+** 5 **X** 2 = 5 **X** 3 **X** 2 **X** 5
9. (60 **÷** 2) **X** 3 = 3 **X** 3 **X** 3 **X** 0 **+** 15 **+** (5 **X** 15)
10. (120 **X** 4) **+** 7 **+** 3 = (7 **X** 7) **X** (2 **X** 5)
11. (91 **+** 3 **+** 6) **X** 3 = 2 **X** 5 **X** 1 **X** 3 **X** (2 **X** 5)
12. (16 **X** 4) **−** 8 = 5 **+** 5 **X** (3 **X** 3) **+** 6
13. 0 **X** 5 **+** 15 **−** 4 = 3 **−** 3 **+** 3 **+** 8
14. 16 **X** 3 **+** 12 **−** (2 **X** 20) = (2 **X** 2) **X** 6 **+** 10 **−** (2 **X** 7)
15. 21 **+** (3 **X** 3) **−** 3 **−** 1 = 3 **+** 1 **X** 2 **+** 20

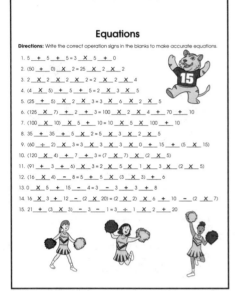

Page 380

Rounding and Estimating

Rounding is expressing a number to the nearest whole number, ten, thousand or other value. **Estimating** is using an approximate number instead of an exact one. When rounding a number, we say a country has 98,000,000 citizens instead of 98,347,425. We can round off numbers to the nearest whole number, the nearest hundred or the nearest million—whatever is appropriate.

Here are the steps: 1) Decide where you want to round off the number. 2) If the digit to the right is less than 5, leave the digit at the rounding place unchanged. 3) If the digit to the right is 5 or more, increase the digit at the rounding place by 1.

> **Examples:** 587 rounded to the nearest hundred is 600.
> 535 rounded to the nearest hundred is 500.
> 21,897 rounded to the nearest thousand is 22,000.
> 21,356 rounded to the nearest thousand is 21,000.
>
> When we estimate numbers, we use rounded, approximate numbers instead of exact ones.
>
> **Example:** A hamburger that costs $1.49 and a drink that costs $0.79 total about $2.30 ($1.50 plus $0.80).

Directions: Use rounding and estimating to find the answers to these questions. You may have to add, subtract, multiply or divide.

1. Debbi is having a party and wants to fill 11 cups from a 67-ounce bottle of pop. About how many ounces should she pour into each cup? **6 ounces**
2. Tracy studied 28 minutes every day for 4 days. About how long did she study in all? **120 minutes**
3. About how much does this lunch cost? $1.19 $0.39 $0.49 **$2.00**
4. The numbers below show how long Frank spent studying last week. Estimate how many minutes he studied for the whole week.
Monday: 23 minutes Tuesday: 37 minutes Wednesday: 38 minutes Thursday: 12 minutes **110 minutes**
5. One elephant at the zoo weighs 1,417 pounds and another one weighs 1,789 pounds. About how much heavier is the second elephant? **400 lbs.**
6. If Tim studied a total of 122 minutes over 4 days, about how long did he study each day? **30 minutes**
7. It's 549 miles to Dover and 345 miles to Albany. About how much closer is Albany? **200 miles**

Page 381

Rounding

Directions: Round off each number, then estimate the answer. You can use a calculator to find the exact answer.

Round to the nearest ten.	Estimate	Actual Answer
1. 86 + 9 =	9	9.56
2. 237 + 488 =	730	725
3. 49 × 11 =	500	539
4. 309 + 412 =	720	721
5. 625 − 218 =	410	407

Round to the nearest hundred.		
6. 790 − 70 =	700	720
7. 690 − 70 =	7	9.86
8. 2,177 − 955 =	1,200	1,222
9. 4,792 + 3,305 =	8,100	8,097
10. 5,210 × 90 =	520,00	468,900

Round to the nearest thousand.		
11. 4,078 + 2,093 =	6,000	6,171
12. 5,525 − 3,065 =	3,000	2,460
13. 6,047 − 2,991 =	2	2.02
14. 1,913 × 4,216 =	8,000,000	8,065,208
15. 7,227 + 8,449 =	15,000	15,676

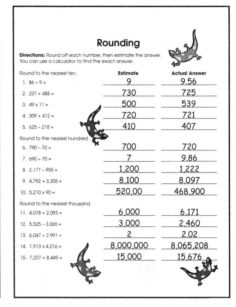

Page 382

Decimals

A **decimal** is a number that includes a period called a **decimal point**. The digits to the right of the decimal point are a value less than one.

one whole one tenth one hundredth

The place value chart below helps explain decimals.

hundreds	tens	ones	tenths	hundredths	thousandths
6	3	2 .	4		
	4	7 .	0	5	
		8 .	0	0	9

A decimal point is read as "and." The first number, 632.4, is read as "six hundred thirty-two and four tenths." The second number, 47.05, is read as "forty-seven and five hundredths." The third number, 8.009, is read as "eight and nine thousandths."

Directions: Write the decimals shown below. Two have been done for you.

1. **1.4**   2. **1.16**   3. **1.78**

4. six and five tenths **6.5**
5. twenty-two and nine tenths **22.9**
6. thirty-six and fourteen hundredths **36.14**
7. forty-seven hundredths **0.47**
8. one hundred six and four tenths **106.4**
9. seven and three hundredths **7.03**
10. one tenth less than 0.6 **0.5**
11. one hundredth less than 0.34 **0.33**
12. one tenth more than 0.2 **0.3**

Page 383

Adding and Subtracting Decimals

When adding or subtracting decimals, place the decimal points under each other. That way, you add tenths to tenths, for example, not tenths to hundredths. Add or subtract beginning on the right, as usual. Carry or borrow numbers in the same way. Adding 0 to the end of decimals does not change their value, but sometimes makes them easier to add and subtract.

> **Examples:**
> 39.40 + 6.81 = 46.21
> 0.064 + 0.470 = 0.534
> 3.56 − .09 = 3.47
> 6.83 − 2.14 = 4.69

Directions: Solve the following problems.

1. Write each set of numbers in a column and add them.
a. 2.56 + 0.6 + 76 = **79.16**
b. 93.5 + 23.06 + 1.45 = **118.01**
c. 3.23 + 91.34 + 0.85 = **95.42**
2. Write each pair of numbers in a column and subtract them.
A. 7.89 − 0.56 = **7.33** B. 34.56 − 6.04 = **28.52** C. 7.6 − 3.24 = **4.36**
3. In a relay race, Alice ran her part in 23.6 seconds. Cindy did hers in 24.7 seconds and Erin took 20.09 seconds. How many seconds did they take altogether? **68.39 seconds**
4. Although Erin ran her part in 20.09 seconds today, yesterday it took her 21.55 seconds. How much faster was she today? **1.46 seconds**
5. Add this grocery bill: potatoes—$3.49; milk—$2.09; bread—$0.99; apples—$2.30 **$8.87**
6. A yellow coat cost $47.59, and a blue coat cost $36.79. How much more did the yellow coat cost? **$10.80**
7. A box of Oat Boats cereal has 14.6 ounces. A box of Sugar Circles has 17.85 ounces. How much more cereal is in the Sugar Circles box? **3.25 ounces**
8. The Oat Boats cereal has 4.03 ounces of sugar in it. Sugar Circles cereal has only 3.76 ounces. How much more sugar is in a box of Oats Boats? **0.27 ounces**

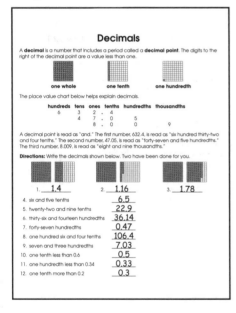

Page 384

Mulitplying Decimals by Two-Digit Numbers

To multiply by a 2-digit number, just repeat the same steps. In the example below, first multiply 4 times 9, 4 times 5 and 4 times 3. Then multiply 2 times 9, 2 times 5 and 2 times 3. You may want to place a 0 in the ones place to make sure this answer, 718, is one digit to the left. Now add 1,436 + 7,180 to get the final answer.

> **Example:**
> 359 × 24 = 6
> 359 × 24 = 36
> 359 × 24 = 1,436
> 359 × 24 = 1,436 − 80
> 359 × 24 = 1,436 − 180
> 359 × 24 = 1,436 + 7,180 = 8,616

When one or both numbers in a multiplication problem have decimals, check to see how many digits are right of the decimal. Then place the decimal point the same number of places to the left in the answer. Here's how the example above would change if it included decimals.

35.9 × 0.24 = 8.616
3.59 × 24 = 86.16

The first example has one digit to the right of the decimal in 35.9 and two more in 0.24, so the decimal point is placed three digits to the left in the answer: 8.616. The second example has two digits to the right of the decimal in 3.59 and none in 24, so the decimal point is placed two digits to the right in the answer: 86.16. (Notice that you do not have to line up the decimals in a multiplication problem.)

Directions: Solve the following problems.

1. Jennie wants to buy 3 T-shirts that cost $15.99 each. How much will they cost altogether? **$47.97**
2. Steve is making $3.75 an hour packing groceries. How much will he make in 8 hours? **$30**
3. Justin made 36 cookies and sold them all at the school carnival for $0.75 each. How much money did he make? **$27**
4. Last year, the carnival made $467. This year it made 2.3 times as much. How much money did the carnival make this year? **$1,074.10**
5. Troy's car will go 21.8 miles on a gallon of gasoline. His motorcycle will go 1.7 times as far. How far will his motorcycle travel on one gallon of gas? **37.06 miles**

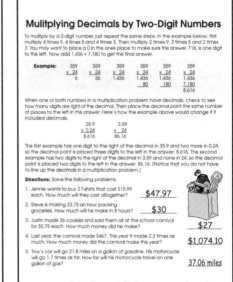

Page 385

Multiplying Decimals

In some problems, you may need to add zeros in order to place the decimal point correctly.

Examples:

0.34	0.0067	0.046
x 0.08	x 4	x 0.07
0.0272	0.0268	0.00322

Directions: Solve the following problems.

1. 0.15 x 0.02 = **0.003**
2. 0.67 x 0.08 = **0.0536**
3. 7.3 x 0.06 = **0.438**
4. 3.59 x 0.08 = **0.2872**
5. 0.061 x 0.014 = **0.000854**

6. 7.10 x 0.042 = **0.2982**
7. 5.05 x 0.08 = **0.404**
8. 8.75 x 0.067 = **0.58625**
9. 0.0647 x 0.3 = **0.01941**
10. 3.62 x 0.003 = **0.01086**

11. 1.07 x 0.05 = **0.0535**
12. 3.03 x 0.07 = **0.2121**
13. 0.02 x 0.02 = **0.0004**
14. 0.501 x 0.03 = **0.01503**
15. 0.321 x 0.09 = **0.02889**

16. The players and coaches gathered around for refreshments after the soccer game. Of the 30 people there, 0.50 of them had fruit juice and 0.30 of them had soft drinks. How many people had each type of drink?

fruit drink **15**
fruit juice **6**
soft drink **9**

Page 386

Dividing Decimals by Two-Digit Numbers

Dividing by a 2-digit divisor (34 in the example below) is very similar to dividing by a 1-digit divisor. In this example, 34 will divide into 78 twice. Then multiply 34 x 2 to get 68. Subtract 68 from 78. The answer is 10, which is smaller than the divisor, so 2 was the right number. Now bring down the next 8. 34 goes into 108 three times. Continue dividing as with a 1-digit divisor.

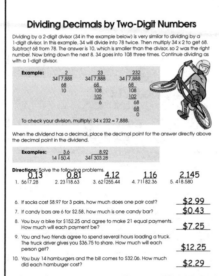

Example:
$$34\overline{)7,888}$$

To check your division, multiply: 34 x 232 = 7,888.

When the dividend has a decimal, place the decimal point for the answer directly above the decimal point in the dividend.

Examples:
$$14\overline{)50.4} = 3.6 \qquad 34\overline{)303.28} = 8.92$$

Directions: Solve the following problems.

1. 56)7.28 = **0.13**
2. 23)18.63 = **0.81**
3. 62)255.44 = **4.12**
4. 71)82.36 = **1.16**
5. 4)8.580 = **2.145**

6. If socks cost $8.97 for 3 pairs, how much does one pair cost? **$2.99**
7. If candy bars are 6 for $2.58, how much is one candy bar? **$0.43**
8. You buy a bike for $152.25 and agree to make 21 equal payments. How much will each payment be? **$7.25**
9. You and two friends agree to spend several hours loading a truck. The truck driver gives you $36.75 to share. How much will each person get? **$12.25**
10. You buy 14 hamburgers and the bill comes to $32.06. How much did each hamburger cost? **$2.29**

Page 387

Dividing With Zeros

Sometimes you have a remainder in division problems. You can add a decimal point and zeros to the dividend and keep dividing until you have the answer.

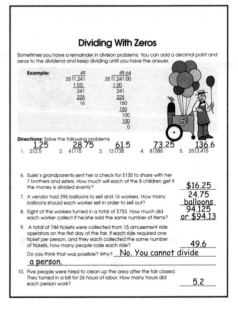

Example:
$$25\overline{)1,241} \qquad 25\overline{)1,241.00} = 49.64$$

Directions: Solve the following problems.

1. 2)2.5 = **1.25**
2. 4)115 = **28.75**
3. 12)738 = **61.5**
4. 8)586 = **73.25**
5. 25)3,415 = **136.6**

6. Susie's grandparents sent her a check for $130 to share with her 7 brothers and sisters. How much will each of the 8 children get if the money is divided evenly? **$16.25**
7. A vendor had 396 balloons to sell and 16 workers. How many balloons should each worker sell in order to sell out? **24.75 balloons**
8. Eight of the workers turned in a total of $753. How much did each worker collect if he/she sold the same number of items? **94.125 or $94.13**
9. A total of 744 tickets were collected from 15 amusement ride operators on the first day of the fair. If each ride required one ticket per person, and they each collected the same number of tickets, how many people rode each ride? **49.6**
Do you think that was possible? Why? **No. You cannot divide a person.**
10. Five people were hired to clean up the area after the fair closed. They turned in a bill for 26 hours of labor. How many hours did each person work? **5.2**

Page 388

Dividing Decimals by Decimals

When a divisor has a decimal, eliminate it before dividing. If there is one digit right of the decimal in the divisor, multiply the divisor and dividend by 10. If there are two digits right of the decimal in the divisor, multiply the divisor and dividend by 100.

Multiply the divisor and dividend by the same number whether or not the dividend has a decimal. The goal is to have a divisor with no decimal.

Examples:
$$2.3\overline{)10.15} \times 10 = 23\overline{)890} \qquad 4.11\overline{)67.7} \times 100 = 411\overline{)6,770}$$
$$4.9\overline{)35.67} \times 10 = 49\overline{)356.7} \qquad 0.34\overline{)789} \times 100 = 34\overline{)78,900}$$

After removing the decimal from the divisor, work the problem in the usual way.

Directions: Solve the following problems.

1. 3.5)10.15 = **2.9**
2. 6.7)415.4 = **62**
3. 0.21)924 = **4,400**
4. 73)50.37 = **0.69**

5. The body can burn only 0.00015 of an ounce of alcohol an hour. If an average-sized person has 1 drink, his/her blood alcohol concentration (BAC) is 0.0003. How many hours will it take his/her body to remove that much alcohol from the blood? **2 hrs.**

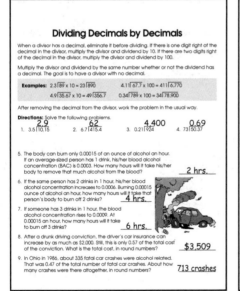

6. If the same person has 2 drinks in 1 hour, his/her blood alcohol concentration increases to 0.0006. Burning 0.00015 ounce of alcohol an hour, how many hours will it take that person's body to burn off 2 drinks? **4 hrs.**
7. If someone has 3 drinks in 1 hour, the blood alcohol concentration rises to 0.0009. At 0.00015 an hour, how many hours will it take to burn off 3 drinks? **6 hrs.**
8. After a drunk driving conviction, the driver's car insurance can increase by as much as $2,000. Still, this is only 0.57 of the total cost of the conviction. What is the total cost, in round numbers? **$3,509**
9. In Ohio in 1986, about 335 fatal car crashes were alcohol related. That was 0.47 of the total number of fatal car crashes. About how many crashes were there altogether, in round numbers? **713 crashes**

Page 389

Decimals and Fractions

A **fraction** is a number that names part of something. The top number in a fraction is called the **numerator**. The bottom number is called the **denominator**. Since a decimal also names part of a whole number, every decimal can also be written as a fraction. For example, 0.1 is read as "one tenth", and can be written $\frac{1}{10}$. The decimal 0.56 is read as "fifty-six hundredths" and can also be written $\frac{56}{100}$.

Examples:
$$0.7 = \frac{7}{10} \quad 0.34 = \frac{34}{100} \quad 0.761 = \frac{761}{1,000} \quad \frac{5}{10} = 0.5 \quad \frac{58}{100} = 0.58 \quad \frac{729}{1,000} = 0.729$$

Even a fraction that doesn't have 10, 100 or 1,000 as the denominator can be written as a decimal. Sometimes you can multiply both the numerator and denominator by a certain number so the denominator is 10, 100 or 1,000. (You can't just multiply the denominator. That would change the amount of the fraction.)

Examples:
$$\frac{3 \times 2}{5 \times 2} = \frac{6}{10} = 0.6 \qquad \frac{4 \times 4}{25 \times 4} = \frac{16}{100} = 0.16$$

Other times, divide the numerator by the denominator.

Examples:
$$\frac{3}{4} = 4\overline{)3.00} = 0.75 \qquad \frac{5}{8} = 8\overline{)5.000} = 0.625$$

Directions: Follow the instructions below.
1. For each square, write a decimal and a fraction to show the part that is colored. The first one has been done for you.

a. $\frac{25}{100}$ 0.25
b. $\frac{60}{100}$ 0.60
c. $\frac{32}{100}$ 0.32

2. Change these decimals to fractions.
a. 0.6 = $\frac{6}{10}$
b. 0.54 = $\frac{54}{100}$
c. 0.751 = $\frac{751}{1,000}$
d. 0.73 = $\frac{73}{100}$
e. 0.592 = $\frac{592}{1,000}$
f. 0.2 = $\frac{2}{10}$

3. Change these fractions to decimals. If necessary, round off the decimals to the nearest hundredth.
a. $\frac{3}{10}$ = 0.3
b. $\frac{89}{100}$ = 0.89
c. $\frac{473}{1,000}$ = 0.473
d. $\frac{4}{5}$ = 0.8
e. $\frac{35}{50}$ = 0.7
f. $\frac{7}{9}$ = 0.78
g. $\frac{1}{3}$ = 0.33
h. $\frac{23}{77}$ = 0.30
i. $\frac{12}{63}$ = 0.19
j. $\frac{4}{16}$ = 0.25

Page 390

Equivalent Fractions and the Lowest Term

Equivalent fractions name the same amount. For example, $\frac{1}{2}$, $\frac{3}{6}$, and $\frac{5}{10}$ are exactly the same amount. They all mean half of something. (And they are all written as the same decimal: 0.5.) To find an equivalent fraction, multiply the numerator and denominator of any fraction by the same number.

Examples: $\frac{3 \times 3}{4 \times 3} = \frac{9}{12} \quad \frac{9 \times 4}{12 \times 4} = \frac{36}{48}$ Thus, $\frac{3}{4}$, $\frac{9}{12}$ and $\frac{36}{48}$ are all equivalent fractions.

Most of the time, we want fractions in their lowest terms. It's easier to work with $\frac{3}{4}$ than $\frac{36}{48}$. To find a fraction's lowest term, instead of multiplying both parts of a fraction by the same number, divide.

Examples: $\frac{36 \div 12}{48 \div 12} = \frac{3}{4}$ The lowest term for $\frac{36}{48}$ is $\frac{3}{4}$.

If the numerator and denominator in a fraction can't be divided by any number, the fraction is in its lowest term. The fractions below are in their lowest terms.

Examples: $\frac{34}{61} \quad \frac{3}{5} \quad \frac{7}{9} \quad \frac{53}{90} \quad \frac{78}{83} \quad \frac{3}{8}$

Directions: Follow the instructions below.

1. Write two equivalent fractions for each fraction. Make sure you multiply the numerator and denominator by the same number. The first one is done for you.

a. $\frac{1 \times 3}{2 \times 3} = \frac{3}{6}$ $\frac{1 \times 4}{2 \times 4} = \frac{4}{8}$
b. $\frac{2 \times 2}{3 \times 2} = \frac{4}{6}$ $\frac{2 \times 3}{3 \times 3} = \frac{6}{9}$
c. $\frac{3 \times 2}{5 \times 2} = \frac{6}{10}$ $\frac{3 \times 3}{5 \times 3} = \frac{9}{15}$
d. $\frac{8 \times 2}{9 \times 2} = \frac{16}{18}$ $\frac{8 \times 3}{9 \times 3} = \frac{24}{27}$

2. Find the lowest terms for each fraction. Make sure your answers can't be divided by any other numbers. The first one has been done for you.

a. $\frac{2 \div 2}{36 \div 2} = \frac{1}{18}$
b. $\frac{12 \div 1}{25 \div 1} = \frac{12}{25}$
c. $\frac{12 \div 4}{16 \div 4} = \frac{3}{4}$
d. $\frac{3 \div 3}{9 \div 3} = \frac{1}{3}$
e. $\frac{25 \div 5}{45 \div 5} = \frac{5}{9}$
f. $\frac{11 \div 11}{44 \div 11} = \frac{1}{4}$

Page 391

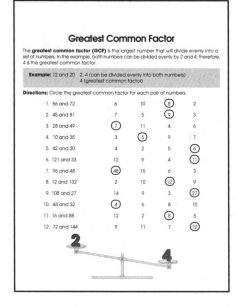

Greatest Common Factor

The **greatest common factor (GCF)** is the largest number that will divide evenly into a set of numbers. In the example, both numbers can be divided evenly by 2 and 4; therefore, 4 is the greatest common factor.

Example: 12 and 20   2, 4 (can be divided evenly into both numbers)
4 (greatest common factor)

Directions: Circle the greatest common factor for each pair of numbers.

1. 56 and 72	6	10	(8)	2
2. 45 and 81	7	5	(9)	3
3. 28 and 49	(7)	11	4	6
4. 10 and 35	3	(5)	9	7
5. 42 and 30	4	2	5	(6)
6. 121 and 33	12	9	4	(11)
7. 96 and 48	(48)	15	6	3
8. 12 and 132	2	10	(12)	9
9. 108 and 27	14	9	3	(27)
10. 44 and 32	(4)	6	8	10
11. 16 and 88	12	2	(8)	5
12. 72 and 144	9	11	7	(72)

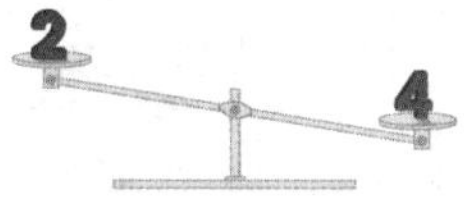

Page 392

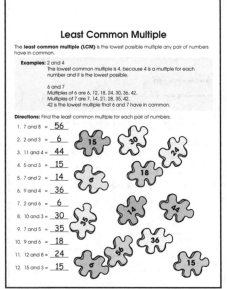

Least Common Multiple

The **least common multiple (LCM)** is the lowest possible multiple any pair of numbers have in common.

Examples: 2 and 4
The lowest common multiple is 4, because 4 is a multiple for each number and it is the lowest possible.

6 and 7
Multiples of 6 are 6, 12, 18, 24, 30, 36, 42.
Multiples of 7 are 7, 14, 21, 28, 35, 42.
42 is the lowest multiple that 6 and 7 have in common.

Directions: Find the least common multiple for each pair of numbers.

1. 7 and 8 = 56
2. 2 and 3 = 6
3. 11 and 4 = 44
4. 5 and 3 = 15
5. 7 and 2 = 14
6. 9 and 4 = 36
7. 2 and 6 = 6
8. 10 and 3 = 30
9. 7 and 5 = 35
10. 9 and 6 = 18
11. 12 and 8 = 24
12. 15 and 3 = 15

Page 393

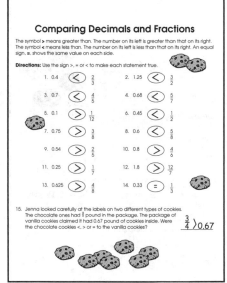

Comparing Decimals and Fractions

The symbol **>** means greater than. The number on its left is greater than that on its right. The symbol **<** means less than. The number on its left is less than that on its right. An equal sign, **=**, shows the same value on each side.

Directions: Use the sign >, = or < to make each statement true.

1. 0.4 (<) $\frac{2}{3}$
2. 1.25 (<) $\frac{3}{2}$
3. 0.7 (<) $\frac{4}{5}$
4. 0.68 (<) $\frac{5}{7}$
5. 0.1 (>) $\frac{1}{12}$
6. 0.45 (<) $\frac{1}{2}$
7. 0.75 (>) $\frac{3}{8}$
8. 0.6 (<) $\frac{5}{8}$
9. 0.54 (>) $\frac{2}{5}$
10. 0.8 (>) $\frac{4}{6}$
11. 0.25 (>) $\frac{1}{7}$
12. 1.8 (>) $\frac{12}{7}$
13. 0.625 (>) $\frac{4}{8}$
14. 0.33 (=) $\frac{1}{3}$

15. Jenna looked carefully at the labels on two different types of cookies. The chocolate ones had $\frac{3}{4}$ pound in the package. The package of vanilla cookies claimed it had 0.67 pound of cookies inside. Were the chocolate cookies <, > or = to the vanilla cookies? $\frac{3}{4}$ > 0.67

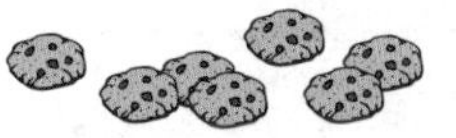

Page 394

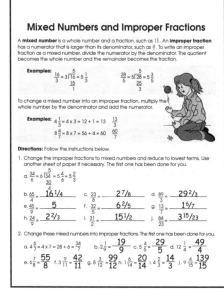

Mixed Numbers and Improper Fractions

A **mixed number** is a whole number and a fraction, such as $1\frac{3}{4}$. An **improper fraction** has a numerator that is larger than its denominator, such as $\frac{7}{4}$. To write an improper fraction as a mixed number, divide the numerator by the denominator. The quotient becomes the whole number and the remainder becomes the fraction.

Examples: $\frac{16}{3} = 3\overline{)16} = 5\frac{1}{3}$ $\frac{28}{5} = 5\overline{)28} = 5\frac{3}{5}$

To change a mixed number into an improper fraction, multiply the whole number by the denominator and add the numerator.

Examples: $4\frac{1}{3} = 4 \times 3 = 12 + 1 = 13 \quad \frac{13}{3}$
$8\frac{4}{7} = 8 \times 7 = 56 + 4 = 60 \quad \frac{60}{7}$

Directions: Follow the instructions below.

1. Change the improper fractions to mixed numbers and reduce to lowest terms. Use another sheet of paper if necessary. The first one has been done for you.

a. $\frac{34}{6} = 6\overline{)34} = 5\frac{4}{6} = 5\frac{2}{3}$
b. $\frac{65}{4}$ = $16\frac{1}{4}$ c. $\frac{23}{8}$ = $2\frac{7}{8}$ d. $\frac{89}{3}$ = $29\frac{2}{3}$
e. $\frac{45}{9}$ = 5   f. $\frac{32}{5}$ = $6\frac{2}{5}$ g. $\frac{13}{7}$ = $1\frac{6}{7}$
h. $\frac{24}{9}$ = $2\frac{2}{3}$ i. $\frac{31}{2}$ = $15\frac{1}{2}$ j. $\frac{84}{23}$ = $3\frac{15}{23}$

2. Change these mixed numbers into improper fractions. The first one has been done for you.

a. $4\frac{6}{7} = 4 \times 7 = 28 + 6 = \frac{34}{7}$ b. $2\frac{1}{9} = \frac{19}{9}$ c. $5\frac{4}{5} = \frac{29}{5}$ d. $12\frac{1}{4} = \frac{49}{4}$
e. $6\frac{7}{8} = \frac{55}{8}$ f. $3\frac{9}{11} = \frac{42}{11}$ g. $8\frac{3}{12} = \frac{99}{12}$ h. $1\frac{6}{14} = \frac{20}{14}$ i. $4\frac{2}{3} = \frac{14}{3}$ j. $9\frac{4}{15} = \frac{139}{15}$

Page 395

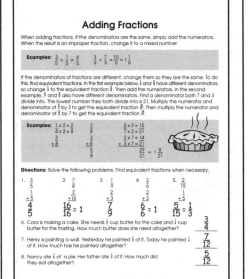

Adding Fractions

When adding fractions, if the denominators are the same, simply add the numerators. When the result is an improper fraction, change it to a mixed number.

Examples: $\frac{3}{5} + \frac{1}{5} = \frac{4}{5}$ $\frac{3}{9} + \frac{7}{9} = \frac{10}{9} = 1\frac{1}{9}$

If the denominators of fractions are different, change them so they are the same. To do this, find equivalent fractions. In the first example below, $\frac{1}{4}$ and $\frac{3}{8}$ have different denominators, so change $\frac{1}{4}$ to the equivalent fraction $\frac{2}{8}$. Then add the numerators. In the second example, $\frac{5}{7}$ and $\frac{2}{3}$ also have different denominators. Find a denominator both 7 and 3 divide into. The lowest number they both divide into is 21. Multiply the numerator and denominator of $\frac{5}{7}$ by 3 to get the equivalent fraction $\frac{15}{21}$. Then multiply the numerator and denominator of $\frac{2}{3}$ by 7 to get the equivalent fraction $\frac{14}{21}$.

Examples: $\frac{1 \times 2}{4 \times 2} = \frac{2}{8}$; $\frac{2}{8} + \frac{3}{8} = \frac{5}{8}$ $\frac{5 \times 3}{7 \times 3} = \frac{15}{21}$; $\frac{2 \times 7}{3 \times 7} = \frac{14}{21}$; $\frac{15}{21} + \frac{14}{21} = \frac{29}{21} = 1\frac{8}{21}$

Directions: Solve the following problems. Find equivalent fractions when necessary.

1. $\frac{3}{5} + \frac{1}{5} = \frac{4}{5}$
2. $\frac{7}{8} + \frac{2}{16} = \frac{16}{16} = 1$
3. $\frac{1}{9} + \frac{2}{3} = \frac{7}{9}$
4. $\frac{2}{6} + \frac{2}{3} = \frac{6}{6} = 1$
5. $\frac{2}{15} + \frac{1}{5} = \frac{5}{15} = \frac{1}{3}$

6. Cora is making a cake. She needs $\frac{1}{2}$ cup butter for the frosting and $\frac{1}{4}$ cup butter for the frosting. How much butter does she need altogether? $\frac{3}{4}$

7. Henry is painting a wall. Yesterday he painted $\frac{1}{3}$ of it. Today he painted $\frac{1}{4}$ of it. How much has he painted altogether? $\frac{7}{12}$

8. Nancy ate $\frac{1}{6}$ of a pie. Her father ate $\frac{1}{4}$ of it. How much did they eat altogether? $\frac{5}{12}$

Page 396

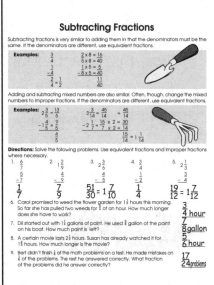

Subtracting Fractions

Subtracting fractions is very similar to adding them in that the denominators must be the same. If the denominators are different, use equivalent fractions.

Examples: $\frac{3}{4} - \frac{1}{4} = \frac{2}{4} = \frac{1}{2}$ $\frac{2 \times 8}{5 \times 8} = \frac{16}{40}$; $\frac{1 \times 5}{8 \times 5} = \frac{5}{40}$; $\frac{16}{40} - \frac{5}{40} = \frac{11}{40}$

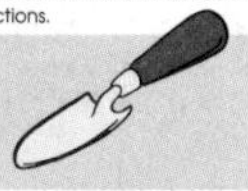

Adding and subtracting mixed numbers are also similar. Often, though, change the mixed numbers to improper fractions. If the denominators are different, use equivalent fractions.

Examples: $2\frac{3}{5} = \frac{13}{5}$; $-1\frac{4}{5} = \frac{9}{5}$; $\frac{4}{5}$ $3\frac{3}{14} = \frac{45}{14} = \frac{45}{14}$; $-2\frac{1}{7} = \frac{15}{7} \times 2 = \frac{30}{14}$; $\frac{15}{14} = 1\frac{1}{14}$

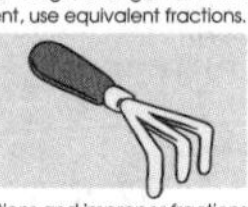

Directions: Solve the following problems. Use equivalent fractions and improper fractions where necessary.

1. $\frac{6}{7} - \frac{5}{7} = \frac{1}{7}$
2. $1\frac{2}{9} - \frac{4}{9} = \frac{7}{9}$
3. $2\frac{3}{6} - \frac{4}{5} = \frac{51}{30} = 1\frac{7}{10}$
4. $\frac{3}{4} - \frac{1}{2} = \frac{1}{4}$
5. $2\frac{1}{3} - \frac{3}{4} = \frac{19}{12} = 1\frac{7}{12}$

6. Carol promised to weed the flower garden for $1\frac{1}{2}$ hours this morning. So far she has pulled two weeds for $\frac{3}{4}$ of an hour. How much longer does she have to work? $\frac{3}{4}$ hour

7. Dil started out with $1\frac{1}{4}$ gallons of paint. He used $\frac{3}{8}$ gallon of the paint on his boat. How much paint is left? $\frac{7}{8}$ gallon

8. A certain movie lasts $2\frac{1}{2}$ hours. Susan has already watched it for $1\frac{2}{3}$ hours. How much longer is the movie? $\frac{5}{6}$ hour

9. Bert didn't finish $\frac{1}{8}$ of the math problems on a test. He made mistakes on $\frac{1}{6}$ of the problems. The rest he answered correctly. What fraction of the problems did he answer correctly? $\frac{17}{24}$ problems

Page 397

Multiplying Fractions

To multiply two fractions, multiply the numerators and then multiply the denominators. If necessary, change the answer to its lowest term.

Examples: $\frac{3}{4} \times \frac{2}{3} = \frac{6}{12} = \frac{1}{2}$ $\frac{1}{6} \times \frac{4}{5} = \frac{4}{40} = \frac{1}{10}$

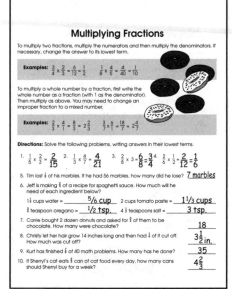

To multiply a whole number by a fraction, first write the whole number as a fraction (with 1 as the denominator). Then multiply as above. You may need to change an improper fraction to a mixed number.

Examples: $\frac{2}{3} \times \frac{4}{1} = \frac{8}{3} = 2\frac{2}{3}$ $\frac{3}{7} \times \frac{7}{1} = \frac{18}{7} = 2\frac{4}{7}$

Directions: Solve the following problems, writing answers in their lowest terms.

1. $\frac{1}{5} \times \frac{2}{3} = \frac{2}{15}$ 2. $\frac{1}{3} \times \frac{4}{7} = \frac{4}{21}$ 3. $\frac{2}{3} \times 3 = \frac{6}{3} = 2$ 4. $\frac{3}{4} \times \frac{1}{2} = \frac{2}{12} = \frac{1}{6}$

5. Tim lost $\frac{1}{8}$ of his marbles. If he had 56 marbles, how many did he lose? **7 marbles**

6. Jeff is making $\frac{5}{6}$ of a recipe for spaghetti sauce. How much will he need of each ingredient below?

$1\frac{1}{2}$ cups water = **$\frac{5}{6}$ cup** 2 cups tomato paste = **$1\frac{1}{3}$ cups**

$\frac{3}{5}$ teaspoon oregano = **$\frac{1}{2}$ tsp.** $4\frac{1}{2}$ teaspoons salt = **3 tsp.**

7. Carrie bought 2 dozen donuts and asked for $\frac{3}{4}$ of them to be chocolate. How many were chocolate? **18**

8. Christy let her hair grow 14 inches long and then had $\frac{1}{4}$ of it cut off. How much was cut off? **$3\frac{1}{2}$ in.**

9. Kurt has finished $\frac{7}{8}$ of 40 math problems. How many has he done? **35**

10. If Sherryl's cat eats $\frac{2}{3}$ can of cat food every day, how many cans should Sherryl buy for a week? **$4\frac{2}{3}$**

Page 398

Dividing Fractions

Reciprocals are two fractions that, when multiplied together, make 1. To divide a fraction by a fraction, turn one of the fractions upside down and multiply. The upside-down fraction is a reciprocal of its original fraction. If you multiply a fraction by its reciprocal, you always get 1.

Examples of reciprocals: $\frac{2}{3} \times \frac{3}{2} = \frac{6}{6} = 1$ $\frac{9}{11} \times \frac{11}{9} = \frac{99}{99} = 1$

Examples of dividing by fractions: $\frac{1}{2} \div \frac{2}{3} = \frac{1}{2} \times \frac{3}{2} = \frac{3}{4}$ $\frac{2}{5} \div \frac{5}{7} = \frac{2}{5} \times \frac{7}{5} = \frac{14}{10} = 1\frac{2}{5}$

To divide a whole number by a fraction, first write the whole number as a fraction (with a denominator of 1). (Write a mixed number as an improper fraction.) Then finish the problem as explained above.

Examples: $4 \div \frac{2}{1} = \frac{4}{1} \times \frac{6}{2} = \frac{24}{2} = 12$ $3\frac{1}{2} \div \frac{2}{5} = \frac{7}{2} \times \frac{5}{2} = \frac{35}{4} = 8\frac{3}{4}$

Directions: Solve the following problems, writing answers in their lowest terms. Change any improper fractions to mixed numbers.

1. $\frac{1}{3} \div \frac{2}{5} = \frac{5}{6}$ 2. $\frac{6}{7} \div \frac{1}{3} = \frac{18}{7} = 2\frac{4}{7}$ 3. $3 \div \frac{1}{4} = \frac{12}{1} = 4$ 4. $1\frac{1}{2} \div \frac{2}{3} = \frac{3}{8}$

5. Judy has 8 candy bars. She wants to give $\frac{1}{3}$ of a candy bar to everyone in her class. Does she have enough for all 24 students? **Yes**

6. A big jar of glue holds $3\frac{1}{2}$ cups. How many little containers that hold $\frac{1}{4}$ cup each can you fill? **14 containers**

7. A container holds 27 ounces of ice cream. How many $4\frac{1}{2}$-ounce servings is that? **6 servings**

8. It takes $2\frac{1}{2}$ teaspoons of powdered mix to make 1 cup of hot chocolate. How many cups can you make with 45 teaspoons of mix? **18 cups**

9. Each cup of hot chocolate also takes $\frac{2}{3}$ cup of milk. How many cups of hot chocolate can you make with 12 cups of milk? **18 cups**

Page 399

Review

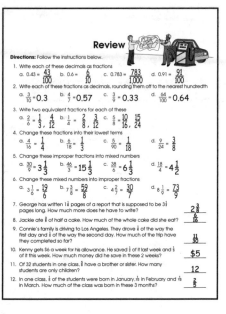

Directions: Follow the instructions below.

1. Write each of these decimals as fractions.
   a. $0.43 = \frac{43}{100}$ b. $0.6 = \frac{6}{10}$ c. $0.783 = \frac{783}{1,000}$ d. $0.91 = \frac{91}{100}$

2. Write each of these fractions as decimals, rounding them off to the nearest hundredth
   a. $\frac{3}{10} = 0.3$ b. $\frac{4}{7} = 0.57$ c. $\frac{3}{9} = 0.33$ d. $\frac{64}{100} = 0.64$

3. Write two equivalent fractions for each of these
   a. $\frac{2}{6} = \frac{1}{3}, \frac{4}{12}$ b. $\frac{1}{4} = \frac{2}{8}, \frac{3}{12}$ c. $\frac{5}{8} = \frac{10}{16}, \frac{15}{24}$

4. Change these fractions into their lowest terms
   a. $\frac{4}{16} = \frac{1}{4}$ b. $\frac{6}{24} = \frac{1}{4}$ c. $\frac{5}{90} = \frac{1}{18}$ d. $\frac{9}{24} = \frac{3}{8}$

5. Change these improper fractions into mixed numbers
   a. $\frac{30}{9} = 3\frac{3}{9}$ b. $\frac{46}{3} = 15\frac{1}{3}$ c. $\frac{38}{6} = 6\frac{1}{3}$ d. $\frac{18}{4} = 4\frac{1}{2}$

6. Change these mixed numbers into improper fractions
   a. $3\frac{1}{6} = \frac{19}{6}$ b. $7\frac{3}{8} = \frac{59}{8}$ c. $4\frac{2}{7} = \frac{30}{7}$ d. $8\frac{1}{9} = \frac{73}{9}$

7. George has written $1\frac{1}{8}$ pages of a report that is supposed to be $3\frac{3}{8}$ pages long. How much more does he have to write? **$2\frac{3}{8}$**

8. Jackie ate $\frac{3}{8}$ of half a cake. How much of the whole cake did she eat? **$\frac{3}{16}$**

9. Connie's family is driving to Los Angeles. They drove $\frac{1}{4}$ of the way the first day and $\frac{3}{8}$ of the way the second day. How much of the trip have they completed so far? **$\frac{11}{18}$**

10. Kenny gets $6 a week for his allowance. He saved $\frac{1}{3}$ of it last week and $\frac{1}{2}$ of it this week. How much money did he save in these 2 weeks? **$5**

11. Of 32 students in one class, $\frac{3}{8}$ have a brother or sister. How many students are only children? **12**

12. In one class, $\frac{1}{4}$ of the students were born in January, $\frac{1}{16}$ in February and $\frac{1}{16}$ in March. How much of the class was born in these 3 months? **$\frac{2}{5}$**

Page 400

Review

Directions: Follow the instructions below.

Add.

1. $\frac{4}{16} + \frac{5}{8} = \frac{14}{16} = \frac{7}{8}$ 2. $\frac{1}{3} + \frac{1}{6} = \frac{3}{6} = \frac{1}{2}$ 3. $\frac{2}{10} + \frac{4}{5} = \frac{10}{10} = 1$ 4. $\frac{3}{5} + \frac{9}{10} = \frac{15}{10} = 1\frac{1}{2}$

Subtract.

1. $\frac{15}{2} - \frac{3}{9} = \frac{9}{18} = 1\frac{2}{1}$ 2. $\frac{3}{4} - \frac{1}{8} = \frac{5}{8}$ 3. $\frac{4}{7} - \frac{2}{14} = \frac{6}{14} = \frac{3}{7}$ 4. $\frac{3}{5} - \frac{1}{10} = \frac{5}{10} = \frac{1}{2}$

Multiply.

1. $\frac{1}{2} \times \frac{4}{16} = \frac{4}{32} = \frac{1}{8}$ 2. $\frac{1}{3} \times \frac{4}{9} = \frac{4}{27}$ 3. $\frac{5}{12} \times \frac{1}{4} = \frac{5}{48}$ 4. $\frac{3}{16} \times \frac{3}{4} = \frac{9}{64}$

Divide.

1. $\frac{3}{5} \div \frac{1}{3} = \frac{9}{5} = 4\frac{2}{5}$ 2. $4 \div \frac{1}{2} = \frac{8}{1} = 8$ 3. $\frac{1}{4} \div \frac{1}{3} = \frac{3}{4}$ 4. $3\frac{3}{4} \div \frac{1}{3} = \frac{45}{4} = 11\frac{1}{4}$

Write >, < or = to make the statements true.

1. $0.5 \; < \; \frac{5}{8}$ 2. $0.8 \; = \; \frac{4}{5}$ 3. $0.35 \; < \; \frac{4}{5}$ 4. $1.3 \; > \; \frac{7}{8}$

Page 401

Trial and Error

Often, the quickest way to solve a problem is to make a logical guess and test it to see if it works. The first guess, or trial, will probably not be the correct answer—but it should help figure out a better, more reasonable guess.

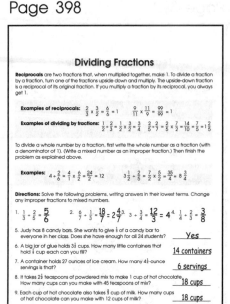

Directions: Use trial and error to find the solutions to these problems.

1. Mr. McFerrson is between 30 and 50 years old. The sum of the digits in his age is 11. His age is an even number. How old is Mr. McFerrson?

   He is 38 years old.

2. The key for number 5 does not work on Rusty's calculator. How can he use his broken calculator to subtract 108 from 351?

   Sample answer: Add 10 to each number and subtract 118 from 361, equalling 243.

3. Tasha likes to swim a certain number of miles each day for 3 days straight. Then, she increases her mileage by 1 for the next 3 days, and so on. Over a nine day period, Tasha swims a total of 27 miles. She swims equal mileage Monday, Tuesday and Wednesday. She swims another amount on Thursday, Friday and Saturday. She swims yet a third amount on Sunday, Monday and Tuesday. How many miles does Tasha swim each day?

   2 Monday **2** Tuesday **2** Wednesday
   3 Thursday **3** Friday **3** Saturday
   4 Sunday **4** Monday **4** Tuesday

Page 402

Trial and Error

Directions: Use trial and error to complete each diagram so all the equations work.

Example:

$6 , 7 \;\Rightarrow\; \frac{+}{\times} \; \frac{13}{42}$

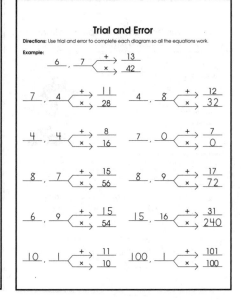

$7 , 4 \;\Rightarrow\; \frac{+}{\times} \; \frac{11}{28}$ $4 , 8 \;\Rightarrow\; \frac{+}{\times} \; \frac{12}{32}$

$4 , 4 \;\Rightarrow\; \frac{+}{\times} \; \frac{8}{16}$ $7 , 0 \;\Rightarrow\; \frac{+}{\times} \; \frac{7}{0}$

$8 , 7 \;\Rightarrow\; \frac{+}{\times} \; \frac{15}{56}$ $8 , 9 \;\Rightarrow\; \frac{+}{\times} \; \frac{17}{72}$

$6 , 9 \;\Rightarrow\; \frac{+}{\times} \; \frac{15}{54}$ $15 , 16 \;\Rightarrow\; \frac{+}{\times} \; \frac{31}{240}$

$10 , 1 \;\Rightarrow\; \frac{+}{\times} \; \frac{11}{10}$ $100 , 1 \;\Rightarrow\; \frac{+}{\times} \; \frac{101}{100}$

ANSWER KEY

Page 403

Choosing a Method

This table explains different methods of computation that can be used to solve a problem.

Method		
Mental Math	– Calculating in your head.	– Use with small numbers, memorized facts and multiples of tens, hundreds, thousands, and so on.
Objects/Diagram	– Drawing or using an object to represent the problem.	– Use to model the situation.
Pencil and Paper	– Calculating the answer on paper.	– Use when a calculator is not available and the problem is too difficult to solve mentally.
Calculator	– Using a calculator or computer to find the solution.	– Use with large numbers or for a quick answer.
Trial and Error	– Making a guess at the answer and trying to see if it works.	– Use when unsure what to do or if none of the methods above work.

Directions: Circle the method of computation that seems best for solving each problem. Then solve the problem.

1. The School Days Fun Fair has 38 booths and 23 games. How many booths and games total are in the fair?
   - (Paper and Pencil)   Answer: __61__
   - Objects/Diagram

2. The lemonade stand was stocked with 230 cups. On the first day, 147 drinks were sold. How many cups were left?
   - Objects/Diagram   Answer: __83__
   - (Paper and Pencil)

3. There are 3 cars in the tram to transport people from the parking lot to the fair. Each car can seat 9 people. How many people can ride the tram at one time?
   - (Objects/Diagram)   Answer: __27__
   - Trial and Error

Page 404

Choosing a Method

Directions: Write what method you will use for each problem. Then find the answer.

1. Jenna receives an allowance of $3.50 a week. This week, her mother pays her in nickels, dimes and quarters. She received more dimes ~~coin~~ did her mom use to pay her?

   Answers may include:

   Method: __Trial and Error__
   Answer: __8 quarters, 13 dimes, 4 nickels__

2. You are buying your lunch at school. There are 4 people in front of you and 7 people behind you. How many people are standing in line? (Hint: it's not 11 people.)
   Method: __mental math__
   Answer: __12 people__

3. A runner can run 1 mile in 12 minutes. He ran for 30 minutes today. How far did he run?
   Method: __calculator__
   Answer: __2.5 miles__

4. A family of four goes out to dinner. They decide to order a 16-cut pizza. Each person likes something different on his/her pizza, but each will eat equal amounts. Maria likes pepperoni and sausage, Tony likes ham and pineapple, Mom likes cheese only and Dad likes mushrooms. Maria is allergic to mushrooms, so her slices can't be next to Dad's. Mom detests pineapple, so her slices can't be next to Tony's. How will the restaurant arrange their pizza?
   Method: __objects/diagram__
   Answer: __starting at top of pizza: Dad's, Mom's, Maria's, Tony's__

5. The Petting Zoo has 72 animals in aquariums, 32 animals in cages and 57 animals fenced in. How many animals does the Petting Zoo have?
   Method: __pencil and paper__
   Answer: __161__

Page 405

Multi-Step Problems

Some problems take more than one step to solve. First, plan each step needed to find the solution. Then solve each part to find the answer.

Example: Tickets for a bargain matinee cost $4 for adults and $3 for children. How much would tickets cost for a family of 2 adults and 3 children?

Step 1: Find the cost of the adults' tickets.

Step 2: Find the cost of the children's tickets.

Step 3: Add to find the sum of the tickets.

2 adults	×	$4 each ticket	=	$8 total
3 children	×	$3 each ticket	=	$9 total
$8 adults	+	$9 children	=	$17 total

The tickets cost $17 total.

Directions: Write the operations you will use to solve each problem. Then find the answer.

Operations: __1. Add the miles they've gone; 2. Subtract from total miles.__
Answer: __29__

Operations: __1. Devise a formula: number of mi. ÷ mph = time; 2. Add the time totals; 3. Convert to hours.__
Answer: __3 hrs. and 5 min.__

Operations: __1. Find total cost of raspberries; 2. Add to the cost of blueberries and strawberries.__
Answer: __$5.89__

Page 406

Hidden Questions

When solving a story problem, you may find that some information you want is not stated in the problem. You must ask yourself what information you need and decide how you can use the data in the problem to find this information. The problem contains a hidden question to find before you can solve it.

Example: Chris and his mother are building a birdhouse. He buys 4 pieces of wood for $2.20 each. How much change should he get back from $10?

Step 1: Find the hidden question:
What is the total cost of the wood? $2.20 × 4 = $8.80

Step 2: Use your answer to the hidden question to solve the problem. $10.00 – $8.80 = $1.20

Directions: Write the hidden questions. Then solve the problems.

1. Chris used 3 nails to attach each board to the frame. After nailing 6 boards, he had 1 nail left. How many nails did Chris have before he started?
   Hidden Question: __How many nails had he used?__
   Answer: __19 nails__

2. Chris sawed a 72-inch post into 3 pieces. Two of the pieces were each 20 inches long. How long was the third piece?
   Hidden Question: __How long where the 2 pieces total?__
   Answer: __32 inches long__

3. It took Chris and his mom 15 hours to make a birdhouse. They thought it would take 3 days. How many hours early did they complete the job?
   Hidden Question: __How many hours are in 3 days?__
   Answer: __57 hours early__

4. It takes Chris 15 hours to make a birdhouse and 9 hours to make a birdfeeder. He worked for 42 hours and made 1 birdhouse and some birdfeeders. How many birdfeeders did Chris make?
   Hidden Question: __How much time total did he spend on birdfeeders?__
   Answer: __3 birdfeeders__

Page 407

Logic Problems

Directions: Use the clues below to figure out this logic problem.

Three friends all enjoy sports. Each of their favorite sports involves a ball. Two of these sports are played on courts, and one is played on a field.

- Rachel likes to run, and doesn't have to be a good catcher.
- Melinda is a good jumper.
- Betsy is also a good jumper, but she is a good ball handler.

Which sport does each girl play?

Melinda __Volleyball__
Betsy __Basketball__
Rachel __Soccer__

Page 408

A Cool Logic Problem

A family with five children went to the ice-cream shop. The children all ordered different flavors.

Directions: Use the clues and the chart to help you write which child ate which flavor of ice cream. Write a dot in the chart for the correct answer. Cross out all the other boxes in that row and column.

- No person had ice cream with the same first initial as his/her name.
- Neither of the twins, Corey and Cody, like peanut butter. Corey thinks vanilla is boring.
- The children are the twins, Vicki, the brother who got chocolate and the sister who got chocolate chip.

	Rocky Road	Chocolate Chip	Vanilla	Chocolate	Peanut Butter
Corey	•	✗	✗	✗	✗
Cody	✗	✗	•	✗	✗
Randa	✗	✗	✗	✗	•
Vicki	✗	•	✗	✗	✗
Paul	✗	✗	✗	•	✗

Who ate which flavor?

Corey __Rocky Road__
Cody __Vanilla__
Randa __Peanut Butter__
Vicki __Chocolate Chip__
Paul __Chocolate__

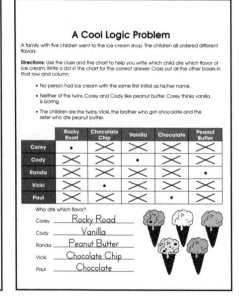

Page 409

Perimeter

The **perimeter** is the distance around a shape formed by straight lines, such as a square or triangle. To find the perimeter of a shape, add the lengths of its sides.

Examples:

For the square, add 8 + 8 + 8 + 8 = 32. Or, write a formula using **P** for **perimeter** and **s** for the **sides**:
P = 4 x s
P = 4 x 8
P = 32 inches

For the rectangle, add 4 + 5 + 4 + 5 = 18. Or, use a different formula, using **l** for **length** and **w** for **width**. In formulas with parentheses, first do the adding, multiplying, and so on, in the parentheses:
P = (2 x l) + (2 x w)
P = (2 x 5) + (2 x 4)
P = 10 + 8
P = 18

For the triangle, the sides are all different lengths, so the formula doesn't help. Instead, add the sides: 3 + 4 + 5 = 12 inches.

Directions: Find the perimeter of each shape below. Use the formula whenever possible.

1. Find the perimeter of the room pictured at left. P = __42 ft.__

2. Brandy plans to frame a picture with a sheet of construction paper. Her picture is 8 in. wide and 13 in. long. She wants the frame to extend 1 in. beyond the picture on all sides. How wide and long should the frame be? What is the perimeter of her picture and of the frame?
Length and width of frame: __14 in. long, 9 in. wide__
Perimeter of picture: __42 in.__
Perimeter of frame: __46 in.__

3. A square has a perimeter of 120 feet. How long is each side? __30 ft.__
4. A triangle with equal sides has a perimeter of 96 inches. How long is each side? __32 in.__
5. A rectangle has two sides that each 14 feet long and a perimeter of 50 feet. How wide is it? __11 ft.__

Page 410

Perimeter

Directions: Find the perimeter of each shape below.

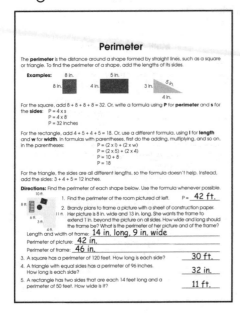

1. P = __12__
2. P = __32__
3. P = __128__
4. P = __18__
5. P = __16__
6. P = __14__
7. P = __25__
8. P = __21__

Page 411

Area: Squares and Rectangles

The **area** is the number of square units that covers a certain space. To find the area, multiply the length by the width. The answer is in square units, shown by adding a superscript 2 (^{2}) to the number.

Examples:

For the rectangle, use this formula: A = l x w
A = 8 x 5
A = 40 in.^{2}

For the square formula, **s** stands for side: A = s x s (or s^2)
A = 3 x 3 (or 3^2)
A = 9 in.^{2}

Directions: Find the area of each shape below.

1. Find the area of a room which is 12 feet long and 7 feet wide. A = __84 ft.^{2}__
2. A farmer's field is 32 feet on each side. How many square feet does he have to plow? __1,024 ft.^{2}__
3. Steve's bedroom is 10 feet by 12 feet. How many square feet of carpeting would cover the floor? __120 ft.^{2}__
4. Two of Steve's walls are 7.5 feet high and 12 feet long. The other two are the same height and 10 feet long. How many square feet of wallpaper would cover all four walls?
Square feet for 12-foot wall = __90 ft.^{2}__ x 2 = __180 ft.^{2}__
Square feet for 10-foot wall = __75 ft.^{2}__ x 2 = __150 ft.^{2}__
5. A clothes shop moved from a store that was 35 by 22 feet to a new location that was 53 by 32 feet. How many more square feet does the store have now?
Square feet for first location = __770 ft.^{2}__
Square feet for new location = __1,696 ft.^{2}__ Difference = __926 ft.^{2}__
6. A school wanted to purchase a climber for the playground. The one they selected would need 98 square feet of space. The only space available on the playground was 12 feet long and 8 feet wide. Will there be enough space for the climber? __No__

Page 412

Area: Triangles

Finding the area of a triangle requires knowing the size of the base and the height. For the triangle formula, use **b** for **base** and **h** for **height**. Multiply ½ times the size of the base and then multiply by the height. The answer will be in square units.

Example:

A = ½ x b x h
A = ½ x 4 x 6
A = 12 in.^{2}

Directions: Apply the formula to find the area of each triangle below.

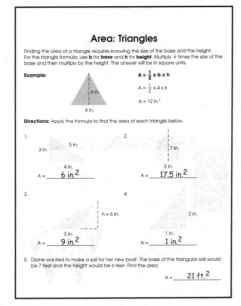

1. A = __6 in.^{2}__
2. A = __17.5 in.^{2}__
3. A = __9 in.^{2}__
4. A = __1 in.^{2}__

5. Diane wanted to make a sail for her new boat. The base of the triangular sail would be 7 feet and the height would be 6 feet. Find the area.
A = __21 ft.^{2}__

Page 413

Area Challenge

When finding the area of an unusual shape, first try to divide it into squares, rectangles or triangles. Find the area of each of those parts, then add your answers together to find the total area of the object.

Directions: Find the area of each shape below.

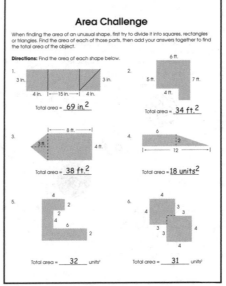

1. Total area = __69 in.^{2}__
2. Total area = __34 ft.^{2}__
3. Total area = __38 ft.^{2}__
4. Total area = __18 units^2__
5. Total area = __32__ units^2
6. Total area = __31__ units^2

Page 414

Volume

Volume is the number of cubic units that fills a space. A **cubic unit** has 6 equal sides, like a child's block. To find the volume (**V**) of something, multiply the length (**l**) by the width (**w**) by the height (**h**), or **V = l x w x h**. The answer will be in cubic units (^{3}). Sometimes it's easier to understand volume if you imagine a figure is made of small cubes.

Example: V = l x w x h
V = 4 x 6 x 5
V = 120 in.^{3}

Directions: Solve the following problems.

1. What is the volume of a cube that is 7 inches on each side? __343 in.^{3}__
2. How many cubic inches of cereal are in a box that is 10 inches long, 6 inches wide and 4.5 inches high? __270 in.^{3}__
3. Jeremy made a tower of five blocks that are each 2.5 inches square. How many cubic inches are in his tower? __78.125 in.^{3}__
4. How many cubic feet of gravel are in the back of a full dump truck that measures 7 feet wide by 4 feet tall by 16 feet long? __448 in.^{3}__
5. Will 1,000 cubic inches of dirt fill a flower box that is 32 inches long, 7 inches wide and 7 inches tall? __Yes__
6. A mouse needs 100 cubic inches of air to live for an hour. Will your pet mouse be okay for an hour in an airtight box that's 4.5 inches wide by 8.25 inches long by 2.5 inches high? __No__
7. Find the volume of the figures below. 1 cube = 1 inch^3

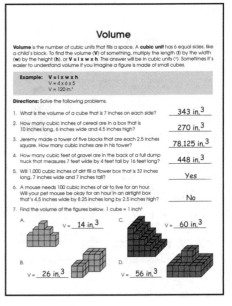

A. V = __14 in.^{3}__
B. V = __26 in.^{3}__
C. V = __60 in.^{3}__
D. V = __56 in.^{3}__

Page 415

Geometric Patterns

Geometric patterns can be described in several ways. **Similar shapes** have the same shape but in differing sizes. **Congruent shapes** have the same geometric pattern but may be facing in different directions. **Symmetrical shapes** are identical when divided in half.

Directions: Use the terms **similar, congruent** or **symmetrical** to describe the following patterns.

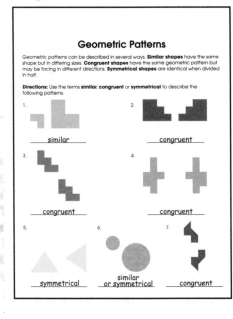

1. similar
2. congruent
3. congruent
4. congruent
5. symmetrical
6. similar or symmetrical
7. congruent

Page 416

Angles

Angles are named according to the number of degrees between the lines. The degrees are measured with a protractor.

Examples:

straight angle (measures 180°)   right angle (90°)   acute angle (less than 90°)   obtuse angle (more than 90°)

Directions: Study the examples. Then follow the instructions below.

1. Use a protractor to measure each angle below. Then write whether it is straight, right, acute or obtuse.

A. Degrees: 60°   Kind of angle: acute   C. Degrees: 120°   Kind of angle: obtuse

B. Degrees: 180°   Kind of angle: straight   D. Degrees: 90°   Kind of angle: right

2. The angles in this figure are named by letters. Write the number of degrees in each angle and whether it is straight, right, acute or obtuse.

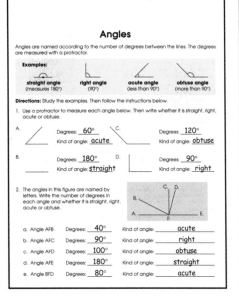

a. Angle AFB   Degrees: 40°   Kind of angle: acute
b. Angle AFC   Degrees: 90°   Kind of angle: right
c. Angle AFD   Degrees: 100°   Kind of angle: obtuse
d. Angle AFE   Degrees: 180°   Kind of angle: straight
e. Angle BFD   Degrees: 80°   Kind of angle: acute

Page 417

Types of Triangles

The sum of angles in all triangles is 180°. However, triangles come in different shapes. They are categorized by the length of their sides and by their types of angles.

Equilateral: Three equal sides   **Acute:** Three acute angles

Isosceles: Two equal sides   **Right:** One right angle

Scalene: Zero equal sides   **Obtuse:** One obtuse angle

One triangle can be a combination of types, such as isosceles and obtuse.

Directions: Study the examples. Then complete the exercises below.

1. Read these directions and color in the correct triangles.
   Color the right scalene triangle blue.
   Color the obtuse scalene triangle red.
   Color the equilateral triangle yellow.
   Color the right isosceles triangle green.
   Color the acute isosceles triangle black.

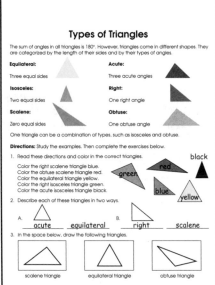

2. Describe each of these triangles in two ways.

A. acute   equilateral   B. right   scalene

3. In the space below, draw the following triangles.

scalene triangle   equilateral triangle   obtuse triangle

Page 418

Finding Angles

All triangles have three angles. The sum of these angles is 180°. Therefore, if we know the number of degrees in two of the angles, we can add them together, then subtract from 180 to find the size of the third angle.

Directions: Follow the instructions below.

1. Circle the number that shows the third angle of triangles A through F. Then describe each triangle two ways. The first one has been done for you.

A. 60°, 60°   45° 50° (60°)   equilateral, acute
B. 35°, 55°   27° (90°) 132°   scalene, right
C. 30°, 120°   (30°) 74° 112°   isosceles, obtuse
D. 15°, 78°   65° (87°) 98°   scalene, acute
E. 28°, 93°   61° (59°) 70°   scalene, obtuse
F. 12°, 114°   60° 50° (54°)   scalene, obtuse

2. Find the number of degrees in the third angle of each triangle below.

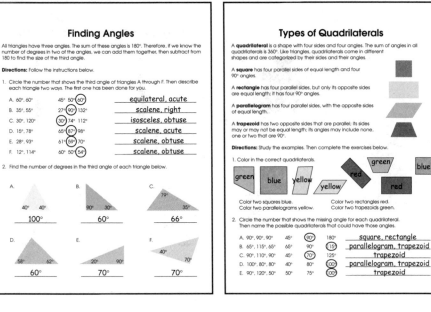

A. 40° 40° → 100°
B. 90° 30° → 60°
C. 79° 35° → 66°
D. 58° 62° → 60°
E. 20° 90° → 70°
F. 40° 70° → 70°

Page 419

Types of Quadrilaterals

A **quadrilateral** is a shape with four sides and four angles. The sum of angles in all quadrilaterals is 360°. Like triangles, quadrilaterals come in different shapes and are categorized by their sides and their angles.

A **square** has four parallel sides of equal length and four 90° angles.

A **rectangle** has four parallel sides, but only its opposite sides are equal length; it has four 90° angles.

A **parallelogram** has four parallel sides, with the opposite sides of equal length.

A **trapezoid** has two opposite sides that are parallel; its sides may or may not be equal length; its angles may include none, one or two that are 90°.

Directions: Study the examples. Then complete the exercises below.

1. Color in the correct quadrilaterals.

green, blue, yellow, yellow, red, green, blue, red

Color two squares blue.   Color two rectangles red.
Color two parallelograms yellow.   Color two trapezoids green.

2. Circle the number that shows the missing angle for each quadrilateral. Then name the possible quadrilaterals that could have those angles.

A. 90°, 90°, 90°   45° (90°) 180°   square, rectangle
B. 65°, 115°, 65°   65° 90° (115)   parallelogram, trapezoid
C. 90°, 110°, 90°   45° (70°) 125°   trapezoid
D. 100°, 80°, 80°   40° 80° (100)   parallelogram, trapezoid
E. 90°, 120°, 50°   50° 75° (100)   trapezoid

Page 420

Length in Customary Units

The **customary system** of measurement is the most widely used in the United States. It measures length in inches, feet, yards and miles.

Examples:

12 inches (in.) = 1 foot (ft.)
3 ft. (36 in.) = 1 yard (yd.)
5,280 ft. (1,760 yds.) = 1 mile (mi.)

To change to a larger unit, divide. To change to a smaller unit, multiply.

Examples:
To change inches to feet, divide by 12.	24 in. = 2 ft.
To change feet to inches, multiply by 12.	3 ft. = 36 in.
To change inches to yards, divide by 36.	108 in. = 3 yd.
To change feet to yards, divide by 3.	12 ft. = 4 yd.

27 in. = 2 ft. 3 in.
4 ft = 48 in.
80 in. = 2 yd. 8 in.
11 ft. = 3 yd. 2 ft.

Sometimes in subtraction you have to borrow units.

Examples:
```
   3 ft. 4 in. = 2 ft. 16 in.
 - 1 ft. 11 in.  - 1 ft. 11 in.
                   1 ft. 5 in.
```
```
   3 yd.      = 2 yd. 3 ft.
 - 1 yd. 2 ft.  - 1 yd. 2 ft.
                  1 yd. 1 ft.
```

Directions: Solve the following problems.

1. 108 in. = 9 ft.
2. 68 in. = 5 ft. 8 in.
3. 8 ft. = 3 yd. 2 ft.
4. 3,520 yd. = 2 mi.

5. What form of measurement (inches, feet, yards or miles) would you use for each item below?

a. pencil   inches   b. vacation trip   miles
c. playground   yards or feet   d. wall   feet or yards

6. One side of a square box is 2 ft. 4 in. What is the perimeter of the box?   9 ft. 6 in.
7. Jason is 59 in. tall. Kent is 5 ft. 1 in. tall. Who is taller and by how much?   Kent, 2 in.
8. Karen bought a doll 2 ft. 8 in. tall for her little sister. She found a box that is 29 in. long. Will the doll fit in that box?   No
9. Dan's dog likes to go out in the backyard, which is 85 ft. wide. The dog's chain is 17 ft. 6 in. long. If Dan attaches one end of the chain to a pole in the middle of the yard, will his dog be able to leave the yard?   No

Page 421

Length in Metric Units

The **metric system** measures length in meters, centimeters, millimeters, and kilometers.

Examples:
A **meter (m)** is about 40 inches or 3.3 feet.
A **centimeter (cm)** is ⅟₁₀₀ of a meter or 0.4 inches.
A **millimeter (mm)** is ⅟₁₀₀₀ of a meter or 0.04 inches.
A **kilometer (km)** is 1,000 meters or 0.6 miles.

As before, divide to find a larger unit and multiply to find a smaller unit.

Examples:
To change cm to mm, multiply by 10.
To change cm to meters, divide by 100.
To change mm to meters, divide by 1,000.
To change km to meters, multiply by 1,000.

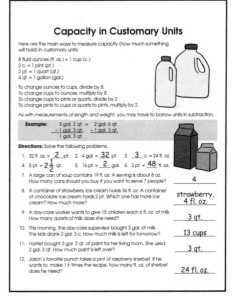

Directions: Solve the following problems.

1. 600 cm = __6__ m   2. 12 cm = __120__ mm   3.47 m = __4,700__ cm   4.3 km = __3,000__ m

5. In the sentences below, write the missing unit: m, cm, mm or km.
   a. A fingernail is about 1 __mm__ thick.
   b. An average car is about 5 __m__ long.
   c. Someone could walk 1 __km__ in 10 minutes.
   d. A finger is about 7 __cm__ long.
   e. A street could be 3 __km__ long.
   f. The Earth is about 40,000 __km__ around at the equator.
   g. A pencil is about 17 __mm__ long.
   h. A noodle is about 4 __mm__ wide.
   i. A teacher's desk is about 1 __m__ wide.

6. A nickel is about 1 mm thick. How many nickels would be in a stack 1 cm high? __10__
7. Is something 25 cm long closer to 10 inches or 10 feet? __10 inches__
8. Is something 18 mm wide closer to 0.7 inch or 7 inches? __0.7 inch__
9. Would you get more exercise running 4 km or 500 m? __4 km__
10. Which is taller, something 40 m or 350 cm? __40 m__

Page 422

Weight in Customary Units

Here are the main ways to measure weight in customary units:

16 ounces (oz.) = 1 pound (lb.)
2,000 lb. = 1 ton (tn.)
To change ounces to pounds, divide by 16.
To change pounds to ounces, multiply by 16.

As with measurements of length, you may have to borrow units in subtraction.

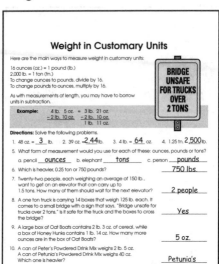

Example: 4 lb. 5 oz. = 3 lb. 21 oz.
           – 2 lb. 10 oz.   – 2 lb. 10 oz.
                            1 lb. 11 oz.

Directions: Solve the following problems.

1. 48 oz. = __3__ lb.   2. 39 oz. = __2.44__ lb.   3. 4 lb. = __64__ oz.   4. 1.25 tn. = __2,500__ lb.
5. What form of measurement would you use for each of these: ounces, pounds or tons?
   a. pencil __ounces__   b. elephant __tons__   c. person __pounds__
6. Which is heavier, 0.25 ton or 750 pounds? __750 lbs.__
7. Twenty-two people, each weighing an average of 150 lb., want to get on an elevator that can carry up to 1.5 tons. How many of them should wait for the next elevator? __2 people__
8. A one ton truck is carrying 14 boxes that weigh 125 lb. each. It comes to a small bridge with a sign that says, "Bridge unsafe for trucks over 2 tons." Is it safe for the truck and the boxes to cross the bridge? __Yes__
9. A large box of Oat Boats contains 2 lb. 3 oz. of cereal, while a box of Honey Hunks contains 1 lb. 14 oz. How many more ounces are in the box of Oat Boats? __5 oz.__
10. A can of Peter's Powdered Drink Mix weighs 2 lb. 5 oz. A can of Petunia's Powdered Drink Mix weighs 40 oz. Which one is heavier? __Petunia's__
11. A can of Peter's Drink Mix is 12 cents an ounce. How much does it cost? __$4.44__
12. How many 5-oz. servings could you get from a fish that weighs 3 lb. 12 oz.? __12__

Page 423

Weight in Metric Units

A **gram (g)** is about 0.035 oz.
A **milligram (mg)** is ⅟₁₀₀₀ g or about 0.000035 oz.
A **kilogram (kg)** is 1,000 g or about 2.2 lb.
A **metric ton (t)** is 1,000 kg or about 1.1 tn.

To change g to mg, multiply by 1,000.
To change g to kg, divide by 1,000.
To change kg to g, multiply by 1,000.
To change t to kg, multiply by 1,000.

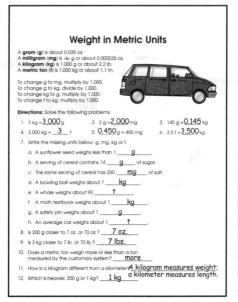

Directions: Solve the following problems.

1. 3 kg = __3,000__ g   2. 2 g = __2,000__ mg   3. 145 g = __0.145__ kg
4. 3,000 kg = __3__ t   5. __0.450__ g = 450 mg   6. 3.5 t = __3,500__ kg

7. Write the missing units below: g, mg, kg or t.
   a. A sunflower seed weighs less than 1 __g__.
   b. A serving of cereal contains 14 __g__ of sugar.
   c. The same serving of cereal has 250 __mg__ of salt.
   d. A bowling ball weighs about 7 __kg__.
   e. A whale weighs about 90 __t__.
   f. A math textbook weighs about 1 __kg__.
   g. A safety pin weighs about 1 __g__.
   h. An average car weighs about 1 __t__.

8. Is 200 g closer to 7 oz. or 70 oz.? __7 oz.__
9. Is 3 kg closer to 7 lb. or 70 lb.? __7 lbs.__
10. Does a metric ton weigh more or less than a ton measured by the customary system? __more__
11. How is a kilogram different from a kilometer? __A kilogram measures weight; a kilometer measures length.__
12. Which is heavier, 300 g or 1 kg? __1 kg__

Page 424

Capacity in Customary Units

Here are the main ways to measure capacity (how much something will hold) in customary units:

8 fluid ounces (fl. oz.) = 1 cup (c.)
2 c. = 1 pint (pt.)
2 pt. = 1 quart (qt.)
4 qt. = 1 gallon (gal.)

To change ounces to cups, divide by 8.
To change cups to ounces, multiply by 8.
To change cups to pints or quarts, divide by 2.
To change pints to cups or quarts to pints, multiply by 2.

As with measurements of length and weight, you may have to borrow units in subtraction.

Example: 3 gal. 2 qt. = 2 gal. 6 qt.
           – 1 gal. 3 qt.   – 1 gal. 3 qt.
                            1 gal. 3 qt.

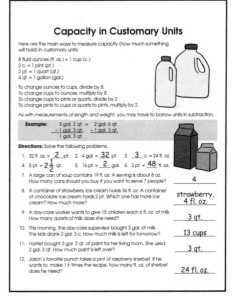

Directions: Solve the following problems.

1. 32 fl. oz. = __2__ pt.   2. 4 gal. = __32__ pt.   3. __3__ c. = 24 fl. oz.
4. 5 pt. = 2½ qt.   5. 16 pt. = __2__ gal.   6. 3 pt. = __48__ fl. oz.
7. A large can of soup contains 19 fl. oz. A serving is about 8 oz. How many cans should you buy if you want to serve 7 people? __4__
8. A container of strawberry ice cream holds 36 fl. oz. A container of chocolate ice cream holds 2 pt. Which one has more ice cream? How much more? __strawberry, 4 fl. oz.__
9. A day-care worker wants to give 15 children each 6 fl. oz. of milk. How many quarts of milk does she need? __3 qt.__
10. This morning, the day-care supervisor bought 3 gal. of milk. The kids drank 2 gal. 3 c. How much milk is left for tomorrow? __13 cups__
11. Harriet bought 3 gal. 2 qt. of paint for her living room. She used 2 gal. 3 qt. How much paint is left over? __3 qt.__
12. Jason's favorite punch takes a pint of raspberry sherbet. If he wants to make 1½ times the recipe, how many fl. oz. of sherbet does he need? __24 fl. oz.__

Page 425

Capacity in Metric Units

A **liter (L)** is a little over 1 quart.
A **milliliter (mL)** is ⅟₁₀₀₀ of a liter or about 0.03 oz.
A **kiloliter (kL)** is 1,000 liters or about 250 gallons.

Directions: Solve the following problems.

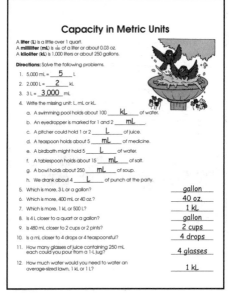

1. 5,000 mL = __5__ L
2. 2,000 L = __2__ kL
3. 3 L = __3,000__ mL
4. Write the missing unit: L, mL or kL.
   a. A swimming pool holds about 100 __kL__ of water.
   b. An eyedropper is marked for 1 and 2 __mL__.
   c. A pitcher could hold 1 or 2 __L__ of juice.
   d. A teaspoon holds about 5 __mL__ of medicine.
   e. A birdbath might hold 5 __L__ of water.
   f. A tablespoon holds about 15 __mL__ of salt.
   g. A bowl holds about 250 __mL__ of soup.
   h. We drank about 4 __L__ of punch at the party.
5. Which is more, 3 L or a gallon? __gallon__
6. Which is more, 400 mL or 40 oz.? __40 oz.__
7. Which is more, 1 kL or 500 L? __1 kL__
8. Is 4 L closer to a quart or a gallon? __gallon__
9. Is 480 mL closer to 2 cups or 2 pints? __2 cups__
10. Is a mL closer to 4 drops or 4 teaspoonsful? __4 drops__
11. How many glasses of juice containing 250 mL each could you pour from a 1-L jug? __4 glasses__
12. How much water would you need to water an average-sized lawn, 1 kL or 1 L? __1 kL__

Page 426

Temperature in Customary and Metric Units

The customary system measures temperature in Fahrenheit (F°) degrees.

The metric system uses Celsius (C°) degrees.

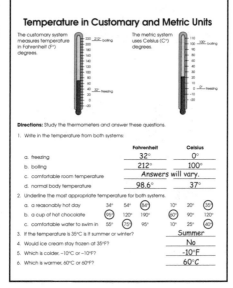

Directions: Study the thermometers and answer these questions.

1. Write in the temperature from both systems:

	Fahrenheit	Celsius
a. freezing	32°	0°
b. boiling	212°	100°
c. comfortable room temperature	Answers will vary.	
d. normal body temperature	98.6°	37°

2. Underline the most appropriate temperature for both systems.
   a. a reasonably hot day   34°   54°   (84°)   10°   20°   (35°)
   b. a cup of hot chocolate   (95°)   120°   190°   (60°)   90°   120°
   c. comfortable water to swim in   55°   (75°)   95°   10°   (40°)
3. If the temperature is 35°C is it summer or winter? __Summer__
4. Would ice cream stay frozen at 35°F? __No__
5. Which is colder, –10°C or –10°F? __–10°F__
6. Which is warmer, 60°C or 60°F? __60°C__

Page 427

Review

Directions: Complete the following exercises.

1. 372 in. = 10.33 yd. 31 ft.
2. 4 km = 4,000 m
3. 1.25 lb. = 20 oz.
4. 2,000 mg = 2 g
5. 1 qt. = 32 oz.
6. 10,000 mL = 10 L
7. Todd has a board that is 6 ft. 3 in. long. He needs to cut it to 4 ft. 9 in. How much should he cut off? 18 in. (1 ft. 6 in.)
8. In a contest, Joyce threw a ball 12 yd. 2 ft. Brenda threw the ball 500 in. Who threw the farthest? Brenda
9. Would you measure this workbook in mm or cm? cm
10. Which is heavier, a box of books that weighs 4 lb. 6 oz. or a box of dishes that weighs 80 oz.? 80 oz.
11. A 1-lb. package has 10 hot dogs. How much of an ounce does each hot dog weigh? 1.6 oz.
12. Would the amount of salt (sodium) in 1 oz. of potato chips be 170 g or 170 mg? 170 mg.
13. If someone ate half of a gallon of ice cream, how many fluid ounces would be left? 64 fl. oz.
14. You want to serve 6 fl. oz. of ice cream to each of 16 friends at your party. How many quarts of ice cream should you buy? 3 qt.
15. Would you measure water in a fish pond with L or kL? kL
16. Would popsicles melt at 5°C? Yes
17. Would soup be steaming hot at 100°F? Yes

Page 428

Ratios

A **ratio** is a comparison of two quantities. For example, a wall is 96 in. high; a pencil is 8 in. long. By dividing 8 into 96, you find it would take 12 pencils to equal the height of the wall. The ratio, or comparison, of the wall to the pencil can be written three ways: 1 to 12; 1:12; $\frac{1}{12}$. In this example, the ratio of triangles to circles is 4:6. The ratio of triangles to squares is 4:9. The ratio of circles to squares is 6:9. These ratios will stay the same if we divide both numbers in the ratio by the same number.

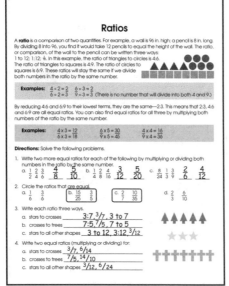

Examples: $\frac{4 \div 2}{6 \div 2} = \frac{2}{3}$ $\frac{6 \div 3}{9 \div 3} = \frac{2}{3}$ (There is no number that will divide into both 4 and 9.)

By reducing 4:6 and 6:9 to their lowest terms, they are the same—2:3. This means that 2:3, 4:6 and 6:9 are all equal ratios. You can also find equal ratios for all three by multiplying both numbers of the ratio by the same number.

Examples: $\frac{4 \times 3}{6 \times 3} = \frac{12}{18}$ $\frac{6 \times 5}{9 \times 5} = \frac{30}{45}$ $\frac{4 \times 4}{9 \times 4} = \frac{16}{36}$

Directions: Solve the following problems.

1. Write two more equal ratios for each of the following by multiplying or dividing both numbers in the ratio by the same number.
   a. $\frac{1}{2}$ $\frac{2}{4}$ $\frac{3}{6}$ $\frac{4}{8}$ $\frac{5}{10}$ b. $\frac{1}{4}$ $\frac{2}{8}$ $\frac{4}{16}$ $\frac{3}{12}$ $\frac{5}{20}$ c. $\frac{8}{24}$ $\frac{1}{3}$ $\frac{3}{9}$ $\frac{2}{6}$ $\frac{4}{12}$
2. Circle the ratios that are equal.
   a. $\frac{1}{6}$ $\frac{3}{6}$ b. $\frac{15}{25}$ $\frac{3}{5}$ (circled) c. $\frac{2}{7}$ $\frac{10}{35}$ (circled) d. $\frac{2}{3}$ $\frac{6}{10}$
3. Write each ratio three ways.

   a. stars to crosses 3:7, 3/7, 3 to 7
   b. crosses to trees 7:5, 7/5, 7 to 5
   c. stars to all other shapes 3 to 12, 3:12, 3/12
4. Write two equal ratios (multiplying or dividing) for:
   a. stars to crosses 3/7, 6/14
   b. crosses to trees 7/5, 14/10
   c. stars to all other shapes 3/12, 6/24

Page 429

Missing Numbers in Ratios

You can find a missing number (n) in an equal ratio. First, figure out which number has already been multiplied to get the number you know. (In the first example, 3 is multiplied by 3 to get 9; in the second example, 2 is multiplied by 6 to get 12.) Then multiply the other number in the ratio by the same number (3 and 6 in the examples).

Examples: $\frac{3}{4} = \frac{9}{n}$ $\frac{3}{4} \times \frac{3}{3} = \frac{9}{12}$ $n = 12$ $\frac{1}{2} = \frac{n}{12}$ $\frac{1}{2} \times \frac{6}{6} = \frac{6}{12}$ $n = 6$

Directions: Solve the following problems.

1. Find each missing number.
   a. $\frac{1}{2} = \frac{n}{12}$ $n =$ 6 b. $\frac{1}{5} = \frac{n}{15}$ $n =$ 3 c. $\frac{3}{2} = \frac{18}{n}$ $n =$ 12
   d. $\frac{5}{8} = \frac{n}{32}$ $n =$ 20 e. $\frac{8}{3} = \frac{16}{n}$ $n =$ 6 f. $\frac{n}{14} = \frac{5}{7}$ $n =$ 10

2. If a basketball player makes 9 baskets in 12 tries, what is her ratio of baskets to tries, in lowest terms? 3:4
3. At the next game, the player has the same ratio of baskets to tries. If she tries 20 times, how many baskets should she make? 15 baskets
4. At the third game, she still has the same ratio of baskets to tries. This time she makes 12 baskets. How many times did she probably try? 16 times
5. If a driver travels 40 miles in an hour, what is his ratio of miles to minutes, in lowest terms? 2:3
6. At the same speed, how far would the driver travel in 30 minutes? 20 mi.
7. At the same speed, how long would it take him to travel 60 miles? 1 hr. 30 min.

Page 430

Proportions

A **proportion** is a statement that two ratios are equal. To make sure ratios are equal, called a proportion, we multiply the cross products.

Examples of proportions: $\frac{1}{5} = \frac{2}{10}$ $\frac{1}{2} \times \frac{10}{5} = \frac{10}{10}$ $\frac{3}{7} = \frac{15}{35}$ $\frac{3}{7} \times \frac{35}{15} = \frac{105}{105}$

These two ratios are not a proportion: $\frac{4}{3} \neq \frac{5}{6}$ $\frac{4}{3} \times \frac{6}{5} = \frac{24}{15}$

To find a missing number (n) in a proportion, multiply the cross products and divide.

Examples: $\frac{n}{30} = \frac{1}{6}$ $n \times 6 = 1 \times 30$ $n \times 6 = 30$ $n = \frac{30}{6}$ $n = 5$

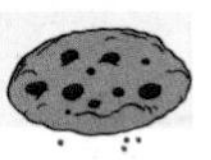

Directions: Solve the following problems.

1. Write = between the ratios if they are a proportion. Write ≠ if they are not a proportion. The first one has been done for you.
   a. $\frac{1}{2}$ = $\frac{6}{12}$ b. $\frac{13}{18}$ ≠ $\frac{20}{22}$ c. $\frac{2}{6}$ = $\frac{5}{15}$ d. $\frac{5}{6}$ = $\frac{20}{24}$
2. Find the missing numbers in these proportions.
   a. $\frac{2}{5} = \frac{n}{15}$ $n =$ 6 b. $\frac{3}{8} = \frac{9}{n}$ $n =$ 24 c. $\frac{n}{18} = \frac{4}{12}$ $n =$ 6
3. One issue of a magazine costs $2.99, but if you buy a subscription, 12 issues cost $35.88. Is the price at the same proportion? Yes
4. A cookie recipe calls for 3 cups of flour to make 36 cookies. How much flour is needed for 48 cookies? 4
5. The same recipe requires 4 teaspoons of cinnamon for 36 cookies. How many teaspoons is needed to make 48 cookies? (Answer will include a fraction.) $5\frac{1}{3}$
6. The recipe also calls for 2 cups of sugar for 36 cookies. How much sugar should you use for 48 cookies? (Answer will include a fraction.) $2\frac{2}{3}$
7. If 2 kids can eat 12 cookies, how many can 8 kids eat? 48

Page 431

Percents

Percent means "per 100." A percent is a ratio that compares a number with 100. The same number can be written as a decimal and a percent. To change a decimal to a percent, move the decimal point two places to the right and add the % sign. To change a percent to a decimal, drop the % sign and place a decimal point two places to the left.

Examples: 0.25 = 25% 0.1 = 10% 1.456 = 145.6% 32% = 0.32 99% = 0.99 203% = 2.03

A percent or decimal can also be written as a ratio or fraction.

Example: $0.25 = 25\% = \frac{25}{100} = \frac{1}{4} = 1:4$

To change a fraction or ratio to a percent, first change it to a decimal. Divide the numerator by the denominator.

Examples: $\frac{1}{3} = 3\overline{)1.00}$ $0.33\frac{1}{3} = 33\frac{1}{3}\%$ $\frac{2}{5} = 5\overline{)2.0}$ $0.4 = 40\%$

Directions: Solve the following problems.

1. Change the percents to decimals.
   a. 3% = 0.03 b. 75% = 0.75 c. 14% = 0.14 d. 115% = 1.15
2. Change the decimals and fractions to percents.
   a. 0.56 = 56 % b. 0.03 = 3 % c. $\frac{3}{4}$ = 75 % d. $\frac{1}{5}$ = 20 %
3. Change the percents to ratios in their lowest terms. The first one has been done for you.
   a. 75% = 75/100 = 3/4 = 3:4 b. 40% = 40/100 = 2/5 = 2:5
   c. 35% = 35/100 = 7/20 = 7:20 d. 70% = 70/100 = 7/10 = 7:10
4. The class was 45% girls. What percent was boys? 55%
5. Half the shoes in one store were on sale. What percent of the shoes were their ordinary price? 50%
6. Kim read 84 pages of a 100-page book. What percent of the book did she read? 84%

Page 432

Percents

To find the percent of a number, change the percent to a decimal and multiply.

Examples: 45% of $20 = 0.45 x $20 = $9.00 125% of 30 = 1.25 x 30 = 37.50

Directions: Solve the following problems. Round off the answers to the nearest hundredth where necessary.

1. Find the percent of each number.
   a. 26% of 40 = 10.4 b. 12% of 329 = 39.48
   c. 73% of 19 = 13.87 d. 2% of 24 = 0.48
2. One family spends 35% of its weekly budget of $150 on food. How much do they spend? $52.50
3. A shirt in a store usually costs $15.99, but today it's on sale for 25% off. The clerk says you will save $4.50. Is that true? No
4. A book that usually costs $12 is on sale for 25% off. How much will it cost? $9.00
5. After you answer 60% of 150 math problems, how many do you have left to do? 60
6. A pet store's shipment of tropical fish was delayed. Nearly 40% of the 1,350 fish died. About how many lived? 810
7. The shipment had 230 angelfish, which died in the same proportion as the other kinds of fish. About how many angelfish died? 92
8. A church youth group was collecting cans of food. Their goal was 1,200 cans, but they exceeded their goal by 25%. How many cans did they collect? 1,500

Page 433

Probability

Probability is the ratio of favorable outcomes to possible outcomes in an experiment. You can use probability (P) to figure out how likely something is to happen. For example, six picture cards are turned facedown—3 cards have stars, 2 have triangles and 1 has a circle. What is the probability of picking the circle? Using the formula below, you have a 1 in 6 probability of picking the circle, a 2 in 6 probability of picking a triangle and a 3 in 6 probability of picking a star.

Example: $P = \dfrac{\text{number of favorable outcomes}}{\text{number of trials}}$ $P = \frac{1}{6} = 1:6$

Directions: Solve the following problems.

1. A class has 14 girls and 15 boys. If all of their names are put on separate slips in a hat, what is the probability of each person's name being chosen? — **1:29**

2. In the same class, what is the probability that a girl's name will be chosen? — **14:29**

3. In this class, 3 boys are named Mike. What is the probability that a slip with "Mike" written on it will be chosen? — **3:29**

4. A spinner on a board game has the numbers 1–8. What is the probability of spinning and getting a 4? — **1:8**

5. A paper bag holds these colors of wooden beads: 4 blue, 5 red and 6 yellow. If you select a bead without looking, do you have an equal probability of getting each color? — **No**

6. Using the same bag of beads, what is the probability of reaching in and drawing out a red bead (in lowest terms)? — **1:3**

7. In the same bag, what is the probability of not getting a blue bead? — **2:1**

8. In a carnival game, plastic ducks have spots. The probability of picking a duck with a yellow spot is 2:15. There is twice as much probability of picking a duck with a red spot. What is the probability of picking a duck with a red spot? — **4:15**

9. In this game, all the other ducks have green spots. What is the probability of picking a duck with a green spot (in lowest terms)? — **3:5**

Page 434

Possible Combinations

Today the cafeteria is offering 4 kinds of sandwiches, 3 kinds of drinks and 2 kinds of cookies. How many possible combinations could you make? To find out, multiply the number of choices together.

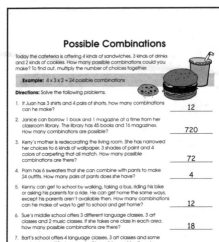

Example: $4 \times 3 \times 2 = 24$ possible combinations

Directions: Solve the following problems.

1. If Juan has 3 shirts and 4 pairs of shorts, how many combinations can he make? — **12**

2. Janice can borrow 1 book and 1 magazine at a time from her classroom library. The library has 45 books and 16 magazines. How many combinations are possible? — **720**

3. Kerry's mother is redecorating the living room. She has narrowed her choices to 6 kinds of wallpaper, 3 shades of paint and 4 colors of carpeting that all match. How many possible combinations are there? — **72**

4. Pam has 6 sweaters that she can combine with pants to make 24 outfits. How many pairs of pants does she have? — **4**

5. Kenny can get to school by walking, taking a bus, riding his bike or asking his parents for a ride. He can get home the same ways, except his parents aren't available then. How many combinations can he make of ways to get to school and get home? — **12**

6. Sue's middle school offers 3 different language classes, 3 art classes and 2 music classes. If she takes one class in each area, how many possible combinations are there? — **18**

7. Bart's school offers 4 language classes, 3 art classes and some music classes. If Bart can make 36 possible combinations, how many music classes are there? — **3**

8. AAA Airlines schedules 12 flights a day from Chicago to Atlanta. Four of those flights go on to Orlando. From the Orlando airport you can take a bus, ride in a taxi or rent a car to get to Disneyworld. How many different ways are there to get from Chicago to Disneyworld if you make part of your trip on AAA Airlines? — **12**

Page 435

Review

Directions: Solve the following problems. Round answers to the nearest hundredth where necessary.

1. Write an equal ratio for each of these:
   a. $\frac{1}{7} = \frac{2}{14}$ b. $\frac{5}{8} = \frac{15}{24}$ c. $\frac{15}{3} = \frac{30}{6}$ d. $\frac{6}{24} = \frac{12}{48}$

2. State the ratios below in lowest terms.
   a. cats to bugs = **4:6 = 2:3**
   b. cats to dogs = **4:5**
   c. dogs to all other objects = **5:10 = 1:5**

3. If Shawn drives 45 miles an hour, how far could he go in 40 minutes? — **30 miles**

4. At the same speed, how many minutes would it take Shawn to drive 120 miles? — **2 hrs. 40 min.**

5. Mr. Herman is building a doghouse in proportion to his family's house. The family's house is 30 ft. high and the doghouse is 5 ft. high. If the family house is 42 ft. wide, how wide should the doghouse be? — **7 ft.**

6. The family house is 24 ft. from front to back. How big should Mr. Herman make the doghouse? — **4 ft.**

7. Change these numbers to percents:
   a. 0.56 = **56%** b. $\frac{4}{5}$ = **80%** c. 0.04 = **4%** d. $\frac{3}{8}$ = **37.5%**

8. Which is a better deal, a blue bike for $125 at 25% off or a red bike for $130 at 30% off? — **red bike**

9. If sales tax is 6%, what would be the total price of the blue bike? — **$99.38**

10. Richard bought 6 raffle tickets for a free bike. If 462 tickets are sold, what is Richard's probability of winning? — **6:462 = 1:77**

11. Lori bought 48 tickets in the same raffle. What are her chances of winning? — **48:462 = 8:77**

Page 436

Comparing Data

Data (**datum**—singular) are gathered information. The **range** is the difference between the highest and lowest number in a group of numbers. The **median** is the number in the middle when numbers are listed in order. The **mean** is the average of the numbers. We can compare numbers or data by finding the range, median and mean.

Example: 16, 43, 34, 78, 8, 91, 26

To compare these numbers, we first need to put them in order: 8 16 26 34 43 78 91. By subtracting the lowest number (8) from the highest one (91), we find the range: 83. By finding the number that falls in the middle, we have the median: 34 (If no number fell exactly in the middle, we would average the two middle numbers.)
By adding them and dividing by the number of numbers (7), we get the mean: 42.29 (rounded to the nearest hundredth).

Directions: Solve the following problems. Round answers to the nearest hundredth where necessary.

1. Find the range, median and mean of these numbers: 19, 5, 84, 27, 106, 38, 75.
   Range: **101**   Median: **38**   Mean: **50.57**

2. Find the range, median and mean finishing times for 6 runners in a race. Here are their times in seconds: 14.2, 12.9, 13.5, 10.3, 14.8, 14.7.
   Range: **4.5**   Median: **13.85**   Mean: **13.4**

3. If the runner who won the race in 10.3 seconds had run even faster and finished in 7 seconds, would the mean time be higher or lower? — **Lower**

4. If that runner had finished in 7 seconds, what would be the median time? — **13.85 (same)**

5. Here are the high temperatures in one city for a week: 65, 72, 68, 74, 81, 68, 85. Find the range, median and mean temperatures.
   Range: **20**   Median: **72**   Mean: **73.29**

6. Find the range, median and mean test scores for this group of students: 41, 32, 45, 36, 48, 38, 37, 42, 39, 36.
   Range: **16**   Median: **38.5**   Mean: **39.4**

Page 437

Tables

Organizing data into tables makes it easier to compare numbers. As evident in the example, putting many numbers in a paragraph is confusing. When the same numbers are organized in a table, you can compare numbers in a glance. Tables can be arranged several ways and still be easy to read and understand.

Example: Money spent on groceries:
Family A: week 1 — $68.50; week 2 — $72.25; week 3 — $67.00; week 4 — $74.50.
Family B: week 1 — $42.25; week 2 — $47.50; week 3 — $50.25; week 4 — $53.50.

	Week 1	Week 2	Week 3	Week 4
Family A	$68.50	$72.25	$67.00	$74.50
Family B	$42.25	$47.50	$50.25	$53.50

Directions: Complete the following exercises.

1. Finish the table below, then answer the questions.
   Data: Steve weighs 230 lb. and is 6 ft. 2 in. tall. George weighs 218 lb. and is 6 ft. 3 in. tall. Chuck weighs 225 lb. and is 6 ft. 1 in. tall. Henry weighs 205 lb. and is 6 ft. tall.

	Henry	George	Chuck	Steve
Weight	205 lbs.	218 lbs.	225 lbs.	230 lbs.
Height	6 ft.	6 ft. 3 in.	6 ft. 1 in.	6 ft. 2 in.

   a. Who is tallest? **George**   b. Who weighs the least? **Henry**

2. On another sheet of paper, prepare 2 tables comparing the amount of money made by 3 booths at the school carnival this year and last year. In the first table, write the names of the games in the left-hand column (like **Family A** and **Family B** in the example). In the second table (using the same data), write the years in the left-hand column. Here is the data: fish pond—this year $15.60, last year $13.50; bean-bag toss—this year $13.45, last year $10.25; ring toss—this year $23.80, last year $18.80. After you complete both tables, answer the following questions.
   a. Which booth made the most money this year? — **ring toss**
   b. Which booth made the biggest improvement from last year to this year? — **ring toss**

Page 438

Bar Graphs

Another way to organize information is a **bar graph**. The bar graph in the example compares the number of students in 4 elementary schools. Each bar stands for 1 school. You can easily see that School A has the most students and School C the least. The numbers along the left show how many students attend each school.

Example:

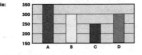

Directions: Complete the following exercises.

1. This bar graph will show how many calories are in 1 serving of 4 kinds of cereal. Draw the bars the correct height and label each with the name of the cereal. After completing the bar graph, answer the questions. Data: Korn Kernals—150 calories; Oat Floats—160 calories; Rite Rice—110 calories; Sugar Shapes—200 calories.

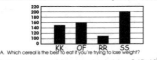

A. Which cereal is the best to eat if you're trying to lose weight? — **Rite Rice**

B. Which cereal has nearly the same number of calories as Oat Floats? — **Korn Kernals**

2. On another sheet of paper, draw your own graph, showing the number of TV commercials in 1 week for each of the 4 cereals in the graph above. After completing the graph, answer the questions. Data: Oat Boats—27 commercials; Rite Rice—15; Sugar Shapes—35; Korn Kernals—28.

A. Which cereal is most heavily advertised? — **Sugar Shapes**

B. What similarities do you notice between the graph of calories and the graph of — **Sugar Shapes is highest in sugar and advertisements**

Page 439

Picture Graphs

Newspapers and textbooks often use pictures in graphs instead of bars. Each picture stands for a certain number of objects. Half a picture means half the number. The picture graph in the example indicates the number of games each team won. The Astros won 7 games, so they have $3\frac{1}{2}$ balls.

Example:

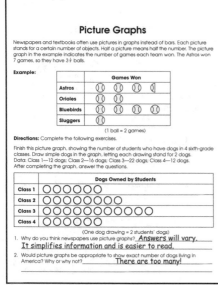

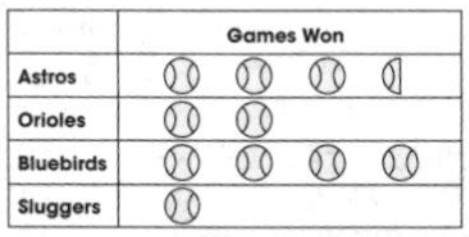
Games Won
Astros
Orioles
Bluebirds
Sluggers

(1 ball = 2 games)

Directions: Complete the following exercises.

Finish this picture graph, showing the number of students who have dogs in 4 sixth-grade classes. Draw simple dogs in the graph, letting each drawing stand for 2 dogs. Data: Class 1—12 dogs; Class 2—16 dogs; Class 3—22 dogs; Class 4—12 dogs. After completing the graph, answer the questions.

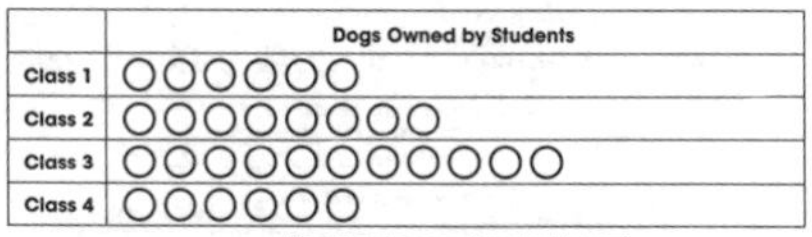
Dogs Owned by Students
Class 1
Class 2
Class 3
Class 4

(One dog drawing = 2 students' dogs)

1. Why do you think newspapers use picture graphs? Answers will vary. It simplifies information and is easier to read.
2. Would picture graphs be appropriate to show exact number of dogs living in America? Why or why not? There are too many!

Page 440

Line Graphs

Still another way to display information is a line graph. The same data can often be shown in both a bar graph and a line graph. Nevertheless, line graphs are especially useful in showing changes over a period of time.

The line graph in the example shows changes in the number of students enrolled in a school over a 5-year period. Enrollment was highest in 1988 and has decreased gradually each year since then. Notice how labeling the years and enrollment numbers make the graph easy to understand.

Example:

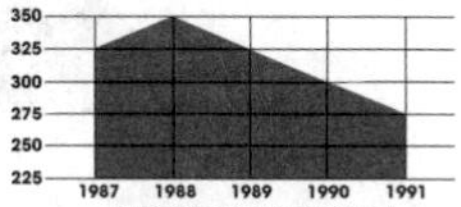
350
325
300
275
250
225
1987
1988
1989
1990
1991

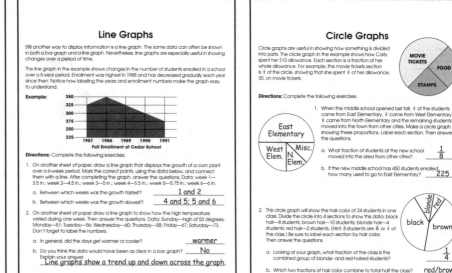

Fall Enrollment at Cedar School

Directions: Complete the following exercises.

1. On another sheet of paper, draw a line graph that displays the growth of a corn plant over a 6-week period. Mark the correct points, using the data below, and connect them with a line. After completing the graph, answer the questions. Data: week 1—3.5 in.; week 2—4.5 in.; week 3—5 in.; week 4—5.5 in.; week 5—5.75 in.; week 6—6 in.
   a. Between which weeks was the growth fastest? 1 and 2
   b. Between which weeks was the growth slowest? 4 and 5; 5 and 6
2. On another sheet of paper draw a line graph to show how the high temperature varied during one week. Then answer the questions. Data: Sunday—high of 53 degrees; Monday—51; Tuesday—56; Wednesday—60; Thursday—58; Friday—67; Saturday—73. Don't forget to label the numbers.
   a. In general, did the days get warmer or cooler? warmer
   b. Do you think this data would have been as clear in a bar graph? No
   Explain your answer. Line graphs show a trend up and down across the graph.

Page 441

Circle Graphs

MOVIE TICKETS
FOOD
STAMPS

Circle graphs are useful in showing how something is divided into parts. The circle graph in the example shows how Carly spent her $10 allowance. Each section is a fraction of her whole allowance. For example, the movie tickets section is $\frac{1}{2}$ of the circle, showing that she spent $\frac{1}{2}$ of her allowance, $5, on movie tickets.

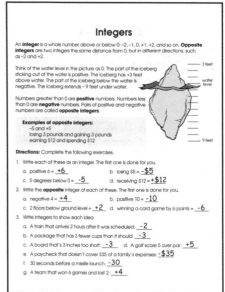

Directions: Complete the following exercises.

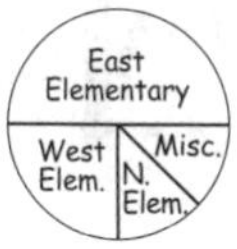
East Elementary
West Elem.
N. Elem.
Misc.

1. When the middle school opened last fall, $\frac{1}{2}$ of the students came from East Elementary, $\frac{1}{4}$ came from West Elementary, $\frac{1}{8}$ came from North Elementary and the remaining students moved into the town from other cities. Make a circle graph showing these proportions. Label each section. Then answer the questions.
   a. What fraction of students at the new school moved into the area from other cities? $\frac{1}{8}$
   b. If the new middle school has 450 students enrolled, how many used to go to East Elementary? 225

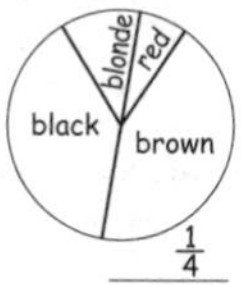
blonde
red
black
brown

2. This circle graph will show the hair color of 24 students in one class. Divide the circle into 4 sections to show this data: black hair—8 students; brown hair—10 students; blonde hair—4 students; red hair—2 students. (Hint: 8 students are $\frac{8}{24}$ or $\frac{1}{3}$ of the class.) Be sure to label each section by hair color. Then answer the questions.
   a. Looking at your graph, what fraction of the class is the combined group of blonde- and red-haired students? $\frac{1}{4}$
   b. Which two fractions of hair color combine to total half the class? red/brown

Page 442

Comparing Presentation Methods

Tables and different kinds of graphs have different purposes. Some are more helpful for certain kinds of information. The table and three graphs below all show basically the same information—the amount of money Mike and Margaret made in their lawn-mowing business over a 4-month period.

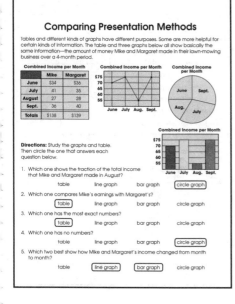

Combined Income per Month

	Mike	Margaret
June	$34	$36
July	41	35
August	27	28
Sept.	36	40
Totals	$138	$139

Combined Income per Month

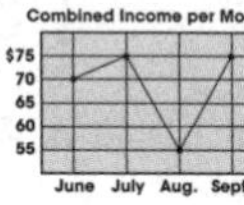
$75
70
65
60
55
June
July
Aug.
Sept.

Combined Income per Month

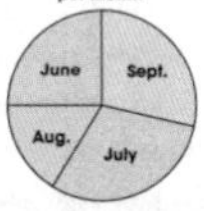
June
Sept.
Aug.
July

Combined Income per Month

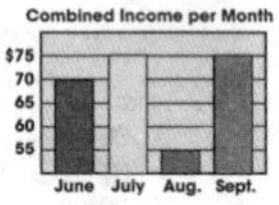
$75
70
65
60
55
June
July
Aug.
Sept.

Directions: Study the graphs and table. Then circle the one that answers each question below.

1. Which one shows the fraction of the total income that Mike and Margaret made in August?
   table — line graph — bar graph — (circle graph)
2. Which one compares Mike's earnings with Margaret's?
   (table) — line graph — bar graph — circle graph
3. Which one has the most exact numbers?
   (table) — line graph — bar graph — circle graph
4. Which one has no numbers?
   table — line graph — bar graph — (circle graph)
5. Which two best show how Mike and Margaret's income changed from month to month?
   table — (line graph) — (bar graph) — circle graph

Page 443

Graphing Data

Directions: Complete the following exercises.

1. Use the following information to create a bar graph.

Cities	Population (in 1,000's)
Dover	20
Newton Falls	12
Springdale	25
Hampton	17
Riverside	5

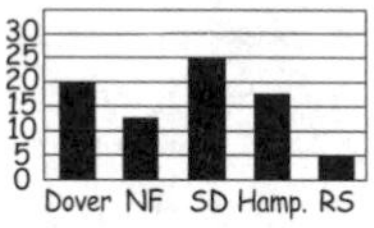
30
25
20
15
10
5
0
Dover
NF
SD
Hamp.
RS

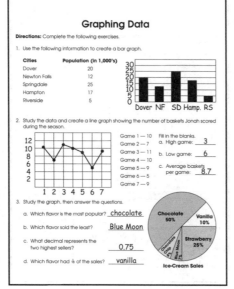

2. Study the data and create a line graph showing the number of baskets Jonah scored during the season.

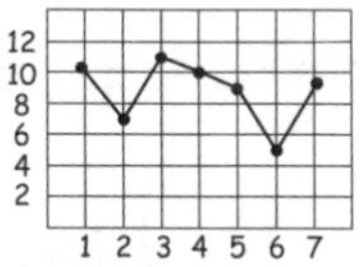
12
10
8
6
4
2
1
2
3
4
5
6
7

Game 1 — 10
Game 2 — 7
Game 3 — 11
Game 4 — 10
Game 5 — 9
Game 6 — 5
Game 7 — 9

Fill in the blanks.
   a. High game: 3
   b. Low game: 6
   c. Average baskets per game: 8.7

3. Study the graph, then answer the questions.
   a. Which flavor is the most popular? chocolate
   b. Which flavor sold the least? Blue Moon
   c. What decimal represents the two highest sellers? 0.75
   d. Which flavor had $\frac{1}{10}$ of the sales? vanilla

Chocolate 50%
Vanilla 10%
Strawberry 25%
Chocolate Chip 8%
Blue Moon 7%

Ice-Cream Sales

Page 444

Integers

An **integer** is a whole number above or below 0: –2, –1, 0, +1, +2, and so on. **Opposite integers** are two integers the same distance from 0, but in different directions, such as –2 and +2.

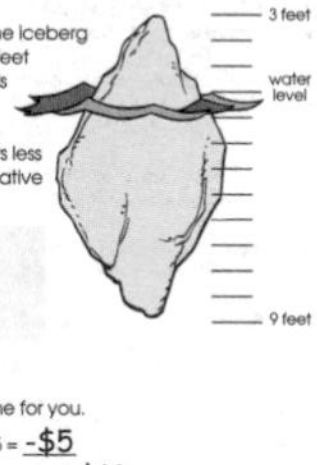
3 feet
water level
9 feet

Think of the water level in the picture as 0. The part of the iceberg sticking out of the water is positive. The iceberg has +3 feet above water. The part of the iceberg below the water is negative. The iceberg extends – 9 feet under water.

Numbers greater than 0 are **positive** numbers. Numbers less than 0 are **negative** numbers. Pairs of positive and negative numbers are called **opposite integers**.

Examples of opposite integers:
–5 and +5
losing 3 pounds and gaining 3 pounds
earning $12 and spending $12

Directions: Complete the following exercises.

1. Write each of these as an integer. The first one is done for you.
   a. positive 6 = +6
   b. losing $5 = -$5
   c. 5 degrees below 0 = -5
   d. receiving $12 = +$12
2. Write the **opposite** integer of each of these. The first one is done for you.
   a. negative 4 = +4
   b. positive 10 = -10
   c. 2 floors below ground level = +2
   d. winning a card game by 6 points = -6
3. Write integers to show each idea.
   a. A train that arrives 2 hours after it was scheduled: -2
   b. A package that has 3 fewer cups than it should: -3
   c. A board that's 3 inches too short: -3
   d. A golf score 5 over par: +5
   e. A paycheck that doesn't cover $35 of a family's expenses: -$35
   f. 30 seconds before a missile launch: -30
   g. A team that won 6 games and lost 2: +4

Page 445

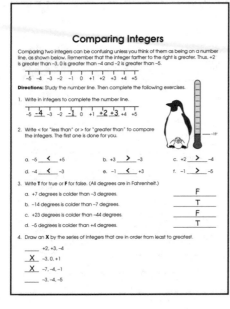

Comparing Integers

Comparing two integers can be confusing unless you think of them as being on a number line, as shown below. Remember that the integer farther to the right is greater. Thus, +2 is greater than –3. 0 is greater than –4 and –2 is greater than –5.

–5 –4 –3 –2 –1 0 +1 +2 +3 +4 +5

Directions: Study the number line. Then complete the following exercises.

1. Write in integers to complete the number line.

–5 **–4** –3 **–2** **–1** 0 +1 **+2** **+3** +4 +5

2. Write < for "less than" or > for "greater than" to compare the integers. The first one is done for you.

a. –5 **<** +5
b. +3 **>** –3
c. +2 **>** –4
d. –4 **<** –3
e. –1 **<** +3
f. –1 **>** –5

3. Write **T** for true or **F** for false. (All degrees are in Fahrenheit.)

a. +7 degrees is colder than –3 degrees. **F**
b. –14 degrees is colder than –7 degrees. **T**
c. +23 degrees is colder than –44 degrees. **F**
d. –5 degrees is colder than +4 degrees. **T**

4. Draw an **X** by the series of integers that are in order from least to greatest.

_____ +2, +3, –4
X –3, 0, +1
X –7, –4, –1
_____ –3, –4, –5

Page 446

Adding Integers

The sum of two positive integers is a positive integer.
   Thus, +4 + +1 = +5.
The sum of two negative integers is a negative integer.
   Thus, –5 + –2 = –7.
The sum of a positive and a negative integer has the sign of the integer that is farther from 0.
   Thus, –6 + +3 = –3.
The sum of opposite integers is 0.
   Thus, +2 + –2 = 0

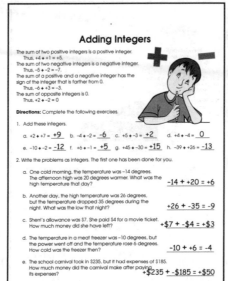

Directions: Complete the following exercises.

1. Add these integers.

a. +2 + +7 = **+9**
b. –4 + –2 = **–6**
c. +5 + –3 = **+2**
d. +4 + –4 = **0**
e. –10 + –2 = **–12**
f. +6 + –1 = **+5**
g. +45 + –30 = **+15**
h. –39 + +26 = **–13**

2. Write the problems as integers. The first one has been done for you.

a. One cold morning, the temperature was –14 degrees. The afternoon high was 20 degrees warmer. What was the high temperature that day? **–14 + +20 = +6**

b. Another day, the high temperature was 26 degrees, but the temperature dropped 35 degrees during the night. What was the low that night? **+26 + –35 = –9**

c. Sherri's allowance was $7. She paid $4 for a movie ticket. How much money did she have left? **+$7 + –$4 = +$3**

d. The temperature in a meat freezer was –10 degrees, but the power went off and the temperature rose 6 degrees. How cold was the freezer then? **–10 + +6 = –4**

e. The school carnival took in $235, but it had expenses of $185. How much money did the carnival make after paying its expenses? **+$235 + –$185 = +$50**

Page 447

Subtracting Integers

To subtract an integer, change its sign to the opposite and add it. If you are subtracting a negative integer, make it positive and add it: +4 – –6 = +4 + +6 = +10. If you are subtracting a positive integer, make it negative and add it: +8 – +2 = +8 + –2 = +6.

More examples: –5 – –8 = –5 + +8 = +3
   +3 – +7 = +3 + –7 = –4

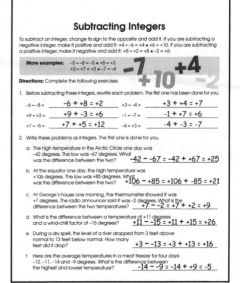

Directions: Complete the following exercises.

1. Before subtracting these integers, rewrite each problem. The first one has been done for you.

–6 – –8 = **–6 + +8 = +2**
+3 – –4 = **+3 + +4 = +7**
+9 – +3 = **+9 + –3 = +6**
–1 – +7 = **–1 + +7 = +6**
+7 – +5 = **+7 + +5 = +12**
–4 – +3 = **–4 + –3 = –7**

2. Write these problems as integers. The first one is done for you.

a. The high temperature in the Arctic Circle one day was –42 degrees. The low was –67 degrees. What was the difference between the two? **–42 – –67 = –42 + +67 = +25**

b. At the equator one day, the high temperature was +106 degrees. The low was +85 degrees. What was the difference between the two? **+106 – +85 = +106 + –85 = +21**

c. At George's house one morning, the thermometer showed it was +7 degrees. The radio announcer said it was –2 degrees. What is the difference between the two temperatures? **+7 – –2 = +7 + +2 = +9**

d. What is the difference between a temperature of +11 degrees and a wind-chill factor of –15 degrees? **+11 – –15 = +11 + +15 = +26**

e. During a dry spell, the level of a river dropped from 3 feet above normal to 13 feet below normal. How many feet did it drop? **+3 – –13 = +3 + +13 = +16**

f. Here are the average temperatures in a meat freezer for four days: –12, –11, –14 and –9 degrees. What is the difference between the highest and lowest temperature? **–14 – –9 = –14 + +9 = –5**

Page 448

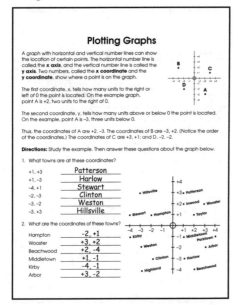

Plotting Graphs

A graph with horizontal and vertical number lines can show the location of certain points. The horizontal number line is called the **x axis**, and the vertical number line is called the **y axis**. Two numbers, called the **x coordinate** and the **y coordinate**, show where a point is on the graph.

The first coordinate, x, tells how many units to the right or left of 0 the point is located. On the example graph, point A is +2, two units to the right of 0.

The second coordinate, y, tells how many units above or below 0 the point is located. On the example, point A is –3, three units below 0.

Thus, the coordinates of A are +2, –3. The coordinates of B are –3, +2. (Notice the order of the coordinates.) The coordinates of C are +3, +1; and D, –2, –2.

Directions: Study the example. Then answer these questions about the graph below.

1. What towns are at these coordinates?

+1, +3 Patterson
+1, –3 Harlow
–4, +1 Stewart
–2, –3 Clinton
–3, –2 Weston
–3, +3 Hillsville

2. What are the coordinates of these towns?

Hampton –2, +1
Wooster +3, +2
Beachwood +2, –4
Middletown +1, –1
Kirby –4, –1
Arbor +3, –2

Page 449

Ordered Pairs

Ordered pairs is another term used to describe pairs of integers used to locate points on a graph.

Directions: Complete the following exercises.

1. Place the following points on the graph, using the ordered pairs as data.

+3, +3
–2, +4
+1, –2
+4, +4
–4, –4
+2, +3
–1, +4

2. Create your own set of ordered pairs. Use your home as the center of your coordinates—zero. Let the x axis serve as East and West. The y axis will be North and South. Now select things to plot on your graph—the school, playground, grocery store, a friend's house, and so on.

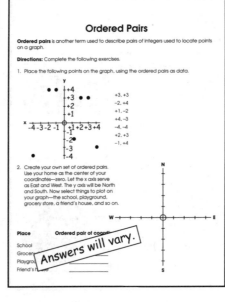

Place	Ordered pair of coord...
School	
Groce...	*Answers will vary.*
Playgro...	
Friend's H...	

Page 450

Review

Directions: Complete the following exercises.

CERTIFICATE
Congratulations to

_____
(Your Name)
for finishing this workbook!

_____
(Date)

1. Write the **opposite** integers of the following:

a. 14 degrees above 0 **–14**
b. Spending $21 **+$21**

2. Write integers to show these ideas.

a. 4 seconds after the launch of the space shuttle **+4**
b. A lake 3 feet below its usual level **–3**
c. 2 days before your birthday **–2**

3. Write < for "less than" or > for "greater than" to compare these integers.

–2 **>** –4
+2 **>** –3
–1 **<** +1

4. Add the integers.

–14 + –11 = **–25**
–6 + +5 = **–1**
–7 + +7 = **0**

5. Subtract the integers.

–4 – –5 = **+1**
+3 – –6 = **+9**
+7 – +2 = **+5**

6. Write **T** for true or **F** for false.

a. The x coordinate is on the horizontal number line. **T**
b. Add the x and y coordinates to find the location of a point. **F**
c. Always state the x coordinate first. **T**
d. A y coordinate of +2 would be above the horizontal number line. **T**
e. An x coordinate of +2 would be to the right of the vertical number line. **T**

AUTHOR'S PURPOSE

Magazines and Internet web sites, as well as books, all have specific purposes for their existence. While your child is reading or watching television, ask him/her what is the purpose of the story, show, news bit or commercial. Discriminating among authors' purposes makes a more informed citizen and consumer.

CAUSE AND EFFECT

Invite your child to read the newspaper front page, circling the causes of an event and underlining the effects.

Have your child write cause-and-effect statements for his/her daily activities. For example: I hit the snooze button on my alarm clock, so I was late for school. I practiced fielding ground balls over the weekend, so I did much better at baseball practice.

CLASSIFYING

Give your child several category names, and invite him/her to provide several examples. For example: Modes of Transportation—car, train, bicycle, airplane, wheelchair, horse and buggy. See how many examples he/she can come up with for each category. Then provide your child with several examples and ask him/her to name the category. For example: sugar, candy, honey, fruit—Sweet Things.

COMPREHENSION

As you read with your child, encourage him/her to picture in his/her mind what is happening. This will help your child recall the story using the "mind's eye" as well as the ear. Discuss details of the story. Ask your child about the sequence of events. Ask him/her to retell the story, noting details from the beginning, middle and end.

Invite your child to write a different ending or new chapter to a story. If your child can do this in a logical manner, he/she has grasped the plot or ideas presented.

Ask your child questions about the story before you begin reading. For example: What do you think the illustration on the book cover means? Will this be an adventure story? A true story? What do you think the title means? What do you think will happen to (character's name)?

Your child is now reading "chapter books." These books have very few pictures. Check your child's comprehension by having him/her draw pictures representing the action or the problem for each chapter. Before starting each new chapter, ask your child to predict what will happen.

DECIMALS

Have your child use money to understand the concept of decimals as part of a whole. Use dollar bills and a variety of coins. Ask your child to find various fractions, or parts, of a dollar. You and your child can write out "money problems" for each other to figure out. Also, use money as a cross-reference with fractions. Example: 25 cents is 0.25 of a dollar. 25 cents is also $\frac{25}{100}$ of a dollar.

ESTIMATING

Take your child to the grocery store with you. While shopping, ask him/her to compare the prices of similar items of varying sizes and determine which is the better bargain. Invite your child to look at labels, pointing out that many are listed with customary and metric measurements. Ask him/her to estimate the total cost of the items by rounding numbers and averaging. Tell your child how much money you have to spend, and ask him/her to estimate the amount of change you should receive.

Take the family out to dinner and have your child estimate the bill and calculate the appropriate amount to leave for a tip.

Take your child to a shopping mall in which several stores are having sales. Ask your child to estimate how much 40%, 25%, 15%, and so on, off an item would be. Then calculate the sale price.

FACT/OPINION

Use the editorial section of a newspaper or magazine. Have your child read an article or letter and classify each sentence as either fact or opinion.

Many advertisements are confusing or misleading. Teach your child that everything in an ad may not be factual. Much of the appeal of ads is opinion. Cut ads from magazines and newspapers and listen to ads on television and radio. Help your child sort through the information. Ask him/her to point out the parts that are facts and those that are opinions. By realizing the difference and separating the two, your child will be able to make better judgments about which products to buy.

FRACTIONS

Cut up fruits, vegetables and other foods to help your child with the concept of fractions. Example: 8 sections of one whole orange 1/8, 8/8; 2 halves of an apple 1/2, 2/2; 6 pieces of pizza 1/6, 6/6.

Your child can also use toy blocks in sets of 10, with a total of 100. Place the blocks on the floor and explain that this represents one whole. Select different fractions for your child to find.

GEOMETRY

Have your child cut out geometric shapes from cereal boxes, wallpaper scraps, construction paper, and so on. Invite him/her to create unique designs, and discuss the differences and similarities among the shapes.

Invite the whole family to join in measuring activities. See how quickly each family member can find the perimeter and area of his/her bedroom. Then figure out the volumes. Invite your child to figure out how many square feet of living space are in your home, and how much space is used as storage areas.

Design a flower bed or plant a vegetable garden. Ask your child to figure the dimensions needed for each plant, what percentage of the garden will be used for flowers, the ratio of edible plants to flowering plants, whether you will plant in straight lines or in geometric patterns, and so on.

GIVING DIRECTIONS

Ask your child if he/she has ever tried to assemble a game, toy or other item and had difficulty following the directions. Invite your child to write more specific, easier-to-understand directions for any of those with which he/she had trouble. Once he/she has rewritten the directions, read them together. Do the directions make more sense?

Show your child the importance of giving clear directions by preparing a simple recipe together. Point out how the steps must be followed in order. Then invite him/her to write a simple recipe for you to follow. Encourage your child to include all the necessary steps, then see if you can create the recipe from his/her directions.

GRAPHING

With your child, collect data at home of birds, insects, flowers, plants, and so on, which you see in your backyard. Do this on several different occasions, then find the ratio between the sets of data.

Invite your child to make charts of games, books or music owned by different family members. Any topic will work! Arrange the data into charts or line graphs.

Have your child record the ages of all the family members, including grandparents, aunts, uncles and cousins. Then have him/her calculate the mean age of the family. Point out to your child how this differs from the median age, using the same set of numbers.

HOMOPHONE CHALLENGE

Homophones are words that are pronounced the same but are spelled differently and have different meanings, like "pear" and "pair." Challenge your child to a contest to see who can write the most homophones.

MAIN IDEA

Show your child that the chapters or units in his/her textbooks are grouped according to the main idea: The Human Body, Space, and so on.

Invite your child to group things into categories to see if the concept, or main idea, is understood. Examples: wild animals, sports played outside, board games, books about famous American women.

Ask your child questions while reading together, such as, "What is the most important thing the author is saying in this paragraph?" "Can you tell what the author means in this sentence?"

MAKING INFERENCES

Guide your child to "figure out" what an author means, even when it is not directly stated in the writing. Practice by describing a situation to your child and having him/her tell you what is happening. Start out with simple situations, then move on to more complicated situations.

POETRY

Share your favorite poems with your child. Borrow books of poetry from the library to read together. Make up poems together, taking turns with every other line.

There are many different types of poetry besides haiku, diamanté and descriptive poetry. Try different poetry styles with your child.

Metaphor and Simile Poems: Have your child use metaphors and similes to create poetry. Poems can rhyme but it's not necessary.

Example: Metaphor

> The clouds in the sky,
> Are popcorn rolling by.

Example: Simile

> Elephants' noses
> Are like firemen's hoses.
> They squirt and they shower,
> With plenty of power.

Let your child illustrate his/her poems for greater visual effect or write his/her best poems with glittery pens on fancy paper. Poetry can be printed in fancy type on the computer with graphics added. Frame the best ones and hang them for all to enjoy.

Verb Poems: Many action words can be arranged on paper so the shape represents the action. Encourage your child to create his/her own action verb poems.

Example: ping ping ping ping; $p_o{}^u r_i{}^n g$

Limericks: Limericks are short, funny, five-line poems. The first, second and fifth lines rhyme. The second and third lines rhyme as well. Edward Lear (1812–1888) first popularized limericks. Read the example below and other limericks out loud together.

Example: There is a fat cat in my town
            Whose fur is all spotted with brown;
            He spends his days,
            In a variety of ways,
            Strolling in the park with a clown.

Have your child use this sentence as the first line and complete the limerick. Then have him/her write another one of his/her own.

There was an old horse from Bellaire

Tanka: Tanka is an extension of haiku. Tankas complete the poet's thoughts by adding two extra lines at the end of seven syllables each. Remember, haiku has three lines of five, seven and five syllables, respectively.

Example: Snow is falling down.
            Crystals collect on the ground.
            Winter has arrived.
            Snowmen will soon decorate
            The yards of children in town.

Have your child begin by composing a haiku. Then have him/her add two additional lines to make the poem a tanka.

CHANGING PROSE TO POETRY

Often, colorful writing in essays, narratives, speeches and advertisements can be easily transformed into poetry. Read the example with your child. Then look for other topics and create your own poem together.

Example: HOUSE FOR SALE: This lovely home is situated on rolling ground in the country. Horses frolic in the pasture by day, and retire to a well-kept barn at night. Lush forests surround the estate and offer plentiful wildlife along the winding paths.

Poem: I would love to live in a house,
          Surrounded by nature and silence.
          I would ride my horse through the woods,
          And enjoy the sights and sounds of the forest.
          I dream of being at peace,

          Relaxed and care-free.
          Alone in my beautiful house,
          Surrounded by nature and silence.

POINT OF VIEW

Learning to look at issues from more than one point of view can help your child see both sides. Read editorials in your local newspaper together. Discuss whose point of view is stated. Ask your child to present an opposing point of view to the one read. Even if he/she agrees with the writer, it is good practice. If you and your child feel strongly about an issue, write an editorial together and send it to your local newspaper. Remember to add reasons, facts and examples to your editorial.

PROBLEM SOLVING/LOGIC PROBLEMS

As you go about your daily business, point out the problem solving to be done. Have your child help you work through the problems, whether they are while cooking, fixing something or creating a budget. He/she may help you map out the order for going around town to shop, taking your children to activities, doing your banking, and so on.

There are also books and magazines with word problems such as crossword puzzles, logic problems and diagramming logic puzzles. If your child enjoys the logic problems in this book, he/she may enjoy flexing his/her mind on one of these during leisure time.

PROOFREADING

The first draft of a story, whether hand-written or typed on a computer, should be one in which the writer doesn't worry about mechanics. He/she needs to create the characters, the setting and the plot. Most stories take several revisions before they are finished. When the story is completed, you can guide your child in proofreading before making a final copy.

Help your child proofread other letters and reports he/she writes. Proofreading consists of checking for grammatical errors, misspellings, punctuation mistakes, capitalization errors and substituting synonyms for overused words. Using a spell checking program on a computer is helpful, but it will not find and correct every error.

Make the corrections together until your child is able to handle proofreading on his/her own. Ask your child to help you check your written work, like memos, letters and reports. This gives your child more practice and could be quite helpful to you.

READING EXTENSIONS

Colonial America

Have your child research famous colonial women such as Betsy Ross, Pocahontas and Sacajawea. Write an informational paragraph about each woman's accomplishments. Invite your child to read more about the Puritans and the Quakers, then complete a Venn diagram comparing the two groups.

Have your child make a time line of important Colonial American events. He/she can include events such as the arrival at Plymouth Rock, the first Thanksgiving, the Revolutionary War and the signing of the Declaration of Independence.

Weather

Collect the daily newspaper weather map for 1 week. Have your child go on a scavenger hunt for weather information such as: Yesterday's High; Tomorrow's Forecast; Temperature in Paris, France; Pollen Count; Pollution Index.

Give your child weather math problems to solve such as: compute the average daily temperature forecast for 1 week; change the high and low temperatures for the week from Fahrenheit to Celsius.

Invite your child to research earthquakes and compare them to weather phenomena such as tornadoes, hurricanes and thunderstorms. Which is the most devastating force of nature? Compare damage in casualties and dollar amounts for each for a 10-year period in the United States. Ask your child to record his/her findings.

Australia

Ask your child to find a picture of the Australian flag and compare it to the United States flag. How are the flags alike? Different? What symbols are on the flags, and what do they represent? Invite your child to write a brief paragraph comparing and contrasting the two flags.

Have your child research the number of sheep in Australia vs. the number of people. Have him/her create bar and circle graphs showing this information.

Invite your child to do additional research on the Aborigine culture. What is their diet? What traditions do they have? What dangers do they face in the future?

Have your child create a habitat display on an Australian animal. Divide a poster board into four equal sections. In the top left section, have him/her write an informational report about the animal. In the top right, have him/her make a web of animals to whom it is related. In the bottom left, have your child write a poem about the animal. Finally, in the last section, your child can draw the animal.

Kites

Invite your child to read more about Benjamin Franklin's kite and key experiment; then write a one-paragraph informational essay about what was discovered. How was this discovery later applied in the world of science?

Have your child go to the library and check out a book illustrating different types of kites, including box kites, stunt kites, flat kites and sled kites. Have your child describe what makes the kites alike and what makes them different?

Many kite terms are also weather terms. Encourage your child to find the definitions for the following words: drag, lift, turbulence, upwind, wind speed and downwind. Ask your child to explain how these terms apply to kite flying. Or better yet, take your child out to fly a kite, and ask him/her to use these terms in the process!

RECALLING DETAILS

Write main ideas on index cards, such as "summer vacation." Then ask your child to write several details about the idea, such as "no school," "playing with friends," "camping," "riding bikes," and so on.

Write a simple sentence for your child. Example: The cat ran down the street. Show your child how adding details makes the sentence more interesting. Example: The fluffy white cat ran quickly down the noisy street. Ask him/her to add details to several simple sentences. Point out that these details are describing words, or adjectives.

RESEARCH/LOCATING INFORMATION

Have your child choose a topic that interests him/her. Help your child brainstorm a project he/she could do to find and present information about that topic. The project may include a written report, a speech, a demonstration, a model, a web page, an interview, etc. Help your child map out a "plan of attack" in obtaining, organizing and presenting the information. If there's not enough information about the chosen topic, help your child brainstorm again about researchable topics. Or, if there is too much information, you may need to help your child focus on a subtopic to research.

Then, allow your child to research and organize data independently. Check to make sure he/she is finding the needed information and is organizing it for easy use later. Make as many of the following resources available to your child as possible: newspapers, CD-ROMs, the Internet, encyclopedias, dictionaries, topical magazines or journals, indexes, etc. Your local public library should have all these resources available to you.

Have your child talk to his/her teacher about sharing the information/project with the rest of the class or turning it in for extra credit.

SUMMARIZING PLOTS

The plot is the action in a story. To summarize a plot, tell about the most important parts in order. After your child finishes reading a book or watching a video, ask him/her to summarize the plot for you and make a recommendation whether he/she thinks you would enjoy it too.

TESTS

Have your child create his/her own test using any or all of the formats covered in this book. Have him/her look at past tests to analyze what he/she might do differently on the next one. There are practice tests for many of the national standardized tests. If your child's school does not have access to them, they can give you a way to contact a company directly.

USING A DICTIONARY/VOCABULARY BUILDING

Encourage your child to learn the spelling and definitions of new words. Select a "word a day" and write it on a sheet of paper. Have your child look up the word and use it in a sentence. At the end of each week, review the new words for the week.

Another way to learn new words is to ask your child to open a dictionary at random and begin reading the words on that page. Stop at the first new word. Learn how to pronounce it and use it in a sentence.

Have your child think of synonyms for words he/she may "overuse." For example: Cold can be converted to frosty, icy, freezing, chilly, cool, and so on.

WORD ORIGINS

Help your child research your family name and your family tree. When and how did your ancestors arrive in America? Have any changes been made to the spelling of your surname?

Invite your child to find words that originate from Native American words. The states of Florida, Ohio and New Jersey have many towns and lakes named by Native Americans. Ask your child to trace the names to a specific tribe.

Guide your child to see that, although Latin is not a spoken language, many of the words in the English language are derived from Latin words. For example, the words "amiable," "fictitious," "liquid," "major," "omit" and "poet" all have Latin origins. Invite your child to trace these and other words to the Latin words from which they are derived.

WRITING

Read the editorial section of your local newspaper with your child. This section includes opinion essays. Invite your child to write a sample "Letter to the Editor" describing something about which he/she feels strongly. If it is currently relevant in your community, help him/her send it to the paper.

Have your child keep a daily journal during a vacation. He/she can record sights, sounds and smells; favorite destinations; and so on. Collect and read brochures about various places and activities. At the end of the vacation, have your child reread his/her journal and write a short essay about vacation highlights.

WRITING DIRECTIONS

Being able to write and give clear directions is a useful skill for everyone. Encourage your child to practice writing directions for various tasks, like painting a room or planting a garden. Remind your child to think about what steps need to be done, in what order they should be done and what equipment or tools are needed.

Directions from one location to another also need to be very clear. Ask your child to give the exact directions from your home to the library, post office, mall or other location. Watch for vague words or phrases, like "turn by the yellow house" or "go past the blue car." Travel to that destination together following the directions exactly. Did you make it?

Before your child begins a task, ask him/her to write each step in order. Then ask him/her to follow the directions exactly as written. This is the best way to determine if any steps or information have been omitted. Have him/her go back and add any missing information or clarify any steps that are unclear.

WRITING AN INVITATION

An invitation needs to include the time, date and place for an event; the reason for the invitation; and whether the receiver should indicate his/her ability to attend (RSVP). Invitations may be written in paragraph form, but it is often much easier to follow the example to the right.

Let your child create an invitation for your next birthday bash or other get-together. He/she can decorate the cards by hand, or use a computer to create an original card. Be sure to include all relevant information.

You're Invited!
We're having a party for Mom and Dad's
50th Anniversary!

Date: September 10, 2001
Time: 5:00 P.M.-9:00 P.M.
Place: McFrange Party Center
RSVP: Mary at 555-1234 by
            September 1 2001

Dinner will be served promptly at 5:30 P.M.

No gifts please.

WRITING A THANK YOU NOTE

Saying thank you in writing is a good habit for children to learn. Children should write thank you notes, not only for gifts, but also for thoughtful actions like an invitation from a friend's parents for dinner or an overnight visit. Help your child use proper form when composing a thank you note, even though it may be informal in nature or sent via e-mail.

December 28, 2000

Dear Grandma,

I received your package in the mail yesterday. I love the quilt you made for my new bedroom. It will match perfectly. I have decorated my room with wildlife, and your choice of the Canadian goose is perfect. Thank you for thinking of me.

Love,

Zach